The Greenwood Encyclopedia of
Multiethnic American Literature

The Greenwood Encyclopedia of

MULTIETHNIC AMERICAN LITERATURE

Volume I

A – C

Edited by Emmanuel S. Nelson

GREENWOOD PRESS

Westport, Connecticut • London

Library of Congress Cataloging-in-Publication Data

The Greenwood encyclopedia of multiethnic American literature / edited by Emmanuel S. Nelson.
   p. cm.
   Includes bibliographical references and index.
   ISBN 0–313–33059–X (set : alk. paper) — ISBN 0–313–33060–3 (v. 1 : alk. paper) — ISBN 0–313–33061–1 (v. 2 : alk. paper) — ISBN 0–313–33062–X (v. 3 : alk. paper) — ISBN 0–313–33063–8 (v. 4 : alk. paper) — ISBN 0–313–33064–6 (v. 5 : alk. paper)
   1. American literature—Minority authors—Encyclopedias. 2. Minorities—United States—Intellectual life—Encyclopedias. 3. Pluralism (Social sciences) in literature—Encyclopedias. 4. United States—Literatures—Encyclopedias. 5. Ethnic groups in literature—Encyclopedias. 6. Minorities in literature—Encyclopedias. 7. Ethnicity in literature—Encyclopedias. I. Nelson, Emmanuel S. (Emmanuel Sampath), 1954–
   PS153.M56G74 2005
   810.9'920693—dc22   2005018960

British Library Cataloguing in Publication Data is available.

This book is included in the *African American Experience* database from Greenwood Electronic Media. For more information, visit www.africanamericanexperience.com.

Library of Congress Catalog Card Number: 2005018960
ISBN: 0–313–33059–X (set)
      0–313–33060–3 (vol. I)
      0–313–33061–1 (vol. II)
      0–313–33062–X (vol. III)
      0–313–33063–8 (vol. IV)
      0–313–33064–6 (vol. V)

First published in 2005

Greenwood Press, 88 Post Road West, Westport, CT 06881
An imprint of Greenwood Publishing Group, Inc.
www.greenwood.com

Printed in the United States of America

The paper used in this book complies with the Permanent Paper Standard issued by the National Information Standards Organization (Z39.48–1984).

10 9 8 7 6 5 4 3 2 1

For Trevor again, with love

Set Contents

List of Entries   ix

Guide to Related Topics   xxiii

Preface   xxxix

Introduction *by Paul Lauter*   xliii

The Encyclopedia   1

Selected Bibliography   2373

Index   2381

About the Advisory Board   2457

About the Editor and Contributors   2459

List of Entries

Abinader, Elmaz
Abish, Walter
Abolition
Abu Jaber, Diana
Acker, Kathy
Acosta, Oscar Zeta
Adamic, Louis
Adams, Elizabeth Laura
Addonizio, Kim
African American Autobiography
African American Biography
African American Children's
   Literature
African American Critical Theory
African American Detective Fiction
African American Drama
African American Film
African American Folklore
African American Gay Literature
African American Lesbian
   Literature
African American Musicals
African American Novel
African American Poetry

African American Pulp Fiction
African American Science Fiction
African American Short Story
African American Slave Narrative
African American Stereotypes
African American Travel
   Narrative
African American Young Adult
   Literature
Afrocentricity
Ager, Waldemar
Agosín, Marjorie
*Aiiieeeee! An Anthology of Asian
   American Writers*
Alameddine, Rabih
Alarcón, Francisco X.
Albert, Octavia Victoria Rogers
Alexander, Meena
Alexie, Sherman Joseph, Jr.
Alfaro, Luis
Algren, Nelson
Ali, Agha Shahid
Alishan, Leonardo
Alkalay-Gut, Karen

Allen, Paula Gunn
Allen, Richard
Allen, Samuel W.
Allen, Woody
Alvarez, Julia
Amanuensis
America Is in the Heart
American Indian Movement
Amish Literature
Anaya, Rudolfo
Angel Island
Angelou, Maya
Ansa, Tina McElroy
Antin, Mary
Anti-Semitism
Anzaldúa, Gloria E.
Apess, William
Apple, Max
Arab American Autobiography
Arab American Novel
Arab American Poetry
Arab American Stereotypes
Ardizzone, Anthony
Arenas, Reinaldo
Armenian American Literature
Armenian Genocide
Arte Público Press
Asayesh, Gelareh
Asimov, Isaac
Assimilation
Attaway, William
Auster, Paul
Austin, Doris Jean
Autobiography of Malcolm X, The
Autobiography of Miss Jane Pittman,
The
Baca, Jimmy Santiago
Bacho, Peter
Baker, Houston A., Jr.
Baker, Nikki
Baldwin, James
Bambara, Toni Cade
Bamboo Ridge
Baraka, Amiri
Barolini, Helen

Barrax, Gerald
Barresi, Dorothy
Basque American Literature
Beckham, Barry
Behrman, S. N.
Bell, James Madison
Bell, Marvin
Bell, Thomas
Bellow, Saul
Beloved
Belton, Don
Bennett, Gwendolyn
Bennett, Hal
Bernardi, Adria
Bernstein, Charles
Berryman, John
Berssenbrugge, Mei-Mei
Bessie, Alvah
Bibb, Henry
Bilingualism
Black Arts Movement
Black Boy
Black Elk [Hehaka Sapa]
Black Nationalism
Blaeser, Kimberly M.
Blatty, William Peter
Bless Me, Ultima
Bloom, Harold Irving
Blues, The
Bluest Eye, The
Bodenheim, Maxwell
Bonner, Marita Odette
Bontemps, Arna
Border Narratives
Born in East L.A.
Boudinot, Elias
Bourjaily, Vance
Boyesen, Hjalmar Hjorth
Bradley, David
Braga, Thomas J.
Brainard, Cecilia Manguerra
Braithwaite, William Stanley
Brer Rabbit
Breslin, Jimmy
Broadside Press

Brodsky, Joseph (Iosif)
Broner, E(sther) M(asserman)
Brooks, Gwendolyn
Broumas, Olga
Brown, Cecil M.
Brown, Claude
Brown, Frank London
Brown Girl, Brownstones
Brown, John
Brown, Linda Beatrice
Brown, Rosellen
Brown, Sterling
Bruce-Novoa, Juan
Bruchac, Joseph
Bryant, Dorothy
Budy, Andrea Hollander
Bukiet, Melvin Jules
Bukoski, Anthony
Bullins, Ed
Bulosan, Carlos
Bumbalo, Victor
Burk, Ronnie
Burnshaw, Stanley
Buslett, Ole Amundsen
Butler, Octavia Estelle
Cabrera Infante, Guillermo
Cahan, Abraham
Calcagno, Anne
Caldwell, Ben
Calisher, Hortense
Calof, Rachel Bella Kahn
Campo, Rafael
Candelaria, Cordelia Chávez
Cane
Cano, Daniel
Canon
Cantú, Norma Elia
Cao, Lan
Caponegro, Mary
Capotorto, Rosette
Cappello, Mary
Caribbean (Anglophone) American
    Autobiography
Caribbean (Anglophone) American
    Novel

Caribbean (Anglophone) American
    Poetry
Carpatho-Rusyn Literature
Castedo, Elena
Castillo, Ana
Castillo, Rafael C.
Catacalos, Rosemary
Cavello, Diana
Ceremony
Cerenio, Virginia
Cervantes, Lorna Dee
Cha, Theresa Hak Kyung
Chabon, Michael
Chan, Jeffrey Paul
Chandra, Sharat G. S.
Chang, Diana
Chase-Riboud, Barbara
Chávez, Denise
Chee, Alexander
Chernin, Kim
Chesnutt, Charles Waddell
Chief Seattle
Childress, Alice
Chin, Frank
Chin, Marilyn Mei Ling
Chinese American Autobiography
Chinese American Drama
Chinese American Novel
Chinese American Poetry
Chinese American Stereotypes
Chinese Exclusion Act
Chmelka, Donald F.
Chock, Eric
Choi, Sook Nyul
Choi, Susan
Chong, Ping
Chu, Louis
Christian, Barbara
Ciresi, Rita
Cisneros, Sandra
Civil Rights Movement
Clarke, Cheryl
Cleage, Pearl
Cleaver, (Leroy) Eldridge
Cliff, Michelle

Clifton, Lucille
Cobb, Ned
Cohen, Sarah Blacher
Coleman, Wanda
Collins, Katherine Conwell
Collins, Merle
Colon, Jesus
Colonialism and U.S. Ethnic
    Literatures
Color Purple, The
Colored Museum, The
Colter, Cyrus
Comden and Green
Confessions of Nat Turner, The
Conjure
Conley, Robert J.
Cook-Lynn, Elizabeth
Cooper, Anna Julia
Cooper, J. (Joan) California
Corso, Gregory Nunzio
Cortez, Jayne
Covino, Peter
Crafts, Hannah
Crasta, Richard / Avatar Prabhu
Crawford, Janie
Crèvecoeur, J. Hector St. John de
Cruz, Nilo
Cruz, Victor Hernández
Cuban American Autobiography
Cuban American Novel
Cuban American Poetry
Cullen, Countee
Culture Clash
Cumpian, Carlos
Curiel, Barbara Brinson
Curran, Mary Doyle
Czech American Literature
Dahl, Dorthea
Dahlberg, Edward
Dame, Enid
Danner, Margaret Esse
Danticat, Edwidge
davenport, doris
Davis, Angela Yvonne
Davis, Frank Marshall

Davis, Ossie
De Burgos, Julia
De Casas, Celso A.
Dee, Ruby
Delaney, Lucy Ann
Delany, Martin Robinson
Delany, Samuel R.
De la Peña, Terri
Del Castillo, Ramon
DeLillo, Don
Demby, William E.
Dent, Tom [Thomas Covington
    Dent]
Der Hovanessian, Diana
DeRosa, Tina
Derricotte, Toi
DeSalvo, Louise
Diaspora
Diaz, Junot
di Donato, Pietro
di Prima, Diane
Divakaruni, Chitra Banerjee
Dixon, Melvin
Dizon, Louella
Doctorow, E. L.
Dodson, Owen Vincent
Domini, John
Dominican American Novel
Dominican American Poetry
Donohue, Maura Nguyen
Dorris, Michael
Douglass, Frederick
Dove, Rita
Down These Mean Streets
Dreiser, Theodore
Du Bois, Shirley Graham
Du Bois, W. E. B.
Dumas, Henry
Dunbar, Paul Laurence
Dunbar-Nelson, Alice
Dunne, Finley Peter
Duplechan, Larry
Dutchman
Dybek, Stuart
Eady, Cornelius

Eastman, Charles Ohiyesa
Eat a Bowl of Tea
Eaton, Edith Maude
Eaton, Winnifred
Elaw, Zilpha
Elder, Lonne, III
Eleni
Elkin, Stanley
Ellis Island
Ellis, Trey
Ellison, Ralph Waldo
Elman, Richard M.
Endore, Guy
Englander, Nathan
Engle, Margarite
Epstein, Joseph
Epstein, Leslie
Equiano, Olaudah
Erdrich, Louise
Espada, Martin
Espaillat, Rhina [Polonia]
Espinosa, María
Esteves, Sandra María
Ethnicity
Eugenides, Jeffrey
Eurocentrism
Evans, Mari
Everett, Percival L.
Faigao-Hall, Linda
Fair, Ronald L.
Falk, Marcia
Fante, John
Farrell, James T.
Fast, Howard
Fauset, Jessie Redmon
Faust, Irvin
Fearing, Kenneth
Federman, Raymond
Feinberg, David B.
Feldman, Irving
Feminism and U.S. Ethnic
    Literatures
Fences
Ferber, Edna
Fernández, Roberta

Fernandez, Roberto G.
Ferro, Robert
Fiedler, Leslie
Field, Edward
Fields, Julia
Fierstein, Harvey Forbes
Figueroa, José Angel
Filipino American Novel
Filipino American Poetry
Finkelstein, Norman
Finnish American Literature
Fisher, Rudolph
Fitzgerald, F. Scott
Flaherty, Joe
Flanagan, Thomas
Flores-Williams, Jason
Flowers, A. R.
Fontes, Montserrat
Foote, Julia A. J.
Forché, Carolyn
Fornes, Maria Irene
Franco American Literature
Frank, Waldo
Franklin, J. E.
Fraxedas, J. Joaquin
Freeman, Joseph
Fried, Emanuel
Friedman, Bruce Jay
Friedman, Sanford
Fries, Kenny
Fuchs, Daniel
Funaroff, Sol
Gage, Nicholas
Gaines, Ernest J.
Gaines, Patrice
Galarza, Ernesto
Gambone, Philip
Ganesan, Indira
García, Cristina
Garcia, Richard
Garcia-Camarillo, Cecilio
Gardaphé, Fred L.
Garvey, Marcus
Gaspar, Frank Xavier
Gates, Henry Louis, Jr.

Gawande, Atul
Geisel, Theodor Seuss ["Dr. Seuss"]
Gelbart, Larry
Gerber, Merrill Joan
German American Literature
Ghose, Zulfikar
Giardina, Denise
Gibran, Gibran Kahlil
Gildner, Gary
Gilgun, John
Gillan, Maria Mazziotti
Ginsberg, Allen
Gioia, Dana
Gioseffi, Daniela
Giovanni, Nikki
Giovannitti, Arturo
Giunta, Edvige
Glancy, Diane
Glickman, Gary
Glück, Louise
Glück, Robert
Godfather, The
Gold, Herbert
Gold, Michael
Golden, Marita
Goldreich, Gloria
Goldstein, Rebecca
Gomez, Jewelle
Gómez-Peña, Guillermo
Gonzáles, Jovita
Gonzalez, N. V. M.
Gonzalez, Ray
Gonzales-Berry, Erlinda
Goodman, Allegra
Gordon, Mary
Gotanda, Philip
Graham, Jorie
Greek American Autobiography
Greek American Fiction
Greek American Poetry
Green, Gerald
Greenberg, Joanne [Goldenberg]
Greenlee, Sam
Griggs, Sutton Elbert
Grimké, Angelina Weld

Grossman, Allen
Gunn, Bill
Guy, Rosa Cuthbert
Ha Jin
Hagedorn, Jessica Tarahata
Hagopian, Richard
Hahn, Gloria
Hale, Janet Campbell
Haley, Alex
Halper, Albert
Hamill, Pete
Hamilton, Virginia
Hammon, Jupiter
Hansberry, Lorraine
Hansen, Joyce
Hardy, James Earl
Harjo, Joy
Harlem Renaissance
Harper, Frances Ellen Watkins
Harper, Michael S.
Harris, E. Lynn
Harrison, Juanita
Hart, Moss
Hashmi, Alamgir
Hawai'i Literature
Hawaiian Literature
Hayden, Robert
Haynes, Lemuel
Hayslip, Phung Le Ly
Hazo, Samuel J.
Heard, Nathan C.
Heath Anthology of American
    Literature, The
Hecht, Anthony
Hecht, Ben
Hegi, Ursula
Hejmadi, Padma [Padma Perera]
Heller, Joseph
Heller, Michael
Hellman, Lillian
Helprin, Mark
Hemphill, Essex
Henderson, George Wylie
Henry, Gordon, Jr.
Henson, Josiah

Hernández, David
Herron, Carolivia
Hershman, Marcie
Highway, Tomson
Hijuelos, Oscar
Hill, Joe [Joel Emanuel Hägglund/
    Joseph Hillström]
Himes, Chester Bomar
Hinojosa-Smith, Rolando
Hirsch, Edward
Hobson, Laura Z.
Hoffman, Eva Wydra
Hogan, Linda
Hollander, John
Holocaust, The
Holocaust Narratives
Holt, John Dominis, IV
Hongo, Garrett Kaoru
hooks, bell
Horton, George Moses
Hosseini, Khaled
House Made of Dawn
House on Mango Street, The
Houston, Jeanne (Toyo) Wakatsuki
Howard, Richard
Howe, Irving
Hua, Chuang
Hughes, Langston
Hunger of Memory
Hunter, Kristin. *See* Lattany, Kristin
    [Hunter]
Hurst, Fannie
Hurston, Zora Neale
I Know Why the Caged Bird Sings
Identity
Ignatow, David
Immigration
Inada, Lawson Fusao
Indian American Film. *See* South
    Asian American Film
Indian American Literature. *See*
    South Asian American Literature
Internment
Invisible Man
Iranian American Literature

Irish American Autobiography
Irish American Drama
Irish American Novel
Islas, Arturo, Jr.
Italian American Autobiography
Italian American Film
Italian American Gay Literature
Italian American Humor
Italian American Lesbian Literature
Italian American Novel
Italian American Poetry
Italian American Stereotypes
Iyer, Pico
Jackson, Angela
Jackson, Elaine
Jacobs, Harriet
Jaffe, Daniel M.
Janda, Victoria
Janson, Drude Krog
Janson, Kristofer
Japanese American Autobiography
Japanese American Novel
Jasmine
Jason, Sonya
Jazz
Jeffers, Lance
Jen, Gish [Lillian C. Jen]
Jerome, V. J. [Isaac Jerome
    Romaine]
Jewish American Autobiography
Jewish American Gay Literature
Jewish American Lesbian
    Literature
Jewish American Musicals
Jewish American Novel
Jewish American Poetry
Jewish American Stereotypes
Jewish American Theater
Jim Crow
Jimenez, Francisco
Joans, Theodore "Ted"
Johnson, Charles Richard
Johnson, E. Pauline
    [Tekahionwake]
Johnson, Helene

Johnson, James Weldon
Johnson, Simon
Jones, Edward P.
Jones, Gayl
Jong, Erica
Jordan, June
Joy Luck Club, The
Kadi, Joanna
Kadohata, Cynthia
Kang, Younghill
Kaplan, Johanna
Karmel, Ilona
Katz, Judith
Kaufman, Bob
Kaufman, George Simon
Kazin, Alfred
Keckley, Elizabeth
Kelley, Samuel L.
Kelley, William Melvin
Kenan, Randall
Kennedy, Adrienne
Kennedy, William
Kenny, Maurice
Kerouac, Jack
Kessler, Milton
Killens, John Oliver
Kim, Myung Mi
Kim, Richard E.
Kim, Yong Ik
Kimmelman, Burt
Kincaid, Jamaica
King, Martin Luther, Jr.
King, Thomas
King, Woodie, Jr.
Kingston, Maxine Hong
Kirchner, Bharti
Klein, Abraham Moses
Klepfisz, Irena
Knight, Etheridge
Koch, Kenneth
Koestenbaum, Wayne
Komunyakaa, Yusef
Konecky, Edith
Kopit, Arthur
Korean American Literature

Kostelanetz, Richard Cory
Kramer, Aaron
Kramer, Larry
Kubiak, Wanda
Kubicki, Jan
Kumar, Amitava
Kumin, Maxine
Kunitz, Stanley
Kushner, Tony
Kwong, Dan
Lahiri, Jhumpa
Lakshmi, Vijay
Lapine, James
La Puma, Salvatore
Larsen, Nella
Lattany, Kristin [Hunter]
Laurence, Patricia Ondek
Laurents, Arthur
Laviera, Tato
Lawson, John Howard
Laxalt, Robert
Lazarus, Emma
Leavitt, David
Lebow, Barbara
Lee, Andrea
Lee, C. Y. (Chin Yang)
Lee, Chang-rae
Lee, Cherylene
Lee, Don L. *See* Madhubuti, Haki R.
Lee, Gus
Lee, Jarena
Lee, Li-Young
Lentricchia, Frank
Lester, Julius
lê thi diem thúy
Levertov, Denise
Levin, Meyer
Levine, Philip
Levins Morales, Aurora
Lifshin, Lyn
Lim, Shirley Geok-lin
Liminality
Limón, Graciela
Lithuanian American Literature
Liu, Aimee

Locke, Alain
Lopate, Phillip
López, Josefina
López Torregrosa, Luisita
Lord, Bette Bao
Lorde, Audre
Louie, David Wong
Love Medicine
Lowe, Pardee
Lowenfels, Walter
Lum, Darrel H. Y.
Lum, Wing Tek
Lumpkin, Grace
Luther Standing Bear
M. Butterfly
Mackey, Nathaniel
Mackus, Algimantas
Madgett, Naomi Long
Madhubuti, Haki R.
Mailer, Norman
Majaj, Lisa Suhair
Major, Clarence
Malamud, Bernard
Malcolm X [aka Malcolm Little; Islamic name El-Hajj Malik El-Shabazz]
Maltz, Albert
Mamet, David
Mandelbaum, Allen
Manfredi, Renée
Mangione, Jerre (Gerlando)
Mann, Emily
Markfield, Wallace
Marotta, Kenny
Marrant, John
Marshall, Paule
Martí, José
Martínez, Demetria
Marvin X
Maso, Carole
Mathews, John Joseph
Mazza, Cris
McBride, James
McCall, Nathan
McCarthy, Mary

McCluskey, John A., Jr.
McCunn, Ruthanne Lum
McDermott, Alice
McDonald, Janet
McElroy, Colleen
McGrath, Thomas
McHale, Tom
McKay, Claude
McKnight, Reginald
McMillan, Terry
McNickle, William D'Arcy
McPherson, James Alan
Medina, Pablo
Mehta, Ved Parkash
MELUS
Mena, María Christina
Mencken, H. L.
Meriwether, Louise
Merkin, Daphne
Mexican American Autobiography
Mexican American Children's Literature
Mexican American Drama
Mexican American Gay Literature
Mexican American Lesbian Literature
Mexican American Poetry
Mexican American Stereotypes
Meyers, Bert [Bertrand]
Mezey, Robert
Middle Passage
Middle Passage, The
Miller, Arthur
Miller, E. Ethelbert
Miller, May
Millican, Arthenia Jackson Bates
Milner, Ron
Min, Anchee
Mirikitani, Janice
Mitchell, Loften
Mohr, Nicholasa
Momaday, Navarre Scott
Monardo, Anna
Montalvo, José
Moody, Anne

Moore, Opal
Mora, Pat
Moraga, Cherríe
Morales, Rosario
Mori, Toshio
Morrison, Toni
Moskowitz, Faye Stollman
Mosley, Walter
Moss, Howard
Mostwin, Danuta
Motley, Willard
Mourning Dove (Hum-Ishu-Ma;
   Christine Quintasket)
Mueller, Lisel
Mukherjee, Bharati
Mulatto
Mullen, Harryette
Multiculturalism
Mumbo Jumbo
Muñoz, Elías Miguel
Mura, David
Murayama, Milton
Murray, Albert
Murray, Pauli
Myers, Walter Dean
Nabokov, Vladimir
Nahai, Gina Barkhodar
Nair, Meera
Najarian, Peter
Narayan, Kirin
Native American Autobiography
Native American Creation Myths
Native American Drama
Native American Mythology
Native American Novel
Native American Oral Texts
Native American Oratory
Native American Poetry
Native American Reservation
Native American Stereotypes
Native Son
Nava, Michael
Navarro, Joe
Naylor, Gloria
Neal, Larry

Negritude
Nemerov, Howard
Neo-Slave Narrative
Neugeboren, Jay
New Negro
Newman, Lesléa
Ng, Fae Myenne
Ng, Mei
Nigam, Sanjay
Niggli, Josephina Maria
Niño, Raúl
Nishikawa, Lane
Nissenson, Hugh
No-No Boy
Norstog, Jon
Norwegian American Literature
Notes of a Native Son
Novak, Michael
Nugent, Richard Bruce
Nuyorican
Nyburg, Sidney Lauer
Nye, Naomi Shihab
Occom, Samson
O'Connor, Edwin
O'Connor, Mary Flannery
Odets, Clifford
O'Hara, Frank
Okada, John
Okita, Dwight
Olsen, Tillie
Olson, Charles
O'Neill, Eugene Gladstone
Ong, Han
Oppen, George
Oppenheimer, Joel Lester
Ornitz, Samuel
Ortiz, Simon J.
Ortiz Cofer, Judith
Ortiz Taylor, Sheila
Osbey, Brenda Marie
Ostriker, Alicia
Owens, Louis
Ozick, Cynthia
Pakistani American Literature. *See*
   South Asian American Literature

Paley, Grace
Pan-Africanism
Paradise
Paredes, Américo
Parini, Jay
Parker, Dorothy (Rothschild)
Parker, Gwendoyn M.
Parks, Gordon
Parks, Rosa
Parks, Suzan-Lori
Passing
Pedagogy and U.S. Ethnic
    Literatures
Pellowski, Anne
Perdomo, Willie
Perelman, S. J.
Pérez Firmat, Gustavo
Peter Blue Cloud
Peterson, Louis Stamford
Petry, Ann
Picano, Felice
Piercy, Marge
Pietri, Pedro
Pietrzyk, Leslie
Pillin, William
Pineda, Cecile
Piñero, Miguel
Plumpp, Sterling
Pocahontas [Matoaka]
Polish American Literature in
    Polish
Polish American Novel
Polish American (Literary)
    Stereotypes
Polish Émigré Writers in the United
    States
Polite, Carlene Hatcher
Ponce, Mary Helen
Portuguese American Literature
Postcolonialism and U.S. Ethnic
    Literatures
Potok, Chaim
Potter, Eliza
Powers, James Earl
Preciado Martin, Patricia

Prida, Dolores
Prince, Mary
Prince, Nancy Gardner
Prose, Francine
Puerto Rican American
    Autobiography
Puerto Rican American Drama
Puerto Rican American Gay
    Literature
Puerto Rican American Lesbian
    Literature
Puerto Rican American Novel
Puerto Rican American Poetry
Puerto Rican Stereotypes
Puzo, Mario
Quin, Mike
Quiñonez, Naomi Helena
Race
Rachlin, Nahid
Racism
Rahman, Aishah
Rahv, Philip
Raisin in the Sun, A
Rakosi, Carl
Rama Rau, Santha
Ramos, Luis Arturo
Ramos, Manuel
Randall, Dudley
Randall, Margaret
Raphael, Lev
Ray A. Young Bear
Rechy, John
Redding, J. Saunders
Reed, Ishmael
Reich, Tova Rachel
Revard, Carter
Reyes, Guillermo
Reznikoff, Charles
Rice, Elmer
Rice, Sarah Webb
Rich, Adrienne Cecile
Richardson, Willis
Ridge, John Rollin [Yellow Bird]
Riggs, Lynn
Rishel, Mary Ann Malinchak

Rivera, Edward
Rivera, José
Rivera, Tomás
Robbins, Doren Gurstein
Rodgers, Carolyn
Rodríguez, Joe D.
Rodríguez, Luis J.
Rodriguez, Richard
Rodríguez Matos, Carlos A.
Roethke, Theodore
Rogers, Will
Roiphe, Anne Richardson
Rolfe, Edwin
Rølvaag, Ole Edvart
Rosca, Ninotchka
Rose, Wendy
Rosen, Norma
Rosenfeld, Isaac
Rossi, Agnes
Rosten, Leo
Roth, Henry
Roth, Philip
Rothenberg, Jerome
Rudman, Mark
Ruiz, Ronald
Ruiz de Burton, Maria Amparo
Rukeyser, Muriel
Russian American Literature
Sáenz, Benjamin Alire
Said, Edward W.
Saiki, Patsy Sumie
Saint, Assotto [Yves François Lubin]
Sakamoto, Edward
Salaam, Kalamu ya
Salinas, Luis Omar
Salinger, J. D.
Sanchez, Sonia
Sandburg, Carl
Sanders, Dori
Sanford, John
Santiago, Danny [Daniel James]
Santos, Bienvenido N.
Sapia, Yvonne V.
Sapphire

Saracino, Mary
Saroyan, William [Sirak Goryan]
Schaeffer, Susan Fromberg
Schoolcraft, Jane Johnston
Schulberg, Budd
Schuyler, George Samuel
Schwartz, Delmore
Schwerner, Armand
Scott-Heron, Gil
Seacole, Mary
Seattle. *See* Chief Seattle
Segal, Lore [Groszmann]
Seguín, Juan N.
Séjour, Victor
Senna, Danzy
Sephardic Literature
Shakir, Evelyn
Shamsie, Kamila
Shange, Ntozake
Shankar, S.
Shapiro, Alan
Shapiro, David
Shapiro, Karl
Shaw, Irwin
Shea, Suzanne Strempek
Shepherd, Reginald
Sherman, Martin
Shockley, Ann Allen
Sholevar, Bahman
Shulman, Alix Kates
Signifying
Šilbajoris, Rimvydas
Silko, Leslie Marmon
Simon, Kate
Simon, Neil
Simpson, Louis
Sinclair, Jo (Ruth Seid)
Singer, Isaac Bashevis
Sklarew, Myra
Slave Narrative. *See* African American Slave Narrative
Slavery
Slesinger, Tess
Slovak American Literature
Slovene American Literature

Smith, Anna Deavere
Smith, Barbara
Sone, Monica
Song, Cathy
Song of Solomon
Sontag, Susan
Sopranos, The
Sorrentino, Gilbert
Soto, Gary
Souls of Black Folk, The
South Asian American Film
South Asian American Literature
Spence, Eulalie
Spencer, Anne
Spewack, Bella Cohen
Spiegelman, Art
Spirituals
Stein, Gertrude
Stern, Elizabeth Gertrude Levin
Stern, Gerald
Stewart, Maria W.
Strand, Mark
Street, The
Suárez, Mario
Suarez, Virgil
Suleri Goodyear, Sara
Sundaresan, Indu
Suri, Manil
Swados, Elizabeth
Swedish American Literature
Syrkin, Marie
Sze, Arthur
Sze, Mai-mai
Tafolla, Carmen
Talented Tenth, The
Talese, Gay
Tan, Amy
Tapahonso, Luci
Tar Baby
Tarn, Nathaniel
Tate, Claudia
Taylor, Mildred
Tea Cake
Tenorio, Arthur
Tharoor, Shashi

Their Eyes Were Watching God
Thelwell, Michael Miles
Thomas, Bigger
Thomas, Joyce Carol
Thomas, Lorenzo
Thomas, Piri
Thurman, Wallace
Tillman, Katherine Davis Chapman
Tolson, Melvin Beaunorus
Tomasi, Mari
Toole, John Kennedy
Toomer, Jean
Torres, Daniel
Torres, Omar
Touré, Askia M.
Toussaint L'Ouverture, François
  Dominique
Tracks
Trickster, African American
Trickster, Native American
Trilling, Lionel
Troupe, Quincy Thomas, Jr.
Truth, Sojourner
Tubman, Harriet
Turkish American Literature
Turner, Nat
Ty-Casper, Linda
Uchida, Yoshiko
Uhry, Alfred
Umpierre, Luz María
Underground Railroad
Up from Slavery
Uris, Leon Marcus
Urrea, Luis Alberto
Uyemoto, Holly
Valdés, Gina
Valdez, Luis
Valerio, Anthony
Vallejo, Mariano Guadalupe
Vando, Gloria
Vásquez, Richard
Vaz, Katherine
Vazirani, Reetika
Véa, Alfredo, Jr.
Verghese, Abraham

Vietnamese American Literature
Villa, José García
Villarreal, José Antonio
Villaseñor, Victor
Viramontes, Helena María
Viscusi, Robert
Vizenor, Gerald
Wade-Gayles, Gloria
Waldo, Octavia
Walker, Alice
Walker, David
Walker, Margaret
Walker, Rebecca Leventhal
Wallant, Edward Lewis
Walrond, Eric
Walter, Mildred Pitts
Walters, Anna Lee
Ward, Douglas Turner
Washington, Booker T.
Wasserstein, Wendy
Way to Rainy Mountain, The
Webb, Frank J.
Weidman, Jerome
Welch, James
Wells-Barnett, Ida B.
Wesley, Richard
West, Cornel
West, Dorothy
West, Nathanael
Wheatley, Phillis
Whitehead, Colson
Whiteness
Whitfield, James Monroe
Whitman, Albery Allson
Whitman, Ruth
Wideman, John Edgar
Wilkes, Paul
Williams, Crystal
Williams, John A.
Williams, Samm-Art
Williams, Sherley Anne

Wilson, August
Wilson, Harriet E.
Winnemucca, Sarah
Winwar, Frances
Wist, Johannes B.
Wolf, Emma
Wolfert, Ira
Womack, Craig S.
*Woman Warrior: Memoirs of a
    Girlhood among Ghosts, The*
Womanism
Women of Brewster Place, The
Wong, Jade Snow
Wong, Nellie
Woo, Merle
Wouk, Herman
Wounded Knee
Wright, Richard
Wright, Sarah Elizabeth
Wynter, Sylvia
Yamada, Mitsuye
Yamamoto, Hisaye
Yamanaka, Lois-Ann
Yamashita, Karen Tei
Yamauchi, Wakako
Yankowitz, Susan
Yau, John
Yep, Laurence
Yerby, Frank
Yew, Chay
Yezierska, Anzia
Yglesias, Helen
Yiddish Literature
Young, Al
Younger, Walter Lee
Yurick, Sol
Zamora, Bernice
Zarrin, Ali
Zitkala-Ša
Zolynas, Al
Zukofsky, Louis

Guide to Related Topics

African American Literature
Abolition
Adams, Elizabeth Laura
African American Autobiography
African American Biography
African American Children's
Literature
African American Critical Theory
African American Detective Fiction
African American Drama
African American Film
African American Folklore
African American Gay Literature
African American Lesbian
Literature
African American Musicals
African American Novel
African American Poetry
African American Pulp Fiction
African American Science Fiction
African American Slave Narrative
African American Short Story
African American Stereotypes
African American Travel Narrative

African American Young Adult
Literature
Afrocentricity
Albert, Octavia Victoria Rogers
Allen, Richard
Allen, Samuel W.
Amanuensis
Angelou, Maya
Ansa, Tina McElroy
Attaway, William
Austin, Doris Jean
Autobiography of Malcolm X, The
Autobiography of Miss Jane Pittman,
The
Baker, Houston A., Jr.
Baker, Nikki
Baldwin, James
Bambara, Toni Cade
Baraka, Amiri
Barrax, Gerald
Beckham, Barry
Bell, James Madison
Beloved
Belton, Don

Bennett, Gwendolyn
Bennett, Hal
Bibb, Henry
Black Arts Movement
Black Boy
Black Nationalism
Blues, The
The Bluest Eye
Bonner, Marita Odette
Bontemps, Arna
Bradley, David
Braithwaite, William Stanley
Brer Rabbit
Broadside Press
Brooks, Gwendolyn
Brown, Cecil M.
Brown, Claude
Brown, Frank London
Brown Girl, Brownstones
Brown, John
Brown, Linda Beatrice
Brown, Sterling
Bullins, Ed
Butler, Octavia Estelle
Caldwell, Ben
Cane
Chase-Riboud, Barbara
Chesnutt, Charles Waddell
Childress, Alice
Christian, Barbara
Civil Rights Movement
Clarke, Cheryl
Cleage, Pearl
Cleaver, (Leroy) Eldridge
Clifton, Lucille
Cobb, Ned
Coleman, Wanda
Collins, Kathleen Conwell
Color Purple, The
Colored Museum, The
Colter Cyrus
Confessions of Nat Turner, The
Conjure
Cooper, Anna Julia
Cooper, J. (Joan) California

Cortez, Jayne
Crafts, Hannah
Crawford, Janie
Cullen, Countee
Danner, Margaret Esse
davenport, doris
Davis, Angela Yvonne
Davis, Frank Marshall
Davis, Ossie
Dee, Ruby
Delaney, Lucy Ann
Delany, Martin Robinson
Delany, Samuel R.
Demby, William E.
Dent, Tom [Thomas Covington Dent]
Derricotte, Toi
Dixon, Melvin
Dodson, Owen Vincent
Douglass, Frederick
Dove, Rita
Du Bois, Shirley Graham
Du Bois, W. E. B.
Dumas, Henry
Dunbar, Paul Laurence
Dunbar-Nelson, Alice
Duplechan, Larry
Dutchman
Eady, Cornelius
Elaw, Zilpha
Elder, Lonne, III
Ellis, Trey
Ellison, Ralph Waldo
Equiano, Olaudah
Evans, Mari
Everett, Percival L.
Fair, Ronald L.
Fauset, Jessie Redmon
Fences
Fields, Julia
Fisher, Rudolph
Flowers, A. R.
Foote, Julia A. J.
Franklin, J. E.
Gaines, Ernest J.

Gaines, Patrice
Garvey, Marcus
Gates, Henry Louis, Jr.
Giovanni, Nikki
Golden, Marita
Gomez, Jewelle
Greenlee, Sam
Griggs, Sutton Elbert
Grimké, Angelina Weld
Gunn, Bill
Haley, Alex
Hamilton, Virginia
Hammon, Jupiter
Hansberry, Lorraine
Hansen, Joyce
Hardy, James Earl
Harlem Renaissance
Harper, Frances Ellen Watkins
Harper, Michael S.
Harris, E. Lynn
Harrison, Juanita
Hayden, Robert
Haynes, Lemuel
Heard, Nathan C.
Hemphill, Essex
Henderson, George Wylie
Henson, Josiah
Himes, Chester Bomar
hooks, bell
Horton, George Moses
Hughes, Langston
Hurston, Zora Neale
I Know Why the Caged Bird Sings
Invisible Man
Jackson, Angela
Jackson, Elaine
Jacobs, Harriet
Jazz
Jeffers, Lance
Jim Crow
Joans, Theodore "Ted"
Johnson, Charles Richard
Johnson, Helene
Johnson, James Weldon
Jones, Edward P.

Jones, Gayl
Jordan, June
Kaufman, Bob
Keckley, Elizabeth
Kelley, Samuel L.
Kelley, William Melvin
Kenan, Randall
Kennedy, Adrienne
Killens, John Oliver
King, Martin Luther, Jr.
King, Woodie, Jr.
Knight, Ethridge
Komunyakaa, Yusef
Larsen, Nella
Lattany, Kristin [Hunter]
Lee, Andrea
Lee, Jarena
Lester, Julius
Locke, Alain
Lorde, Audre
Mackey, Nathaniel
Madgett, Naomi Long
Madhubuti, Haki R.
Major, Clarence
Malcolm X [aka Malcolm Little; Islamic name El-Hajj Malik El-Shabazz]
Marrant, John
Marvin X
McBride, James
McCall, Nathan
McCluskey, John A., Jr.
McDonald, Janet
McElroy, Colleen
McKay, Claude
McKnight, Reginald
McMillan, Terry
McPherson, James Alan
Meriwether, Louise
Middle Passage
Middle Passage, The
Miller, E. Ethelbert
Miller, May
Millican, Arthenia Jackson Bates
Milner, Ron

Mitchell, Lofton
Moody, Anne
Moore, Opal
Morrison, Toni
Mosley, Walter
Motley, Willard
Mulatto
Mullen, Harryette
Mumbo Jumbo
Murray, Albert
Murray, Pauli
Myers, Walter Dean
Native Son
Naylor, Gloria
Neal, Larry
Negritude
Neo-Slave Narrative
New Negro
Notes of a Native Son
Nugent, Richard Bruce
Osbey, Brenda Marie
Pan-Africanism
Paradise
Parker, Gwendolyn M.
Parks, Gordon
Parks, Rosa
Parks, Suzan-Lori
Passing
Peterson, Louis Stanford
Petry, Ann
Plumpp, Sterling
Polite, Carlene Hatcher
Potter, Eliza
Prince, Mary
Prince, Nancy Gardner
Rahman, Aishah
Raisin in the Sun, A
Randall, Dudley
Redding, J. Saunders
Reed, Ishmael
Rice, Sarah Webb
Richardson, Willis
Rodgers, Carolyn
Saint, Assotto (Yves François
   Lubin)

Salaam, Kalamu ya
Sanchez, Sonia
Sanders, Dori
Sapphire
Schuyler, George Samuel
Scott-Heron, Gil
Seacole, Mary
Séjour, Victor
Senna, Danzy
Shange, Ntozake
Shepherd, Reginald
Shockley, Ann Allen
Signifying
Slavery
Smith, Anna Deavere
Smith, Barbara
Song of Solomon
Souls of Black Folk, The
Spence, Eulalie
Spencer, Ann
Spirituals
Stewart, Maria W.
Street, The
Talented Tenth, The
Tar Baby
Tate, Claudia
Taylor, Mildred
Tea Cake
Their Eyes Were Watching God
Thomas, Bigger
Thomas, Joyce Carol
Thomas, Lorenzo
Thurman, Wallace
Tillman, Katherine Davis Chapman
Tolson, Melvin Beaunorus
Toomer, Jean
Touré, Askia M.
Toussaint L'Ouverture, François
   Dominique
Trickster, African American
Troupe, Quincy Thomas, Jr.
Truth, Sojourner
Tubman, Harriet
Turner, Nat
Underground Railroad

Up from Slavery
Wade-Gayles, Gloria
Walker, Alice
Walker, David
Walker, Margaret
Walker, Rebecca Leventhal
Walrond, Eric
Walter, Mildred Pitts
Ward, Douglas Turner
Washington, Booker T.
Webb, Frank J.
Wells-Barnett, Ida B.
Wesley, Richard
West, Cornel
West, Dorothy
Wheatley, Phillis
Whitehead, Colson
Whitfield, James Monroe
Whitman, Albery Allson
Wideman, John Edgar
Williams, Crystal
Williams, John A.
Williams, Samm-Art
Williams, Sherley Ann
Wilson, August
Wilson, Harriet E.
Womanism
Women of Brewster Place, The
Wright, Richard
Wright, Sarah Elizabeth
Yerby, Frank
Young, Al
Younger, Walter Lee

Afghan American Literature
Hosseini, Khaled

Amish American Literature
Amish American Literature

Arab American Literature
Abinader, Elmaz
Abu Jabar, Diana
Alameddine, Rabih
Arab American Autobiography

Arab American Novel
Arab American Poetry
Arab American Stereotypes
Blatty, William Peter
Bourjaily, Vance
Gibran, Gibran Khalil
Hazo, Samuel J.
Kadi, Joanna
Majaj, Lisa Suhair
Nye, Naomi Shihab
Said, Edward W.
Shakir, Evelyn

Armenian American Literature
Alishan, Leonardo
Armenian American Literature
Armenian Genocide
Der Hovanessian, Diana
Hagopian, Richard
Najarian, Peter
Saroyan, William [Sirak Goryan]

Basque American Literature
Basque American Literature
Laxalt, Robert

Caribbean American (Anglophone) Literature
Caribbean (Anglophone) American Autobiography
Caribbean (Anglophone) American Novel
Caribbean (Anglophone) American Poetry
Cliff, Michelle
Collins, Merle
Danticat, Edwidge
Guy, Rosa Cuthbert
Kincaid, Jamaica
Marshall, Paule
McKay, Claude
Saint, Assotto [Yves François Lubin]
Thelwell, Michael Miles
Wynter, Sylvia

Carpatho-Rusyn American Literature
Carpatho-Rusyn Literature
Jason, Sonya

Chilean American Literature
Castedo, Elena
Reyes, Guillermo

Chinese American Literature
Aiiieeeee! An Anthology of Asian
    American Writers
Angel Island
Berssenbrugge, Mei-Mei
Chan, Jeffery Paul
Chang, Diana
Chee, Alexander
Chin, Frank
Chin, Marilyn Mei Ling
Chinese American Autobiography
Chinese American Drama
Chinese American Novel
Chinese American Poetry
Chinese American Stereotypes
Chinese Exclusion Act
Chong, Ping
Chu, Louis
Eat a Bowl of Tea
Eaton, Edith Maude
Eaton, Winnifred
Ha Jin
Hua, Chuang
Jen, Gish [Lillian C. Jen]
Joy Luck Club, The
Kingston, Maxine Hong
Kwong, Dan
Lee, C. Y. (Chin Yang)
Lee, Cherylene
Lee, Gus
Lee, Li-Young
Lim, Shirley Geok-lin
Liu, Aimee
Lord, Betty Bao
Louie, David Wong
Lowe, Pardee

M. Butterfly
McCunn, Ruthanne Lum
Min, Anchee
Ng, Fae Myenne
Ng, Mei
Sze, Arthur
Sze, Mai-mai
Tan, Amy
The Woman Warrior: Memoirs of a
    Girlhood among Ghosts, The
Wong, Jade Snow
Wong, Nellie
Woo, Merle
Yau, John
Yep, Laurence
Yew, Chay

Cuban American Literature
Arenas, Reinaldo
Cabrera Infante, Guillermo
Campo, Rafael
Cruz, Nilo
Cuban American Autobiography
Cuban American Novel
Cuban American Poetry
Engle, Margarite
Fernandez, Roberto G.
Fornes, Maria Irene
Fraxedas, J. Joaquin
García, Cristina
Hijuelos, Oscar
Martí, José
Medina, Pablo
Muñoz, Elías Miguel
Pérez Firmat, Gustavo
Prida, Dolores
Suarez, Virgil
Torres, Omar

Czech American Literature
Chmelka, Donald F.
Czech American Literature

Dominican American Literature
Agosín, Marjorie

Alvarez, Julia
Díaz, Junot
Dominican American Novel
Dominican American Poetry
Espaillat, Rhina [Polonia]
Gonzalez, Ray

Filipino American Literature
America Is in the Heart
Bacho, Peter
Brainard, Cecilia Manguerra
Bulosan, Carlos
Cerenio, Virginia
Dizon, Louella
Faigao-Hall, Linda
Filipino American Novel
Filipino American Poetry
Gonzalez, N. V. M.
Hagedorn, Jessica Tarahata
Ong, Han
Rosca, Ninotchka
Santos, Bienvenido N.
Ty-Casper, Linda
Villa, José García

Finnish American Literature
Finnish American Literature
Franco American Literature
Crèvecouer, J. Hector St. John de
Forché, Carolyn
Franco American Literature
Kerouac, Jack

German American Literature
Dreiser, Theodore
Geisel, Theodor Seuss ["Dr. Seuss"]
German American Literature
Hegi, Ursula
Mencken, H. L.
Mueller, Lisel
Roethke, Theodore

Greek American Literature
Broumas, Olga
Catacalos, Rosemary

Eleni
Eugenides, Jeffrey
Gage, Nicholas
Greek American Autobiography
Greek American Fiction
Greek American Poetry

Hawaiian Literature
Bamboo Ridge
Chock, Eric
Hawai'i Literature
Hawaiian Literature
Holt, John Dominis, IV
Hongo, Garrett Kaoru
Lum, Darrel H. Y.
Lum, Wing Tek
Miyamoto, Kazuo
Murayama, Milton
Saiki, Patsy Sumie
Sakamoto, Edward
Song, Cathy
Yamanaka, Lois-Ann

Iranian American Literature
Asayesh, Gelareh
Iranian American Literature
Nahai, Gina Barkhodar
Rachlin, Nahid
Sholevar, Bahman
Zarrin, Ali

Irish American Literature
Breslin, Jimmy
Curran, Mary Doyle
Dunne, Finley Peter
Farrell, James T.
Fitzgerald, F. Scott
Flaherty, Joe
Flanagan, Thomas
Gilgun, John
Gordon, Mary
Hamill, Pete
Irish American Autobiography
Irish American Drama
Irish American Novel

Kennedy, William
McCarthy, Mary
McDermott, Alice
McGrath, Thomas
McHale, Tom
O'Connor, Edwin
O'Connor, Mary Flannery
O'Hara, Frank
O'Neill, Eugene Gladstone
Powers, James Earl
Quin, Mike
Toole, John Kennedy

Italian American Literature
Addonizio, Kim
Ardizzone, Anthony
Barolini, Helen
Barresi, Dorothy
Bernardi, Adria
Bryant, Dorothy
Bumbalo, Victor
Calcagno, Anne
Caponegro, Mary
Capotorto, Rosette
Cappello, Mary
Cavello, Diana
Ciresi, Rita
Corso, Gregory Nunzio
Covino, Peter
DeLillo, Don
DeRosa, Tina
DeSalvo, Louise
di Donato, Pietro
di Prima, Diana
Domini, John
Fante, John
Ferro, Robert
Gambone, Philip
Gardaphé, Fred L.
Giardina, Denise
Gillan, Maria Mazziotti
Gioia, Dana
Gioseffi, Daniela
Giovanitti, Arturo
Giunta, Edvige

Godfather, The
Italian American Autobiography
Italian American Film
Italian American Gay Literature
Italian American Humor
Italian American Lesbian Literature
Italian American Novel
Italian American Poetry
Italian American Stereotypes
La Puma, Salvatore
Lentricchia, Frank
Manfredi, Renée
Mangione, Jerre (Gerlando)
Marotta, Kenny
Maso, Carole
Mazza, Cris
Monardo, Anna
Parini, Jay
Picano, Felice
Puzo, Mario
Rossi, Agnes
Saracino, Mary
Sopranos, The
Sorrentino, Gilbert
Talese, Gay
Tomasi, Mary
Valerio, Anthony
Viscusi, Robert
Waldo, Octavia
Winwar, Frances

Japanese American Literature
Gotanda, Philip
Houston, Jeanne (Toyo) Wakatsuki
Inada, Lawson Fusao
Internment
Japanese American Autobiography
Japanese American Novel
Kadohata, Cynthia
Mirikitani, Janice
Mori, Toshio
Mura, David
Nishikawa, Lane
No-No Boy
Okada, John

Okita, Dwight
Sone, Monica
Uchida, Yoshiko
Uyemoto, Holly
Yamada, Mitsuye
Yamamoto, Hisaye
Yamashita, Karen Tei
Yamauchi, Wakako

Jewish American Literature
Abish, Walter
Acker, Kathy
Agosín, Marjorie
Algren Nelson
Alkalay-Gut, Karen
Allen, Woody
Antin, Mary
Apple, Max
Asimov, Isaac
Auster, Paul
Behrman, S. N.
Bell, Marvin
Bellow, Saul
Bernstein, Charles
Berryman, John
Bessie, Alvah
Bloom, Harold Irving
Bodenheim, Maxwell
Broner, E(sther) M(asserman)
Brown, Rosellen
Budy, Andrea Hollander
Bukiet, Melvin Jules
Burnshaw, Stanley
Cahan, Abraham
Calisher, Hortense
Calof, Rachel Bella Kahn
Chabon, Michael
Chernin, Kim
Cohen, Sarah Blacher
Comden and Green
Dahlberg, Edward
Dame, Enid
Doctorow, E. L.
Elkin, Stanley
Elman, Richard M.

Endore, Guy
Englander, Nathan
Epstein, Joseph
Epstein, Leslie
Espinosa, María
Falk, Marcia
Fast, Howard
Faust, Irvin
Fearing, Kenneth
Federman, Raymond
Feinberg, David B.
Feldman, Irving
Ferber, Edna
Fiedler, Leslie
Field, Edward
Fierstein, Harvey Forbes
Finkelstein, Norman
Frank, Waldo
Freeman, Joseph
Fried, Emanuel
Friedman, Bruce Jay
Friedman, Stanford
Fries, Kenny
Fuchs, Daniel
Funaroff, Sol
Gelbart, Larry
Gerber, Merrill Joan
Ginsberg, Allen
Glickman, Gary
Glück, Louise
Glück, Robert
Gold, Herbert
Gold, Michael
Goldreich, Gloria
Goldstein, Rebecca
Goodman, Allegra
Graham, Jorie
Green, Gerald
Greenberg, Joanne [Goldenberg]
Grossman, Allen
Halper, Albert
Hart, Moss
Helprin, Mark
Hecht, Anthony
Hecht, Ben

Heller, Joseph
Heller, Michael
Hellman, Lillian
Herron, Carolivia
Hershman, Marcie
Hirsch, Edward
Hobson, Laura Z.
Hoffman, Eva Wydra
Hollander, John
Holocaust, The
Holocaust Narratives
Howard, Richard
Howe, Irving
Hurst, Fannie
Ignatow, David
Jaffe, Daniel M.
Jerome, V. J. [Isaac Jerome
    Romaine]
Jewish American Autobiography
Jewish American Gay
    Literature
Jewish American Lesbian
    Literature
Jewish American Musicals
Jewish American Novel
Jewish American Poetry
Jewish American Stereotypes
Jewish American Theater
Jong, Erica
Kaplan, Johanna
Karmel, Ilona
Katz, Judith
Kaufman, George Simon
Kazin, Alfred
Kessler, Milton
Kimmelman, Burt
Klein, Abraham Moses
Klepfisz, Irena
Koch, Kenneth
Koestenbaum, Wayne
Konecky, Edith
Kopit, Arthur
Kostelanetz, Richard Cory
Kramer, Aaron
Kramer, Larry

Kumin, Maxine
Kunitz, Stanley
Kushner, Tony
Lapine, James
Laurents, Arthur
Lawson, John Howard
Lazarus, Emma
Leavitt, David
Lebow, Barbara
Lester, Julius
Levertov, Denise
Levin, Meyer
Levine, Philip
Lifshin, Lyn
Lopate, Phillip
Lowenfels, Walter
Lumpkin, Grace
Mailer, Norman
Malamud, Bernard
Maltz, Albert
Mamet, David
Mandelbaum, Allen
Mann, Emily
Markfield, Wallace
Merkin, Daphne
Meyers, Bert [Bertrand]
Mezey, Robert
Miller, Arthur
Moskowitz, Faye Stollman
Moss, Howard
Nemerov, Howard
Neugebaren, Jay
Newman, Lesléa
Nissenson, Hugh
Nyburg, Sidney Lauer
Odets, Clifford
Olsen, Tillie
Oppen, George
Oppenheimer, Joel Lester
Ornitz, Samuel
Ostriker, Alicia
Ozick, Cynthia
Paley, Grace
Parker, Dorothy (Rothschild)
Perelman, S. J.

Piercy, Marge
Pillin, William
Potok, Chaim
Prose, Francine
Rahv, Philip
Rakosi, Carl
Randall, Margaret
Raphael, Lev
Reich, Tova Rachel
Reznikoff, Charles
Rice, Elmer
Rich, Adrienne Cecile
Robbins, Doren Gurstein
Roiphe, Ann Richardson
Rolfe, Edwin
Rosen, Norma
Rosenfeld, Isaac
Rosten, Leo
Roth, Henry
Roth, Philip
Rothenberg, Jerome
Rudman, Mark
Rukeyser, Muriel
Salinger, J. D.
Sanford, John
Schaeffer, Susan Fromberg
Schulberg, Budd
Schwartz, Delmore
Schwerner, Armand
Segal, Lore [Groszmann]
Sephardic Literature
Shapiro, Alan
Shapiro, David
Shapiro, Karl
Shaw, Irwin
Sherman, Martin
Shulman, Alix Kates
Simon, Kate
Simon, Neil
Simpson, Louis
Sinclair, Jo (Ruth Seid)
Singer, Isaac Bashevis
Sklarew, Myra
Slesinger, Tess
Sontag, Susan

Spewack, Bella Cohen
Speigelman, Art
Stein, Gertrude
Stern, Elizabeth Gertrude
   Levin
Stern, Gerald
Strand, Mark
Swados, Elizabeth
Syrkin, Marie
Tarn, Nathaniel
Trilling, Lionel
Uhry, Alfred
Uris, Leon Marcus
Wallant, Edward Lewis
Wasserstein, Wendy
Weidman, Jerome
West, Nathanael
Whitman, Ruth
Wolf, Emma
Wolfert, Ira
Wouk, Herman
Yankowitz, Susan
Yezierska, Anzia
Yglesias, Helen
Yiddish Literature
Yurick, Sol
Zukofsky, Louis

Korean American Literature
Cha, Theresa Hak Kyung
Choi, Sook Nyul
Choi, Susan
Hahn, Gloria
Kang, Younghill
Kim, Myung Mi
Kim, Richard E.
Kim, Yong Ik
Korean American Literature
Lee, Chang-rae

Lithuanian American Literature
Lithuanian American Literature
Mackus, Algimantas
Šilbajoris, Rimvydas
Zolynas, Al

Mexican American Literature
Acosta, Oscar Zeta
Alarcón, Francisco X.
Alfaro, Luis
Anaya, Rudolfo
Anzaldúa, Gloria E.
Arte Público Press
Baca, Jimmy Santiago
Bless Me, Ultima
Border Narratives
Born in East L.A.
Bruce-Novoa, Juan
Burk, Ronnie
Candelaria, Cordelia Chávez
Cano, Daniel
Cantú, Norma Elia
Castedo, Elena
Castillo, Ana
Castillo, Rafael C.
Catacalos, Rosemary
Cervantes, Lorna Dee
Chavez, Denise
Cisneros, Sandra
Culture Clash
Cumpian, Carlos
Curiel, Barbara Brinson
De Casas, Celso A.
Del Castillo, Ramón
Fernández, Roberta
Flores-Williams, Jason
Fontes, Montserrat
Galarza, Ernesto
Garcia, Richard
Garcia-Camarillo, Cecillio
Gómez-Peña, Guillermo
Gonzáles, Jovita
Gonzales-Berry, Erlinda
Hinojosa-Smith, Rolando
House on Mango Street, The
Hunger of Memory
Islas, Arturo, Jr.
Jimenez, Francisco
Limón, Graciela
López, Josefina
Martínez, Demetria

Mena, María Cristina
Mexican American Autobiography
Mexican American Children's
  Literature
Mexican American Drama
Mexican American Gay Literature
Mexican American Lesbian
  Literature
Mexican American Poetry
Mexican American Stereotypes
Montalvo, José
Mora, Pat
Moraga, Cherríe
Nava, Michael
Navarro, Joe
Niggli, Josephina Maria
Niño, Raúl
Ortiz Taylor, Sheila
Paredes, Américo
De la Peña, Terri
Pineda, Cecile
Ponce, Mary Helen
Preciado Martin, Patricia
Quiñonez, Naomi Helena
Ramos, Luis Arturo
Ramos, Manuel
Rechy, John
Rivera, Tomás
Rodrígues, Joe D.
Rodriguez, Richard
Rodríguez-Matos, Carlos A.
Ruiz, Ronald
Ruiz de Burton, Maria Amparo
Sáenz, Benjamin Alire
Salinas, Luis Omar
Santiago, Danny [Daniel James]
Seguín, Juan N.
Soto, Gary
Suárez, Mario
Tafolla, Carmen
Tenorio, Arthur
Urrea, Luis Amberto
Valdés, Gina
Valdez, Luis
Vallejo, Mariano Guadalupe

Vásquez, Richard
Véa, Alfredo, Jr.
Villarreal, José Antonio
Villaseñor, Victor
Viramontes, Helena María
Zamora, Bernice

Native American Literature
Alexie, Sherman Joseph, Jr.
Allen, Paula Gunn
American Indian Movement
Apess, William
Black Elk [Hehaka Sapa]
Blaeser, Kimberley M.
Boudinot, Elias
Bruchac, Joseph
Ceremony
Chief Seattle
Conley, Robert J.
Cook-Lynn, Elizabeth
Dorris, Michael
Eastman, Charles Ohiyesa
Erdrich, Louise
Glancy, Diane
Hale, Janet Campbell
Harjo, Joy
Henry, Gordon, Jr.
Highway, Tomson
Hogan, Linda
House Made of Dawn
Johnson, E. Pauline
    [Tekahionwake]
Kenny, Maurice
King, Thomas
Love Medicine
Luther Standing Bear
Mathews, John Joseph
McNickle, William D'Arcy
Momaday, Navarre Scott
Mourning Dove (Hum-Ishu-Ma;
    Christine Quintasket)
Native American
    Autobiography
Native American Creation
    Myths

Native American Drama
Native American Mythology
Native American Novel
Native American Oral Texts
Native American Oratory
Native American Poetry
Native American Reservation
Native American Stereotypes
Occom, Samson
Ortiz, Simon J.
Owens, Louis
Peter Blue Cloud
Pocahontas [Matoaka]
Ray A. Youngbear
Revard, Carter
Ridge, John Rollin [Yellow Bird]
Riggs, Lynn
Rogers, Will
Rose, Wendy
Schoolcraft, Jane Johnston
Silko, Leslie Marmon
Tapahonso, Luci
Tracks
Trickster, Native American
Vizenor, Gerald
Walters, Anna Lee
Way to Rainy Mountain, The
Welch, James
Winnemucca, Sarah
Womack, Craig S.
Wounded Knee
Zitkala-Ša

Norwegian American Literature
Ager, Waldemar
Boyesen, Hjalmar Hjorth
Buslett, Ole Amundsen
Dahl, Dorthea
Janson, Drude Krog
Janson, Kristofer
Johnson, Simon
Norstog, Jon
Norwegian American Literature
Rølvaag, Ole Edvart
Wist, Johannes B.

Polish American Literature
Bukoski, Anthony
Dybek, Stuart
Gildner, Gary
Janda, Victoria
Kubiak, Wanda
Kubicki, Jan
Mostwin, Danuta
Olson, Charles
Pellowski, Anne
Pietrzyk, Leslie
Polish American Literature in
    Polish
Polish American Novel
Polish American (Literary)
    Stereotypes
Polish Émigré Writers in the United
    States
Shea, Suzanne Strempek

Portuguese American Literature
Braga, Thomas J.
Gasper, Frank Xavier
Portuguese American Literature
Vaz, Katherine

Puerto Rican American Literature
Colon, Jesus
Cruz, Victor Hernández
De Burgos, Julia
Down These Mean Streets
Espada, Martin
Estevas, Sandra María
Figuero, José Angel
Hernández, David
Laviera, Tato
López Torregrosa, Luisita
Mohr, Nicholasa
Morales Levins, Aurora
Morales, Rosarío
Nuyorican
Ortiz Cofer, Judith
Perdomo, Willie
Pietri, Pedro
Piñero, Miguel

Puerto Rican American
    Autobiography
Puerto Rican American Drama
Puerto Rican American Gay
    Literature
Puerto Rican American Lesbian
    Literature
Puerto Rican American Novel
Puerto Rican American Poetry
Puerto Rican American
    Stereotypes
Rivera, Edward
Rivera, José
Sapia, Yvonne V.
Thomas, Piri
Torres, Daniel
Umpierre, Luz María
Vando, Gloria

Russian American Literature
Brodsky, Joseph (Iosif)
Nabakov, Vladimir
Russian American Literature

Slovak American Literature
Bell, Thomas
Laurence, Patricia Ondek
Novak, Michael
Rishel, Mary Ann Malinchak
Slovak American Literature
Wilkes, Paul

Slovene American Literature
Adamic, Louis
Slovene American Literature

South Asian American Literature
Alexander, Meena
Chandra, Sharat G. S.
Crasta, Richard / Avatar
    Prabhu
Divakaruni, Chitra Banerjee
Ganesan, Indira
Ghose, Zulfikar
Gawande, Atul

Hashmi, Alamgir
Hejmadi, Padma [Padma
    Perera]
Iyer, Pico
Jasmine
Kitchner, Bharti
Kumar, Amitava
Lahiri, Jhumpa
Lakshmi, Vijay
Mehta, Ved Parkash
Mukherjee, Bharati
Nair, Meera
Narayan, Kirin
Nigam, Sanjay
Rama Rau, Santha
Shamsie, Kamila
Shankar, S.
South Asian American Film
South Asian American Literature
Suleri Goodyear, Sara
Sundaresan, Indu
Suri, Manil
Tharoor, Shashi
Vazirani, Reetika
Verghese, Abraham

Swedish American Literature
Hill, Joe [Joel Emanuel Hägglund/
    Joseph Hillström]
Sandburg, Carl
Swedish American Literature

Turkish American Literature
Turkish American Literature

Vietnamese American Literature
Cao, Lan
Donohue, Maura Nguyen
Hayslip, Phung Le Ly
lê thi diem thúy
Vietnamese American Literature

General Topics
Anti-Semitism
Assimilation
Bilingualism
Canon
Colonialism and U.S. Ethnic
    Literatures
Diaspora
Ellis Island
Ethnicity
Eurocentrism
Feminism and U.S. Ethnic
    Literatures
*Heath Anthology of American
    Literature, The*
Identity
Immigration
Liminality
MELUS
Multiculturalism
Pedagogy and U.S. Ethnic
    Literatures
Postcolonialism and U.S. Ethnic
    Literatures
Race
Racism
Whiteness

Preface

Certain foundational texts, such as encyclopedias, sourcebooks, and dictionaries, are indispensable for legitimizing as well as institutionalizing any distinct and emergent field of knowledge. Such books collect, organize, and present primary data about the subject. By doing so, they help define the new discipline, create a necessary knowledge base, and provide an epistemological framework that can be shared by students and scholars in the field. They serve as instruments of basic research and as foundations for advanced inquiry; they facilitate dialogue within and across disciplines. Such works, therefore, are vital for the relatively young field of multiethnic literary studies. Those of us who are committed to this field must continue to consolidate its gains, expand its knowledge base, and claim its intellectual grounds. This illustrated, five-volume *The Greenwood Encyclopedia of Multiethnic American Literature* is intended as a major contribution to that ongoing project.

This reference work is unique in its scope. Though there are quite a few sourcebooks and reference volumes devoted to individual ethnic traditions—such as African American, Native American, and Jewish American literatures—this multivolume *Encyclopedia* is the first reference work that seeks to offer a comprehensive introduction to a spectacularly diverse range of ethnic American writing. The more than 1100 entries in the five volumes address topics as diverse as Arab American poetry, Italian American autobiography, Mexican American lesbian narratives, the Polish American novel, Turkish American writing, and Vietnamese American literature. A large majority of the entries—about one thousand of them—are on individual authors. Some of those authors are major figures with international name recognition; others are lesser-known or emerging new artists. These author entries range in length from about five hundred to two thousand words, depending on the relative importance of the writers. In the considerably daunting task of choosing the approximately one thousand authors who are included in this *Encyclopedia,* I was ably guided by the eight advisory board members who have expertise in a wide range of ethnic American literary traditions. Their guidance is also reflected in the inclusion of myriad other topics, such as the several entries on various ethnic stereotypes (e.g., Chinese American Stereotypes); individual seminal texts (e.g., Ralph Ellison's *Invisible Man,* Sandra Cisneros's *The House on Mango Street,* N. Scott Momaday's *The Way to Rainy Mountain*); place names that are prominent in ethnic histories (e.g., Wounded Knee, Ellis Island); major historical events (e.g., the Armenian Genocide, the Holocaust); key pieces of legislation affecting ethnic populations (e.g., Chinese Exclusion Act); and general topics that have compelling relevance to our deeper understanding of ethnic American experiences (e.g., Assimilation, Civil Rights Movement, Colonialism, Ethnicity, Feminism, Identity, Immigration, Multiculturalism, Postcolonialism).

Yet the central objective of this *Encyclopedia* is not to define or redefine an ethnic literary canon; its primary goal is to provide reliable, thorough, and up-to-date information on hundreds of ethnic authors, texts, topics, and traditions. Advanced scholars will find it a useful research tool. Its user-friendly style, format, and level of complexity, however, make it accessible to a much broader audience that includes high school students and their teachers, community college as well as undergraduate students, and intellectually curious general readers and patrons of public libraries. For example, if you are a scholar researching the subgenre of neo-slave narratives that have proliferated in recent African American writing, you will find here a succinct entry on that topic. If, on the other hand, you are a student researching the works of an individual author, such as Maxine Hong Kingston or Bernard Malamud, you will be able to locate in this *Encyclopedia* concisely crafted entries on their lives and works; those entries will also direct you to others in this *Encyclopedia* that you will find useful. Similarly, if you are an instructor interested in introducing your students to Japanese American autobiography or Cuban American writing, you will find not only lively overviews of those specific subjects but also useful entries on a range of closely related topics. And if you are a general reader curious about Norwegian American literature or Native American creation myths or Italian American film or Puerto Rican American stereotypes or the literature of Hawai'i, you will find in this *Encyclopedia* thoughtful and accessible commentaries on those subjects.

Accessibility, in fact, is a salient feature of this reference work: I have made every effort to make it as user-friendly as possible. The entries, for example, are arranged in alphabetical order. If you have a particular author or topic in mind, you may go directly to that entry. You may also consult the two elaborate tables of contents: the first one lists all entries alphabetically; the second lists them, alphabetically, under various topical categories. You will also find the index useful. It is located at the end of Volume 5 of the *Encyclopedia*. Look under Leslie Marmon Silko, for instance, to find the main entry for that author, and to find any other substantive discussion of her in the book.

Furthermore, the entries themselves are designed to facilitate cross-referencing. For example, whenever an author who is also the subject of an entry is first mentioned within another entry, his or her name appears in bold. Similarly, whenever a topic or concept (e.g., Civil Rights Movement, Immigration, Race) on which there is a separate entry is first mentioned within another entry, the words appear in bold. Many entries also conclude with the "*see also*" feature: the entry on James Baldwin, for example, invites the reader to see also the longer entry African American Novel to gain an understanding of Baldwin's significance in a wider context.

Over three hundred scholars have contributed to this *Encyclopedia,* so the entries reflect a wide spectrum of styles, perspectives, and approaches. However, the entries themselves generally follow a standard format. An entry on an individual author, for example, begins with the author's name (last name first), followed parenthetically by the year of birth and, when applicable, the year of death. The opening line is always a phrase that identifies the author's ethnic background and the genre(s) in which he or she has published. The rest of the entry offers a judicious discussion of the author's major works and themes. When the title of a text by the author is first mentioned, its year of publication is indicated parenthetically. If brief quotations from primary sources are introduced, page numbers are not included, largely because multiple editions of works are often available and page numbers would therefore be misleading. However, direct quotations from secondary sources are parenthetically documented and the sources listed in the Further Reading section that follows almost all entries. Entries on general topics (e.g., Portuguese American Literature, South Asian American Film) also follow a standard pattern; they allude to major events, figures, and texts and relevant historical and cultural background information. Those entries, too, conclude with a Further Reading section.

All Further Reading sections direct interested readers to the most useful secondary materials available on the topics. Given the constraints of space, the contributors were specifically instructed to list only the most seminal and accessible secondary sources. Entries on topics that have received substantial critical attention (e.g., Jewish American Novel) have several entries listed in the Further Reading section. However, entries on authors who are yet to be discovered by a wide audience (e.g., Richard Crasta, Gelareh Asayesh) list only a couple of book reviews. On very rare occasions an entry on an individual author (e.g., Opal Moore, Adria Bernardi) does not have a Further Reading section, because he or she is a little-known or emerging artist whose work has not yet received any attention in venues that can be accessed relatively easily.

I would like to take this opportunity to thank all the contributors to this project. They have been immensely generous in sharing their knowledge and expertise; it is their participation—their enthusiastic and professional handling of the assignments—that has allowed me to gather and edit this massive, multivolume *Encyclopedia* in less than eighteen months. The members of the advisory board—Ken Cerniglia, Roberta Fernández, Thomas Gladsky, Guiyou Huang, Arnold Krupat, Paul Lauter, Ann Shapiro, Loretta Woodard—were particularly helpful, and I want to express my special gratitude to Paul Lauter, whose lively and provocative introduction follows this preface. Finally, I would like to thank George Butler, who commissioned this project and served as its developmental editor for Greenwood Press; Cynthia Harris of Harris Editorial Services for gathering the many photographs that grace the pages of the *Encyclopedia*; and Greenwood's editorial staff, who expertly guided this large work to its successful completion.

Introduction

Paul Lauter

When in 1782 some of the founders of the United States selected *E pluribus unum* as the motto on the new nation's Great Seal, they may have chosen even more wisely than they knew. They were very likely thinking of thirteen disputatious colonies being bound up into a single nation, or at most of an America constituted, as J. Hector St. John de Crèvecoeur wrote, also in 1782, of a "mixture of English, Scotch, Irish, French, Dutch, Germans, and Swedes." "From this promiscuous breed," Crèvecoeur had continued, "that race now called Americans have arisen." But in fact, long before Europeans arrived in what they thought of as the "new world," this hemisphere was already inhabited by enormously diverse groups of Native Americans, speaking a huge range of distinctive and mutually unintelligible languages, and with a multitude of cultures, religions, forms of organization, food, and folkways. Some were hunters and gatherers, moving from place to place through forest or across plains; others constructed careful dwellings within forbidding cliffs or on protected mesas, maintaining control over fertile oases of green amid an austere landscape; still others built large, complex, and often very rich cities, complete with elaborate temples and playing fields; yet others lived where nature was extraordinarily fruitful, providing salmon, furs, and fruit in sufficient abundance to sustain a large class of artisans and artists. The artistic productions of Native Americans were as varied as the terrain they inhabited. Thus "America," well before the arrival of Europeans, was, as we would now call it, a "multicultural" world.

When the Europeans did come—first probably from Scandinavia, then from Italy, Spain, Portugal, France, Holland, and finally England and elsewhere in Western Europe—they, too, were a more diverse cast than Crèvecoeur's phrasing indicates. Differing in language, religion, and attitudes toward the native populations, toward the land, and toward the future, they were often at war, and even in peaceful times engaged in struggles over power, property, and cultural authority. By the time the United States was constituted as a nation in 1776, moreover, something like 10 percent of its population came not from Europe or from among native peoples, but from Africa. These people, too, came from differing nations or tribes in west and central Africa, and carried with them to the new world differing languages, customs, and memories.

Thus, when the Constitution of the new United States was established in 1791, the country that would come to be called "America" was by any account a "multicultural" nation. To be sure, certain elements of culture were more dominant than others. While German was the common language in many parts of Pennsylvania and Dutch in New York—just as, later, French would be in some of Louisiana, Swedish in parts of the Midwest, and Spanish in the Southwest—English became the language of public discourse and of schooling everywhere throughout the United States. English jurisprudence—including the presumption of innocence and trial by a jury of one's peers—provided a basis for much of the legal structure of the United States, though such peculiar American legal institutions as the Southern "slave codes," the Chinese Exclusion Acts, the colonial statutes governing Puerto Rico and the Philippines, and the executive decisions that brought about the internment of Japanese Americans during World War II would have profound effects on culture and society. Likewise, throughout the nineteenth century and much of the twentieth, American literature was seen solely as a branch of English stock. Only within the last forty years or so have we come to appreciate the fact that writers in America were composing texts throughout that period in many languages other than English and, perhaps more important, even when writing in English were working out of artistic imperatives arising from a wide range of cultures and historical experiences.

The variety of subjects, artistic styles, and distinctive qualities that, we now see, have characterized American culture from its beginnings was seldom widely appreciated, and certainly not within the academic world, before the 1960s. Certainly there were some critics and anthologists, particularly those on the political left, who had earlier promoted a more diverse idea of American writing. Still, had you studied American literature in the 1950s—as I did at New York University, Indiana University, and Yale University—or at other predominantly white colleges and universities, you would seldom have encountered a writer of color. I knew only of three—Richard Wright, James Baldwin, and Ralph Ellison—but nary a Native American or Latino or Asian American author, and hardly any white women apart from Emily Dickinson and Marianne Moore. Autobiographies of Benjamin Franklin and Henry Adams graced most American literature curricula, but not such works as Frederick Douglass's *Narrative* (1845), Harriet Jacobs's *Incidents in the Life of a Slave Girl* (1861), or other slave narratives, most of which were not even in print in 1960. Many writers who today are familiar to any student of American literature, such as Langston Hughes, Zora Neale Hurston, Kate Chopin, and Mary Wilkins Freeman, existed on the far margins of cultural knowledge, if they existed at all. Indeed, the titles of widely used anthologies of the time, such as *12 American Authors* (1962), reflected the narrow conceptions of American literature then dominant. Similarly, had you studied music, you would have learned about Bach cantatas, Beethoven symphonies, and Verdi operas, but not about African American spirituals or the extraordinarily creative work then being produced by such jazz musicians as Charlie Parker and Dizzy Gillespie, much less the blues or Chicano *corridos*.

It has become a truism to assert—either with something of a sigh of regret or with delight—that the social movements of the 1960s changed forever how American culture can be thought about. It is an often-told tale, and one I will not repeat at length here. It is, however, worth underlining that a central political demand of the civil rights and feminist movements of the time readily translated itself into cultural and educational terms. The demand was for access: to the voting booth, to the front of the bus, to public accommodations, to jobs from which one had been largely excluded by virtue of race, ethnicity, or gender. "Where are the blacks?" and "Where are the women"? were among the questions of the moment. And those questions might be, and were, quickly focused on curricula, reading lists, critical texts, and anthologies, as well as upon the student bodies and faculties of educational institutions. Once asked, such questions and similar ones about other ethnic and minority groups, including gay people, could steadily if not readily be answered. There was something of a model for entry into the canon provided by the phenomenal explosion of highly regarded writing by and study of Jewish American authors in the 1950s: Bernard Malamud, Norman Mailer, Grace Paley, Saul Bellow, among many others. And there was the work of scholars who had, for example, long been investigating the texts of African Americans, especially at the traditionally black colleges; others slowly but surely picked up their knowledge and their distinctive insights about what fully constituted American literature and culture. Moreover, the increasing study of ethnic and minority writing helped foster the publication and wide dissemination of important new works by new authors, such as *The Way to Rainy Mountain* (1969) by N. Scott Momaday (Kiowa) and *The Bluest Eye* (1970) by Toni Morrison. Dialectically, the success of such works encouraged the study of earlier texts that had emerged from particular ethnic or minority cultures. Thus, even when the movements for social change began to falter during the 1970s, the processes of reconstructing American literature continued apace.

By about 1980, it had become possible to think of producing an anthology that significantly represented the many cultures that, together, constituted the newly emerging multicultural conception of American literature. Anthologies, like encyclopedias, are in their nature consolidations of particular cultural moments. The anthology that a group of us initially at The Feminist Press planned to produce as part of a project modestly called "Reconstructing American Literature" would, we hoped, make more fully visible the literatures and histories of the full spectrum of the people of America by making their works better known, accessible, and teachable. Out of mind, out of sight, we argued, and the supporters of the project—the federal Fund for the Improvement of Post-Secondary Education, the Rockefeller Foundation, and the Eli Lilly Endowment—apparently agreed. The *Heath Anthology of American Literature*, which emerged from that project, took nearly another decade to produce, and it became part of a general shift in the study of American literature from its earlier narrow focus on a very limited number of authors, literary forms, styles, and texts to the much more diverse and pluralistic conceptions characteristic of American literary study today.

Multiculturalism is the name we give to the study of that *pluribus* that has so distinctively constituted the United States. It is not that America is altogether exceptional in being made up by a variety of cultures. To the contrary, in recent times nations across the world that once saw themselves as monocultural have discovered the true multiplicity of cultures, languages, and histories shaping their character; indeed, a major problem of twenty-first-century politics from Chechnya to Sri Lanka to Central Africa has to do with violent struggles of minority peoples to throw off what they regard as the oppressive yoke of dominant groups. In the United States, the reality of a relatively peaceful multiculturalism today needs to be seen in the context of the sometimes violent clashes between groups: the displacement and, often, extermination of native peoples by Europeans; the capture, transportation, and enslavement of Africans; the struggles over title to land between Spanish- and English-speaking peoples in the Southwest and in California; the discrimination embodied in the phrase "No Irish need apply"; the attacks on Chinese laborers on the West Coast. These and other such events have deeply seared the historical experience not only of minority communities in America, but also, less observably perhaps, of the nation as a whole. As Toni Morrison has pointed out, for example, the very absence of African Americans from many American literary texts, which suggests a certain need to bury or displace elements of our history, is a central feature of much canonical literature in this country.

But multiculturalism is by no means constituted by the study of conflict and oppression. In part it has to do with the celebration of what is or was distinctive in the cultures and histories of groups of people now resident in America. The ethnic parades and festivals, the display and consumption of foodways and fabrics, the study and transmission of a group's original language illustrate the processes of often colorful celebration that many ethnic Americans have maintained. These are of value in and of themselves. But more fundamentally, they express what Randolph Bourne pointed to in his important 1916 essay "Trans-National America." "Each national colony in this country," he wrote, "seems to retain in its foreign press, its vernacular literature, its schools, its intellectual and patriotic leaders, a central cultural nucleus. . . . The influences at the centre of the nuclei are centripetal. They make for the intelligence and the social values which mean an enhancement of life. And just because the foreign-born retains this expressiveness he is likely to be a better citizen of the American community" (*Heath* 1720).

Still, the concerns of multiculturalism as an area of academic study go deeper. We ask: What, if anything, in the social and historical experience of a group of people persists and significantly shapes the cultural productions of artists from among them? What, if anything, in the forms of works of art marks them as distinctive to a particular ethnic group? Are there characteristic tropes, master narratives, sets of events and characters, evident functions that distinguish the cultural works of any particular group? How do region, ideas about gender and sexuality, religious practices, persistent class barriers inflect ethnic artistic and intellectual practices? How, if at all, do relationships with a "home" country affect how people think and act and create, and how does that change from one generation to the next? How do ideas, images, characters from one ethnic background, indeed from majority backgrounds, get incorporated into and transformed in other ethnic writings; indeed, to what extent are "ethnic" texts necessarily hybrid in practice? What, to paraphrase Maxine Hong Kingston, is ethnic: the time period, the region—or the movies? (6). Above all, perhaps, what are the roles of writers and performers in the struggles of ethnic communities for survival, visibility, progress? Such questions, and others, constitute a vast academic field, within which this *Encyclopedia* is designed to play an important role for a number of reasons.

First, answering any of these questions demands a considerable range of knowledge, often of languages and of cultures to which one was not raised. No one could be at home in each of the multiple cultures that now constitute America. Thus multiculturalism is a collective enterprise, for which an encyclopedia, like an archive or library, is an essential tool.

Second, though most of the works with which this *Encyclopedia* is concerned are written primarily in English, there remains a problem of "translation." In part that has to do with the fact that significant authors—for example, Jimmy Santiago Baca, Víctor Hernández Cruz, and Gloria Anzaldúa—write both in Spanish and in English and mix into predominantly English texts many Spanish words and phrases. That produces a sometimes difficult, occasionally irritating, but generally productive experience of disorientation for non-Spanish speakers. The use of Spanish or Yiddish or Italian words and phrases, and even of dialects, may serve as a proxy for identity, a counter toward verisimilitude, or even a challenge to the "outside"—that is, non-ethnic—reader. But "translation" has more generally to do with the fact that common cultural knowledge in one group is often the stuff of mystery or at least of puzzlement to people from another. I have often been surprised, for example, by how often students need "translation" not only of such Yiddish terms as *mohyl* or *schnurrer* but of concepts about the status of men and women, the nature of daily rituals, the roles of the rabbinate in the orthodox Jewry sometimes portrayed by Henry Roth or Rebecca Goldstein, among many others. Similarly, teaching James Baldwin's story "Sonny's Blues" confronts many students with altogether unfamiliar but crucial musical idioms that need "translation," such as the playing of "Bird," the theatrics of a Harlem street-corner preacher, or the jukebox of a fifties black bar.

In many ways this process of what I have been calling "translation" is continuous with the need for understanding distinctive historical contexts upon which works of ethnic literature may in some measure depend. Most literary texts come more richly alive when they are understood within as well as beyond the historical moments of their creation, whether we speak of *Macbeth* or of *MacBird*. But Louise Erdrich's novel *Tracks* (1988) will be peculiarly puzzling for one unfamiliar with the impact of the Dawes Severalty Act of 1887 upon Indian land tenure. The events unfolding in Sui-Sin Far's (Edith Eaton's) 1909 story "In the Land of the Free" seem simply arbitrary and incomprehensible if one is ignorant of the Chinese Exclusion Act and its daily implementation. Even the title of John Okada's novel *No-No Boy* will make no sense to anyone unfamiliar with the range of responses within the Japanese-American community to their internment during World War II. The compelling texture of Bernard Malamud's story "The Lady of the Lake" (1958) dissolves before ignorance of the debates among Jews in the 1940s and 1950s about authenticity and the denial of Jewish identity.

Identity is, of course, a significant element in ethnic writing and criticism; indeed, forming one's identity as a hyphenated American, or in opposition to that very classification of "hyphenated American," probably constitutes the single largest category of ethnic fiction. Ethnic identity, it is now generally understood, is not a fact of nature but a social construction—as is expressed in the title of George Sanchez's important study, *Becoming Mexican American* (1993). As Sanchez demonstrates, the content of the name "Mexican American" changes over time, as relationships with the country of residence, the country of origin, and second- or third-generation community, as well as within the immigrant, change. There is, then, a certain contingency to ethnic identity: it must always be historically grounded, often regionally inflected. The meanings of "Italian" or "Italian American" have changed radically from the moment of Sacco and Vanzetti, to the moment of *Christ in Concrete*, to the moment of Tony Soprano. Yet there are cultural continuities; what are these? The very name preferred by inhabitants of an ethnic or racial category change: Negro, black, African American.

Are there cultural continuities, and if so are they the products of material conditions, of ideology, or of stereotypes imposed by the majority society?

To be sure, we resist stereotypes, yet we use them all the time. In the United States in particular a deep chasm exists between its fundamental individualistic ideology and the harsh facts of racial and ethnic stereotyping, which sees not individuals but instances of a group. Paradoxically, ethnic writers face precisely this tension: can, should, must, will their ethnic characters, particularly central figures in fictions about growing up, be taken as "representative," as expressive of some distinctively Polish or Chinese or Indian set of characteristics? Few would now argue that such characteristics, *if* they exist at all, are products of one's genetic inheritance. But might they be products of one's 1950s Washington Heights inheritance? Or, to return to Kingston's formulation, are they effects of ethnicity, time and place . . . or the movies?

It can, in fact, be argued that certain central tropes and certain distinctive stylistic features play peculiarly significant roles in different ethnic literatures. Henry Louis Gates Jr. and Houston Baker Jr., for example, have called attention to the importance of the Signifying Monkey and of the call-and-response pattern in African American cultural productions of many kinds. As Gates puts it, "the Signifying Monkey exists as the great trope of Afro-American discourse, and the trope of tropes, his language of Signifyin(g) is his verbal sign in the Afro-American tradition." "Signifyin(g)" is the practice in black vernacular of using innuendo, needling, ridiculing, parodying a previous statement to put down an opponent, to gain status and attention, or to establish one's voice as potent. Gates links the practice to "the tension between the oral and the written modes of narration that is represented as finding a voice in writing," a central phenomenon of many African American texts. The "call-and-response" pattern, Baker argues, characterizes not only African American religious practice but many other forms of black "expressive culture." It points to the strong oral and folk elements that inform the most sophisticated and elaborate African American written works. One might also point to the centrality of the theme of struggling for freedom in many African American texts. Indeed, in one of the earliest moments of African American literary production, Phillis Wheatley bases her authority to speak to the students at Cambridge University about democratic responsibility or to the Earl of Dartmouth about liberty on her identity as an African *and* an American.

Among Mexican Americans, the border takes on a particular cultural weight—no surprise given its proximity to where most Mexican immigrants initially lived as well as its overnight transformation after the Treaty of Guadalupe Hidalgo. Moreover, the role of the border in limiting and controlling workers or enabling them to migrate makes it a constant presence in the experience and thus in the culture of Mexican Americans. But in recent years, the "Borderland" has come to name not just a geographical space but a state of consciousness, a *mestizaje* sense of betweenness. As

Gloria Anzaldúa has phrased it, "The new *mestiza* copes by developing a tolerance for contradictions, a tolerance for ambiguity. She learns to be an Indian in Mexican culture, to be Mexican from an Anglo point of view. She learns to juggle cultures." The inhabitant of the "Borderlands" thus comes to represent postmodern hybridity not only in terms of nationality but of gender, sexuality, race, or ethnicity. And the language spoken or written by such a *mestizaje* figure is, not surprisingly, an intermingling of, in this instance, English with Spanish.

In significant numbers of Native American texts, a distinguishing stylistic feature is repetition, and the fundamental trope is one of disease or disorder and efforts to restore or maintain health. In Leslie Silko's (Laguna) novel *Ceremony* (1977), for example, the central figure Tayo participates in a series of ceremonies, old and new, designed to cure him of the anomie, violence, and decline imposed by absorption in white culture, and particularly in war. Analogous patterns emerge in other contemporary Indian fictions, such as Louise Erdrich's (Chippewa) *Love Medicine* (1984) and N. Scott Momaday's (Kiowa) *House Made of Dawn* (1968). But one can trace such patterns of disruption and renewal far back into the oral cultures of many Native peoples, in which highly repetitive chants form part of a purification ritual. Critics have suggested that such a trope reflects not only the need of people living in arid or uncertain natural conditions to renew fertility, but also the role imported disease has played in decimating Native peoples, as well as the pervasiveness of alcoholism in the last two centuries among Indians on and off the reservation. The roots of a trope may thus reach out into mythic and historical, as well as contemporary social and personal, origins, as the structure of Momaday's *The Way to Rainy Mountain* illustrates.

But to what extent might such a trope, or those of the borderland or of the signifying trickster, function across ethnic cultures? Charles Chesnutt, for example, develops a fascinating instance of illnesses being cured by trickster figures in his story "Sis Becky's Pickaninny" (1899). And a large number of recent writers have adopted the border metaphor to talk about gay sexuality, among many other topics. In what degree and in what ways are such tropes or certain stylistic qualities distinctive to particular ethnic groups? Can they be rearticulated in differing contexts, for differing purposes, under differing historical skies? Gates traces the figure of the Signifyin(g) Monkey back to complex African origins, but in what ways is the Monkey distinct from trickster figures such as Coyote who inhabit many Native American oral and written texts? Or the tricksters who are also, maybe, curers in such stories as Malamud's "The Last Mohican" (1958) or "The Magic Barrel" (1958)?

Such questions remain on the agenda for the study of multicultural literatures. So, in fact, does the exploration of such literatures to identify other key tropes or elements of style—if any—common to writers of a particular ethnicity. This is no easy task for a student working within one particular ethnic culture; the difficulties are multiplied when one launches into what we might call "comparative multiculturalism," bringing into conversation two or more traditions. That is so, first, because of significant cultural differences among groups, native or immigrant, within the United States. Class training, levels of literacy, family structures, religious affiliations, among other things, have differed enormously and have thus quite differently promoted assimilation, intermingling, continuing ethnic identification, the very production of art or literature. The expectations and assumptions about ethnic culture one forms from the study of one or two groups may, or may well not, carry over fruitfully into the study of others. And second, as I have suggested, multiculturalism is a youthful field of study, barely thirty years of age, as compared with the eighty or ninety years in which mainly white and primarily male American literature has been studied, and the 150 or so years in which English literature has been formally analyzed. It is only now that the tools critical to our trade are being crafted, and so we look at this *The Greenwood Encyclopedia of Multiethnic American Literature* not as the end but as the beginning of our work.

Works Cited

Anzaldúa, Gloria. *Borderlands/La Frontera: The New Mestiza*. San Francisco: Aunt Lutie Books, 1987.

Baker, Houston A., Jr. *Blues, Ideology, and Afro-American Literature: A Vernacular Theory*. Chicago: U of Chicago P, 1984.

Gates, Henry Louis, Jr. *The Signifying Monkey: A Theory of Afro-American Literary Criticism*. New York: Oxford UP, 1988.

Kingston, Maxine Hong. *The Woman Warrior*. New York: Random House, 1975.

Lauter, Paul, et al., eds. *The Heath Anthology of American Literature*. Lexington, MA: D.C. Heath, 1990.

Morrison, Toni. *Playing in the Dark: Whiteness and the Literary Imagination*. Cambridge, MA: Harvard UP, 1992.

A

ABINADER, ELMAZ (1954–) First-generation Arab American writer, poet, performance artist, and political activist. Abinader's work extends over an array of literary genres, in which she not only explores her cultural and often conflicted identity as an Arab American, but vividly traces the histories that forge her deep-rooted ties to her heritage. Her memoir *Children of the Roojme: A Family's Journey from Lebanon* (1991) resulted from her postdoctoral fellowship in the humanities, which she pursued with **Toni Morrison** as her advisor after having completed her MFA in poetry at Columbia University and her PhD in creative writing at the University of Nebraska.

Children of the Roojme acts as a strong testimonial to the hardships and cross-Atlantic encounters experienced by four generations of the Abinader family. It follows their journeys of **immigration** from their northern town in Lebanon to the United States, depicting the cultural adjustment they had to negotiate in relocating to a small western Pennsylvania town and their immense loss and yearning for the land and people they left behind. This memoir offers an honest portrayal of the harsh conditions encountered by its characters during the first half of the twentieth century, with nostalgic ruminations on the homeland being superseded by accounts of World War I and the Ottoman rule over Lebanon, along with famine and poverty.

Abinader has written and performed a number of plays, such as the three-act, one-woman *Country of Origin* (1997), which portrays the lives of three Arab American women (Abinader's grandmother, mother, and herself as a young girl) coping with cultural pressures on the individual as well as the

Elmaz Abinader. *Photo by Anthony Byers. Courtesy of Elmaz Abinader.*

communal level. In 1999 this play was the winner of two Drammies, Portland's Critic's Circle Awards for Theater. Other performances include *Under the Ramadan Moon* (2000), which focuses on Arab and **Arab American stereotypes**, in addition to the more recent *When Silence Is Frightening* and *Thirty-two Mohammeds*.

In 2000 Abinader won the PEN Oakland Josephine Miles Literary Award for Multicultural Poetry for her book *In the Country of My Dreams* (1999). This collection fuses myriad cross-cultural concerns and synthesizes a heritage and a history rooted in the real rather than the imaginary. The tone that ultimately emanates from this book of poetry is a celebratory one of optimism and hope. Abinader, however, does not shy away from voicing her political beliefs: her opposition to the U.S. wars in the Middle East, particularly in Iraq, and her reactions to the September 11, 2001, events and the racial profiling of Arabs emanating from them. Her writings have appeared in *The Poetry of Arab Women*, edited by Nathalie Handal, and in the anthology *Writers on America*, published by the United States State Department, as well as in *Creative Nonfiction*'s project titled the "Living Issue," featuring various writers' essays on the events of September 11, 2001.

Abinader has been the recipient of an Academy of American Poets Award and a Fulbright Senior Scholarship in Egypt, and she won the 2002 Goldie Award for Literature. She lives in Oakland, California, and teaches at Mills College.

Further Reading

Handal, Nathalie, ed. " Introduction." *The Poetry of Arab Women: A Contemporary Anthology.* New York: Interlink, 2001. 1–62.

Majaj, Lisa Suhair. "Two Worlds: Arab-American Writing." *Forkroads: A Journal of Ethnic American Literature* 1.3 (1996): 64–80.

Carol Fadda-Conrey

ABISH, WALTER (1931–) Jewish American novelist, poet, and short story writer. Walter Abish is the author of three novels, three collections of short stories, and a book of poems. The recipient of many distinguished awards and grants, Abish is known for his interest in language, literary experimentation, as well as various forms of cultural, social, and political hegemony. Abish's work deals with the effects of globalization on culture, and often interrogates elements of nationalism and national **identity** construction. Inherent in these concerns is the symbiotic relationship between fiction and history, or the extent to which the imagination, narrative, and revision contribute to perceptions of the past as well as to perceptions of self.

Walter Abish is very much a postmodern writer. Oftentimes the style, structure, and language of his texts convey more meaning than the details of their narratives, which are frequently fragmented to delineate the confusion indigenous to a fractured consciousness. In his short introduction to *99: The New Meaning* (1990), Abish states that the "orchestrated," selected fragments of published works by other writers found in the text are devised to "probe certain familiar emotional configurations afresh," and to "arrive at an emotional content that is not [his] by design." Experimentation with alliteration, letter limitation, and narrative detachment propel the narrative of *Alphabetical Africa* (1974), replete with inane characters, war and genocide, corruption, as well as social, political, and historical commentary. In Abish's *How German Is It* (1980), for which he won the PEN/Faulkner Award, the text's style strives for precision; however, the novel's structure betrays this quest. The text's details are splintered and offer a disjointed chronology so as to create an obvious tension between the style and structure of the novel that reflects contemporary Germany's desire to put its ugly past behind it and move on in a new, orderly fashion. The more the text's style seeks order, however, the more a tension develops out of the silences and omissions that are naturally a part of Germany's attempt to conceal its history. Eventually, attempts at concealment manifest themselves in the form of questions, such as: How deeply rooted in the old Germany is the new one? Can contemporary Germany ignore its past's influence on the present? Can Germany resist the infiltration of American ideology into its contemporary culture and, if not, will the American influence on Germany inspire or quell the desire to dominate the world once again? These questions are, of course, answered by such discoveries as the mass grave near the school in Brumholdstein and the wish of some characters in the book to bury the communal grave with cement. The novel's strategy, then, demonstrates that the more Germans want to break with their past, the more they are in fact linked to it. Those who want to hide the evidence of the atrocities associated with Nazi Germany are in fact accomplices in past acts of racist genocide.

Eclipse Fever (1993), Abish's first novel after the publication of *How German Is It*, is a complicated, commanding illustration of the corruption and self-indulgence inherent in the affluent and intellectual communities of Mexico City. An otherwise disconnected narrative is held together by themes of self-gratification, thievery, and social and cultural oppression. Among the many storylines in the novel is the tale of an American developer, Preston

Hollier, who plans to despoil precious Mexican antiquities while posing as an advocate of the restoration and conservation of the Mayan pyramids and artifacts. Hollier's web of depravity includes government officials and museum administrators, and this contributes to one of the text's central themes: that Mexican heritage is fading among cultural, financial, and political hegemony. Throughout the novel, mistaken identities mark the confusion propagated by fraudulent individuals and institutions.

In *Double Vision* (2004) Walter Abish recounts two momentous occasions in his life. First, the autobiographical account details Abish's return to Vienna (the city of his birth), and tells of the boyhood confusion spawned by his family's forced exile to Italy then France before sailing to Shanghai. In 1948 the Chinese Red Army forced the Abish family to move to Israel. The second part of the memoir tells of Abish's first visit to Germany. As suggested by its title, the author's attempts to negotiate situations of double-consciousness are at the heart of the book. Abish tries to reconcile his pride in his Austrian heritage with the Austria that welcomed the Nazis, and he must confront the real Germany beyond the Germany he had only envisioned before. Walter Abish purposely wrote *How German Is It* without ever setting foot on German soil because he was most interested in exploring what constitutes "Germanness," or the qualities that make up the Germany of the world's imagination. Curiously, Abish changes little with regard to his perception of Germany once he surveys its physical, social, and cultural landscapes first-hand.

Further Reading

Klinkowitz, Jerome. "Fictive Empowerment through Cultural Criticism in the Works of Walter Abish, Raymond Federman, and Michael Stephens." *Powerless Fictions?: Ethics, Cultural Critique, and American Fiction in the Age of Postmodernism*. Ed. Ricardo Miguel Alfonso. Atlanta: Rodopi, 1996. 63–84.

Peyser, Thomas. "How Global Is It?: Walter Abish and the Fiction of Globalization." *Contemporary Literature* 40.2 (1999): 240–62.

Alex Ambrozic

ABOLITION   In Western Europe and the Americas, abolition refers to the movement responsible for generating the psychological climate necessary for ending the transatlantic slave trade and chattel **slavery**. With the disappearance of slavery in the Roman Empire and the emergence of medieval serfdom, slavery was virtually unknown in Western Europe until 1442, when the Portuguese brought back slaves from the west coast of Africa. With further European exploration and annexation of colonies in North and South America, the need for labor created a huge market for slaves. Between the fifteenth and sixteenth centuries, an estimated total of fifteen million Africans were transported to the Americas in the most dehumanizing conditions. Although abolitionist pressure first succeeded in halting this traffic during the early decades of the 1800s, widespread smuggling continued until about 1862. With mounting international pressure, slavery was abolished in the British West Indies by 1838 and in French possessions ten years later. The situation in the United States was more complex because the institution of slavery was a domestic rather than a colonial affair. It provided the social and economic base of the plantations of eleven Southern states, and it completely shaped the way of life in the South. Abolitionists were repulsed by the brutality and immorality in Southern plantations and, therefore, attacked its whole way of life. The South, in turn, reacted by increasing its system of slave control and calling for oppressive legislation, especially after the **Nat Turner** (1800–31) revolt. Fueled by his religious ardor, Turner saw himself called upon by God to lead his people out of bondage. On the night of August 21, 1831, together with seven fellow slaves in whom he confided, Turner murdered his master, Joseph Travis, and his family. They marched on to Jerusalem, Virginia, to capture the county's armory, but were crushed by a force of about three thousand men. Turner's rebellion dispelled the white Southern myth that slaves were contented with their situation or too subdued to show opposition. By this time, abolitionists came to realize their inability in

Individual portraits of Charles Sumner, Henry Ward Beecher, Wendell Phillips, William Lloyd Garrison, Gerrit Smith, Horace Greeley, and Henry Wilson, c. 1866. *Courtesy of the Library of Congress.*

changing American public opinion through persuasion or even through such ambitious projects as the resettlement of freed black slaves in Liberia by the American Colonization Society, founded in 1817. Many abolitionists took part in other social reform movements, but because of the millions of chattel slaves toiling in the South, the issue of slavery eclipsed other causes. Probably the most famous abolitionist was William Lloyd Garrison (1805–79), founder of the New England Anti-Slavery Society in 1832. In 1833 he helped organize the American Anti-Slavery Society. Not only did Garrison denounce slavery, he was repulsed by the notion that the Constitution of the United States tolerated it as well. He earned recognition as the most radical of American antislavery advocates through the editorials he wrote for his newspaper, *The Liberator* (1831–65), which circulated widely both in England and the United States.

Other individuals influenced by or in opposition to Garrisonian abolitionism included such men and women as Theodore Dwight Weld, James Birney, Gerrit Smith, Theodore Parker, Julia Ward Howe, Arthur Tappan and his brother Lewis, Salmon P. Chase, and Lydia Maria Child. Each one had his or her own personal stance on the institution of slavery but was, without a doubt, more conciliatory than Garrison. Whereas a few abolitionists belonged to the clergy (Weld and Parker) or the world of letters (John Greenleaf Whittier, James Russell Lowell, and Harriet Beecher Stowe), others came from the free black community as was the case with such prominent and educated former slaves as **Frederick Douglass**. Contrary to what is often assumed, abolition was not a popular cause even in the North since some of its advocates experienced continual persecution and assault. Such was the case with the antislavery editor Elijah P. Lovejoy (1802–37), who died in defense of his right to print antislavery material in the *St. Louis Observer* of St. Louis, Missouri; he later relocated to Alton, Illinois, under mounting pressure from a number of important men who had requested him to moderate the tone of his editorials. Because he had refused to abide by their request, on the night of November 7, 1837, a mob attacked the newspaper's headquarters and Lovejoy was killed in its defense. Although this occurrence shocked many people in the North, it also strengthened abolitionist sentiment there.

Whether they adhered to Garrisonian abolitionism or not, abolitionist leaders were often scorned and ridiculed. On occasion, they were regarded as a group of people who were working out their own personal maladjustments in American society or, instead, as individuals who manipulated the institution of slavery so as to assert their superiority. As a New England cultural elite that was proud of being on the forefront of noble causes, its enemies, however, tried everything to minimize their impact. The goal of the abolitionists was to attack slavery with words. Such an attitude was in sharp contrast with the behavior of those whose hatred of such verbal attacks actually drove them to murder and assault. In addition to their New England backgrounds, abolitionist leaders shared a common Calvinist self-righteousness as well as a prominent social status and an excellent education. Ordinary citizens, however, were often more inclined to abhor blacks and rally for the maintenance of the institution of slavery, while securing their own advancement within the system. The individuals who looked after their own egoistical needs have been forgotten long ago. But the legacies left by a number of men and women who devoted or sacrificed their lives and careers to such a noble cause—as the following sketches will show—are the ones whose memory we still wish to recall today.

After leaving his studies in 1834, Theodore Dwight Weld (1803–95) worked for the American Anti-Slavery Society, recruiting and training such prominent abolitionists as James G. Birney, Harriet Beecher Stowe, and Henry Ward Beecher to work for the cause. Most of Weld's pamphlets were published anonymously. His most notorious pieces are *The Bible Against Slavery* (1837) and *Slavery As It Is* (1839), with the latter often said to have partly influenced Stowe's novel, *Uncle Tom's Cabin* (1852). James G. Birney (1792–1857), another famous opponent of slavery, was twice the presidential candidate of the abolitionist Liberty Party. In 1819 he was elected to the Alabama legislature. During his tenure, he fought for inclusion of provisions into the state constitution empowering the legislature to either emancipate or prohibit the sale of slaves brought into the state. In 1837 he served as executive secretary of the American Anti-Slavery Society and in 1840 he was appointed to the position of vice president of the World Anti-Slavery Convention in England, where he wrote *The American Churches, the Bulwarks of American Slavery*, published in the same year.

Gerrit Smith (1797–1874) became an abolitionist in 1835, after witnessing the disruption of an antislavery meeting by a mob in Utica, New York. He is still remembered for, his role of leadership in the organization of the antislavery Liberty Party in 1840; his home village, Peterboro, New York, which became a station on the **Underground Railroad**; and his funding, after 1850, of the legal expenses of individuals charged with infractions of the Fugitive Slave Law. Most notorious is his close friendship with **John Brown**, to whom he gave a farm in Essex County, New York and, on occasion, supplied with funds for the abolitionist cause. As a Unitarian theologian, Theodore Parker (1810–60) believed that the moral truths of Christianity should be applied to the social problems of his time. Parker was an advocate of prison reform, temperance, women's education, and other such causes, with abolition still being regarded as his major concern. His contributions to the movement range from his speeches against slavery, his assistance of runaway slaves, and his written abolitionist tract, *A Letter to the People of the United States Touching the Matter of Slavery* (1848). He also served on the secret committee that aided John Brown. Julia Ward Howe (1819–1910), an author and lecturer, is best known for her "Battle Hymn of the Republic," which was composed to the rhythm of the folksong "John Brown's Body." It was first published in *The Atlantic Monthly* in 1862.

Arthur Tappan (1786–1865) and his brother Lewis provided the monetary funds, which they earned as successful businessmen, in support of missionary societies, colleges, and theological seminaries. It was the abolitionist cause, however, to which Arthur Tappan devoted himself during the latter part of his life. His contributions include his assistance in founding several abolitionist journals, his role as founder and first president of both the New York City Anti-Slavery Society and the American Anti-Slavery Society, and his support of the Liberty Party in the 1840s, which was motivated by his belief that abolition was possible through the political process. When the Fugitive Slave Law of 1850 came into effect, both brothers became more radical. In his determination to disobey the law, Arthur Tappan supported the

Underground Railroad and lived to witness the Emancipation Proclamation of 1863 fulfill much of his life's work for the cause.

In the 1830s Salmon P. Chase (1808–73) practiced law in Cincinnati, Ohio, where he became notorious for his courtroom work on behalf of fugitive slaves and white persons who had assisted them. He is also noted for using his prestige in dealing with Reconstruction measures aimed at uplifting emancipated slaves after his 1864 appointment as chief justice to the Supreme Court.

Lydia Maria Child's (1802–80) devotion to abolitionism is said to have started in 1831 when she met Garrison. Child's most widely read work, *An Appeal in Favor of That Class of Americans Called Africans* (1833), relates the history of slavery and denounces the inequality of employment and educational opportunities for blacks. As a result, she was ostracized socially and suffered financial distress when her magazine failed in 1834. The book, nonetheless, succeeded in drawing a great number of members for the abolitionist movement. Although she is remembered for her editing of the *National Anti-Slavery Standard* (1841–43) and for recording the recollections of slaves who had been set free, her home was a sanctuary in the Underground Railroad in that she assisted runaway slaves. John Greenleaf Whittier (1807–92), too, endorsed Garrisonian abolitionism, especially after experiencing discouragement from his lack of literary recognition. His pamphlet "Justice and Expediency" made him a leading figure in the abolitionist movement, a cause that he passionately embraced for a decade. James Russell Lowell (1819–91) published *Conversations on Some of the Old Poets* (1845), which included a plea for abolition. He wrote about fifty antislavery articles for various periodicals between 1845 and 1850, but his most powerful pieces of writing on abolition were his *Biglow Papers*, which he began to serialize on June 17, 1846. Written in New England dialect, Lowell used satire to denounce the Mexican war, which the United States used as an excuse to increase its area of slavery. Often regarded as the greatest literary contribution to the abolitionist cause and responsible for bringing about the Civil War is Harriet Beecher Stowe's (1811–96) *Uncle Tom's Cabin; or, Life Among the Lowly*. Before appearing as a book, it was submitted for serial publication in the *National Era*, an antislavery paper based in Washington, DC.

After escaping from Baltimore to New England in the late 1830s, at a Nantucket, Massachusetts, antislavery convention in 1841, Frederick Douglass (1817?–95) was asked to give an account of his feelings and experiences as a bondsman. His audiences found his poignant and fiery speeches so riveting that he eventually became an agent for the Massachusetts Anti-Slavery Society and a staunch advocate of abolition. Douglass felt impelled to write his autobiography in 1845, which he revised and completed in 1882, as *Life and Times of Frederick Douglass*. He wrote it mostly to convince those skeptics who doubted such an articulate speaker could ever have been a slave. Douglass' slave narrative became a classic in American literature as well as a primary source written from the slave's perspective.

His own antislavery newspaper, the *North Star*, which he published from 1847 to 1860 at Rochester, New York, was also instrumental in strengthening the abolitionist cause.

A number of factors combined to give the abolitionist movement an increased momentum. In addition to the issue of permitting or outlawing slavery in the new Western territories, most of these abolitionists expressed their opposition to the Fugitive Slave Law of 1850, which put runaway slaves at the mercy of ruthless hunters. A martyr in the cause, John Brown (1800–59) was repulsed by this measure. He did not rest until he created the conditions for establishing a sanctuary for runaway slaves in the Maryland and Virginia mountains. On the night of October 16, 1859, Brown and a group of sixteen whites and five blacks unsuccessfully raided the federal arsenal at Harpers Ferry, Virginia. Brown believed that escaped slaves would join his rebellion and eventually form an army of emancipation. He was tried for murder, slave insurrection, and treason against the state and was convicted and hanged.

Over time thanks to the efforts of these abolitionists and as the gulf between the North and the South widened, American society—especially the South—came to understand that its entire way of life based on cheap labor provided by slaves was irretrievably threatened when President Abraham Lincoln was elected to the White House. The Civil War (1861–65), which began as an attempt to preserve the Union and halt Southern Confederate impulses, finally resulted in the emancipation of almost four million blacks. Even if the Civil War outlawed slavery on American soil, a whole new series of challenges and difficulties awaited the liberated African Americans during the Reconstruction period and afterwards. Under the pressure of worldwide public opinion, slavery was finally abolished in the Western hemisphere by 1900.

Further Reading

Adler, Mortimer. *The Annals of America*. Chicago: Encyclopaedia Britannica, 1976.

The New Encyclopaedia Britannica. 15th ed. Chicago: Encyclopaedia Britannica, 1988.

Zinn, Howard. *A People's History of the United States*. New York: Harper & Row, 1980.

Reinaldo Francisco Silva

ABU JABER, DIANA (1960–)   Arab American novelist. Abu Jaber's contribution to Arab American literature has mainly consisted of two novels that illustrate, often in a humorous light, the difficulties of forming an Arab American **identity**. She is currently recognized as one of the most important young writers in the emerging genre of Arab American literature.

Born in Syracuse, New York, to a Jordanian father and an American (Irish-German) mother, she and her family moved to Jordan for two years when Abu Jaber was a child. In 1986 she earned a PhD in creative writing from SUNY Binghamton. Her first novel, *Arabian Jazz* (1993), published when Abu Jaber was thirty-three years old, won the Oregon Book Award and was a finalist for the national PEN/Hemingway Award. The novel also won her simultaneous praise and criticism from the American and Arab American reading audience.

Arabian Jazz is set in upstate New York, where the author herself was raised, and traces the saga of the Ramoud family. Matussem Ramoud, the father, is a widower, an Arab American who lost his wife years ago. His two daughters, Jemora and Melvina, have both recovered from the loss of their mother in very different ways. Melvina has thrown herself into her work and nursing career, while Jem—who is approaching thirty—feels lost, both in terms of her career (she works in an unfulfilling and unsatisfying job) and personally. She has not married and is feeling pressured to do so, but cannot devote her life to someone else when she is unsure of her own identity.

Further complicating Jem's crisis is the atmosphere in the local Arab community. Although Jem feels bonded to the Arab language and Arab culture, she cannot help but feel disconnected at times by characters such as her overbearing paternal aunt, who is aggressively hunting for Arab husbands for her nieces.

When *Arabian Jazz* was published the depictions of the potential bridegrooms and their aggressive mothers (one of whom insists on inspecting the teeth of any prospective daughter-in-law) was viewed as humorous by some readers and as stereotypical and offensive by others. Some readers considered the depiction of Jem's aunt and other Arab characters, such as Jem's ill-mannered and womanizing uncle, to be poorly drawn and superficially developed. The publication of the book, and the wide media attention it received, highlighted a major rift in the Arab American literary community, prompting debate about the responsibility (or lack thereof) of Arab artists in representing the community.

Jem's sense of being a cultural misfit continues to plague her, and is only reconciled when a distant cousin comes to visit them in New York. Before Nader's arrival, Jem had considered a move to Jordan to reconcile her cultural ambiguity. Nader, who was born in Jordan but who has traveled the world extensively, however, helps Jem understand that she does not need to make a physical journey to understand her identity, and that perhaps her identity can be reconciled in any place she chooses to call home.

Identity is also the theme of Abu-Jaber's second novel, *Crescent* (2003), the tale of an Iraqi American orphan, raised by her uncle, a master storyteller. Sirine, who is thirty-nine years old, is a chef in a small Middle Eastern restaurant in Los Angeles, where she has earned a reputation for her cuisine. Food is the single strand that connects her to her culture, and she is masterful at it, finding solace and peace working in the kitchen among the aroma of spices and smells.

She is satisfied with her life until she meets Hanif, a handsome Iraqi immigrant and a professor at the local university, who starts frequenting the restaurant. Sirine suddenly wants to know more about her ethnic heritage, as an Arab and specifically as an Iraqi. The obstacles that present themselves during the development of the romance leave Sirine questioning her roots and even her desire to identify herself as an Arab.

Like *Arabian Jazz*, *Crescent*'s storyline is often humorous, which is an unusual approach in the emerging genre of Arab American literature, given the often-political nature of Arab-American identity. Abu-Jaber's contribution to the genre also lies in her ability to navigate the tenuous terrain of identity crises, especially of female protagonists. (*See also* Arab American Novel)

Further Reading

De Haven, Tom. "Arabian Jazz." *New York Times Book Review* (July 18, 1993): E9.

Salaita, Steven. "Sand Niggers, Small Shops, and Uncle Sam: Cultural Negotiation in the Fiction of Joseph Geha and Diana Abu-Jaber." *Criticism* 43.4 (2001): 423–444.

Shalal-Esa, Andrea. "Diana Abu-Jaber: The Only Response to Silencing . . . Is to Keep Speaking." *Al Jadid* 8.39 (Spring 2002): 4–6.

Susan Muaddi Darraj

ACKER, KATHY (1948–1997)   Jewish American performance artist, avant-garde novelist, and poet. Kathy Acker grew up in an upper-middle-class Jewish household in New York City, and her writing expresses a resistance to and reworking of not only traditional notions of appropriate Jewish femininity and sexual conservatism, but of traditional notions of literary genre and narrative form.

Concrete information about Kathy Acker is, not incidentally, hard to discern: Acker's body of written work, like her physical body, the subject of her performative persona, is malleable, hard to define, and often impossible to locate within any specific literary or social genre. As a result of the combination of narrative styles—including philosophical theory, popular cultural references, drawings, and extracted chunks of **canon**ical texts— that may be present within any one of Acker's novels, Acker's proponents and detractors have ascribed to her such divergent monikers as punk, postmodern, postfeminist, poststructuralist, and plagiarist, none of which fully encompasses the range and scope of Acker's literary project. Part of the confusion stems from Acker's multiple authorial positions in works like *The Childlike Life of the Black Tarantula: By the Black Tarantula* (1973) and *The Adult Life of Toulouse Lautrec: By Henri Toulouse Lautrec* (1975) as well as her appropriation of extant famous literary titles—*Great Expectations* (1983) and *Don Quixote* (1986) for example.

Like her primary literary influences, William S. Burroughs and **Allen Ginsberg**, Acker's writing is both experimental and infused with her status and physical image as a counter-cultural icon. In the 1960s she was loosely affiliated with the Dadaist FLUXUS group, an art movement founded upon anarchist social principles. In college at Brandeis University and later at the

11

University of California, San Diego, she studied with the Marxist psychologist Herbert Marcuse and the poet **Jerome Rothenberg** before turning to fiction as her primary source of creative expression. But Acker's work is equally influenced by her experiences working as a stripper in New York during her twenties, and by her performative manipulation of her body through tattooing, piercing, bodybuilding, and ultimately the double mastectomy that she underwent in 1996 after being diagnosed with breast cancer.

Acker's best-known novel, *Blood and Guts in High School* (1978), is nonlinear and allows the reader to enter the text at any given point. Made up of several of Acker's performance pieces, *Blood and Guts* chronicles the life of protagonist Janey Smith. In Germany, where it was printed under the title *Tough Girls Don't Cry*, it was banned for its sexually descriptive content. This banning is merely one example of the controversy that remained constant during Acker's career; while living in England, she was charged with plagiarism for incorporating, verbatim, several pages of Harold Robbins's novel *The Pirate* in *The Adult Life of Toulous Lautrec*. But piracy and appropriation are major themes that Acker actively demonstrates in her works by placing the familiar writing of other authors in unfamiliar contexts, and by changing the genders of famous literary characters as well as the time periods of more canonical literary texts. The resulting pastiche emerges from fragments of extant texts; for example, Acker's final novel, *Pussy, King of the Pirates* (1996), loosely based on Robert Louis Stevenson's *Treasure Island*, is a female pirate narrative that journeys from a whorehouse in Alexandria to a city that may (or may not) be located in the future.

Perhaps one of Acker's greatest achievements is the tenacity of her writing as evidenced by the fact that many of her novels—even those written decades ago—remain in print. Acker's genius is apparent in writing that blurs the academic and the personal, the intellectual and the physical, and, ultimately, the marginal and the mainstream.

Further Reading

King, Noel. "Kathy Acker on the Loose." *Meanjin* 55.2 (1996): 334–40.

Moran, Joe. *Star Authors: Literary Celebrity in America*. London: Pluto Press, 2000.

Laura Wright

ACOSTA, OSCAR ZETA (1935–1974?)   Chicano memoirist, fiction writer, lawyer, and activist. In 1974 Acosta made his last known contact with civilization when he telephoned his son from Mexico. Acosta's famous disappearance and presumed death has only added to the legend that began to crystallize around the Acosta-inspired character Dr. Gonzo, Hunter S. Thompson's Samoan sidekick in *Fear and Loathing in Las Vegas* (1971). Acosta's unique place in Chicano letters and American cultural history resides in the turmoil that surrounded his life, recorded in two semifictional memoirs, *The Autobiography of a Brown Buffalo* (1972) and *The Revolt of the Cockroach People* (1973). Acosta draws his deepest inspiration in this work from the psychological trauma of a reckless lifestyle and from the social trauma of a vexed period in U.S. history. Together the memoirs chronicle Acosta's ethnic awakening and artistic emergence, from self-doubting war-on-poverty lawyer to bona fide Chicano activist, during the late 1960s and early 1970s.

Acosta was born in El Paso, Texas, to a working class *mestizo* family. (Acosta claimed direct descent from the *indios* of Durango, Mexico, on his father's side of the family.) His family moved to the San Joaquin valley in California while Acosta was still a young child, and after a relatively normal childhood he joined the Air Force to perform in its military band. While still a young man Acosta converted to the Baptist faith, and traveled to Panama, where he was a missionary at a lepers colony. He eventually worked his way through college and San Francisco Law School, taking a job at the East Oakland Legal Aid Society. Around this time Acosta began writing poetry, drama, and fiction, including the short story, "Perla is a Pig" (1970), which was first published in the avant-garde Chicano journal *Con Safos*. (This work was posthumously published in *Oscar "Zeta" Acosta: The Uncollected Works* [1996].)

The Autobiography of a Brown Buffalo recounts these and other moments in Acosta's early life, but the memoir begins *in medias res*, as the burnt-out lawyer teeters on the verge of a psychological breakdown. In response to the crisis, Buffalo Zeta Brown, the semifictional persona who narrates Acosta's life story, undertakes a spiritual odyssey in search of his roots in El Paso and Mexico, a journey in keeping with the now-classic arc of bohemian vagabondage. *Brown Buffalo* culls its narrative from several Beat Generation mainstays—dank, seedy bars peopled with social misfits, free-love hippie communes, separatist bunkers loaded with acid rock LPs and paramilitary firearms, Mexican red-light district *cantinas*—only to find each locale devoid of lasting meaning. The narrative repeatedly projects the psychological onto the social, so that the repair of the fractured self suggests the possibility of communal rebirth; in the words of Ramón Saldívar, *Brown Buffalo* articulates a "shared desire, itself related to the historical moment of the late 1960s and early 1970s, to fashion out of the instability and fragmentation of social life a utopian vision of collective action" (74). The memoir ends with Brown Buffalo's profound conversion experience, in which he rejects both U.S. and Mexican officialdom to proclaim himself a member of the Chicano community.

The Revolt of the Cockroach People takes up where *Brown Buffalo* left off: in the heat of the Chicano Movement of Los Angeles. Buffalo Zeta Brown, who has rededicated himself to his legal career, this time working on behalf of Chicano activists, uncovers hypocrisy and corruption in the institutional pillars of society: the church, the schools, and the courts. Buffalo handles several controversial cases, representing demonstrators whose social protests land them in jail. The memoir recounts several key moments in the Chicano Movement, from the incarceration of the "Saint Basil Twenty-One" to school walkouts to the Chicano Moratorium riots to the suspicious death of Chicano journalist Rubén Salazar ("Roland Zanzibar" in the memoir) at the hands of the Los Angeles police. It is this latter tragedy that leads Buffalo to reject the law in favor of a career—or more precisely a vocation—in writing. As Michael Hames-García notes, Acosta saw "extralegal pressure [as] necessary to transform the system, to eliminate the repressive legal features of society, and to project a radical vision of justice that could serve the interests of Chicanos" (483). We must situate Acosta's writing alongside his other, more radical gestures, if we are to grasp the full significance of his life's work. (*See also* Mexican American Autobiography)

Further Reading

Hames-García, Michael. "Dr. Gonzo's Carnival: The Testimonial Satires of Oscar Zeta Acosta." *American Literature* 72 (2000): 463–93.

Lee, A. Robert. "Chicanismo's Beat Outrider?: The Texts and Contexts of Oscar Zeta Acosta." *The Beat Generation: Critical Essays*. Ed. Kostas Myrsiades. New York: Peter Lang, 2002. 259–80.

Saldívar, Ramón. *Chicano Narrative: The Dialectics of Difference*. Madison: U of Wisconsin P, 1990.

Stavans, Ilan. *Bandito: Oscar "Zeta" Acosta and the Chicano Experience*. New York: Icon, 1995.

Michael Soto

ADAMIC, LOUIS (1898–1951)   Slovenian American novelist, publicist, and political activist. With his twenty books of documentary prose and fiction, some 500 articles, and his public lectures—particularly those focusing on the role of immigrants in the development of the nation—Adamic has played a prominent part not only in American ethnic literature but also in the prehistory of American **multiculturalism.**

Born in Blato, Slovenia, he emigrated to the United States at fifteen. He worked for a Slovenian immigrant newspaper in New York, served in the army, traveled all over the States, and worked his way through various jobs. Having improved his English, he began to publish original material and his translations from Slavic authors in *Pearson's Magazine*, Haldeman-Julius publications, *Our World*, *The Living Age*, *American Mercury*, and various Slovenian American journals. In 1929 he became a freelance writer and moved back to New York, married a young Jewish intellectual, and finished his first two major works: *Dynamite: A History of Class Violence in America, 1830–1930* (1931), which—although it evoked contradictory public response—was later used in some eighty U.S. colleges; and *Laughing in the Jungle* (1932), an anecdotic autobiographic narrative including social commentary and tragicomic portraits of people who had been part of his immigrant experience.

Back from a visit to Yugoslavia, Adamic wrote *The Native's Return* (1934), a Book-of-the-Month Club selection for February 1934, in which he condemned King Alexander's dictatorship and predicted his assassination.

The book was prohibited in Yugoslavia and an immediate success in the United States. His next major work was *Grandsons* (1935), one of his few works of fiction. Its topic represents a link between the American "jungle" of his early autobiography and his four later books on social and intercultural relations within the country. This novel about third-generation immigrants and their lack of a feeling of rootedness demonstrates the tragic results of their inferiority complex, imposed by the American success mentality and exaggerated individualism.

Adamic continued his determined investigation of the United States and published *My America* (1938), a compilation of his articles written since 1934. During the war years, he was engaged in political activism but still managed to accomplish his major writing project, the Nation of Nations series. The first volume, titled *From Many Lands* (1940)—a collection of portraits of mostly ordinary immigrants—won the John Anisfield Award as "the most significant book of 1940 on **race** relations in the contemporary world." The series further included *Two-Way Passage* (1941), *What's Your Name?* (1942), and *A Nation of Nations* (1945). Although Adamic consistently stressed the significance of ethnic heritage, he also considered with great sensitivity the many faces of its stigma. His social criticism exposes nationwide ignorance, **racism**, and xenophobia as tools of exploitative capitalism. Adamic argued for pluralism, for a dynamic, ever-evolving American culture that not only respects and protects its cultural diversity but also gains vitality from it.

In *Two-Way Passage*, Adamic suggested that qualified American immigrants should help the postwar Europe by spending the first postwar years in their native lands to share their know-how and democratic values. This brought him an invitation for dinner with the Roosevelts and Churchill in January 1942. Alarmed at subsequent world tensions, Adamic published *Dinner at the White House* (1946), in which he challenged U.S. and British foreign policy. Churchill sued him for libel; Adamic lost his publisher but remained general editor for nine of the Peoples of America Series (1946–50), published by Lippincott. Upon the Tito-Stalin split in 1948, Adamic sided with the former, visited his native land for a second time, and wrote *The Eagle and the Roots* (1952) to clarify the split. Facing a wide range of political opponents, he now also became a target of the House Un-American Activities Committee. On September 5, 1951, Adamic was found shot in his burning farmhouse. His death was proclaimed a suicide, which evoked considerable doubt in the media. His posthumously published book contains only chapters on postwar Yugoslavia and President Tito's life. A book-sized chapter on the contemporary U.S. domestic and foreign policy, the psychosis of the emerging McCarthy era, and the U.S. motives for entering the Korean War has remained unpublished.

Adamic's life is a unique experience of a boy from the Slovenian countryside, with scarce formal education, who became a nationally recognized, award-winning American writer and the guest of presidents Roosevelt and

Truman. His writing brought him an honorary doctorate from Temple University, Philadelphia (1941); the Yugoslav Order of Brotherhood and Unity (1944); and correspondent membership of the Serbian Academy of Sciences and Arts (1949). His endorsements from renowned authors such as Upton Sinclair, Sinclair Lewis, **H. L. Mencken**, Sherwood Anderson, and **F. Scott Fitzgerald** contributed largely to his outstanding literary career.

Adamic's writing reveals an author who is equally convincing in his sincere attempt to understand class violence, social change, or inner and outer conflicts relating to ethnic and cultural diversity. Throughout his lifetime, feeling simultaneously an insider and outsider, Adamic was seeking a balance between his role of a watchful observer and that of an activist. Probably his most characteristic feature is that he actually managed to remain detached from stereotypes and from any preformulated ideology. Numerous American authors in the field of multicultural studies, including Werner Sollors, have considered his views. Although written in English, most of Adamic's books include a treatment of Slovenian-related subjects in a way that fosters an integration of the literary heritage and cultural values of his two homelands. Therefore his writing has been fully accepted in the Slovenian literary canon as well. (*See also* Slovene American Literature)

Further Reading

Christian, Henry A. *Louis Adamic: A Checklist*. Kent, OH: Kent State UP, 1971.

McWilliams, Carey. *Louis Adamic and Shadow-America*. Los Angeles: Arthur Whipple, 1935.

Petrič, Jerneja. *Svetovi Louisa Adamiča*. Ljubljana: Cankarjeva založba, 1981.

Shiffman, Dan. *Rooting Multiculturalism: The Work of Louis Adamič*. Madison–Teaneck: Farleigh Dickinson University Press; London: Associated University Press, 2003.

Stanonik, Janez, ed. *Louis Adamič: Simpozij/Symposium*. Ljubljana: Univerza Edvarda Kardelja, 1981.

Žitnik, Janja. *Pero in politika: Zadnja leta Louisa Adamiča*. Ljubljana: Slovenska matica, 1993.

Janja Žitnik

ADAMS, ELIZABETH LAURA (1909–)   African American memoirist. With the publication of *Dark Symphony* (1942) Elizabeth Laura Adams sustained the genre of African American women's spiritual biographies while also presenting the first African American memoir on the subject of Catholic conversion. Though primarily flourishing in the last quarter of the nineteenth century, this genre continues to interest readers and produced an arena for spiritual expression.

Dark Symphony (1941) was criticized as short on anecdotes, and Adams responded by saying that her memoir was a search for spiritual peace and was concerned with internal matters of the soul and heart and not with external worldly events, although Adams's battle with racial discrimination is a recurrent motif. Criticism was markedly split along racial lines. White reviewers praised her work whereas African American reviewers found it dull and inauthentic.

After a pleasant and intellectual childhood, Adams was disappointed in her ambitions for a writing career, an education, and a musical career as a concert violinist. Within *Dark Symphony* (1942), she attributes her strength in dealing with life's disappointments to her strong religious upbringing and religious faith. She also explores how her alienation from the Methodist church manifested in her childhood. Displays of screaming and spiritual dancing that alarmed her timid sensibilities coupled with the humiliation suffered by adult criticism of her failure to memorize assigned scriptures turned Adams against the church, though she admired religious music during the services.

Her parents, Daniel Henderson and Lula Josephine Holden Adams, taught her to ignore racial epithets and find refuge in religion, poetry, classical music, and the arts. Raised in a strong patriarchal household, her attraction to Catholicism was stymied until her father, a Mason, died. Adams details her conversion, which occurred just after her father died at the beginning of the Great Depression.

Gaining her mother's permission, she converted with plans to join a convent, but had to go to work to support her mother after she divorced her second husband. She provided support for her mother until her death in 1952 by doing domestic and secretarial work and sometimes bringing home supplemental income with her writing. Despite rejections she suffered at the hands of the Catholic Church because of her race, she clung tenaciously to her belief that she could eliminate racial prejudice by working through the church.

Her stories, articles, and poems were published by *The Torch*, a Catholic journal, and are much like *Dark Symphony*; they marry themes of religion and spirituality with **race**. Imbued with her positive attitude that racial inequality would be eradicated from society through perseverance, the narrative of *Dark Symphony* alternates between her adult and childhood voices and appeals to readers of all ages.

Further Reading

Rellihan, Heather. "Elizabeth Laura Adams." *African American Autobiographers: A Sourcebook.* Ed. Emmanuel S. Nelson. Westport, CT: Greenwood Press, 2002. 1–4.

Rebecca Tolley-Stokes

ADDONIZIO, KIM (1954–) Italian American poet, writer of short stories, and teacher. She is the author of four books of poetry: *The Philosopher's Club* (1994); *Jimmy & Rita* (1997); *Tell Me* (2000), which was a finalist for the 2000 National Book Award; and *What Is This Thing Called Love* (2004). A collection of short stories, *In the Box Called Pleasure*, was published in 1999. With Dorianne Laux, she coauthored *The Poet's Companion: A Guide to the Pleasures of Writing Poetry* (1997), a complex and passionate guidebook to the writing of poetry, and coedited with Cheryl Dumesnil *Dorothy*

Parker's Elbow: Tattoos on Writers, Writers on Tattoos (2002), a collection of poems, memoirs, and short stories about tattoos, their fascination, and their permanence. In 2004 *Swearing, Smoking, Drinking, & Kissing* was released, a word/music CD with poems by Kim Addonizio and Susan Browne. Kim Addonizio has been the recipient of two fellowships from the National Endowment for the Arts, a Pushcart Prize, a Commonwealth Club Poetry Medal, and the John Ciardi Lifetime Achievement Award.

Addonizio writes realist poetry in a personal, lyrical mode that is both passionate and fearless. She feels no qualms about saying what most people would not dare and, as a result, her work is characterized by a refreshing sense of penetrating directness and heartbreaking intensity. Addonizio's most important themes include single motherhood, interpersonal relationships, and Italian American and working class **identity**. Her book *Tell Me* includes some of her most representative poems, such as "Virgin Spring," "Therapy," and "The Promise," which chronicle wry and redemptive feminist visions, in lucid and visceral language, that portray female speakers perservering against overwhelming odds.

In her post-postmodern, postfeminist short stories, her prose is at the same time aggressive, lucid, edgy, and experimental, and the characters—all women—are obsessed, drunk, desperate, lonely, unconventional, fiercely independent, continuously redefining their body politics. In stories like "The Gift," the fixity of sexual identity is challenged when a woman, who finds a dildo in the street and takes it home, wakes up to find herself in a young man's body. In "But," the dream of romantic love and marriage is shattered in a story of violence, sex, alcohol, and drugs. In "Bedtime Story," the reassuring fairy-tale that induces sleep and sweet dreams upon children is transformed into a surreal nightmare in which a woman becomes so lonely when her lover leaves, after thousands or years of enchainment and violent sexual intercourse, that she eats herself up until only her head is left. A mixture of sexuality, obsessions, loneliness, pleasure, and lust, her stories are an exploration of the self and of the human condition at the turn of the third millennium. (*See also* Italian American Poetry)

Further Reading

Giunta, Edvige. *Writing with an Accent: Contemporary Italian American Women Authors.* New York: Palgrave/St. Martin's Press, 2002.

Caterina Romeo

AFRICAN AMERICAN AUTOBIOGRAPHY   Any discussion of autobiography involves historical and literary considerations; therefore, it is appropriate at the beginning of this essay to cite important dates in African American history and literature. Africans arrived in the New World as early as 1492 when Pedro Alonzo Nino, who was of African descent, was one of the explorers who sailed with Christopher Columbus. Thirty-four years later, in 1526, the first African slaves arrived in territory that eventually became part of the United States (in present day South Carolina).

Twenty Africans in 1619 arrived in Jamestown, Virginia, as indentured servants and were the first Africans to settle in North America. When did the African American literary tradition begin? Many individuals mistakenly believe that it originated with Phillis Wheatley, author of "On Messrs. Hussey and Coffin" (1767), her first published poem; and *Poems on Various Subjects, Religious and Moral* (1773), the first book of verse published by an African American. However, the African American literary tradition began decades earlier, in 1746, when Lucy Terry, at the age of sixteen, wrote "Bars Fight," the earliest known work by an African American. Since Terry's poem was not published until 1855, **Jupiter Hammon**'s poem "An Evening Thought," written on December 25, 1760 and published in 1761, is acknowledged as the first poem published by an African American. Yet the first published work by an African American is not a poem; it is an autobiography. *A Narrative of the Uncommon Sufferings and Surprizing Deliverance of Briton Hammon, a Negro Man* (1760) marks the beginning of African American prose and, more specifically, the inception of African American autobiography. Since then, autobiography has maintained an influential position in African American literature as thousands of black men and women have written or dictated their life stories.

Eighteenth- and Nineteenth-Century Autobiographies

Spiritual Narratives

Although it is not known whether Hammon wrote or dictated his fourteen-page autobiography, his *Narrative* recounts the traumatic events that transpire after his master allows him to go to sea and he is captured by Native Americans; Hammon ends his autobiography praising God. Thus Hammon's *Narrative* blends the theme of **slavery** and two motifs that were popular in colonial American literature: Native American captivity and Christian conversion. Unlike Hammon, a number of eighteenth- and nineteenth-century African American autobiographers focused primarily on sacred concerns. Spiritual narratives were created by former slaves, including *A Brief Account of the Life, Experiences, Travels, and Gospel Labours of George White* (1810); *The Life, Experience and Gospel Labors of the Rt. Rev. Richard Allen* (1833); and *Memoir of Old Elizabeth* (1863). A number of spiritual narratives were written by African Americans who had never been enslaved; among these works is *The Life and Religious Experience of Jarena Lee, a Coloured Lady, Giving an Account of Her Call to Preach the Gospel* (1836), which is the first autobiography written by an African American woman. Other spiritual autobiographies authored by free blacks include *A Narrative of the Lord's Wonderful Dealings with John Marrant* (1785); *A Journal of the Rev. **John Marrant*** (1790); *Memoirs of the Life, Religious Experience, Ministerial Travels and Labours of Mrs. Zilpha Elaw* (1846); *A Narrative of the Life and Travels of Mrs. **Nancy Prince*** (1850); **Julia A. J. Foote**'s *A Brand Plucked from the Fire* (1879); and Daniel A. Payne's *Recollections of Seventy Years* (1888). Spiritual narratives dominated

African American literary production in the late eighteenth century, yet they were eclipsed by slave narratives in the nineteenth century. Although liberation was a paramount concern in both types of autobiographies, spiritual narrators endeavored to be free of sin, and slave narrators sought emancipation from servitude.

Slave Narratives

Hammon's autobiography is the first **African American slave narrative**. The slave narrative, defined as a first-person, written or oral testimony of African American bondage, is the earliest form of African American autobiography. Hammon's *Narrative* was followed by *A Narrative of the Most Remarkable Particulars in the Life of James Albert Ukawsaw Gronniosaw, an African Prince, as Related by Himself* (1772); and the two-volume *The Interesting Narrative of the Life of Olaudah Equiano, or Gustavus Vassa, the African Written by Himself* (1789). Gronniosaw and **Equiano** provide rare, firsthand accounts of life in Africa prior to their arrival in America, and as their titles reveal, Gronniosaw dictated his life story and Equiano wrote his. Thus Equiano's *Interesting Narrative*, the most widely read eighteenth-century slave narrative, is apparently the first full-length autobiography written by an African American and is recognized as the prototype of the slave narrative. William Andrews estimates that approximately seventy slave narratives were published as books or pamphlets between 1760 and 1865 and that at least fifty book-length slave narratives were published from 1865 to 1930 ("Slave Narrative" 667–68), whereas Frances Smith Foster opines that the total number of slave narratives written or dictated over the years in formats ranging from interviews of a single page to books is at least 6,000 (ix).

Gronniosaw's *Narrative* begins with the phrase "I was born," a convention that was frequently employed in subsequent slave narratives. James Olney identifies additional definitive features found in many slave narratives including testimonials written by white **abolition**ists, editors, and so forth verifying the authenticity and accuracy of the autobiographies; memories of "first observed whipping"; descriptions of Christian masters or mistresses; accounts of literacy efforts; details of slave auctions; descriptions of failed as well as successful escape attempts; and selections of new surnames (152–53). Foster has identified "four chronological phases" found in many slave narratives: (1) "the loss of innocence" as one becomes aware of "what it means to be a slave"; (2) "realization of alternatives to bondage and the formulation of a resolve to be free"; (3) "the escape"; and (4) "freedom obtained" (85).

In addition to the autobiographies by Hammon, Gronniosaw, and Equiano, other noteworthy slave narratives include *The Confessions of Nat Turner* (1831); *Narrative of the Life and Adventures of Henry Bibb, An American Slave, Written by Himself* (1849); *The Fugitive Blacksmith; or, Events in the History of James W. C. Pennington* (1849); *Narrative of Sojourner Truth* (1850); *Twelve Years a Slave: Narrative of Solomon Northrup* (1853); *J. W. Loguen, as a Slave and as a Freeman. A Narrative of Real Life* (1859); *Running a Thousand Miles for Freedom; or the Escape of William and Ellen Craft from Slavery* (1860); and **Elizabeth Keckley**'s *Behind the Scenes; or, Thirty Years a Slave and Four Years in the White House* (1868). Three slave narratives have attained the status of classics in African American autobiography: *Narrative of the Life of **Frederick Douglass**, an American Slave, Written by Himself* (1845); *Narrative of William Wells Brown, a Fugitive Slave, Written by Himself* (1847); and **Harriet Jacobs**'s *Incidents in the Life of a Slave Girl, Written by Herself* (1861).

Narrative of the Life of Frederick Douglass, an American Slave, Written by Himself is the preeminent slave narrative. Although Douglass had escaped to the North by the time his *Narrative* was published, he was still a fugitive slave until his freedom was purchased in 1846. Unlike Brown, Douglass does not identify himself as a fugitive slave in the title of his first autobiography; instead he describes himself as an American slave. Thus *Narrative*'s title contains an indictment against the nation that professed to be the land of liberty while it concurrently enslaved African Americans. Douglass expressed this idea in a more vehement manner in his famous 1852 speech "What to the Slave Is the Fourth of July?" in Rochester, New York. Although *Narrative*'s title also includes the phrase "Written by Himself," many of Douglass's contemporaries doubted that Douglass, who was self-educated, could write such an eloquent autobiography; however, if they heard his speech in Rochester or at any other rally sponsored by abolitionists, they realized that Douglass was an exceptional orator as well. Douglass's *Narrative*, along with autobiographies by Brown, Jacobs, and others, became powerful weapons for abolitionists. In Chapters One through Nine of the *Narrative*, Douglass shows how a human being is made a slave as he depicts slavery's horrors, including the beating of his Aunt Hester, which he witnesses as a boy and considers his initiation into slavery. In Chapter Ten, Douglass reveals how a slave is transformed into a man as he resolves, prior to his successful escape in Chapter Eleven, that although his slave status is unchanged, he no longer views himself as a bondman. Douglass provides more details about his life as a slave and as an abolitionist in two additional autobiographies, *My Bondage and My Freedom* (1855) and *The Life and Times of Frederick Douglass* (1881).

Douglass's *Narrative* overshadowed all other slave narratives, including the aforementioned works by Brown and Jacobs. Brown wrote several short autobiographies including the 36-page *Memoir of William Wells Brown, an American Bondman, Written by Himself* (1859), and like Douglass, he also wrote three book-length autobiographies. *Narrative of Williams Wells Brown* ranked second in popularity and sales only to Douglass's *Narrative*. Brown's second book-length autobiography, *Three Years in Europe: Or Places I Have Seen and People I Have Met* (published in London, 1852), was published in Boston as *The American Fugitive in Europe, Sketches of Places and People Abroad* (1855). Brown, with the publication of his second autobiography, followed the tradition established as early as John Marrant, who as previously mentioned, published autobiographies in 1785 and 1790. Unlike Marrant's autobiographies, each of Brown's autobiographies was full-length. Thus Marrant and Brown paved the way for nineteenth-century African American autobiographers such as Douglass and twentieth-century African American autobiographers such as **Langston Hughes**, **W. E. B. Du Bois**, **Maya Angelou**, and **Chester Himes** who published multiple autobiographies. Indeed Angelou has carried Marrant and Brown's tradition into the twenty-first century as her sixth autobiography was published in 2002. Brown's third book-length autobiography, *My Southern Home, or the South and Its People* (1880), is regarded as a bridge between slave narratives and early twentieth-century African American fiction and nonfiction. Jacobs's *Incidents in the Life of a Slave Girl* is not the first American slave narrative by a female; *The History of Mary Prince, a West Indian Slave, Related by Herself* (1831) holds that distinction. Jacobs, who hid in a crawl space for seven years rather than become her master's concubine, wrote the only known full-length African American female slave narrative in order to draw attention to the multitude of African American mothers who were still enslaved. Thus Jacobs, like Douglass and Brown, as well as the other slave narrators, wrote and spoke for the silent, enslaved masses.

The influence of the slave narratives can be seen in the earliest African American novels including William Wells Brown's *Clotel: Or the President's Daughter, A Narrative of Slave Life in the United States* (1853); **Frank J. Webb's** *The Garies and Their Friends* (1857); and **Frances E. W. Harper's** *Iola Leroy: Or, Shadows Uplifted* (1892). Evoking themes of slavery is not a convention that is limited to nineteenth-century fiction. Twentieth-century African American novels such as **Arna Bontemps's** *Black Thunder* (1936); **Margaret Walker's** *Jubilee* (1966); **Ernest J. Gaines's** *The Autobiography of Miss Jane Pittman* (1971); **Alex Haley's** *Roots* (1976); **Octavia Butler's** *Kindred* (1979); **Barbara Chase-Riboud's** *Sally Hemings* (1979) and its sequel, *The President's Daughter* (1994); **Sherley Anne Williams's** *Dessa Rose* (1986); **Toni Morrison's** *Beloved* (1987); Chase-Riboud's *Echo of Lions* (1989); **Charles Johnson's** *Middle Passage* (1990); and **Louise Meriwether's** *Fragments of the Ark* (1994) are neo-slave narratives that consider slavery's myriad experiences or effects. Early twenty-first-century **neo-slave narrative**s include Lalita Tademy's *Cane River* (2001); **Hannah Craft's** *The Bondwoman's Narrative* (written in the 1850s but unpublished until 2002); David Anthony Durham's *Walk Through Darkness* (2002); and **Edward P. Jones's** *The Known World* (2003).

Twentieth- and Twenty-first-Century Autobiographies

Obviously identity is of paramount concern to African American autobiographers. During the eighteenth and nineteenth centuries, slaves produced autobiographies that proclaimed their personhood in a society that primarily viewed them as property. After slavery was abolished, African American autobiography, while continuing to present realistic images of black life in America, began providing a panoramic view of African American life as opportunities for blacks increased and became more diverse with each subsequent decade.

1900 to 1950

During the first half of the twentieth century, the last slave narrative was published—**Booker T. Washington**'s *Up from Slavery* (1901). Washington's autobiography, which details his birth into slavery less than a decade before the Emancipation Proclamation was issued, his founding of Tuskegee Institute, and his Atlanta Exposition Address in 1895, was the most popular African American autobiography until the 1940s. After *Up from Slavery*'s publication, the next two significant African American autobiographies were authored by William Pickens, who encouraged black Americans to ignore Washington's philosophy of industrial education and tolerance of racial discrimination in favor of W. E. B. Du Bois's philosophy of academic education as well as political and civil rights. Although Pickens, who was a college administrator, journalist, orator, National Association for the Advancement of Colored People (NAACP) official, and government official, was not born into slavery, his parents were. Pickens's first autobiography, *The Heir of Slaves* (1911) was expanded into *Bursting Bonds* (1923). **James Weldon Johnson**, a NAACP colleague of Pickens and Du Bois, wrote his autobiography, *Along This Way* (1933), after readers mistakenly believed that his novel, *The Autobiography of an Ex-Colored Man* (1912), was his life story. Du Bois, the foremost African American intellectual of the twentieth century, wrote two autobiographies: *Dusk of Dawn* (1940) and the posthumously published *The Autobiography of W. E. B. Du Bois* (1968). In addition to Du Bois's first autobiography, the 1940s marked the publication of Langston Hughes's *The Big Sea* (1940), **Zora Neale Hurston**'s *Dust Tracks on a Road* (1942), and **Richard Wright**'s *Black Boy* (1945). *The Big Sea* begins ironically as the twenty-one-year-old Hughes, on board the S.S. *Malone,* tosses his books into the Atlantic Ocean in an effort to be free of his unhappy past, before the ship sails to Africa. Hughes's autobiography evokes Foster's previously mentioned chronological phases of slave narratives: developing awareness, resolving to be free, escaping, and gaining freedom (85). In Part One of *The Big Sea*, "Twenty-one," Hughes writes that although he has attained adulthood, others exert too much control over him. In an effort to take charge of his life, he signs on board the ship as a mess boy in order to see Africa, the land of his dreams. In Part Two, "The Big Sea," Hughes celebrates his independence as he experiences life's ups and downs. Hughes was not the only member of the **Harlem Renaissance** to publish his autobiography; previously mentioned autobiographies by Johnson and Du Bois as well as **Claude McKay**'s *A Long Way From Home* (1937) preceded his, and Hurston's *Dust Tracks* and Walter White's *A Man Called White* (1948) followed *The Big Sea*. However in the third section of *The Big Sea*, "Black Renaissance," Hughes provides the most detailed written account of the Harlem Renaissance by one of its participants. Hughes focuses on his travels in his second autobiography, *I Wonder as I Wander* (1956). Both autobiographies employ the travel motif established in Brown's aforementioned *The American Fugitive*.

Hurston's *Dust Tracks*, along with her works of fiction, has received renewed interest since Alice Walker traveled to Florida in 1973 and placed a marker on Hurston's unmarked grave. Hurston's autobiography is of particular interest to subsequent generations of African American women writers who view her as a literary foremother and to scholars interested in Harlem Renaissance personalities. *Dust Tracks* was not the first noteworthy twentieth century autobiography by an African American woman; **Ida Wells-Barnett**'s *Crusade for Justice* was written in 1928, six years before her death, but it remained unpublished until 1970. *Crusade for Justice* focuses on Wells Barnett's public life as a journalist, social activist, feminist, and anti-lynching crusader rather than on her private life as a wife and mother.

Wright's *Black Boy*, one of the earliest Book-of-the-Month Club (BOMC) selections by an African American, was the most popular black autobiography since *Up from Slavery*. Indeed the BOMC influenced the autobiography's publication. When the publishing company received Wright's manuscript that was titled *American Hunger*, it submitted the manuscript to the BOMC for selection consideration. The BOMC accepted the book only after the publisher agreed to delete Part Two, "The Horror and the Glory," which was an account of Wright's years in Chicago. Thus in 1945, only Part One, "Southern Nights" (later titled *Black Boy* by Wright) was published. "The Horror and the Glory" was published posthumously in 1977 as *American Hunger*, and the complete autobiography was first published in 1991. Like Hughes, Wright opts for a memorable beginning when he describes how as a four year old, he sets his house on fire. More importantly *Black Boy* documents how **racism** affects African Americans.

1950 to the Present

Three of the most widely read African American autobiographies of the latter half of the twentieth century are **The Autobiography of Malcolm X** (1965); **I Know Why the Caged Bird Sings** (1970), by Maya Angelou; and *Having Our Say: The Delany Sisters' First 100 Years* (1993), by Sarah Delany and A. Elizabeth Delany (with Amy Hill Hearth). These three autobiographies were adapted for the screen and stage. Malcolm X's *Autobiography* was made into a feature film in 1992, which Spike Lee wrote the screenplay for, directed, and produced; *Caged Bird* was transformed into a 1979 made-for-television film with a screenplay by Angelou; and *Having Our Say* became a Broadway play that debuted in 1995 and was produced by Camille Cosby and Judith Rutherford James. Malcolm X's *Autobiography*, as told to Alex Haley and published posthumously, traces Malcolm X's childhood, conversion to Islam, and trip to Mecca. *Autobiography* was published ten years after **Rosa Parks** refused to sit at the back of a bus, ten years after fourteen-year-old Emmett Till was lynched, five years after African American college students staged a sit-in at a Woolworth's lunch counter, four years after "freedom riders" rode South, two years after **Martin Luther King Jr.** delivered his "I Have a Dream" speech during the March on Washington, and two years after four little girls were killed in the bombing of the Seventeenth Street Baptist Church in Birmingham, Alabama. Following in the tradition of Frederick Douglass and Richard Wright, Malcolm X audaciously protested the abuse of African Americans. Indeed the turbulence of the **Civil Rights Movement** of the 1950s and 1960s is documented in such African American autobiographies as **Anne Moody**'s *Coming of Age in Mississippi* (1968); Coretta Scott King's *My Life with Martin Luther King, Jr.* (1969); Charlayne Hunter-Gault's *In My Place* (1992); *Rosa Parks: My Story* (1992, with Jim Haskins); Melba Beals's *Warriors Don't Cry* (1994); and Vernon Jordan's *Vernon Can Read!* (2001, with Annette Gordon-Reed). After Malcolm X's *Autobiography*, arguably the most memorable African American autobiography by a male, is Arthur Ashe's *Days of Grace* (1993, with Arnold Rampersad) where Ashe reveals that living as a black person in America was a greater burden than living with AIDS. Additional exceptional African American male autobiographies published during the second half of the twentieth century and beyond include **Claude Brown**'s *Manchild in the Promised Land* (1965); **Eldridge Cleaver**'s *Soul on Ice* (1967); Adam Clayton Powell Jr.'s *Adam by Adam* (1971); Chester Himes's *The Quality of Hurt* (1971) and *My Life of Absurdity* (1976); **John E. Wideman**'s *Brothers and Keepers* (1984); Ben Carson's *Gifted Hands* (1990, with Cecil Murphey); **Henry Louis Gates**'s *Colored People* (1994); **Nathan McCall**'s *Makes Me Wanna Holler* (1994); Colin Powell's *My American Journey* (1995, with Joseph E. Persico); Marcus Mabry's *White Bucks and Black-Eyed Peas* (1995); Dwayne Wickham's *Woodholme* (1995); **James McBride**'s *The Color of Water* (1996); Kweisi Mfume's *No Free Ride* (1996, with Ron Stodghill II); **Amiri Baraka**'s *The Autobiography of Leroi Jones/Amiri Baraka* (1997); **James A. McPherson**'s *Crabcakes* (1998); **E. Lynn Harris**'s *What Becomes of the Brokenhearted* (2003); and Andre Leon Talley's *A.L.T.* (2003).

Angelou's first autobiography, *I Know Why the Caged Bird Sings*, ushered in the contemporary era of autobiographies by African American women. *Caged Bird* contains many memorable incidents such as the Sunday when an overzealous Sister Monroe hits Rev. Thomas on the back of his head with her purse and Thomas's dentures land by the young Maya's right shoe. Such humorous events are overshadowed by Angelou's recollections of her innocent uncle hiding in the potato and onion bins in order to escape a lynching mob and her mother's boyfriend raping her when she is eight years old. After the rapist is murdered, Angelou refrains from speaking until Mrs. Flowers encourages her to break her silence. Angelou's five additional autobiographies are *Gather Together in My Name* (1974), *Singin' and Swingin' and Gettin' Merry Like Christmas* (1976), *The Heart of a Woman* (1981), *All God's Children Need Travelin' Shoes* (1986), and *A Song Flung Up to*

Heaven (2002). Other important autobiographies by African American women include **Nikki Giovanni**'s *Gemini* (1971), **Marita Golden**'s *Migrations of the Heart* (1983), **Pauli Murray**'s *Song in a Weary Throat* (1987), Bebe Moore Campbell's *Sweet Summer* (1989), Jill Nelson's *Volunteer Slavery* (1983), **Patrice Gaines**'s *Laughing in the Dark* (1994); Veronica Chambers's *Mama's Girl* (1996), Rosemary Bray's *Unafraid of the Dark* (1998), and **June Jordan**'s *Soldier* (2001).

With the publication of the Delanys's *Having Our Say*, African American middle-class life is emphasized. Other works that also focus on black middle-class or upper-class lifestyles are Lorene Cary's *Black Ice* (1991), Lawrence Otis Graham's *Member of the Club* (1995), **Gwendolyn Parker**'s *Trespassing* (1997), and **Rebecca Walker**'s *Black White and Jewish* (2001). Affluent African American life is also represented in the autobiographies of athletes and entertainers. Indeed during the latter half of the twentieth century and the beginning of the twenty-first century, this subgenre of African American autobiography has proliferated and, in addition to the previously mentioned Ashe autobiography, is represented by such works as Muhammad Ali's *The Greatest* (1975, with Richard Durham); Sidney Poitier's *This Life* (1980) and *The Measure of a Man* (2000); Kareem Abdul Jabbar's *Giant Steps* (1983, with Peter Knobler); Diahann Carroll's *Diahann!* (1986, with Ross Firestone); Tina Turner's *I, Tina* (1986, with Kurt Loder); Smokey Robinson's *Smokey* (1989, with David Ritz); Hank Aaron's *I Had a Hammer* (1991); Patti LaBelle's *Don't Block the Blessings* (1996, with Laura Randolph); Eric Davis's *Born to Play* (1999, with Ralph Wiley); and Quincy Jones's *Q* (2001).

In conclusion African American autobiography has documented black life from the colonial period to the present time. Although the goal of accurate portrayals of African Americans has remained constant since 1760, each autobiography provides a glimpse into the diversity of the African American experience.

Further Reading

Andrews, William L. ed. *African-American Autobiographies: A Collection of Critical Essays*. Englewood Cliffs, NJ: Prentice Hall, 1973.

———. "Secular Autobiography." *The Oxford Companion to African American Literature*. Ed. William L. Andrews, Frances Smith Foster, and Trudier Harris. New York: Oxford UP, 1997. 34–7.

———. "Slave Narrative." *The Oxford Companion to African American Literature*. Ed. William L. Andrews, Frances Smith Foster, and Trudier Harris. New York: Oxford UP, 1997. 667–70.

———, ed. *To Tell a Free Story: The First Century of Afro-American Autobiography, 1760–1865*. Urbana: U of Illinois P, 1986.

———. "Toward a Poetics of American Autobiography." *Afro-American Literary Study in the 1990s*. Ed. Houston A. Baker Jr. and Patricia Redmond. Chicago: U of Chicago P, 1989. 78–97.

Andrews, William L., Frances Smith Foster, and Trudier Harris, eds. *The Oxford Companion to African American Literature*. New York: Oxford UP, 1997.

Braxton, Joanne M. *Black Women Writing Autobiography: A Tradition within a Tradition*. Philadelphia: Temple UP, 1989.

Butterfield, Stephen. *Black Autobiography*. Amherst: U of Massachusetts P, 1974.

Davis, Charles T., and Henry Louis Gates Jr., eds. *The Slave's Narrative*. New York: Oxford UP, 1985.

Dudley, David L. *My Father's Shadow: Intergenerational Conflict in African American Men's Autobiography*. Philadelphia: U of Pennsylvania P, 1991.

Foster, Frances Smith. *Witnessing Slavery: The Development of Ante-bellum Slave Narratives*. Westport, CT: Greenwood Press, 1979.

Franklin, V. P. *Living Our Stories, Telling Our Truths: Autobiography and the Making of the African-American Intellectual Tradition*. New York: Oxford UP, 1995.

Nelson, Emmanuel S., ed. *African American Autobiographers: A Sourcebook*. Westport, CT: Greenwood Press, 2002.

Olney, James. "'I Was Born': Slave Narratives, Their Status as Autobiography and as Literature." *The Slave's Narrative*. Ed. Charles T. Davis and Henry Louis Gates Jr. New York: Oxford UP, 1985. 148–75.

Sekora, John, and Darwin T. Turner, eds. *The Art of Slave Narratives: Original Essays in Criticism and Theory*. Macomb: Western Illinois UP, 1982.

Linda M. Carter

AFRICAN AMERICAN BIOGRAPHY   Biography as a life story of an individual written by another person is an ancient art, exemplified in Plutarch's *Parallel Lives* (second century A.D.) and English biographies such as Samuel Johnson's *Lives of the Poets* (1779–81) and James Boswell's *Life of Samuel Johnson* (1791). However, American biography began only toward the end of the eighteenth century, and African American biography appeared even later with the **abolition** of **slavery**, though African American autobiographies were already well established early. African American biography was born as an offshoot of the **slave narrative**. Following the lead of early American biographers such as Mason Locke Weems (1759–1825) who glorify their subjects and minimize or deny their flaws, African American biographers commemorate the lives and deeds of famous African men and women who fought against slavery, **racism**, and exploitation, and for freedom, justice, and equality. Most of the early African American biographies are exemplary biographies that sing of the glorious accomplishments of their subjects in the face of heavy odds, revealing little about their personal lives. The origins of African American biography thus lie in the common human instinct for celebrating the lives of one's own people who have fought for justice. Frances A. Rollin's *The Life and Public Services of **Martin R. Delany*** (1868) is the earliest known African American biography. Written under the pseudonym of Frank, it is clearly an adulatory biography of a freeborn black man and a Union Army officer who himself provided the material, sat for interviews, and approved the final product before publication. Although there are biographies of African American subjects written by white writers as well as biographies of white subjects written by black writers, this appraisal is limited to African American subjects by African American writers.

When former slaves began to write accounts of their lives, they told of the horrors of slavery to excite the sympathies of their readers and to further the cause of abolition. The classic texts are **Frederick Douglass**'s *Narrative of the Life of Frederick Douglass* (1845) and **Harriet Jacobs**'s *Incidents in the Life of a Slave Girl, Written by Herself* (1861). Written under the pseudonym of Linda Brent, Jacob's narrative was considered fiction until the 1980s when Jean Fagin Yellin discovered correspondence between Jacobs and the narrative's editor that proved its authenticity. The impulse that gave rise to the slave narratives is also behind the early African American biographies. As close allies of the slave narratives, early African American biographies retell the stories of the lives of the African American heroes, offering role models for African Americans to emulate.

A good biography, as Thomas Carlyle puts it in his essay on Robert Burns, represents the subject as a "living unity" and reveals "all the inward springs and relations" of the subject (*Scottish and Other Miscellanies*, J. M. Dent, 1950: 3–4). Carlyle further points out that a good biography shows the relationship between the subject and the society—"the effect of society on him" and "his effect on society" (4). In his interview with Anne Marie Deer Owens, the African American biographer Arnold Rampersad states that "we [biographers] make human beings come alive—we put them in a broader social context." Biographies can, in general, be divided into the following five main categories: (1) biographies that tend to glorify their subjects as heroes or role models, magnifying their strengths and glossing over their shortcomings and following the maxim "De mortuis nil nisi bonum" (speak no evil of the dead); (2) biographies that present a particular thesis or point of view; (3) biographies written in a partisan spirit where the subjects are either glorified or debunked due to their authors' party affiliations; (4) biographies that reinterpret the subjects in light of newly discovered facts; and (5) biographies that assess the subjects dispassionately without suppressing details of their personalities and make the subjects come alive in their milieu—the cultural and sociopolitical realities of the times in which they lived—so the reader can, to use Boswell's words, "see him live, and live o'er each scene with him."

African American biographies can be divided into biographies that appeared before 1966 and those that appeared after 1966, with the coming of the civil rights era. The number of African American biographies written before 1966 that merit critical attention is relatively small; however, since 1966 the biographical interest in African American figures has caught up. Today, African American biography thrives, as evident from the authoritative studies of David Levering Lewis, Arnold Rampersad, Margaret Walker, and Thadious Davis.

Some two decades after Rollin's biography of Martin Delany, three Frederick Douglass biographies appeared, in 1891, 1899, and 1907, respectively.

Frederick May Holland's *Frederick Douglass: The Colored Orator* (1891) is an avowedly partisan portrait. As the author states in the "Preface," his "plain duty is to try and vindicate Douglass, even at the expense of a great philanthropist [William Lloyd Garrison] whom all delight to honor." **Charles W. Chesnutt**'s *Frederick Douglass* (1899) falls into the category of biographies that tend to glorify their subjects. To Chesnutt, Douglass is the champion of oppressed people and an example of the heights to which they can reach, as well as a source of inspiration to future generations. **Booker T. Washington**'s *Douglass* (1907) belongs in the category of biographies that expound a particular point of view. Washington seems to recreate Douglass in his own image, arguing that Douglass believes in the same principles as he himself does. His Douglass did not ask for social equality, opposed black migration from the South, and advocated establishing industrial colleges all over the South so that black people could learn useful trades to be of service to the people there.

Sutton E. Griggs's *The Triumph of Simple Virtues or the Life of John L. Webb* (1926) is an exemplar of an adulatory biography. This biography shows Webb as a role model who embodied the characteristics of industry, thrift, economy, and community spirit. Griggs's biography omits any mention of the subject's family, inner life, any crisis or racial incidents encountered by him. **Pauli Murray**'s *Proud Shoes: The Story of an American Family* (1956) is a celebration of the achievements of the author's maternal grandparents, Robert and Cornelia Fitzgerald, both of whom were one-eighth black (what was then known as an "octoroon"). The author proudly observes that both Robert and Cornelia, who could pass for white, did not, choosing to suffer racial prejudice instead. The biography relies on the diary kept by Robert Fitzgerald, as he served in the Union army and navy during the Civil War, before moving to North Carolina to serve as a teacher of the freedmen.

Two more Douglass biographies appeared in the late 1940s. They are Shirley Graham's *There Was Once a Slave: The Heroic Story of Frederick Douglass* (1947) and Benjamin Quarles's *Frederick Douglass* (1948). Writing mainly about the life and work of Douglass after he escaped from slavery, Graham gives a fictionalized account of Douglass, dwelling only on Douglass's positive qualities and making him a superhuman figure. That Graham conjures up events is clear from her account that the Cedar Hill house in Washington, DC that Douglass later bought had caught the attention of Douglass and Anna as they were escaping slavery by boat, and the sight of the house had made him remark, "Look! Some day we'll have a house like that!" By contrast, Quarles's critical biography, written as his doctoral dissertation, sees Douglass objectively as an individual of many positive qualities but not without human weaknesses. Quarles portrays Douglass in the context of the part he played in the **abolition**ist movement, Civil War, Reconstruction era, and Republican Party. He describes Douglass's close association with William Lloyd Garrison and their later parting. Unlike earlier Douglass biographers, Quarles deals with Douglass's personal and domestic life and his relations with two white women, Julia Griffiths who assisted him on his journal *The North Star* and Helen Pitts whom he married after his wife Anna Murray's death. Even though he had access to her letters, Quarles does not reveal the true nature of the German journalist Otilla Assing's relationship with Douglass. He dismisses the subject with a noncommittal statement: "Their friendship was close, as her letters denote."

Edmond David Cronon's *Black Moses: The Story of Marcus Garvey and the Universal Negro Improvement League* (1955) is a well-documented biography, written with sympathy but without adulation. According to Cronon, **Marcus Garvey** was "a sincere and dedicated visionary," "an unparalleled propagandist and organizer of the Negro masses," who became a scapegoat for the Black Star demise due to the "financial chicanery of his two-faced associates." His accomplishment lies in giving black people collective race pride in the years when black soldiers came back from World War I to find that they were treated the same way as they were before.

Francis L. Broderick's *W. E. B. Du Bois: Negro Leader in a Time of Crisis* (1959) is an example of a denunciatory biography. It attacks **W. E. B. Du Bois**'s personality, activities, and works. Broderick describes Du Bois's personality as "handicapped . . . by righteous, tempestuous arrogance." He was driven by "racist tendencies," and his Pan-Africanism was a "type of racial nationalism." Du Bois's style in his literary works "fell between sociological prose and vague grandiloquence."

Since 1966 African American biography has come out of the stranglehold of hero worship and "speak no evil of the dead" mould, and its best practitioners have started treating their subjects as individual human beings, showing their strong points and imperfections. Modern African American biographies are, generally speaking, written with imaginative sympathy and fidelity to facts but without adulation of their subjects. They reveal their subjects' complex motivations and the contradictions between their public stance and private behavior. As Arnold Rampersad puts it, in their approach to their subjects modern biographers follow "the criteria of exhaustiveness, factuality, skepticism, and frankness" (*Yale Review* 73:8). To illustrate the modern art in biography, consider some major African American biographies written by African American men and women.

Margaret Walker in *Richard Wright: Daemonic Genius* (1988) expounds the thesis that Wright was a compulsive genius who was driven by the "demons of anger, ambivalence, alienation, and aberration" to creativity. Thadious M. Davis in *Nella Larsen: Novelist of the Harlem Renaissance* (1994) has put together a complete life story of **Nella Larsen**, who wrote *Quicksand* and *Passing*, unraveling the details of her life when she disappeared from the literary scene after she is accused of having plagiarized a short story in 1930. Davis reveals that Larsen lived the rest of her life out of the public eye, worked primarily as a nurse, and died in isolation in the spring of 1964, "alienated from her writerly self" for thirty years.

David Levering Lewis and Arnold Rampersad offer perhaps the best examples of genuine biography that present the manifold aspects of the life and work of W. E. B. Du Bois and **Langston Hughes**, respectively, in their true character, "warts and all," but not without imaginative sympathy and factual evidence. These two modern biographers set themselves apart from traditional biographers in that they portray their subjects in all aspects of their lives, in their mightiness and nadir, triumphs and failures, passions and peccadilloes. Lewis's Du Bois is not only Du Bois the genius but also a flawed individual with quirks and contradictions; Rampersad brings Hughes to life as he explores the connection between his life and the socio-political realities of his world. Their contributions as biographers have been duly recognized, with Lewis winning the Pulitzer Prize twice for his multi-volume biography of Du Bois, and Rampersad the National Book Award for his biography of Langston Hughes.

Arnold Rampersad's two-volume biography of Langston Hughes—*The Life of Langston Hughes, Volume I: 1902–1941* and *The Life of Langston Hughes, Volume II: 1941–1967*—is an objective study that interprets Hughes's life through the people who knew him, his correspondence, and his works. The first volume appeared in 1986 and the second volume appeared in 1988. The last chapter of the first volume titled, "The Fall of a Titan," exemplifies Rampersad's art as a biographer. It recaptures for the reader the activities of Hughes in 1940 and the incidents of his life that year. It shows the vulnerable side of Hughes: his professional jealousy of **Richard Wright** when he heard from his friend **Arna Bontemps** about the soaring sales of *Native Son*, while he was still struggling to sell his *Big Sea*; cancellation of his readings from *Big Sea* at the expensive Vista del Arroyo Hotel on November 15 because the evangelist Aimee Semple McPherson and her followers threatened to picket the hotel if the luncheon reading by the writer of "Goodbye Christ " took place; Hughes's taking steps to repudiate his radical past by sending a statement that he has abjured the radicalism of his younger days; his venereal infection in December; and the news about his eviction from his Harlem home because his subtenant had fallen $98.00 behind in the rent. On the question of his subject's sexuality, the biographer has not found even "a single person" to testify that Hughes was gay.

David Levering Lewis's two-volume biography of W. E. B. Du Bois—*W. E. B. Du Bois: Biography of a Race 1868–1919* (1994) and *W. E. B. Du Bois: The Fight for Equality and the American Century 1919–1963* (2000) is a biography of epic proportions. This monumental work is the result of Lewis's study of the 115,000 Du Bois documents at the University of Massachusetts and innumerable other sources. To Lewis, Du Bois was "an extraordinary man of color in a racialized century," who believed in his own destiny. Lewis quotes from Du Bois's twenty-fifth birthday entry in which he spells out his life's purpose: "to make a name in science, to make a name in literature and thus to raise my **race**." This biography traces the life of its subject—activist, scholar, editor, historian, sociologist, cofounder of the National Association for the Advancement of Colored People (NAACP), Pan-Africanist, and leading civil rights leader until his death at the age of ninety-five in Ghana where he had become a citizen hardly a year before. Lewis points out that Du Bois reluctantly assumed the role of an adversary to Booker T. Washington when the latter in his famous Atlanta Compromise Speech virtually gave up the civil rights of African Americans in exchange for industrial and vocational education for them. The second volume opens with Du Bois's tenure as the editor of the NAACP magazine, *The Crisis*, during the Red Summer of 1919 at the height of racial tensions, and it traces his career as a leader who relentlessly fought racism and **colonialism**. Lewis also points out inconsistencies between Du Bois's ideology and practice. Although he was an outspoken feminist, Du Bois was in practice a patriarchal husband who spent little time with his first wife, Nina, and his daughter, Yolande, and had a number of "parallel marriages" to other women.

African American biography has come of age in the hands of stalwarts like Arnold Rampersad and David Levering Lewis as it is now depicting subjects as complex individual human beings, not "stainless" creatures. In the twenty-first century, reinterpretation of African American lives is on the rise, making history intensely alive with the artistry of the present day biographers.

Further Reading

Edel, Leon. *Literary Biography*. London: Rupert Hart-Davis, 1957.

Rampersad, Arnold. "Biography, Autobiography, and Afro-American Culture." *Yale Review* 73 (Autumn 1983): 1–16.

Weintraub, Stanley. *Biography and Truth*. Indianapolis: Bobbs-Merrill, 1967.

Harish Chander

AFRICAN AMERICAN CHILDREN'S LITERATURE   This is a body of literature about African American children that focuses on their present-day lives, cultural experiences, and history and serves to enlighten, inspire, and expand the knowledge of the child audience. In the beginning were the **African American slave narrative**s and talking animal tales. The folktales that Joel Chandler Harris heard from slaves in the early 1860s were told in black families long before and after this, finally passing into print over a century later in works by black authors such as William J. Faulkner, **Julius Lester**, and **Virginia Hamilton**. **Frederick Douglass**'s first autobiography, *Narrative of the Life of Frederick Douglass*, published in 1845, passed into children's hands in 1947 with Shirley Graham's biography, *There Was Once a Slave: The Heroic Story of Frederick Douglass*.

The postwar 1940s were particularly important for reclaiming the stories of earlier African Americans. Former slaves told their stories to members of the Works Progress Administration in 1939, and these later passed into children's hands in books like Julius Lester's *To Be a Slave* (1968), Virginia Hamilton's *The People Could Fly* (1985), and *Many Thousand Gone; African Americans from Slavery to Freedom* (1993). Dorothy Sterling's *Freedom Train:*

The Story of Harriet Tubman (1950) and **Ann Petry**'s *Harriet Tubman, Conductor on the Underground Railroad* (1955) emerged to fill a gap in textbook materials that ignored African Americans. Publishers opened their doors to early civil rights activists such as Shirley Graham, who produced the first biography of Paul Robeson in 1946.

The earliest example of African American children's literature was **W. E. B. Du Bois**'s *The Brownies' Book* (1920–21), published during the **Harlem Renaissance**, when black editors such as **James Weldon Johnson** wanted to refute stereotypes and promote social realism, and African American writers were inspired to create black art forms: literature inspired by black, not white, writers.

In the 1930s, after Du Bois issued a call for books for African American children, two prominent members of the Harlem literary establishment, **Langston Hughes** and **Arna Bontemps**, in *Popo and Fifina: Children of Haiti* (1932) found a way to connect adult aims for African American art with a children's audience. Hughes's poetic language effectively complemented Bontemps's understanding of both childhood playfulness and parental concerns. Bontemps, the father of six children, produced more books about the black child, each important for its authenticity. From a total use of standard English in *Popo and Fifina*, he reverted to moderate use of regional Alabama dialect in *You Can't Pet a Possum* (1934), finally producing in *Sad Faced Boy* (1937) an early version of black English for the three Southern black children of this story, who are visiting the North. In Bontemps's work, for the first time, black children could read books written by an adult positioned firmly in the segregated worlds of both rural Alabama and urban Harlem.

In the 1940s Ellen Tarry produced books such as *Hezakiah Horton* (1942) and *My Dog Rinty* (1946) in which Northern black families in Harlem could be seen advancing economically, but their story still pictured a segregated world; Hezekiah dreams of some day owning an automobile, but learns he can only become the white man's chauffeur.

In books of the 1950s and 1960s, other black authors spoke of the problem of integrating schools and neighborhoods. Lorenze Graham's *South Town* (1958) reveals a quiet, even-handed father figure, Ed Williams, who is nevertheless reduced to hatred by the bigotry of his white employer. Jessie Jackson also produced authentic stories about African American children. His *Call Me Charley* (1945) is important historical fiction today, as is Graham's *South Town* and **Mildred Pitts Walter**'s later novel about school desegregation after the Supreme Court ruling of 1954, *Girl on the Outside* (1982).

Bontemps's *Lonesome Boy* (1955) took a different path, producing a theme that would also emerge in Virginia Hamilton's *Zeely* (1969): Solipsism could result in unproductive self-absorption. (Bontemps's Bubber loses himself in his trumpet playing, and Hamilton's Elizabeth deludes herself that her neighbor Zeely is an African queen.) Both authors were emphasizing the need for black children to engage in meaningful relationships in family and community, and both were revealing a direct line of influence from values espoused by Du Bois (equality, justice, and self-esteem). Hamilton, who grew up in a house where Du Bois's magazine, *The Crisis*, was a staple, was dramatizing that children take pride in native materials and forms out of which family members carve, whittle, and create (oak tables, pine sculptures, dramas, history—and most of all storytelling).

Like Bontemps, Hamilton was also positioned firmly in both urban and rural worlds, having grown up on a midwestern farm and moved to New York City in 1959, where she met her future husband, Arnold Adoff, and encountered Warren Miller's *The Cool World* that same year. Two decades later, Hamilton would reference this novel about black urban street life and the "wall" that black Americans confronted in *Sweet Whispers, Brother Rush* (1982), her first novel to focus heavily on black vernacular in the same way Miller reproduced both naturalistic setting and language. But she had previously used ideas expressed by Miller and others when she wrote biographies of two prominent African Americans often up against the wall: *W. E. B. Du Bois* (1972) and *Paul Robeson* (1974). Two of her early novels also used the "wall" as centerpiece. *The Planet of Junior Brown* (1971) focused on emotional, physical, and mental struggles of black homeless boys in the modern urban world, and *M. C. Higgins the Great* (1974) ended with the boy, M. C., building a wall to avert human disaster (a sliding slag heap, caused by strip mining near his Appalachian home).

Other black children's authors were also championing authenticity at this time. Artist John Steptoe, like Bontemps, wanted to produce dialogue he had heard black children speak, and *Stevie* (1969), *Uptown* (1970), and *Train Ride* (1971) became worthy successors to Bontemps's works, filled as they were with authenticity of language, urban setting, and economic circumstances. The children in these books often appear as miniature adults—serious, belligerent, solemn—with the figures, heavily outlined in black, adding a bright intensity.

In *Black Pilgrimage* (1971) Tom Feelings told about turning down jobs illustrating children's books in the 1960s because he felt that writers were presenting a distorted view of African American life. Returning from a visit to Ghana, Feelings and his wife, Muriel, published *Zamani Goes to Market* (1970), a story of an African family. Soon afterward, they produced two more books from their African experience, an alphabet and a counting book, all three books providing positive representations of the black heritage and revealing a new method of illustration that Feelings conceived in Africa for portraying the black child. He combined black ink, white tempera with tissue paper overlay, and a final ink wash in order to reveal for children the feeling of the hot sun upon the black skin.

Feelings's attitude that children needed more books with positive—and authentic—black images was echoed by many other black writers in the 1970s, particularly by members of the Council on Interracial Books for Children, founded in 1965 and dedicated to promoting literature reflecting multicultural realities and to fighting for the elimination of racist attitudes; thus it paved the way for more black writers and illustrators to tell their own stories. Once the idea of cultural differences gained the attention of publishers, the doors opened even wider for authors and artists such as Arnold Adoff, Ashley Bryan, Carole Byard, **Lucille Clifton**, Leo Dillon, Tom and Muriel Feelings, **Nikki Giovanni**, Eloise Greenfield, **Rosa Guy**, Sharon Bell Mathis, John Steptoe, Mildred Taylor, and Carmille Yarbrough in the 1970s; for Jeannette Caines, Donald Crews, Pat Cummings, Valerie Flournoy, Joyce Hansen, Angela Johnson, Patricia and Frederick McKissack, **Walter Dean Myers**, Jerry Pinkney, Eleanora Tate, and **Joyce Carol Thomas** in the 1980s; for Floyd Cooper, Donald Crews, Christopher Paul Curtis, Carol Fenner, Sharon Draper, Deborah Hopkins, Elizabeth Howard, Mary Lyons, Christopher Myers, Andrea Davis Pinkney, Gloria Pinkney, Brian Pinkney, James Ransome, Faith Ringgold, Rita Williams-Garcia, Jacqueline Woodson, and Sharon Wyeth in the 1990s; and Jaime Adoff, Brian Collier, Javaka Steptoe, and Brenda Woods in the early 2000s.

In 1974 Virginia Hamilton became the first African American writer to win the Newbery Award (American Library Association), and in 1978 Mildred Taylor became the second black writer to do so. By the end of the 1990s, many black writers, such as Christopher Paul Curtis, Carol Fenner, Patricia McKissack, and Walter Dean Myers, had won Newbery Awards and Honor Awards, and many artists, such as Jerry Pinkney, Faith Ringgold, Christopher Myers, and Brian Pinkney, had won in the Caldecott category. In the early 1970s, the American Library Association instituted the Coretta Scott King Award for distinguished writing and illustration of children's books by African American authors.

Writing from the black perspective about the cultural fabric of black life in America, these notable writers and artists have recorded their own African American experiences and have remembered or imagined fascinating stories of their ancestors. **Slavery** stories fill many of their books, as do stories of racial conflicts of all kinds in American life, past and present. Often these writers focus on growing up black in America in a particular place, era, or family.

What makes African American children's literature unique is the strong sense of family—especially the extended family—and community and the importance for cultural survival of keeping and transmitting the knowledge of family and cultural history. What gives African American children's literature its particular artistic strength is the medley of richly varied ethnic voices. African American traditions, values, beliefs, idioms, people, and stories flow through these works; in this way writers and artists of so many diverse black communities are able to inscribe readers into their own cultural worlds, giving this particular branch of American children's literature its own unique identity.

Some artists use the theme of the flying African and the tradition of quilt-stories to reclaim African American history, as in Faith Ringgold's *Tar Beach* (1991) and *Aunt Harriet's Underground Railroad in the Sky* (1992), and bright colors to display the elaborate quilt designs. Others such as Tom

Feelings eliminate primary colors in order to emphasize expression and activity. In *The Middle Passage: White Ships/Black Cargo* (1995) he uses black and white for symbolic power and imaginative evocation, abstract designs for graphic energy, and realism for stronger reader identification. Hamilton uses storytelling as a cultural way of knowing, ethnic feminist beliefs in the supernatural exerting magical and mystical power, ecology as a natural part of the African American world view, and "rememory" time as a way of seeing and knowing the world—a concept similar in many ways to the way **Toni Morrison** evokes the term. Morrison, Hamilton, Ringgold, Rita Williams-Garcia, and Christopher Myers all use the African fractal design of constantly evolving inner stories (or images) to illuminate the vast repositories of the black imagination. And Walter Dean Myers in *Shadow of the Red Moon* (1995) and Hamilton in her *Justice Trilogy* (1980–81) have used **race**s of fantasy children struggling for survival to expand beyond their own ethnic worlds in America.

Further Reading

Harris, Violet. "From *Little Black Sambo* to *Popo and Fifina*: Arna Bontemps and the Creation of African-American Children's Literature." *Lion and the Unicorn* 14 (1990): 108–27.

Johnson, Dianne, ed. *The Best of the Brownies' Book*. New York: Oxford UP, 1996.

———. "A Selected Bibliography for the Study of African American Children's Literature. *African American Review* 32 (Spring 1998): 157.

———. *Telling Tales: The Pedagogy and Promise of African American Literature for Youth*. Westport, CT: Greenwood Press, 1990.

Johnson, Dianne, and Lewis, Catherine. "Introduction" for special issue on African American Children's Literature. *African American Review* 32 (Spring 1998): 5–7.

Mickenberg, Julia. "Civil Rights, History, and the Left: Inventing the Juvenile Black Biography." *MELUS* 27 (Summer 2002): 65–94.

Mikkelsen, Nina. "Diamonds within Diamonds within Diamonds: Ethnic Literature and the Fractal Aesthetic." *MELUS* 27 (Summer 2002): 95–116.

———. "Insiders, Outsiders, and the Question of Authenticity: Who Shall Write for African American Children?" *African American Review* 32 (Spring 1998): 33–50.

Nina Mikkelsen

AFRICAN AMERICAN CRITICAL THEORY   This is a body of writing that focuses on the humanistic study of black life in the United States employing frameworks of analysis that reflect disciplinary or academic strands of Western thought. African American critical theory conceives of **race** as a simultaneously textual and social phenomenon, and its mode of inquiry derives not only from aesthetics but from historiography, political philosophy, linguistics and semiotics, structural anthropology, and the law.

W. E. B. Du Bois's *The Souls of Black Folk* (1903) is African American critical theory's foundational text. The book is a model of the dynamic interplay of research and imagination that constitutes informed theoretical inquiry. Specifically, Du Bois's central metaphorical concept of "double-consciousness" retains its critical salience because it shows how the segregated socioeconomic logic of the U.S. "color-line" conditions yet does not exhaust the psychic and expressive dimensions of black existence. Beyond the formal end to legalized segregation, the concept remains a viable method of understanding the flexible, long-term effects racial domination has on the culture and psyche of blackness. This conceptual mode of thinking race distinguishes African American critical theory from historical determinism or purely sociological analysis.

A genealogy of the field continues with what Winston Napier has termed the "onset of theory" in black intellectual life in the early 1970s. Though not without its antecedents in *The Souls of Black Folk*, Du Bois's subsequent reflections on **colonialism** and class, and the cultural criticism of **James Baldwin** and **Ralph Ellison** in the 1950s and 1960s, African American critical theory began to recognize and call itself as such—a paradigm of knowledge-production—in conjunction with the institutionalization of black studies departments and programs of study in the U.S. academy. Within the intellectual space afforded by hard-fought institutional legitimacy, the field developed as the formulation of a putatively distinct Black Aesthetic, itself the discursive articulation of the **Black Arts Movement**'s ideological praxis. Edited by Addison Gayle Jr., *The Black Aesthetic* (1971) is the landmark post–**Civil Rights Movement** anthology, and its opening section gives voice to the theoretical project that would effectively shape Black Arts advances in music, poetry, drama, and fiction. Contributions by Hoyt W. Fuller, **Larry Neal**, and Gayle himself argue that the Black Aesthetic singularly achieves what Neal deems the "integral unity of culture, politics, and art." Ron (later Maulana) Karenga's essay theorizes a "black cultural nationalism" in relation to the Black Power revolution.

A different sort of revolution occurred in the late 1970s and early 1980s when structuralist (Roland Barthes), poststructuralist (Jacques Derrida), and deconstructive (Paul de Man) challenges to Western semiotics, linguistics, and philosophy more generally were taken up by young, some would say maverick, black literary critics like **Houston A. Baker Jr**. and **Henry Louis Gates Jr**. At once fed up with rigidly sociological interpretations of minority literatures and disillusioned by the racially essentialist politics of the Black Aesthetic, Baker and Gates not only pushed to legitimize African American texts in the U.S. academy but brought those texts into conversation with theories that would elucidate their distinctively "literary" or figural qualities. Such conversation, as Baker explains in *Blues, Ideology, and Afro-American Literature* (1984), uncouples the sign of blackness (signifier) from actual black bodies (signified) in order to denaturalize racialized categories of being. Indeed, the very textuality of race assures that new, diverse, and often unexpected meanings circulate under and through the sign of race. The use of Derrida's notion of *différance* to locate the interstices of identity slippage in racial discourse is taken up more deliberately in

Gates's oeuvre, and in three publications in particular: *"Race," Writing, and Difference* (1986), the edited volume whose contributions originally appeared in two special issues of *Critical Inquiry*; the Yale School–inspired *Figures in Black* (1987); and *The Signifying Monkey* (1988), which undoes poststructuralism's Eurocentric orientation through a provocative Yoruban-trickster recasting of Derrida's "Structure, Sign, and Play in the Discourse of the Human Sciences" (1966).

The emergence of black feminist thought roughly paralleled the "linguistic turn" in African American critical theory. Seemingly removed from Baker's and Gates's preoccupations, what intellectuals like **bell hooks** (Gloria Watkins), in *Ain't I a Woman* (1981), and **Angela Yvonne Davis**, in *Women, Race, and Class* (1981), so forcefully demanded was for black nationalists and white feminists alike to recognize that their respective political projects ignored a black feminist standpoint entirely. Black feminists thus attempted to theorize an experiential—or "intersectional," as Kimberlé Crenshaw would later call it from the perspective of critical legal studies—account of the multiple social categories that inform the construction of black womanhood. In addition to hooks's and Davis's historical monographs, this kind of theoretical venture is most compellingly outlined and detailed in Gloria T. Hull, Patricia Bell Scott, and **Barbara Smith**'s *All the Women Are White, All the Blacks Are Men, But Some of Us Are Brave* (1982), the pedagogically influential and self-consciously interdisciplinary anthology of essays devoted to the institutional affirmation of "Black Women's Studies." Smith's own contribution to the book, "Toward a Black Feminist Criticism" (originally published in 1977), is widely regarded as the inaugurating model of black feminist literary criticism, especially for its reading of topoi of lesbian desire in **Toni Morrison**'s novel *Sula* (1974).

With the possible exception of Deborah E. McDowell's theory-oriented critique of Smith in "New Directions for Black Feminist Criticism" (1980), collected in her *The Changing Same* (1995), African American critical theory remained divided between deconstructive and feminist camps through the mid-1980s, with neither side really acknowledging the valuable insight or even points of contention being offered up by the other. In 1987, however, a flurry of articles published in prominent academic journals sparked the field's own version of the "theory wars." Black feminist **Barbara Christian**'s strategically titled "The Race for Theory" was the clarion call of sympathetic colleagues who were troubled by the masculinist tone of Baker's and Gates's work as well as their ostensible subordination of African American literary texts—indeed, the historical and cultural particularities of black life in the United States—to "hegemonic" (white) philosophical interventions. Christian implies that the professional race to "apply" theory to the study of discrete racial formations inflicts symbolic violence upon the experiential basis for the African American condition. In a more direct engagement, the winter 1987 issue of *New Literary History* saw Joyce A. Joyce spar with Baker and Gates in a series of four full-length articles. With titles such as "'What's Love Got to Do with It?'" (Gates), "In Dubious Battle" (Baker), and "'Who the Cap Fit'" (Joyce), these pieces declare that the lines of disagreement are clearly drawn and that the stated differences in opinion are simply irrevocable.

What the theory wars managed to ignore most tellingly, perhaps, was the extent to which black feminist thought is profoundly theoretical on its own terms and how deconstructive interpretations of African American literary texts tend to pay a good amount of attention to black expressive culture's historical conditions of possibility. Thus, the lack of understanding across critical perspectives might be more convincingly attributed to frustration over the differentially gendered hierarchy of authoritative "voice" within the field itself. Rather than choose between competing institutional positions, Hortense J. Spillers, a black feminist literary critic and cultural theorist, negotiated those positions in a new analytic as she displaced the masculinist tone of previous and other scholars' work. "Mama's Baby, Papa's Maybe," collected in her *Black, White, and in Color* (2003), was published in 1987 as well, yet in it Spillers proposes a generous and enduring theory of embodied subjectivities, racialized writing techniques, and black kinship protocols both under and in the wake of U.S. **slavery**. Here Spillers organizes close, historical readings of textual material within a structured, not always explicit, bricolage of theories that must themselves be reconfigured to adequately address the African American condition: Lévi-Straussian anthropology, Freudian and Lacanian psychoanalysis, Althusserian ideological critique. Though far from being solely responsible for moving African American critical theory, now fully engaged with the ideals of deconstruction and **feminism** alike, beyond the theory wars, Spillers is generally considered to be an exemplary scholar of the field's revived mode of inquiry.

In addition to Spillers's unique theoretical vision, which has lately attended to questions of diasporic hybridity and academic institutionality, that mode of inquiry has been heavily influenced by recent developments in critical legal studies, queer studies, and cultural studies. Derrick A. Bell, in *And We Are Not Saved* (1987), and Patricia J. Williams, in *The Alchemy of Race and Rights* (1991), have examined how the supposedly neutral character of American law in fact has embedded within its structure a logic of differential treatment toward people of color. To complement black feminists' early theorizations of lesbian desire, revisited in Evelynn Hammonds's "Black (W)holes and the Geometry of Black Female Sexuality" (1994), male critics have made available readings of gay black masculinities that are informed by the first wave of queer studies in the U.S. academy: Marlon B. Ross's "Some Glances at the Black Fag" (1994), Phillip Brian Harper's *Are We Not Men?* (1996), and Robert Reid-Pharr's edited volume *Black Gay Man: Essays* (2001).

If critical work on the law exposes race to be a fictive but hardly benign social construct, and if queer work on gender and sexuality locates overlapping and divergent identities within the very category of race, then cultural studies situates these findings in popular, mass-mediated, and commodified social relations. hooks's *Black Looks* (1992) and Ann duCille's *Skin Trade* (1996) highlight the political and socioeconomic stakes of mass consumption when white Americans "eat the [black] Other." Tricia Rose's *Black Noise* (1994) identifies popular resistance to white hegemony in the way hip-hop artists produce and promote their craft vis-à-vis the culture industry's dictates. And Hazel V. Carby, the U.S.-based black cultural studies practitioner most attuned to the discourse's origins in the Birmingham Centre for Contemporary Cultural Studies and the British New Left, is one of a minority of scholars who wish to disseminate African American critical theory's methodological and pedagogical interests beyond the borders of the nation-state.

With such developments lending the field a vibrancy and acumen that promise even more innovative work to come, younger intellectuals whose scholarship is explicitly conversant with the genealogy of African American critical theory have flourished. Sandra Adell articulates an incisive critique of her forefathers, from Du Bois to Baker and Gates, in *Double-Consciousness/Double Bind* (1994). Lindon Barrett's *Blackness and Value* (1999) juxtaposes philosophical notions of value with literal and figural enactments of racial violence; his analysis takes its cue from **Ann Petry**'s novels *The Street* (1946) and *The Narrows* (1953). J. Martin Favor gainfully recontextualizes theories of identity and performance in his study of **Harlem Renaissance** literature, *Authentic Blackness* (1999). Maurice O. Wallace delineates a cross-generational masculinity study with an eye toward black visual culture in *Constructing the Black Masculine* (2002). If these intellectuals' output is any indication of African American critical theory's being self-reflexively legitimized as a paradigm of knowledge-production, it is also a sure sign that their students across the disciplines will have access to what has come to be one of the most productive and stimulating modes of thinking about race, culture, society, and self in the contemporary U.S. academy.

Further Reading

Baker, Houston A., Jr. *Blues, Ideology, and Afro-American Literature: A Vernacular Theory.* Chicago: U of Chicago P, 1984.

Gates, Henry Louis, Jr., ed. *"Race," Writing, and Difference.* Chicago: U of Chicago P, 1986.

———. *The Signifying Monkey: A Theory of Afro-American Literary Criticism.* New York: Oxford UP, 1988.

Gayle, Addison, Jr., ed. *The Black Aesthetic.* Garden City, NY: Doubleday, 1971.

Harper, Phillip Brian. *Are We Not Men? Masculine Anxiety and the Problem of African-American Identity.* New York: Oxford UP, 1996.

hooks, bell. *Black Looks: Race and Representation.* Boston: South End, 1992.

Hull, Gloria T., Patricia Bell Scott, and Barbara Smith, eds. *All the Women Are White, All the Blacks Are Men, But Some of Us Are Brave: Black Women's Studies.* New York: Feminist Press, 1981.

McDowell, Deborah E. *"The Changing Same": Black Women's Literature, Criticism, and Theory.* Bloomington: Indiana UP, 1995.

Napier, Winston, ed. *African American Literary Theory: A Reader.* New York: New York UP, 2000.

Spillers, Hortense J. *Black, White, and in Color: Essays on American Literature and Culture.* Chicago: U of Chicago P, 2003.

Kinohi Nishikawa

AFRICAN AMERICAN DETECTIVE FICTION   Since the beginning of the twentieth century African American writers have used and expanded the conventions of the detective fiction genre in order to expose racial discrimination and to criticize the existing social and political order. Stephen F. Soitos has shown in his groundbreaking study, *The Blues Detective* (1996), that African American writers have altered the existing formulas to their own ends, first by changing the persona of the detective in such a way that his or her blackness plays an important role in the investigation. In addition, African American writers have introduced the element of "double-consciousness" or the awareness of racial inequities into detective fiction through the use of masks, disguises, and the figure of the **trickster**, which derives from African mythology. The inclusion of such black vernacular elements as dialect, music, food, and the religious practices of hoodoo results in what Soitos calls a "blackground." This blackground contributes to transforming "a Euro-American popular culture form to express African American cultural identity "(51).

Pauline Hopkins's serialized novel *Hagar's Daughter* (1901–02), which features Venus Johnson, a black maid-turned-sleuth who teams up with black detective Henry Smith to solve a murder, is the earliest known use of black detective fiction in order to expose and criticize racial discrimination. John Edward Bruce, author of the serialized, unfinished novel *The Black Sleuth* (1908–09), introduced an element of **Afrocentricity** and racial pride in the genre with his protagonist, the African-born detective Sadipe Okukeno who, as a member of the racially diverse International Detective Agency, is successful in tracking down jewel thieves. Whereas these two early examples of African American detective fiction pitted black detectives against racist whites, **Rudolph Fisher**, a member of the **Harlem Renaissance**, featured only black characters in *The Conjure Man Dies* (1932) which is set in Harlem and in which a team of four black detectives solves the murder of N'Gana Frimbo, a practitioner of hoodoo. While employing conventions of the traditional detective novel like the locked-room murder mystery originated by Edgar Allen Poe, Fisher reinterpreted the genre for African Americans by setting his novel in a black environment replete with hoodoo and black vernacular elements such as black dialect and language rituals like "playing the dozens," music, and dance. **Chester Himes**, arguably the most important and innovative writer of African American detective fiction, also set his ten novels in Harlem. Having written several naturalistic novels portraying the fate of blacks in a racist society, Himes, who had tried to escape the **racism** of his homeland by moving to France in 1953, turned to detective fiction at the behest of the French publisher Marcel Duhamel. Between 1957 and his death in 1984 Himes wrote ten detective novels that transformed the conventions of the hard-boiled detective genre and gave expression to the author's absurdist and ultimately pessimistic vision of American society. All novels, with the exception of *Run Man, Run* (1966), form a cycle that has been called Himes's Harlem domestic series and that features the team of Coffin Ed Johnson and Grave Digger Jones. Whereas law and order is restored in a conventional hard-boiled narrative, Himes's increasingly dark novels no longer hold out hope for such a resolution: At the end of his posthumously published novel *Plan B* (1993) both detectives are killed. Himes's reputation has consistently been stronger in Europe, especially in France where all of his detective novels were first published, than in his native land. However, this should come as no surprise considering his devastating depiction of a United States torn asunder by racial strife. Whereas Himes stretched the conventions of the genre nearly to their limits, such postmodernist writers as **Ishamel Reed** (*Mumbo Jumbo*, 1972; *The Last Days of Louisiana Red*, 1974) and **Clarence Major** (*Reflex and Bone Structure*, 1975) exploded them so that their works need to be considered antidetective novels.

Since the 1980s there has been a veritable explosion of African American detective fiction. More black writers than ever have turned to the genre to explore racial problems, and more and more readers have discovered it. Although generally less prone to experimentation, this new wave of African American authors continues to makes use of such elements as double-consciousness and black vernacular. The most prominent, critically acclaimed, and—in part thanks to the endorsement of former President Clinton—widely read author is **Walter Mosley**. He is best known for his Easy Rawlins series that so far encompasses nine volumes. The cycle is set in post–World War II Los Angeles and features private investigator Ezekiel "Easy" Rawlins and his sidekick Raymond "Mouse" Alexander. Each novel takes place during a historical or cultural turning point, and the protagonist's development mirrors the societal changes. In order to balance the darkness of the Rawlins books, which Mosley has characterized as dramas verging on tragedy, he began a new series in 2001 featuring Fearless Jones and his friend Paris Minton, a retiring bookseller who is the narrator of the books (*Fearless Jones*, 2001; *Fear Itself*, 2003). Mosley has called these novels dramas verging on comedy or comic noir. In addition to several futuristic novels, Mosley has published two collections of short stories revolving around the inner-city philosopher Socrates Fortlow and his two-legged dog, Killer (*Always Outnumbered, Always Outgunned*, 1997; *Walkin' the Dog*, 1999). The commercial and critical success of Mosley has partially been responsible for the recent wave of African American writers of detective fiction. Although male authors have held their own (Gar Anthony Haywood, Hugh Holton, Robert O. Greer, and Gary Phillips), there has been a profusion of female writers who combine racial themes with those of gender. Prominent among them are **Nikki Baker**; Charlotte Carter; Nora DeLoach; Grace Edwards; Barbara Neely; Valerie Wilson Wesley; Paula Woods, who edited *Spooks, Spies, and Private Eyes* (1995); and Eleanor Taylor Bland, the editor of *Shades of Black* (2004), a collection of black crime and mystery stories. The commercial and critical success of these writers is an indication of the detective genre's continuing effectiveness in combining entertainment with social criticism.

Further Reading

Soitos, Stephen F. *The Blues Detective: A Study of African American Detective Fiction.* Amherst: U of Massachusetts P, 1996.

Karl L. Stenger

AFRICAN AMERICAN DRAMA African American drama is the second-oldest genre in the African American literary canon. African American drama dates to 1823 when Mr. Brown, a ship steward and West Indian native, produced a play he penned, *The Drama of King Shotaway*, at his Lower Manhattan African Grove Theatre. *The Drama of King Shotaway* recounts the 1795 insurrection of black Caribs of St. Vincent's Island in the West Indies. The play is thought to be based upon Brown's eyewitness account of the rebellion.

The year 1823 was also the time of the African Grove's demise (Brown had founded the theater in 1816), and five decades would elapse before another African American drama would appear on a stage. Between the African Grove's final curtain call and that time, however, there was another important milestone in the African American dramatic tradition: the minstrel show.

Born in 1832, the minstrel show was an extremely popular dramatic form in which white actors donned blackface make-up and parodied African American dress, dance, speech, and song. The typical minstrel show featured "shuffling, irresponsible, wide-grinning, loud-laughing Negroes in a musical rendition of darky life on the Old Plantation" (Woll 1).

The early minstrel shows were popular, perhaps not because of the stereotyped characterization of African Americans, but for the romanticized images of plantation life they depicted. For the white audience, these shows were a nostalgic reminder of those antebellum days of the past. Regardless of the reasons for the minstrel show's popularity, African Americans found them offensive, not only for their use of racist **African American stereotypes** such as the coon, Sambo, and Mammy, but for the message they sent: that although free, African Americans yearned for the world of **slavery** that gave them the security of protection. Thus, many African American activists of the time, such as **Frederick Douglass** and **Martin Delaney**, not only wrote articles and essays to rebut and revise the defamatory images propagated by the minstrel show but also to defend African American character and contentment with freedom.

Despite its controversy, the minstrel show has been credited with launching the careers of many African American actors of the time. After the Civil War, finding the minstrel show as the only mainstream outlet for their stage talent, African American performers developed competing versions of the minstrel show. By 1870 several troupes of African American minstrels billed as "real and original" existed and employed 1,490 African American actors.

Thirty-three years after *The Drama of King Shotaway*, William Wells Brown's penned two plays, *Experience, or How to Give a Northern Man a Backbone* (1856) and *The Escape, or A Leap for Freedom* (1857). The two plays, the former which tells the story of a white preacher who condemns slavery after being sold into slavery and the latter which relates the story of a newlywed couple who escape slavery when they learn that their master plans to separate them so he can take the wife as his concubine, were never produced. Instead, Brown performed readings of them at **abolition**ist meetings.

In 1880 Pauline Hopkins's *Peculiar Sam, or the Underground Railroad* (1879) became the second play by an African American dramatist to be produced on stage. Her play was performed in Boston by the Hopkins Colored Troubadours. This play was followed three years later by John Patterson Sampson's *The Disappointed Bridge, or Love at First Sight* (1883) and a play that chronicles Haitian history by dramatist William Edgar Easton. Easton's *Dessalines* (1893) is a semibiography of General Dessalines, who became the first Haitian king after helping the country win its independence. Six years later in 1899, **Paul Laurence Dunbar** penned two plays, *Robert Herrick*, a comedy of manners about the poet for which the play is named, and *Winter Roses*, a play about a widower who reunites with his first love after many years.

Joseph Seamon Cotter Sr.'s *Caleb, the Degenerate* (1903), a play that examines **Booker T. Washington**'s philosophy, is the first African American drama of the twentieth century. In 1910 **Katherine Davis Chapman Tillman** became the second woman to write a play. Her *Fifty Years of Freedom, or From Cabin to Congress* is a commemoration of the fiftieth anniversary of the Emancipation Proclamation. William Edgar Easton's *Christophe* (1911) completes his examination of Haitian history; the play dramatizes Dessalines's removal from power. Like Easton, **W. E. B. Du Bois** penned an homage play. His *The Star of Ethiopia* (1913) pays tribute to the gifts Africa has given to the world.

During the early 1900s social protest plays became a common means for dramatists to voice their antipathy toward the American racial climate. In 1916 **Angelina Weld Grimké** penned *Rachel*, the first social protest play by an African American female playwright. Hailed as a pioneering work in the use of racial propaganda to enlighten white Americans to the plight of African Americans, *Rachel* is the story of a young woman who during the course of the play's plot becomes increasingly aware of the racial violence and prejudice to which African Americans are subjected.

Alice Dunbar-Nelson used her *Mine Eyes Have Seen* (1918) to voice her objection to the treatment that African American soldiers received after their return from World War I. In the play she extols their loyalty to the war. Like, Dunbar-Nelson, Mary Burrill chose to bring attention to the mistreatment of the African American soldier. Her *Aftermath* (1919) dramatizes the tragic killing of an African American soldier after his return to racist America. She brings attention to a woman's right to access to contraceptives in *They That Sit in Darkness* (1919).

Although **Marita Bonner**'s *The Purple Flower* (1927) is not as critically acclaimed as Grimké's *Rachel*, it, too, calls attention to **race**. It is an allegorical treatment of American **race** relations in which African-Americans are depicted as wormlike creatures living in a valley trying to climb the Hill of Somewhere to reach the purple flower of Life-at-Its-Finest; whites are depicted as sundry devils living on the side of the hill who try to keep the worms from getting to the top of the hill.

In 1923 **Willis Richardson**'s *The Chip Woman's Fortune* (1923) had the distinction of being the first African American drama to be produced on Broadway. The play narrates the attempt of a young man to rob an old woman of her life's savings so that he can rid himself of his debt. Following in Richardson's footsteps were Garland Anderson, Frank Wilson, and **Wallace Thurman**. Anderson's *Appearances*, which relates the story of an African American bellhop who is tried and exonerated of killing a white woman, debuted on Broadway in 1925. Wilson's *Meek Mose* (1928), which concerns an African American activist whose community loses faith in him after he is unsuccessful in his attempts to help them retain the land from which they are being forced to move by white citizens who want the land for their own use, was followed in 1929 by Thurman's *Harlem*, which is a sordid depiction of life in Harlem.

In addition to his Broadway play, Richardson also wrote a number of other plays, including *Mortgaged* (1924), *Compromise* (1925), and *The Broken Banjo* (1925). Just as prolific as Richardson was Randolph Edmonds. Edmonds is credited with penning fifty plays; most of them were published in the collections *Shades and Shadows* (1930), *Six Plays for a Negro Theatre* (1934), and *The Land of Cotton and Other Plays* (1940).

Other notable writers of the time period include Georgia Douglass Johnson, **Eulalie Spence**, and Dr. John Frederick Matheus. Johnson wrote two one-act plays: *Blue Blood* (1926), which is about a mulatto's couple discovery that they have the same father, and *Plumes* (1927), which depicts a mother's decision to use her life's savings to grandly bury her dead daughter instead of using the money for an operation that will save her own life. Spence continues the examination of the family with her plays *Undertow* (1927) and *The Fool's Errand* (1927). The former is the story of a man, his wife, and his lover; the latter is a depiction of the ridicule a young, unmarried woman receives when she is mistakenly presumed pregnant. Matheus is best known for the plays '*Cruiter* (1926) and *Ti-Yette* (1930).

The Great Depression caused a waning in the production of African American dramaturgy. However, because of the efforts of the Federal Theatre Project, many playwrights were able to continue their craft.

As a part of the Roosevelt administration's WPA, Congress created the Federal Theatre Project. The Federal Theatre Project established sixteen segregated African American units for the production of plays by or about African Americans. The Federal Theatre Project was instrumental in helping young, emerging African American playwrights; not only did it provide them an opportunity to concentrate on their creative efforts, but it also gave them a chance to participate in stage procedures and productions on a large scale.

Not only did the Federal Theatre Project provide unprecedented opportunities for the playwrights, but it also provided opportunities for the audience as well. The nominal prices charged for tickets made it possible for more African Americans to attend performances, and the increased degree of artistic freedom practiced by the project made it possible for the playwrights to project a new and recognizable image for those African Americans.

One of the project's plays that was especially appealing to audiences was the New Jersey Unit's *The Trial of Dr. Beck*. Written by Allison Hughes, it was so successful that after it closed in New Jersey it did a four-week run on Broadway. In the play, Dr. Beck, a handsome and distinguished-looking mulatto, is accused of murdering his wealthy dark-skinned wife, Amanda, and the play unfolds through the evidence at his trial. *The Trial of Dr. Beck* was hailed by the African American community for its emphasis on the need in the African American community for a reevaluation of its self-image. Many saw it as a daring assault on the fact that a social hierarchy based on skin color had been established in the African American community.

Other noteworthy Federal Theatre Project plays are the New York Unit's productions of Frank Wilson's *Walk Together Children* (1936), a dramatization of the conflict between two African American labor unions; **Arna Bontemps** and **Countee Cullen**'s adaptation of **Rudolph Fisher**'s *Conjur Man Dies* (1936), an examination of superstitions of Harlem citizens; and J. Augustus Smith's *Turpentine* (1936), which is an exploration of the conditions in Southern labor camps, and *Just Ten Days* (1937), a play about a family's attempt to avoid eviction from their home. The Seattle Unit produced *Go Down Moses* (1937), a depiction of **Harriet Tubman**'s life; *Natural Man* (1937), an account of the John Henry myth; and *Swing, Gates, Swing* (1937), a musical. The Chicago Unit's most significant production was Theodore Ward's *Big White Fog* (1938), a moving depiction of a family who find that the injustice, poverty, and prejudice they hoped to escape when they left the South remain impediments in Chicago.

A number of African American plays were also produced on Broadway during the Depression years. Two plays with Broadway curtain calls were J. Augustus Smith's *Louisiana* (1933) and Hall Johnson's *Run, Little Chillun!* (1933). Both plays concern voodoo and Christianity. Dennis Donoghue's

Legal Murder (1934) examines the Scottsboro Boys Case, and **Langston Hughes**'s *Mulatto* (1935) is an examination of miscegenation. In addition to *Mulatto*, Hughes penned three additional plays during the Depression years: *Little Ham* (1935), *The Emperor of Haiti* (1935), and *Don't You Want to Be Free?* (1937), the latter play having had 135 performances by its final curtain call.

Like the Depression Era, the 1940s was a decade of decline for African American drama. Because of World War II, a number of writers turned their attention to the war effort instead. In spite of the war, a number of dramatists did continue to write, and during this time one of the most renowned theater groups in African American theater history was founded. In 1940 in the basement of the public library on 135th Street in Harlem, Frederick O'Neal and Abram Hill founded the American Negro Theater. Not only is it recognized for its successful productions of **Owen Dodson**'s *Garden of Time* (1939), Hill's *On Striver's Row* (1940), and their adaptation of Philip Yordan's *Anna Lucasta* (1940)—which set a record when it later played on Broadway for 957 performances—but it is also known for having trained actors Harry Belafonte and Sidney Poitier and actress **Ruby Dee**. Unfortunately, the American Negro Theatre's success also led to its demise, for its best actors left after having found mainstream commercial work.

By the 1950s, African American dramatists had become more skilled at the technique of writing plays, and this ability was exhibited in the plays. The plays of this decade were more sophisticated in their development of character and theme. Common themes included interracial relationships, poverty, integration, segregation, the African American church, and life in the urban North/ghetto. Because most of the African American community was concerned with these issues, many of the plays explored those subjects in some form. One such play was **Louis Peterson**'s *Take a Giant Step* (1953), which depicts the **identity** crisis of a youth who seeks relationships within the African American community after having grown up in a white neighborhood. Another play is Charles Sebree's *Mrs. Patterson* (1954), which dramatizes an African American girl's desire to become as rich as a white lady she knows. A final play is **James Baldwin**'s *The Amen Corner* (1955). This play, which played Broadway in 1965, is a critique of the power the African American church has over its congregants' lives.

The most well-known play of the 1950s is **Lorraine Hansberry**'s *A Raisin in the Sun* (1959). Not only was it the first play by an African American woman to have a run on Broadway, but it was also the first noncomical Broadway play to be directed by an African American, Lloyd Richards. Many critics considered *A Raisin in the Sun* to have presented the most realistic exploration of African American domestic life of its time. In its dramatization of the Younger family, *A Raisin in the Sun* gave America a glimpse of the struggles and frustrations of the urban African American family.

Other plays penned by African American women during the 1950s were *Florence* (1950) and *Wedding Band* (1956) by **Alice Childress** and *A Bolt from the Blue* (1950) by Gertrude Jeannette.

African American dramas of the early 1960s were musical in nature. Two well-known musical satires are **Ossie Davis**'s *Purlie Victorious* (1961), which satirizes white-created African American stereotypes, and C. Bernard Jackson's *Fly Blackbird* (1962), a satire of the sit-in movement. Although not a satire, **Loften Mitchell**'s *Ballad for Bimshire* (1963) provides commentary on the ideas of **racism**, nationalism, and **colonialism**. The other musicals of the period came from the pen of Langston Hughes. His *Black Nativity* (1961), *Jerico-Jim Crow* (1963), *Tambourines to Glory* (1963), and *Prodigal Son* (1965) are all light-hearted examinations of various aspects African American life

Despite the proliferation of musicals in the early 1960s, a vast number of nonmusicals were also penned during this time. **Adrienne Kennedy**'s *Funnyhouse of a Negro* (1963) is a traditional drama that narrates the attempts of a young girl to come to terms with her mixed heritage. Likewise, Lorraine Hansberry's *The Sign in Sidney Brustein's Window* (1964); **Douglas Turner Ward**'s *Day of Absence* (1965) and *Happy Ending* (1965); and **Lonne Elder**'s *Ceremonies in Dark Old Men* (1965) are also conventional works. Ward's one-act satirical dramas were produced Off-Broadway on a single bill and set a record for 504 performances. Elder's play was nominated for the Pulitzer Prize for drama, and although it did not win that coveted prize, it did win the Outer Critics Circle and Drama Desk awards.

Beginning in the mid-1960s, a Black Theater Movement, growing out of the civil rights struggle, began to flourish. The founders of the movement called for more positive images in plays by African American playwrights and advocated the use of drama as a weapon in the Black Power struggle. The plays of this movement were controversial, as well as shocking and militant. In addition, they presented confrontation and revolution as the sole means of resolving racial problems.

Despite their militancy, the plays of this decade did more than just advocate African American rights and political activism; they also emphasized the dynamism of African American culture. Like "black power," pride in blackness, too, was a common theme of the plays. To the playwrights involved in the Black Theater Movement, it was essential that African American theater become more black-oriented, consciously drawing on African American community culture.

The best-known figure and playwright of the Black Theatre Movement is **Amiri Baraka** (formerly known as Leroi Jones), who founded and directed the Black Arts Repertory Theatre and School (BARTS) in Harlem. Not only were Baraka and BARTS instrumental in changing the focus of African American theater from one of racial integration to one of separation, but with plays like ***Dutchman*** (1964), *The Slave* (1964), and *The Toilet* (1964), Baraka brought an increasing racial consciousness and political militancy to African American theater. *Dutchman* is a warning to African American men who may desire white women. In the play a young African American, Clay, is seduced and murdered by a white woman, Lula. *The Slave* has a newly converted black militant as its protagonist. In an attempt to prove his militancy, the protagonist kills his white wife and children. *The Toilet* dramatizes the brutal beating of a white homosexual by a group of black boys. They beat him because he sends a love letter to the leader of their group.

In addition to Amiri Baraka, **Ed Bullins** was an instrumental figure in the Black Theater Movement. Like Baraka, Bullins penned a number of plays, including *Clara's Old Man* (1965), *The Electronic Nigger* (1968), and *A Son Come Home* (1968). These dramas, which played Off Broadway on a triple bill, were lauded for their realism. *Clara's Old Man* is an account of African American life in the ghetto; *The Electronic Nigger* is a satire of the African American who refuses to think for himself but allows the white man to think for him; and *A Son Come Home* examines the estranged relationship between a mother and her son.

The Black Theater Movement influenced a number of playwrights, including **Ben Caldwell**, **Ron Milner**, and Jimmy Garrett. Caldwell's *The Job* (1966) is a work that enjoins African Americans to protest government unemployment-opportunity projects, and his *Prayer Meeting, or the First Militant Minister* (1967) is the story of a preacher who becomes a militant. Milner's *The Monster* (1968) is about a confrontation between college students and their dean who have divergent ideas, and Garrett's *And We Own the Night* (1967) is a brutal depiction of a militant who kills his mother because he views her as being an adversary of the Black Revolution.

The 1970s were a very high point for African American drama. During the decade an African American play won the coveted Pulitzer Prize for drama.

In 1970 with *No Place to Be Somebody*, Charles Gordone became the first African-American to win the Pulitzer Prize for drama. Set in a New York City bar, the play examines the thwarted ambitions of the bar's patrons (which includes hustlers, prostitutes, artists, and ex-cons) and its owner, Johnny Williams. Subtitled "A Black-Black Comedy," *No Place to Be Somebody* was hailed for its brutal and honest examination of the individual and communal struggle for identity.

In addition to *No Place to Be Somebody*, a number of other African American plays received awards during the 1970s. Most notable of those plays are J. E. Gaines's *Don't Let It Go to Your Head* (1970), Philip Hayes Dean's *Sty of the Blind Pig* (1971), **J. E. Franklin**'s *Black Girl* (1971), Mario Van Peebles's *Ain't Supposed to Die a Natural Death* (1971), Richard Wesley's *The Black Terror* (1971), and Joseph A. Walker's *The River Niger* (1976), all of which received Drama Desk Awards in their respected years of production. J. E. Gaines's *What If It Had Turned up Heads* (1971), Paul Carter Harrison's *The Great McDaddy* (1974), Leslie Lee's *The First Breeze of Summer* (1976), and **Ntozake Shange**'s *for colored girls who have considered suicide/when the rainbow is enuf* (1976) were recipients of the Obie Award, and Steve Carter's *Eden* was an Outer Critics Circle Award recipient.

Two Pulitzer Prizes for drama were awarded to African American playwrights during the 1980s. Twelve years after Charles Gordone accepted the

Pulitzer for *No Place to Be Somebody*, Charles Fuller accepted it for *A Soldier's Play* (1981).

Set in 1944 at Fort Neal, Louisiana, *A Soldier's Play* is a mystery play that through the course of the plot attempts to uncover the murderer of Sgt. Vernon Waters, the leader of the African American company at the segregated World War II army base. The officer in charge of the investigation initially believes Waters's death is a hate crime, but as the story unfolds he realizes that Waters was killed by one of his own men.

In spite of the critical acclaim *A Soldier's Play* received, it was heavily criticized in the African American community. Many African Americans disapproved of the play because of its portrayal of black-on-black crime. Amiri Baraka, in particular, saw the play as "catering to the desires of the white power structure rather than to the needs of the oppressed blacks." Like *A Soldier's Play*, Fuller's *Zooman and the Sign* (1980) was also criticized. It, too, is an examination of black-on-black crime. In the play, the protagonist, Zooman, terrorizes a neighborhood into silence about his unintentional murder of a neighborhood girl.

The second play to win the Pulitzer Prize for drama during the 1980s is **August Wilson**'s *Fences* (1987). *Fences* focuses on the conflict between Troy Maxson, who is an ex-con and former Negro League baseball player, and his son Corey. Corey wishes to play football but, believing that Corey will suffer the same hardships as he did as a professional player, Troy refuses to allow Corey to "waste" his life on sports. In addition to winning the Pulitzer Prize, *Fences* also won a New York Drama Critics Circle Award and a Tony Award.

Many critics have proclaimed the 1980s as the decade of August Wilson. Other than George Wolfe's **The Colored Museum** (1986), which satirizes the African American experience in America, the two other bright spots of the decade are plays Wilson penned. Wilson's *Ma Rainey's Black Bottom* (1982) launched his career when it opened on Broadway in 1984. His *Joe Turner's Come and Gone* premiered on Broadway in 1988, giving him the distinction of having two plays run simultaneously on Broadway (the play debuted while *Fences* was still enjoying its stint at the 46th Street Theatre). *Ma Rainey's Black Bottom* is a play about a group of musicians and ends in the murder of one of them; *Joe Turner* is a about a group of boardinghouse residents, all who are in search of someone or something.

August Wilson's dramaturgy also ushered in the 1990s. His *The Piano Lesson*, a play about the estranged relationship between a brother and sister, won the Pulitzer Prize for drama in 1990. That play was followed by *Two Trains Running* (1992) and *Seven Guitars* (1996). The former focuses on the disintegration of the city, and the latter is a murder mystery that focuses on the events leading to the protagonist's death.

If the 1980s and 1990s are Wilson's decades, the early twenty-first century is the decade of **Suzan-Lori Parks**. In 2002 Parks became the first African American female playwright to win the Pulitzer Prize for drama with her *Top Dog/Under Dog*, a tragic story about two brothers, Lincoln and Booth. Parks followed *Top Dog/Under Dog* with *Fucking A* (2003). In the play Parks focuses on a character type she used in an earlier play, *In the Blood* (1999). Both plays have as their protagonist a modern day Hester Prynne. *Fucking A* is the story of a female abortionist who has an A branded into her skin according to the law of the community in which she lives; *In the Blood* focuses on a young mother who has five illegitimate children and is daily reminded of her sins by the scarlet As that are painted on the walls of the makeshift home in which she and her children live.

The past 181 years have been a time of metamorphosis for African American drama. The genre has evolved tremendously in every aspect. Because of the universal issues they depict and the refined craft of the playwrights, African American dramaturgy is seen and enjoyed by audiences of all nationalities. (*See also* African American Musicals)

Further Reading

Craig, E. Quita. *Black Drama of the Federal Theatre Era*. Amherst: U of Massachusetts P, 1980.

Elam, Harry, J., Jr., and David Krasner, eds. *African American Performance and Theater History*. New York: Oxford UP, 2001.

Euba, Femi. *Archetypes, Imprecators and Victims of Fate: Origins and Developments of Satire in Black Drama*. Westport, CT: Greenwood Press, 1989.

Hatch, James V., and Ted Shine, eds. *Black Theater U.S.A.: Forty Plays by Black Americans (1847–1974)*. New York: Free Press, 1974.

Hay, Samuel. *African American Theatre: A Historical and Critical Analysis*. New York: Cambridge UP, 1994.

Patterson, Lindsay, ed. *The Anthology of the American Negro in the Theater*. New York: Publishers Co., 1967.

Peterson, Bernard L. *Early Black American Playwrights and Dramatic Writers: A Biographical Directory and Catalog of Plays, Films and Broadcasting Scripts*. Westport, CT: Greenwood Press, 1990.

Sampson, Henry T. *Blacks in Blackface: A Source Book on Early Black Musical Shows*. Metuchen, NJ: Scarecrow Press, 1980.

Sanders, Leslie Catherine. *The Development of Black Theater in America: From Shadows to Selves*. Baton Rouge: Louisiana State UP, 1987.

Toll, Robert. *Blacking Up: The Minstrel Show in Nineteenth-Century America*. New York: Oxford UP, 1974.

Williams, Mance. *Black Theatre in the 1960s and 1970s: A Historical-Critical Analysis of the Movement*. Westport, CT: Greenwood Press, 1985.

Woll, Allen. *Black Musical Theatre: From Coontown to Dreamgirls*. Baton Rouge: Louisiana State UP, 1989.

Yolanda W. Page

AFRICAN AMERICAN FILM   The beginning of the twentieth century saw the Great Migration of African Americans from rural areas to cities. According to film scholar Thomas Cripps, the mass introduction of black people into urban areas coincided with the entrée of black iconography into moving pictures. Unfortunately, the same images of African Americans that had been prevalent in literature, advertising, and the popular imagination made their way into film ("Emerging Images" 8). As early as 1894, the Edison Motion Picture Company featured a series of shorts depicting blacks as faithful and long-suffering servants, clowning buffoons, and dimwitted thieves. In addition, it became quite common to see vignettes of black people dancing happily, stealing watermelons, or fleeing from ghosts.

These early portrayals of blacks were created for white audiences by white filmmakers. The most infamous example is D. W. Griffith's epic *Birth of a Nation* (1915). An adaptation of Thomas Dixon Jr.'s racist play *The Clansman*, *Birth of a Nation* capitalized on the negative stereotypes of black people in the South. From the doting mammy figure to the devious **mulatto** to the sinister black rapist, the film prompted African Americans to take their imagery in their own hands. In an essay titled "Chicago Origins," Davarian L. Baldwin marks that city as the birthplace of black-owned theaters and production companies. The concentration of blacks in cities and their desire for positive images of themselves made it possible for companies like the Peter P. Jones Photoplay Company and the William Foster Photoplay Company to release documentaries of black life and short films known as "uplift" comedies in order to combat the damage done by negative images (4–9).

By 1919 there were more than one hundred black-owned theaters, such as Robert T. Mott's Pekin Theater in Chicago (Musser 13–14). These theaters were a place where African American patrons could be treated with dignity and respect. Theaters, particularly in the South, were still segregated, and black patrons were relegated to separate entrances and balcony seating. In addition, blacks who did not have access to black-owned theaters attended Midnight Rambles, which were special midnight or other late hour exhibitions of movies that occurred after white patrons left the theaters.

The demand for **race** movies, or movies with black subject matter and casts, grew and the Lincoln Motion Picture Company was created to fill the void. George Johnson was the director of the company and his brother Noble Johnson was one of the first black movie stars. In 1918 the Lincoln Motion Picture Company refused to let Oscar Micheaux direct the film adaptation of his novel, *The Homesteader*. An enterprising man, Micheaux withdrew his script and started his own production house. Oscar Micheaux remains the most famous historical figure of early black film production. With films like *Body and Soul* (1924) starring Paul Robeson and *Within Our Gates*, Micheaux's company was in business from 1918 to 1948 and was the only black company to survive the advent of sound in 1929.

In the 1920s Hal Roach introduced a film serial aimed at children called *Our Gang*. Roach's serial featured a number of black children, and his most recognizable character was Buckwheat. Although the portrayals of the children were still quite stereotypical and one dimensional, they did at least feature several black children in many of the episodes. The *Our Gang* series moved from the silver screen to the television screen and was renamed the *Little Rascals*. Several generations of American children were familiar with the series during its production or while in was in syndication.

As America entered the Great Depression in the 1930s, the movies became an increasingly popular means of escapism. The Hollywood production system had by this time begun producing full scale "talkies," or motion pictures with sound. Because the equipment used to show sound films and the production of the films themselves was quite expensive, the enervated black film production houses were forced out of business. This left a dearth of race movies for black audiences, and for a while there were several films produced by major Hollywood studios that were aimed at black audiences. In particular, Hollywood turned to musicals to showcase the new sound technology and in 1929 produced *Hallelujah* and *Hearts in Dixie*, the first all-black musicals. Still, the films produced by the major studios catered to the stereotypical ideas about blacks, which had their roots the antebellum South. Although such films showcased the talents of African American singers, dancers, and actors the characterizations still drew heavily from the negative historical references to blacks as jezebels and thieves, or the plantation imagery of contented mammies and servants.

Perhaps the next turning point for media images of blacks came during World War II. Black soldiers were being courted by the U.S. government, and for the first time the short films used to recruit or train black enlisted men featured characters that looked like them. Jennifer Barker credits the National Association for the Advancement of Colored People (NAACP) for putting pressure not only on the government but on Hollywood movie houses to more fairly represent blacks especially as they were giving their lives for their country (11). In 1943 *Stormy Weather* with Bill "Bojangles" Robinson and Lena Horne, as well as *Cabin in the Sky* featuring Horne and Ethel Waters, represented the scope of the commitment to revise the negative stereotypes of blacks. Both films featured strong talent and musical numbers but still relied on simple depictions of African American people. There was not another major Hollywood film featuring a black cast until 1954 with Otto Preminger's *Carmen Jones*. The legendary Dorothy Dandridge played Carmen and was the first black woman to receive an Oscar nomination for Best Actress. Although she did not win, *Carmen Jones* remains a milestone in Dandridge's career and in the history of blacks in Hollywood.

The history of black people in American can be closely associated with their positioning in motion pictures. The 1950s marked the beginning of the film career of Sidney Poitier. Poitier became the filmic symbol of the **Civil Rights Movement**. While Black people were fighting for their right to equal protection under the law and equal access to housing, employment, and dignity, Poitier's screen roles were reflective of the dream of the integration. He often portrayed characters who had to prove that they were just as good, or better, than the white characters, and he often dramatized the professional roles (physicians, detectives) to which real life blacks aspired. Poitier was the first African American to win an Academy Award for Best Actor in *Lilies of the Field* (1963).

The period in African American cinematic history from the late 1960s through the mid-1970s is marked by the Black Exploitation era in film. Faced with the flight of mainstream audiences to suburbs during this time period the Hollywood film industry struggled with ways to fill urban movie theaters. The success of Melvin Van Peebles's *Sweet Sweetback's Baadasssss Song* and Gordon Parks Jr.'s *Shaft*, both released in 1971, are commonly thought to have resuscitated Hollywood's interest in black audiences. The success of these films spawned a legion of films that imitated their style and subject matter. Known as Blaxploitation films, these movies, which featured black urban culture and popular sound tracks, continue to influence black film, fashion, language, and culture today.

The quality of black films fell in the 1980s, which rarely featured films with complex treatments of African Americans. Comedic talent like Richard Pryor and Eddie Murphy achieved notoriety in buddy and cop films, and the only black woman to star in films in that era was Whoopi Goldberg. In 1985, fresh from her success as a stand-up comic, Goldberg played the role of Celie in Steven Spielberg's controversial adaptation of **Alice Walker**'s novel *The Color Purple*. Though nominated for eleven Academy Awards, the film failed to win in any category. *The Color Purple* received less than favorable press in the African American community and was the target of protests by the NAACP because of what was perceived as negative portrayals of African American men. Goldberg went on the star in several films and became one of the most prolific black actresses in Hollywood history.

At the close of the twentieth century African American cinema once again began to embrace its independent roots. Filmmakers like Spike Lee, John Singleton, and Tim Reid led the way in establishing a black directorial presence in Hollywood. Lee's *Do the Right Thing* (1989), *Malcolm X* (1992), and *Bamboozled* (2000) are evidence of the director's attempts to document the complex coexistence of African Americans with racism, classism, and poverty in this country. Working truly outside of Hollywood, directors such as Julie Dash, Charles Burnett, and Cheryl Dunye likewise began to explore the complex characters, history, and culture of African Americans.

Although there is currently a wealth of black-owned production houses, black directors, black producers, and black talent there still remains a scarcity of complex imagery of African Americans. This is due in large part to the capriciousness of the Hollywood movie machine and to the difficulty black films still have in finding distribution deals. The history of African American cinema is indeed one of triumph, but also of tragedy. Those involved in the industry still have much work to do to overcome the still prevalent one-dimensional images of black people in film However, the spirit of early black film pioneers continues to prevail, and African American cinema is becoming a cinema that is as rich and diverse as the people it reflects. (*See also* African American Stereotypes)

Further Reading

Baldwin, Davarian L. "Chicago Origins." *African Americans in Cinema: The First Half Century.* Ed. Phyllis R. Klotman. DVD. Urbana and Chicago: U of Illinois P, 2003.

Barker, Jennifer. "Segregation at the Movies." *African Americans in Cinema: The First Half Century.* Ed. Phyllis R. Klotman. DVD. Urbana and Chicago: U of Illinois P, 2003.

Bogle, Donald. *Toms, Coons, Mulattoes, Mammies, and Bucks: An Interpretive History of the Blacks in American Films.* 4th Edition. New York: Continuum, 2001.

Bowser, Pearl, Jane Gaines, and Charles Musser. *Oscar Micheaux and His Circle: African American Filmmaking and Race Cinema of the Silent Era.* Bloomington: Indiana UP, 2001.

Cripps, Thomas. "Emerging Images." *African Americans in Cinema: The First Half Century.* Ed. Phyllis R. Klotman. DVD. Urbana and Chicago: U of Illinois P, 2003.

———. *Slow Fade to Black: The Negro in American Film, 1900–1942.* Reprint. New York: Oxford UP, 1993.

Diawara, Manthia. *Black American Cinema.* New York: Routledge. 1993.

Musser, Charles. "Early Silent Film." *African Americans in Cinema: The First Half Century.* Ed. Phyllis R. Klotman. DVD. Urbana and Chicago: U of Illinois P, 2003.

Tarshia L. Stanley

AFRICAN AMERICAN FOLKLORE   A rich conglomeration of oral and written materials and expressive styles, folklore refers to tales (or in more popular parlance, "lies"), dances, songs, chants, riddles, proverbs, sermons, jokes, and games. These are communal forms by which the speakers and their audiences explore issues historically and topically important to African Americans. Rooted primarily in West African antecedents, folklore has been altered and amplified over time by European, Anglo-American, Native American, and Caribbean influences. The themes, motifs, and recurrent character types range from the humorous and fantastic to the ironic and troublingly real. According to such culturally literate commentators as **James Weldon Johnson**, folklore illuminates the contributions of black Americans to the diverse texture of contemporary society. Its variety and originality dispel the myth that a politicized consciousness was the only fruit of four hundred years of racial subjugation.

One popular folkloric arrangement considers the transactions between a master figure and a slave or underdog. This imbalance, along with the possibility of its subversion, offers a prime occasion for the japes of such **tricksters** as **Brer Rabbit**, the clever slave John, the consummate survivor Shine, and the **Signifying** Monkey. Other folk scenarios seek justifications for natural or social phenomena using the standard etiological tale (the "why" or creation story) configured to fit the cultural and historical referents of the time. The unpredictability of human nature and the vicissitudes of fortune are also powerfully examined topics that recur frequently.

Whether written, spoken, or sung, the content of folklore often oscillates between an examination of the daily struggles of life and their more mythical alternatives. The homeliest character may become the most exalted, or vice versa. Undeserved failures and spectacular windfalls serve as reflections upon the nation's past or present, especially in the context of its race relations. Such folktales as "Why the Sister in Black Works Hardest" and "De Reason Niggers Is Working So Hard" (both from **Zora Neale Hurston**'s 1935 *Mules and Men*) appear more facetious than bitter in tone, but do not fail to make an implicit commentary on the injustices of white supremacist ideology and its combined socioeconomic toll on the lives of the African American populace.

Whatever its goal, be it entertainment or instruction, black folklore offers a platform for the revivification of the vernacular tradition. This process involves a consolidation of linguistically dexterous forms of orality (or "orature"). Through words, folklore encourages an active recourse to, and experimentation with, topics of enduring cultural breadth. Thus, artistic improvisation and political mobilization are combined and distilled into material that is "double-voiced." Furthermore, complex strategies of resistance may be veiled in rhetoric that takes advantage of the material's very simplicity, humor, or seeming artlessness. Folklore presents an informal and often subtly coded platform upon which to broach sensitive issues— sin, trickery, sexual indiscretions, social reversals, wish-fulfillment myths, the scatological and taboo—without the accountability that a single-author work would have. From spirituals and work songs to blues and rap, music especially offers an occasion for emotional release and a more indirect medium for critical engagement.

Many events and fictional settings point to the American South as the epicenter of folkloric activity. This tendency has changed over time, especially after the Great Migration, to include major urban areas. As expected, much of the early folk material illuminates a rural/agrarian base, both in terms of the source of transmission (versions of dialect, for instance) and an improvisational quality that contrasts the highly rehearsed performances of nineteenth-century blackface minstrelsy. Such variety is also a function of the personality, style, and discursive situation of the speakers. Hurston's storefront porch in Eatonville, Florida, Joel Chandler Harris' fire-lit cabin corner, and **Charles W. Chesnutt**'s breezy plantation piazza all stand as sites of dialogue between worker and coworker, youth and age, pundit and simpleton, and especially Northern white and Southern black.

While they mine the often highly asymmetrical relations of power between groups and individuals, some strains of folklore also question and subvert heavily stylized epochs in American history. They do so by using the viewpoint of the black layperson. For instance, the age of antebellum slavery, euphemized as the "old plantation days" of contented slaves and benevolent masters, finds counterdiscursive engagement in a variety of sources, from work songs, hollers, and the banned ring shouts to the kind of thinly veiled creative resistance described in **Toni Morrison**'s *Beloved* (1987). Members of a chain gang sing while they work, but their garbled lyrics and imprecise harmonies are disguised insults directed at their overseers and the punitive conditions that constitute their daily lives.

By signifying upon fugitive slave narratives, folklore has reemerged in such pivotal modern fictions as **Ralph Ellison**'s *Invisible Man* (1952), Morrison's *Tar Baby* (1981), as well as in the known and lesser-known works of **Richard Wright** (*Native Son* [1940]; *Lawd Today!* [1963]). "New" readings of folklore that focus on its treatment of class and gender, or its intertextuality with later or earlier works, have contributed to a systematic (and systemic) reworking of what theorists call an "unracialized" canon of Western literature and criticism. The new order favors a distinctly black mode of analysis. Although not immune to charges of racial essentialism, one notable example is the work of **Henry Louis Gates Jr.** in *The Signifying Monkey: A Theory of Afro-American Literary Criticism* (1988).

Folklore is principally concerned with vivid, evocative portraiture that grapples with the concerns of Afro-Americans by means of a *communal* voice. This does not mean that individuals lack the opportunity to distinguish themselves through their craft. One only has to think of the verbal sparring technique known as "the dozens" in order to observe this duality. A witty crescendo of competing insults is unleashed in an informal setting to the delight of listeners and passers-by. The open invitation to participate is what differentiates such exchanges from formal debate or more esoteric speech-acts that circulate within a select group (for instance, "jiving" and urban slang).

As "orature," early folk forms may have posed problems in terms of standardization for collection and literary publication. The variations between these forms, however, offer room for each speaker's creative investments and the compiler's particular editorial tastes. Hurston's *Mules and Men* is widely considered to be the first anthology of African American folklore assembled by a black individual. Replete with the personal intensity of autobiography and the tension experienced by an outsider entering an exclusive (and not always hospitable) creative community, Hurston's text writes back to earlier attempts at "local color" storytelling by such white Southerners as Thomas Nelson Page (*In Ole Virginia* [1887]) and Harris, the self-effacing but talented Georgian journalist.

Like *Mules*, such titles as **Julius Lester**'s *Black Folktales* (1970) and the collaborative effort of **Harlem Renaissance** notables **Langston Hughes** and **Arna Bontemps** (*A Book of Negro Folklore* [1958]) offer broad, eclectic selections from which themes, patterns of exposition, and familiar rhetorical devices may be (re)established and compared. Stories of talking animals prove to be more than mere fables; they often plunge into overt violence in order to make a point about human fallibility and the oft-hidden efficacies of the imagination. In one version of the Tar Baby story, Brer Fox mentions skinning, drowning, and making a "bobbycue" out of Brer Rabbit.

Fantastic hypertrophia, or exaggeration intermingled with the supernatural, is a technique whereby the miraculous or unexpected is rendered commonplace. One of the most famous examples of this is the story of the flying Africans that Nobel laureate Morrison harnessed for *Song of Solomon* (1977). This particular author has suggested that an atmosphere of enchantment—of "haints," inherited magic and ancestral wisdom—has always characterized her experience of growing up in black communities. The need to perpetuate this intimate legacy found expression in the Folklore Division of the Federal Writers' Project (1936–40). Even the best-selling *Norton Anthology of African American Literature* (1997) includes a section on folklore that headlines "The Vernacular Tradition."

Finally, whether ritualized or not, language remains the revolutionary medium through which the logically impossible can and does materialize: slaves take flight from abusive masters back to Africa ("All God's Chillen Had Wings"), humans bargain with immortals ("Why Women Always Take Advantage of Men"), and animals glibly converse with humans ("You Talk Too Much, Anyhow"). Although many of these folktales prove lighthearted, some very purposefully construct and elevate human culture-heroes as models of racial resilience and ultimate survival: wise-cracking slaves, clever or brawny "representative men" (the John Henry archetype), even the amoral Badman (pimp, hustler, agitator, crook). *Invisible Man's* enigmatic Rinehart, while far from virtuous, personifies a fluid world of possibilities. This remains both the territory and appeal of folklore.

Further Reading

Abrahams, Roger D., ed. *African American Folktales: Stories from Black Traditions in the New World.* New York: Random House, 1998.

Hurston, Zora Neale. "Characteristics of Negro Expression." *Double-Take: A Revisionis Harlem Renaissance Anthology.* Ed. Venetria K. Patton and Maureen Honey. New Brunswick, NJ: Rutgers UP, 2001. 61–73.

Levine, Lawrence. *Black Culture and Black Consciousness—Afro-American Folk Thought from Slavery to Freedom.* New York: Oxford UP, 1977.

Nancy Kang

AFRICAN AMERICAN GAY LITERATURE   The heterosexist ideologies of the African American community as well as the **racism** of the white gay community have historically often kept African American gay male literature invisible. Yet African American gay males have a rich literary history in which they have used poetry, fiction, drama, and autobiography to express a proud and resistant **identity** and to render their lives visible. Although African American gay writers have often been asked to identify first as "black" or as "gay," most have highlighted the interconnection between their **race** and sexual orientation. Indeed, many gay male African Americans writers publishing in the 1980s and 1990s have placed their work in the tradition of civil rights activism. They have reimagined themselves as "revolutionaries" who are furthering the work of earlier women and men by remaking history and opening up a dialogue about social values regarding sexuality, gender relations, community life, and family. In addition, these writers have also challenged the authority of "white" models of gay identity in the United States and the long history of eroticizing the black male body from a colonial perspective.

The dating of an African American gay literary history depends on how one defines the marker "gay." Prior to World War II most Americans, regardless of race, did not self-identify as "gay," which was still understood more as a sinful action or a gender "deviance," not an identity based on sexual orientation. The expression of same-sex desire and attraction among black men, however, has a longer history, one that is traceable back to at least 1646 when the "Negro," Jan Creoli, was sentenced to death in New Netherlands (Manhattan) for committing sodomy. In *The Autobiography of a Runaway Slave*, the Cuban Esteban Montejo testifies to homosexuality among slaves and even to loving male couples and families prior to abolition, and his account repudiates homophobic myths that homosexuality was a disease imposed by whites or the result of "dysfunctional" matriarchal families.

The first flowering of a self-conscious expression of homoerotic desire, however, occurred during the **Harlem Renaissance**. The younger generation of bohemian writers, **Richard Bruce Nugent**, **Wallace Thurman**, **Claude McKay**, **Langston Hughes**, **Countee Cullen**, encouraged by **Alain Locke**, sought to express the full lived experience of African Americans and challenged the cultural practices among middle-class political leaders to portray only a respectable "**New Negro**" who would win white acceptance. During the 1920s and 1930s, Harlem had a thriving gay community, and despite the objection of leaders such as **W. E. B. Du Bois,** who feared the depiction of homosexuality would only reaffirm white society's fantasy of black people as overly sexual primitives, many Harlem Renaissance writers depicted—directly or indirectly—homoerotic scenes. The painter Bruce Nugent published the first known gay short story, "Sadji" (1925), in Locke's landmark New Negro anthology, but he is remembered more for his 1926 story "Smoke, Lilies, and Jade," which appeared in the avant-garde literary journal *Fire!!!* and that narrates an explicit homoerotic celebration of black male beauty.

In contrast to Nugent, most Harlem Renaissance artists referred to homosexuality in coded form. The poet Countee Cullen, who, three months after his marriage to W. E. B. Du Bois's daughter Yolande, escaped to Paris with his best man and friend, Harold Jackman, penned numerous poems with homoerotic undertones, such as "The Shroud of Color," "For a Poet," "The Black Christ," "Tableau," and "Every Lover." Although African American literary critics in the past silenced questions about Langston Hughes' sexuality because of his importance as a father of a "black aesthetic," Hughes also wrote layered poems in which the overt subject of race decoys readers away from the homoerotic subtext, such as in "Young Sailor" and "I Loved My Friend." In his 1951 poem, "Café 3 A.M.," Hughes openly denounces the persecution of lesbians and gays, and in his 1963 collection *Something in Common and Other Stories*, he included a story with gay characters, "Blessed Assurance."

Written after the peak of the Harlem Renaissance, Wallace Thurman's 1932 roman a clef novel, *Infants of the Spring*, offers a fictionalized account of the Harlem Renaissance bohemian crowd who were "in the life," particularly Richard Bruce Nugent, who served as the model for the sexually open artist Paul. In the implied attraction between the main character, Raymond, and the white Villager, Stephen, the "bisexual" Thurman discloses his desire to dispense with categories that limit sexual expression. Similarly, Claude McKay's 1928 *Home to Harlem* includes an implied homoerotic subtext in the intimate friendship between the main character, Jake, and the Jamaican-born (like McKay) poet intellectual, Ray, amid what is an otherwise stereotypical depiction of bulldykes and pansies in Harlem. In his later autobiography, *A Long Way from Home* (1937), however, McKay would be much more open about his friendship and cohabitation with a white gay hustler Michael when he lived in Harlem.

The 1940s and 1950s post–World War II period of "integrationist" optimism in African American literature was also a time of strict gender and sexual conformity. Cold war ideologies that linked the threat of communism to homosexuality and the assimiltionist tendencies of a rising black middle class pressured many gay writers to adopt once again the mask of invisibility. Bayard Rustin, a key civil rights activist, who was arrested in 1952 on moral charges during a police witch hunt, had to distance himself from **Martin Luther King Jr.**'s Southern Christian Leadership Conference .

Yet, representations of homosexuality did not disappear from African American writing. Indeed, they intensified, appearing in the works of **Chester Himes**, **Willard Motley**, **William Demby**, William Yarby, **Owen Dodson**, as well as **Richard Wright** and **Ralph Ellison**. Although only the playwright Owen Dodson's semiautobiographical novel *Boy at the Window* (1951) alludes to homosexuality in a positive light, other novels such as Himes's prison potboiler, *Cast the First Stone* (1952), and Demby's novel of small town alienation, *Beetlecreek* (1950), have characters who struggle with internalized homophobia and self hatred, and thus testify to the lived experience of many African Americans.

During the 1950s also appeared the groundbreaking work of **James Baldwin**, the most defining figure in gay African American literature whose legacy has fostered the writing of so many later voices. While living as an expatriate in Paris, Baldwin wrote the first African American public defense of homosexuality, "The Preservation of Innocence" (1949), for *Zero*, a Moroccan journal. In his first coming-of-age novel, *Go Tell It on the Mountain* (1953), Baldwin's protagonist wrestles with an emerging homosexual awareness, but in his 1956 *Giovanni's Room*, Baldwin wrote openly about the struggle for gay self-acceptance, although choosing white characters as his protagonists. To avoid a critical backlash, Baldwin initially had to deny that *Giovanni's Room* was a homosexual novel, and that he himself was gay. In his novels dating from the 1960s and 1970s, however, Baldwin focused with increasing openness on gay subject matter, depicting the troubled relationship between the bisexual black musician Rufus and the white writer Vivaldo in *Another Country*. His subsequent novels *Tell Me How Long the Train's Been Gone* (1968) and *Just Above My Head* (1979) continued to set the groundwork for a subsequent generation of gay writers.

During the civil rights era the struggle to reclaim black manhood often became equated with imitating a heterosexist patriarchal ideal. Gay men within the **Black Arts Movement** of the 1960s and 1970s often became figures of ridicule who lacked the strength and virility to overthrow an oppressive, white, racist society. Black writers and activists such as **Amiri Baraka** pointed to homosexuals as figures of an emasculation by white men and, therefore, what "authentic" black men were not. Yet the recurrence of gay "degenerates" in plays such as *The Toilet* (1964) testify to a more conflicted relation to homosexuality, and Baraka's autobiographically based *The System of Dante's Hell* (1965) tells the story of a self-hating black gay man in Chicago who is finally "converted" to heterosexuality by a prostitute named Peaches. Not all African Americans associated with the more radical wings of the Black Power Movement, however, shared this homophobia. Huey Newton, the founder of the Black Panthers, sought to build coalitions with gay activists and to implement a more inclusive understanding of the black community.

Whereas the post-Stonewall era of the 1970s saw the growth of white gay fiction published by large commercial establishments, gay African American writing did not reach a similar level of intensity until the growth of black gay grassroots organizations and gay publishing houses and journals. The New York-based writing collective Other Countries (founded in 1986) put out two anthologies, *Other Countries Journal: Black Gay Voices* (1988) and the Lambda award-winning *Sojourner: Black Gay Voices in the Age of AIDS* (1993). Michael Smith, the founder of Black and White Men Together (BWMT), edited the volume *Black Men/White Men: A Gay Anthology* (1983), though it has subsequently been criticized for its white perspective. Two anthologies, however, have been especially important in giving African American gay males a voice: Joseph Beam's *In the Life: A Black Gay Anthology* (1986), which announced that "Black Men loving Black men is the revolutionary act of the eighties" and **Essex Hemphill**'s *Brother to Brother: New Writings by Black Gay Men* (1991), which similarly connected art to politics and called for a reconstitution of family, community, and nation that includes black voices. The poet **Assotto Saint** also founded his own Galiens Press to release, in addition to his work, two seminal anthologies of African American gay poetry, *The Road Before Us* (1991) and *Here to Dare* (1992).

For this new generation of gay African American writers, the goal of representing themselves as self-identified gay men required developing their own idiom and aesthetic tradition. Many of the poems, essays, and short stories in *Brother to Brother* were self-avowedly experimental in form and drew on African diasporic oral traditions and black gay subcultural practices, such as SNAP!. In speaking out about a distinctive black gay selfhood that was not the same as the dominant media image of gays as middle-class whites, these writers also introduced a number of themes that would recur in the fiction of other writers in the 1990s and beyond. Some of these would include, finding a home within the African American community, the complications of a loving interracial relationship, black men's internalization of the values of a white homosexual community, the homophobia of the black church, surviving the tragedy of AIDS, the double lives of many black men concealing their sexuality, the relation between sexuality and patriarchal norms of masculinity, and the fight against heterosexist standards that structure social values.

Although **E. Lynn Harris**'s novels, starting with *Invisible Life* (1991), have been among the most commercially successful works of fictions by an African American gay author, since the 1980s, there has been a wide array of fictional production. A number of novelists have dealt with the possibilities or problems of interracial love. **Larry Duplechan**'s *Eight Days a Week* (1985) and *Blackbird* (1987) deal with the relationship between Johnny Ray and his white gay lover Keith, although critics have been divided on whether the black man's attraction to the white lover is a sign of his colonized mind or a reversal of the racial objectification within **colonialism**. In addition, Canaan Parker's *The Color of Trees* (1992), which is set on an elite prep school campus, deals with a love that transcends color and class differences, and **Melvin Dixon**'s *Vanishing Room* (1991) focuses on the racism of the white male lover. In contrast, another group of writers has sought to reflect a more black-centered consciousness in which characters live and work amidst a largely black population. **James Earl Hardy**'s B-Boy Blues Series has characters who embrace **Afrocentricity** as part of black gay self-acceptance. Other novelists have dealt specifically with the homophobia in black families, including Steve Corbin's *Fragments that Remain* (1993) and award-winning author Brian Keith Jackson's second novel, *Walking Through Mirrors* (1998), which deals with a gay New Yorker's return home to Louisiana for his father's funeral.

The last two decades have also seen a number of African American gay fiction writers becoming a part of the literary canon. In 1989 **Randall Kenan** published *A Visitation of Spirits*, an autobiographical-based book of magic realism that recalls James Baldwin's *Go Tell It on the Mountain* in dealing with a young man's troubled relation with a homophobic black church. Many of the short stories in his National Book Critics Award–nominated *Let the Dead Bury the Dead*, such as the often anthologized "The Foundations of the Earth," deal with key themes such as the homophobia in the African American community as well as the losses from AIDS. One of the earliest writers to deal with the problem of AIDS was the innovative science fiction writer **Samuel Delany** in *Flight from Neveryon* (1985). Even in his earliest works, such as *The Jewels of Aptor* (1962), the short story "Aye, and Gomorrah . . ." (1967), and *The Einstein Intersection* (1967), Delany explored through his outcast characters sexual and gender difference. In his novels *Dhalgren* (1975) and *Tales of Neveryon* (1979), homoeroticism had become directly expressed in his fiction. The writings of Gary Fisher, a graduate student who died of AIDs in the mid-1990s, have been edited by **Don Belton**, the author of another black gay classic, *Almost Midnight* (1986), into a moving collection called *Gary in Your Pocket: Stories and Notebooks of Gary Fisher* (1996), which has engendered increasing scholarly conversation.

Marlon Rigg's document *Tongues Untied* (1989) and his essay "Black Macho Revisited: Reflections of a SNAP! Queen" have become classics in gender and African American studies courses, and inspired the formation of Pomo Afro Homos (Postmodern African American homosexuals), a performance art group that produced *Fierce Love: Stories from Black Gay Life* (1991) and that was the first gay group to be funded (though not without controversy) by the National Endowment of the Arts. In his satirical play, *The Colored Museum*, playwright and director, George C. Wolfe included among his eleven exhibits (or scenes) "The Gospel according to Miss Roj," a spunky black SNAP! queen who talks back to the indifference and oppression of the African American and gay communities.

In recent years there have been an increasing diversity of gay African American literature, demonstrating that there is no single gay African American experience. The 1990s saw the release of a numerous powerful memoirs, such as Gordon Heath's *Deep Are the Roots: Memoirs of a Black Expatriate* (1992), Bill T. Jones's *Last Night on Earth* (1995), Alvin Ailey's *Revelations* (1995), and the drag entertainer RuPaul's *Lettin' It All Hang Out* (1995), and transgendered Lady Chablis's *Hiding My Candy* (1996). Several anthologies have also appeared in the late 1990s and early 2000s giving voice to recognized and little-known writers from the past and the present, such as *Go the Way Your Blood Beats: An Anthology of Lesbian and Gay Fiction by African American Writers* (1996), *Shade: An Anthology of Fiction by Gay men of African Descent* (1996), and one of the most thorough and scholarly representations of twentieth-century African American gay literature, *Black Like Us: A Century of Lesbian, Gay and Bisexual African American Fiction*, edited by Devon Carbado, Dwight McBride, and Donald Weise (2002). Finally the scope of African American literature is broadening to include more transnational voices, such as Jamaican American Thomas Glave who explores the situation of gays and lesbians in Jamaica.

Further Reading

Carbado, Devon, Dwight McBride, and Donald Weise. *Black Like Us: A Century of Lesbian, Gay, and Bisexual African American Fiction*. San Francisco: Cleis Press, 2002.

Chauncey, George. *Gay New York: Gender, Urban Culture and the Marketing of the Gay Male World 1890–1940*. New York: Basic Books, 1994.

Nelson, Emmanuel S., ed. *Critical Essays: Gay and Lesbian Writers of Color*. New York: Haworth Press, 1994.

Nero, Charles. "Toward a Black Gay Aesthetic: Signifying in Contemporary Gay Literature." *Brother to Brother: New Writings by Black Gay Men*. Boston: Alyson Publications, 1991. 229–50.

Reid-Pharr, Robert. *Black Gay Man: Essays*. New York: New York UP, 2001.

Schwarz, A. B. Christa. *Gay Voices of the Harlem Renaissance*. Bloomington, IN: Indiana UP, 2003.

Stephen Knadler

AFRICAN AMERICAN LESBIAN LITERATURE   With the **Harlem Renaissance** (1920s), African American literature came into its own, connected to a politics and an aesthetics that were uniquely Negro and deeply American and that looked to stake out not only the humanity and freedom of African Americans but also an identity replete with intellectual and artistic traditions. The literature of the Harlem Renaissance put into fictional form **W. E. B. Du Bois**'s theories about the double-consciousness of African Americans. It also celebrated African heritage and its contribution to contemporary art forms such as **jazz**. Famous for its sexual permissiveness, the Harlem Renaissance fostered many authors who explored same-sex desire. These were mostly male authors such as Langston Hughes and **Countee Cullen** who considered only desire between men. However, one of the most famous literary suggestions of African American lesbianism dates from the Harlem Renaissance: **Nella Larsen**'s *Passing* (1929).

As its title indicates, *Passing* belongs to a common subgenre of African American literature popular in the Harlem Renaissance: the passing novel that tells the tale of light-skinned African Americans who pass for white. Larsen's novella indeed focuses on two light-skinned African American women, Irene who does not pass for white and Clare who does. A possible relationship between Irene and Clare haunts the text. Critics note that the very unclear and unknown quality of desire between women in the novel points to how in the first half of the twentieth century African Americans may have passed not only racially but also sexually, asking us not to identify lesbian characters but to think about the many desires and identities that intersect and that mask one another in the first centuries of African American literature and culture.

As the Harlem Renaissance gave way to the Protest Era with the **Civil Rights Movement**, the **Black Arts Movement**, and the Black Power Movement, the great focus of the African American community turned to the urgent need to secure equal rights. The fight against **racism**, particularly institutional racism, became the single most important issue in African American politics, culture, and artistic production. The reliance of the Civil Rights Movement on Christian ministers and of the Black Power Movement on Muslim clerics established for both profoundly heterosexist value systems. A fear of taking attention away from the movement's antiracist message blocked serious consideration of the ways that race, gender, sexuality, and class implicate one another, of the ways in which the Civil Rights Movement might not only support but also be supported by women's rights and lesbian rights. Furthermore, throughout African American history the mother stands as the holder of tradition, the connection to Mother Africa, so women who might be perceived as untraditional threaten the entire community. African American lesbian writers found no place to express their sexuality that was not considered marginal or even antithetical to the Civil Rights Movement and the great literature that surrounded it. At the same time, the women's and homosexual movements that emerged in the 1960s prioritized gender and sexuality, respectively, over **race**, ignoring the ways that by virtue of their different races some women experience different oppressions, and refusing to acknowledge the racism within their own ranks. Thus African American lesbian authors often kept their lesbianism hidden in their lives and in their works well into the 1970s.

A certain reticence to identify African American authors or characters as lesbian may also, however, indicate not homophobia or fear of coming out, but rather an attempt to express desire between women outside the category "lesbian" that can be taken to be marked white by its allusion to European history (the Greek island of Lesbos) and by its connection to a predominantly white movement. Perhaps the most important example of this, after Larsen's *Passing*, can be found in **Alice Walker**'s epistolary novel, *The Color Purple* (1982). Walker refers to herself as a womanist, a term that for her expresses a primary commitment to women that may take any form, from political activism to erotic relationships, but that also always attends to race. Set in rural Georgia in the early twentieth century, *The Color Purple* recounts the troubled lives of sharecropping families through a series of letters written by Celie and her sister Nettie. Although Celie marries, leaves, and then reconnects with Mr.___, she finds herself through a relationship with Shug, a blues singer with whom both she and her husband are in love. To both Celie and Shug, the relationship that they share is of primary importance in their erotic and emotional lives, but to neither is it exclusive nor does it stop both women from having subsequent relationships with men. The relationship between Shug and Celie provides an essential alternative to the sexual violence and abuse that Celie suffers with men, but Celie learns not to turn away from men but to embrace them differently. Celie's relationship with Shug brings her to consciousness about her power as an African American woman and allows her to formulate an identity that cannot be organized by any single marker.

Prior to *The Color Purple*, however, a few novels by African American women had begun to claim lesbianism for themselves. The first novel written by an African American woman with a self-identified lesbian protagonist is **Ann Allen Shockley**'s *Loving Her* (1974), though Shockley did not label her own sexual identity. Over a decade later, Shockley's second novel, *Say Jesus and Come to Me* (1985), depicts African American women negotiating their lesbianism and their Christianity. **Rosa Guy**'s *Ruby* (1976) offers another early portrayal an African American protagonist whose primary love relationship was with another girl, but *Ruby* ends with an apparent universal turn to heterosexual adulthood.

Around the same time, African American lesbian poetry provided a space for much more radical expressions of lesbianism. Pat Parker, in *Child of Myself* (1971), *Pit Stop* (1974), *Womanslaughter* (1978), and *Jonestown and Other Madness* (1985), playfully and explicitly describes lesbian lovemaking, coming out of the closet, and black lesbian feminist politics. **Cheryl Clarke** has devoted herself to assuring that Parker's work continues to be remembered while also publishing her own poetry. In collections including *Living as a Lesbian* (1986) and *Experimental Loves* (1996), Clarke writes with openness, humor, sensuality, and profanity about lesbianism in a violent, underprivileged, urban environment that is nonetheless marked by hope as well as by struggle.

The most well-known African American lesbian writer, **Audre Lorde**, in her "autobiomythography" *Zami: A New Spelling of My Name* (1982), comes up with a novel way to negotiate the apparent disjoints between African American and lesbian identification. By 1982 Lorde was already an accomplished poet and essayist who in *The First Cities* (1968), *Cables to Rage* (1970), *From a Land Where Other People Live* (1973), *The New York Head Shop and Museum* (1974), *Coal* (1976), and *The Black Unicorn* (1978) expressed herself as an African American lesbian. In *Zami*, she traces how she came to that identity and what it means to her. Zami describes Lorde's coming of age in a Granadian immigrant family in New York in the 1950s. Lorde/Zami initially connects to her Caribbean heritage rather than to any African American community or identity. She finds in this community a strong assertion of women's sexuality and power, although not any women lovers. The relative invisibility of African American lesbians in New York in the 1950s also contributes to Lorde/Zami's discovering her sexuality with white women and in the burgeoning lesbian community. After an initial exuberance at the acceptance and exploration of her sexuality, however, Lode/Zami finds the racism of white lesbians as stifling as the homophobia of the African American community. She continues to search for a community and an identity where she can be black and lesbian without needing to prioritize either. This she finally finds with another black lesbian, Afrekete, and also with the change of her name to Zami. "Zami" is a term used in parts of Grenada to refer to lesbians and thus asserts the existence of a historical Afro-Caribbean lesbian community. Furthermore, Lorde argues that the very tradition of black mothering is one of "black dykes," so that even married mothers who never have sexual relationships with other women can be part of a community and a history of Afro-Caribbean and African American lesbians. But as a young African American lesbian in New York in the 1950s, Lorde remains a lonely trailblazer, establishing rather than joining a community. By the time that *Zami* reached the presses, however, and certainly aided by the novel's tremendous critical and popular success, an African American lesbian community did exist. And thanks to Lorde, Walker, Parker, and others a variety of identity positions seem increasingly available to African American lesbian writers.

Also in the 1980s, another lesbian straddling Caribbean and African American communities, **Michelle Cliff**, began to publish semiautobiographical novels and essay and poetry collections. In *Claiming an Identity They Taught Me to Despise* (1980), *Abeng* (1984), *The Land of Look Behind* (1985), *No Telephone to Heaven* (1987), *Bodies of Water* (1990), *Free Enterprise* (1993), and *The Store of a Million Items* (1998), Cliff describes the experiences of an Afro-Caribbean girl discovering her cultural and sexual identities between New York and Jamaica. Cliff's work joins a growing body of not only novels and poetry but also critical and anthological work by African American lesbians. These women brought the issues of African American lesbian literature and its relative absence into the critical debates surrounding feminism and lesbianism and also African American studies. Literary and cultural critics such as **Barbara Smith**, Ann Allen Shockley, Cheryl Clark, and **Jewelle Gomez** wrote about how although women, lesbians, and African Americans made great steps forward in the arenas of civil rights and artistic recognition between the 1950s and the 1980s, African American lesbians still often found themselves in the untenable position of needing to proclaim themselves wither lesbian or African American, as if the two could be separated.

In the 1990s African American lesbian writing again turned away from predominantly lesbian-themed novels but now rather than avoiding explicit lesbianism or the term "lesbian," authors such as Helen Elaine Lee, April Sinclair, **E. Lynn Harris**, and Sapphire integrate lesbian characters and themes into their treatment of the multiple questions of race, class, gender, place, sexuality, religion, motherhood, and family on which African American literature turns. At the same time, a growing body of literature also focuses on lesbian characters involved not only in staking out a place for themselves to exist but also in negotiating the many parts of their lives as African American lesbians. Jewelle Gomez in *The Gilda Stories* (1991) and *Don't Explain* (1998) plays with history and literary genre in a series of romance-science fiction-historical-vampire stories that consider how to articulate African American lesbianism even as they do so. The first novel by Odessa Rose, *Water in a Broken Glass* (2000), traces a young African American sculptor's coming out in the context of her homophobic family but also in an out and proud African American lesbian and gay community. Laurinda D. Brown's first novel, *Fire and Brimstone* (2001), depicts a relationship between a single mother and a minister as the two explore what it means to be an African American family and to have religion in the South. Lesbianism has become not the unspoken and unspeakable shadow but rather one of the many spoken pieces of African American literature.

Further Reading

Carbado, Devon, Dwight McBride, and Donald Weisse, eds. *Black Like Us: A Century of Lesbian, Gay, and Bisexual African American Fiction*. San Francisco: Cleis Press, 2002.

McKinley, Catherine, and Joyce DeLaney, eds. *Afrekete: An Anthology of Black Lesbian Writing*. New York: Anchor Books, 1995.

Nelson, Emmanuel S., ed. *Critical Essays: Gay and Lesbian Writers of Color*. New York: Haworth Press, 1993.

Smith, Barbara. *The Truth That Never Hurts: Writings on Race, Gender, and Freedom*. New Brunswick, NJ: Rutgers UP, 1998.

Smith, Barbara, ed. *Home Girls: A Black Feminist Anthology*. New York: Kitchen Table Women of Color Press, 1983.

Keja Lys Valens

AFRICAN AMERICAN MUSICALS Popular theatrical productions combining music, dance, and acting staged by black composers, lyricists, and performers. The roots of the African American musical reach back to Africa. Music and dance were central elements of tribal rituals; they survived the **Middle Passage** and were adapted to the American environment during **slavery**. In the 1840s minstrelsy introduced imitations of black music, dance, and speech to the popular stage; white performers in blackface enacted racial caricatures that dominated working-class entertainment in the nineteenth century. Only after the Civil War did careers as performing artists became a serious possibility for black Americans.

Minstrelsy's combination of music and comedy also shaped the first black musicals. *The Creole Show* (1890), *The Octoroons* (1895), *Black Patti's Troubadours* (1896), and *Oriental America* (1896) followed minstrel conventions, but Bob Cole and Billy Johnson's ground-breaking *A Trip to Coontown* (1898), the first black show produced and performed exclusively by African Americans, substituted minstrelsy's episodic structure with an integrated plot ("book musical"). Alex Rogers, J. A. Shipp, and composer Will Marion Cook's *In Dahomey* (1903), Rogers and Bert Williams's *Abyssinia* (1906), and Cole and J. Rosamond Johnson's *The Red Moon* (1909) soon followed. Poet **Paul Laurence Dunbar** and Cook's musical comedy *Clorindy, or the Origin of the Cakewalk* (1898) was the first black musical performed on Broadway (Casino Theatre Roof Garden).

Between 1890 and 1915, approximately thirty shows were produced in black New York neighborhoods and on Broadway (Riis xxi). Though the majority of them did not differ substantially from white shows, important additions were made, such as new dance styles in *Clorindy* and the comedy and cakewalking talents of Bert Williams and George Walker in *In Dahomey*. Williams and Walker also appeared in *The Policy Players* (1899), *The Sons of Ham* (1900), and *Bandanna Land* (1907), and Williams became the first African American performer to work with the famous Ziegfeld *Follies*.

Early musicals revolved around a fairly narrow corpus of themes. *In Dahomey* and *Abyssinia* satirized the Back to Africa movement; *The Cannibal King*

(1900), *Jes' Lak White Fo'ks* (1901), and *Brown Sugar* (1927) commented on black-white relations. *Who's Stealing?* (1918), *Africana* (1922), *Liza* (1922), *Come Along Mandy* (1924), *The Chocolate Dandies* (1924), and *Lucky Sambo* (1925) featured sweet-talking dandies and gambling "coons." Additional topics included love relationships, ethnic stereotypes, and Old South nostalgia.

Flournoy Miller, Aubrey Lyles (book), Noble Sissle (lyrics), and composer Eubie Blake's *Shuffle Along* (1921) transported the black musical into the **Jazz** Age. It combined the story of two crooked politicians trying to manipulate the result of their mayoral campaigns with an appealing love plot. The show enjoyed extended runs at the Sixty-Third Street Theater and on Broadway, featuring performances by Josephine Baker and Paul Robeson. *Runnin' Wild* (1923), written by Miller, Lyles and James P. Johnson, became famous for the Charleston, the dance that defined the Roaring Twenties. *Hot Chocolates* (1929), written by Fats Waller, Andy Razaf, and Harry Brooks, showcased Louis Armstrong, the rising star of the jazz trumpet, on "Ain't Misbehavin'."

The themes and figures of the black musical during the **Harlem Renaissance** and earlier periods met with opposition from **W. E. B. Du Bois** and others, who favored overt political engagement and advocated social protest theater as means of battling the remnants of minstrel imagery and racist attitudes. The significance of black musical theater in the 1920s, however, lay less in sociopolitical messages than in expressing the sense of cultural exuberance and social change diagnosed in Alain Locke's introduction to *The New Negro* anthology (1925).

As the Great Depression took its toll on black musical theater in the 1930s, and as television and movies attained cultural prominence in the 1940s and 1950s, only few significant musicals were produced: **Arna Bontemps**/Harold Arlen/**Countee Cullen**'s *St. Louis Woman* (1946), **Langston Hughes**'s *Simply Heavenly* (1957), *Black Nativity* (1961), and *Tambourines to Glory* (1963). Hughes's works are sacred/gospel musicals (Hay 53–55). Continuing the rich African American religious tradition and capitalizing on the popularity of gospel music, the subgenre has inspired Vinette Carroll's *Trumpets of the Lord* (1963) and *Your Arms Too Short to Box with God* (1976), **Ron Milner**'s *Don't Get God Started* (1987), as well as Vy Higgerson's *Mama I Want to Sing, Part I* (1982) and *Part II* (1990) and *Let the Music Play Gospel* (1989).

Since the 1970s, African American musicals have increasingly included social themes, as in Runako Jahi's *A Place to Be Me* (1989), Michael Mathews's *Momma Don't* (1990), Karmyn Lott's *Stop and Think* (1989), Micki Grant's *Don't Bother Me I Can't Cope* (1972), Richard Wesley's *The Dream Team* (1989), Melvin Van Pebbles's *Ain't Supposed to Die a Natural Death* (1971), and the 1973 Broadway version of **Lorraine Hansberry**'s *A Raisin in the Sun*. Vernel Bagneris's *One Mo' Time* (1979), **Loften Michell** and Rosetta LeNoire's *Bubbling Brown Sugar* (1976), and Honi Coles/Bobby Shorts's *Black Broadway* (1980) restaged shows from the 1920s and 1930s, featuring performers from the bygone era like Avon Long, Joseph Attles, and Josephine Premice in *Bubbling Brown Sugar*.

Musical tributes such as Donald McKayle's *Sophisticated Ladies* (1981) and Julian Swain's *Mood Indigo* (1981), both celebrating Duke Ellington, have also enjoyed substantial popularity in recent decades. Elmo-Terry Morgan's championing of female blues and jazz singers in *The Song of Sheba* (1988), Josh Greenfield's *I Have a Dream* (1989) and Clarence Cuthbertson/George Broderick's *Faith Journey* (1994; both about Martin Luther King), Queen Esther Marrow's *Truly Blessed* (1989; about Mahalia Jackson), Reenie Upchurch's *Yesterdays* (1990; about Billie Holiday), and Charles C. Wolfe's *Jelly's Last Jam* (1992; about Jelly Roll Morton) complete the list of musical biographies of seminal black historical figures. (*See also* African American Drama)

Further Reading

Graziano, John. "Black Musical Theater and the Harlem Renaissance Movement." *Black Music in the Harlem Renaissance*. Ed. Samuel A. Floyd. Knoxville: U of Tennessee P, 1993. 87–110.

Hay, Samuel A. *African American Theatre: An Historical and Critical Analysis*. Cambridge: Cambridge UP, 1994.

Riis, Thomas L. *Just Before Jazz: Black Musical Theater in New York, 1890 to 1915*. Washington, DC: Smithsonian Institution P, 1989.

Woll, Allen. *Black Musical Theater: From Coontown to Dreamgirls*. Baton Rouge: Louisiana State UP, 1989.

Daniel T. Stein

AFRICAN AMERICAN NOVEL African American novels, here defined as novels written by African Americans, are often distinct from—while remaining a significant part of—the broader tradition of American novels. Given the history of slavery, **Jim Crow** segregation, the **Civil Rights Movement**, and persistent systemic racial inequity in the United States, African American writers have had particularly fertile ground for crafting novels of social and political critique. With eighteenth-century philosophers such as Immanuel Kant, David Hume, and Thomas Jefferson arguing that people of African descent did not have the intellectual capacity to create art or literature, the stakes for producing literature were high for the first African American novelists writing in the nineteenth century. At a basic level, that early African American literature by its very existence claimed a place for African Americans in the human family. Many African American writers further chose, and continue to choose, racial oppression or racial **identity** as their subject matter and use their novels not only to expose the cruelties and inconsistencies of the U.S. racial system, but also to present African American characters who are at the very least the social, intellectual, economic, or moral equals of their fictional white counterparts. Twentieth-century African American novels often engage intraracial (rather than in*ter*racial) identity, black pride and black power, and a transcontinental connection with people of the African diaspora. Not all African American novels, however, center on **race**. Indeed, African American novels range over a wide spectrum of genres, from science fiction to satire to romance, and engage a plethora of topics restricted only by the limits of the human imagination. Arguably, then, *the* African American Novel does not exist, for African American novels are as varied as the authors themselves.

Rising to prominence between the late eighteenth century and the middle of the nineteenth century, **African American slave narrative**s such as those by **Olaudah Equiano, Frederick Douglass**, William and Ellen Craft, and **Harriet Jacobs** were the first extended narrative publications written by African Americans to find a wide audience in the United States. These slave narratives played a fundamental role in the abolitionist movement of the mid-nineteenth century by providing firsthand accounts of the experience of the oppressed under the rule of **slavery** and by evidencing the literary, aesthetic, and intellectual equality of African Americans. The earliest African American novels, published in England because their authors could not find a publisher within the United States, were influenced in both form and content by these popular slave narratives, as well as by sentimental fiction, the genre that produced the first best-sellers in the United States. Sentimental fiction usually follows a youthful female protagonist through various adventures to a resolution in marriage. For example, the earliest published African American novel, William Wells Brown's *Clotel; or, the President's Daughter* (1853), is the story of three generations of the mulatto descendents of Thomas Jefferson and his slave, (presumably) Sally Hemings. The novel unfolds through the lives of the women as they move from slavery to freedom and ultimately to marriage. However, throughout the novel, Brown (himself an escaped ex-slave) also incorporates real-life stories of the brutality of slavery, advertisements for runaway slaves, and newspaper accounts of slave escapes and captures, digressions from fiction that link his novel closely to the slave narrative.

Brown's novel is also an early use of the trope of the "tragic mulatto/a," one that figures prominently in African American novels up through the **Harlem Renaissance**. The tragic mulatto/a is a light-skinned African American who, because of his or her "mixed" racial heritage, often passes for white and/or is romantically involved with a white person. He or she usually suffers a lamentable fate due to the vagaries of the U.S. race system and his or her individual struggle with racial, familial, and national identity. **Frank J. Webb**'s *The Garies and Their Friends* (1857), another of the earliest African American novels, offers readers both a male and female tragic **mulatto**. The Garies move to Philadelphia to escape the racism of the South; however, they find themselves under attack because of their interracial marriage. Marie, the light-skinned female protagonist, dies during childbirth while hiding from an angry white mob that has already murdered her husband. In the novel's second half, the couple's orphaned son passes for white, and as an adult becomes involved with a white woman. White **racism** and greed prove his demise: His racial identity is exposed and he dies, presumably from a broken heart after being rejected by his white fiancée. Both mother and son ultimately fall to racism for challenging the color line that separates "black" from "white."

Because the story is set largely in the North, *The Garies* also has a point in common with another early African American novel, **Harriet E. Wilson**'s *Our Nig; or, Sketches from the Life of a Free Black* (1859). *Our Nig* is the semiautobiographical story of a mixed race little girl abandoned by her white mother in the North. Although Frado is not a slave, the narrative follows a trajectory quite similar to African American slave narratives such as Harriet Jacobs's *Incidents in the Life of a Slave Girl* (1861): Little Frado is treated just as harshly as Southern slaves, and she exits the novel alone and trying to support her child with the proceeds of her novel. Although in many points similar to Jacobs's slave narrative, like *The Garies*, *Our Nig* primarily exposes white Northern racism and belies the illusion of the North as an emancipatory and benevolent refuge for escaped slaves. These early novels illustrated that African Americans were savvy and courageous enough to critique even the region of the United States touted as a haven because not overtly ruled by the law of slavery.

This tendency toward exposing both racism and prejudice through characters who suffer under their influence survives in many African American novels today. Even in the 1850s, however, not all writers let their protagonists pay the price for the destructive nature of racism. Other writers, such as **Martin R. Delany**, considered the father of American black nationalism, provided a contrasting model of resistance within the fledging African American novel tradition. In his serialized novel *Blake, or the Huts of America* (1859), Delaney fictionalized the leaders of slave revolts embodied by men such as Gabriel Prosser, Denmark Vesey, and Nat Turner, men who led or planned slave revolts in 1800, 1822, and 1831, respectively. The novel thus provides one of the earliest militant black characters willing to risk his life to liberate himself and his people by throwing off the shackles of slavery.

With the dissolution of the Confederacy and the beginning of Reconstruction, the focus of many African American novels shifted. Gone was the abolitionist interest in slave narratives and novelistic representations of slave life. Although African American authors continued to use slavery and the Old South as a backdrop for their fiction, many turned their thoughts forward toward the goal of racial uplift. Their texts were written not only to illustrate the ills of slavery, but as importantly, to emphasize the success of those who had once been slaves. The goal of many African American novels, then, was not just to confirm the basic possession of humanity for nonwhites while denouncing slavery and racism, but to illustrate the refined sensibilities, advanced education, and irreproachable morals of those labeled second-class citizens. African American novelists paid significant attention to representing "the best" in African American life in order to justify their claims for equal rights, equal representation, and equal protection under the law. Although *de jure* slavery was dead, the stakes in these decades continued to be high, as the country was negotiating the relationships between African Americans and whites in a post-bellum, industrializing world.

Between 1883 and 1896, the courts were crystallizing custom into law by establishing the legal rights of Jim Crow segregation. African Americans were struggling for equal opportunities in education and political representation, in addition to legal protection against lynch mobs. This period between the Civil War and the turn of the twentieth century saw the publication of many novels written by African American women activists. Believing that African American women would lead the race forward into racial equality, these novelists, including writers such as **Frances E. W. Harper**, Pauline E. Hopkins, Amelia E. Johnson, and Emma Dunham Kelley, wrote sentimental fiction that presented moral, educated African American families, and, specifically, African American heroines. Johnson and Kelley wrote fiction with a decidedly religious theme for a Sunday school audience: Their novels often followed their heroines, who were not always overtly marked as African American, through their quests for spiritual salvation, a goal usually attainted by novel's end. In comparison, Hopkins and Harper, two of the most well-known African American women of the era and highly public figures in the world of magazine journalism, gave readers heroines who often faced moral sexual dilemmas stemming from the lingering complexities of slavery and the U.S. race system. Their heroines, ranging from a reincarnated African goddess to a woman who resists the sexual assaults of a string of slave owners, triumph with their sexual virtue in tact.

This impulse to exonerate African American women from the charge of lasciviousness arose from the racist belief that African American women were biologically incapable of being sexually virtuous, an idea with roots in the ideology of slavery. In response, African American women novelists offered black and white readers alike representations of moral, virtuous black women worthy of membership in the "Cult of True Womanhood" that held sway at the time, and the marriage of these virtuous women at novels' end was the ultimate evidence of their sexual morality. These female protagonists also further acquitted themselves and set a positive example by working toward racial uplift. For instance, in Harper's *Iola Leroy, or Shadows Uplifted* (1893), the light-skinned Iola rejects the option of passing as white and instead marries a (light-skinned) black man. The two close the novel in wedded bliss teaching and preaching to underprivileged African American children in the South. Similarly, in Hopkins's *Contending Forces* (1900), Sappho, who has been raped and impregnated by her white uncle, ultimately marries the (light-skinned) African American hero of the text; the two set off to Europe to open a university for African Americans. Although the novels of this era (opposed to earlier novels such as *Blake* or *The Garies and Their Friends*) offered virtuous, moral, educated, upwardly mobile African Americans, they have also been criticized for presenting very few positive dark-skinned characters. Many suggest in response that these light-skinned characters, no longer tragic mulattas, serve to remind white readers of the artificiality of the color line and, furthermore, allow whites to sympathize with the characters, an important consideration as a significant portion of the intended audience was white.

African American men writers, too, were open to these charges. **Charles Chesnutt**, perhaps the most famous African American writer of these decades, often used light-skinned protagonists in his short stories and novels. His novel *The House Behind the Cedars* (1900) shares themes from earlier works: the tragic mulatta, passing, racial uplift, and the evils of the slave system. Rena Walden, the daughter of a white ex-slave owner and a mulatta, passes for white until she is forsaken by her white fiancé when her racial heritage is discovered. Her brother, John, however, succeeds in passing as white and exits the novel unscathed by his racial choice. Another of Chesnutt's novels, *The Marrow of Tradition* (1901), also centers on light-skinned African Americans, but also continues the narrative representation of strong, rebellious African American men who resist racism through violence, here in the Wilmington, North Carolina, race riot of 1898. Like Delaney's before him, Chesnutt's novel critiques white hegemonies that continued to oppress African Americans while questioning the method of racial classification in the United States. Although Chesnutt continued to write well into the 1920s, during his lifetime he published no novels after 1905. His style, reminiscent of the local color fiction of the 1880s and 1890s, and his settings isolated him from the new fiction that blossomed in the **Harlem Renaissance**. In short, Chesnutt's work did not represent the politically charged voice of the "**New Negro**."

The Harlem Renaissance, an explosive period of literary, artistic, and philosophical production that reached its peak in the 1920s, witnessed a new racial consciousness. Many of the themes and tropes in African American novels, however, remained the same. For instance, passing continued as one of the most prevalent tropes in African American novels: Novelists such as **Jessie Redmon Fauset**, **James Weldon Johnson**, **Nella Larsen**, and **George Schuyler** all used the trope. Whereas many early passing narratives centered on protagonists who did not know they were passing (they were raised as white), passing novels of the Harlem Renaissance more often provide readers with characters who pass intentionally in order to challenge Jim Crow segregation. Female passers in these novels often pass to marry white men and hence achieve better socioeconomic positions; others pass for access to better jobs. No matter what impetus spurs these characters to adopt a white identity, passing novels of this period usually condemn passing as an act of self- and racial betrayal. The female characters are often twentieth-century versions of the tragic mulatta. Male passers, as well, suffer from their choice to pass. James Weldon Johnson's unnamed male narrator in *Autobiography of an Ex-Colored Man* (1912) feels he has sacrificed his "birthright" for materialistic gains garnered from passing as white. Although he fares better than many of his female counterparts, he struggles with guilt and psychological displacement. In short, these novels expressed the new racial consciousness of the Harlem Renaissance by advocating both a pride in and responsibility for claiming one's blackness no matter what the shade of skin. They thus evince the continued philosophy of racial uplift; indeed, many of these passers would be considered a part of **W. E. B. Du Bois**'s "**talented tenth**," the educated, culturally and economically successful African Americans who had a responsibility to raise up their racial family. They can only do that by proclaiming their blackness.

Not all authors, however, advocated this racial responsibility or resolved the fates of their passers tragically. **Wallace Thurman**'s *Infants of Spring* (1932) satirizes many of the well-known figures of the Harlem Renaissance, and George Schuyler, in *Black No More* (1931), offers readers a satiric spin on passing that ultimately runs its white supremacist characters into a lynch mob who believes them to be black. By novel's end, it is difficult, if not impossible, to accurately identify any character's "true" racial identity in a world where dark skin has gained the cultural currency previously reserved for whites. Additionally, African American authors of the period grappled with a plethora of other narrative themes, structures, and styles. **Claude McKay**'s *Home to Harlem* (1928) delved into the controversy of primitivism that circulated through the period, and **Zora Neale Hurston** combined her university training in anthropology with her narrative genius as a folklorist and novelist to produce novels such as *Jonah's Gourd Vine* (1934) and *Their Eyes Were Watching God* (1937). These novels represented a rural African American life that stood in stark opposition to McKay's urban novel. Diverging from the traditional novel structure, **Jean Toomer** wrote *Cane* (1923), a combination of poems, vignettes, and musings, that engaged all of modernism's fragmentation and play with language while continuing to focus on themes of racial identity, lynching, and the differences between life in Northern urban centers and Southern rural towns.

The heyday of the Harlem Renaissance and the **Jazz** Age faded with the onset of the Great Depression, and, while African American writers such as Hurston and Langston Hughes continued to write through the 1930s or beyond, a new group of African American novelists grew to maturity. Although these decades produced black women writers such as **Ann Petry**, who carried forward traditions from the black women writers of the Harlem Renaissance, the period is perhaps better known for its male writers. Indeed, even Petry's *The Street* (1946) is often contextualized in relation to **Richard Wright**'s *Native Son* (1940). Wright, one of the most prominent African American writers of the 1940s and 1950s, is kept company by **Ralph Ellison** and **James Baldwin**, all at one time expatriots in Paris, although not always friends. Like their predecessors a hundred years earlier, their novels continue to critique racism and racial violence in the United States; however, their social protest evinces a racial consciousness changed radically by the Depression, World War II, and socialism. The novels, variously fusions of urban realism, naturalism, and modernism, offer protagonists who struggle psychologically to find their place in a white-dominated society that sees them, *if it sees them,* as "boys," with only few rights that whites need respect. *Native Son* tells the story of Bigger Thomas, a young Black man who tries to improve his condition by working within the Jim Crow system. After Bigger accidentally kills his rich, white employer's daughter, his fate is sealed as he flees from the white mob intent on lynching him. Ellison's masterpiece *The Invisible Man* (1951) offers the story of an unnamed narrator who negotiates the social and psychological invisibility of the black man in the United States. Fleeing the 1940s Harlem riots, the narrator ultimately goes underground, living beneath the city in a room electrified with 1,369 light bulbs powered by stolen electricity. Baldwin's *Go Tell It on the Mountain* (1952) fuses an analysis of the psychological impact of the Great Migration northward and the urban North/rural South split with an investigation of the role religion has played in the African American consciousness. These protagonists all search for identity and independence in a racist world. **Chester Himes**, another expatriot and best known for his detective fiction, wrote the widely acclaimed novel *If He Hollers Let Him Go* (1945), which highlights another psychological reaction to the pervasive racism of World War II America: The novel's protagonist lives in constant fear of doing or saying the wrong thing in a racist world. His fears are ultimately justified when he is falsely accused of having raped a white woman.

The racial unrest and social protest of the 1940s and 1950s matured in the **Civil Rights Movement** of the following decades. Although African Americans were certainly writing novels during the 1960s, the decade witnessed a stronger wave of black autobiography, essays, and poetry that focused directly on issues of black power, racism, equality, and the failings of democracy. The 1970s, in comparison, birthed novels that not only critiqued the inequity of the American social structure and continued to expose the high psychological and physical costs of racism, but that also reclaimed and rewrote African American history in powerful ways. **Margaret Walker**'s *Jubilee* (1966), an intergenerational account of African American women, ushered in other narrative explorations of history, including **Ernest Gaines**'s *The Autobiography of Miss Jane Pittman* (1971), **Gayl Jones**'s *Corregidora* (1975), and **Alex Haley**'s *Roots* (1976). These texts harken back to the slave narratives of the mid-nineteenth century as they situate contemporary social conditions as developing from America's distinct racial history. This narrative reclamation and exploration of history has continued through the last two decades of the twentieth century and includes novels such as **Sherley Anne Williams**'s *Dessa Rose* (1986), a tale of African Americans who went West to escape slavery and Southern persecution; **Toni Morrison**'s *Beloved* (1988), the fictionalized account of the escaped slave Margaret Garner who killed her child; Lalita Tademy's *Cane*

River (2001), an intergenerational account of one family's women; and Alice Randall's *The Wind Done Gone* (2001), a parody of Margaret Mitchell's best seller *Gone With the Wind* (1936). Evincing the U.S. public's interest in its racial past, many of these fictionalized histories have been made into major motion pictures and television series. The novelists of these decades, however, were not all concerned with exploring or reframing the past. Many were interested in representing a present replete with new forms of racism, violence, and identity crises. Thus rose "gangsta" literature and authors such as Iceberg Slim and Donald Goines, whose novels focus on the lives of young, black, inner-city youths raised in a world of violence. Goines, who wrote his first two novels in jail, was shot to death in 1974.

The last two decades of the twentieth century—the post–Civil Rights era—have witnessed another burgeoning of African American novelists. A substantial black readership and expanded black middle class have allowed African American novelists to broaden their scope. In addition to Nobel and Pulitzer Prize winner Toni Morrison, writers such as **Toni Cade Bambara**, **David Bradley**, **Paule Marshall**, **Gloria Naylor**, **Alice Walker**, and **John Edgar Wideman** write what might be classified as "literary" fiction that explores African American identity, the African **diaspora**, or the complex relationship between race and gender. These novels often experiment with temporal linearity, narrative voice, and poetic language. In another vein, and following in the tradition of George Schuyler, **Charles R. Johnson** and **Ishmael Reed** write satiric novels often set in historical periods in ways that reflect upon contemporary racial identity and politics. **Octavia Butler** and **Samuel R. Delany** write science fiction, and, continuing in the tradition of James Baldwin, **E. Lynn Harris** and James Earl Hardy explore black male homosexuality. Walter Mosley writes hard-boiled detective fiction, and Terri McMillan and Elizabeth Atkins Bowman keep romance readers busy. Following the tradition of Iceberg Slim and Donald Goines, writers such as Shannon Holmes, Sister Souljah, Nikki Turner, Carl Weber, and Teri Woods write "hip-hop" novels, a genre attracting many younger readers. Hip-hop fiction, a new "urban realism" with a specific and dynamic link to hip-hop music, offers a dramatic record of street life, drugs, gangs, or coming-of-age difficulties for urban youth. And the passing novel survives still, as witnessed by **Danzy Senna**'s *Caucasia* (1998), Elizabeth Atkins Bowman's *Dark Secret* (2000), and Alice Randall's *The Wind Done Gone* (2001).

Regardless of era, genre, style, subject, or intended audience, taken together African American novels reflect the trope of the "talking book," a trope that connects the written text to the complex oral and musical traditions that circulate in African American culture. Writers, from Harriet Jacobs to **Langston Hughes** to Zora Neale Hurston to Ishmael Reed to Alice Walker to Sister Souljah, incorporate not only in their dialogue but in the very structure of their novels the rhythms, sounds, values, and traditions of African American storytelling. Furthermore, as **Henry Louis Gates Jr.**, has suggested, African American books "talk" to each other. That is, the stories, themes, and characters in African American fiction carry forward with them what has come before in African American culture and combine it with ever developing styles, structures, and stories. Contemporary authors continue to revise and retell in new settings stories of triumph, defeat, despair, and surviving humanity in the face of continued racism and social inequity, and thus African American novels not only talk to each other, but also talk to contemporary readers of all races, ethnicities, and nationalities.

Further Reading

Carby, Hazel V. *Reconstructing Womanhood*. New York: Oxford UP, 1996.

Christian, Barbara. *Black Women Novelists: The Development of a Tradition, 1892–1976*. New York: Greenwood Press, 1980.

Dickson-Carr, Darryl. *African American Satire: The Sacredly Profane Novel*. Columbia: U of Missouri P, 2001.

Fabi, M. Giulia. *Passing and the Rise of the African American Novel*. Urbana and Chicago: U of Illinois P, 2001.

Gates, Henry Louis, Jr. *The Signifying Monkey: A Theory of African-American Literary Criticism*. Oxford: Oxford UP, 1988.

Graham, Maryemma, ed. *The Cambridge Companion to the African American Novel*. London: Cambridge UP, 2004.

Greene, J. Lee. *Blacks in Eden: The African American Novel's First Century*. Charlottesville: UP of Virginia, 1996.

Hubbard, Dolan. *The Sermon and the African American Literary Tradition*. Columbia: U of Missouri P, 1996.

Nelson, Emmanuel S., ed. *Contemporary African American Novelists*. New York: Greenwood Press, 1999.

Tate, Claudia. *Domestic Allegories of Political Desire: The Black Heroine's Text at the Turn of the Century*. Oxford: Oxford UP, 1993.

Julie Cary Nerad

AFRICAN AMERICAN POETRY   Historically, the beginning of African American poetry is strongly rooted in the oral traditions of an oppressed people, who were largely denied an opportunity and the occasion to create literary expression. As a resistance to their denial, the earliest voices, from the eighteenth century to the twenty-first century, have found ways in which to express their experiences, either by adapting traditional forms to suit their needs or by creating new aesthetic forms, which have allowed for a wider range of creativity and freedom. From the beginning of the eighteenth century, though, poets have encountered numerous problems, such as choice of subject matter, themes, forms of expression, securing a publisher, authenticating authorship, and appealing to a wider audience. However, by envisioning a world of justice and equality, and by cultivating their own art out of a spirit of human necessity, both old and new voices, with innumerable stories to tell, have created a rich legacy of poetry within the larger context of American culture, spanning over two hundred and fifty years. The quest for freedom remains a defining theme of this poetic tradition.

Eighteenth-Century Beginnings

New England slave Lucy Terry, who converted to Christianity in 1735, was one of the earliest voices to emerge with "Bars Fight" (1746), a historical account of the Indian raid on Deerfield, Massachusetts, composed in rhymed tetrameter couplet. Though not recognized for its literary merits, Terry's work set the pace for an important poetic tradition. After Lucy Terry, the two early poets of note, whose poetry reflects a strong influence of American Wesleyanism and the revolutionary fervor for liberty ensuing from the radical implications of the American Revolution, were **Jupiter Hammon** and **Phillis Wheatley**. Hammon, a slave all of his life and the first African American to publish a poem—"An Evening Thought" (1761), a repetitive shout-hymn with the word "salvation" occurring in every stanza—yearned for salvation from this world, but rather than lose his soul fighting against the system of **slavery**, accepted enslavement on earth instead. Hailed as the Sable Muse of London society, Phillis Wheatley, a Senegal-born woman who used traditional modes and models such as John Milton, Alexander Pope, John Dryden, and William Blake, wrote, around age twenty, the first volume of poetry by an African American, *Poems on Various Subjects, Religious and Moral* (1773), which reflected her New England education and a heavy emphasis on the Bible and the classics. It included several elegies in honor of prominent persons, such as Mr. George Whitefield, odes to political leaders and heroes, such as General George Washington, reflective poems, and more general subjects on nature, religion, education, and biblical incidents. Given her upbringing and training in the Wheatley household, she did not write any protest poetry against slavery, like the poets in the nineteenth century, but her works do reflect a strong growing social conscience.

Nineteenth-Century Poetry

A more articulate tradition of protest through poetry began to emerge in the nineteenth century. And although the **abolition**ist movement had emerged from its comatose state, several poets had a more personal interest in the struggle. Concerned with his own human rights and the struggle against slavery and racism, **George Moses Horton**, a North Carolinian slave and America's first African American professional poet, expressed his protest in his volume of poems, *The Hope of Liberty* (1829), published in an effort to buy his freedom. Unlike Jupiter Hammon and Phillis Wheatley, Horton's tone is distinctly different, and his poetry is void of their heavy religiosity and pious sentimentality.

Like George Moses Horton, other poets devoted themselves to the cause of abolition. **James M. Whitfield**, one of black America's most forceful and angry abolitionist poets, makes a scathing indictment of injustices in his best-known work, *America, and Other Poems* (1853), especially in the title poem "America," dedicated to **Martin R. Delany**, where he states it was a "land of blood, and crime, and wrong" (Barksdale and Kinnamon 223). **Frances Ellen Watkins Harper**, an abolitionist orator and poet, echoes Whitfield in the "wrong" and injustices done to blacks in her familiar volume, *Poems on Miscellaneous Subjects* (1854), which reveals the inhumane practices and abuses of slavery, as she pleas in the poem "Bury Me in a Free Land" not to be buried "in a land where men are slaves." Other contemporaries such as **James Madison Bell**, and **Albery A. Whitman**, continued the protest begun by Horton. John W. Holloway, James Edwin Campbell, James David Corrothers, and Daniel Webster Davis mimicked the dominant stereotypes of the popular plantation tradition with dialect poems. Though not totally oblivious to problems of their day, such poets as Ann Plato, and Henrietta Cordelia Ray, chose the route of romantic escapism and wrote about nature, platonic love, and religious ideals.

With the financial assistance of Wilbur Wright, **Paul Laurence Dunbar** self-published his first volume of poems, *Oak and Ivy* (1893), and launched his career as America's first black nationally known poet and also as one of America's finest lyricists. *Majors and Minors* (1895) garnered him the favorable attention of literary critic William Dean Howells, who also arranged to have *Lyrics of Lowly Life* (1896) published. Disappointed over Howells' endorsement of his dialect poetry, for which he earned national fame and captured white America with poems exhibiting freshness, humor, and catchy rhythms, Dunbar, unfortunately, spent the last years of his life brooding over the critics' neglect of his poetry in Standard English for that of "a jingle in a broken tongue" (Barksdale and Kinnamon 360). Nevertheless, he published eleven volumes of poetry and is remembered for some of his most anthologized poems, "We Wear the Mask" and "Sympathy," both of which vividly portray the frustrations of the black man's dismal plight, including Dunbar's own.

At the turn of the century, several African American poets adopted a number of popular literary traditions or literary trends of the era and were influenced by experiments with local color, regionalism, realism, and naturalism, rejecting, as did other American poets, sentimentality, didacticism, romantic escape, and poetic diction. In this atmosphere of literary freedom, African American women poets like **Angelina Weld Grimké** wrote with brevity on nature, loss of love, racial issues, and, sometimes, eroticism. Covering a range of themes, **Helene Johnson** wrote on Negro pride, culture, love, and the love of **jazz** music, and **Gwendolyn Bennett** wrote of the nostalgia for Africa, the beauty of black women, and the nurturing practices and traditions within African American culture. Traditional in form, **Alice Moore Dunbar-Nelson**'s poetry explored a woman's heart and was precisely crafted. Called the most modernist, original, and unconventional of her contemporaries, **Anne Spencer**'s poetry focused on nature's beauty, friendship, and love, and she exhibited a command of slant rhymes, sinister rhythms, and obscure symbolism. The spirited, ambitious, dynamic Georgia Douglass Johnson, whose home was one of the greatest literary salons in Washington, DC, published four volumes of poetry centering on romance (often eroticism) and sociopolitical issues. Though her third collection, *An Autumn Love Cycle* (1928), garnered her critical acclaim, her critical reception, and that of other African American women poets during the first three decades of the twentieth century, was sorely diminished.

During such an outpouring from the women, two poets' works emerged as robust, militant racial poetry with a political intent. A native of Chicago, Fenton Johnson, who exhibited a keen racial consciousness, produced three volumes of poetry, *A Little Dreaming* (1913), *Visions of the Dark* (1915), and *Songs of the Soil* (1916), using a lyrical Victorian style, dialect in both personal and traditional idioms, free verse forms, and urban realism. Like **Carl Sandburg**, Edgar Lee Masters, and other midwestern authors, Johnson wrote of the despair and fatalism prevalent of his own urban experiences. His poem "Tired" captures his despair and melancholy mood when he states, " I am tired of building up somebody else's civilization . . . I am tired of civilization" (Barksdale and Kinnamon 456). Though a prolific writer, **W. E. B. Du Bois**, known for his scholarly historical and sociological works and his call for racial equality and social justice, wrote little poetry. His most anthologized work, "A Litany of Atlanta," uses as series of supplications and responses with vivid imagery to dramatize the black's plea for freedom and justice, and provides a valuable link to the existing protest prevalent in both the 1800s and the 1900s.

New Negro Renaissance

First known as the **New Negro** Movement, African American poetry flourished during the **Harlem Renaissance** of the 1920s, and was enriched by numerous young aspiring talents, who were vocal and interested in new themes, styles, and tones of writing. In *The New Negro* (1925), according to mentor, critic, and interpreter of the Harlem Renaissance **Alain Locke**, a growing racial awareness among African American writers promoted a new self-awareness in their culture and heritage, uninhibited by fear or shame. So as to influence the prevailing views about themselves and their community through their creativity, these artists moved to urban areas, including Harlem, New York, and Chicago, to produce works that were culturally affirming.

The first and most radical voice to emerge during the 1920s was **Claude McKay**, and the first great literary achievement during this period was his *Harlem Shadows* (1922). A master of the sonnet, the Jamaican-born poet was most noted for his poems expressing anger and rage, which were rich in animal imagery and metaphors, as in "If We Must Die," composed in the wake of the 1919 race riots. Unlike his contemporaries, **Countee Cullen**, a romantic poet influenced by John Keats and Percy Bysshe Shelley, wrote mostly nonracial poetry on love, youth, spring, and death. Ambivalent about his own racial identity, the few poems that do celebrate blackness, such as "Heritage," reveal his confusion while exploring the problem of racism and the meaning of Africa, though not apparent from the titles of his collections, *Color* (1925), *Copper Sun* (1927), and *Ballad of a Brown Girl* (1927). Expressing his sentiments at being labeled a "Negro poet" in "Yet Do I Marvel," Cullen was, nevertheless, one of the most prize-winning poets nationwide, one of several to benefit from publishing opportunities for promising writers, and one of the best-known poets of the twenties.

Other poets who came into prominence during the Harlem Renaissance, celebrating a full expression of their own cosmology and cultural myths, were **James Weldon Johnson**, **Sterling A. Brown**, and **Langston Hughes**. Writing works rich in folk heritage, they explored the **blues**, spirituals, tales, proverbs, and sayings. James Weldon Johnson's classic anthologies *The Book of American Negro Poetry* (1922) and *The Book of Negro Spirituals* (1925) are landmarks in the study of African American culture. Beginning as a writer of sentimental poems in black dialect, Johnson, who criticized Paul Laurence Dunbar's use of it, abandons dialect, which he claims "[was] not capable of giving expression to the varied conditions of Negro life in America" (Johnson 42), and became a poet who crafted black folk materials and speech patterns into an art form. Relying heavily upon imagery, rhythm, idiom, and a great sympathy for subject matter, Johnson draws on the stock material of black preachers in *God Trombones: Seven Negro Sermons in Verse* (1927).

Langston Hughes, the most prolific, versatile, and experimental artist of the New Negro Renaissance, was poet laureate of Harlem, and a folk poet, who, unlike James Weldon Johnson, combined work songs, blues, **jazz**, and ballads to depict the harsh realities of the common man. In his first two volumes, *The Weary Blues* (1926) and *Fine Clothes to the Jew* (1927), Hughes captures the heartbeat of black life and recreates the jazzy, exotic world of Harlem nights in such poems as "The Weary Blues," "Bound No'th Blues," "Lenox Avenue Midnight," and "Jazzonia." Always a poet for the people, Hughes continued to capture the sounds, colors, and rhythms of his people throughout the urban blight of the 1950s and 1960s.

Sterling A. Brown, like Langston Hughes, was a master adaptor of folk forms and experimented with blues, work songs, spirituals, and ballads, combining these forms with folk speech to create a sensitive portrayal of the black experience in the rural South. To create a new poetic language that accurately captured the plight of his people, Brown skillfully uses free verse forms, and fuses the blues song with the ballad to create the blues-ballad, as is evident in some of his finest poems, "John Henry," "The Odyssey of Big Boy," and "Ma Rainey" in his significant first work, *Southern Roads* (1932). Of his folk poetry, James Weldon Johnson notes, "He has deepened its meanings and multiplied its implications . . . developed a unique technique . . . and worked it into original and genuine poetry" (247).

Over the next three decades, from 1930 to 1960, the major voices that elevated African American poetry to a new level of consciousness and maturity were **Melvin B. Tolson**, **Robert Hayden**, **Margaret Walker**, and **Gwendolyn Brooks**, joined by **Samuel W. Allen**, **May Miller**, **Margaret Esse Danner**, **Dudley Randall**, **Owen Dodson**, **Frank Marshall Davis**, Frank Horne, and others. Stretching the boundaries of language, they explored the subject of history, and aligned themselves with international affairs and socialistic movements. Melvin Tolson used classical imagery, extensive historical allusions, and racial symbolism in his works, *Rendezvous with America* (1944), which includes his award-winning poem, "Dark Symphony"; *Libretto for the Republic of Liberia* (1953); and *Harlem Gallery* (1965).

An award-winning poet of voice, symbol, and lyricism, Robert Hayden, like Countee Cullen, felt that a poet, whether black or white, should not be restricted to racial themes that would evaluate him as a black poet, and that a poet should be able to make any valid statements about any aspect of a man's experience. To prove how such freedom enriched and deepened his own poetry, Hayden wrote, among others, "**Frederick Douglass**," "Runagate Runagate," and "Middle Passage." Margaret Walker, unlike Hayden, fully embraced her racial material and struck a new cord in the title poem of her first volume of poetry, " For My People." A celebration of black people, Walker's prose poem vibrates with racial consciousness and social protest, energetic movement of language, parallelism of words and phrases, and the absence of major punctuation marks, charting new paths in African American poetry.

Pulitzer Prize–winning poet Gwendolyn Brooks and former poet laureate of Illinois was one of the most prolific poets of the twentieth century. She was the author of over twenty works, including her first, *A Street in Bronzeville* (1945); *Annie Allen* (1949), which received the Pulitzer Prize in 1950, the first such prize by a black author; *The Bean Eaters* (1961); *Selected Poems* (1963); *In the Mecca* (1968); *Riot* (1969); and *Family Pictures* (1970). Moving from traditional forms, including ballads, sonnets, lyric stanzas, conventional rhyme, and rhythm of the blues, to unrestricted free verse, her works depict, with brevity, black, ordinary people struggling to survive the harsh realities of the urban North, particularly Chicago.

The Black Arts Movement

During the 1960s, after the advent of **Malcolm X**'s assassination, many of the poets of the Black Arts Movement, inspired by his example, achieved a new black renaissance, while politically, socially, and creatively engaged in the struggle for justice and equality. Fueled by their energy and determination, they helped to sustain the **Civil Rights Movement**, by calling for self-reliance, pride in their black heritage and culture, and reaffirming a racial consciousness utilizing black life as a model for their art, exhibited in their poetic style and diction. Complementing such established writers as Gwendolyn Brooks, Margaret Walker, Robert Hayden, **Dudley Randall**, and Owen Dodson were **Amiri Baraka** (LeRoi Jones), **Larry Neal, Askia M. Touré** (Rolland Snellings), **Etheridge Knight, Sonia Sanchez**, A. B. Spellman, **Haki R. Madhubuti** (Don L. Lee), Johari Amini (Jewel Latimore), **Nikki Giovanni**, David Henderson, and **Tom Dent**.

Three of the earliest visionaries and revolutionaries of the Black Arts Movement, Amiri Baraka (LeRoi Jones), Larry Neal, Askia M. Touré (Rolland Snellings), capture with vigor and pride the spirit of the struggle for black liberation and equality. An acclaimed poet, activist, playwright, editor, jazz critic, and cofounder of the Black Arts Repertory Theatre/School along with Larry Neal, Amiri Baraka is considered the "Dean of Revolutionary Poetry" (Reid 71) and one of the most influential poets for a whole generation of young black writers. In the late 1950s and early 1960s, he gained a reputation as a poet, editor, and jazz critic among the artists of Greenwich Village. Baraka's first published collection, *Preface to a Twenty Volume Suicide Note* (1961), reveals his emerging political views, and the poem "Black Art" (1965) served as his poetic/political manifesto of the Black Arts literary movement. In more than twelve volumes of poetry, including *The Dead Lecturer* (1964), *Black Magic Poetry* (1969), *In Our Terribleness* (1970), *It's Nation Time* (1970), *Spirit Reach* (1972), and *Reggae or Not!* (1981), Baraka emerged over the years with a strong, nationalistic, frequently militant voice, utilizing onomatopeia, obscenity, hyperbolic imagery, rhetorical questions, unusual syntax, and signification. What has resulted is a poetry that is experimental and improvisational, evoking a sense of jazz and explosiveness.

Two other poets of note are Larry Neal and Askia M.Touré (Rolland Snellings). Characterized as a spiritual journeyman of the Black Arts Movement, Larry Neal was one of its most influential critics, scholars, editors, and philosophers. In his manifesto and seminal essay, "The Black Arts Movement," he asserts that the movement is "the aesthetic and spiritual sister of the Black Power concept . . . [and] the Black Arts Movement proposes a radical reordering of the Western cultural aesthetic" (Donalson 926). Utilizing the rhythm of black music, in his two collections of poetry, *Black Boogaloo: Notes on Black Liberation* (1969) and *Hoodoo Hollerin' Bebop Ghosts* (1974), Neal often engages African American history, language, and mythology. Another architect of the Black Arts Movement, poet and political activist Askia Touré, has continued to combine his compassion for justice and artistic expression in such works as his long poem *Juju: Magic Songs for the Black Nation* (1970), *Songhai* (1973), and *From the Pyramids to the Projects: Poems of Genocide and Resistance* (1990).

The political and social upheavals of the 1950s and 1960s brought about by the Civil Rights Movement ushered in an outpouring of African American poetry. The assassination of **Martin Luther King Jr.**, inspired poetry from Haki R. Madhubuti (Don L. Lee), Nikki Giovanni, Sam Allen, **Mari Evans**, and **Quincy Troupe**. In the wake of the Black Power Movement, with its bold language of racial confrontation, black pride, use of free verse, and unconventional poetic structure, the works of Baraka, Neal, and Touré, along with such eminent poets as Madhubuti, Giovanni, Evans, Troupe, Etheridge Knight, June Jordan, Ray Durem, Sonia Sanchez, and **Clarence Major**, among others, left no poetic innovation untested and no theme untouched. Speaking of the existing body of poetry written by these poets, Margaret Reid notes, "This poetry written expressively for Black people by Black people . . . defied all traditional standards as poets sought to free themselves artistically and politically from . . . imposed restrictions" (97).

Contemporary African American Poetry

Since the 1970s, contemporary African American poets have produced works that draw heavily upon the blues and jazz, features of call-and-response, the dozens, the rap, **signifying**, and folktales. Though no longer in the throes of a cultural and political revolution like the 1960s, these poets continued to affirm their blackness, which was transformed into a performance that speaks to the power of black music and speech, as in the works of Haki R. Madhubuti, Sonia Sanchez, Amiri Baraka, Nikki Giovanni, Askia Touré, **Jayne Cortez**, Eugene Redmond, and Ted Joans. Whereas the works of these poets absorbed full musical forms, oratory and performance, other poets like Alvin Aubert, Pinki Gordon Lane, and **Naomi Long Madgett** avoided a prescribed poetic form and enhanced their poetry by more subdued means. **Lucille Clifton**, **Audre Lorde**, Jay Wright, and **Michael S. Harper** explored more personal and individualized goals. **Rita Dove** credits the Black Arts Movement for her acceptance in America depicting a message other than a politically charged one in her well-known work, the 1987 Pulitzer Prize–winning *Thomas and Beulah* (1986). During the late 1970s and 1980s, like Dove, who earlier published her first book of poems with a major press, *The Yellow House on the Corner* (1980), a large group of poets also published their first poem, chapbook, or book of poetry, and would go on to become some of the most accomplished poets of the twentieth century. Among them were **Yusef Komunyakaa**, **Melvin Dixon**, Delores Kendrick, **Cornelius Eady**, **Toi Derricotte**, Gloria Oden, **Sherley Anne Williams**, and Thylias Moss. Writing in the 1990s, the voices of Elizabeth Alexander, Thomas Sayers Ellis, Kevin Young, Sharan Strange, Carl Phillips, Natasha Trethewey, and **Harryette Mullen**, to name a few, write of both public issues and concerns in contemporary life. Other young poets like Ras Baraka, Kevin Powell, Jabari Asim, and Esther Iverem seek to revisit the ideals of the Black Arts Movement in the language of a hip-hop nation, keeping the spirit of a bygone revolution alive and anew.

At the close of the twentieth century, African American poetry has experienced an expansive, renewal phase that some have called the "Third

Renaissance." Evidence of such a renewal was obvious at the 1994 Furious Flower Conference, the first of its kind to focus solely on poetry, dedicated to Gwendolyn Brooks and hosted at James Madison University in Virginia, where four generations of poets met to read, discuss, and celebrate black poetry. Such a gathering symbolized the importance of poetic expression as a continuous medium and signaled the dynamics of its future growth and development. Poets who launched their writing careers in the1960s and early 1970s are continuing to write with such skill and force. First-rate examples are **Gerald W. Barrax**'s *Leaning Against the Sun* (1992); Haki R. Madhubuti's *Claiming the Earth: Race, Rage, Redemption* (1994); Sonia Sanchez's *Wounded in the House of a Friend* (1995); Amiri Baraka's *Funk Lore: New Poems (1984–95)* (1996); and Askia M. Touré's *Dawnsong!* (2000). African American poets receiving some of the nation's most prestigious achievements and top honors during this time were Derek Walcott, with his 1992 Nobel Prize for Literature (for his epic poem *Omeros*); Rita Dove's 1993 appointment as Poet Laureate of the United States; and Gwendolyn Brooks's naming by the National Endowment for the Humanities as the Jefferson Lecturer for 1994. A few other poets deserve mention as well. Eugene Redmond is the first and only poet laureate of his native East Saint Louis, Illinois (1976), Pinki Gordon Lane, is the first African American to be named Louisiana's poet laureate, and one of the youngest is Marilyn Nelson of Connecticut.

During this renaissance, a new group of young poets emerged and have been published in such anthologies as *In the Tradition: An Anthology of Young Black Writers* (1992), edited by Kevin Powell and Ras Baraka; *On the Verge: Emerging Poets and Artists* (1993), edited by Thomas Sayers Ellis and Joseph Lease; *Every Shut Eye Ain't Sleep: An Anthology of Poetry by African Americans Since 1945* (1994), edited by Michael Harper and Anthony Walton; *The Garden Thrives: Twentieth-Century African American Poetry* (1996), edited by Clarence Major; *African American Literature: A Brief Introduction and Anthology* (1996), edited by **Al Young**; *Trouble the Water: 250 Years of African-American Poetry* (1997), edited by Jerry W. Ward Jr.; and *Beyond the Frontier: African American Poetry for the 21st Century* (2002), edited by **E. Ethelbert Miller**. Shaping their work in relation to hip-hop culture, many of the younger award-winning poets published in these works, such as Tony Medina, Jessica Care Moore, Ras Baraka, Ruth Foreman, Kevin Powell, Charlie Braxton, Carl Redux Rux, Suheir Hammad, Saul Williams, and Jacquie Jones, have turned toward popular culture, presenting new challenges for critics in understanding their art. This was never more apparent than at the second historic 2004 Furious Flower Conference, also dedicated to Gwendolyn Brooks and hosted at James Madison University, which ushered in the promise of black poetic expression during the twenty-first century. Many of these new voices, like the poets in the 1970s and 1980s, have debuted their first poems and books of poetry: Angela Shannon's *Singing the Bones Together* (2003), F. Kelly Norman Ellis' *Tougaloo Blues* (2003), **Opal Moore**'s *Lot's Daughters* (2004), and Geoffrey Johnson's *smells* *i see: a collection of poetry and prose* (2004), to name a few. As James Weldon Johnson affirms in *The Book of Negro American Poetry* (1922), "Much ground has been covered, but more will yet be covered" (47). Committed to the ideals of beauty and liberation, this "ground" will continue to be "covered" by new voices inspired by the muses of long ago, sounding a clarion call for more humanism, for more critics to understand the beauty of poetic expression, and especially for more readers to understand the power and wisdom of poetry from its earliest conception to the present.

Further Reading

Barksdale, Richard, and Keneth Kinnamon. *Black Writers of America: A Comprehensive Anthology.* New York: Macmillan, 1972.

Bell, Bernard. W., ed. *Modern and Contemporary Afro-American Poetry.* Boston: Allyn and Bacon, 1972.

Bolden, Tony. *Afro-Blue: Improvisations in African American Poetry and Culture.* Urbana: U of Illinois P, 2004.

Bontemps, Arna, ed. *American Negro Poetry.* New York: Hill and Wang, 1963.

Donalson, Melvin. *Cornerstones: An Anthology of African American Literature.* New York: St. Martin's Press, 1996. 926–37.

Gabbin, Joanne V. "Forward." *Dictionary of Literary Biography.* Vol. 41: *Afro-American Poets Since 1955.* Eds. Trudier Harris and Thadious M. Davis. Detroit: Gale, 1985. xi–xv.

———. "Poetry." *The Oxford Companion to African American Literature.* Ed. William L. Andrews, Frances Smith Foster, and Trudier Harris. New York: Oxford UP, 1997. 592.

Hayden, Robert. *Kaleidoscope: Poems by American Negro Poets.* Harcourt, Brace & World, 1967.

Henderson, Stephen. *Understanding the New Black Poetry: Black Speech and Black Music as Poetic References.* New York: Morrow, 1973.

Hughes, Langston. *New Negro Poets, U.S.A.* Bloomington: Indiana University, 1964.

Jackson, Blyden, and Louis Rubin. *Black Poetry in America.* Baton Rouge: Louisiana State UP, 1974.

Johnson, James Weldon, ed. *The Book of American Negro Poetry.* New York: Harcourt, Brace, 1922 [reprint 1931].

Major, Clarence, ed. *The New Black Poetry.* New York: International, 1969.

Redding, J. Saunders. *To Make a Poet Black.* Chapel Hill: U of North Carolina P, 1939.

Redmond, Eugene B. *Drumvoices: The Mission of Afro-American Poetry.* Garden City, NY: Anchor, 1976.

Reid, Margaret Ann. *Black Protest Poetry: Polemics from the Harlem Renaissance and the Sixties.* New York: Peter Lang, 2001.

Robinson, William, Jr., ed. *Early Black American Poets.* Dubuque, IA: William C. Brown, 1969.

Wagner, Jean. *Black Poets of the United States: From Paul Laurence Dunbar to Langston Hughes.* Urbana: U of Illinois P, 1973.

Loretta G. Woodard

AFRICAN AMERICAN PULP FICTION   The moniker "pulp fiction" refers to the short fiction serialized in magazines that were printed on inexpensive, inferior paper. This short fiction made the leap to book-length work and was produced for mainstream audiences from the late 1930s through the latter part of the 1960s. Pulp fiction was infamous for its book jackets, which were highly artistic affairs featuring technicolors and lusty scenes. They were marketed mainly to a male audience and could be found in venues not usually associated with bookstores. They could be easily obtained at book vending machines, dime stores, and even at general merchandising stores on military bases. The flamboyant book covers and the simple yet provocative story lines earned pulp fiction a lowbrow reputation among literary critics. Thus genre of literature known as Black Pulp Fiction, or Ghetto Pulp Fiction, gets its name because of its quick and inexpensive production and its sensational storylines. It is most closely associated with the work produced by writers like Iceberg Slim and Donald Goines.

According to Susanne B. Dietzel there are three categories of African American pulp fiction. The foremost category is "ghetto realism or cautionary tales modeled after formulaic gangster fiction" (611). Beginning in 1969 Robert Lee Maupin, a.k.a. Robert Beck, a.k.a. Iceberg Slim, wrote novels with a decidedly street culture influence. Although he spent a brief period at Tuskeegee Institute in the 1930s, Slim was a pimp by the time he was eighteen. Over the next twenty-five years Slim was in and out of jail and it was not until he decided to pursue a more legitimate line of work that he began his series of novels immortalizing the lifestyle of those engaged in inner-city prostitution. His first work *Pimp: The Story of My Life* was autobiographical and has sold more six million copies since its initial run. Slim's works are pulp fiction classics. Like the original pulp fiction, the storylines of Slim's novels are scintillating—fraught with sex, violence, and apathy. Slim's novels were published by Holloway House, which specialized in inexpensive, sensationalist melodrama for the African American audience.

Donald Goines began his writing in prison. He hailed from a prosperous family in Detroit, but eventually became a heroin addict. Crippled by his reliance on drugs, Goines became a career thief, pimp, and bootlegger. Goines penned his semiautobiographical work *Whoreson* (1972) after reading the work of Iceberg Slim. Holloway House also published Goines's work and went on to release nearly twenty of his books. Goines also published a serial featuring the antihero Kenyatta. The four-book series followed Kenyatta as he tried to reclaim the urban streets and rid them of prostitution and drugs. Kenyatta was a militant black leader, a reflection of the turbulent times of the Black Power Movement during which Goines wrote.

Both Robert Beck and Donald Goines worked to illuminate the kind of underworld that could be the black streets of 1960s and 1970s America. The tales they contrived were one reflection of poor, urban America in the initial throes of drugs abuse and embittered by the ongoing trauma of prostitution and petty crime. Their readership was enormous, and although they were quite popular, academic critics have virtually ignored them because of the perception that pulp fiction is subliterary.

African American pulp fiction has experienced a rebirth as the characters and language of the novels have been resuscitated in popular rap and hip-hop music. Artists like Tupak Shakur, Ice T, and Ice Cube cite the work of Iceberg Slim. As a result of this revival, in the late 1990s Norton Publishing launched Old School Books, which reissued the work of Beck, Goines, and other unsung writers in the tradition. Additionally, Syndicate Media Group began printing novels written by new writers in this same vein. Beginning with *Streetsweeper* (2000), Syndicate Media began a campaign to reinvigorate this category of black pulp fiction by packaging the new works with an accompanying CD. Showcasing the work of hip-hop and rap artists, the book/CD was marketed in music stores rather than bookstores. The novels also featured pages of glossy ads featuring sneakers and clothing. Syndicate's venture met with much criticism, particularly as they began contracting with prison libraries to carry the books.

The second and "standard" tradition of African American pulp fiction consists of "political action thrillers, mysteries and detective stories" (Dietzel 611). The tales are concerned with preservation of the black community via historical and cultural awareness. There is often a hero who is passionate about and concerned with the perpetuation of the community. The characters are often confronted with an unjust judicial and economic system and must devise ways to overcome and survive. These novels promote an understanding of the entangled structures of **racism** and classism and offer broad-spectrum and sometimes vague solutions.

Novels concerned with love and romance and those with family-driven plotlines round out the genre known as African American pulp fiction. In this category there is a uniquely autonomous African American world with minimal intrusion from other cultures unless it is specific to the plotline. The storylines in these private worlds are largely concerned with white-collar blacks who have achieved some form of the American dream. Dietzel compares these novels to **Booker T. Washington**'s *Up from Slavery* in that they venerate the African American tradition of struggle and persistence (611). They also indulge the fantasies of black women for romance. Again, the protagonists in these novels are usually removed from the everyday cares of average African Americans and conduct their trysts and liaisons in a safe and contained black space where concerns with **race** rarely intrude.

Further Reading

Davis, Anthony C. "The New Sons of Iceberg Slim." *Black Issues Book Review* 3.5 (2001): 56.

Dietzel, Susanne B. "Pulp Fiction." *The Oxford Companion to African American Literature.* Ed. William L. Andrews, Frances Smith Foster, and Trudier Harris. New York: Oxford UP, 1997. 610–12.

Osborne, Gwendolyn. "The Legacy of Ghetto Pulp Fiction." *Black Issues Book Review* 3.5 (2001): 50–52.

Tarshia L. Stanley

AFRICAN AMERICAN SCIENCE FICTION   Also called AfroFuturism. From its early days as "scientifiction," named in the 1920s by Hugo Gernsback, who was a first-generation American and writer for an electronics magazine, the field of science fiction was dominated by white males writing for a predominantly white male readership. Popularized by the pulp fictions of the early twentieth century, by 1970, when the Science Fiction Research Association was founded to expand the study of science fiction, science fiction had already captured a large share of the contemporary fiction market and emerged as a significant genre.

Although there is much critical debate regarding the defining characteristics of the genre, a text is generally viewed as a work of science fiction when the narrative is set in a future time; a futuristic setting is used as a basis for speculation about the application or impact of new science or technology on humankind; travel through time or space is used as a motif or device for discovery of some universal truth; and there is a cautionary social commentary embedded in the narrative that comments on the past, the present, and the future. Typically **Martin Delany**'s *Blake, or the Huts of America* (1857) is considered the first African American science fiction novel when science fiction is broadly defined as either imaginative or speculative fiction, terms made popular by literary scholars interested in expanding the canon of science fiction. However, because the term science fiction did not come into use until the late 1920s, it is perhaps more accurate to say that **George Schuyler**'s satiric *Black No More: Being an Account of the Strange and Wonderful Workings of Science in the Land of the Free, A.D. 1933–1940*, published in 1931, is the first African American science fiction novel.

In Schuyler's novel, a Harlem-based scientist, Dr. Julius Crookman, discovers a way to permanently whiten black skin while researching a cure for vitiligo, a disease affecting skin pigmentation. Crookmans new scientific process, involving nickel-plating and electricity, makes it possible for black Americans to turn themselves white in just three days. As black characters turn themselves white, violence erupts across the country, and to protect the secret of their identities and capitalize on the value of their new white skins, some of those now passing for white join white-supremacy hate groups that participate in **racism** and violence against black men, including lynching, mutilation, and torture. In the end of the novel, white skin ceases to be the final determinant of racial **identity** when scientists discover a genetic indicator showing that the majority of white Americans have, as one of the white characters in the novel puts it, "dusky" ancestors and so, the character concludes, all are "niggers" now.

Schuyler continued to write science fiction under the pen name of Samuel I. Brooks, and his work was serialized in black newspapers. His second and third novels appeared in sixty-three newspaper installments as the story of a black researcher and scientist, Dr. Beldsidus, who creates a futuristic black utopia in the hidden interior of Africa. Dr. Beldsidus and his army of black geniuses and engineers use sophisticated germ warfare and cyclotrons, a futuristic proton impacting weapon of mass destruction, to ground Euro-American air defenses and render the armies and navies of the world completely without power. Under the guidance of Dr. Beldsidus, Africa emerges as the uncontested supreme world superpower. Primarily remembered in the twenty-first century as an essayist, Schuyler produced more than twenty such novels before his death in 1977.

Although literary scholars use the term speculative fictions or alternative histories to discuss African American science fiction as part of a larger literary tradition, contemporary African American writers of science fiction prefer Mark Dery's 1993 moniker "AfroFuturism" for the speculative fictions and alternative histories that rely upon the conventions of science fiction. Paul D. Miller, a writer and musician who goes by the professional name of D. J. Spooky, defines AfroFuturism as a "zone" and it is in this zone that "core aspects of African-American identity and it's unfolding in America" are "translated" and "fade in the algorithm of life in the liquid parade of the modern mindstream . . . subtle to the point of formlessness" (413–14). In essence, as a literary and cultural aesthetic, AfroFuturismcritiques as it revises, interrogates as it creates, and defines as it redefines the very definition of what it means to be human in the modern world. Both the form of the fiction and the fiction itself are impacted by this postmodern perspective.

In contemporary America, the names most commonly associated with the genre of African American science fiction are those of **Samuel R. Delany**, **Octavia Butler**, Steve Barnes, and Charles Saunders. Delany and Butler, in particular, have radically redefined the genre. Delany and Butler populate their worlds with characters that are without fixed racial or gender roles, and identity is determined by a character's words, deeds, and thoughts more than by their physical appearance. The physical body is an extension of identity, not the prime determinant, and the main characters are in conflict with the social structure that seeks to delineate the character's place in the man-made world. The main characters seek to transcend the world made by man.

Additionally, what sets AfroFuturism apart from mainstream American science fiction is an insistence on multi**ethnicity**. Instead of the racial tokenism common to even the best of mainstream American science fiction, African American writers of science fiction create characters with "a plethora of identities," and racial and gender "ambiguity is a positive attribute" (Brooks and Hampton 70). Butler, for example, in her *Parable* series, populates her texts with interracial, bilingual families traveling through an interracial, bilingual dystopia in search of a new beginning. In her *Patternmaster* series, characters can change gender as well. Identity is a composite of experience, memory, and emotion, and a single character can carry the archetypal memories of many races.

As the field of African American science fiction has expanded into paraliterary genres such as comic books, graphic novels, and movies, multiethnic mixed-blood characters abound. For example, Milestone Media, an African American–owned comic book company (1992–96), created a line of science fiction comics with a large cast of characters from a variety of ethnic backgrounds including multiethnic characters. Hardwire, Icon, and Xombi are mutants created by scientific disaster or are humans augmented by new cyborg weapons technology, fighting to create a livable world in the Dakota Universe. Movies such as *Underworld* (2003), in which African American producer, writer, actor, and stuntman Kevin Grioux played the part of the werewolf Raze, depict a world dominated by vampires who track the increasingly technological werewolves using sophisticated databases and futuristic laptop computers. In turn, the werewolves use genetic research to uncover the truth about a mythological common human ancestor who gave rise to both vampires and werewolves. In *Underworld*, there are black and white vampires and black and white werewolves, and the sexual taboo is the mixing of supernatural species, not colors. Color does not determine identity, and the key event of the movie is a Romeo-Juliet style romance between a werewolf and a vampire that is then played out over the course of a thousand years until individual characters choose to separate themselves from their "group" and act on the basis of their own heartfelt conclusions. Peace is achieved only when the three bloodlines again become mixed as one and the resulting mix is stronger.

African American novels, comics, graphic novels, and movies fit into a pattern of Afrofuturism or African American science fiction that emphasizes the need for self-knowledge and an acceptance of **multiculturalism** that goes beyond the embracing of "otherness" so often found in popular American science fiction. Instead of populating a text with representatives of different **race**s, African American science fiction celebrates the diversity that is part of each person's bloodline. Shared blood is shared history, and the texts' heroes recognize that there are worlds within as well as without. That level of self-knowledge, writer Greg Tate explains, comes from an individual pursuit of self-awareness; one must accept that identity is "not something that's given to you, institutionally; it's an arduous journey that must be undertaken by the individual" ("Black to the Future" 766). In African American science fiction identity is not restricted to a single racial identity, and "the final frontier" is not restricted to "space," as Captain James T. Kirk of *Star Trek* might say. Instead, the real journey—the one that requires true boldness—is the journey within.

Further Reading

Brooks, Wanda, and Gregory Hampton. "Black Women Writers and Science Fiction." *NCTE English Journal* 92.6 (June 2003): 70–75.

Dery, Mark. "Black to the Future: Interviews with Samuel R. Delany, Greg Tate, and Tricia Rose." *South Atlantic Quarterly* 92.4 (Fall 1993): 735–78.

Miller, Paul D. "Yet Do I Wonder." *Dark Matter: A Century of Speculative Fiction from the African Diaspora.* Ed. Sheree R. Thomas. New York: Warner Books, 2000. 408–14.

Scholes, Robert, and Eric Rabkin. *Science Fiction: History, Science, Vision.* New York: Oxford UP, 1977.

Darcy A. Zabel

AFRICAN AMERICAN SHORT STORY   Like autobiographies, novels, and poetry written by black Americans, the African American short story participates in a call-and-response dialogue with literary movements and social trends. Whereas critics have readily developed theories of black autobiography (William Andrews), novels (**Henry Louis Gates Jr.**), and poetry (Steven Henderson), few have extended the same to the African American short story. To date, there are only three sources that offer comprehensive analyses of black short fiction: Robert A. Bone's *Down Home: A History of Afro-American Short Fiction from Its Beginnings to the Harlem Renaissance* (1975), Peter Bruck's *The Black American Short Story in the 20th Century: A Collection of Critical Essays* (1977), and Wolfgang Karrer's *The African American Short Story, 1970–1990: A Collection of Critical Essays* (1993). These compilations, groundbreaking in their study of the African American short story, are nonetheless lacking in one area: their overall treatment of stories by black women.

The publishing history of the black short story suggests that the omissions made by Bone, Bruck, and, to a much lesser degree, Karrer, are not the product of sexism, but are, instead, the result of limited access to black women's stories. Typically published in any number of black periodicals—the *Anglo African Magazine* (1859), *Colored American Magazine* (1900), *Crisis* (1910), or *Opportunity* (1923), for example—black women's short stories became more accessible when scholars anthologized these texts. Such groundbreaking compilations include Elizabeth Ammons's *Short Fiction by Black Women, 1900–1920* (1991), Marcy Knopf's *The Sleeper Wakes: Harlem Renaissance Stories by Black Women* (1993), Judith Hamer's *Centers of the Self: Stories by Black Women from the Nineteenth Century to the Present* (1995), and Bill Mullen's *Revolutionary Tales: African American Women's Short Stories from the First Story to the Present* (1995). Taken together, short stories by black men and women offer gendered approaches to historical events, sociological forces, and literary movements affecting the nation at large.

In line with overarching trends in black writing, African American short fiction articulates the diverse perspectives within the black American literary tradition. Nineteenth-century poet, novelist, and short fiction writer **Frances Ellen Watkins Harper**—like **Frederick Douglass** and **Harriet Jacobs**—used her position on the margins to mask subversive messages about the world in which she lived. Most black writers employed masking, an African American literary and social convention, to hide their frustration with **race** or gender oppression behind the socially acceptable guise of subservience. The first short story written by a black man approached this practice of literary masking differently. A saga of miscegenation, rape, murder, and revenge, **Victor Séjour**'s "Le Mulâtre" [The Mulatto] (1837), tells the harrowing tale of Georges, a slave pushed to homicide when met with his "master's" ultimate betrayal. Where other early texts, mostly **African American slave narrative**s, dealt with the horrifying effects of institutionalized **slavery** indirectly, Séjour attacked the "peculiar institution" head on, relating with graphic detail slavery's psychological effects on blacks and whites alike.

In contrast, "The Two Offers" (1859), the first short story published by a black woman, masked Harper's message about the personal freedoms yearned for by free and escaped blacks before the Civil War. Published in the *Anglo-African Magazine*, a black periodical directed to an audience of free and literate Northern blacks, "The Two Offers" dramatizes the lives of Laura Lagrange and Janette Alston, cousins who attempt to define themselves in relation to the tenets of the Cult of True Womanhood. Despite the intense racial milieu out of which this story was written, Harper leaves the race of her characters ambiguous. In so doing, she shifts the centripetal theme of her narrative from race to gender. As a result, Harper creates a critical space where her black female readership can insert themselves into the roles of Laura and Janette and fantasize about living their lives as women, not chattel.

At the turn of the century, as **Booker T. Washington**, **W. E. B. Du Bois**, and **Anna Julia Cooper** assessed where blacks had been and where the twentieth century might take them, **Charles Chesnutt** and Pauline Hopkins fictionalized this postbellum America where Reconstruction, the "Negro Problem," and lynching permeated the lives and politics of black Americans. Without question, Charles Chesnutt stands as the most prolific and highly regarded master of the African American short story. A fair-skinned black man who could pass for white, Chesnutt's choice to align himself racially and politically with African Americans demonstrated a profound act of resistance—a defiance that finds its way into his short stories. Chesnutt's tales play upon plantation tradition literature and its promotion of the time "befo' de wah" when the white, paternalistic slave system maintained order and racial caste. In *The Conjure Woman* (1899), Chesnutt's (Uncle) Julius McAdoo recasts Joel Chandler Harris's Uncle Remus as a forked-tongued trickster—a figure who manipulates whites by playing upon the stereotypes they have of blacks. Chesnutt's other stories, "The Wife of His Youth" (1899) and "Baxter's Procrustes" (1904), demonstrate Chesnutt's evolving sensibilities regarding race and the publishing industry. Following **Paul Laurence Dunbar**'s *Folks from Dixie* (1898), Chesnutt published the second collection of short stories written by an African American author.

Although not nearly as productive as fellow "race woman" **Alice Dunbar-Nelson** (the former wife of Paul Laurence Dunbar who published over forty-five stories during her lifetime), Pauline Hopkins's stint as editor of the *Colored American Magazine* allowed her to promote black literary achievement and ensure its place in print. Before black literature was readily accepted for publication by white publishing houses, most authors published their work in black periodicals. The *Colored American Magazine* was one such monthly. In it, black writers **Angela W. Grimké**, Pauline Hopkins, and Ruth Todd, among others, all published short stories; these include Grimke's "Black Is, As Black Does" (1900), Hopkins's "As the Lord Lives, He Is One of Our Mothers' Children" (1903), and Todd's "The Taming of a Modern Shrew" (1904). By manipulating literary conventions, classical tropes, and themes related to race and gender, these writers continued the work begun by Frances Ellen Watkins Harper and anticipated the work of **Jessie Redmon Fauset**, editor of the *Crisis* (a major literary artery of the **Harlem Renaissance**) from 1919 to 1926.

In the twentieth century, the disenfranchisement of black Americans continued to impact the short fiction of African American writers. Disillusioned by the crop lien system and devastated by the boll weevil, blacks at the turn of the century migrated North to places like Harlem, Chicago, and Washington, DC. The literary and cultural renaissance that emerged in Harlem and Chicago allowed **Langston Hughes**, **Zora Neale Hurston**, **Jean Toomer**, **Richard Wright**, **Gwendolyn Brooks**, and others to evaluate the costs and benefits of the African American's ascent North. Rendered with the imagistic eye of literary modernists, Jean Toomer's *Cane* (1923) paints a rich picture of black life in both North and South. A "prose poem" that combines short stories, poems, and sketches, *Cane* allowed Toomer to personally explore the images and psychology of race in the North and South. From the tragic beauty of "Fern" to the visceral intensity of "Blood-Burning Moon," Toomer's *Cane* articulates with artistic detail the lives of Southern blacks before migration and captures their new lives in the North.

The short stories of Langston Hughes and Zora Neale Hurston portray the wonder and tragedy of black life in Harlem and beyond. Hailed as the "poet laureate of Harlem," Hughes's "Jess B. Semple Stories" (1943–65) uses the sardonic wit of its protagonist, Simple, to capture the rhythm and pulse of Harlem and its people. With Hughes's classic "laugh-to-keep-from-crying" tone, *The Ways of White Folks* (1934) exposes the tensions between blacks and whites during the era when "the Negro was in vogue." Even though Hughes focuses primarily on Harlem life in his stories, folklorist and author Zora Neale Hurston returned South to reverently recreate the beauty and brilliance of black Southern oral culture. Her short stories "Sweat" (1926) and "The Gilded Six Bits" (1933) explore abusive and adulterous marriages through the eyes of both men and women. Criticized by **Richard Wright** for her use of dialect, Hurston's recognition of the wisdom of black culture reconnected cosmopolitan Harlemites with their folk roots and preserved a myriad of folkways for future generations.

Less renowned than the Harlem Renaissance but just as important, the Chicago Renaissance of the 1930s and 1940s produced literature, art, music, and photography that articulated the experiences of blacks that migrated to the Midwest. Richard Wright's naturalistic collection *Uncle Tom's Children* (1938) paints black life as a losing battle against external, institutionalized, racist forces. The short story "Big Boy Leaves Home" (1938), for example, casts the North as a refuge from the violence of the South, a depiction that contrasted sharply with the prevailing "milk-and-honey" myth of the day. In contrast, Gwendolyn Brooks's *Maud Martha* (1953), while classified as a novel or novella, contains a series of chapters that, when read as self-contained stories, depicts life in Chicago from a more hopeful point of view. "We're the Only Colored People Here" for example, anthologized in Langston Hughes's *The Best Short Stories by Black Writers, 1899–1967* (1967), reveals the different ways in which African American men and women view their "intrusion" upon white spaces. In "Maud Martha Spares the Mouse," Brooks rewrites the violent opening scene of Richard Wright's *Native Son* (1940)—again, through the sympathetic eyes of a black woman. Read as a series of vignettes or as a short story cycle, *Maud Martha* serves as a useful foil to Wright's bleak depiction of life in Chicago.

With the end of World War II (1939–45), African Americans decided to hold the nation accountable for the freedoms it promoted overseas yet perverted within its borders. The "Double V" campaign of black newspapers, which promoted victory at home and abroad, set the stage for the **Civil Rights Movement** led publicly by **Martin Luther King Jr.** Through localized acts of resistance, black servicemen fought against America's prejudices and lobbied for holding the country accountable for her hypocrisy. These same sentiments emerge in the work of **Ralph Ellison**, **Ann Petry**, and **James Baldwin**—writers whose short stories hold a naturalistic mirror to America's institutionalized injustices and reveal the societal strongholds that prevent blacks from realizing the American dream. Ellison's "Flying Home" (1944) manipulates classical and African American myths—of Icarus, the Phoenix, and the Flying Africans—to describe the tragedy of Todd, a Tuskegee Airman grounded symbolically by a buzzard, but literally by the pervasive prejudice of whites. As Ellison portrays the relationship between Todd, an accomplished airman, and Jefferson, a black farmer, he identifies the emotions—anger, shame, and disgust—that distance working-class blacks from educated ones. "Flying Home" critiques the American racial machine that paints black men, even those fighting for their country, as second-class citizens.

Published in 1942 in the *Crisis*, "On Saturday the Siren Sounds at Noon" launched Ann Petry's literary career and positioned her as a writer whose naturalistic fiction rewrote, within a feminist context, the tradition mastered by Wright. In this account, Petry gives voice to a black man's pain and identifies the seemingly inescapable forces that plague blacks in the urban centers of the North. Author of the award-winning novel *The Street* (1946),

Petry's collection *Miss Muriel and Other Stories* (1971), set in her native New England, expands the sense of place typically associated with black literature and breathes life into Petry's experiences in the family pharmacy business. In another story that, like "Flying Home," addresses the place of a black man in America's military, James Baldwin's "Sonny's Blues" (1957) recalls the troubled relationship between Sonny and his brother, an unnamed narrator who attempts to piece together the events leading up to Sonny's death. Included in his 1965 collection *Going to Meet the Man*, this story evaluates the push and pull of familial structures, **jazz** culture, and social pressures on both Sonny and black men as a whole.

Weary of adopting the American dream and, by extension, an American aesthetic at the expense of the black American idiom, the stories of **Amiri Baraka**, **John Edgar Wideman**, **Alice Walker**, and **Toni Cade Bambara** invoke black aesthetics, vernacular speech, and signifying—an African American form of irony—to ground black literature within the context of black life. Best known for his drama, Baraka embraces an experimental style throughout *Tales* (1967), the first collection of short stories by a black American to do so since Toomer's *Cane*. *Tales* combines poetry and autobiography to portray, with extreme intensity, periods of philosophical crisis or emotional epiphany among African Americans. Wideman signifies on the theoretical stability of history and rewrites African Americans into the fabric of America's chronicled past. In 1981 and 1989 Wideman published his first two books of short stories, *Damballah* and *Fever*. In the title stories, Wideman fictionalizes events and persons and writes a new history in the process. "Fever" revisits the 1793 yellow fever epidemic in Philadelphia, Pennsylvania, highlighting its effects on African Americans; "Damballah" (the serpent deity) recounts the enslavement of Orion, an African renamed Ryan by his white masters, and promotes the power of storytelling in keeping the memories of the elders and ancestors alive.

The short stories of Alice Walker and Toni Cade Bambara give voice to otherwise marginalized groups—particularly women, children, and the elderly—and use domestic imagery and vernacular speech to transform everyday experiences into art. "To Hell With Dying," originally published in 1967 and reprinted in Walker's collection *In Love and Trouble* (1973), sings a blues song about the power of ritual and youth against death. "Everyday Use," published in the same compilation, uses sisters' divergent views on the function of a family quilt to highlight the practical beauty of black women's domestic arts. With a literary voice that captures the rhythm and cadence of black speech, Toni Cade Bambara's short story collections *Gorilla My Love* (1972) and *The Sea Birds Are Still Alive* (1977) speak for sassy black girls ("Gorilla My Love"), the elderly in love ("My Man Bovanne"), the strength of family ("Raymond's Run"), the politics of living with a politician ("The Organizer's Wife"), and war refugees from Asia ("The Sea Birds Are Still Alive).

Ernest Gaines, **Toni Morrison**, **Paule Marshall**, and **Edwidge Danticat** stand at the vanguard of a body of black short fiction writers where the desire for self-representation remains ever strong and an expanding sense of identity ever present. Gaines's collection *Bloodline* (1968) immerses readers in the stressful maturation journeys of black boys during the 1940s, 1950s, and 1960s. Set in his home state of Louisiana, Gaines articulates with sensitivity, color, and wit the black man's vexed relationship with social and historical forces—a portrayal that adds texture to the often one-dimensional representations of black men in American fiction. The American Short Story Collection adapted "The Sky Is Gray," from *Bloodline*, into film. In another more experimental racial critique, "Recitatif" (1983), Toni Morrison's first and only foray into short story writing, chronicles the strained relationship between Twyla Benson and Roberta Fisk, women who become friends during their stints as not-quite-orphans at St. Bonaventure's orphanage. An experiment in the removal of overt racial categories (we know that Twyla and Roberta are black and white, but we don't know which is which) the tale's racial ambiguity pushes readers to examine their personal practices of racial classification and reveals the prerequisites for intimate interpersonal relationships between blacks and whites.

Paule Marshall's two short story collections, the award-winning *Soul Clap Hands and Sing* (1961) and *Reena and Other Stories* (1983) include two of her most popular and representative works, "Barbados" and "To Da-Duh in Memoriam." Included in *Soul Clap*, a collection that takes its title from William Butler Yeats's "Sailing to Byzantium," Barbados chronicles the new life of Mr. Watford, a man who, after becoming quite wealthy in the United States, returns home to Barbados where he must reckon with class conflicts and heartbreak. "To Da-Duh in Memoriam," originally published in 1967 and reprinted in *Reena*, introduces generational conflicts that emerge in Marshall's later works and establishes Da-Duh, her grandmother, as a guiding, ancestral force in her literary oeuvre. In *Krik? Krak!* (1995), Edwidge Danticat continues the diasporic themes introduced by Marshall, but shifts the cultural center to her Haitian homeland. With a title taken from the call-and-response of Haitian storytelling where the leader calls out "Krik?" and the listeners respond "Krak!" Danticat's collection speaks for poor people with rich dreams whose stories, like those of black America, yearn to be heard.

Further Reading

Andrews, William L. *To Tell a Free Story: The First Century of Afro-American Autobiography, 1760–1865*. Urbana: U of Illinois P, 1986.

Clarke, John Henrik. *Black American Short Stories: One Hundred Years of the Best*. New York: Hill and Wang, 1993.

Gates, Henry Louis, Jr. *The Signifying Monkey: A Theory of Afro-American Literary Criticism*. Oxford: Oxford UP, 1988.

Glasrud, Bruce A., and Laurie Champion, eds. *The African American West: A Century of Short Stories*. Boulder: U of Colorado P, 2000.

Henderson, Stephen. *Understanding the New Black Poetry*. New York: William Morrow, 1973.

Hughes, Langston, ed. *The Best Short Stories by Black Writers, 1899–1967*. Boston: Little, Brown, 1967.

Major, Clarence, ed. *Calling the Wind: Twentieth-Century African American Short Stories*. New York: Harper Collins, 1993.

Naylor, Gloria, ed. *Children of the Night: The Best Short Stories by Black Writers, 1967 to the Present*. Boston: Little, Brown, 1995.

Rowell, Charles H., ed. *Ancestral House: The Black Short Story in the Americas and Europe*. Boulder, CO: Westview, 1995.

Shanna Greene Benjamin

AFRICAN AMERICAN SLAVE NARRATIVE   The slave narrative is a unique genre of African American literature that has helped both to spur other genres and to bring to public attention the trials and talents of African Americans who were enslaved in the United States for hundreds of years. An autobiographical form, the slave narrative is contingent, as its name suggests, on telling the story of an African American who triumphed over **slavery** by escaping that historical institution in one way or another. Most slave narratives were written by the former slave himself or herself; in other cases, the former slave being illiterate or semi-literate, a ghostwriter was used to pen the "as-told-to" story. In one particular case, oral histories of former slaves who survived beyond the Civil War years were recorded by workers in the Federal Writers Project of the 1930s in a singular effort to capture those voices before they were silenced forever. Today transcripts of those interviews can be read in the volume *Remembering Slavery*. The voices of those interviewed have been preserved on tape.

There are other instances when a tale that fits closely into the genre of slave narrative is written and marketed as simply an autobiography or even as an autobiographical novel. Such is the case with **Harriet Wilson**'s 1859 narrative, *Our Nig*, which tells the story of an African American woman who found herself as an indentured servant throughout her childhood in the North. Wilson's narrative is similar to the typical slave narrative in that it exposes Northern **racism**. Wilson was never legally a slave, however, and she was freed from her indentured servant status once she reached adulthood, which marks a significant difference from those writers who were presumed to have been born into slavery for life.

An Early Narrative

Although the slave narrative dates back as early as 1789 with Olaudah Equiano's *The Interesting Narrative of the Life of Olaudah Equiano, or Gustavus Vassa, the African*, the majority of slave narratives originate in the nineteenth century, especially in the decades directly preceding and encompassing the Civil War. Equiano's narrative, however, is extremely important, as it sets the stage for a new genre and as its setting is remarkably different from the standard slave narrative of the century following his. Equiano writes of his actual capture into slavery in his own native Africa and of his subsequent sale to European slave traders. We read in *The Interesting Narrative* of Equiano's miserable experiences on the slave boat, his survival of the infamous **Middle Passage**, his being sold from one person to another, and finally his ability to purchase his own freedom at the age of twenty-one. Equiano's narrative also conveys the message that human freedom is a basic right and that slavery must be abolished. The fact that Equiano wrote his narrative on his own, and that he wrote it well, served to foster some discussion on inherent racial abilities.

Abolitionism and the Nineteenth Century

The nineteenth century is the time period most closely associated with the slave narrative. It was during this century that the ugliness and social evils of slavery were taking their strongest hold. Unlike Equiano, the slaves of the nineteenth century were American born and had been raised in a predominately pro-slavery culture. They had been indoctrinated into Christianity in a twisted way that made slavery seem justified, and they had been raised with the supposition that they were indeed members of an inferior—if not a cursed—race. Still, there existed the basic human desire to be free, to be the master of one's own destiny, and to dream of greater possibilities. It was such a desire that drove some of the enslaved to risk all—including their very lives—and attempt escape. Those who were successful in such attempts often found themselves helped by both black and white **abolition**ists along the **Underground Railroad**. It was staunch white abolitionists such as William Lloyd Garrison who encouraged many escaped slaves to tell their stories, largely as a way to persuade other voting members of the United States to join the fight for the abolition of slavery. Some of these escaped slaves were able to write their own stories; some needed assistance. Many were convinced to testify publicly to the truth of their tales. Some became standard members of the antislavery lecture circuit.

The titles of these slave narratives were often long and cumbersome, as well as descriptive. For example, in 1842 Lunsford Lane's narrative was published under the title, *The Narrative of Lunsford Lane, Formerly of Raleigh, N.C., Embracing an Account of His Early Life, the Redemption by Purchase of Himself and Family from Slavery, and His Banishment from the Place of His Birth for the Crime of Wearing a Colored Skin.* Truly, the reader is set up to expect not only a narrative of Lane's life as a slave but also a tale of deeply ingrained racial prejudice.

As the nineteenth-century slave narrative became more popular and more widely used for the political agenda of the abolitionist groups, the larger readership began to demand proof of the veracity of the tale and proof of the identity of the author. There certainly was the possibility of an unscrupulous white writer fashioning a false slave narrative in the hopes of taking financial advantage of the newest wave of the publishing world.

Beyond that, however, was the biased supposition that a black writer could not automatically be believed. In order to continue to find a steady market for the slave narrative and, in turn, to continue to spread the message of the need for abolition, it became the fashion to include testimonials to the veracity of a given work at the end of the narrative. These testimonials were largely written by white citizens who were considered to be upstanding members of the community. Often a preface written by an especially prominent white citizen was also included; such prefatory statements served as authenticating devices that were intended to validate the slave narratives and testify to their essential truthfulness. All of this set the stage for some of the most important writers of the genre, including **Frederick Douglass**, **Harriet Ann Jacobs**, **Sojourner Truth**, and William Wells Brown.

Frederick Douglass

Frederick Douglass became famous with the 1845 publication of his *Narrative of the Life of Frederick Douglass, an American Slave, Written by Himself*. Douglass's book remains one of the most famous of all slave narratives, often being the only text of the genre that appears in a mainstream anthology of literature. Douglass's narrative contains a preface by William Lloyd Garrison and tells the tale of what seemed to many of his contemporaries to be the portrayal of an uncommonly intelligent and industrious African American man. It is precisely this perception that made Douglass's book a best seller in his homeland as well as abroad.

Douglass's story has some similarities to that of Equiano's. Both men are filled with a sense of outrage at their situations, both men are able to procure an informal education, both men are able to learn a trade, and both men find themselves in a position to secure their own freedom. In Douglass's case, this involved saving the money to run North with his wife. Also like Equiano, Douglass was committed to working toward the abolition of slavery. Douglass formally joined the abolitionist movement and became one of its most famous lecturers, even traveling to England to preach against slavery. His narrative became one of the steady tomes of the abolitionist movement.

Douglass presents to the reader tales of the physical brutality of slavery that became pivotal in his fight for the freedom of all. He also presents the human aspects of the enslaved, convincing educated white readers that they had more in common with the black man than they had previously thought possible. This helped to set the stage for further acceptance of future slave narratives.

Harriet Ann Jacobs

When Harriet Ann Jacobs's slave narrative was published sixteen years after Douglass's, it marked a critical change in the face of slavery as it was presented to the genteel white readership. Whereas Douglass's narrative illustrates all of the physical brutality of slavery, especially as it touched men's lives, Jacobs's *Incidents in the Life of a Slave Girl, Told by Herself* (1861) forced readers to look carefully at the sexual politics of slavery, something most had refused to do prior to this time. Jacobs exposes the cruelties of repeated sexual harassment and attempted and actual rapes that occurred between the slaveholder and the enslaved woman or even the enslaved girl.

The events surrounding the publication of Jacobs's narrative were also critical to the development of this genre. Jacobs's abolitionist friends certainly urged her to tell her tale, as had the friends of Douglass, but Jacobs did not at first think of writing her own story. She had planned to tell the tale to Harriet Beecher Stowe and let her write it. This plan failed miserably, though, when Stowe decided that Jacobs's tale was unbelievable. After all, who could fathom that a good Christian white man would attempt to abuse sexually a black slave? Stowe went to Jacobs's employer asking for verification of Jacobs's story, which put Jacobs in the uncomfortable position of having her employer hear about this very personal part of her previous life from a stranger, for Jacobs had never revealed this part of her past to her employer. The embarrassment worked out well for the development of African American literature, however, as Jacobs eventually wrote her own story, adding to the growing evidence that intellect and talent were not reserved for members of one racial group alone. With her famous and well-respected contemporaries Amy Post and Lydia Maria Child supporting her efforts, Jacobs found success with the publication of her narrative and also found herself a free woman. Today many scholars see Douglass's and Jacobs's narratives as complementary examples of the slave narrative.

Sojourner Truth

Sojourner Truth's slave narrative represents yet a different style of the genre. Born into slavery as Isabella, Sojourner Truth took on her new name upon her escape from slavery. Though highly intelligent and absolutely committed to doing what she saw as the work of the Lord through her preaching, Truth was illiterate. A physically strong woman who paid for her strength with an unusual degree of physical abuse from her master, Truth had a tale to tell but no means with which to do so on her own. She had survived slavery, she had answered a calling from God, and she had joined the lecture circuit as an outspoken advocate of not only abolition but women's rights as well. When it became evident that Truth's tale must be written down, the white abolitionist Olive Gilbert acted as Truth's ghostwriter. *The Narrative of Sojourner Truth* was originally written in 1850. With the help of other white women friends, Truth continued to work on the narrative until it was reprinted in 1884 under the title *The Narrative of Sojourner Truth; a Bondswoman of Olden Time, with a History of Her Labors and Correspondence Drawn from Her "Book of Life."* As the title suggests, this volume contains much more than Truth's simple slave narrative. It also contains letters and testament to Truth's spiritual journey. The writing of spiritual autobiography was to become yet another important part of African American literature.

William Wells Brown

In 1847 William Wells Brown published his slave narrative, *The Narrative of William W. Brown, a Fugitive Slave,* which, like Douglass's narrative published two years prior, became incredibly successful both in the United States and abroad. Brown's narrative tells of his days of captivity and of his attempts at escape. It also gives the reader a good understanding of what happens to a slave who is caught attempting to escape. Of course, Brown did eventually succeed in escaping. Like Douglass and Truth, he began to lecture against slavery, and, like Jacobs, he eventually had his freedom purchased for him through the help of friends.

The difference between Brown and most of the other writers of the slave narrative is that he saw himself as a creative writer as well as a reporter on the conditions of the enslaved. Brown went on to write several books, including the well-known novel *Clotel; or, the President's Daughter* (1853). He also published drama, a travel book, and history books focusing on African Americans in U.S. history. Brown is considered to be the first African American novelist, playwright, and travel writer in the United States. Brown's slave narrative set the stage for his later works. It also opened the door for other African Americans to see themselves as creative writers and as true literary figures rather than simply as vehicles for the abolitionist movement.

Reconstruction and Beyond

Although slavery technically ended in the United States with the Civil War, the genre of the slave narrative did not. Several former slaves penned the tales of their days as slaves. Among these writers was **Elizabeth Keckley**, who had worked in the Lincoln White House as Mary Todd Lincoln's dressmaker. These works began to take on a different focus than had the antebellum slave narratives, however. Keckley's *Behind the Scenes, or Thirty Years a Slave and Four Years in the White House* (1868) includes a good deal of the intimacy of the Lincoln household to which she was privileged, bringing her a somewhat different audience than her predecessors had had.

Another post–Civil War slave narrative is **Booker T. Washington**'s famous *Up from Slavery* (1901), which has the dubious distinction of significantly changing the focus of the slave narrative. Washington's premise is that, as slavery is dead, the African American must embrace his or her possibilities and go cheerfully forth, trying to assimilate smoothly into an already established society. Washington's style was unthreatening to his white audience, and he was rewarded for such with much praise, so much so that other writers of the slave narrative attempted to follow his lead.

Today much discussion revolves around how useful Washington's narrative actually was to the cause of true freedom and equality, with many scholars taking the view that Washington may have done more harm than good to the social causes of his race.

Of course, there are also the oral histories of former slaves compiled by the writers of the Works Project Administration. Although these remain a fascinating study, it is interesting to note the near desperation that seems to come from some of the former slaves as they craft their words carefully so as not to offend. Although slavery had officially ended, these former slaves well knew that racism was far from over and that it was perfectly possible to endanger their own lives and those of their families by saying the "wrong thing."

Overview

African American literature is still in a place of discovery. New texts by African American writers are still being recovered, and among these are possible samples of slave narratives, such as **Hannah Crafts**'s *The Bondswoman's Narrative*, a nineteenth-century work that has recently been brought to publication by literary scholar **Henry Louis Gates Jr.** What exists in the way of slave narratives at this point in time is a rich variety of personal styles and personal concerns, coupled with a common need to tell the true tales of slavery so that slavery will first be ended and then be kept dormant forever. The reader sees the personality of the author and the uniqueness of the author's situation in the slave narrative. The careful reader, though, is also cognizant that some slave narratives were altered significantly by the white editors who were attempting to help get the narrative published. Lydia Maria Child, for instance, convinced Harriet Ann Jacobs to delete a chapter she had devoted to the infamous slave rebellion of **Nat Turner.** Child also convinced Jacobs to rearrange her chapters so that the book ended on a more optimistic note. The wise reader of the slave narrative keeps in mind the political situation of the nineteenth-century United States.

The slave narratives teach much about history. They also served historically to prove the point that African Americans could indeed read, write, think, and calculate as well as could any other people. In addition, they helped the cause of abolition, and, after the Civil War, they underlined the arguments for equal rights for all. As we look beyond the nineteenth century, we also see the slave narrative as an important step toward the type of **African American autobiography** that emerged in the twentieth century.

Further Reading

Andrews, William L. *To Tell a Free Story: The First Century of Afro-American Autobiography, 1760–1865.* Urbana: U of Illinois P, 1986.

Davis, Charles T., and Gates, Henry Louis, Jr. *The Slave's Narrative.* New York: Oxford UP, 1990.

Foster, Frances Smith. *Witnessing Slavery: The Development of the Ante-Bellum Slave Narratives.* Madison: U of Wisconsin P, 1994.

Terry D. Novak

AFRICAN AMERICAN STEREOTYPES   From the first attempts to categorize human beings several hundred years ago, simplified perceptions of racial difference have plagued society. The "scientifically" sanctioned concept of **race** both enabled and encouraged individuals to manufacture certain assumptions and stereotypes about African Americans. With the notable exception of an enlightened few, most spurned the notion of racial equality. Even Thomas Jefferson, who proclaimed in the Declaration of Independence "that all men are created equal," did not truly believe that African Americans were inherently equal to whites. Like many of his contemporaries, Jefferson believed that an indelible color line had been drawn between the two **race**s. In his acclaimed *Notes on the State of Virginia* (1787), Jefferson asserted that African Americans' physical, mental, and moral characteristics offered indisputable evidence of their innate inferiority.

In the hands of Southern apologists for **slavery**, Jefferson's pseudoscientific theories were substantive proof of African Americans' suitability as slaves. Some advocates of slavery went so far as to suggest that the differences between the two races were so insurmountable that white society was doing "the Negro" a favor by enslaving him. These and other champions of the "positive good" theory argued that slavery was not, as the abolitionists would have everyone believe, an incomprehensible evil but an essential good. In short, they depicted slavery not as the "peculiar institution" it was reputed to be, but as a mutually beneficial relationship between slave owners and their slaves.

Repudiating the "positive good" theory, Harriet Beecher Stowe's *Uncle Tom's Cabin* (1852) sought to portray the African American as the unfortunate victim of a barbarous system. Unfortunately, her stereotypical portrayal of Tom and other slaves as "simple" and "childlike" served to legitimize the prejudice and limited views of those already convinced of the inferiority of African Americans. In her attempt to subvert the stereotype of the African American as lazy, shiftless, and uncivilized, Stowe, inadvertently, created a pejorative tag that survives to this day. Whereas the hero of Stowe's immensely popular novel was the embodiment of forbearance and goodness, the name "Uncle Tom" came to represent something very different. Uncle Tom became a trope, the incarnation of a shiftless, unscrupulous character who catered to whites and betrayed his black brethren.

Not surprisingly, the character (or, more accurately, caricature) of Uncle Tom became a mainstay on the minstrel circuit, which was famed for its patronizing portrayals of African Americans. Drawing on popularly held stereotypes of blacks, minstrel performers exaggerated what they considered to be "the Negro's eccentricities." Donning flashy clothes, and using greasepaint or burnt cork to darken their skins, the actors hammed it up for their white audiences. The handbills and posters advertising the minstrel shows—with their monstrous images of African Americans with protruding lips and misshapen heads—underscored the physical and intellectual differences between blacks and whites to an even greater degree. The figure depicted in these advertisements, and on the stage, was a grotesque caricature of the African American—freakish and inhuman. Although minstrel troupes thought nothing of caricaturing slaves, they were, however, more conscientious in their depictions of the institution of slavery. Playing to the Southern crowd, the performers were careful to limit their portraitures to contented slaves, which would explain their fascination with the character of Uncle Tom, the "happy darkie."

Like *Uncle Tom's Cabin*, Mark Twain's *Adventures of Huckleberry Finn* (1885) sought to expose the perils of slavery. Despite his efforts to the contrary, Twain, like Stowe, failed to fully dignify the slave. Although Twain endowed Jim with many consummate qualities, he nonetheless reinforced the stereotype of the slave as a gullible, superstitious creature. In addition, Jim's placid acceptance of the young Huck's absolute authority over him cemented the slave's status as an indiscriminate piece of property.

However their works were interpreted, Stowe and Twain endeavored to humanize African Americans, not further degrade them. The same cannot be said for Thomas Dixon's *The Clansman* (1905)—the anti–African American novel upon which the film *Birth of a Nation* (1915) was based. A former Baptist minister, Dixon envisioned the novel as an evangelical effort to revolutionize the African American stereotype. Scandalized by American society's acceptance of Stowe's positive rendering of Uncle Tom, Dixon felt it was time they heard the whole truth. Dixon's version of the "truth," as depicted in *The Clansman*, characterized the African American male as a vicious brute, unable to control his animal urges. With its unflattering portraits of African Americans and its valiant portrayals of the Ku Klux Klan, *The Clansman* provided a strong impetus for the forces of racial bigotry. By Dixon's own admission, the explicit purpose of *The Clansman*, and *The Leopard's Spots* (1902) before it, was to sway public opinion against the African American. As the catalyst for the hugely successful film *Birth of a Nation* Dixon's novel did just that.

Woven into the social fabric by writers whose works were fervently devoted to degrading African Americans, racial stereotypes resonated deeply in the American psyche. The myths perpetuated by the media advocated the continued exploitation and oppression of African Americans. Eminent magazines like *Harper's*, *Scribner's*, *Century*, and *The Atlantic Monthly* were replete with epithets such as "nigger," "darkey," "coon," "pickaninny," "mammy," "buck," and "yaller hussy." At the same time, reports of rape and other alleged crimes perpetrated by African Americans leapt from the inflammatory headlines of local and national newspapers. Even when the stories proved to be unfounded, the newspapers, concerned more with increasing circulation than ascertaining the truth of what they printed, never bothered with retractions.

The influx of immigrants during the latter half of the nineteenth and early twentieth centuries also contributed to many Americans' disdain for African Americans. With the number of immigrants rapidly increasing, Americans became that much more conscious of the multiple racial populations within their midst. What aided the immigrants in their **assimilation** into American society was their positioning of themselves against members of the African American community. With the proliferation of the anti–African American sentiment they encountered from the moment of their arrival, it did not take long for the newcomers to figure out that ascension up the social ladder was best accomplished by stepping firmly on the lowest wrung.

At the turn of the century, a strong opposition to racial determinism and inequality was launched by the African American intellectual community. Repudiating the oft-recited allegations of "Negro" inferiority, **W. E. B. Du Bois** and his contemporaries ardently insisted that African Americans had important contributions to make to American society. Du Bois's efforts to uplift members of his race made a significant impact on **Alain Locke** and other seminal figures of the **Harlem Renaissance**. Intent on proving that African Americans were not intellectually or culturally inferior to whites, they sought to establish a new image for their people—one that both challenged and subverted the old. Through self-confidence and self-actualization, the "**New Negro**" hoped to shrug off the image of subservience and submissiveness that had characterized the "Old Negro." Only then could members of the African American community hope to emancipate themselves from the chains of bigotry that continued to bind them.

Determined to reclaim the image of the African American from the mire of racist literature, writers like **Richard Wright** took pleasure in undermining the all-too-familiar stereotypes. An indictment of Stowe's classic novel, Wright's *Uncle Tom's Children* (1938) offered a stark look at racial oppression and its ravaging effects on the African American community. Published two years later, *Native Son* (1940) reinvented the character of the African American male in **Bigger Thomas**, a crude, violent man, who lashes out at a society that has persecuted him. As a protest writer, Wright took issue with African American writers who, in his mind, continued to pander to white audiences. In a biting critique of *Their Eyes Were Watching God* (1937), Wright rebuked **Zora Neale Hurston** for perpetuating the very stereotypes that African Americans had been struggling against their whole lives. Likening Hurston's "quaint" portrayal of "Negro" life and lore to a literary minstrel show, Wright dismissed the novel as unworthy. So obsessed was he with purging stereotyped images from African American culture that Wright failed to appreciate the intrinsic value of Hurston's elegantly written and enormously influential work.

Like their African American foremother, Zora Neale Hurston, **Toni Morrison** and **Alice Walker** also came under fire for failing to eradicate racist stereotypes from their literary works. Morrison's depiction of Cholly Breedlove in *The Bluest Eye* (1970) and Walker's portrayal of Mr. ___ in *The Color Purple* (1982) were said to reinforce the stereotype of the African American male as archetypal rapist. What was most disturbing to Morrison's and Walker's detractors was that the once "spoiler of white women" was now preying on members of his own race, and, even worse, his own family. What such critics failed to appreciate was that these male characters were themselves victims of a racist society.

Recognizing how stereotypes negatively influence people's perceptions of "otherness," the African American community continues to wage a war against reductive notions of race. Fortunately, the battle has not been at the expense of its rich literary tradition.

Further Reading

Baker, Lee D. *From Savage to Negro: Anthropology and the Construction of Race, 1896–1954*. Berkeley: U of California P, 1998.

Franke, Astrid. *Keys to the Controversies: Stereotypes in Modern American Novels*. New York: St. Martin's Press, 1999.

Fredrickson, George M. *The Black Image in the White Mind: The Debate on Afro-American Character and Destiny, 1817–1914*. New York: Harper & Row, 1971.

Gossett, Thomas, F. *Race: The History of an Idea in America*. New York: Oxford UP, 1997 [orig. pub. 1963].

Jordan, Winthrop D. *White Over Black: American Attitudes Toward the Negro, 1550–1812*. Chapel Hill: U of North Carolina P, 1968.

Lively, Adam. *Masks: Blackness, Race and the Imagination*. Oxford: Oxford UP, 2000.

Toll, Robert C. *Blacking Up: The Minstrel Show in Nineteenth-Century America*. New York: Oxford UP, 1974.

Carol Goodman

AFRICAN AMERICAN TRAVEL NARRATIVE   African American travel writing generally refers to nonfiction accounts of visits to or limited sojourns in places outside of the United States written by African American authors. Although scholars disagree about which was the first African American travel account, the tradition dates back at least to the early nineteenth century and includes the writings of fugitive slaves, international political activists, musicians, soldiers, missionaries, and scholars who visited every corner of the globe. The list of African American literary travelers includes many of the most significant figures in African American literature. Authors such as William Wells Brown, **Frederick Douglass**, **Ida B. Wells-Barnett**, **W. E. B. Du Bois**, **Booker T. Washington**, **Langston Hughes**, **Zora Neale Hurston**, **James Baldwin**, and **Richard Wright** all traveled outside of the United States and wrote about their experiences. Not all of these literary travelers, however, devoted book-length accounts specifically to their travels. A considerable amount of what critics now consider African American travel writing, particularly those texts written before World War II, is not found in conventional travel books, defined here as books that are specifically and primarily devoted to documenting foreign travels. However, because travel writing is a hybrid genre with limits that are not always easy to define, texts from a variety of other genres can also be classified as travel writing.

African American travel accounts are taken from a wide variety of sources, including autobiographical materials, personal letters, notes, diaries, dispatches, travel guides, official reports, lectures, and ethnographies. What all of these diverse texts have in common is that they are written records of African American travelers' journeys to foreign lands. Examining these accounts can reveal a great deal about how African American writers at different historical moments understood their individual and group identities in relation to America and the world outside its borders. Because African Americans have frequently had their mobility restricted within the United States—first by **slavery** and later by segregation—foreign travel has often been a symbol of freedom and independence. In describing their encounters with cultures that are different, and sometimes similar, to their own, African American literary travelers often reveal their own troubled relationship with the United States and their sense of being both allied with and excluded from American **identity**.

Travel writing by African Americans has only recently begun to receive widespread scholarly attention. In the past, studies of travel writing focused mostly on white male travelers, and studies of African American literature paid little attention to African American travel accounts. The recent increase in critical attention devoted to African American travel writing is an effect of both the expansion of the field of travel studies, influenced by postcolonial and feminist criticism to focus new attention on travel writings by women and people of color, and the popularity of broader, more international approaches to African American literary scholarship stimulated in part by the influence of Paul Gilroy's *The Black Atlantic* (1993), which advocated viewing African American literature and culture as part of an international black cultural formation that Gilroy termed "the black Atlantic." The publication of two recent anthologies of black travel writing offers evidence of the newfound interest in these texts. *A Stranger in the Village: Two Centuries of African-American Travel Writing* (1998), edited by Farah J. Griffin and Cheryl J. Fish, focuses specifically on the travel writings of African Americans, whereas Alasdair Pettinger's *Always Elsewhere: Travels of the Black Atlantic* (1998) focuses more broadly, including writings by black travelers from the Caribbean and Europe as well as from the United States. As the editors of both of these anthologies make clear, there is no fixed set of characteristics that unites the writings of all African American travelers. According to Griffin and Fish, African American travel writing must be examined "in the context of the genre of travel writing and the particular occasions and historical time frame that led each writer to take a journey and record his or her experiences of it" (Griffin and Fish xiii–xiv).

African American literary travelers have embarked on their journeys for a wide variety of reasons. Many have traveled to support a cause, as in the case of the fugitive slave author William Wells Brown who published the first conventional travel narrative by an African American, *Three Years in Europe, or Places I Have Seen and People I Have Met* (1852), which documented his travels through Great Britain as an **abolition**ist lecturer. Others traveled as missionaries, like Amanda Smith, whose autobiography, *The Story of the Lord's Dealings with Mrs. Amanda Smith, the Colored Evangelist* (1893), details her travels in Europe, Africa, and Asia. There are also those who traveled as anthropologists, like Zora Neale Hurston, whose *Tell My Horse* (1938) documents her trip to Haiti. Still others, like Langston Hughes, whose autobiographies *The Big Sea* (1940) and *I Wonder As I Wander* (1964) provide lengthy accounts of his international wanderings, made numerous journeys to destinations all over the world for a variety of different reasons, ranging from tourism to war reportage.

One common feature of many of African American travel accounts is that their authors often embarked with the hope that foreign travel would provide a temporary respite from **racism**. Many found that this was the case and used their writings to call attention to the disparity between the courteous and respectful treatment that they received in foreign countries and the hostility and oppression they had become accustomed to in the United States. These writers often commented on feeling a new sense of freedom and self-respect during their visits to foreign land that they had never felt on American soil. This theme is most prominently echoed in a number of African American accounts of European travel, dating back to the antebellum writings of fugitive slaves, including William Wells Brown, and sometimes continuing, to a much lesser extent, to the accounts of contemporary tourists. France in particular developed a reputation among many African Americans as a welcoming place, as well as a meeting ground for other blacks from around the world. Not everyone felt at home while abroad, however. Some travelers have written about the feeling of becoming an object of curiosity to local people in regions with no black population and little experience with black visitors. **James Baldwin** memorably captured these feelings in his essay "Stranger in the Village" (1953), from which Fish and Griffin take the title of their anthology.

Although African American travelers have documented their journeys to every part of the globe, it is perhaps not surprising that the greatest number of African American travel accounts deal with journeys to the African continent. For nearly two centuries African Americans have journeyed to Africa, many seeking a spiritual and cultural connection with the continent they view as an ancestral homeland. Although some writers find the connection they seek, others write about the contrast between their idealized image of Africa and their experience with the realities of that continent. The earliest account of African travel written by a black American is Paul Cuffe's *A Brief Account of the Settlement and Present Situation of the Colony of Sierra Leone, in Africa* (1812). Although there were other early accounts of Africa, including Robert Campbell's *A Pilgrimage to My Motherland* (1859), as well as shorter pieces published in magazine and newspaper articles, the publication of travel books about Africa became more common as African nations moved toward and achieved independence from European colonialism. Since then, many African American literary travelers have sought to observe life in Africa, some seeking a spiritual home and others hoping to see prosperous, independent black nations. These accounts include Eslanda Goode Robeson's *African Journey* (1945), Era Bell Thompson's *Africa: Land of My Fathers* (1954), Hoyt Fuller's *Journey to Africa* (1971), and, more recently, **Maya Angelou**'s *All God's Children Need Traveling Shoes* (1986) and Eddy L. Harris's *Native Stranger* (1992). The most prominent African American to publish a book-length African travel account was Richard Wright, who wrote *Black Power* (1954) about his trip to what was then the Gold Coast and would soon become Ghana. An international traveler, Wright also wrote two other books of travel, *Pagan Spain* (1957), which was based on his travels through that country, and *The Color Curtain* (1955), an account of the Bandung Conference in Indonesia in 1955.

Scholars have only recently begun to reconstruct a tradition of African American travel writing, and new texts are being written every year. As more and more of these texts are written, rediscovered, republished, and analyzed, they will help to challenge our understanding of the way that African Americans have perceived their relationship to the outside world, as well as to the United States, the country that they have, sometimes ambivalently, called home.

Further Reading

Baldwin, Katherine Anne. *Beyond the Color Line and the Iron Curtain: Reading Encounters Between Black and Red, 1922–1963.* Durham, NC: Duke UP, 2002.

Gilroy, Paul. *The Black Atlantic: Modernity and Double Consciousness.* Cambridge, MA: Harvard UP, 1993.

Griffin, Farah Jasmine, and Cheryl J. Fish, eds. *A Stranger in the Village: Two Centuries of African-American Travel Writing.* Boston: Beacon Press, 1998.

Pettinger, Alasdair, ed. *Always Elsewhere: Travels of the Black Atlantic.* London and New York: Cassell, 1988.

Smith, Virginia Whatley, ed. *Richard Wright's Travel Writings: New Reflections.* Jackson: U of Mississippi P, 2001.

Todd Dapremont

AFRICAN AMERICAN YOUNG ADULT LITERATURE Historically, most critics of literature for young people have focused on literature by white American authors and illustrators that represents African Americans. However, whether the representations of African Americans in literature by white artists are well rounded and accurate or stereotyped and deceptive, the audience for these books is multiracial. African American young adult literature is best described as a body of literature for ages ten through eighteen produced by African American authors and illustrators that is appreciated by a multiracial audience from many age groups.

Young people have always appropriated narrative, oral and written, for their entertainment, but literature for children and young adults emerged as a distinct and independent form only in the late eighteenth century. This genre blossomed in England and the United States in the nineteenth century; it encompasses a wide range of work that appeals to all ages of young people and includes acknowledged classics of world literature, picture books, and easy-to-read stories, poetry, novels and short fiction, and the lullabies, fairy tales, fables, folk songs, and folk narratives from oral tradition. It is only since the 1960s that this genre has been studied and taught as two distinct but overlapping categories: children's literature as meant for preschool and elementary school children, and young adult literature designed for readers approximately ten through eighteen years of age.

African Americans began to publish for children during the so-called Golden Age of children's literature, when a profusion of books designed specifically for a young audience were published in the late nineteenth century. Despite their abundance, however, these works represented only a portion of the literate youth in America. There were few depictions of African American children in textbooks, periodicals, stories, and poems, and very few of these were unbiased. Mrs. A. E. Johnson's *Clarence and Corinne; or, God's Way* (1890) could be seen as the first African American young adult novel because its author was African American, but the book features white teenagers. More properly seen as the first African American book for young people, **Paul Laurence Dunbar**'s *Little Brown Baby* (1895) is a germinal text in the genre. A collection of dialect poems that celebrate African American folk culture, *Little Brown Baby* is neither didactic nor religious. Intending to delight his young readers, Dunbar also placed African American people and culture in a positive light. After the turn of the century, African American young adult literature expanded with the development of an educated African American middle class. **W. E. B. Du Bois**'s visionary magazine *The Brownies' Book* (1920–21) offered African American children an entertainment alternative to *St. Nicholas* (1873–1945), the prevailing popular magazine for children, which featured a poem titled "Ten Little Niggers" as late as 1920. Recognizing the urgent need for characters black children could respect and emulate, Du Bois, the only black founder of the National Association for the Advancement of Colored People and the editor of that organization's *The Crisis* (1919–26), experimented with "Children's Numbers," an annual children's issue of *The Crisis*. These issues were so successful that in 1920, Du Bois, along with business manager Augustus Granville Dill and literary editor **Jessie Redmon Fauset**, established a new magazine aimed specifically at children aged six to sixteen. Incorporating a variety of popular forms, such as fiction, folk and fairy tales, poetry, drama, biography, and photography and illustrations by African American artists, *The Brownies' Book* offered nonreligious, nondidactic entertainment that inspired self-esteem, confidence, and racial pride.

Du Bois and Dill also published two biographies for children, Elizabeth Ross Haynes's *Unsung Heroes* (1921) and Julia Henderson's *A Child's Story of Dunbar* (1921), and thereby pioneered another important form of African American young adult literature. Haynes published twenty-two biographies, and many of them introduced children to African Americans rarely depicted in their school texts, figures that are now well known, like **Frederick Douglass** and Harriet Tubman. Several African American writers, among them **Arna Bontemps,** Shirley Graham, and Carter G. Woodson, published biographies of notable African Americans. Committed to educating African American youth about and for the advancement of their race, Woodson founded the Associated Press, which continues today. He published a significant number of African American collections of poetry and folklore, readers, biographies and histories for young adults. Like Woodson, librarians, classroom teachers, and postsecondary educators have worked to ensure that African American young adult literature flourishes and reaches an audience. During her thirty-seven-year career with the New York City Public Library as a children's/young adult librarian, storyteller, and administrator, Augusta Baker (1911–98) added appropriate books to the library's collection, encouraged authors and illustrators, and worked with publishers to get this literature produced and distributed. Following Baker, African American members of the American Library Association Glyndon Greer and Mabel McKissack established the Coretta Scott King Award for African American authors and illustrators of books for children and young adults in 1969. Also in the late 1960s, the Council on Interracial Books for Children began holding contests in order to identify and support promising young artists. These awards have garnered wide professional and public recognition for many of their winners; for example, the first winner of the Council Award, **Kristin Lattany**'s *The Soul Brothers and Sister Lou* (1969), sold over a million copies.

With the growing support of educators, librarians, and publishers, African American young adult literature became an established and expanding tradition that reflected contemporary social and cultural consciousness. **Langston Hughes** collaborated with Bontemps on the short novel *Popo and Fifina* (1932), and Hughes's *The Dream Keeper* (1932) is a classic collection of poetry for young people. Bontemps created an extensive body of work, including biography, fiction, and poetry. The poetry anthology he edited, *Golden Slippers* (1941), includes poetry by respected authors such as Dunbar, Hughes, **Countee Cullen**, **Claude McKay**, and **James Weldon Johnson**. **Gwendolyn Brooks**'s poetry collection *Bronzeville Boys and Girls* (1956) was also an important book for African American young adults. These books gained wide popularity in part because of their literary quality and in part because they offer authentic portrayals of African Americans engaged in the daily life of their society and culture. They are, however, exceptions, since most African American young adult literature from the 1930s through the 1950s offered an integrationist approach to racial difference and the problems of bigotry. Jesse Jackson's *Call Me Charlie* (1945) and Lorenz Bell Graham's *South Town* (1958) and *North Town* (1965) are some of the many books about African American experiences written for young adults of all races. These novels tried to instill a social conscience that afforded awareness and tolerance of racial difference without taking into account cultural difference.

In the 1960s this "social conscience" literature promoting an ideology of assimilation gave way to more culturally conscious young adult literature that reflects African American social and cultural traditions and experiences. Since the late 1960s, African American young adult literature is most often "culturally conscious," with its focus on African American perspective and setting. Over the last thirty years, dozens of African American writers have gained wide popularity through a variety of works that present the range of African American experiences. They offer a tradition of resistance to **racism** and discrimination even as they provide aesthetic experience; they entertain and educate even as they engender racial pride. These books cover multiple forms and genres and are joined by magazines such as *Ebony Jr.* (1973–85), which offered positive representations of African Americans in art and literature and provided a forum for young writers to publish their work, and *Footsteps*, which has been published since 1999 and includes a variety of art and text, such as reprints of Jacob Lawrence's work or an interview with baseball great Hank Aaron.

As with these illustrated magazines, illustrated texts for young adults are popular and serve a variety of purposes. Illustrations are able to depict African Americans as individuals with a rich and diverse culture. Ashley Bryan's linecut illustrations for his four volumes of African folktales and his collections of African American **spirituals**, *I'm Going to Sing* (1976) and *Walk Together Children* (2 vols. 1974, 1982), and Brian Pinkney's illustrations for Patricia McKissack's collection of African American folktales, *The Dark Thirty* (1992), are notable examples. Illustrated collections of African American poetry are also important in this genre, such as Romare Bearden's collages of poems by Langston Hughes in *The Block* (1995) and the many titles by Arnold Adoff, among them *All the Colors of the Race* (1982) illustrated by John Steptoe. Illustrated books provide readers of all ages with positive images of African Americans and the rich diversity of their history and culture, and offer a literary experience that can aid in the understanding and interpretation of life experience.

African American literature for young adults also plays important educational and cultural roles. The adolescent years are timely years for dealing with issues of discrimination, prejudice, and cultural differences since adolescents often perceive themselves as a "culture" apart from the mainstream. Authors of young adult fiction who deal with themes of diversity in race, religion, gender, or class can touch young readers in a profound way. Since the 1960s African American young adult fiction has grown into a vast and diverse body of work read by a wide audience. African American writers of young adult literature offer stories of the inner city and rural America, such as **Walter Dean Myers**'s stories about Harlem in *Fallen*

Angels (1989) or June Jordan's urban landscape in *His Own Where* (1972), and **Mildred Taylor**'s continuing saga of the Logans, set in rural Mississippi. African American young adult writers set their fiction in the past, the present and the future, such as **Julius Lester**'s slave narrative *To Be a Slave* (1968), **Virginia Hamilton**'s realistic novel *M. C. Higgins the Great* (1974), or Octavia Butler's futuristic fantasy *The Parable of the Sower* (1993). These writers deal with themes about and alongside racism, such as **Rosa Guy**'s exploration of a lesbian relationship between two black teenagers in *Ruby* (1976), Sharon Bell Mathis's *Listen for the Fig Tree* (1973) about the experience of a blind girl, or **Joyce Carol Thomas**'s short stories representing the African American teenager in the midst of various ethnic groups in *A Gathering of Flowers* (1990). Further, poets and novelists who write mainly for adults are widely read by young adults and taught in their classrooms, among them **Maya Angelou**, **Alice Walker**, **Toni Cade Bambara**, **Lorraine Hansberry**, **James Baldwin**, **Lucille Clifton**, and **Zora Neale Hurston**.

Young adult novels written by and about African Americans provide one method for beginning to break down barriers created through culture and **ethnicity** even as they generate respect for those cultures and ethnic backgrounds. Now more than a century old, African American young adult literature is a tradition that performs essential functions in the growth and development of its readers, and its benefits go far past simply making visible the formerly absent African American, or countering negative portrayals of African Americans with positive ones.

Further Reading

Baker, Augusta. "The Changing Image of the Black in Children's Literature." *Horn Book* 51 (February 1975): 79–88.

Bontemps, Arna. "Special Collections of Negroana." *Library Quarterly* 14 (July 1944): 187–206.

Harris, Violet J. "African American Children's Literature: The First One Hundred Years." *Journal of Negro Education* 59.4 (1990): 540–55.

Johnson-Feelings, Dianne. *The Best of "The Brownies' Book."* New York: Oxford UP, 1996.

———. *Telling Tales: The Pedagogy and Promise of African American Literature for Youth*. Westport, CT: Greenwood Press, 1990.

Kutenplon, Deborah, and Ellen Olmstead, eds. *Young Adult Fiction by African American Writers, 1968–1993: A Critical and Annotated Guide*. New York: Garland, 1996.

Rollins, Charlemae. "Promoting Racial Understanding through Books." *Negro American Literature Forum* 2 (1968): 71–76.

Sims, Rudine. *Shadow and Substance: Afro-American Experience in Contemporary Children's Fiction*. Urbana, IL: National Council of Teachers of English, 1982.

Tolson, Nancy. "Making Books Available: The Role of Early Libraries, Librarians, and Booksellers in the Promotion of African American Children's Literature." *African American Review* 32.1 (1998): 9–16.

Roxanne Harde

AFROCENTRICITY   Panafricanist critical perspective associated with Molefi Kete Asante, a professor in the department of African American studies at Temple University. As articulated in Asante's trilogy—*The Afrocentric Idea* (1987), *Afrocentricity* (1988), and *Kemet, Afrocentricity and Knowledge* (1990)—Afrocentric thought has sought to create an African center for Africans in the **diaspora**, to reaffirm the contribution of Africans to world civilization, to show and reject the bias of European thought on Africa, and to reconnect African Americans and Africans in the diaspora to the original homeland.

In *Afrocentricity*, Asante names "intelligence" and "boldness" as central characteristics of Afrocentricity, as they shape relationships with others and the universe and create "intellectual activism"(x). Afrocentricity thus becomes the struggle to resist victimization and to claim a place in the center of world civilization, placing Africa at the core of African American existence and partaking of human regeneration. Reminiscent of Franz Fanon's ideas on cultural liberation, Asante's Afrocentricity calls on African Americans to reconnect with their African ancestry and heritage as a condition of their liberation. Only then can they influence the rest of the world through the transformative force of Afrocentricity.

Afrocentricity is nationalistic (because it speaks first to its people), circular (not linear), activist and transformative (because it transforms old attitudes and beliefs into new ones), inclusive (because it recognizes diversity within the African cultural experience), and spiritual (since it helps to sanctify African history and cultures and reconnects African Americans to their ancestral roots). On the spiritual level, Asante encourages African Americans to make pilgrimages not to Mecca or other such places of foreign creeds, but to Africa and to African American places of historical significance. Afrocentricity recognizes the transformative power of other religions such as Christianity, Judaism, Islam, and Hinduism, but since "all religions represent the deification of someone's nationalism"(Asante 2), the African diaspora needs to adopt Afrocentricity as its religion and *Njia* (Kiswahili for the Way) as its spiritual expression. This is a sine qua non if Africans in the diaspora are to develop a collective black consciousness capable of transforming the world.

Early influences on Asante include **Booker T. Washington** and **W. E. B. Du Bois**, who, in the Post-Reconstruction period, disagreed on how to uplift the black **race** facing violence, **racism**, and segregation. Washington had a very strong sense of purpose and strived to help African Americans achieve economic development in the **Jim Crow** South. For Asante, the two men essentially shared the same goals but differed in strategies. Asante asserts that the two Post-Reconstruction leaders were not Afrocentric because their ideologies were not rooted in African history and culture; Afrocentric discourse must blend history, culture, economics, and politics. Both, however, were pioneers of Afrocentricity because they loved their people and worked tirelessly for the liberation of the black people.

Other pioneers include writers of the **Harlem Renaissance** and founders of the **Negritude** Movement, as well as Cheikh Anta Diop, Elijah Muhammad, **Malcolm X**, and Maulana Karenga. In general, the Harlem Renaissance worked to dispel the old **African American stereotypes**, to promote race consciousness and pride, and to show, as Arthur Schomburg did, the contribution of Africans to world civilization. **Marcus Garvey**, a true Afrocentric activist, promoted the oneness of all Africans and the centrality of African history, culture, dignity, self-respect, and respect by others. Like Du Bois, Garvey forcefully called for African liberation from European colonization. Garvey's work through the Universal Negro Improvement Association fostered a strong sense of black consciousness in America, Africa, and the Caribbean islands.

The Négritude Movement, influenced by the Harlem Renaissance and associated with Aimé Césaire, Léopold Senghor, Léon Damas, and Jacques Rabemananjara, all from French colonies, helped to establish cultural unity among Africans on the continent and the West Indies and sought to redeem African cultures and values from the ravages of colonial discourse. In his work, Cheikh Anta Diop methodically questioned the foundations of Eurocentric explanations of the history of humanity and established an Afrocentric view of world civilization.

Asante particularly credits Karenga with articulating an African American ideology called *Kawaida*, a theory of liberation and social change that is anchored in African culture and that has inspired the African American holiday *Kwanzaa*. *Kawaida* underlies Asante's concept of *Njia*, the knowledge of African history, culture, values, and myths that have influenced world civilization, and the main source of African spirituality.

Further Reading

Asante, Molefi Kete. *Afrocentricity.* Trenton, NJ: Africa World Press, 1988.

Karenga, Maulana. *Introduction to Black Studies.* Los Angeles: U of Sankore P, 1993.

Aimable Twagilimana

AGER, WALDEMER (1869–1941) Norwegian American novelist, essayist, and journalist. Waldemar Ager was a well-known figure in Norwegian American cultural life throughout its most dynamic years in the early twentieth century, writing in Norwegian in multiple genres and lecturing tirelessly on temperance to Norwegian American audiences. Implicit as theme or subtext in much of Ager's work is his support of Norwegian language and cultural preservation. With O. E. Rølvaag and others, Ager rejected complete assimilation as a goal and advocated instead the retention of a uniquely Norwegian American subculture that would embody the best of Norwegian culture, arguing that this would make for the best possible American citizens.

Ager immigrated to Chicago with his family in 1885 where he learned the printing trade and first began writing. In 1892 he joined the staff of *Reform*, a Norwegian language news and temperance weekly published in Eau Claire, Wisconsin, eventually becoming its owner. For decades Ager wrote articles, short stories, and poetry for *Reform* and used its pages to support prohibition, female suffrage, and other social movements, as well as to thoughtfully respond to nativist pressures to Americanize.

Ager's longer works often responded to this pressure also, particularly in the World War I era. *Oberst Heg og hans gutter* (1916; *Colonel Heg and His Boys*, 2000) is an informal, eclectic history of the celebrated Wisconsin Fifteenth Regiment. Its subtitle, "A Norwegian Regiment in the American Civil War," pointedly asserts that those of distinct ethnic background can be exemplary citizens, in wartime or otherwise. *Paa veien til smeltepotten* (1917; *On the Way to the Melting Pot*, 1995) is a bitingly satirical look at errant **assimilation**. In the Norwegian American world Ager delineates, children are embarrassed at their parents' foreignness, parents are entranced by their children's command of English, and virtually all try to outdo each other in aping and impressing the Anglo-American characters. Lars Olson, an enterprising new arrival, follows the typical path. Fixated on material gain and shallow status seeking, his fiancée Karoline, who has preserved her Norwegian cultural integrity, rejects him and returns to Norway.

Gamelandets sønner (1926; *Sons of the Old Country*, 1983) treats the Norwegian American experience with gentler humor. Set in the multiethnic logging region of central Wisconsin in the 1850s, emigration is portrayed as generally positive for the diverse ensemble of Norwegian American characters, providing them with second chances or a chance to mature, with the final chapters showing the immigrants fighting in the Civil War for the Union. In *Hundeøine* (1929; *I Sit Alone*, 1931) Christian Pedersen, the embittered immigrant narrator, lives on the prairie not as a pioneer but as a psychological refugee. Pedersen's self-conscious angst as he reviews his life seems both specific to his immigrant experience as well as related to the more general cultural upheavals portrayed in mainstream modern literature.

By Ager's death, Norwegian language fluency in the United States was almost extinct; as with Prohibition his cause proved too optimistic for numerous complex reasons. Ironically, after decades of relative inaccessibility, Ager's writing is today becoming better known through the English translations that recent interest in ethnic literature has spurred. (*See also* Norwegian American Literature)

Further Reading

Haugen, Einar Ingvald. *Immigrant Idealist: A Literary Biography of Waldemar Ager, Norwegian American*. Northfield, MN: Norwegian-American Historical Association, 1989.

Øverland, Orm. *The Western Home: A Literary History of Norwegian America*. Northfield, MN: Norwegian-American Historical Society, 1996.

Sue Barker

AGOSÍN, MARJORIE (1955–)   Chilean American Jewish poet, short story writer, essayist, editor, literary critic, and human rights activist. Marjorie Agosín has had a prolific and active career and is associated with many identities and literary movements, from Latina feminist to Jewish **diaspora** writer to human rights activist. She has more than thirty books to her credit. Although she has lived and worked most of her life in the United States, she writes almost exclusively in her native language of Spanish, but has managed to find an English-language audience through very thorough and continuous translations of her writing.

Pervasive in her poetry and prose is a questioning of oppressive convention and lifeless routines. Her writing is infused with both eroticism and feminism and with a critique of the upper classes of both North and South America. One of her early books, *Brujas y algo más—Witches and Other Things* (1986), became quite popular for this very mixture. Published in a bilingual edition with translations into English by Cola Franzen, it includes poems that celebrate witches and question traditional fairy tales. The poem "Cuentos de hadas y algo más—Fairy Tales and Something More" is a good example of her humor and social criticism. In a satirical style comparable to Anne Sexton's, Agosín portrays the seven dwarves, who did not keep Snow White as an ornament but rather had her doing chores during the day and who knows what during the night. Yet, unlike in Sexton, the poetic **identity** in Agosín's work extends beyond the self to include a political statement on the condition of women in general.

When dealing with women of different social classes or life circumstances, Agosín takes on the position of witness, of one who knows or sees and cannot keep silent. She documents the injustices caused by oppressive regimes or oppressive social norms. She has dedicated whole books to these issues and to individual and group efforts to combat different oppressions. For example, *Circles of Madness: Mothers of the Plaza de Mayo* (1992) draws attention to the mothers of the disappeared in the seventies and eighties in Argentina. Another book along these lines is *Scraps of Life: Chilean Arpilleras* (1989), which spotlights the subversive work of everyday Chilean women who documented the horrors of the U.S.-backed Pinochet regime on cloth. However, Agosín's work is not strong in documenting the mistreatment that people of color in the United States, including Latino groups, have undergone both historically and in contemporary times. Her writing is stronger in dealing with the racially, politically, culturally, and economically marginal peoples of Latin America, especially of the Southern Cone region where she is from. She does have one well-known poem titled "La mesa de billar en New Bedford, Mass." ("The Billiard Table in New Bedford, Mass.") about a highly publicized rape in North America.

In much of her work she chronicles her experience of being regarded as the "other," in situations ranging from her childhood as a Jewish minority in Chile, to her racist and xenophobic white high school classmates and teachers in Georgia, to the North American Jewish community that regarded

Latin American Jews as second-class, to her adult career in academia where relations with other professors are cold. She turns the othering around, by holding a mirror up to the mainstream white culture, documenting its many peculiarities, so that this mainstream itself comes off as strange through the eyes of Agosín. It is perhaps this aspect of her writing that has eased her acceptance by other Latina and Latino writers in the United States. Yet Agosín also explores how she herself is privileged as a very light-skinned, blonde Latina Jewish woman, whose childhood included perks such as an indigenous nanny. At the same time, she consistently questions privilege and the complacency of those who benefit from social systems that exploit others.

Currents of joy, love, and optimism run through her work, reflected both in the erotic writing and in the political. Sensual experiences abound. Her work is about affirmation of life as well as denunciation of injustice.

Further Reading

Mujica, Barbara. "Marjorie Agosín Weaves Magic with Social Vision." *Americas* 45.1 (January/February 1993): 44–49.

Scott, Nina M. "Marjorie Agosín as Latina Writer." *Boundaries: Latina Writing and Critical Readings.* Amherst: U of Massachusetts P, 1989. 235–49.

Isabel R. Espinal

AIIIEEEEE! AN ANTHOLOGY OF ASIAN AMERICAN WRITERS (1974)

Edited by **Frank Chin**, **Jeffery Paul Chan**, **Lawson Fusao Inada**, and Shawn Wong—all writers themselves—*Aiiieeeee!* was one of the first anthologies of Asian American literature. Chin, Chan, and Wong also formed the Combined Asian Resources Project (CARP) to recover and republish key Asian American texts such as **Carlos Bulosan**'s *America Is in the Heart* (1973), **John Okada**'s *No-No Boy* (1976), and **Louis Chu**'s *Eat a Bowl of Tea* (1979). Through their recovery and anthology work, the *Aiiieeeee!* editors sought to establish the existence of an Asian American literary tradition that was distinct from the exoticized works preferred by those few readers and publishers who even knew of Asian American writers (indeed, because the texts featured in *Aiiieeeee!* did not meet the expectations of white publishers, the anthology was published by an African American press, Howard University). In addition to excerpts from the aforementioned novels by Bulosan, Okada, and Chu, the editors included work by writers such as **Diana Chang**, **Toshio Mori**, **Hisaye Yamamoto**, and **Wakako Yamauchi**.

The *Aiiieeeee!* editors conceptualized an Asian American **identity** that rejected "Americanization," or the acceptance of white cultural standards. Nonetheless, this identity was rooted in America; for example, the preface argues that "Asian American" refers only to American-born people of Asian descent. This distinction was meant to counter stereotypes of Asian Americans as inassimilable foreigners and exotics, exemplified by the racist Asian caricature who screams, "aiiieeeee!" when angered or hurt—the editors subvert this caricature through appropriation by using this cry to title their anthology. Despite this initial concern with place of birth, the editors are substantially more interested in Asian American "sensibility," or political orientation. The sensibility of the *Aiiieeeee!* writers opposes the work of "Americanized" Asians like **Jade Snow Wong**, author of *Fifth Chinese Daughter* (1950), or **C. Y. Lee**, author of *Flower Drum Song* (1957), who (the editors claim) stereotypically represent obedient, passive Asian Americans from a white perspective. Taking a central tenet of the **Black Arts Movement**, the editors argue that the *Aiiieeeee!* writers express their oppositional sensibility through developing a new language capable of representing the experiences of "the people."

In further considering the ways that *Aiiieeeee!* defines Asian America, it is important to note that the anthology primarily features work by Chinese and Japanese Americans. However, the editors helped to challenge the even greater invisibility of Filipino American writing by including three such examples along with a separate introduction to Filipino American literature that discusses its colonial and antiimperialist history and influences. Men are more heavily represented than women, and the editors privilege themes of Asian American manhood, such as the threat of emasculation by white racists and by those Asian American women who internalize white standards. Nonetheless, *Aiiieeeee!* was pivotal in recovering and reconstructing Asian American literature for a new generation of readers and activists. (*See also* Chinese American Poetry)

Further Reading

Li, David Leiwei. *Imagining the Nation: Asian American Literature and Cultural Consent*. Palo Alto, CA: Stanford UP, 1998.

Cheryl Higashida

ALAMEDDINE, RABIH (1959–) Arab American fiction writer and painter. Rabih Alameddine's fiction vividly portrays a rich array of thematic concerns that mirror many of the main issues faced by the Arab American community such as cultural displacement, in-between identities, and the struggle against **racism**. His characters are often suspended between two or more worlds that are at odds with each other—most often America on the one hand and Lebanon on the other.

Although acknowledging the critical need for categorizing ethnic literatures, Alameddine posits that such labeling could possibly further the marginalization of the ethnic voice. He states in an interview, "I think and hope that my work transcends that [kind of categorization] because if it doesn't, then I would have failed" (25).

Born in Jordan to Lebanese parents, Alameddine has lived in Kuwait, Lebanon, England, and the United States. He currently lives in San Francisco and Beirut, and is the recipient of a Guggenheim Fellowship. Alameddine is the author of two novels, *Koolaids: The Art of War* (1998) and *I, the Divine: A Novel in First Chapters* (2001), as well as the collection of short stories titled *The Perv: Stories* (1999).

In *Koolaids*, Alameddine's first novel, an intensely fragmented narrative consisting mainly of a dizzying patchwork of journal entries, first-person narrations, and excerpts from emails and letters, he creates a world in which the novel's characters, many of whom straddle both the American and Lebanese worlds, are in the process of constantly creating a space from within which they define, and consequently articulate, their sexual and ethnic/racial identities. One of the characters, Mohammad, a Muslim Lebanese American painter living in San Francisco, watches his lovers and friends die one after another from AIDS while he himself struggles with this disease. In this novel, Alameddine deftly parallels the horrors of the Lebanese Civil War (1975–90) and the AIDS crisis in the United States during the eighties, creating in the process a poignant link between two different kinds of trauma and emotional survival.

Koolaids was followed in 1999 by *The Perv*, a collection of eight short stories that handle the theme of exile and displacement from a variety of perspectives, giving voice to those Lebanese who had left their home country and live abroad, as well as those who had opted or were compelled to stay behind. The thematic leitmotifs permeating all these stories revolve around the Lebanese war, the AIDS crisis, exile, and memory, to name a few. The story titled "The Changing Room," for instance, is written from the first-person point of view of a Lebanese boy ostracized by his schoolmates at an English boarding school due to his **ethnicity** and homosexuality, and "A Flight to Paris" features a frank but short rapport between two strangers on a flight from the United States to Paris: The first passenger is a Lebanese woman voicing her anxieties about her gay son and the graphic book he's written about his sexual exploits, and the second is a gay American man confessing his unreleased grief over his deceased lover who had died of AIDS. Alameddine's second novel, *I, the Divine*, was published in 2001. This novel, subtitled *A Novel in First Chapters* and written mainly from the first-person perspective of the main narrator Sarah, is solely composed of first chapters that introduce, then reconstruct and retell Sarah's story. This form of reconstructing the past reveals deeply rooted identity dilemmas faced by Sarah, an Arab American whose perpetual feeling of alienation define and dictate her narrative perspective. Born to an American mother and a Lebanese father, Sarah's sense of cultural identity is irreversibly fragmented due to her sense of not fitting in either of her parents' cultures. The notion of a stable and tangible homeland, representing a specific personal and collective history, is dramatically undermined in the novel. By putting into question the reliability of the narrator, this novel brings up the driving forces dictating the suppression of personal as well as collective memories, such as the traumas inherent in being subjected to rape and civil war.

Although Alameddine is far from comfortable about being a representative of any one literary category, including Arab American, gay, or Lebanese literatures, his voice nevertheless adds a necessary complexity to these categories, highlighting their multilayered and multi-voiced characteristics. (*See also* Arab American Novel)

Further Reading

Alameddine, Rabih. "Transcontinental Detachment: What Shelf Are You On?" Interview with Carol Fadda-Conrey. *Al-Jadid: A Review & Record of Arab Culture and Arts* 9.44 (2003): 24+.

Hout, Syrine C. "Of Fathers and the Fatherland in the Post-1995 Lebanese Exilic Novel." *World Literature Today: A Literary Quarterly of the University of Oklahoma* 75.2 (2001): 285–93.

Carol Fadda-Conrey

ALARCÓN, FRANCISCO X. (1954–)   Chicano poet, scholar, and educator. Internationally acclaimed poet Alarcón has published ten volumes in poetry for adults, four volumes for children, and several textbooks for teaching Spanish at the college and high school levels. His poetry has been published in more than forty anthologies and translated into Spanish. Alarcón received both the Danforth and Fulbright fellowships, and has been awarded more than twenty-five literary prizes including the 1998 Carlos Pellicer-Robert Frost Poetry Honor Award by the Third Binational Border Poetry Contest, the 1993 American Book Award, the 1993 PEN Oakland Josephine Miles Award, and the 1984 Chicano Literary Prize. In 2002 he received the Fred Cody Lifetime Achievement Award from the Bay Area Book Reviewers Association (BABRA) in San Francisco and the same year was one of the three finalists nominated for the state poet laureate of California.

He was born in Wilmington, California where he spent the first six years of his life, continued his primary education in Guadalajara, Mexico, and returned to the United States at the age of eighteen. He completed his undergraduate studies at California State University, Long Beach and his graduate studies at Stanford University. This binational and bilingual upbringing clearly influenced the scope of his poetic and professional vision. He currently teaches at the University of California, Davis where he directs the Spanish for Native Speakers Program.

Alarcón's children's books have received numerous accolades and reflect a genuine warmth and sense of play in their language and in the images produced in collaboration with artist Maya Christina Gonzalez. Each of the four collections corresponds to a different season, is written entirely bilingually as we see in one title: *Laughing Tomatoes and Other Spring Poems/ Jitomates Risueños y Otros Poemas de Primavera* (1997). They all contain familiar themes and references that are at once culturally specific to Latina/o families as well as universal: food, plants, weather, and dreams, for example.

Since the mid-1980s, Alarcón has developed an evolving poetic voice; a recently published anthology, *From the Other Side of Night/Del otro lado de la noche: New and Selected Poems* (2002), brings together poems from throughout his career that highlight a range of themes central to Alarcón's body of work: poems that express solidarity with Central American refugees as well as other U.S. Latina/os, explorations of **identity**, social justice, desire, myth, and history. This retrospective anthology traces the development of the literary work that has shaped Alarcón's reputation as a poet of love and justice.

According to critic Manuel de Jesus Hernandez-G, the three most important collections in Alarcón's writing career are *Body in Flames/Cuerpo en llamas* (1990), *De amor oscuro/Of Dark Love* (1991), and *Snake Poems: An Aztec Invocation* (1992). These three collections most clearly reflect the evolution of a unified erotic and activist vision. The personal and the public are intimately connected: love and politics are closely linked and experienced in the same physical and poetic body. *Body in Flames* weaves together erotic poems and concerns with explicitly political ones. Indeed, in claiming an unequivocally gay Chicano poetic voice, these two aspects are already deeply intertwined, and what is most intimate is inscribed with social meanings. In many ways, Alarcón explores the same territories which Chicana lesbian writers such as **Cherríe Moraga** and **Gloria Anzaldúa** do, claiming a poetic voice in which politics, spirituality, and sexuality are lived and understood together and expressed with the same intensity and importance. *Of Dark Love* is the most extended meditation on love, noteworthy because of its exploration of a classically European poetic form, the sonnet cycle, and its contrast to the typically explicit political concerns that characterize what critic Rafael Perez-Torres calls classic Chicano poetry. *Snake Poems* reflects the indigenous influences in Mexican culture, voiced in Nahuatl translations, and a spare minimalism, which places them squarely in an American literary tradition.

Alarcón's poetic vision is wide-ranging, democratic, and intensely personal. Like other Latina/o poets of his generation such as **Lorna Dee Cervantes** and **Martín Espada**, Alarcón writes of love and justice, and of politics and desire as interanimating forces that create beauty in poetry and in the world. (*See also* Mexican American Gay Literature, Mexican American Poetry)

Further Reading

Foster, David W. "The Poetry of Francisco X. Alarcón: The Queer Project of Poetry." *Chicano/Latino Homoerotic Identities*. Ed. David William Foster. New York: Garland Publishing, 1999. 175–95.

González, Marcial. "The Poetry of Francisco X. Alarcón: Identifying the Chicano Persona." *Bilingual Review* 19.2 (May–August 1994): 179–87.

Hernandez-G, Manuel de Jesus. "Alarcón, Francisco X." *Latin American Writers on Gay and Lesbian Themes: A Bio-Critical Sourcebook*. Ed. David William Foster. Westport, CT: Greenwood Press, 1994. 7–13.

Eliza Rodriguez y Gibson

ALBERT, OCTAVIA VICTORIA ROGERS (1853–1889?) African American teacher, scholar, social activist, and author. In her only published work, *The House of Bondage, or Charlotte Brooks and Other Slaves* (1890), Octavia Albert narrates the life stories of several former African American slaves and provides a brief record of the accomplishments of African Americans in the post-Reconstruction era. *The House of Bondage* is a unique blend of journalism, **slave narrative**, historiography, biography, and social commentary. In contrast to the plantation fiction that was widely popular at the time, Albert's text emphasizes the barbarity of American slavery, detailing physical, psychological, and spiritual hardships. The narrator claims that the horrors of the Spanish Inquisition cannot compare to the punishments meted out under American **slavery**. The text catalogs cruelties regularly recounted in slave narratives, including vicious physical beatings, the separation of families through sale, masters' disregard of slave marriages, and the use of dogs as a form of punishment. Highlighting Albert's own investment in Christianity, the narrator also laments—as do her characters—the inability of slaves to practice their Protestant religion in a largely Catholic Louisiana. Slaves were prohibited from song, forced to work on Sundays, and banned from religious meetings or public forms of worship. Although the text insists that violence against African Americans did not stop with emancipation, the latter section of the text includes images of successful African American businessmen, soldiers, and politicians in post-Reconstruction America.

Albert herself was born a slave in Oglethorp, Georgia, in 1853. After emancipation, she studied at Atlanta University to become a teacher, a profession she understood as an extension of her mission as a Christian and member of the African Methodist Episcopal Church. While teaching in Georgia, she met A. E. P. Albert, a fellow teacher and future minister in the Methodist Episcopal Church. They married in 1874 and soon moved to Louisiana where, in her role as the minister's wife, Albert began her interviews. Recorded in *The House of Bondage*, these interviews, along with Albert's astute social commentary, serve as both a record of the past and a reflection on the future: in her vision, America must amend the wrong of slavery and uplift the downtrodden. The nation must also become fully integrated, as a reflection of God's kingdom in heaven.

Shortly after her death, the *South-western Christian Advocate* (the Methodist Episcopal Church's newspaper, which boasted an interracial readership) serialized her text as a tribute to her good works and noble contributions to the community and church. The following year, A. E. P. Albert and their daughter, Laura T. F. Albert, were successful in having *The House of Bondage* issued in book form and jointly published in New York and Cincinnati. The book was reprinted in 1988 as part of the Schomburg Library of Nineteenth-Century Black Women Writers series.

Further Reading

Foster, Frances Smith. "Introduction." *The House of Bondage, or Charlotte Brooks and Other Slaves*. Octavia Victoria Rogers Albert. New York and Oxford: Oxford UP, 1988 [orig. pub. 1890]. xxvii–xliii.

Ravi, Geetha. "Octavia Victoria Rogers Albert." *African American Authors, 1745–1945: A Bio-Bibliographical Critical Sourcebook*. Ed. Emmanuel S. Nelson. Westport, CT: Greenwood Press, 2000. 6–12.

Julie Cary Nerad

ALEXANDER, MEENA (1951–)   Indian American poet, novelist, literary critic, and professor of English. Meena Alexander is primarily known for her poetry, but she has also written several critically acclaimed novels and has contributed criticism to a wide range of scholarly journals. Born in Allahabad, India, Alexander completed a baccalaureate degree at the University of Khartoum in 1969 and a doctorate at the University of Nottingham in 1973. After lecturing in English and French at several Indian universities, she taught as an assistant professor at Fordham University from 1980 to 1987. In 1987, she joined the faculty at Hunter College of the City University of New York where she has continued to teach. Currently she is a Distinguished Professor of English at Hunter College and the City University of New York Graduate Center.

Critics such as John Oliver Perry have asserted that Alexander's work places her in the top ranks of Indian poets writing in English. She has published nine volumes of poetry. In the first four of these volumes—*The Bird's Bright Wing* (1976), *Without Place* (1977), *I Root My Name* (1977), and *Stone Roots* (1980)—she has treated Indian subjects, exploring issues related to family and community, as well as the postcolonial concerns about borrowed **identity**, cultural uncertainty, and linguistic and literary autonomy. In the process, she has developed a personal symbology that provides a suggestive complement to the growing store of symbolism connected to Indian nationalism and, more broadly, to the common elements of South Asian cultures.

In her fifth collection, *House of a Thousand Doors* (1989), Alexander combined prose passages with her poetry and began to shift her focus from India itself to the Indian diaspora. In her subsequent collections—*The Storm* (1989), *Night Scene: The Garden* (1992), *River and Bridge* (1995), and *The Shock of Arrival: Reflections on Postcolonial Experience* (1996), in which she again has combined prose passages and poetry—she has explored the themes associated with migration. These include the immigrant's continuing sense of geographical and cultural dislocation; the need to find compromises between competing cultural values and demands; the sense that creating a hybrid cultural identity may ultimately leave one with no identity at all; the need to assimilate despite physical and cultural markers of difference; and the sense that the present is less a bridge between the past and the future than a limbo in which the self languishes when the past represents lost certainties and the future seems to present alternatives too remote or extravagant to be realized. Alexander has also become increasingly concerned with feminist issues, with the relationships between women of different generations, and with the triple burden of being a woman of color who is trying to write meaningfully about a cultural transition that presents hazards on all three levels—gender, **ethnicity**, and literary disclosure.

Nampally Road (1991), Alexander's first novel, is a slender volume at just 120 pages, but it is as packed with eccentric characters and cultural revelations as any Indian street. Autobiographical in its basic situation, the novel focuses on a young woman named Mira who, after earning her doctorate overseas, returns to India to assume a teaching position at a university. She rents a room from a female doctor who is known as the "Little Mother" because of her extraordinary compassion, which is shown in her continuing commitment to caring for indigent patients. The doctor's house is located next door to a loud cinema, and both her office and the movie theater generate a great deal of traffic, placing Mira in contact with much of the broad and complex spectrum of Indian social classes. At the same time, Mira becomes romantically involved with a politically radical labor organizer named Ramu. In the midst of a series of dramatic clashes with the police, Mira finds something of a doppelganger in a young woman named Rameeza Be. While detained by the police who have killed her activist husband, Rameeza Be has been gang-raped by her interrogators. The crimes against her become a focal point of the volatile protests against the whole economic and political system that operates largely to oppress the great masses of ordinary people and to protect the narrow interests of the corporate and political bosses. Ultimately, Rameeza Be comes under the care of the "Little Mother" and begins her physical and psychological recovery. In her response to Rameeza Be's experiences, Mira recognizes her deep sympathy for the victims of oppression but admits her inability or unwillingness to commit herself completely to their cause.

In her second novel, *Manhattan Music* (1997), Alexander provides a portrait of a community of Indian immigrants in the New Jersey suburbs of New York City. Interestingly, this community includes the same sort of diversity in ethnicity, socioeconomic class, and religious affiliation that has so often led to eruptions of terrible violence in India itself. Here the tensions are somewhat undercut by the vulnerability in the immigrant status of the characters and by the surprising variety of geographic locations from which they have emigrated. For some, the West Indies or any of dozens of other places were simply temporary stops on their way to the United States. But others have had long family histories in places outside of India and now view themselves as more West Indian than Indian. In this manner, Alexander conveys the tremendous complexities that exist beyond the simple truisms about **multiculturalism**.

Alexander has also written an autobiographical volume, *Fault Lines: A Memoir* (1993), in which she explores, with both directness and subtlety, the effects of migration on her own psyche. The title refers both to geographical and cultural boundaries that are difficult to cross and to the historical legacy of assumed culpability that is the burden of women of color. Her contributions to criticism include the book *Women in Romanticism: Mary*

Wollstonecraft, Dorothy Wordsworth, and Mary Shelley (1989). (*See also* South Asian American Literature)

Further Reading

Ali, Zaniab, and Dharini Rasiah. "Meena Alexander." *Words Matter: Conversations with Asian American Writers*. Ed. King-Kok Cheung. Honolulu: U of Hawai'i P/ UCLA Asian American Studies Center, 2000. 69–91.

Bahri, Deepika, and Mary Vasudeva. "Observing Ourselves among Others: Interview with Meena Alexander." *Between the Lines: South Asians and Post-Coloniality*. Ed. Deepika Bahri and Mary Vasudeva. Philadelphia: Temple UP, 1996. 35–53.

Dave, Shilpa. "The Doors to Home and History: Post-Colonial Identities in Meena Alexander and Bharati Mukherjee." *Amerasia Journal* 19.3 (1993): 103–13.

———. "*Nampally Road* by Meena Alexander." *A Resource Guide to Asian American Literature*. Ed. Sau-ling Cynthia Wong. New York: Modern Language Association of America, 2001. 13–20.

Duncan, Erika. "A Portrait of Meena Alexander." *World Literature Today* 73 (Winter 1999): 23–28.

Mukerji, Sumitra. "Towards the Creation of a Vital Aesthetics: A Survey of Contemporary Indian English Poetry and Criticism with Special Reference to Meena Alexander." *Journal of the School of Languages* 3 (1993): 1113–23.

Perry, John Oliver. "Contemporary Indian Poetry in English." *World Literature Today* 68 (Spring 1994): 261–72.

Rustomji-Kerns, Roshni. "An Interview with Meena Alexander." *Weber Studies* 15 (Winter 1998): 18–27.

Shankar, Lavina Dhingra. "Postcolonial Diasporics 'Writing in Search of a Homeland' Meena Alexander's *Manhattan Music, Fault Lines,* and *The Shock of Arrival.*" *Lit: Literature Interpretation Theory* 12 (September 2001): 285–312.

Sultana, Rebecca. "Rewriting Nationalism: A Comparison of *The Tiger's Daughter* and *Nampally Road.*" *Conference of College Teachers of English Studies* 64 (September 1999): 62–70.

Martin Kich

ALEXIE, SHERMAN JOSEPH, JR. (1966–) Poet, novelist, screenwriter, essayist, and comedian. Alexie's writing is highly regarded for its precision in representing the experience of being American Indian in the contemporary moment. In his work, Alexie scripts the confrontation of pain, poverty, and alienation alongside the ability to access laughter, humor, and comedy. Alexie's representations of the tragic through the comic, through the capacity to laugh in the midst of hostility overtly link up much of Alexie's work with narratives of resistance rooted in other ethnic cultural traditions, from the African American **blues** in *Reservation Blues* (1995) to the safe space of the basketball court in *Ten Little Indians* (2003).

Alexie was born in Spokane, Washington, to a father from the Coeur d'Alene tribe and a mother with ancestors from the Spokane, Flathead, and Colville tribes. Registered Spokane/Coeur d'Alene Indian, he was raised on the Spokane reservation in Wellpinit, Washington. As a teenager, he traveled some fifteen miles off the **Native American reservation** to attend a white high school, before returning to a reservation that was hamstrung by chronic alcoholism, poverty, and other material effects of an institutionalized **racism**. Alexie attended college at Gonzaga and Washington State universities in eastern Washington. His mentor, poet Alex Kuo, encouraged Alexie to write his first collection of stories and poetry, *The Business of Fancydancing*, which was first published in 1992. Since leaving Washington State University in 1991, Alexie has published some twenty works of fiction, poetry, screenplays, and essays, including the critically acclaimed *The Lone Ranger and Tonto Fistfight in Heaven* (1993) and *Reservation Blues* (1995).

Writer Sherman Alexie gestures while speaking to students at North Seattle Community College, April 17, 2000. *AP/ Wide World Photos.*

Clear in much of Alexie's writing is that any understanding of American Indian life must grapple with the bloody history of the American continent's conquest by white folk. Embedded in so many of Alexie's narratives are the losses experienced after Christopher Columbus's "discovery of the new world" in 1492, puritan preacher and educator Cotton Mather's sermons of "America's God-given rights" in the late 1600s, the implicit and explicit policies of Manifest Destiny in the early nineteenth century and the Indian wars later in that century, and the debilitating conditions of reservation life into the contemporary era. Precisely because this history of conquest—and resistance and resilience of many kinds—is embedded in his work, not only does Alexie's writing speak to other ethnic American literary traditions, but it also resonates with literatures produced in other colonized contexts, from South Asia to sub-Saharan Africa, the Caribbean, and the Spanish Americas.

The Lone Ranger and Tonto Fistfight in Heaven is Alexie's first sustained prose work. The collection of twenty-two short pieces follows Victor Joseph and Thomas Builds-the-Fire, two friends coming of age on the Spokane Indian Reservation. Thomas proudly embraces his Indian heritage and sees his existence as built through the sum total of stories passed down by his ancestors. His role—indeed his only means of living in the world—is to continue the story-telling tradition. Thomas states plainly, "I learned a thousand stories before I took my first thousand steps. They are all I have. It's all I can do." Victor, on the other hand, finds himself in the middle of what he sees as two opposing worlds, unable to fully identify with either. He cannot fully ground himself in a purified Indian worldview of an idealized heritage; but he is also increasingly uncomfortable in identifying with the capitalist-driven popular culture of the Brady Bunch and rock and roll. Victor's struggle to resolve this tension highlights the ways in which neither world can be purified of its opposite; rather, these forms of identification are always relational and contaminated.

Thomas and Victor reappear in Alexie's first conventional novel, *Reservation Blues*. The narrative here follows the short-lived career of an all-Indian rock band calling itself Coyote Springs. Each chapter opens with an epigraph composed of lyrics from one of the band's songs, and the content of the lyrics—grappling with familial and tribal heritage, poverty, desolation—resonate with the various themes found in the narrative. One of the comedic and fanciful elements of the narrative is found in the novel's opening. A black man appears on the reservation for the first time in its history. The man turns out to be Robert Johnson (1911–38), the famous guitarist from the early 1900s, widely regarded as one of the musicians who gave birth to the modern blues. In the story, Johnson looks for and receives spiritual salvation in the tribe's maternal figure, Big Mom. The mixing of ethnic traditions here is expanded upon when Thomas finds Johnson's guitar and pledges to "change the world with it." Thus the African American tradition of using music to grapple with the daily terrors of enslavement and racism is imported into Indian culture.

Since 1995, along with publishing several novels and short story collections, much of Alexie's work has been in other media. He recorded the lyrics from the *Reservation Blues* epigraphs with singer-songwriter Jim Boyd on a critically acclaimed album of the same name. In 1998, the film adaptation of *Lone Ranger and Tonto* was released and distributed across the United States. Titled *Smoke Signals* (dir. Chris Eyre), the film is understood to be the first major motion picture written, directed, starring, and produced by American Indians. And in 2003, Alexie directed a small video production of an adaptation of *The Business of Fancydancing*. Alexie has also moved into the realm of live performance. For four consecutive years (1998–2001), Alexie was crowned the World Heavyweight Poetry Bout champion and during these years focused some energy on the genre of stand-up comedy as well.

With Alexie's multifaceted work, one finds the importance of seeing how traditional fixed identities are enmeshed in shifting social contexts, how the comic is enmeshed in the tragic. His growing corpus of work leads a new generation of American Indian voices into wider national critical and cultural discourses. These discourses ask incisive questions about the centrality of histories of conquest, resistance, and resilience, and provide frames for representing racial and ethnic difference in new and profoundly moving ways. (*See also* Native American Novel, Native American Poetry)

Further Reading

Coulombe, Joseph L. "The Approximate Size of His Favorite Humor: Sherman Alexie's Comic Connections and Disconnections in *The Lone Ranger and Tonto Fistfight in Heaven.*" *American Indian Quarterly* 26.1 (2002): 94–115.

Evans, Stephen F. "'Open Containers': Sherman Alexie's Drunken Indians." *American Indian Quarterly* 25.1 (2001): 46–72.

Keith Feldman

ALFARO, LUIS (1963?–)   Chicano writer, director, performance artist, and activist. Widely acknowledged as a major figure in contemporary American theater, as well as in Latina/o literature, Luis Alfaro is codirector of the Latino Theater Initiative at the Mark Taper Forum in Los Angeles. A writer of fiction, poetry, and theater, director, performance artist, and activist, Alfaro has received numerous awards including a MacArthur "genius" grant, the NEA/TCG Fellowship for playwriting, and the Kennedy Center Fund for New American Plays, and he also won the 1998 National Hispanic Playwriting Competition. His writing has been published almost exclusively in anthologies such as *Men on Men 4* (1992), *Blood Whispers: LA Writers on AIDS* (1994), *Uncontrollable Bodies* (1994), *Goddess of the Americas* (1997), *Urban Latino Cultures* (1999), *Out of the Fringe* (2000), and *Another City: Writing from Los Angeles* (2001). His work has received attention in both scholarly journals and the popular press such as *Aztlán*, *Theatre Journal*, and *The Advocate*. His spoken word CD *Downtown* was released in 1994, and his plays include *Straight as a Line* (1994) and *Bitter Homes and Gardens* (2000). He collaborated with three Chicana poets, Sandra Muñoz, Marisela Norte, and Alma Cervantes, to write, direct, and produce *Black Butterfly, Jaguar Girl, Piñata Woman,* and *Other Superhero Girls like Me* about the everyday lives of teenage girls in East Los Angeles. His solo-performance work has been seen throughout the United States, England, and Mexico. His short film *Chicanismo* (1999) was produced by the Public Broadcasting Service and nominated for an Emmy Award. As an activist, Alfaro works with at-risk youth, cofounded three nonprofit arts organizations, and chaired the Gay Men of Color Consortium.

Born and raised in Los Angeles, Alfaro often infuses his work with memories of growing up Chicano in the city. Expressing his aesthetic and political vision, in interviews he often speaks of his writing and creative work coming from his activism. Crossing the boundaries of genre, art, and activism, his work illuminates contemporary Chicana/o experience in all of its *mestizaje* or cultural mixture. Alfaro is deeply invested in the relationship between language and the body. Critics regard the performative aspect of his work as key to fully understanding its significance—especially as it complicates recurring themes of memory and **identity**, undoing racial and sexual stereotypes that inscribe meaning on the bodies of his characters. This is no small thing as the bodies in many of Alfaro's works are often marginalized: queer, brown, and working-class.

The breadth and energy of Alfaro's work ensures that the intersecting spheres of literature, performance, and theater are forever changed. His work crosses cultural, aesthetic, and political boundaries, simultaneously making connections while stressing the difference that one's body can make. (*See also* Mexican American Gay Literature, Mexican American Drama)

Further Reading

Allatson, Paul. "Siempre Feliz en Mi Falda: Luis Alfaro's Simulative Challenge." *GLQ: Journal of Gay and Lesbian Studies* 5.2 (1999): 199–230.

Muñoz, José. "Memory Performance: Luis Alfaro's 'Cuerpo Politizado'." *Corpus Delecti: Performance Art of the Americas*. Ed. Coco Fusco. London: Routledge, 2000.

Roman, David. "Latino Performance and Identity." *Aztlán* 22 (1997) 151–67.

Roman, David, and Susan Bennet, eds. "Latino Performance." [Special issue of *Theatre Journal*] 52.1 (2000).

Eliza Rodriguez y Gibson

ALGREN, NELSON (1909–1981) Jewish American writer. Known as the "poet of the Chicago slums," Nelson Algren wrote about drifters, prostitutes, thieves, con men, and addicts. He worked as a journalist most of his life, writing essays, articles, and reviews, but his reputation was established through his fiction, which includes numerous short stories and novels such as *A Walk on the Wild Side* (1956), *Never Come Morning* (1942), and the 1950 National Book Award–winning *The Man with the Golden Arm* (1949).

Born Nelson Ahlgren Abraham on March 28, 1909, in Detroit, Michigan, Algren worked as a salesman and migratory worker in the South and Southwest during the Depression. It was a job at a gas station in Rio Hondo, Texas, in 1933 that led to the writing of his first published story. His career as an author and journalist began in 1941 and lasted forty years. He received a variety of awards and grants, and the Nelson Algren fiction contest was established by *Chicago Magazine* in 1982 in the author's memory, and has been continued by the *Chicago Tribune* since 1986. In 1983, the PEN American Center established the PEN/Nelson Algren Fiction Award. Algren wrote four novels and contributed short stories, essays, articles, and reviews to numerous periodicals, including *Story, Nation, Life, Saturday Evening Post, Atlantic, Chicago Tribune, Partisan Review, Playboy,* and *Rolling Stone*. His novel *The Man with the Golden Arm* was produced as a film under the same title by United Artists, in 1955, and *A Walk on the Wild Side* was produced as a film under the same title by Columbia Pictures, in 1962.

Algren's fictional world embodies a vision of hopelessness. His novels explore the seamy side of town, the effects of extreme poverty and social indifference. Algren's work engages in social criticism, but according to Chester E. Eisinger in *Fiction of the Forties*, the criticism "is not in any sense ideological. It is a compound of resentment and perversity, of feelings; it is a conviction that the respectable classes ought to have their noses rubbed in the poverty and degradation of American life as an antidote to their self-satisfaction; it is a conviction that the poor are just as good as the rich, and more fun to boot; it is sheer sentimental sympathy for the under-dog" (9).

Algren's first novel, *Somebody in Boots* (1935), is considered uneven and less satisfying than Algren's later works, and it was not very successful commercially. This led Algren to focus on short stories and journalism for nearly five years. When his second novel, *Never Come Morning*, was published in 1942 it received immediate critical acclaim. *Never Come Morning* is set in a Polish community in Chicago and examines physical conquest and brutality. Bruno Bicek is a boxer who turns to crime and murder after his street gang rapes his girlfriend, and the novel is a harsh critique of the American myth of fairness and democracy—a myth Algren believed covered the reality of the strong taking from the weak. *Never Come Morning* established Algren as a "Chicago novelist" and a practitioner of the American realist style.

What followed was Algren's most productive decade as a fiction writer. Between 1947 and 1956 he published a short story collection, *The Neon Wilderness*; a lengthy prose poem, *Chicago: City on the Make*; and two highly acclaimed novels, *The Man with the Golden Arm* and *A Walk on the Wild Side*. It was also during this period that Algren began the extensive travels through Europe, Central America, and the U.S. that influenced much of his nonfiction in the 1960s and 1970s. Through Simone de Beauvoir he met members of prominent Parisian literary circles, including Jean-Paul Sartre. Algren's primary residence, however, remained Chicago.

Algren's best novel, *The Man with the Golden Arm*, continues Algren's examination of society's underbelly. It portrays the downfall of Frankie Machine, a card-dealing morphine addict running from the law, and takes up the central conflict between self-sacrifice and self-preservation. Considered by many to be the first serious American treatment of the drug addict, the novel was almost universally praised.

Algren died of a heart attack on May 9, 1981, just weeks before his formal induction into the prestigious American Academy and Institute of Arts and Letters.

Further Reading

Cox, Martha H., and Wayne Chatterton. *Nelson Algren.* Boston: Twayne, 1975.

Drew, Bettina. *Nelson Algren: A Life on the Wild Side.* New York: Putnam, 1989.

Eisinger, Chester E. *Fiction of the Forties.* Chicago: U of Chicago P, 1963.

J. P. Steed

ALI, AGHA SHAHID (1949–2001) Indian American poet, translator, and teacher. Born in Kashmir, he migrated to the United States in 1975. Agha Shahid Ali identified himself as "Kashmiri-American-Kashmiri." This self-designation points not only to the shape of his ethnic life in the United States, but also to his writing, which emphasizes, among other themes, migration, loss, memory, and recovery. Agha Shahid Ali occupies a prominent place in the tradition of Indian poets writing in English in the United States. He brought the plight of Kashmir torn by strife and war to the attention of American poetry readers. He is also credited with introducing the classical Urdu-Persian poetic form, the ghazal, to American literature. In considering his writing life in its entirety, it becomes readily apparent that his greatest achievement lies in his rendering, in well-crafted verse, narratives of dislocation and complex cross-cultural connections.

His poetic voice speaks with eloquence and wit of the multiple histories that constitute his home in India and Kashmir and that have characterized the world throughout time; his poetic voice represents equally well the lives of expatriates and others in situations of exile in relation to an original home. In Agha Shahid Ali's writing, rigorous form serves the concerns of complex content. Thus, for example, Ali wrote verse in Western forms such as sonnets and the difficult sestina and canzone, as well as in the Eastern form of the ghazal; these forms frequently serve as vehicles for emotions, ideas, and conditions originating in geographies and experiences that may be historically and culturally at a distance from the structures themselves.

The eclectic subject matter and use of form can be traced back, in great part, to the poet's personal history, including his family origins. Agha Shahid Ali was born in New Delhi on February 4, 1949, into a Muslim family; he spent most of his childhood and young adulthood in Kashmir. His father, Agha Ashraf Ali, was a notable educator in Srinagar, the capital of Kashmir, and he, along with Shahid's mother, provided a culturally rich and diverse environment for Shahid and his siblings. Shahid spoke English, Kashmiri, and Urdu; while growing up, he was exposed to diverse literary traditions, including Urdu, Persian, Arabic, Hindu, and English. Building upon such an education, he was later author of the study on Eliot, *T. S. Eliot as Editor* (1986). Then in *The Rebel's Silhouette: Selected Poems by Faiz Ahmed Faiz* (1992), Ali translated into English the work of Faiz, the great twentieth-century, politically revolutionary Pakistani Urdu poet of the ghazal. Ali greatly admired and emulated Faiz in his own work. *The Rebel's Silhouette* is a rare and valuable accomplishment, for Ali not only succeeds in translating a complexly structured poetry from one language into another, but also he is effective in rendering into a foreign tongue the cultural and political contexts to which Faiz's poetry belongs.

It was Ali's mother, Sufia, who was particularly responsible for cultivating the love of the ghazal in her children. Agha Shahid Ali's own collection of ghazals, *Call Me Ishmael Tonight: A Book of Gazals* (2003), was published posthumously. Earlier, he had edited *Ravishing Disunities: Real Ghazals in English* (2000). Although the bulk of this innovative volume of verse consists of contributions by American poets, in the introduction Ali provides an important but brief background and lesson in the writing of the ghazal. The paradox of unity-in-disunity and a general tone of sadness are significant attributes of the ghazal for Ali; the tone is best understood as the sentiment that characterizes a relationship of longing between lover and beloved and that underlies the history of the form. These two attributes are preoccupations of Ali's own thought and writing as well.

Sufia continued to be a strong figure throughout her son's life and creative work. His early collection of poetry *The Half-Inch Himalayas* (1987) focuses on a double loss central to the consciousness of the diasporic poet: separation from his homeland simultaneous with inevitable and frequently unfortunate transformations of that homeland. In *The Half-Inch Himalayas*, Ali relies on maternal vision and matrilineal history to weave memory, sentiment, location, and history in order to identify and reproduce the culture and place of his and his family's origins. Thus, in several poems, nostalgic narratives of Kashmir intersect with tales of his mother's and grandmother's attachment to their own and ancestral pasts in India. It is important to note that two significant poems, "Homage to Faiz Ahmed Faiz" and "In Memory of Begum Akhtar" are included in this volume. A great admirer of Begum Akhtar, a master singer of ghazals who also influenced his aesthetics, Ali published early on in his career *In Memory of Begum Akhtar and Other Poems* (1979).

The collection of poems titled *The Country Without a Post Office* (1997) emerged in response to the plight of Kashmir, his beloved homeland, ravaged by strife, but the specific impulse behind the creation of this volume can be traced back to an incident a few years earlier: A friend in Kashmir saw on the street a heap of undelivered mail; there he found a letter to Ali, written by his father. His other volumes of poetry are *Bone Sculpture* (1972), *A Walk Through the Yellow Pages* (1987), *A Nostalgist's Map of America* (1991), and *The Beloved Witness: Selected Poems* (1992). *Rooms Are Never Finished* (2001) was the last collection and was a finalist for the National Book Award.

His last poetry is a dialogue with death and departure. He returns to memories of his mother and to Kashmir; he turns his attention to spaces of transition, such as hotel rooms and airports. Playing on the doubleness of his name, "Shahid," meaning both witness and beloved, he documents the moments of his final departure. Death is envisioned as the meeting of disparate, yet familiar, worlds as well as a release from the longing that inhabits poetry and life itself. As such it is also the ultimate affirmation of the ghazal. Agha Shahid Ali died in December 2001 from a brain tumor. (*See also* South Asian American Literature)

Further Reading

Catamaran Magazine: South Asian American Writing. 1.1 (2003). Special Issue devoted to Agha Shahid Ali.

Katrak, Ketu. "South Asian American Writers: Geography and Memory." *Amerasia Journal* 22.3 (1996): 121–38.

Needham, Lawrence. "'The Sorrows of a Broken Time': Agha Shahid Ali and the Poetry of Loss and Recovery." *Reworlding: The Literature of the Indian Diaspora*. Ed. Emmanuel S. Nelson. Westport, CT: Greenwood Press, 1992. 63–76.

Krishna Lewis

ALISHAN, LEONARDO (1951–2005)   Iranian American writer, poet, and literary critic of Armenian descent. He writes in English and Persian. He was born to Armenian parents in Tehran and came to America in 1973 to pursue his higher education. For a long time he taught Persian literature and comparative literature at the University of Utah, Salt Lake City.

He has participated in numerous conferences including the meetings of the Middle East Studies Association, the Southern Comparative Literature Association, Armenian Studies Association, the American Oriental Society, and the Center for Iranian Research and Analysis where he has presented papers on subjects ranging from classical Persian and Armenian literature to contemporary literary studies in comparative literature. He has been invited for guest lectures and seminars to a number of academic institutions, among them the University of California at Berkeley, University of British Columbia, University of Chicago, University of Texas, Columbia University, New York University, and the University of Armenia at Yerevan.

For Iranian Americans, he is a sought-after poet and critic who knows Persian poetry from ancient times to the present and who can quote an obscure Persian poet of the past and pinpoint the cultural, mythological, and Islamic elements in the piece. He is in love with his birthplace Iran, especially the Iran of yesteryears, which he compares to a beautiful woman in her youth shining like a morning star ("I Saw Susa," 2003). He has translated into English a number of contemporary Persian poems by Nima Yushij, Mehdi Akhavan-Sales, and Ahmad Shamlu among them.

He is known in American literature as the sensitive soul whose heart goes for all human sufferings, whose poetry has won him prestigious awards—Academy of American Poets Award (1977), New England Poetry Club's Daniel Varujan Award (1981), Lullwater Review Poetry Prize (2002), People Before Profits Poetry Prize (2003)—who has mastered the Japanese genres of haiku, senryu, and tanka and can create in those forms, new to many, by skillfully blending his most personal sentiments, his culture, and his heritage. He is a humanitarian. He dreams of sewing all the small and big flags of the small and big nations "into the biggest blanket and tent."

For the Armenian American literature, Alishan is that third-generation survivor of the genocide who lives gripped by the nightmare of genocide, struggling in vain to tell the world the story of that colossal tragedy, his grandmother's story. His strongest literary creations are about his "Granny" and bearing witness to her agony. He shares her agony; he is a part of it. "Gayané, the living martyr" appears in his poetry and fiction in the statue of Mary, with granny's face, burning in a church in Van where Armenians are locked and set on fire by the Turkish persecutors ("Ecce Homo," 2000). She appears as a mad woman who sees Turkish horsemen around her deathbed in a mental hospital in London ("An Exercise on a Genre for the Genocide and Exorcisms," 1992). She is a ladybug living on the Persian rug in his bedroom talking to him, nagging on him why he is so inept to tell the world her story and about the tragedy that befell her nation

("The Lady-Bug and the Persian Rug," 1994). She governs his life and his emotions, his dreams and his waking thoughts. It is through her that Alishan sees the Armenian suffering from the genocide.

Alishan strives to find that proper means of expression for best picturing the inexplicable truth of genocide. "There is no proper genre for giving an artistic expression to the genocide," he complains. "[T]he artist is caught between serving his art and convincing people of his own people's collective catastrophe. He plays both the role of the detached artist and the passionate propagandist. Consequently, there is a chaotic confusion of genres and roles, resulting in a frustrated failure."

His poetry, fiction, and essays are published widely in national and international journals. He has published two collections of poetry, *Dancing Barefoot on Broken Glass* (1991) and *Through a Dewdrop* (2000). (*See also* Armenian American Literature, Armenian Genocide)

Rubina Peroomian

ALKALAY-GUT, KAREN (1945–) Jewish American poet, performer, and professor of English literature living in Israel. Born in London during the Blitz, Alkalay-Gut grew up in Rochester, New York, where she received her PhD in English literature. For the past thirty years she has been teaching poetry at Tel Aviv University and chairing the Israel Association of Writers in English. Alkalay-Gut has published a number of works, including a biography of the Victorian writer Adelaide Crapsey and numerous articles on poets and poetry as well as twenty volumes of verse. The poet has also put out a compact disc with the rock group Thin Lips. She is presently completing *Open Secret: Poetry and Popular Culture*, a work about the intersections between poetics and everyday life in Israel.

In *The Love of Clothes and Nakedness* (1999), one of her most popular volumes of poetry, Alkalay-Gut composes existential odes to clothing past and present. The clothes featured in the poet's work become allegorical figures for the experiences of a diverse body of women. The clothes in *The Love of Clothes and Nakedness* have memories and hopes for the future, as well as worries about the violent present. In this short work—only eighty pages—Alkalay-Gut establishes herself as one of the seminal voices speaking about the experiences of women living in Israel.

So Far, So Good (2004), another volume of verse, continues where *The Love of Clothes and Nakedness* leaves off. In this retrospective and semiautobiographical look at the most dramatic and dangerous moments of a woman's life, Alkalay-Gut moves between events mundane and transcendent. Searching for an apartment and surviving the sudden death of a loved one become personal conduits to looking at the universalities of being a woman in a complicated and often threatening national landscape. *In My Skin* (2000) is Alkalay-Gut's most obviously political volume of poetry. It engages on myriad levels with the histories both of the state of Israel and of the Jewish people. Her work in this volume touches on the plight of Palestinians and

Israelis, immigrants and "natives," women and men, in a nation perpetually at war.

In her essay "Getting Women to Talk about Themselves: My Role Models of the Previous Generation," Alkalay-Gut moves forward with her commitment to documenting the pain that violent conflict carries by writing about the absence of women's stories in the telling of history. She relates her mother's never-recorded tales of being a young Jewish woman in Poland during the **Holocaust**. Beside her mother's narrative of loss and escape in Eastern Europe, the poet places the stories told to her of early pioneer life in Israel conveyed to her by her mother-in-law. Juxtaposing these poignant yet unwritten stories with tales of women—Israeli and Palestinian—during the Intifada allows Alkalay-Gut to make a potent statement about the political importance of recovering and disseminating accounts of women's lives during times of hardship. Perhaps, she contends, these untold stories might have an effect not simply on popular understanding of the costs of conflict on the everyday lives of families but could also become what she calls a "weapon" against war and its dehumanizing power. As a result of her meditations on war and the absence of women's stories, Alkalay-Gut began writing a daily, uncensored diary about her life in the always complicated landscape of Israel.

Alkalay-Gut's writing is interesting not simply because it explicitly engages with questions of gender identity and the difficulties of negotiating daily life in Israel, but also because her work is at the center of debates about language and expatriate life in the nation. The poet was raised in the United States but has spent most of her life teaching and writing in Israel. Choosing to write in English in a nation that has sought to anoint Hebrew as the supreme and only language of the region, Alkalay-Gut finds her work marginalized within the dominant Israeli literary culture. For this reason, her work has become representative of the concerns of many expatriates in Israel. In "Double Diaspora: English writers in Israel," Alkalay-Gut meditates on the position of the English writer in a Hebrew culture. Writers in English, she argues, have had little or no chance of finding audience or arenas for publication in Israel. Alkalay-Gut's pessimism about the place of the English writer in Israel is offset, however, by her enthusiasm about the possibilities of the Internet to alter the status of those writing in English. It is incumbent upon members of what she calls the "double diaspora" to use the Internet to get their words out to a global audience that more than ever needs bulletins from inside Israel. (*See also* Jewish American Poetry)

Further Reading

Baym, Nina. Review of *Alone in the Dark: A Life of Adelaide Crapsey. American Studies* 31.1 (Spring 1990): 125–26.

Lurie, Susan. Review of *Alone in the Dark: A Life of Adelaide Crapsey. American Literature* 62.4 (December 1990): 723–24.

Jennifer Glaser

ALLEN, PAULA GUNN (1939–)   Native American poet, novelist, academic, and political activist. Paula Gunn Allen is a prominent figure in Native American scholarship, known particularly for her unique brand of tribal **feminism**. Her poetry collections include *Coyote's Daylight Trip* (1978), *Shadow Country* (1982), and *Life is a Fatal Disease* (1996). The works examine the dilemma of the Indian's position in modern America. Drawing on Allen's personal struggles as a mixed blood, they resonate with an intimate sense of place, native traditions, and rituals.

In the process of exploring Native aesthetics, Allen has written several controversial articles including "Special Problems in Teaching **Leslie Marmon Silko**'s *Ceremony*." The dynamics of what to reveal and what to conceal while trying to teach and clarify Silko's text are interwoven with the practical issues of how to be a responsible tribal member and academic. Allen's articles are often part of a dialogue to create a critical methodology, a tool with which to read Laguna and other Native works. Her *Studies in American Indian Literature: Critical Essays and Course Designs* (1983) is considered a milestone in Native American critical theory.

The Sacred Hoop: Recovering the Feminine in American Indian Traditions (1986) is one of her many works interrogating how that tribal tradition of woman-centeredness has been undermined in the past five hundred years by the distorting influences of white patriarchal colonization. In her revisionist mythic system, she distinguishes between what she perceives as a more limiting white, Christian, heterosexual perception of creation and alternative forms of creativity stemming from a more organic view of the world.

Likewise, her novel, *The Woman Who Owned the Shadows* (1983), is a reflection of her own mixed heritage and her call for women to engender themselves anew, away from negative racial and gender typing. Here the figure of Shadow Woman is both a symbol of refuge as well as imprisonment, embracing both erasure and power. In highlighting the symbolic correlation between her protagonist's culpability in domestic abuse and the internalization of victimhood in some Indians, Allen stresses how the individual and community are interrelated. Both individual and community need to establish the heroic authority of the mythic woman in their lives in order to facilitate healing and the breaking of imposed **Native American stereotypes** through the tradition of storytelling.

Off the Reservation: Reflections on Boundary-Busting, Border-Crossing Loose Canons (1999) is a collection of essays of diverse content. Topics range from personal recollections and family ancestry to critiques of Western social constructs and ecological treatises. The woman-centric angle that pervades Allen's work is evident also in *Pocahontas: Medicine Woman, Spy, Entrepreneur, Diplomat* (2003), which provides a Native interpretation of the history of **Pocahontas**. Allen illuminates Pocahontas's actions by reading her as one in a long line of "Beloved Women," trained in spiritual, diplomatic, and political ways to serve her tribe. In addition to her creative writing work, Allen has also edited important anthologies including *Spider Woman's Granddaughter* (1989), which won her the American Book Award in 1990.

A self-declared Americanist, Allen supports a multiplicity of cultural identities and a diversity of approaches to the issue of writing identity in America. Yet, Allen's critics have criticized her for oversimplifying the Native position and encouraging a mode of cosmic spiritualism that supports the stereotype of Indians perpetuated by New Age holistic banalities. Such controversy is not new to Allen, and she seems to revel in the exchanges and possibilities that emerge from such interaction. She constantly treads on sensitive territory, criticizing Indians blinded by reverse **racism** who deny the multiple cultures and origins present in the all-embracing category they call "whites."

The extent to which one can belong or be set apart from various communities is an issue that is intensely personal to Allen and which is reflected in much of her writing. Of Laguna Pueblo, Sioux, Scottish, and Lebanese descent, she was married with three children before coming out as a lesbian in the 1970s. Raised in a background that includes Catholic, Native American, Maronite, Jewish, and Protestant heritages, Allen is well aware of the often-irreconcilable conflicts that confuse and influence a person. She relates the focus of her own work and those of her contemporaries to the essence of what haunts American writers: the need to discover their own **identity** and realize their purpose amid the plethora of traditions that are available for them to negotiate. (*See also* Native American Novel, Native American Poetry)

Further Reading

Hanson, Elizabeth I. *Paula Gunn Allen.* Boise State University Western Writers
     Series 96. Ed. Wayne Chatterton and James H. Maguire. Boise, ID: Boise State
     U, 1990.

Poh Cheng Khoo

ALLEN, RICHARD (1760–1831)   African American autobiographer, religious leader, and founder and first bishop of the African Methodist Episcopal (AME) Church. Best-known as a founder of the African Methodist Episcopal Church, Allen was also the author of an autobiography, *The Life Experience and Gospel Labors of the Rt. Rev. Richard Allen: To Which Is Annexed the Rise and Progress of the African Methodist Episcopal Church in the United States* (1833), as well as several notable addresses, including "Address to the Free People of Colour in these United States" (1830) and the coauthor with Absalom Jones of *A Narrative of the Proceedings of the Black People, During the Late Awful Calamity in Philadelphia in the Year 1793 and A Refutation of Some Censures Thrown Upon Them in Some Late Publications* (1794).

Born a slave in Philadelphia, Pennsylvania, Allen and his family were sold in 1768 to a Delaware plantation owner named Stokely Sturgis. While still a slave, Allen (along with his owner) converted to Methodism. Following his conversion, his owner agreed to let him hire himself out in order to raise funds to buy his way out of slavery. By 1786, Allen had earned enough money, through manual labor and preaching, to purchase his freedom.

The same year, Allen began to preach to the racially mixed Methodist congregation of St. George's Church in Philadelphia. When white church leaders responded to the growing black presence in their congregation by constructing a segregated balcony for black worshippers, a discouraged Allen joined the Reverend Absalom Jones in founding the Free African Society in 1787. However, after two years, Allen's devotion to Methodism led him to leave the nondenominational FAS to return to St. George's.

Several years later, after an incident in which Jones challenged the segregated seating arrangements at St. George's and was forcibly ejected, Allen and other free blacks left the congregation. Jones and the Free African Society would found the African Church of Philadelphia, a Protestant Episcopal Church. Allen, however, used his own savings to purchase a former blacksmith's shop and a plot of land that would become Bethel African Church, a new place of worship for African American Methodists.

In 1816, Allen organized a convention of African American Methodists to discuss their shared difficulties. The result was the decision to unify their congregations under the newly formed African Methodist Episcopal (AME) Church, ensuring that African American church leaders retained control over their own churches and remained independent of white ecclesiastical authorities In addition to his role in the founding of the AME, which would become a central institution of African American life in the free North, Allen also published articles in the first-ever African American newspaper, *Freedom's Journal*, in which he attacked **slavery** and the American Colonization Society. He also founded the Bethel Benevolent Society and the African Society for the Education of Youth. Allen's legacy of leadership among free African Americans in the North in both secular and religious matters established him as a pivotal figure in early African American history.

Further Reading

George, Carol V. R. *Segregated Sabbaths: Richard Allen and the Emergence of Independent Black Churches*, 1760–1840. New York: Oxford University Press. 1973.

Gould, Philip. "Race, Commerce, and the Literature of Yellow Fever in Early National Philadelphia." *Early American Literature* 35 (2) (2000): 157–86.

Todd Dapremont

ALLEN, SAMUEL W. (1917–)   African American poet, translator, editor, attorney, and teacher. Samuel W. Allen has published four volumes of poetry (one under the pseudonym of Paul Vesey) that bring into play his broad range of experience as an African American intellectual. His other contributions to the literary and legal professions reflect Allen's sense of his role as a socially committed artist and activist. Allen's wide-ranging international experiences, which include periods of residence in France and Germany, center on his actual and imaginative experience of Africa. In his early life, Allen was a prominent interpreter of the Negritude movement, that group of African, Caribbean, and African American writers who sought to increase consciousness of African culture and history.

Born in Columbus, Ohio, in 1917, Allen has led an eventful life, distinguishing himself in both literary and legal endeavors. Son of a prominent clergyman, Allen studied with **James Weldon Johnson** at Fisk University where he encountered the poets of the **Harlem Renaissance**. From an early age, Allen also became steeped in the poetry of the English and European traditions. After graduation from Fisk, he earned a Doctor of Jurisprudence degree from Harvard Law School in 1941 and started a legal career that continued until 1968. After that, he taught at Tuskegee Institute, Wesleyan University, and Boston University.

While studying in Paris, Allen met a number of American expatriate writers, including **Richard Wright** and **James Baldwin**, and others who belonged to the Negritude movement, such as Leopold Senghor. Allen became associated with the journal, *Présence Africaine*, which he helped to edit and in which he published poems. While in Europe, he also began to write essays that explored Pan-African concerns, including "Tendencies in African Poetry" and "Negritude and Its Relevance to the American Negro Writer." Allen defines Negritude as an endeavor to recover a world in which the Negro writer once again has a sense of whole identity and a non-subordinate role. He analyzes the unique position of the African American, more alienated from social power than either the African or Caribbean writer. In other essays, Allen considers the legacy of colonialism and the potential contribution of the poet to renewing formerly colonized national cultures, both in Africa and in Islamic nations.

Allen's poems express the powerful emotions generated by the poet's reflections on African American history. Not infrequently, Allen's poetry returns to the Alabama homeland of his grandparents and to the associated themes of slavery and Reconstruction. In this writing he expresses a wide spectrum of his and others' racial feelings, from rage and bitterness to pride and strength. Allen interprets the history of American society in terms of racial domination. Despite its realism, Allen's poetry holds out the hope of racial progress.

Further Reading

Brittin, Ruth L. "Samuel W. Allen." *Dictionary of Literary Biography*. Vol. 41. Ed. Trudier Harris and Thadious M. Davis. Detroit: Gale, 1985. 8–17.

Mphahlele, Ezekial. *The African Image*. New York: Praeger, 1962. 49–55.

Redmond, Eugene. *Drumvoices: The Mission of Afro-American Poetry: A Critical History*. Garden City, NY: Anchor/Doubleday, 1976.

Stern, Frederick C. "Black Lit., White Crit?" *College English* 35 (March 1974): 637–58.

Jeffrey J. Folks

ALLEN, WOODY (1935–) Jewish American comic, screenwriter, director, actor, playwright, and fiction writer. Born Allen Stewart Konigsberg in Brooklyn, New York, Woody Allen has become a legend in the movie world, having produced, directed, or starred in more than three dozen films. After failed attempts in academic study at New York University and City College of New York, Allen pursued a career as a stand-up comic. He also began writing jokes for newspapers and television, becoming involved with such notables as Bob Hope, Carl Reiner, Mel Brooks, and **Larry Gelbart**, and writing for *The Garry Moore Show, The Sid Caesar Show*, and Alan Funt's *Candid Camera*. Numerous appearances on *The Tonight Show* heightened his fame and also led to his serving as guest host for Johnny Carson.

In 1965, Allen directed his first film, *What's New Pussycat*, which was critically panned but financially successful. It marked the debut of an incredibly prolific and diverse career that has produced such memorable movies as *Crimes and Misdemeanors, Manhattan, The Purple Rose of Cairo, Zelig*, and *Bullets Over Broadway*, garnering Allen fifteen Academy Award nominations along the way. In 1978, one of Allen's most famous works, *Annie Hall*—a highly biographical work about its star, Diane Keaton—won Academy Awards for Best Film, Best Screenplay, Best Director, and Best Actress (Keaton). In 1987, Allen won the Oscar for Best Screenplay for another popular film, *Hannah and Her Sisters*, which was also semi-biographical, based partly on the relationships between Mia Farrow and her two sisters.

Allen has played the central character in many of his films, establishing an onscreen persona as a *schlemiel*—a Yiddish term for a bungling, insecure, often neurotic individual, and a portrayal that seems in many ways to parallel Allen's own **identity**. He is well known for having spent years in Freudian psychoanalysis, an experience that often finds its way into his films, usually through sardonic humor. Allen's personal life also became grist for the tabloids in the 1990s, when he and his lover Mia Farrow separated after she discovered that Allen had been having an affair with Soon-Yi Previn, Farrow's daughter by ex-husband André Previn. (Allen and Previn later married and adopted a daughter.) The highly public vituperation between Allen and Farrow was exacerbated by Allen's failed quest for custody of their child Satchel, as well as for two of his stepchildren. In 1992, when the film *Husbands and Wives* opened, it was regarded by many critics as

Woody Allen in *Annie Hall. United Artists/The Kobal Collection.*

143

autobiographical, presenting as it does a cynical and satirical view of marriage and relationships. Others, however, considered the timing of the film to be merely coincidental, and in fact it was highly praised, winning Oscar nominations for Best Screenplay as well as for Judy Davis's role as Best Supporting Actress.

Allen is renowned for his prolific output, always working on a new film even as he is completing another. He is also an active fiction writer, having published numerous short stories, many of them collected in his three volumes *Without Feathers*, *Getting Even*, and *Side Effects*. In addition, Allen is a talented clarinet player, performing regularly in New York with his New Orleans Jazz Band. The 1996 film *Wild Man Blues* documents one of the occasional short tours his band takes, while *Sweet and Lowdown* (1999) also reflects his interest in **jazz**.

Chief influences on Allen's work are legendary filmmakers Ingmar Bergman and Federico Fellini, for whom he has expressed intense admiration. Films such as *Interiors* (1979)—a notorious failure—*Stardust Memories* (1980), *A Midsummer Night's Sex Comedy* (1982), and *Another Woman* (1988) pay tribute to these mentors.

Further Reading

Benayoun, Robert. *The Films of Woody Allen*. New York: Harmony Books, 1986.

Curry Renee R. *Perspectives on Woody Allen*. New York: G. K. Hall & Co., 1996.

Girgus, Sam B. *The Films of Woody Allen*. New York: Cambridge UP, 1993.

King, Kimball. *Woody Allen: A Casebook*. New York: Routledge, 2001.

Lax, Eric. *Woody Allen: A Biography*. New York: Knopf, 1991.

Pogel, Nancy. *Woody Allen*. Boston: Twayne, 1987.

Karen C. Blansfield

ALVAREZ, JULIA (1950–)   Dominican American novelist and poet, born in New York City and raised there for part of her childhood as well as in the Dominican Republic. Julia Alvarez is one of the most popular Latina authors in the United States and is the first Dominican American to have her work accepted for publication by a major publisher.

Alvarez's family arrived in the United States from the Dominican Republic before she was born and then, homesick, returned to their native land when Alvarez was only three months old. After Rafael Trujillo's dictatorship began to divide the country, making it unstable for thousands of Dominicans, her family returned to the United States. For Alvarez's father, flight from the Dominican Republic was crucial, because he was directly involved in attempts to overthrow Trujillo's government. Upon arriving back in the United States, Alvarez found a world that was far from welcoming to new immigrants, especially those who spoke a different language or did not look "American." Many of her experiences are captured in her first novel, *How the Garcia Girls Lost Their Accents* (1991), which is based on four sisters who come from the Dominican Republic to the United States. The sisters go through life having to balance the cultural demands and expectations at home with the norms in the United States. They have difficulty appeasing their parents, particularly their father, who believes in the values of the Old World Generation (i.e., the Dominican Republic). The sisters find that while they adapt to customs in the United States, they cannot get entirely away from their father's parental grasp. Even as older women, they struggle with the demand to treat him with a respect that is consistent with the way that he would be treated in the Dominican Republic. But, of course, it is not just parent-child conflicts that help define the process of **assimilation**. Alvarez's portrayals of other conflicts that arise as a result of assimilation are brilliantly captured in her novels, poetry, and her prose.

Julia Alvarez. *Photo by Bill Eichner. Reprinted by permission of Susan Bergholz Literary Services, New York. All rights reserved.*

The Woman I Kept to Myself (2004), an autobiographical collection of poems, each thirty lines long, closely examines Alvarez's life as a writer and expounds on her internal struggle to keep stories to herself as her mother would have preferred. It also discusses her own career choice of becoming a writer. Within this collection, one can find descriptions of the pain and sacrifices that she and her family had to go through in the United States as they made decisions on everything from schooling to which neighborhoods in which to live. She details, for example, the taunts from children who made fun of her in and out school when she was growing up. Likewise, in *Homecoming* (1984; 1996), she explores similar themes of how **immigration** often results in some type of loss, whether in the form of identity or in one's connection to their family's ancestry. Not surprisingly, she has also written extensively about this subject in her collections of essays, *Something to Declare* (1998). In the work, she discusses the influence that English and Spanish have had on her life. English opened up a new world for her, helping her understand her parents' secret conversations and eventually allowing her to become a best-selling author. Meanwhile, Spanish permitted her to become more creative in her own writing. Although she writes in English, she attributes the verbal rhythm and word choices to her knowledge of the Spanish language.

Alvarez's novels provide a dignified look at Latinas. The Garcia girls rebel, no doubt, but they rarely do so without some reasoning that the reader cannot understand. This is one of Alvarez's great gifts as a writer—

she is able to depict characters as full, well-rounded individuals who do not base their decisions on hasty judgments, but rather on an oftentimes complicated cultural labyrinth. ¡Yo! (1997) continues to portray the strong-willed character, Yolanda, who was introduced in *How the Garcia Girls Lost Their Accents*, and who provides a commentary on many issues pertaining to women. In her two historical novels, *In the Name of Salome* (2000) and *In the Time of the Butterflies* (1994), Alvarez pays homage to women who have become cultural icons in Dominican history. The former is based on the life of Salome Urena, a **mulatto** woman who becomes the Dominican Republic's most famous poet, and her daughter, Camila, a professor at Vassar College who upon retirement decides to leave the United States and go to Cuba. The latter novel is based on the Mirabal sisters—Las Mariposas—who become involved in clandestine efforts against the government and regime, and one day are brutally murdered. Alvarez's children's books also center on gender, though on a lesser scale. *How Tia Lola Came to (Visit) Stay* (2001) looks at the role of women in an extended family, while *The Secret Footprints* (2000) tells of a mythical female creature, Guapa, who boldly ventures into the world of human beings.

Alvarez's works have appeared in such major publications as *The New Yorker, Ploughshares, American Poetry Review*, and *The New York Times Magazine*. The New York Public Library selected Alvarez as one of fifty poets included in its exhibit, *The Hand of the Poet: Original Manuscripts by 100 Masters, from John Donne to Julia Alvarez*.

She has received numerous awards, including the Hispanic Heritage Award in Literature, the Jessica Nobel-Maxwell Poetry Prize from *American Poetry Review*, and Woman of the Year by *Latina Magazine*. She has been a finalist for the National Book Award, a Robert Frost Poetry Fellow at the Breadloaf Writers' Conference, and has been a recipient of a grant from the National Endowment for the Arts. She is a writer-in-residence at Middlebury College. (*See also* Dominican American Novel, Dominican American Poetry)

Further Reading

Jacques, Ben. "Julia Alvarez: Real Flights of Imagination." *Americas* 53.1 (January–February 2001): 22–29.

Rosario-Sievert, Heather. "Anxiety, Repression, and Return: The Language of Julia Alvarez." *Readerly/Writerly Texts: Essays on Literature, Literary/Textual Criticism, and Pedagogy* 4.1 (Spring–Summer 1997): 125–39.

Rosario-Sievert, Heather. "Conversation with Julia Alvarez." *Review: Latin American Literature and Arts* 54 (Spring 1997): 31–37.

Jose B. Gonzalez

AMANUENSIS   The institution of **slavery** in the United States prevented the proper education of enslaved African Americans. Illiteracy was common within the slave population and almost no self-education opportunities existed. The employment of an amanuensis was a way in which slaves could document their experiences by relating their stories to a person who would record and write down their narrative. However, since the slave narrating the story could not read what the amanuensis wrote, stories related by slaves could be edited or changed in order to cater to a specific audience or book publisher. Thus the employment of an amanuensis to assist in the relaying of a slave's experience could ultimately complicate or call into question the truth of that experience.

Slave narratives were autobiographical or biographical accounts of the lives and experiences of American slaves told by the slaves who suffered through the barbarous treatment and conditions imposed upon them. As a result, the use of slave narratives became an important force in the struggle for social justice and freedom. One aim of the slave narrative was to relay the mistreatment of slaves to a broader audience in order to educate people and create support for the **abolition** of slavery. To ready these stories for publication assistance came in the form of an "editor" who acted as the amanuensis. This was the most common method of recording slave histories and experiences. Famous narratives such as those of Henry Box Brown and **Sojourner Truth** were both recorded by amanuensis. However, the use of the amanuensis or editor could quite easily complicate the reality of the stories the slaves were trying to tell. Though the slaves could share their experiences verbally there was no way for them to read or know of what changes or embellishments the amanuensis could and in some cases did make. Thus a slave would not be aware of places in the text where violence or abuse might be softened or omitted by an editor in order to make the story more palatable to a larger (white) audience. Complicating our understanding of slave narratives, the use of amanuensis calls into question the claims that a book was "biographical" or "autobiographical" as there were no ways to confirm the validity of the tale being told. In some cases an amanuensis or "ghost writer" could fabricate an entire story, but these instances were not common.

However, despite the complications that arose, the use of the amanuensis ultimately ensured the survival of the slave narrative and assisted in communicating the reality of slavery to a wider audience, while creating an historical record based on the stories of the slaves.

Further Reading

Andrews, William. *To Tell a Free Story: The First Century of Afro-American Autobiography, 1760–1865.* Champaign: U of Illinois P, 1986.

Andrews, William, and Henry Louis Gates Jr., eds. *Slave Narratives.* New York: Library of America, 2000.

Foster, Francis Smith *Witnessing Slavery: The Development of Ante-Bellum Slave Narratives.* Westport, CT: Greenwood Press, 1979.

Steven Bruce

AMERICA IS IN THE HEART (1946)   **Carlos Bulosan**'s autobiographical novel presents one of the most vivid documentations of the lives of

Filipinos on the West Coast and in Alaska during the 1930s. Through his protagonist, Allos, Bulosan portrays the racist violence, segregation, and exploitation endured but also fought by the approximately 45,000 Pinoys (Filipinos in America) who worked on the American mainland. Presenting these experiences as a "personal history" (the book's subtitle) lent greater authenticity, force, and mass appeal to the narrative than presenting it as novel would have. Nonetheless, *America Is in the Heart* is a fictionalized account of Bulosan's experiences and those of other Pinoys.

Spanning the end of World War I to the bombing of Pearl Harbor, the book is divided into four parts. Part I, which depicts Allos's childhood in the Philippines, represents Filipino peasant life as it is shaped by capitalist (under) development and the colonial relationship between the Philippines and the United States. Like other peasants, Allos's family loses their land to the native bourgeoisie, but they are not simple victims: Allos is aware of revolts against absentee landlords, and his mother demonstrates fortitude and compassion in her trade. America's impact on Allos's family is clearest in his brother's Western education, a primary reason why they immigrate to the United States for a better life. The remaining three sections take place in America, where, contrary to his expectations, Allos continually encounters racist violence and economic exploitation working in the Alaskan canneries and the fields of the west coast, while gambling dens and dance halls strip Pinoys of their paltry wages. Through meeting other Pinoys who have been radicalized and intellectuals who foster his literary interests, Allos develops his own class and racial consciousness. He becomes involved with unionizing and educating other migrant laborers to fight for their rights, and the novel ends with Allos affirming his faith in America.

America Is in the Heart creates an unresolved tension between Allos's idealistic faith in the potential of American democracy, and the novel's careful documentation of the unrelenting violence faced by Filipinos. Another opposition lies between the nonlinear plot presenting the directionless lives of farm workers denied the American dream of upward mobility, and the trajectory of Allos's political development that can be traced through the sprawling narrative. The production of these tensions can be examined through the text's amalgamation of autobiography, collective history, and the social realist novel. Finally, gender and sexuality are significant themes, for the text explores relationships between Filipino men and white women, which resulted from the gendered imbalance in Filipino labor migration. (*See also* Filipino American Novel)

Further Reading

Alquizola, Marilyn. "Subversion or Affirmation: The Text and Subtext of *America Is in the Heart." Asian Americans: Comparative and Global Perspectives*. Ed. Shirley Hune, et al. Pullman: Washington State UP, 1991.

Lee, Rachel. *The Americas of Asian American Literature: Gendered Fictions of Nation and Transnation*. Princeton, NJ: Princeton UP, 1999.

Mostern, Kenneth. "Why Is America in the Heart?" *Critical Mass: A Journal of Asian American Cultural Criticism* 2 (1995): 35–65.

Cheryl Higashida

AMERICAN INDIAN MOVEMENT This activist movement enjoyed a meteoric rise to fame and an equally swift demise in the late 1960s and early 1970s. Although it may not have accomplished all of its political goals, this movement did raise national awareness of the social and economic problems faced by American Indians; it also created resurgence in popularity of literature by Native American writers.

The actual organization that took the name American Indian Movement (AIM) was founded in Minneapolis, Minnesota, in 1968; however, the term "American Indian Movement" has been applied generally to the series of activist demonstrations by Native Americans that took place during this time period, even though AIM was not directly involved in all of them.

Inspired by the **Civil Rights Movement** gaining prominence in the late 1960s, Chippewa Dennis Banks, in prison for violating parole, decided that he would build a movement to remedy the social and political problems his people faced. Once released, Banks formed AIM, and at the first meeting he invited another Chippewa, Clyde Bellecourt, to help lead the new organization.

One of AIM's early projects included the AIM patrol, which provided attorneys for Indians arrested in the Twin Cities and monitored police treatment of Indians they took into custody. AIM's first "activist" moment came in November 1969 when its members visited a Minnesota school to protest a Thanksgiving play that depicted Indians in stereotypical and insulting ways. During these early days, AIM functioned primarily as a local support group for Minneapolis Indians, providing a place to go if they needed a ride, a job, a loan, or a place to stay. Quickly, local chapters of AIM sprang up in other large cities as interest in the organization spread, and with the addition of Lakota Russell Means to their leadership, AIM began to seek opportunities to address Indian issues on a national level.

One of the first protests to gain national headlines came in November 1969 when a group of Indians occupied Alcatraz Island with the goal of forming a Native American cultural center and university there. While AIM was not directly involved in the occupation, the event raised awareness of the growing discontent among Native Americans with their social and living conditions. However, as would be the pattern for many of these symbolic protests, disagreement among the occupation's leaders led to the group being evacuated in June 1971. But the event sparked other demonstrations at national monuments such as Mount Rushmore, Plymouth Rock, and at nuclear missile sites across the country.

Alcatraz did have a role in inspiring AIM's first national event, however; the shooting death of Richard Oakes, one of the leaders of the Alcatraz occupation, touched off anger and dismay in AIM's ranks. Joining with other Indian organizations, AIM organized a cross-country caravan that traveled through the larger Indian communities in the west, convened in Minneapolis to draft a position paper, and then proceeded to Washington, DC, to present their demands to President Richard Nixon. The caravan took the name of "The Trail of Broken Treaties" to call attention to its primary objective—restoration of Indian treaty rights.

Intended as a peaceful demonstration of Indian unity and an opportunity to call attention to the problem of treaty rights, the caravan was plagued by disorganization and logistical problems. Miscommunication between organizers of the caravan and leaders in Washington contributed to distrust on both sides and the caravan arrived in Washington, DC without a place to stay. In desperation, the Indians took over the Bureau of Indian Affairs (BIA) Building, renaming it "The Native American Embassy." From here, AIM attempted to organize discussions centering on the issue of treaty rights but was thwarted by more miscommunication and the fact that they had chosen the week of the presidential election, which meant most government officials were on the campaign trail. The occupation ended with vandalism to the BIA building and members of the caravan dispersing without accomplishing their goals. However, the occupation once again put AIM in the national spotlight.

Despite this disappointment, AIM had several successes, the most notable of which occurred in Gordon, Nebraska, where AIM came to the aid of the family of Lakota Raymond Yellow Thunder, who was beaten and killed by three white men. AIM used the incident to bring about reform in how police in the reservation border town treated Indians, thereby winning the respect of the reservation Indians.

But AIM's finest moment came in 1972 when the movement went to the Pine Ridge Indian reservation in South Dakota to help the Oglala Sioux reform the current tribal government. This request resulted in AIM's decision to occupy the village of **Wounded Knee**, site of an 1890 massacre of Indians by U.S. soldiers. Here AIM declared itself to be "The Independent Oglala Nation" and broadened their goals from reforming the tribal government to negotiating treaty rights with the U.S. government.

The occupation captured national attention for several weeks and sparked sympathetic donations of food to those barricaded in the small town. Eventually, however, it became an armed standoff between the AIM occupiers and their sympathizers and the FBI and other government agencies. Finally, after ten weeks, an agreement was negotiated and the occupiers left Wounded Knee, many to face criminal charges. The ensuing trials and legal actions served to essentially dismantle AIM by imprisoning or discrediting its leaders.

After Wounded Knee, AIM faded from the spotlight as quickly as it had become a center of media attention, and the Indian movement collapsed, in part due to its own internal inconsistencies and disagreements. Some reform had been achieved, but much remained to be done. But the Movement's lasting effect was not political reform, but rather the sense of pride in being Indian it instilled in tribal communities and reservations.

Further Reading

Mathiesson, Peter. *In the Spirit of Crazy Horse*. New York: Viking, 1983.

Smith, Paul Chaat, and Robert Allen Warrior. *Like a Hurricane: The Indian Movement from Alcatraz to Wounded Knee*. New York: New Press, 1996.

Patti J. Kurtz

AMISH LITERATURE   The Amish are an ethnic religious group that grew out of the Radical Reformation. Named after their leader, Jacob Amman, who led the group to split off from the less conservative Mennonites in 1693, the Amish have retained many traditional religious practices as well as the rural farming and family-oriented lifestyle of their ancestors. The Amish were early immigrants to America. Most arrived from the southern Rhine valley and Switzerland in the early 1700s when Pennsylvania opened its borders to immigrants and refugees from Europe looking for religious freedom and the privilege of owning their own land. Today, the Amish are concentrated in Ohio, Pennsylvania, and Indiana, but are also scattered across the country in Colorado, Delaware, Florida, Idaho, Illinois, Iowa, Kansas, Kentucky, Maine, Maryland, Michigan, Minnesota, Mississippi, Missouri, Montana, New York, North Carolina, Nebraska, Oklahoma, Texas, Virginia, Washington, West Virginia, Wisconsin, and Ontario, Canada, in 333 small settlements, where the majority of Amish families continue to practice small-scale farming. In places where farmland has grown expensive and scarce, and light industry is profitable, more Amish are starting their own businesses (e.g., carpentry, plumbing, construction, or woodwork) or working in factory jobs. The Amish make friendly neighbors, but they take to heart the Biblical injunction to be "in the world but not of it." Therefore, many of their church rules reinforce a sense of "separation from the world." The Amish are easily distinguished from other Americans because of their distinctive plain dress and their rejection of technological developments. All Amish are bilingual. They speak a Low German dialect among themselves and use eighteenth-century High German in their church services, but they are also fluent in English, which they learn in grade school. The Old Order Amish do not own or drive cars, trucks, or tractors with rubber tires, nor do they allow electricity or telephones in their homes. New Order Amish may allow ownership or use of motorized vehicles and a limited array of technological devices, but they do not allow radio or television and continue the practice of plain dress. The Old Order Amish maintain "separation from the world" in a number of other practices as well: They forbid higher education beyond the eighth grade, except in rare instances. They do not accept social security or other government insurance, believing that the community should take care of its own people. Along with a number of other Anabaptist groups, such as the Mennonites, Hutterites, and the Brethren in Christ, the Amish abstain from participation in military service, as they believe that participation in war violates the Biblical injunction "thou shalt not kill."

Although the Amish do not receive higher education, they are literate and well educated in reading, writing, arithmetic, and basic history and geography. They have been sharing news of local congregations and settlements nationwide for over 100 years in the Amish newspaper, *The Budget*. While the Amish have not been traditionally known as producers of literature, in recent years a number of publishing ventures among the Amish—and the achievements of a few writers beyond the Amish community—have led to the development of an "Amish Literature." The first impetus for literature among the Amish has been the growth of Amish schools staffed by Amish teachers. Most Amish communities today have their own one-room schoolhouses and provide and train their own teachers. This increase in private parochial schools among the Amish has precipitated a need for reading materials appropriate for families, school, and teachers. Responding to this need, two Amish farmers, David Wagler and Joseph Stoll, founded Pathway Publishing in 1964. Along with Anabaptist classics, Amish-authored works, and a series of graded readers for Amish school children, Pathway publishes three periodicals for Amish markets on its diesel-powered presses: *The Blackboard Bulletin* (for teachers, parents, and school boards), *The Young Companion* (for Amish youth), and *Family Life* (for families and general readers). The latter two publications have offered some Amish-authored fiction as well as human interest stories, essays, editorials, recipes, and household tips. Many of the articles in these publications are authored anonymously, as individuality is discouraged among the Amish. Selections from the first twenty-five years of *Family Life* (1968–92) have been collected by Brad Igou in *The Amish in Their Own Words* (1999). In addition to these publications, Amish value genealogies and family histories, a number of which have been printed on Amish presses. A genre of literature that thrives among the Amish is the story of the sudden or saintly death, such as Emma King's *Joys, Sorrows, and Shadows* (1992), an account of her aunt's murder in Lancaster County. These works are usually self-published and available only through Amish venues. Collections of memorial poems written in honor of a deceased relative or friend are a related genre. This literature is reinforced by the "Sudden Death Reunion"—an annual gathering of those who have lost a loved one in this way.

Fiction among the Amish is rare, but novels about the Amish are common on tourist bookshelves in Lancaster County, Pennsylvania and Shipshewana, Indiana. Increasingly, some of these are written by ex-Amish or Mennonite authors, joining the ranks of such authors as Joseph W. Yoder, whose *Rosanna of the Amish* (1940; rvsd. 1973; rpt. 1995), a novel allegedly based on the life of the author's Amish mother, is arguably the first in its genre. Mary Christner Borntrager, author of the "Ellie's People" series, was raised Amish. To date, the many novels in this series have sold over half a million copies. Carrie

Bender, the pen name of an Old Order woman from a non-Amish group in Lancaster County, is the author of two popular novel series about the Amish, the "Whispering Brook" and "Miriam's Journal" series, published by Herald Press. Levi Miller, the Amish-born author of *Ben's Wayne* (1989), is now the Director of Herald Press, the Mennonite publisher of most of the aforementioned novels. These novels about the Amish by former Amish or Old Order writers are largely directed at the Christian fiction market. However, a great number of purportedly "Amish novels" are written by authors of Christian and romance genres such as Beverly Lewis or Annette Blair and have little or no authenticity as literary productions by the Amish. As the popular appetite for Amish fiction has grown, there have even been a number of impostors presenting themselves as Amish authors of Amish fiction. For those who would study the representation of the Amish in American popular culture, David Weaver-Zercher's *The Amish in the American Imagination* (2001) offers a valuable guide.

Few Amish authors of serious literature are known outside of the Amish community today, but there are several notable exceptions. The best known of these is David Kline, a writer of literary nonfiction, who got his start writing essays for Pathway Publishing's *Family Life*. Kline collected a number of these essays to create a book of nature-oriented meditations on sustainable agriculture, *Great Possessions: An Amish Farmer's Journal* (1990; rpt. 2001). Wendell Berry wrote the foreword for *Great Possessions*, which was reviewed in such prominent places as *The New York Times Book Review*. It was followed by *Scratching the Woodchuck: Nature on an Amish Farm* (1997), chosen as a Quality Paperback Book Club Alternate selection. David Kline still works on his ancestral farm in Fredericksburg, Ohio, and publishes *Farming Magazine*, devoted to small-scale organic farming and sustainable agriculture. Julia Kasdorf, author of the poetry collection, *Sleeping Preacher* (1992), winner of the Agnes Lynch Starrett Poetry Prize and the Great Lakes Colleges Association Award for New Writing, writes of the Big Valley Amish from whom she is descended in this fine collection. Four of these poems were published by *The New Yorker*. Although Kasdorf's parents left their Amish upbringing, the communal stories of her Amish ancestry are clearly inscribed on Kasdorf's work. The opening poem in this collection, "Green Market, New York," describes the encounter between an Amish pie vendor and the author in an open air market in Manhattan. "She knows I know better than to pay six dollars for this," the poet writes, referring to their common values as she sheepishly buys a pie at tourist prices. Kasdorf does not sentimentalize her roots, but rather portrays the anguish of moving through the world with conflicting loyalties—some to the ethnic group, some to the literary vocation she has chosen. Her biography of Joseph W. Yoder, *Fixing Tradition* (2003), is a valuable contribution to the scanty criticism available on Amish literature. Recently, G. C. Waldrep, a convert to the New Order Amish (he was a member of the Yanceyville, North Carolina New Order Amish group from 1995–2000), was awarded the Colorado Prize for his first book of poetry, *Goldbeater's Skin (2003)*. Unlike the traditional Amish, who do not receive education beyond the eighth grade, Waldrep has a BA degree from Harvard and a PhD in American History from Duke University. His work is widely published in literary reviews and he teaches at the University of Iowa. While his poetry reveals a deeply religious sensibility, it is also informed by his advanced study of contemporary poetry, something almost unheard of in the Amish community. He is also the author of an historical study, *Southern Workers and the Search for Community* (2000). Waldrep is a writer whose work and faith reveal the ways in which converts can shape the literary profile of a community as well as the ways in which the Amish faith and way of life can profoundly shape the work of someone who adopts this lifestyle and culture as an adult.

For many years *Amish Society* (fourth ed., 1993), by John A. Hostetler, an anthropologist who was raised in an Old Order Amish family, has been considered the definitive anthropological study of the Amish. This work should be included in any study of Amish literature for its literary merits, for its accurate information about Amish communities, and as the product of a formerly Amish author. Hostetler also compiled the first general anthology of writings by the Amish: *Amish Roots: A Treasury of History, Wisdom, and Lore* (1989).

Further Reading

Guthrie, Margaret E. Review of David Kline's *Great Possessions*. *The New York Times Book Review* (May 9, 1990): 23.

Hostetler, John A. *Amish Roots: A Treasury of History, Wisdom, and Lore*. Baltimore: Johns Hopkins UP, 1993.

———. *Amish Society*. Fourth ed. Baltimore: Johns Hopkins UP, 1993.

Igou, Brad. *The Amish in Their Own Words*. Scottdale, PA: Herald Press, 1999.

Kasdorf, Julia. *Fixing Tradition: Joseph W. Yoder, Amish American*. Telford, PA: Pandora Press, 2003.

Rukoff, Joanna Smith. "First." Profile of G. C. Waldrep. *Poets & Writers* 32.3 (May/June 2004): 67.

Weaver-Zercher, David. *The Amish in the American Imagination*. Baltimore: Johns Hopkins UP, 2001.

———. *Writing the Amish: The Worlds of John A. Hostetler*. State College: Pennsylvania State UP, 2005.

Ann Hostetler

ANAYA, RUDOLFO (1937–) Mexican American novelist, essayist, and emeritus professor of English at the University of New Mexico. Anaya is renowned for his first work, **Bless Me, Ultima** (1972), a best-selling Chicano novel that remains on high school and college reading lists. *Bless Me, Ultima* was awarded the 1971 Premio Quinto Sol (Fifth Sun Award) and is the first of what Anaya considers his New Mexico trilogy, followed in 1976 by *Heart of Aztlán* and in 1979 by *Tortuga*. In addition to these and other novels, he has written essays, short stories, plays, poetry, and children's books, and edited several anthologies. In 2001 Anaya received the National Medal of Arts, one of the highest civilian awards.

The Trilogy

Bless Me, Ultima

Bless Me, Ultima is a coming-of-age novel in which the child, Antonio Márez Luna of Guadalupe, New Mexico, struggles to reconcile two conflicting heritages: the land-loving farmers on his mother's side, and the wandering *vaquero* (cowboy) men of the *llano* (plains) on his father's side. Ultima, the "last" one, comes to live with the family in the year before Antonio begins first grade in the local Anglo school. She is a *curandera*, or folk healer, also called "*la Grande*," or "the great one." Her powers to heal seem mysterious to the very people she cures; though she is deeply respected she is also somewhat feared. Ultima is an essential element in these formative years for Antonio. She teaches him how to gather and use herbs; she encourages him to respect the earth, whether farmland or *llano*; and she helps him to understand the dreams interspersed throughout the text. Indicated by italicized print, Antonio's dreams express his fears or presage the future, but they sometimes recall events that he remembers only subconsciously, such as his birth.

In the nearly two years that pass in the novel, Antonio faces four deaths, two of them violent and one of them the drowning of his own young friend Florence. He begins school and must speak English for the first time in his young life. He learns to read and becomes successful academically, fueling his mother's hopes that he will be a priest, a learned man. He studies the catechism and receives his first communion, but he also learns the legend of the golden carp, a god-become-fish, a pagan god.

Bless Me, Ultima contains many dichotomies: Catholic/pagan; witchcraft/folk healing; farms/plains; Spanish/English; moon (Luna)/oceans (Márez, or "*mares*"). Narrated from the young Antonio's perspective, but with the retrospection of the adult Antonio, some critics have criticized the novel for a worldview that at times seems rather sophisticated for a seven-year-old boy. Nevertheless, *Bless Me, Ultima* remains an essential text of the Chicano novel of **identity**.

Heart of Aztlán

The second novel of the trilogy, *Heart of Aztlán*, portrays one year in the life of the Chávez family, comprising the father, Clemente; the mother, Adelita; and four of their five children, Jason, Benjie, Juanita, and Ana. They move from their homeland of rural Guadalupe to urban Albuquerque. The fifth son, Roberto, already lives in the Chicano neighborhood of Barelas with his wife. The loss of the family land, sold off to pay debts, initiates the difficult transition from rural to urban, traditional to modern. Clemente gets work at the railroad, replacing a dead worker, and later becomes embroiled in the struggle for workers' rights. The daughters find work to help support the family, and quickly become more independent than tradition allows, undermining Clemente's authority as the patriarch. The *pachuco* or Chicano dude identity attracts both Benjie, who joins a gang and becomes a drug seller and user, and Ana, who drops out of high school. Adelita adapts more readily to change than her husband, who temporarily loses his way, after losing his job and seeking solace in drinking.

Just as Antonio had Ultima as his guide, Clemente has a guide in Crispín, a blind poet-seer who plays a magical blue guitar. Crispín tells Clemente that only by returning to the true "heart of Aztlán" can he find himself and help his people, whether his family, his barrio neighbors, or his abused co-workers at the railroad. The myth of Aztlán is the myth of origin, a kind of Aztec Paradise. Chicanos, or Mexican Americans, trace their heritage to the comingling of the Spanish conquerors and the Aztec Indians. Aztlán is the holy land of origin for the Aztecs, who were instructed by the gods to find their homeland by searching for a cactus upon which an eagle would be mounted, holding a serpent in his beak. That same image is on the Mexican flag today, but for Clemente, Aztlán represents the true source of knowledge and identity, in contrast to the confusion of modern, capitalistic life.

Myth is central to *Heart of Aztlán*, but here myth is used to tell the story of a people, "*la raza*," or "the race." Whereas *Bless Me, Ultima* relates the development of a young boy from a first-person perspective, *Heart of Aztlán* uses a third-person narration to tell the story of the Chávez family, and relates that story to the larger socioeconomic context of many Chicanos. *Bless Me, Ultima* is an early novel of individual Chicano identity; *Heart of Aztlán*, though less popular and less well executed, is one of the earliest novels to deal with the theme of the Chicano movement, and Chicano group identity.

Tortuga

Tortuga (Turtle) completes Anaya's New Mexico trilogy, returning to the first-person narration so successful in *Bless Me, Ultima*. Tortuga is the nickname of the sixteen-year-old protagonist, so called because his paralyzed body is enclosed in a cast reminiscent of a turtle's shell. This may be Anaya's most autobiographical novel: as an adolescent he was paralyzed instantly when he dove into an irrigation canal and hit the bottom, fracturing two vertebrae in his neck. Like his protagonist Tortuga, Anaya suffered through months of therapy.

Tortuga's physical journey is a short one, from his home across the New Mexican desert to the Crippled Children and Orphans Hospital where he meets other crippled children. Among them is Salomón, a paralytic mute who communicates telepathically with Tortuga, serving as Tortuga's guide, instructing him through visitations to his dreams. Salomón also introduces Tortuga the paralyzed teenager to Tortuga Mountain, a "magic mountain" near the hospital, known for its holy water with healing powers. Tortuga's spiritual journey is longer and more arduous than his physical one. He must overcome his alienation and enter fully into life. Human nature and Nature herself provide his path to illumination. Tortuga's experiences with the other patients in the hospital reveal the possibility of true friendship, and the mountain exercises its magic on him. According to Native American legend, Tortuga Mountain is a turtle who once swam freely in the waters that originally covered the desert. One day the waters will return and the turtle will again swim freely. Nature and myth are powerful forces in Anaya's work, and here the connection between the two Tortugas is clear. The protagonist will "swim" free, and he does.

Near the end of the novel Tortuga's identity is revealed—he is nineteen-year-old Benjie from *Heart of Aztlán*, the alienated adolescent who fell from a tower. The connection between the two novels is reinforced when the cured Tortuga receives a package as he prepares to leave the hospital. It is Crispín's blue guitar, willed to Benjie, suggesting that Benjie's journey of enlightenment will eventually take him to the role of seer once held by Crispín.

Other Works

Short Stories

The Silence of the Llano: Short Stories (1982) is a collection of ten short stories, three of which were first published as sections of chapters in each of the novels of the trilogy. "The Christmas Play" originated in *Bless Me, Ultima*, "El Velorio"("The Wake") in *Heart of Aztlán*, and "Salomón's Story" in *Tortuga*. Of the remaining seven stories, two deal with the theme of incest and four treat the theme of mythmaking.

Serafina's Stories (2004) is a Chicano version of *A Thousand and One Nights*, with Serafina, a mission-educated Pueblo Indian, as the Scheherezade whose mesmerizing tales will save her life and the lives of the Indians imprisoned with her.

Novellas

The Legend of the Llorona: A Short Novel (1984) is a retelling of the Llorona, or wailing woman, myth. *Lord of the Dawn: the Legend of Quetzalcoatl* (1987) retells the legend of Quetzalcoatl, the feathered serpent confused with the Spanish conqueror, Hernán Cortés. *Jalamanta: A Message from the Desert* (1996) follows the return of an exiled prophet who brings new wisdom to his village.

The Alburquerque Quartet

Spelled like the original name of the town, which purportedly lost the "r" because an Anglo stationmaster couldn't pronounce it, *Alburquerque* (1992) begins in April, thus beginning a seasonal cycle continued in *Zia Summer*

(1995), which begins in June, and *Rio Grande Fall* (1996), which begins in October, and completed by *Shaman Winter* (1999), which begins in December. *Alburquerque* contains characters familiar to readers of Anaya's earlier novels. Benjie and Cindy from *Heart of Aztlán*, appear as adults, Benjamin Chávez and Cynthia Johnson, the biological parents of the protagonist, Abrán González. Abrán is a fair-skinned boxer who discovers he is adopted and goes on a quest to find his natural parents. Sonny Baca is a minor character in the first novel of the tetrology, but the central character of the remaining three novels, which are sometimes referred to as the Sonny Baca mysteries. *Zia Summer* deals with Sonny's detective work to uncover a conspiracy headed by Raven, leader of the Zia cult and perpetrator of ritual murders. In *Rio Grande Fall* Sonny undergoes a ritual cleansing by a *curandera* and again contends with his "dark twin," Raven. In *Shaman Winter* Sonny must again struggle against Raven, this time confined to a wheelchair after a fierce battle with his archenemy. As in his earlier novels, the action alternates between dreams, or dream time, and real time.

Travel Writing

A Chicano in China (1986) is a travel journal that recounts Anaya's month-long visit to China in 1984 and attempts to make connections between his observations of Chinese life and his own Chicano upbringing.

Children's Books

Anaya has published five children's picture books, *The Farolitos of Christmas* (1995), *Maya's Children* (1996), *Farolitos for Abuelo* (1999), *The Roadrunner's Dance* (2000), and *The Santero's Miracle: A Bilingual Story* (2004), as well as *My Land Sings: Stories from the Rio Grande* (1999), a collection of ten stories for young adults. Like his other works, his children's books are grounded in the culture and legends of New Mexican life.

Plays

Several of Anaya's plays have been produced, but only two have been published: *Who Killed Don José?* and *Billy the Kid*. The former was first published in *New Mexico Plays* in 1989, and both were included in *The Anaya Reader* in 1995.

Poetry

The Adventures of Juan Chicaspatas (1985) is an epic poem about Aztlán and Chicano culture, and the *Elegy of the Death of César Chávez* (2000) memorializes the life of the great labor organizer, founder of the United Farm Workers union.

Edited Works

Anaya has translated, edited, and coedited an impressive number of works, attesting to his central role as a Chicano author and visionary. In 1980 he published *Cuentos: Tales from the Hispanic Southwest*, an English translation of Hispanic folktales. A coedited anthology of short stories, *Cuentos Chicanos—A Short Story Anthology,* followed in 1984. He edited *Voces, An Anthology of Nuevo Mexicano Writers* and coedited *Aztlán, Essays on the Chicano Homeland* (both 1987), and in 1989 edited *Tierra, Contemporary Short Fiction of New Mexico.*

Despite his immense and constant production of work in a range of genres, and the popularity of his Sonny Baca mysteries, Anaya's reputation remains most firmly grounded on his first novel, *Bless Me, Ultima,* and on his role as one of the founding fathers of Chicano literature. He remains one of the most vigorous and influential voices of Mexican American literature, culture, and identity.

Further Reading

Black, Debra B. "Times of Conflict: *Bless Me, Ultima* as a Novel of Acculturation." *The Bilingual Review* 25 (May–August 2000): 146–62.

Dick, Bruce, and Silvio Sirias, eds. *Conversations with Rudolfo Anaya.* Jackson: U of Mississippi P, 1998.

Fernández Olmos, Margarite. *Rudolfo A. Anaya: A Critical Companion.* Westport, CT: Greenwood Press, 1999.

González-T., César A., ed. *Rudolfo A. Anaya: Focus on Criticism.* La Jolla, CA: Lalo Press, 1990.

Linda Ledford-Miller

ANGEL ISLAND Former site of an **immigration** detention center, which operated from 1910 to 1940. Located in the San Francisco Bay, Angel Island is often referred to as the "**Ellis Island** of the West," but the immigration department tellingly viewed it as the "Guard of the Western Gate." Following the Chinese Exclusion Act of 1882, which sought to end the influx of Chinese immigrants, the center was constructed on Angel Island to detain and interrogate those who claimed to be among the few Chinese still permitted entry into the United States, including students, merchants, and diplomats. Many immigrants claimed a right to entry, or re-entry, based on either personal citizenship or citizenship through paternal lineage. Desperate for an opportunity for life in America, some immigrants purchased identities as the children of Chinese Americans; they were called paper sons and daughters. Memorizing coaching books which detailed their assumed family and home, they stepped into new identities.

All Chinese immigrants endured physical and psychological indignities as they were subjected to prison-like conditions, physical examinations, and interrogations regarding their proposals to enter the United States. Some immigrants were detained for a few weeks, while others remained on Angel Island for months or even years.

Many of the immigrants were Cantonese labors from the Guandong province in rural southern China, and driven by economic and political toil, they journeyed to America, drawn by its national myths as a land of opportunity and liberty. Their incarceration at Angel Island destroyed these beliefs and hopes as the Chinese immigrants realized that they were singled out for such treatment.

Some expressed their sorrow and frustration by carving or writing poems on the barracks walls. These poems were discovered in 1970 when the center was designated for demolition. As significant examples of early Chinese American literature, the poems fortunately have been saved and recorded. The majority of Chinese immigrants were laborers with little education, so records of their literary practices and even personal expression are rare and valuable. Written in secret to avoid punishment, the poems call attention to the American cultural myths and the contradictions represented by the very existence of the Angel Island detention center.

Angel Island, now a state park, serves as an important cultural and historical site, and many Chinese American families identify it as their ancestors' point of entry. The landmark is bittersweet, however, as it remains evidence of racial discrimination, but the extraordinary poems left behind articulate the experiences and sentiments of an often silenced population, thereby providing insight into a period of American history from their perspective.

Further Reading

Lai, Him Mark, et al., ed. *Island: Poetry and History of Chinese Immigrants on Angel Island, 1910–1940.* Seattle: U of Washington P, 1991.

Lowe, Felicia, dir. *Carved in Silence.* Felicia Lowe Productions, 1988.

Shan, Te-Hsing. "Carved on the Walls: The Archaeology and Canonization of the Angel Island Chinese Poems." *American Babel: Literatures of the United States from Abnaki to Zuni.* Ed. Marc Shell. Cambridge, MA: Harvard UP, 2002.

Karen Li Miller

ANGELOU, MAYA (1928–)   African American author, autobiographer, poet, playwright, editor, and educator. Originally named Marguerite Johnson, Maya Angelou is particularly well known for her autobiographical novels, which deal with the complexities of racial, economic, and sexual oppression. She has written numerous volumes of poetry and received national honor when she read her poem *On the Pulse of Morning* at the inauguration of President Bill Clinton in 1993. Angelou has enjoyed a multi-faceted career and has worked as a dancer, singer, actress, director, producer, feminist, political activist, talk show guest, and lecturer. She has also received many awards and honorary degrees for her outstanding contributions.

Angelou was born on April 4, 1928, in St. Louis, Missouri, and is the daughter of Bailey Johnson and Vivian Baxter. She lived in California until the divorce of her parents and was then sent to live with her paternal grandparents in Stamps, Arkansas. While in Arkansas, she experienced the trials of discrimination and segregation in the pre-civil rights South, but she also witnessed the strength and fortitude of the black community. After several years, Angelou moved to St. Louis where she lived with her mother's family. She was raped by her mother's boyfriend when still just a young girl, and she dealt with the subsequent beating death of her perpetrator by becoming mute. She eventually returned to live with her grandparents in Arkansas and developed a passion for reading. In 1940, Angelou moved with her mother to San Francisco where she graduated from high school and gave birth as an unwed mother to her son, Guy Johnson. She married Tosh Angelos in 1952 and was divorced soon after. Angelou took private music lessons; studied dance with Martha Graham, Pearl Primus, and Ann Halprin; and studied drama with Frank Silvera and Gene Frankel. During the 1950s, as her career began to flourish, Angelou performed in Off Broadway plays such as *Calypso Heatwave* in 1957 and Jean Genet's *The Blacks* in 1960. In collaboration

Maya Angelou. *AP/Wide World Photos.*

with Godfrey Cambridge, she produced, directed, and performed in *Cabaret for Freedom* (1960). She was also nominated for an Emmy Award for best supporting actress for her role in the television adaptation of **Alex Haley**'s *Roots*.

Angelou was involved as a leader and activist. During the 1960s, she served as northern coordinator for the Southern Christian Leadership Conference, a responsibility she was encouraged to accept by **Martin Luther King Jr.** Angelou married Vusumzi Make, a civil rights activist, and the couple lived in Cairo where Angelou was an associate editor of the *Arab Observer*. After her relationship with Make dissolved, Angelou moved to Ghana, where she worked as an assistant administrator and teacher at the School of Music and Drama at the University of Ghana and as a feature editor of the *African Review*. Angelou returned to the United States where she was appointed by President Gerald Ford to work on the American Revolution Bicentennial Council. She also received the appointment by President Jimmy Carter to serve on the National Commission on the Observance of International Women's Year. During the 1970s, she married the British writer Paul Du Feu, but this union also ended in divorce. In 1981, she became the first Reynolds Professor of American Studies at Wake Forest University in North Carolina, which is a lifetime position.

Angelou published her first autobiography, ***I Know Why the Caged Bird Sings***, in 1970, and wrote five subsequent books on her life. *I Know Why the Caged Bird Sings* deals with her childhood, the rape, her mute period, the many moves she experienced during her younger years, and the birth of her child. Her intense yet lyrical story presents issues regarding gender, **race**, class, power, poverty, sexuality, education, and familial relationships. Her second autobiography, *Gather Together in My Name* (1974), covers the next segment of her life when she works at miscellaneous jobs, such as a cook, cocktail waitress, brothel owner, and dancer. During this dark period in her existence, she experiments with drugs, deals with the kidnapping of her son by a babysitter, and struggles to find meaning in life. In the third addition to her autobiography, *Singin' and Swingin' and Gettin' Merry Like Christmas* (1976), Angelou is torn between the responsibility of motherhood and the desire to further her career. She decides to leave her son in the care of her mother, Vivian Baxter, while she goes on a multination tour with *Porgy and Bess*. Throughout the text, the universal theme of motherhood versus career haunts her as she experiences feelings of guilt for not being home with her son. In *The Heart of a Woman* (1981), the fourth autobiography, Angelou continues to fret over her role as a mother. Although her son is now living with her, she continues to leave him on occasion for various opportunities to work. One of the intense passages in the text deals with the trauma of seeing her unconscious son after he has been injured in a car accident. In the fifth autobiography, *All God's Children Need Traveling Shoes* (1986), the theme of motherhood continues, but another important focus is that of Africa, the home of her ancestors. Angelou acquires a stronger sense of personal identity when she realizes that some of her own traditions correlate with those of Africans. Her connection with Africa helps her to better understand and appreciate her role as a mother. In the final and sixth autobiography to date, *A Song Flung Up to Heaven* (2002), Angelou discusses her return to the United States after having lived many years in Africa. She writes of her association with historical figures such as **Malcolm X** and Martin Luther King Jr., and with icons such as **James Baldwin**. She also tells of beginning to write *I Know Why the Caged Bird Sings,* and says: "I thought if I wrote a book, I would have to examine the quality in the human spirit that continues to rise despite the slings and arrows of outrageous fortune" (212). Angelou's autobiographies draw the reader into the deep pain and struggle of her existence. They chronicle her development as a human being, her familial and personal relationships, and the blossoming of her career. These works also contribute substantially to both black autobiographical tradition and serial autobiography.

Many of Angelou's books of poetry include *Just Give Me a Cool Drink of Water 'fore I Diiie* (1971), *Oh Pray My Wings Are Gonna Fit Me Well* (1975), *And Still I Rise* (1978), *Shaker, Why Don't You Sing* (1983), *Now Sheba Sings the Song* (1987), *I Shall Not Be Moved* (1990), *On the Pulse of Morning* (1993), *The Complete Collected Poems of Maya Angelou* (1994), *Phenomenal Woman: Four Poems for Women* (1995), *A Brave and Startling Truth* (1995), and *From a Black Woman to a Black Man* (1995). Her poetry emerges as a response to a difficult and challenging childhood and provides lessons and wisdom gained during her life of struggle and hardship. She incorporates simple, short lines to make bold statements on social and political issues. In many poems there is a theme of survival and of overcoming oppressive and seemingly overwhelming obstacles. There is also a sense of hope, optimism, and encouragement regarding the possibilities and potential of both men and women on this earth and their ultimate capacity to live together in harmony.

Some of Angelou's other works include plays, screenplays, essays, and children's books. Among her plays are *Cabaret for Freedom*, *The Least of These* (1966), *Ajax* (1974), and *And Still I Rise* (1976). Her screenplays include *Georgia, Georgia* (1972), for which she also wrote the musical score, and *All Day Long* (1974). Her personal essays can be found in *Wouldn't Take Nothing for my Journey Now* (1993) and *Even the Stars Look Lonesome* (1997). Some of her children's books include *Life Doesn't Frighten Me* (1993), *My Painted House, My Friendly Chicken and Me* (1994), and *Kofi and His Magic* (1996).

Throughout her life, Angelou has met obstacles and challenges with perseverance and dignity. Rather than allowing negative and difficult trials to weigh her down, she has, on the contrary, risen and met them head on. The theme of survival is prevalent in her work, as are concerns for **identity**, displacement, motherhood, oppression, and imprisonment.

In her writing, she continues the black tradition of storytelling, and she does so with honesty and frankness combined with wisdom, lyricism, and humor. In addition, her narratives follow the structure of a journey in which she moves from place to place in pursuit of self-understanding, knowledge, and self-identity. She has successfully drawn upon personal experience, both negative and positive, and channeled it in creative output that has enlightened, encouraged, and enriched society. (*See also* African American Autobiography)

Further Reading

Bloom, Harold, ed. *Maya Angelou.* Philadelphia: Chelsea, 2002.

Braxton, Joanne M., ed. *I Know Why the Caged Bird Sings: A Casebook.* New York: Oxford UP, 1999.

Jaquin, Eileen O. "Maya Angelou." *African American Autobiographers: A Sourcebook.* Ed. Emmanuel S. Nelson. Westport, CT: Greenwood Press, 2002. 10–28.

Lupton, Mary Jane. *Maya Angelou: A Critical Companion.* Westport, CT: Greenwood Press, 1998.

Moore, Lucinda. "A Conversation with Maya Angelou at 75." *Smithsonian* 34.1 (April 2003): 96–99.

Deborah Weagel

ANSA, TINA McELROY (1949–) African American fiction writer, essayist, and journalist. A Southern writer best known for her fiction, Ansa locates her novels in mythical Mulberry, Georgia, a close-knit, self-sufficient African American small town. Combining a focus on the internal dynamics of family and community with consistent attention to folkways, ghosts, and spirits, Ansa's novels suggest that the stable, largely affluent social world she envisions must seek and retain vital lessons from the African American past if it is to survive.

Born in Macon, Georgia, and raised in the small African American community of Pleasant Hill, Ansa attended Spelman College and graduated with a degree in English in 1971. She was the first black woman to be hired by the *Atlanta Constitution,* where she worked as a copy editor, editor, feature writer, and news reporter. Her first novel, *Baby of the Family* (1989), won the Georgia Author Series Award and the American Library Association award for best literature for young adults and was named a *New York Times* Notable Book of the Year. Her other major works include *Ugly Ways* (1993) and *The Hand I Fan With* (1996), both of which have begun to garner significant critical attention.

Baby of the Family focuses on heroine Lena's childhood and coming of age at the center of a doting family and community. Because she is born with a "veil" or caul over her face, folk tradition indicates that Lena will possess psychic powers, especially the ability to see and speak to the dead. However, because Lena's mother disdains such folk wisdom, she prevents Lena from being given a potion that would protect the child from the worst aspects of this gift, leaving Lena vulnerable both to the hostile spirits that visit her and the aggression of her peers, who find her odd reactions a sign of insanity. The novel's sequel, *The Hand I Fan With,* which takes its title from an African American rural saying, finds Lena a wealthy forty-five-year-old woman who expends her considerable material and spiritual resources "fanning" or taking care of her community. When she accidentally conjures up Herman, her ideal lover, Lena learns from him that she must use her spiritual gifts to care for herself and that the townspeople will ultimately benefit from learning to be self-sufficient. As Nagueyalti Warren points out, Herman's characterization closely echoes that of Teacake in **Zora Neale Hurston**'s *Their Eyes Were Watching God;* in Ansa's version, however, the past comes only to teach but not to stay, and Herman returns to his spirit form once Lena's transformative journey is complete.

The lessons taught by spirits from the past are more ambiguous in *Ugly Ways,* in which three sisters, all successful career women, return to Mulberry to bury their mother, known to them as Mudear. Initially ruled over by a domineering and unfaithful husband, Mudear used a moment of financial weakness on her husband's part to seize control of the household. Having taken the reins, Mudear becomes a domineering ruler herself, forcing her daughters to wait on her, care for the household, and take care of each other. Told from the point of view of all four women, the novel alternates between presenting the sisters' complaints about their mother's outrageous behavior and Mudear's defense, mounted by the ghost herself. While reviewers agreed in their positive appraisal of the novel, critics have nonetheless been divided in their assessment of Mudear, who has been alternately condemned for creating her daughters' neurotic misery and celebrated for her transgression of conventional roles. In part, this disagreement appears to arise from the novel itself, which is provocative in its refusal to endorse emphatically either Mudear's choices or her daughters' complaints. Instead, *Ugly Ways* asks the reader to weigh both the costs and benefits of a mother whose primary role is as a model of freedom and self-possession, and to imagine how familial bonds might be rethought to avoid the simple substitution of one tyrant for another.

Further Reading

Bennett, Barbara. "Making Peace with the (M)other." *The World Is Our Culture: Society and Culture in Contemporary Southern Writing*. Ed. Jeffrey Folks. Lexington: UP of Kentucky, 2000. 186–200.

Grooms, Anthony. "Big Bad Mudear." *Callaloo* 17 (Spring 1994): 653–55.

Warren, Nagueyalti. "Echoing Zora: Ansa's Other Hand in the Hand I Fan With." *CLA Journal* 46.3 (2003): 362–82.

———. "Resistant Mothers in Alice Walker's *Meridian* and Tina McElroy Ansa's *Ugly Ways*." *Southern Mothers: Fact and Fictions in Southern Women's Writing*. Ed. Nagueyalti Warren. Baton Rouge: Louisiana State UP, 1999. 182–203.

Jane Elliott

ANTIN, MARY (1881–1949) Jewish American writer, public speaker, and **immigration** activist. Mary Antin owes her meteoric success to the arguably most famous immigrant autobiography in America. An instant best seller published when Antin was barely thirty-one, *The Promised Land* (1912) is a landmark literary record of the "new immigration" from South and East Europe and one of the founding texts of Jewish American literature.

Born in Plotzk, Russia, young Mashke (Mary) Antin and her family immigrated in the United States in 1894, joining the hopeful crowds searching for the American dream. Within less than two decades of her arrival in the new country, Antin was a recipient of literary awards, a published poet, a teacher with degrees from Barnard College and Columbia, and a famous immigrant writer. Antin's literary career began with her first autobiographical piece, *From Plotzk to Boston* (1899), an impressive account of the transatlantic journey written by an eleven-year-old child to her relatives in Russia. The warm reception of *Plotzk* paved the way to *The Promised Land*, a triumphant makeover story of an immigrant girl, propelled by education from ethnic obscurity to public prominence. Building her narrative on a series of stark contrasts between oppressive czarist Russia and free and democratic America, Antin professes faith in the progress of the new country and its immigrant nation. The famous opening sentence, "I was born, I have lived, and I have been made over," shows Antin's belief in the need for cultural conversion of immigrants and a replacement of an ethnic past with an American present. Antin's enthusiastic embrace of the new world and her youthful idealization of immigration in America have made *The Promised Land* the ultimate document of **assimilation** in America and its "melting pot" immigration practices. However, recent criticism indicates that Antin's work is less monolithic than initially believed. The polarized and divisive nature of Antin's narrative, along with the poignant images of the difficulties of urban immigration, shows the author's awareness that immigration is a complex process of cultural negotiations.

The Promised Land is a story of an individual achievement of the American dream, which offered an inspiring example for many dispirited and disillusioned immigrants of the time. It was also Antin's powerful argument for immigration, stating boldly that the future of America lies in the talents, patriotism, and educational opportunities of immigrant children. Because the publication of *The Promised Land* coincided with growing immigration controversies of the early 1910s, Antin used her instant celebrity to speak on behalf of unrestricted immigration. In 1914, she published *They Who Knock on Our Gates: A Complete Gospel of Immigration* (1914), a compelling rebuttal of nativist charges against immigrants as an economic burden on America, practitioners of unfamiliar cultural practices, and disloyal voters guilty of "civic indifference." In a number of public lectures that followed, Antin revisited the same topics she explored in *The Promised Land*: her difficult childhood in the settlement of Pale and the importance of education for immigrants. She continued to promote the assimilationist view of immigration, countering Randolph Bourne's call for a transnational America that would internationalize America by preserving immigrants' ethnic characteristics. By 1917, when the immigration quota system was passed, Antin's efforts had become futile. America's interests had shifted toward other topics as the country listened to the reports from the World War I battlefields and prepared for the economic boom of the 1920s. Antin, the outspoken immigration advocate, lost her audience, falling into obscurity and becoming increasingly critical of her work that lost its topicality. The immigration doors to "the promised land" were closed; America lost its interest in immigrant stories, and her exemplary interfaith marriage to Amadeus Grabau, a geologist of German extraction, dissolved. Apart from the two articles published in *Atlantic Monthly*, the disappointed Antin spent the rest of her life in silence, embittered by the betrayal of her immigrant hopes and battling bouts of depression. However, despite the disillusionment of her old age, Antin is remembered for her youthful idealism and enthusiastic belief in America. Along with **Abraham Cahan** and **Anzia Yezierska**, she played a crucial role as a founder of Jewish American literature, responsible also for popularizing the genre of immigrant autobiography and embodying the American dream of the turn-of-the-century America: its myths of swift assimilation, instant success, and radical new beginnings.

Further Reading

Sollors, Werner. "Introduction." *The Promised Land*. Mary Antin. New York: Penguin Books, 1997. xi–l.

Ljiljana Coklin

ANTI-SEMITISM Anti-Semitism is a relatively new term that, in contemporary usage, refers to a variety of phenomena and beliefs manifesting a hatred or fear of Jewish people as well as things associated with Jewish tradition and belief. Originally, the self-chosen name of a movement whose intellectual foundation was grounded in the biases of racial theories in the late-nineteenth and early-twentieth centuries, anti-Semitism has only gradually attained its present meaning. Anti-Semite was once a label proudly self-applied; now the term refers to a wide range of behaviors and attitudes largely regarded as socially unacceptable. Thus, the history of the term itself has lead to disagreement among scholars as to what constitutes anti-Semitism.

Since the era of the composition of the Hebrew Bible, at least, fear or hatred of Jews, on various levels, has been a familiar theme in history and literature. The Book of Exodus opens with Pharaoh's decision to destroy the Jews, who had become slaves in Egypt, and the Book of Esther is an account of Haman's distrust and hatred and his plot to rid the realm of King Ahasuerus of its Jews. In these major biblical figures we already find types of the anti-Semite. Aside from the biblical evidence, little is know about ancient sentiments regarding the Jews before the Classical period.

Hellenized Egyptians reveal anti-Semitic attitudes. Manetho, an Egyptian historian of the second century B.C.E., parodies the Exodus story, claiming that the Jews were leper slaves expelled by Pharaoh and that Moses was a convert priest of Osirus. Classical authors, such as Lysimachus of Alexandria, Horace, and Juvenal, heaped reproach upon the Jews for being enemies of the world in restricting so many bodily pleasures, for clannishness, and for atheism, arising from their refusal to honor imperial gods or the emperor. The Classical period also saw its share of popular uprisings against Jews, such as the riots of Alexandria in 38 B.C.E., and of anti-Semitic governance, such as Hadrian's edicts of 135 C.E. in response to the Bar Kokba rebellion, but the world of Christian Late Antiquity and the Middle Ages brought anti-Semitism into the mainstream.

Anti-Semitic themes were common in the writings of the Church Fathers; Tertullian's tract, *Adversus Judaeos* (circa 200 C.E.), was particularly influential. John Chrysostom, an Eastern Father, preached a series of eight sermons against the Jews in Antioch from 386–87 C.E., sparking violent repression and setting the tone of Jewish-Christian relations in the east until Byzantium was largely overwhelmed by Muslim invasion in the seventh century C.E. Byzantine leaders ordered forced baptisms and conversions time and again, and the repression of the Jews by the government was punctuated only by brief periods of more liberal rule. Seventh-century Jews in Visigoth Spain fared scarcely better, as a series of church councils in Toledo demanded forced conversions and expulsions. Councils throughout Frankish Gaul, modern-day France, forbade Christians to eat or socialize with Jews or to work for Jews.

The initiation of the Crusades in 1096 marked a shift from the regularized repression of Jews marred by occasional violence to the normalization of violence against Jews. Crusaders massacred Jews and pillaged their goods, sometimes even against the wishes of local bishops, and local populaces often rose up against Jewish communities in times of disease, war, or societal misfortune. During this time a trove of legends developed about Jews, legends which served to justify the violent outbursts of the Christians: Jews were accused of spying for foreign powers, of killing Christians, particularly babies, to bake their Passover bread (also known as the blood libel), and of deicide—the murder of Christ. With the coming of the Plague, the Jews were even accused of poisoning the wells with the disease. Such charges were often levied and would ultimately culminate in the deaths of many thousands of Jews during the Middle Ages. They are perhaps most notable because they persist; even the most unbelievable, the blood libel, finds its place in works as diverse as the writings of Martin Luther and the modern propaganda cartoons of the Nazis.

While most anti-Semitic violence was local in character and relatively short-lived, nations, too, took action against the Jews. In 1290 C.E., an edict was issued in England expelling the Jews. This act was repeated many times on the continent. Most notably, Spain ordered expulsion in 1492 C.E. Such expulsions were presented as theologically sound; governments portrayed themselves as acting as instruments of God's exilic curse. Protestant leaders of the Reformation did nothing to cool the anti-Semitism of the age, as the writings of Calvin, Luther, and many of their followers readily attest, and even some Enlightenment and post-Enlightenment philosophers criticized the Jewish faith, even as the Jews began to achieve some legal status and citizenship rights across Europe.

In the late-nineteenth century, a shift occurred in the anti-Semites' justification. Throughout Jewish history, what set Jews apart was their religion: classical authors describe them as clannish and otherworldly because of their religious convictions, Christian authors present them as perverse, unbelieving, and even deicidal because of religious difference, and many modern philosophers describe them as archaic and superstitious because of their form of religion. The nineteenth century and its theories of race gave birth to what many scholars call modern anti-Semitism—that is racial, as opposed to religious, anti-Semitism. Racial anti-Semites view the Jews, so much like themselves in many ways in outward appearance, as a threat to racial purity, and because the races are hierarchical in their ordering, a mixing of **races** upsets the balance.

Such theories come to form an integral part of Adolf Hitler's plan to utilize the resources of Nazi Germany to destroy the Jews, beginning with the Jews of Europe. Hitler gave depression-wracked Germany a scapegoat for its turmoil, just as the clerics of Europe had done in times of war, plague, or famine. According to the Nazi propaganda, the Jews weakened Germany financially, militarily, and, most insidiously, by diluting the pure, virile Aryan blood of the true German—images which could have been drawn from rhetoric many hundreds of years old. However, while the **Holocaust** marks the most horrific outburst of anti-Semitic violence in recorded history, modern anti-Semitism is by no means restricted to continental Europe and, unfortunately, was not brought to an end by the fall of the Nazis.

Anti-Semitism in America and Its Literature

Anti-Semitism in the United States has taken comparatively milder forms; it has, nevertheless, left its mark on the national psyche. While in some locales Jews participated fully in American social and political life, many jurisdictions only allowed Christians to vote, and laws requiring voters to take an oath that they believed in Christ were not rescinded in New Hampshire until 1877. Waves of Eastern European immigrants, like so many waves of immigrants before, were met with prejudice and exclusion from means of advancement in society.

Immigrants of previous generations often resented the newcomers, seeing them as competition for precious jobs. On the other hand, some prominent Americans in the first half of the twentieth century were public proponents of anti-Semitic doctrines. Henry Ford published the *Dearborn Independent*, which, for six years, published anti-Jewish propaganda, charging a Jewish conspiracy with undermining society. His paper published, and made available for mass audiences, the spurious "Protocols of the Elders of Zion," a forged document laying out the organization of the Jewish conspiracy and its plan for world domination, though the document had already been shown to be fraudulent. Only years later would Ford recant, when his finances began to suffer. Charles Lindbergh, a hero to many people, was a firm anti-Semite, opposing the war against Nazi Germany and visiting Hitler. These two are but visible and vocal examples; countless millions of public and private individuals in the United States have publicly expressed anti-Semitic opinions or joined groups with anti-Semitic agendas, from the Ku Klux Klan to anti-Jewish religious groups.

American literary society, too, had its share of notable anti-Semites. Ezra Pound's radio broadcasts during World War II lead to a charge of treason, avoided by a plea of insanity. Later, when Pound was awarded the Bollingen Prize by the Fellows of the Library of Congress for his Pisan *Cantos*, George Orwell raised concern over the anti-Semitic content of the work. More disturbing, perhaps, than overt and infamous cases of anti-Semitism in literature is its seemingly innocuous, unnoticed forms. One scholar, Guy Stern, finds such anti-Semitism in the works of authors as diverse as Katherine Ann Porter, Gore Vidal, T. S. Eliot, and **Amiri Baraka** (Gilman 291–310). Extreme cases such as Pound's taken along with the subtler cases only serve to make this radically clear: American literature is not exempt from the stain of anti-Semitism and must be examined closely for its remnants.

Further Reading

Finzi, Roberto. *Anti-Semitism: From Its European Roots to the Holocaust*. Trans. Maud Jackson. New York: Interlink Books, 1999.

Gilman, Sander L., and Steven T. Katz. *Anti-Semitism in Times of Crisis*. New York: New York UP, 1991.

Lindemann, Albert S. *Esau's Tears: Modern Anti-Semitism and the Rise of the Jews*. Cambridge: Cambridge UP, 1997.

Poliakov, Leon. *The History of Anti-Semitism*, 3 vols. Trans. Richard Howard. New York: Vanguard Press, 1965.

Sartre, Jean-Paul. *Anti-Semite and Jew*. Trans. George J. Becker. New York: Schocken Books, 1948.

James Allen Grady

ANZALDÚA, GLORIA E. (1942–2004) Chicana-tejana cultural theorist, poet, and spiritual activist. Born in the Rio Grande Valley of south Texas to sixth-generation mexicanos and punished in grade school for her inability to speak English without a Spanish accent, Gloria E. Anzaldúa is now internationally recognized as a leading cultural theorist and a highly innovative author. Anzaldúa's redefinition of Chicana/o identities, her use of code-switching (transitions from standard to working-class English to Chicano Spanish to Tex-Mex to Nahuatl-Aztec), and her sophisticated explorations of border issues have played important roles in shaping contemporary U.S. literature. Anzaldúa's writings have challenged and expanded previous views in a variety of additional disciplines, including American studies, composition studies, cultural studies, ethnic studies, **feminism**/feminist theory, literary studies, queer theory, and women's studies. As one of the first openly lesbian Chicana authors, Anzaldúa has played a major role in redefining contemporary Chicano/a and lesbian/queer identities. And as editor or coeditor of three multicultural anthologies, she has played an equally vital role in developing an inclusive feminist movement.

Anzaldúa is a versatile writer and has published poetry, theoretical essays, short stories, autobiographical narratives, interviews, children's books, and multi-genre anthologies. She has won numerous awards, including the Before Columbus Foundation American Book Award, the Lamda Lesbian Small Book Press Award, an NEA Fiction Award, the Lesbian Rights Award, the Sappho Award of Distinction, and the American Studies Association Lifetime Achievement Award. Her works in progress include a collection of short stories; a novel-in-stories; a writing manual; a book of daily meditations; a young-adult novel; and an edited collection titled *Bearing Witness, Reading Lives: Imagination, Creativity, and Cultural Change*.

For Anzaldúa, aesthetic and political issues are deeply intertwined. In her poetry, fiction, and prose she employs concrete, visceral metaphors and images to convey her meanings and impact her readers. Throughout her work she draws on her personal experiences to explore a wide variety of interlocking political, aesthetic, and spiritual issues. These issues include, but are not limited to, the following: the destructive effects of externally imposed labels; the ways interlocking systems of oppression marginalize people who—because of their class, color, gender, language, physical (dis)abilities, religion, and/or sexuality—do not belong to dominant cultural groups; Chicana, Mexican American, Latina, queer, lesbian, and female sexualities and identities; shamanism and other indigenous spiritualities and epistemologies (theories of knowledge); non-Western aesthetics; and homophobia, **racism**, and sexism within both the dominant U.S. culture and Mexican American communities.

Borderlands/La Frontera: The New Mestiza (1987) is Anzaldúa's most widely acclaimed book and was named one of the 100 Best Books of the Century by both *Hungry Mind Review* and *Utne Reader.* Although *Borderlands/La Frontera* resists easy classification, scholars often describe it as a complex cultural autobiography that builds on and expands previous uses of the genre. Anzaldúa herself describes *Borderlands/La Frontera* as "autohistoria-teoría," a term she coined to describe women-of-color interventions into and transformations of traditional western autobiographical forms. Autohistoria-teoría includes both life-story and self-reflection on this story. Writers of autohistoria-teoría blend their cultural and personal biographies with memoir, history, storytelling, myth, and other forms of theorizing. By so doing, they create interwoven individual and collective identities.

Borderlands/La Frontera is divided into two parts. The first half consists of seven mixed-genre essays that combine autobiographical details with history and social protest with poetry and revisionist mythmaking. Anzaldúa uses this unique combination to develop affirmative definitions of herself and her tejana culture. The second half consists of thirty-eight poems, divided into six sections. Like the mixed-genre essays, the poems depict a wide variety of issues and scenes. In poems such as "I Had to Go Down" and "Letting Go," Anzaldúa offers graphic depictions of her writing process. Other poems, such as "Antigua, mi diosa" and "Canción de la diosa de la noche," complement Anzaldúa's revisionist mythmaking in the first half of the book. Still other poems, such as "Cihuatlyotl, Woman Alone" and "Nopalitos," illustrate Anzaldúa's negotiations between individual and collective identities. Anzaldúa also includes storytelling poems ("Holy Relics" and "Interface"), poems about her family and life in south Texas ("Immaculate, Inviolate: Como Ella," "Cervicide"), and love poems ("Compañera, cuando amábamos"). The poetry continues and expands upon the code switching found in the book's first half. Ten poems—including "En el nombre de todas las madres que han perdido sus hijos en la guerra," "No se raje, chicanita," and "Arriba me gente"—are written entirely in Spanish, and almost all of the remaining poems include various forms of code switching.

Borderlands/La Frontera has significantly impacted the ways contemporary scholars think about border issues, the concept of the Borderlands, ethnic/gender/sexual identities, and conventional literary forms. Anzaldúa uses the term "Borderlands" in two complex, overlapping yet distinct ways. First, she builds on previous views of the borderlands as a specific geographical location: the Southwest border between Mexico and Texas. Second, she expands and redefines this concept to encompass psychic, sexual, and spiritual borderlands as well. For Anzaldúa, the borderlands—both in geographical and metaphoric meanings—represent painful yet also potentially transformational spaces where opposites converge, conflict, and transform. Anzaldúa's theory of the "new mestiza" has been equally influential and represents an innovative expansion of previous biologically based definitions of mestizaje. For Anzaldúa, "new mestizas" are people who inhabit multiple worlds because of their gender, sexuality, color, class, bodies, personality, spiritual beliefs, or other life experiences. This theory offers a new concept of personhood that synergistically combines apparently contradictory European American and indigenous traditions. Anzaldúa further develops her theory of the new mestiza into an epistemology and ethics she calls "mestiza consciousness": holistic, relational modes of thinking and acting.

Anzaldúa's three anthologies emerge from and illustrate her desire to create alliances and dialogues among diverse peoples. Her first coedited anthology, *This Bridge Called My Back: Writings by Radical Women of Color* (1981), is a groundbreaking collection of essays, letters, and poems widely recognized as a premiere multicultural feminist text. This multi-genre anthology served as a crucial reminder that U.S. feminism is not and never has been a "white," middle-class women's movement. Anzaldúa's second anthology, *Making Face, Making Soul/Haciendo Caras: Creative and Critical Perspectives by Women of Color* (1990), illustrates her ongoing attempts to develop coalitions between nonacademic and academic social activists. In her preface, Anzaldúa rejects the inaccessible, elitist nature of academic "high" theory and underscores the importance of inventing new theorizing methods, "mestizaje theories," that "create new categories for those of us left out or pushed out of the existing ones." Most recently, Anzaldúa has coedited *this bridge we call home: radical visions for transformation* (2002), a collection of theoretical and creative essays, short stories, poems, email conversations, and artwork offering a bold new vision of women-of-color consciousness for the twenty-first century. This anthology illustrates the growth in Anzaldúa's vision of social change. Written by women and men—both of color and white—*this bridge we call home* challenges readers to transform existing **identity** categories and develop new forms of feminist theorizing and action, or what Anzaldúa calls "spiritual activism." Based on the belief in our radical interrelatedness, spiritual activism includes concrete actions designed to intervene in and transform existing social conditions. This visionary, experientially based way of thinking and acting recognizes the many differences among human beings yet simultaneously insists on our commonalities and uses these commonalities as catalysts for social change.

Anzaldúa has also written two bilingual children's books with a strong female protagonist named Prietita. *Friends from the Other Side/Amigos del otro lado* (1993) explores, in child-appropriate ways, issues concerning undocumented workers, the border patrol, and friendship. *Prietita and the Ghost Woman/Prietita y la Llorona* (1995) revises traditional stories of La Llorona, an important cultural figure in Southwestern/mexicano life. Anzaldúa has also published a collection of interviews, *Interviews/Entrevistas* (2000), offering intimate biographical details and useful information about her theories and writings. Anzaldúa's most recent publications—essays such as "Putting Coylxauhqui Together, A Creative Process," "now let us shift," and "Let us be the healing of the wound"—are informed by her theory of autohistoria-teoría and contain innovative philosophies like "nepantla" and "nepantleras," "nos/otras," "conocimiento," and "new tribalism." These concepts represent important and useful expansions of her earlier theories of the Borderlands, the new mestiza, and mestiza consciousness.

Anzaldúa's ability to create expansive new categories and interconnections makes her work vital to contemporary social actors, thinkers, and scholars. Destabilizing apparently fixed classifications and provocatively crossing sexual, cultural, gender, and genre boundaries, her writing breaks down the categories that lead to stereotyping, over-generalizations, and arbitrary divisions among groups. By so doing, Anzaldúa opens up new spaces where mestizaje connections—alliances between people from diverse sexualities, cultures, genders, and classes—can occur. (*See also* Border Narratives, Mexican American Lesbian Literature)

Further Reading

Alarcón, Norma. "Chicana Feminism: In the Tracks of 'The' Native Woman." *Living Chicana Theory*. Ed. Carla Trujillo. Berkeley: Third Woman P, 1998. 371–82.

Barnard, Ian. "Gloria Anzaldúa Queer Mestizaje." *MELUS: Journal for the Study of the Multi-Ethnic Literature of the United States* 22 (1997): 35–53.

Garber, Linda. "'Caught in the Crossfire between Camps': Gloria Anzaldúa." *Identity Poetics: Race, Class, and the Lesbian-Feminist Roots of Queer Theory*. New York: Columbia UP, 2001. 147–75.

Keating, AnaLouise. *Women Reading Women Writing: Self-Invention in Paula Gunn Allen, Gloria Anzaldúa, and Audre Lorde*. Philadelphia: Temple UP, 1996.

———, ed. *EntreMundos/AmongWorlds: New Perspectives on Gloria E. Anzaldúa*. New York: Palgrave Macmillan, 2005.

Yarbro-Bejarano, Yvonne. "Gloria Anzaldúa's *Borderlands/La frontera*: Cultural Studies, 'Difference,' and the Non-Unitary Subject." *Cultural Critique* 28 (1994): 5–28.

AnaLouise Keating

APESS, WILLIAM (1798–1839?) Native American autobiographer, preacher, writer, and social activist. William Apess stands as the first major Native American author in the nineteenth century. His reputation has been anchored by the publication of *A Son of the Forest* (1829), the first published autobiography by a Native American. *A Son of the Forest* appeared amid the controversy of the Indian Removal Act (1830), which gave the U.S. government the authority to remove Native Americans from their lands east of the

Mississippi to designated Indian reservation territories. Apess's first autobiography takes the form of a spiritual conversion narrative, which details his struggles to create a unified sense of self in a world of bigotry and ignorance. His early childhood was marred by an abusive relationship with his intemperate maternal grandmother, and the majority of his upbringing took place in white foster homes. Apess's writings are noted for their firm belief in the common humanity shared between European colonizers and Native Americans, and the author made apparent the misrepresentation of his people as innately deprived and uncivilized by white culture.

William Apess was born near Coltrain, Massachusetts, to parents of mixed **race**. It is believed that his father was part Peqout, part white, while Apess's mother was believed to be an African American slave. Like many of the stereotypical portrayals of Native Americans, William Apess lived life under severe economic hardship, racial oppression, and severe bouts of alcoholism. What distinguishes Apess's place as an important Native American writer and thinker was his conversion to Christianity in 1818 and his eventual ordination by the Protestant Methodist Church.

Apess's writings counteracted much of the popular stereotypes of Native Americans during the early formation period of the United States. While Indian captivity narratives stereotyped Indians as either brutal savages or preying spies, Apess suggested to readers that Native Americans were just as worthy of Christ's salvation as their white oppressors. His life and his writings made the case for equality among whites and natives. In his second book *The Experiences of Five Christian Indians of the Pequot Tribe* (1833), Apess details his own successful conversion, the conversion stories of four others, and it focuses on different formulaic callings to be messengers of Christ's word. Apess's sermon *The Increase of the Kingdom of Christ* (1831) also reached publication along with the attached document *The Indians: The Ten Lost Tribes*, which argued for Native Americans as being one of the lost tribes of Israel.

As a result of his preaching the gospel and his successful oratory skills, Apess began a career as an advocate for Native American rights. After a visit to the Mashpee tribe in 1833, the tribe rallied behind Apess as a leader of their revolt to attain self-government from corrupt white leaders. Apess documented the peaceful rebellion in his *Indian Nullification of the Unconstitutional Laws of Massachusetts* (1835).

His final published work, and perhaps his most controversial, was his *Eulogy on King Philip, as Pronounced at the Odeon, Federal Street, Boston* (1836). King Philip, actually Metacom, was the Native American leader in a brutal period of armed conflict (1675–1676) with English colonists, which came to be called King Philip's War. Apess's eulogy made the revolutionary claim that Philip was a hero and deserved praise as revolutionary heroes such as George Washington. Apess condemned the hypocrisy and the abusiveness of white culture, which had attempted to demonize Philip for protecting and defending his homeland. In essence, Apess appears to be writing what may be regarded a postcolonial defense in Philip's name.

The final years of William Apess are shrouded in mystery. The location and exact date of his death are not known, but it is believed that he succumbed to alcoholism at the end of his career. Regardless, Apess's life and writings testify to his important place in the development of ethnic American literature. As a writer, preacher, and advocate for his people, Apess cleared an important path for Native Americans to follow. Not only did his work argue for egalitarianism for Native Americans in regard to conversion to God's grace, but he also wrote for a more widespread understanding of social and cultural equality by exposing the hypocrisy, misrepresentations, and violence of white colonizers.

Further Reading

Krupat, Arnold. *Ethnocriticism: Ethnography, History, Literature.* Berkeley: U of California P, 1992.

———. *The Voice in the Margin: Native American Literature and the Canon.* Berkeley: U of California P, 1989.

McQuaid, Kim. "William Apess, Pequot, an Indian Reformer in the Jackson Era." *New England Quarterly* 50 (1977): 605–25.

Murray, David. *Forked Tongues: Speech, Writing, and Representation in North American Indian Texts.* Bloomington: Indiana UP, 1991.

O'Connell, Barry. *On Our Ground: The Complete Writings of William Apess, a Pequot.* Amherst: U of Massachusetts P, 1992.

Ian S. Maloney

APPLE, MAX (1941–) Jewish American fiction writer, memoirist, and editor. Born in Grand Rapids, Michigan, in 1941, Max Apple spoke only Yiddish for the first years of his life. He grew up in a household that included his recently immigrated Lithuanian grandfather and grandmother—the latter of whom, Apple says, "was a great storyteller." For this reason, perhaps, Apple has, from the beginning of his writing career up to the present, focused on **ethnicity** and issues of cultural **identity**.

Apple received his PhD in English from the University of Michigan in 1971, where he fell in love with stories and novels. He published his first collection of fiction *The Oranging of America and Other Stories* in 1976. In his second novel, *Zip: A Novel of the Left and the Right,* (1978) a nice Jewish boy, Ira Goldstein, manages the Puerto Rican boxer, Jesus. Apple explores some of the idiosyncrasies of each culture, as well as the differences and similarities in their acculturation. In later works, Apple has published two nonfiction memoirs about his grandparents, which further explore his ethnic inheritance. *Roommates: My Grandfather's Story* (1994), perhaps Apple's best-selling work, recounts an entire life living alongside his grandfather, focusing on his graduate school days where the two shared a bedroom. This memoir, which the *New York Times* praised for its straightforward prose and its moving detail, was made into a successful full-length movie. In his second memoir, *I Love Gootie: My Grandmother's Story* (1998), Apple describes the divergence between the culture in which his grandmother was raised, and his own. Recalling her craziness and bitterness, Apple connects his own life to the Lithuanian shtetlach, the name for the impoverished Eastern European towns which often had to face pogrom.

Apple's signature story, which appeared in his second collection of short fiction, *Free Agents* (1984) has been widely anthologized, most notably in *Jewish American Literature: A Norton Anthology*, (2001) and *Writing Our Way Home: An Anthology of Contemporary Jewish American Short Fiction* (1992). The title "Eighth Day" refers to the twenty-four-hour period during which Jewish law demands that male infants be circumcised. Central to understanding the writer's relationship to his ethnic and religious identity, the story features a Jewish man who, after marrying a Christian woman, returns to his hometown, South Bend, Indiana, to find the moil—a religious figure that performs circumcisions—in order to be reborn, recircumcized, and to reclaim his Jewish spirituality. Although Apple gently satirizes his characters, he ultimately upholds this religious ritual and others, because, as the concluding line of the story says, "a man is not a chicken."

Apple has published eight books. In addition to those mentioned above, he has published *Propheteers: A Novel* (1987) and *Three Stories* (1983). Apple taught English and Creative Writing at Rice University for twenty-nine years. After his retirement, he and his wife moved to Philadelphia, where Apple occasionally teaches at the University of Pennsylvania's Writer's House.

Further Reading

Nannatta, Dennis. "Satiric Gestures in Max Apple's *The Oranging of America*." *Studies in Contemporary Satire* 7 (1980): 1–7.

Vorda, Allan. "An Interview with Max Apple." *Michigan Quarterly Review* 27.1 (Winter 1988): 69–77.

Wilde, Alan. "Dayanu: Max Apple and the Ethics of Sufficiency." *Contemporary Literature* 26.3 (Fall 1985): 254–85.

Hilene Flanzbaum

ARAB AMERICAN AUTOBIOGRAPHY   In the Arab world, the auto-biography genre has been traditionally popular, especially those of esteemed writers such as Taha Hussein, author of the three-part autobiography *The Days* (1926) and Fadwa Tuqan, author of *A Mountainous Journey* (1985). Among Arab American writers, the genre is still developing and is often marked by its stretch of poetic license, illustrated by the fact that the authors rarely tell their story directly, but opt for a more creative narrative and chronology.

Furthermore, the political scene in the last two decades can be seen as a primary force behind the very recent emergence of this genre in Arab American literature in the 1990s. Undoubtedly, the American involvement in the Arab-Israeli crisis, especially in the 1987 and 2000 Intifadas, and in the 1991 and 2003 Gulf wars in Iraq, created a need among Arab American writers to discuss and explain their lives to an American audience that was increasingly curious.

Leila Ahmed's *A Border Passage* (1999) is probably the most traditional Arab American autobiography published to date. Narrated in a direct, chronological style, the book traces Ahmed's life from her childhood in Cairo to her current role as a professor and a writer in the United States. She weaves her personal experiences with intersecting world and national events, and she highlights the ways in which her journeys and experiences in the Middle East, in Europe, and in the United States shaped her **identity**. She concludes that the world has constructed images of Arabs that are false and misleading; she believes that, as a woman and as a Muslim, she can elucidate and clarify the Arab identity and mentality.

The most controversial autobiography published to date has been **Edward Said**'s *Out of Place* (1999) in which the now-deceased Columbia University professor recounts his childhood in Palestine and his family's exile to Cairo, Egypt, after 1948, the year that hearkened the creation of the state of Israel. The title of Said's book succinctly captures the theme popular among Arab American memoirists, the feeling of being a perpetual outsider in one's adopted homeland. In *Out of Place*, Said, a professor of literature and the author of several seminal works of literary criticism and political analysis such as *Orientalism* (1978) and *The Question of Palestine* (1979), does not cover his entire life, nor even half of it. Instead, he ends the memoir at the point where he is a very young man, focusing mainly on his parents and childhood memories.

He discusses the consciousness of an exile. The person who finds himself in exile will struggle all his life to reconcile his identity, but Said's case is complicated further by the controversy caused in identifying himself as a Palestinian. Because the West Bank and Gaza Strip are Israeli-occupied territories and the crux of the Palestinian-Israeli conflict, this is interpreted as a political statement and not simply a statement of fact.

Out of Place was itself the crux of a controversy, the result of an essay titled "'My Beautiful Old House' and Other Fabrications by Edward Said" by Justus Reid Weiner (*Commentary*, September 1999). Weiner claimed to have spent several years investigating and researching Said's past, and he concluded, in his essay, that Said had crafted a public image as a refugee from Palestine, although he came from a privileged background and lived among Cairo's elite as a young man. Indeed, Weiner even questioned Said's Palestinian roots. The overall point of the essay, as interpreted by many in the Arab American academic and literary community, was to cast doubt upon the portrayal of Palestinians as exiles, as people displaced from their homeland—a central tenet of the Palestinian American identity, which is the Palestinian experience of suffering. As such, many academics and writers leapt to Said's defense, publishing articles that emphasized the right of Palestinians to assert this identity, but the impact was still deeply felt: that the Arab identity is, essentially, a political one because of the unrest in the region.

Fay Afaf Kanafani's autobiography also tells the story of how Palestinian life was impacted in 1948, but from a woman's perspective. *Nadia, Captive of Hope: Memoir of an Arab Woman* (1999) covers Kanafani's difficult childhood in Beirut, Lebanon, including years of sexual abuse at the hands of her own father and the deafening silence of her mother. In fact, the memories were so painful that Kanafani took creative license and chose to write about herself under the name of Nadia—a way to create some distance from these memories in order to recount them truthfully and completely.

Kanafani's memoir is significant because she recounts her emerging awareness of **feminism**. In the memoir, as unjust actions are taken against her, Nadia rebels from an inner sense of empowerment. For example, she was forced into a marriage with a cousin, and moved to Palestine during the tumultuous 1930s and 1940s; in protest, she refused to consummate the marriage. She was eventually raped by her husband, but the crime solidified her understanding of male-female relationships and inequities.

Nadia, Captive of Hope is considered remarkable because of the fact that Kanafani's feminism was not adopted by interactions with other feminists, especially Western feminists. Middle Eastern feminists hear the common accusation that they are being misled or deceived by Western feminist ideology and that Middle Eastern women should resist feminism as another form of western colonialism. However, Kanafani's autobiography is a testament to the insistence by Middle Eastern women's rights activists that their feminism is not imported, but arose from the real need to address the flaws of patriarchal society.

Elmaz Abinader's book *Children of the Roojme: A Family's Journey from Lebanon* (1991) is an unusual, but highly artistic, family autobiography. Considered Abinader's seminal work, *Children of the Roojme* traces the history of the Abinader family and their **immigration** from the Middle East to the United States. The book traces the lives of four generations of her family and offers detailed, rich descriptions of life in Lebanon and the necessary **assimilation** into the culture of the United States. Furthermore, she details the sorrows endured by the Lebanese who suffered through the various wars in the region, poverty, and other crises. It is important for Abinader to paint a portrait of life in the Middle East, to give her readers a sense of the background and experiences of immigrants before they arrive on American shores.

The most nontraditional autobiography to be penned to date by an Arab American writer is *Drops of This Story* (1996), by Palestinian American poet Suheir Hammad. Hammad first made her appearance on the literary scene with a poetry collection, *Born Palestinian, Born Black* (1996), in which the poet, who was born in a Palestinian refugee camp and moved to New York at the age of five, identified her voice with those of African American and other ethnic writers. In her memoir, Hammad uses a fusion style of Arab themes and hip-hop tone, making her one of the first Arab American writers to make a link to other ethnic literary and musical movements. Her writing style is terse and brief with powerful statements delivered in a no-nonsense style. She reflects on her childhood growing up in a New York neighborhood. She also discusses how difficult it was to form and develop the Arab American identity, as well as the specific challenges of being a Palestinian in the United States.

Many of autobiographies by Arab American writers, including those by Said, Ahmed, Kanafani, and even Abinader, focus on the lives of Arabs in the Middle East, then recount the shock of immigration and the ensuing shifts in cultural perspective. Hammad's *Drops of This Story* is one of the first to focus on Arab American life growing up in the United States and the necessary negotiations made between two cultures. (*See also* Arab American Stereotypes)

Further Reading

Armstrong, Paul. "Being 'Out of Place': Edward W. Said and the Contradictions of Cultural Differences." *Modern Language Quarterly* 64.1 (March 2003): 97.

Cherif, Salwa Essayah. "Arab American Literature: Gendered Memory in Abinader and Abu-Jaber." *MELUS* (Winter 2003): 207–28.

Cockburn, Alexander. "Defending the Integrity of Edward Said." *Los Angeles Times* (August 29, 1999): A5.

Crossette, Barbara. "Out of Egypt, A Border Passage." *Migration World Magazine* 28.3 (March 2000): 50.

Fleischmann, Ellen. "Women: *Nadia: Captive of Hope. Memoir of an Arab Woman.*" *Middle East Journal* 54.2 (Spring 2000): 325.

Hassan, Wail. "Arab-American Autobiography and the Reinvention of Identity: Two Egyptian Negotiations." [Special Issue: *The Language of the Self: Autobiographies and Testimonies*] *Alif* 22 (2002).

Handal, Nathalie. "Drops of Suheir Hammad: A Talk with a Palestinian Poet Born Black." *Al Jadid* 3.20 (Summer 1997): 19.

Susan Muaddi Darraj

ARAB AMERICAN NOVEL   The novel genre, along with that of poetry, has been highly popular among Arab American writers. However, many critics agree that there is not yet an established canon of Arab American novels, although such works are starting now to amass and distinguish themselves in theme and style. Most of the first novels by Arab American authors tend to be autobiographical either in whole or in part, as are most early novels. Among the themes that are explored in Arab American novels, **identity** is by far the most common. Characters in the novels struggle with a hyphenated identity, attempting to reconcile both their Arab and American cultures. It is commonly agreed that the Arab American identity, more so than the identities of African American, Latino/a, Asian American, and others, is not just a social and cultural construct, but an intensely political one as well.

Some novels have been written in Arabic, by authors living in America, and then translated into English; some are even written in English and then translated into Arabic for Middle Eastern audiences; most, however, are written in English primarily for the English-speaking audience. Some of these novels have found their way into the American mainstream, such as those penned by **Diana Abu Jaber, Rabih Alameddine**, and **Naomi Shihab Nye**.

It is generally acknowledged that the first Arab American novel is *The Book of Khalid* (1911) by Ameen Rihani, widely regarded as the father of Arab American literature. Born in 1876 in Lebanon, Rihani emigrated to the United States when he was only twelve years old with his father and his uncle. He attended a New York school but was pulled out so that he could help the family business, namely keeping records and writing letters and transactions in English, the basics of which he had mastered by that point. Without a formal education, Rihani turned to English books, and among his favorite writers were William Shakespeare, Percy Shelley, and Victor Hugo. After several years, he attended law school, but dropped out due to his poor health; his father sent him to Lebanon to regain his health. In Lebanon, Rihani studied Arab literature and soon became fluently bilingual. In this sense, he was truly an Arab American writer, one who read and wrote in both languages. Rihani lived in an age marked by orientalism (an image, first definitely described by **Edward Said**, of the Arab world by the West that viewed the Arab and Muslim world as inferior in terms of religion, civilization, and culture). Rihani considered it part of his mission to explain the values of Arab culture and literature to his Western readers; thus, he was aware, as his successors would be, of the political facet of the Arab American identity. He returned to New York in 1899 but continued to travel back and forth between America and the Middle East for the rest of his life.

The Book of Khalid is the first novel to be written by an Arab or by an American of Arab descent in English. It is considered remarkable not for its artistic merit, but rather for its scope: Largely autobiographical, the novel describes the trials of its protagonist, a young man named Khalid, who seeks his identity between East and West. The novel is infused with philosophical and political undertones, making reference to Islam, the Baha'i faith, Christianity, capitalism, life in the Arab world, and related themes. The novel inspired many other Arab American writers of his generation, as well as those who succeeded him. *Jahan* (1917) is the title of another novel Rihani wrote in English, and he also authored several works of fiction in Arabic.

Etel Adnan's *Sitt Marie Rose* (1978) is another novel that gained widespread popular recognition, propelling the Lebanese American writer to the crest of the American literary scene. Like Rihani, Adnan's identity is complex and consists of more than one culture; she grew up in Lebanon, speaking French, English, and Arabic. Her main language, however, was French, and she has written about the fact that she regrets not being able to compose in Arabic. She emigrated to the United States to pursue her college education, settling in California. Like the writing of Rihani and other Arab Americans, Adnan's work has a pronounced political undertone; she also incorporates feminist themes into her novel, emphasizing the way in which women especially suffer due to political games and wars.

Sitt Marie Rose, which focuses on the tragedy of the Lebanese civil war, was translated into six languages. It focuses on Sitt Marie Rose, a young Christian Lebanese teacher. During the Lebanese Civil War, she sympathizes with the many Palestinian refugees who live in Lebanon, feeling connected to them and their plight. Her sympathies, however, are viewed as traitorous and she is kidnapped and executed, in a brutal, vicious manner, before her students. *Sitt Marie Rose* demonstrates the brutality of war in general while specifically exploring the fate of women in a patriarchal society as well as the ways in which the Israeli-Palestinian crisis has affected the Middle East.

Naomi Shihab Nye's *Habibi* (1997) also focuses on the Israeli-Palestinian crisis, but from a very different perspective. *Habibi* is widely acknowledged as the first young adult novel by an Arab American novelist and depicts the crisis from the point of view of a fourteen-year-old Palestinian American girl. Liyana Abboud, the novel's young protagonist, moves to Jerusalem for one year with her Palestinian father, her American mother, and her younger brother. There she learns about Palestinian culture and society and comes to love it; her Palestinian grandmother, whom she addresses as Sitti, proves to be a warm and wise mentor for the young teenager. Liyana also begins to understand the Israeli-Palestinian conflict when she befriends and falls in love with Omer, a Jewish boy. The novel is extraordinary, handling difficult scenes of Israeli-Palestinian violence with grace and skill, highlighting the common humanity that persists in the face of hatred. Nye, one of the most widely recognized and prolific Arab American writers, is herself the daughter of a Palestinian father and an American mother who moved to Jerusalem for one year when she was a teenager. *Habibi* is partly autobiographical and it also exemplifies the manner in which politics fundamentally tends to inform the themes of many Arab American novels.

Rabih Alameddine's *Koolaids: The Art of War* (1999) also deals with politics, although it tackles both Arab and American politics—specifically, the Lebanese Civil War and the American AIDS epidemic. The two events are compared because both are senseless, result in the deaths of thousands of innocents, and force people to contemplate their mortality. Alameddine, a painter and artist, tackles two very difficult subjects in a novel whose form is experimental and new for Arab American literature, especially in its adoption of homosexuality as a major theme. The protagonist, Mohamad, arrives in the United States as a teenager; he lives with an uncle, and is supposed to be finishing his studies, but instead decides to become an artist—a decision his father rejects. In defiance, Mohamad remains in the States, where he is able pursue his chosen profession. He contracts the AIDS virus and eventually dies. But even when he is seriously ill his parents refuse to associate with him; Mohamad's sense of loss of his family, complicated by the deaths of family members in the Lebanese Civil War, is overwhelming, finding expression in his art and in his dreams.

Alameddine, who was born in Jordan but lived in Kuwait and Lebanon, is a painter as well as a writer. His second novel, *I, the Divine: A Novel in First Chapters* (2001), features a female protagonist, Sarah Nour El-Din, who wants to write the story of her life but cannot begin. Thus, Alameddine pens various drafts of her first chapters, which the reader pieces together to form a more complete picture of Sarah's troubled life. The novel is exceptional in its form and in its male author's depiction of a convincing female protagonist.

Diana Abu Jaber's *Arabian Jazz* (1993) is also controversial because it offers a humorous look at the crisis of identity many young Arab Americans feel: her main character, Jemora Ramoud (Jem), is the daughter of a Jordanian father and an American mother. Her mother, however, died when Jem and her sister were young, and they were raised by Matussem, their father, who can only express his grief by playing in his **jazz** band. Jem, who is approaching her thirtieth birthday, feels unsatisfied with her life and struggles to reconcile her identity. Is she an American or an Arab? Should she marry or pursue a career? Should she move to Jordan and seek her identity there or remain in the United States with her family? A visit by a distant cousin, who has grappled with similar issues, helps Jem to realize that home is wherever she chooses to spend her life, and that one is not born with an identity, but must craft it.

Arab American literature in general, the novel in particular, has elicited considerable attention from mainstream publishers in the last decade and especially after the terrorist attacks on the World Trade Center on September 11, 2001. The ensuing war with Iraq that began in March 2003 has also sparked curiosity about Arab civilization at large as well as the culture and lives of Arab Americans. It is to be expected that the political environment, both national and global, will continue to shape Arab American art.

Further Reading

Castro, Joy. "Nomad, Switchboard, Poet: Naomi Shihab Nye's Multicultural Literature for Young Readers: An Interview." *MELUS* 27.2 (Summer 2002): 225–28.

Gabriel, Judith. "Emergence of a Genre: Reviewing Arab American Writers." *Al-Jadid: A Review and Record of Arab Culture and Arts* 7 (Winter 2001): 4–7.

Susan Muaddi Darraj

ARAB AMERICAN POETRY   Arab American Poetry is the oldest form of literature written by people of Arab descent in the United States, undoubtedly connected to the long and rich history of poetry in the Arab world. There are three overlapping periods of Arab American poetry, beginning in the early 1900s. The genre then re-emerged in the 1960s and 1970s, during the same period in which a large number of immigrants from the Middle East arrived in the United States. Finally, there is the current period, the early part of the new millennium. Throughout these periods, Arab American poetry has evidenced two main tendencies. The first is to adapt and assimilate, which is illustrated by poetry that is American in theme and content. The other tendency is to explore one's Arab heritage, either by depicting the immigrant experience or to write about the politics that affect the lives of Arabs both in the Middle East and in the United States.

The tradition of Arab poetry written by American Arabs can be traced back to the Al-Mahjar movement, which emerged in New York at the end of the nineteenth century and which was led by Ameen Rihani and **Kahlil Gibran**. Their colleagues, including Elia Abu-Madi and others, are also widely recognized, but they wrote mostly in Arabic, while the former two poets composed their work in Arabic as well as in English.

The Al-Mahjar poets ("mahjar" translates loosely into English as "émigré"), who numbered about ten men, considered themselves exiles from the Arab world, and their poetry reflected a sense of not belonging in the new world. However, the distance between them and the Middle East also afforded them a level of intellectual freedom they likely would not have enjoyed under the Ottoman Empire; in that light, they could both praise and criticize Arab politics, culture, and society. They established the Pen League, or Al-Rabitah al-Qalamiya, and—influenced mostly by the American and British Romantic writers—experimented with new forms, styles, and content in their own work.

Poets like Gibran, for example, became intrigued by the mystical themes of Romantic poetry and began to explore these themes in their own poems. Gibran is typical of the Mahajar poets; he emigrated to the United States in 1895 when he was only thirteen years old. He initially lived in Boston, in a large Arab American community, but relocated to New York City by 1912 where he helped establish the Mahajar movement by 1920. He was an artist and a philosopher, as well as a poet, and his sense of exile is a marked feature of his work. Gibran's most famous work, and the one that put him on the literary map of the United States, is *The Prophet* (1923), a sequence of twenty-six prose poems. In the book, a wise man has been away from his homeland for many years and is about to return; before he embarks on his journey home, he preaches to a gathered audience about the spiritual and physical mysteries of the world.

The work of Rihani, who also emigrated to the United States as a young man, is wide-ranging in theme, and like Gibran, he was prolific in his writing: his poetry collections include *The Quatrains of Abul'Ala'* (1903), *Myrtle and Myrrh* (1905), *The Luzumiyat of Abul'Ala'* (1918), and *A Chant of Mystics and Other Poems* (1921). A collection of his Arab poetry, published posthumously, was titled *Hutaf al-Awdiya*, or *Hymn of the Valleys* (1955).

While the Mahajar poets found comfort in one another's company, a band of exiles in New York City, their successors have sought to form bonds and forge alliances with other ethnic American writers. It is not unusual to find Arab American poets who trace their literary influences to African American, Asian American, or Latino writers. This trait is especially marked in the Arab American poetry that emerged after the **Civil**

Rights Movement in America during the 1960s, when many ethnic Americans expressed solidarity with African Americans. During this time period, Arab **identity** was also undergoing a major transformation, as the Arab-Israeli conflict reached its climax with the 1967 war, which saw the Israeli occupation of the Palestinian West Bank and Gaza. This war, and other regional wars that followed, including the 1972 war and the Lebanese Civil War, resulted in an influx of immigrants to the United States and had a lasting effect on the writing produced by Arabs in America.

D. H. Melhem, a New York-based Lebanese American poet, was one of the first scholars to write a comprehensive study of the literature of Gwendolyn Brooks, the African American poet. Titled *Gwendolyn Brooks: Poetry and the Heroic Voice* (1987), the study earned Melhem a nomination for a Woodrow Wilson Fellowship in Women's Studies. She also published *Heroism in the New Black Poetry* (1990), which won an American Book Award the following year.

Melhem's poetry spans more than three decades. Her first collection, titled *Notes on 94th Street* (1972), is regarded as the first collection of poetry in English to be published by an Arab American woman, although the poems do not focus specifically on Arab American identity. Rather, the poems illustrate life in New York, evoking the atmosphere of the city's Upper West Side. The collection was followed by *Children of the House Afire: More Notes on 94th Street* (1976); her other collections include *Rest in Love* (1978), an elegy for the poet's mother, and *Country: An Organic Poem* (1998), in which many poems address the immigrant experience. Her most recent collection is *Conversations with a Stonemason* (2003), in which Melhem tackles the subject of preserving humanity in a post-9/11 world.

Samuel Hazo, a poet of Lebanese and Syrian ancestry, was appointed the first State Poet of the Commonwealth of Pennsylvania 1993. A prolific writer, Hazo has published several works of fiction and nonfiction, as well as poetry. His poetry collections include *Once for the Last Bandit* (1972), *Quartered* (1974), *To Paris* (1981), *Nightwords* (1988), *The Holy Surprise of Right Now: Selected and New Poems* (1996), and *As They Sail* (1999). The themes of his poetry are the classic ones: life, death, spirituality, suffering, and aging. While Hazo's early work is written in structured, carefully metered verse, his later work has moved toward a more open and free style of expression. Hazo is also an accomplished translator and has published his translations of Arab poets Nadia Tueni and Adonis.

Just as the Arab-Israeli conflict shaped the consciousness of Arab American poets in the 1960s and 1970s, the Persian Gulf wars between America and Iraq, in 1991 and 2003, as well as the September 11, 2001 attacks on the United States, also influenced the work of a new generation of Arab American poets. These new poets were more assertive about their identity, writing to explain their feelings of being ostracized by American society and their anger at American foreign policy.

Lawrence Joseph, the son of Syrian and Lebanese Catholic immigrants, was born and raised in Detroit, Michigan; since beginning his literary career with the publication of *Shouting at No One* (1983), the winner of the Agnes Lynch Starrett Prize, Joseph has become a highly acclaimed poet. His other poetry collections include *Before Our Eyes* (1993) and *Curriculum Vitae* (1988). Joseph, who is also an essayist and a professor of law, addresses the political identity of Arab Americans directly in his work. His poem, "Sand Nigger," for example, highlights the **racism** faced by Arabs living in the United States.

Another highly regarded and prolific Arab American poet is **Naomi Shihab Nye**, the daughter of an American mother and a Palestinian father. Her bicultural ethnic identity features prominently in her poetry. Her collections include *19 Varieties of Gazelle: Poems of the Middle East* (2002), which was a National Book Award finalist, as well as *Fuel* (1998), *Red Suitcase* (1994), and *Hugging the Jukebox* (1982). Her recent poetry is often political in nature, which Nye considers to be natural, as politics is a force that shapes everyday life. (After the 9/11 attacks on the United States, Nye wrote a lengthy essay titled "Letter from Naomi Shihab Nye to Any Would-Be Terrorists," in which she implores the Arab world to strive for peace and to question the stereotypes about Americans to which they might subscribe.) One of Nye's most important books is the anthology *The Space Between Our Footsteps: Poems & Paintings from the Middle East* (1998), which she edited for young adults, but which has found a popular audience among adults as well. Her writing has been recognized by fellowships from the Lannan Foundation, Guggenheim, and the Library of Congress, as well as by four Pushcart Prizes.

Nye is the first of many Arab American women whose poetry has emerged onto the American literary scene in the last decade. In the seminal anthology *The Poetry of Arab Women* (2000), poet and editor Nathalie Handal collects the voices of many Arab, and especially Arab American, women poets. Among the most prolific is Suheir Hammad, a young Palestinian American known for her hip-hop style and powerful imagery. Hammad, born in a Palestinian refugee camp in Jordan, emigrated to the United States as a child, settling in New York City where she grew up in a diverse neighborhood; her poetry reflects Arab rhythms, as well as Latino, African American, and other ethnic influences. Another poet included in Handal's anthology is Dima Hilal, a young Lebanese American poet whose work is ripe with political and cultural imagery and themes. (*See also* Arab American Stereotypes)

Further Reading
Smith, Dinitia. "*Arab-American Writers*, Uneasy in Two Worlds." *New York Times* (February 19, 2003): E1.

Susan Muaddi Darraj

ARAB AMERICAN STEREOTYPES   By repeatedly disallowing their subjection to negative stereotypes, various ethnic communities, including African Americans, Jewish Americans and Italian Americans, among others, have succeeded in drastically curtailing the racial and ethnic stereotypes that minority groups have historically faced in the United States. Arab Americans, however, remain somehow outside such antiracist awareness and consequently continue to be subjected to increasing levels of derogatory stereotypes. Accepted by the U.S. public as true, these stereotypes engender feelings of hate toward Arabs living in the United States (both as citizens and otherwise) as well as those living in the Arab world. Arabs are often characterized as cheats, liars, dangerous terrorists, and irrational fanatics, and these stereotypes, disseminated widely by the media and other cultural productions, enter into higher levels of circulation in the United States at moments of national crisis, examples of which include the attacks of September 11, 2001, and the subsequent invasions of Afghanistan and Iraq. Even though the inconsistency in the naturalization of the first wave of Arab immigrants in the early twentieth century culminated in the U.S. Census Bureau classifying Arab Americans as white or Caucasian, this group's racial categorization is not stable. Deeply affected by U.S. foreign policy in the Middle East (examples of which include the 1967 Arab-Israeli war and the 1973 oil embargo), Arab Americans still occupy an ambiguous position in terms of **race** and citizenship.

Negative portrayals of Arab Americans have their roots in eighteenth- and nineteenth-century European depictions of the Orient, by which the East becomes "the Other," replete with subjugated women living in harems and mysterious and romanticized settings harboring a "heathen" population. Such images are handled at length by Palestinian American critic **Edward Said** in his groundbreaking book *Orientalism* (1978), which questions the foundations upon which the West has constructed its representation of the East as Other. This Western outlook, Said believes, is propagated in the current cultural stereotyping of, and prejudice against, Arabs generally and Muslim Arabs particularly, in the West.

Drawing on a repertoire of stereotypes revolving around fanatic killers, oil-rich sheikhs, and an unfamiliar religion set against a desert background, cultural representations of Arabs and Arab Americans disregard the diversity of Arab **identity**, whether in cultural, religious, ethnic, or national aspects. The dangerous confluence of Arab and Muslim identities in the U.S. national consciousness (whereby all Muslims are Arab and all Arabs are Muslim) is one example of the extremely limited and simplistic understanding of Arab and Arab American identity. Statistics show that the majority of the Arab American population is Christian and that the majority of Muslims worldwide are located in Indonesia, India, and Malaysia (Shaheen 3, 4).

Starting in 1967 with the Association of Arab-American University Graduates (AAUG), several organizations have been founded by Arab Americans to promote a better understanding of their community and to fight against Arab American stereotypes and discrimination. Such organizations include The National Association of Arab Americans (NAAA), the American-Arab Anti-Discrimination Committee (ADC), and the Arab American Institute (AAI), formed in 1972, 1980, and 1985, respectively. By focusing on issues affecting the representation and the civil rights of Arab Americans, such as negative stereotypes permeating the media, racial profiling, and hate crimes, these groups ensure that Arab Americans retain an important role in their self-representation as U.S. citizens.

Arab American writers repeatedly address their individual and communal subjection to negative stereotypes that not only relegate them to the margins of American society, but also render them invisible. A host of Arab American writers, such as **Joanna Kadi**, **Lisa Suhair Majaj**, and Nada Elia, has focused on this issue of invisibility, noting the manner in which it permeates the various areas of Arab American identity, encompassing the social, cultural, and literary arenas. Poetic challenges to the negative stereotyping of Arab Americans are exemplified in the works of Suheir Hammad and Mohja Kahf, who arm themselves with a distinct ethnic, religious, and racial identity that questions the ambiguity inherent in the current racial categorization of Arab Americans. By featuring in their work the derogatory labels and negative stereotypes targeting Arab Americans, other writers such as Lawrence Joseph and **Diana Abu Jaber** call attention to the false assumptions upon which such stereotypes are constructed, thus reinforcing the need for their eradication. Barbara Nimri Aziz, Arab American journalist and cofounder of the Radius of Arab American Writers Inc., emphasizes the importance of self-representation through writing, thus calling for Arab Americans to emulate other ethnic communities such as Italian Americans, whose writers' association had as one of its doctrines: "Write or be written." Such an act is elemental for Arab Americans because, as Aziz states, "the histories we learn in school, the tales we hear in the street, the claims made on our behalf, all somehow miss the point. Or simply get it wrong. We are really not how others write us. At best we are invisible. What we witnessed and were taught was not and is not our heritage" (xii).

Further Reading

Aziz, Barbara Nimri. Foreword. *Scheherazade's Legacy: Arab and Arab American Women on Writing*. Ed. Susan Muaddi Darraj. Westport, CT: Praeger, 2004. xi–xv.

Elia, Nada. "The 'White' Sheep of the Family: But *Bleaching* Is like Starvation." Ed. Gloria E. Anzaldúa and Analouise Keating. *this bridge we call home: radical visions for transformation*. New York: Routledge, 2002. 223–31.

Ghareeb, Edmund. *Split Vision: The Portrayal of Arabs in the American Media*. Washington, DC: The American-Arab Affairs Council, 1983.

Hammad, Suheir. *Born Palestinian, Born Black*. London: Writers & Readers, 1996.

Kadi, Joanna, ed. *Food for Our Grandmothers: Writings by Arab-American and Arab-Canadian Feminists*. Boston: South End Press, 1994.

Majaj, Lisa Suhair. "Arab-Americans and the Meanings of Race." *Postcolonial Theory and the United States: Race, Ethnicity, and Literature*. Ed. Amritjit Singh and Peter Schmidt. Jackson: UP of Mississippi, 2000. 320–37.

McCarus, Ernest, ed. *The Development of Arab-American Identity*. Ann Arbor: U of Michigan P, 1994.

Shaheen, Jack G. *Reel Bad Arabs: How Hollywood Vilifies a People*. New York: Olive Branch Press, 2001.

Terry, Janice J. *Mistaken Identity: Arab Stereotypes in Popular Writing*. Washington, DC: The American-Arab Affairs Council, 1985.

Carol Fadda-Conrey

ARDIZZONE, ANTHONY (1950–) Italian American fiction writer. Author of three novels—*In the Name of the Father* (1978), *Heart of the Order* (1986), and *In the Garden of Papa Santuzzu* (2000)—Tony Ardizzone has been honored with publication in Best American Short Stories. His collection of short stories, *The Evening News* (1986), won the **Flannery O'Connor** Award for Short Fiction. Ardizzone's fiction displays a myriad set of responses to Italian American cultural values and to their expression. His fiction reveals a search back into the roots of Sicilian folklore to discover the heart of wisdom the fiction of this culture can offer us.

Ardizzone's characters tend to be first- or second-generation Italian Americans, with little or no awareness of the mainstream American culture. The author neither unabashedly celebrates nor denigrates these immigrants. However, in one of his short stories, "Holy Cards," he brings to bear a naturalistic disdain for the insularity and naïveté of some immigrant cultures. In this story, the protagonist, a little boy named Dominic, succumbs to the primitive superstitions and symbolism of his Italian Catholic faith. For example, responding to an image of the Trinity, Dominic thinks that the Holy Spirit must feel weak to be "only a bird." Events and images take on a bizarrely hyperreal significance, and nothing within the Italian American cultural context can serve as a means to greater intellectual development for the boy.

By this token, then, the American cultural side of the Italian American cultural matrix should offer some answers. But in his novel *Heart of the Order*, Ardizzone examines America's national pastime to form the central metaphor of coming to terms with migration from ethnic ghetto to the American big leagues. Protagonist Danilo Boccigalupo (literally "kissed by the wolf") is a talented third baseman and hitter fated to play most of his career in the minors. Having accidentally killed his childhood friend Mickey Meehan with a wild line drive to the Adam's apple, he imagines the ghost of his friend dwells within his own body. For Danny, being Italian American and Catholic means being open to experiencing all the conflicting emotions of his life. One fateful day releases Danny from his curse, but the predestiny that pervades the treatment of his release undercuts the theme of **assimilation** and the freedom from oppressive ideological constructs (like Southern Italian fatalism) it would bring.

However, Ardizzone's collection of folklore woven into *In the Garden of Papa Santuzzu*, reconciles American and Sicilian cultural currents by design. The narrative is constructed as a series of folktales recounted by relatives and descendants of Papa Santuzzu, who becomes an archetype of all ancestors of Southern Italian and Sicilian immigrants. The magical realist tales represent the harsh realities of the tenant farming system of Sicily. Family becomes the rope immigrants cling to as they escape. The same strength of character that allows these characters to survive the harsh landscape empowers them to protest conditions in the new land. Papa Santuzzu's descendants assimilate heroically, taking the best of their culture with them. (*See also* Italian American Novel)

Further Reading

Tamburri, Anthony Julian. *A Semiotic of Ethnicity: In (Re)cognition of the Italian/ American Writer.* Albany: State U of New York P, 1998.

Paul Giaimo

ARENAS, REINALDO (1943–1990)   Cuban writer who spent the final ten years of his life as a refugee in the United States. Reinaldo Arenas has been considered by many scholars and literary critics as one of the most eloquent and daring writers of his generation. Perhaps because he refused to conform to societal expectations, Arenas and his writing became emblems to the ideals of a counter-revolution.

His literary works encompass all genres including novels, plays, short stories, and poetry. He is best known for his "pentagonía" (pentagony), a series of five novels that details the lives of Cubans from Fulgencio Batista's dictatorship to Fidel Castro's revolutionary regime. In each of the novels that are part of his pentagony, the characters die at the end of the story; however, they are "resurrected" in the next installment only to experience the harshness of Fidel Castro's regime. Also well-known is his autobiography *Before Night Falls*, the basis for the 2000 film by the same title.

What makes Arenas's writing distinct from many of his contemporaries is the fact that he was openly critical of Fidel Castro's regime, which promised to expel from the island any remnants of imperialism and the dictatorship that controlled it. However, as an open homosexual, Arenas found that the same revolution he supported was persecuting individuals like himself. Because of his opposition to the ideals of the Socialist, and later Marxist-Leninist regime, Reinaldo Arenas became an enemy of the state and became a target of harassment.

His refusal to conform and his adherence to what he considered to be his freedom of expression and creativity in order to promote the ideals of the revolution are reflected in his writing. His attacks on the regime's goals and false promises fueled his desire to create a counter-discourse that promoted freedom of expression and assertion of an **identity** separate from the revolution. Thus, he attempted to assert his own sense of self by any means necessary. Arenas's reaction, and continued approaches to his writing against the revolutionary government, and Castro's ideology in particular, developed into an attack against the regime's official story. This act of resistance on Arenas's part had as its goal a reappropriation of the discourse of the voiceless, to recount events that allowed for the reconstruction of an identity taken away from those individuals who were persecuted, oppressed, and marginalized.

The characters that Reinaldo Arenas employed in his literary work, such as the homosexual and the child, represented those individuals who were not accepted or welcomed by the regime. His representation of the soldier, the mother, the grandfather, Fidel Castro, and the revolution itself allowed him to attack the regime and at the same time rewrite his own story in a way that those who experienced life as he had would understand. The depiction of these characters in his writing allowed him to reflect on his own experiences and express his concern for the conditions under which many homosexuals lived in Cuba.

His exile in 1980 to the United States through the Port of Mariel allowed him the opportunity to oppose Fidel Castro openly, doing so not only through his writing, but at conferences and in his lectures across the United States, Spain, and the rest of Europe. For the first time Arenas felt he could express in speech what he had been trying to do in his writing. His migration to the Unites States thus afforded him an opportunity to articulate more freely his liberatory politics.

Throughout his exile he continued expressing his opposition to the Cuban revolution in his writing, culminating in the posthumous publication of his autobiography. In *Before Night Falls*, Arenas shares with his readers not only what life was like for a child growing up in the countryside under Fulgencio Batista's dictatorship but also what life was like for homosexuals on the island specifically after the success of Fidel Castro's revolution. His autobiography is perhaps one of the best examples of his literary work because it confronts directly issues pertaining to sexuality, its relationship to identity, and the art of writing itself. It is his last act as a writer and as a political activist to claim for himself and for those who shared similar experiences a sense of self and a reappropriation of what was once denied to them. Thus, Arenas's autobiography can be read as an oppositional act to the patriarchal and authoritative society that oppressed anyone who dared challenge its control. As such, the characters that Arenas presents in his writing, as well as themes such as death, suicide, the sea, writing, and sex, became archetypical ways of reconstructing an identity. (*See also* Cuban American Autobiography)

Further Reading
Soto, Francisco. *Reinaldo Arenas.* New York: Twayne, 1998.

Enrique Morales-Diaz

ARMENIAN AMERICAN LITERATURE   The **Armenian genocide**, more than a catastrophic experience for the victimized nation, brought about an end to the three-thousand-year Armenian presence in the western part of historic Armenia. The land was swept clean of its indigenous people. The few survivors were not allowed to return to their homes, and, uprooted, they took refuge in the four corners of the world. With the influx of the refugees, the pre–World War I Armenian American **diaspora**, small in number and composed mostly of factory workers and shopkeepers, grew substantially and incorporated a new meaning that entailed a new frame of mind, a worldview, and a way of life.

The concept of diaspora, of course, was not new to Armenians. Many were poets and writers, who were engaged in literary activities away from the homeland, away but always near, because the bridges were not burned yet and the option to return was always open. The diaspora was actually a window to the world culture, to new schools of thought, and new literary directions. The genocide of 1915 cancelled all existing conventions and a priori assumptions. Cut off from the homeland and deprived of a collective national existence, Armenians in the diaspora struggled to survive and perpetuate as a nation in exile, a predicament conducive of a particular literary milieu with particular social, political, and cultural determinants reacting on the artist's individuality, intellect, and creative mind. The pre-genocide literary milieu had evolved into its antithesis in the post-genocide diaspora, as had collective national life into dispersion.

Indeed, it was between 1920 and the 1930s that the final dispersion of the Armenian people became a reality, and the full impact of the genocide sank in. Significantly, this period also coincided with the loss of the short-lived Armenian independence (May 1918–December 1920) and the realization of having been denied the freedom to live as a nation. The outcome was a unique psychological state that translated into nostalgic literature permeating pathetic sentimentalism, which stemmed not only from yearning for the lost homeland, but also from that strong sense of inhibition Armenian immigrant writers experienced in foreign, unfamiliar environments. And from that point it is not difficult to pass into the poetry of homesickness, which, as Hagop Oshagan, the renowned diaspora Armenian writer and critic, puts it, is a literary affliction, nonconforming with the prevailing concepts of world literature of the time. But, perhaps, this was the most feasible direction the literature of a nation of victims could take—an uprooted literature that had not yet taken root, or that was reluctant to take root in the new environment, a reason why the American scene was absent and if present, only as an alien and unfriendly environment, the cause of the pain and suffering of an exile. Even Ruben Darbinian, the prominent and long time editor of *Hairenik Monthly*, considered America a temporary station, sort of a haven for the survivors, with nothing interesting to affect literary creations.

In order to survive in the broadest sense and liberate literature and literary creativity from psychological, political, and emotive constraints, it was necessary to confront the Catastrophe to find a way to deal with it, to write it, in other words, to find literary tools to harness the horrifying images and the overpowering experience and bring them down into the realm of language. Very few were able to cross that bridge. The rest remained entrapped in and overwhelmed by the traumatic experience of the past and the hardship to adjust to the present conditions.

The literature produced in this period, thus, mostly in the Armenian language and by immigrant writers, marks the inception of the Armenian American diaspora literature and is followed by a transitional period in which the themes and the style of the Old World gradually give in to the American Armenian reality. Of course, a literary historian would rightfully argue that the inception of the Armenian American literature dates back to the 1880s, coinciding also with the publication of the first periodical, *Aregak* (Sun), in 1888 in Jersey City, but the fact is that the bulk of Armenian American literature of substantial esthetic value owes its development to the influx of intellectuals who reached the United States in 1920s after the genocide.

The Periodical Press

With the scarcity of publications in separate volumes in the initial and the transitional stages, the Armenian periodical press in America remains as an important source of inquiry. It had, in effect, assumed an important role in the cultural development of the community. Mostly organs of Armenian political parties and thus each with a political mission, these periodicals were also dedicated to the preservation of the Armenian culture, language, and **identity** in the New World. On the one hand, they fostered the necessary literary milieu for artistic literature to develop. On the other hand, they reflected the community's literary taste and worked toward refining that taste and giving direction to art. In this dichotomy, it is natural, for socioeconomic reasons, to witness the periodicals succumbing to the average reader's convenience and priority to see his own image, his pains, and anxieties in it in the most simplistic way. It is also understandable why very little of the literature filling the pages of these periodicals is read today and is an integral part of the Armenian literary legacy of all times.

The more important of these periodicals were: *Hairenik* daily newspaper and *Hairenik Weekly* (since 1898, New York, then Boston) and especially its literary monthly (1922–70). The paper particularly echoed the 1894–96 massacres of Armenians in the Ottoman Empire with literary responses that did not necessarily merit aesthetic value, but they appeared alongside the poems of great Armenian poets of Constantinople such as Siamanto and Daniel Varuzhan, who later became victims of genocide. Especially in the 1920s and 1930s, *Hairenik Monthly* was the repository of memoirs and eyewitness accounts of the survivors. Names that frequently appeared in *Hairenik* were: Hagop Oshagan, H. Siruni, Artashes Abeghian, Intra, Hamastegh, Aram Haigaz, Simon Vratsian, Aleksandr Khatisian, Malkhas, Destegul, Ruben Berberian, Levon Shant, Kostan Zarian, Varduhi Kalantar, Arsen Erkat, Sos Vani, Hrand Armen, Suren Saninian, Edvard Boyajian, A. Arpine, Chituni, Armenak Melikian Armenuhi Tikranian, Armen Anush,

Mari Kalaijian, Dzerun Torgomian, and later, Minas Teoleolian (sometimes using also Armen Amatian and Vazken Vanandian pen names), Gurgen Mkhitarian, Gevorg Tonapetian, and others, some of whom did not even live in United States but whose literature certainly impacted the Armenian American life and frame of mind. *Hairenik*, meaning homeland in Armenian, had actually become the reincarnation of the Armenian homeland, the embodiment of its natural beauty, its lifestyle, human relationships, national movements, and the struggle for freedom.

Nor Kir, a monthly, then quarterly (1936–54, New York), had these important names in it: Vahé Haig, Aram Haigaz, Vahé Vahian, Beniamin Nourikian, Andranik Andreasian, Hagop Asaturian, and Suren Manuelian. *Nor Kir* also introduced its readers to Soviet Armenian literature, abundantly publishing works of Soviet Armenian contemporary writers.

Piunik Monthly (1918–20, Boston) strove to gather new voices like Hamastegh, Shahan Natali, Karapet Sital, Vahé Haig, Hovhannes Avagian, Nshan Destegiul, and Arsen Erkat to continue in the footsteps of great Western Armenian writers who fell victim to the genocide.

Paykar Daily (since 1922, Boston), its literary quarterly (1930–31, 1963–68), and its annual volumes (1942–63) were surrounded by intellectuals such as Andranik Andreasian, Vahé Haig, Suren Samuelian, Noubar Agishian, and Zareh Melkonian.

Later on as the Armenian communities grew in America, literary journals were published in Los Angeles (*Navasart Monthly*, and the literary supplement of *Asbarez Daily*) and Montreal, Canada (the literary supplement of *Horizon Weekly*), and the names that often appear in these journals and have some degree of prestige in the field of Armenian literature are: Vahé Oshagan, Hakop Karapents, Garo Armenian, Vehanush Tekian, Vrej Armen, Biuzand Kranian, Jacque Hagopian, Hrant Markarian, Harutiun Berberian, Armen Tonoyan, Boghos Kupelian, Alicia Ghiragossian, Torkom Postachian, Arshavir Mkrtich, Jirayr Attarian, Loucik Melikian, Vanuhi Avetissian, Avetis Gevorgian (Hayordi), Vahé Berberian, Khoren Aramuni, Gevorg Kristinian, Vahram Hajian, and Grish Davtian. They all have their own published volumes in prose or poetry.

During its short life (1995–2000), the quarterly publication *Bats Namak* (Gourgen Arzoumanian, editor) became a stage for both renowned and novice poets and writers, a sort of a meeting place for new ideas in literary presentations and discussions. There appeared poems and prose from Raffi Setian, Marc Nichanian, Vardan Mateossian, Gevorg Manoyan, Raffi Ajemian, Ara Kazanchian, and Gevorg Bedikian.

Characteristically, none of the writers mentioned above are born and educated in the United States. They write in Armenian (only some are bilingual), and although they are to a great extent acculturated and most of them choose their topics from everyday life in America, their protagonists suffer the destiny of a diaspora Armenian with all the problems of culture shock and a dual identity.

The need to provide a forum for the English writers, immigrant or native, and to reach the new generation who did not read or write Armenian anymore, the *Hairenik* group in Boston began to publish the *Hairenik Weekly* in 1934 (renamed *Armenian Weekly* in 1969). Then again, in order to fill a void of scholarly articles on Armenian literature, history, and politics, the publication of *Armenian Review* was initiated (1949), which houses Armenian and non-Armenian literary critics, historians, and social and political scientists. Similar in content are the *Journal of Armenian Studies* (first issued in 1975, then regularly after 1985 as a twice-yearly publication of National Association for Armenian Studies and Research), *Journal of the Society for Armenian Studies* (issued yearly since 1984), and *Armenian Forum* (issued quarterly since 1998).

Ararat (since 1960, New Jersey), an English-language quarterly magazine of literature, history, popular culture, and art, has published works of almost all the Armenian American writers: John Andriasian, David Kherdian, **William Saroyan**, Levon Surmelian, Peter Sourian, Leo Hamalian, Edmond Azadian, Gevorg Dervish, Ara Baliozian, Vahé Oshagan, Tigran Guyumjian, and more recent writers and poets Haig Khachadourian, **Diana Der Hovanissian**, **Leonardo Alishan**, Izabelle Gabrielian, Arleen Vosgi Avakian, Nancy Kricorian, Florence Avakian, David Colonne, Margaret Bedrossian, Arpine Konialian Grenier, and Lou Ann Matossian.

RAFT: A Journal of Armenian Poetry and Criticism (1987–99), a yearly with Vahé Oshagan and Armenologist John Greppin, coeditors, aimed to introduce Armenian poetry old and new in their English original or English translation to English-speaking Armenian and non-Armenian audience. Vahé Oshagan's critical reviews, the literary works of Diana Der Hovanessian, Leonardo Alishan, Raffi Setian, Lorne Shirinian, Nancy Kricorian, Haig Khachadourian, Peter Balakian, and Garik Basmajian appeared regularly.

Diaspora, a journal of transnational studies (Khachig Tololyan, editor), is published three times a year and is dedicated to the multidisciplinary study of the history, culture, social structure, politics, and economics of both the traditional diasporas—Armenian, Greek, and Jewish—and those transnational dispersions. It is a forum for Armenian scholars expert in the field of transnational studies.

The above is only a very short list of Armenian or English language literary periodicals. There are still many that are mushrooming with the growth of the Armenian community and those literary periodicals that have had a longer life belong to church parishes, or compatriotic, cultural, and benevolent organizations. In the latter case articles or literary pieces are bilingual.

As a pattern, the newcomer writer either continues to write in Armenian or after a while, gaining competence in English and with an aim to reach a larger audience of English speakers, switches to English.

Individual Writers of Importance

Hamastegh (1895–1966), born in Kharbert, whose works were first published in *Hairenik*, continued in the pre-genocide tradition of Western

Armenian literature. He immigrated to America when he was sixteen years old but remained attached to the homeland he had left. He portrayed life in his native village and strove to keep the memory of the Old World alive. *Gyughe* (The Village, 1924), *Andzreve* (The Rain, 1929), *Spitak dziavor* (The White Horseman, 1952), *Kaj Nazar ev tasnerek patmvatskner* (The Brave Nazar and Thirteen Stories, 1955), and *Aghotaran* (Chapel, 1957) are some of his works.

Beniamin Nourigian (1894), born in Kharbert, immigrated to America before 1915, and he too continued in the tradition of the pre-genocide Western Armenian literature. His short stories and novels paint the nature and the lifestyle of the Old Country and embody the author's unabated yearning for that life. His works were published in *Nor Kir* and in separate volumes, *Aigekutk* (Harvest, 1937), *Pandukht hoginer* (Migrant Souls, 1959), and *Karot hayreni* (Yearning for the Homeland, 1978).

Vahé Haig (1896–1983), born in Kharbert, immigrated to America in 1920 after he had already made his career as a writer in Constantinople. He continued it in America, and his works were published in many periodicals of the time. His short stories of life in the Old Country were published in *Haireni Tskhan* (Paternal Hearth) in five volumes. He also has essays on historical events of the past, the massacres of Yozgat, and the Armenian community in Fresno.

Aram Haigaz (1900–86), born in Shapin Garahisar, as a fifteen-year-old boy participated in his town's armed self-defense against the Turkish army of executioners. He later described this heroic venture in his work, *Chors tari Kurdistani lernerun mej* (Four Years in the Mountains of Kurdistan, 1973). *Tseghin dzayne* in two volumes (The Voice of the Race, 1949 and 1954), *Chors ashkharh* (Four Worlds, 1962), *Pandok* (Hotel, 1967), and *Karot* (Yearning, 1971) are some of his other works.

Hagop Asadurian (1903–2003), born in Chomakhlu, immigrated in 1920 after spending his early teenage years in orphanages. He was the only survivor of his family. A self-taught man of letters, he became a regular contributor for *Nor Kir* with his poetry, creative prose, and literary criticism. His fictionalized autobiography, *Hovagimin tornere* (The Grand Children of Hovagim, 1965) was a contribution to the fiftieth anniversary of the genocide.

A. Arpiné (1908–2003), born in Marzovan, settled in the United States in 1931. Some of her writings, scattered in periodicals of the 1940s, were published between 1967 and 1980 in three volumes depicting Armenian life, struggles, pain, and happiness in America.

Biuzand Kranian (1912–), born in Aintab, belongs to the generation of Armenians who had lost their language to Turkish oppression. He learned his mother tongue, which was not his mother's tongue, after the family's escape to Aleppo. His literature in prose and poetry reflects the gradual influence of the American culture, lifestyle, and literary trends. The bulk of it is published in two volumes in 1975 and 1980.

Jacque Hagopian (1917–), born in Jerusalem, is the poet of love and life, but most of all he sings the love of his Armenian homeland. With a fiery style, he inspires national pride and aspiration.

Lucik Melikian (1922–), born in Tehran, was a young but renowned writer when she immigrated to the United States. With her experience of the American life, she continued to portray the diaspora Armenian and the reality of the diaspora communities. She is one of the few Armenian immigrant writers who ventured into using the English language in her work. *Forbidden Days of Ramazan* and *From Hunger to Caviar* are her novels in English, the latter dealing with the genocide.

To create Armenian literature using the English language as a medium of artistic expression was a paradox and an issue for long debate, especially among those intellectuals who regarded the phenomenon as a sign of surrender and assimilation. But how is it possible to disqualify Emmanuel Varandyan and disown *The Well of Ararat* (1938), which encompasses Armenian village life in Persia before 1915, evolving past the immigration to America and the whole scope of its impact; or how is it possible to discredit Bedros Margosian (*Of Desert Bondage*, 1940), Marie Sarafian Banker (*Armenian* Romance, 1941), and Nishan Der-Hagopian (*Out of Inferno*, 1949), all of whom depicted the massacres and deportation of Armenians in the Ottoman Empire? Where can you put William Saroyan? He is an Armenian, and his literature belongs to the Armenian literary legacy—even as much as he is American producing in the American mainstream literary world (if such a thing exists).

As time went by and the concept of Armenian American literature as part of the Armenian diaspora literature was shaped, the relevancy of the theme to Armenian life and the diaspora Armenian mindset—context, milieu, and historicity—rather than the language of expression became the norm for categorization. This was a definite sign of acculturation, an attempt to get out of isolation and find a niche for the Armenian American minority—their cultural values, art, and tradition—in mainstream America, to give and to receive. The publication of *Three Words* by *Hairenik Weekly* (1939), the first anthology of short stories and poems by Armenian American writers and translations from Armenian literature, is evidence for that willingness. Also significant is Ruben Darbinian's preface that clearly speaks of the transformation of his initial view—and the initial stance of Armenian intellectuals in America—of America being a temporary station with nothing to offer to the Armenian literature.

Levon-Zaven Surmelian (1907, Trabizond) began to write poetry in Armenian when he was dragging his life in the orphanages. *Luis Zvart* (1924), his first and only collection of poetry, speaks of the pain and deprivations of a young boy who lived through the atrocities and witnessed the demise of his family. He stopped writing in Armenian in the United States. His two major works, *I Ask You, Ladies and Gentlemen* (1945, and the second edition in 1980 with William Saroyan's foreword) and *98.6°* (1950), have the

Armenian genocide as their leitmotif and are based on his own life experience. He continued producing literature in English, translating the Armenian national epic (*Daredevils of Sasun*, 1965) and Armenian legends and folklore (*Apples of Immortality: Folktales of Armenia*, 1968). *Techniques of Fiction Writing: Measure and Madness* is his contribution to literary theory and criticism.

Leon Srabian Herald (1912, Erzinjan) published his first volume of poetry, *This Waking Hour*, in 1925 in America. Since then, he has been a regular contributor to American and Armenian periodicals.

Richard Hagopian's (1914–76) short story "The Burning Acid" (1944 in a volume of short stories, titled *The Dove Brings Peace*) is the story of the death of the nation and the painful birth of the diaspora, communities of dead Armenians (in America) whose predicament—a result of the genocide—is transformed into an unbearable pain, hatred, and frustration burning their souls like acid. The novel *Faraway the Spring* (1952) is life in the Old Country evolving through the story of a genocide survivor who has made home and is raising children in America, but he is a misfit. He can't belong.

Peter Sourian's *The Gate* (1965) is the story of three generations of Armenians rooted in the Ottoman Empire. The father miraculously survives the genocide and attempts to make a new life. His son, a young man, immigrates to America and submerges himself in the mainstream society. He refuses to teach Armenian to his children whom he raises as true Americans. But he is involuntarily drawn back to his heritage.

And finally, Wiliam Saroyan (1908–81), born in Fresno, California, the son of immigrant parents from Bitlis, took his first steps toward fame in American literature in the 1930s. His Armenian background, cultural values, the discriminations against his people in his hometown, Armenian tales, and stories of Turkish persecutions have shaped his outlook on life and influenced his literature.

The Renewed Recourse to the Past

Coinciding with the trend of searching for one's roots in America, the African American movement of the 1960s, the worldwide commemoration of the fiftieth anniversary of the Armenian genocide in 1965, and the heightened political activism of the Armenian diaspora played a pivotal role in sensitizing the new generation and in directing attention to the unhealed wound of genocide. After all, it was all right to look for your ancestors, to have your roots in another part of the world, to have inherited a completely different culture and still be a good citizen—a member of the mainstream. This was a beginning for the new diaspora Armenian reality, which called for a stronger commitment to the cause of national ideology. It kindled self-consciousness and self-recognition among a stratum of youth, who were now thoroughly immersed in the mainstream culture yet still searching for the source of their own particularity.

The echoes of this search reverberate both in the works of immigrant writers and of those born in America; however, there is a significant difference. The American-born writer has not gained enough command of the Armenian language to be able to use it in artistic expression and therefore writes in English. The literature of American-born Armenian writers is readily available to an English reader interested in ethnic literature; the immigrant's literature in Armenian is not, but yet is an equally important part of the Armenian American literature.

Lorne Shirinian, a Canadian Armenian poet and literary critic, published an anthology of the Armenian North American poets (1974) in which he views the new trend as the result of "our fathers' efforts to keep Armenian culture vital in the diaspora, perhaps we can say that now the second and third generations are beginning to experience a new awareness of their heritage" (1). Indeed, there is rarely a piece of poetry in that anthology which does not betray its author's cultural background and ancestry. Archie Minasian, Peter Manuelian, James Magorian, David Kherdian, Helen Pilibosian, Ralph Setian, Alan Hovhaness, Leo Hamalian, Vaughn Koumjian, Mary Avakian Freericks, Harold Bond, Michael Casey, John Vartoukian, Shant Basmajian, Ara Baliozian, Diana Der Hovanessian, Hagop Missak Merjian, Lorne Shirinian, Harry Keyishian, and Vivian Kurkjian, authors chosen for this anthology, were predominantly born in America and have several volumes of poetry and fiction to their credit.

Memoirs—Revival of the Tragic Past

Interest in one's origin and ethnic history kindled the memory of the genocide in the acculturated Armenian youth in America. A renewed interest in the traumatic experience of their parents in the Old Country encouraged memoir writing. In fact, the post-1965 era has seen an upsurge of published memoirs, mostly in English but also in Armenian. Decades after the immediate Armenian language responses, survivors who were in their old age were encouraged by their children to write.

Kerop Bedoukian's memoir, *Some of Us Survived* (1979) reassumes the unique perspective of a nine-year-old boy from Sivas, playing games with death around him. "I forced myself to examine the stinking bodies, to guess their time of death. There came a time, when the body melted completely into the sun under the hot desert sun—I thought this happened in about six days. When I saw a baby still clinging to her dead mother's breast, I knew this death was quite recent."

Alice Muggerditchian Shipley's memoir, *We Walked Then Ran* (1983), delineates an unusual route of escape from Diarbekir to Kharbert, Dersim, Erzinjan, Erzerum, and then to Tbilisi, Baku, Astrakhan, up the Volga River, over the Arctic Ocean and the North Sea to Great Britain and freedom.

John Minassian had a duty. He could not forget what someone said to him in a Turkish prison: "We may not survive, but your generation has a call and a duty." *Many Hills Yet to Climb* (1986) fulfilled that call of duty.

Hovhannes Mugrditchian's *To Armenians With Love, The Memoirs of a Patriot* (1996) is an English rendering of the old man's Armenian manuscript. "For our children and grandchildren, we knew we had to have an English-language version," his son contended.

Bertha (Berjuhi) Nakshian Ketchian wrote her story at the behest of her son and daughter. *In the Shadow of the Fortress: The Genocide Remembered* was published in the English original in 1988. In the introduction she writes, "We—the survivors—are living eyewitnesses of the genocide of Armenians by the Turks. What was documented in writing and pictures at the time is now being denied," and continues, "recognition of the crime does not bring the victims back, but it eases somewhat the pain of the living."

The Armenian genocide survivors had long years to live out and recall the event, to play and replay the traumatic experiences in their mind before it was crystallized into narrative.

Testimonies as Raw Material

In addition to their function as an effective transmitter of memory, the oral and written testimonies of the first-generation survivors served as raw material to inspire literary responses by the second and third generations, who took on the role of storyteller, for they rarely leave the raw material untouched. The material is transformed into a structured and organized memoir or a novel with a specific form and style, embellished by the authors' artistic skills and rich imagination. The most common difficulty in this complicated task is the struggle to overcome emotion, to be able to relive the world of genocide and to produce an authentic expression of the painful saga.

David Kherdian gives one of the earliest examples. *The Road from Home: The Story of an Armenian Girl* (1979) is a touching account of young Veron Dumehjian, David's mother, and her miraculous survival.

Efronia: An Armenian Love Story (1994) is another example. Efronia Katchadourian's memoir of some five hundred pages was translated into English by her son and then turned into a nicely wrought piece of creative literature, a love story, by her non-Armenian daughter-in-law, Stina Katchadourian.

In *Rise the Euphrates* (1994), Carol Edgarian skillfully blends the facts of the Armenian genocide and the traumatic experience of the survivor generation with the attractions and fun and multiple opportunities that American culture can offer a third-generation Armenian American teenager. It comes through clearly in Edgarian's work that no matter how deeply assimilated to the culture and lifestyle of the mainstream, no matter how aloof from the Armenian past, this American-born generation still carries traces of the wounds of the genocide.

Mae M. Derdarian speaks with the voice of her grandmother, adding her own imagination and artistic skill to create a work of art, *Vergeen: A Survivor of the Armenian Genocide* (1996). The author's motivation was not only to tell her grandmother's story, but also, as she notes in the "Acknowledgement" of her book, "to immerse the reader in her story and to refute historical revisionists who deny and distort the facts of the Armenian holocaust." Vergeen cries out to the world and to the deniers, "I was there! I was an eyewitness! I was a victim!"

Lines in the Sand (2001), a novel by Thomas A. Ohanian, is subtitled *Love, Tragedy, and the Armenian Genocide*. It is, according to the author's note, "a work of fiction in a background of history." Most interesting is the juxtaposition of the Armenian and the Jewish tragedies and effacement of the time span between them. "The little black lines of news type became trains carrying Jews, moving through the dense forests. . . . And as the wheels swerved along the curving track the snaking train turned into shifting, moving people. Walking, in the desert. Lines of people. Lines in the sand."

A Sudden Discovery of the Past

Many of the survivors refrained from speaking of their horrible experience, especially to their children. There was this inexplicable sense of reproach for having survived while other members of the family met a torturous death. Then, there was this inner compulsion to leave everything behind and live in the new environment, integrated into the mainstream like everyone else, fearing that if they told their stories, it would set them apart. The prevailing discrimination and prejudice against the newcomers bolstered that mentality. There was also the burden of daily struggle for survival in a new, unfamiliar world. "Victim of America who escaped the Turkish Genocide," David Kherdian writes of his mother. Beyond this, there was the intent to spare their children, to protect them against the paralyzing memory with which they had to live. After the parent's death, through fragmented memorabilia left behind, or because of renewed interest and the usual reverence that creeps into one's heart toward a dead parent, the son or daughter discovered the full scope of the source of that unexplained pain and disposition, the tremendous burden of memory that had weighed so heavily upon the parent.

Virginia Haroutounian's *Orphan in the Sands* (1995) is the story of the author's mother, who only in the final days of her life shared with her daughter her terrible ordeal during and after the genocide. It is also the story of the daughter, who resented her mother's strange behavior, and all her life strove to adjust to it, only to learn in the end that it was the genocide and its aftereffects that caused her unfathomable, peculiar behavior, ruining her mother's and her own life.

David Kherdian speaks of the same experience in a collection of poems and the series dedicated to his father, *Homage to Adana* (1970), Adana being the father's birthplace in the Old Country. The burden of tragic memories had been indirectly yet effectively transmitted, for it fit perfectly into the family atmosphere and the parent-children relationship experienced by the generation born to the survivors of the genocide.

Agop Hacikyan knew very little of the Armenian past when he was growing up in Istanbul. His parents, both survivors of the genocide, kept silent, and their reason, obviously, was not only psychological but also political. The new regime in Turkey had successfully suppressed the historical memory of its citizens. But the conspicuous silence and the occasional references to *aksor* (meaning exile, as survivors referred to the deportation) were factors that spurred Hacikyan to write a series of novels decades later, beginning with *Tomas* (1970) to *A Summer Without Dawn* (2000) translated from the French original (*Eté sans aube* [1991]).

Peter Balakian's *Black Dog of Fate* (1998) is a journey into the past after a sudden discovery of a family secret tied with the Old World. The result, as the author himself puts it, is a "polyphonic, multilayered memoir" in which "personal discovery and history merge."

Vickie Smith Foston comes across the astonishing truth about her roots, heritage, and background. *Victoria's Secret: A Conspiracy of Silence* (2001) is the story of that journey into the past.

Micheline Aharonian Marcom knew very little about her family and the history of her people. *Three Apples Fell from Heaven* (2001) is the result of her search woven into an abstract and complex tapestry wherein the voices of the dead and the living intermingle to evoke a surrealistic tableau of suffering and death.

Children of Der Zor

The memory of the massacres is alive among second- and third-generation Armenian American writers. The pain of a wound that refuses to heal persists. One way or another, the entire nation bears the effects of victimization. An Armenian is a child of Der El-Zor (Der Zor) irrespective of any family connection to those who perished. For Diana Der-Hovanessian, all Armenians are survivors of genocide. It does not matter whether or not one has lost family members in the death marches, "We are children of Der Zor," she writes. (Der Zor was the most notorious of the last concentration camps in the Syrian desert where the deportees, the remnants of survivors reaching there were liquidated.)

Leonardo Alishan remained a child of Der Zor never able to transcend the tragedy that was his grandmother's and became his fate at the age of nine. "I try to be a spectator of that tragedy which culminated in a London hospital room in 1978 where Granny saw Turkish horsemen around her bed before she died. But, alas, I am not the spectator. I am a character caught in that play which never, never, never reaches its equilibrium."

Harold Bond's poem, "Postscript: Marash" (1969), speaks of the burden of the past on the present. The topoi associated with the genocide appear as fragmented images imposing themselves upon everyday life in the New World. Many of Peter Balakian's poems in *Sad Days of Light* (1983) illustrate this duality. Through a commingling of images past and present, Balakian registers the replay of the tragedy of 1915 in his grandmother's mind.

In Search of an Identity (Ethnic?)

The quest for self-identity takes Armenian American imaginative literature along different paths; yet the genocide and the reconstruction of the memory of it remain at the core as the leitmotif. **Peter Najarian**'s *Voyages* (1971) is the site of the painful conflict and attempted reconciliation between the past and the present. There is little reference to the genocide, but it is the ever-present past constantly pressuring the present, defeating the efforts of the characters to rise above the unhappiness, to find their identity and adjust to their adopted country. Najarian's *Daughters of Memory* (1986) is again a search for identity and a quest to revive and perpetuate the memory of the genocide. The conversations and reminiscences among a group of old Armenian women who experienced the genocide in their youth provide the background and trace the history of the Armenian genocide.

Michael Arlen Jr.'s journey to Armenia to rediscover for himself what it meant to be Armenian makes his renowned narrative *Passage to Ararat* (1975) a classic in the search for ethnic identity. Renounced by the father and rediscovered by the son, Armenia, the Armenian culture and heritage, and the Armenian past—the genocide—interfuse to impose their presence as elements of Michael Arlen's identity.

Alicia Ghiragossian, who, being born in South America and living in the United States, writes poetry in Spanish and English, believes that all Armenians have the obsession to tell the world how hard it is to survive when the memories of a lost family and a lost homeland are still fresh. She explains what it means "To be an Armenian" (1998).

Helene Pilibosian tries to capture the life of her parents in their native village in Kharbert. *Carvings from an Heirloom: Oral History Poems* (1983) clearly defines the source by which the author identifies herself.

Peter Balakian's *The Black Dog of Fate* (1998) is another example in which the Armenian component is gradually extracted from a nebulous memory hole to become an important dimension in the diaspora Armenians' self-identity.

The emigrant writers from Middle Eastern countries write in Armenian, but they too portray the painful transition, the make-up of the new diaspora Armenian. The memory of the dead family continues as a part of the Armenian heritage and is leaving an indelible mark on the makeup of an Armenian's identity. With such complex givens of this persisting past, can this be simply called ethnic identity?

Vahé Oshagan (1922–2000), born in Jerusalem, portrays the assimilated, alienated generation in America against a backdrop of national traditions deriving from the past, the roots of this past calling the generation back, demanding action, be it in the most unconventional way, for example, by staging shockingly scandalous scenes or by alluding to generally unacceptable political violence. Oshagan's literature delineates a constant effort to move from the predicament of the victim's psychology toward a complete and free human being. He tries to reach a new synthesis in the new diaspora Armenian with cognition of the past, dedication in the present, and a reinterpretation of Armenianness for the future, that is, one that could carry the strength of the nation and withstand obstruction. His published works of prose and poetry are: *Patuhan* (Window, 1963), *Kaghak* (City, 1963), *Karughi* (Crossroad, 1971), and *Ahazang* (Alarm Bell, 1980) to *Taparakane* (The Wanderer, 1988), *Arvardzanner* (Suburbs, 1990), and *Serundner* (Generations, 1995).

The pain and frustration resulting from the struggle to adjust to one's dual identity and the search for an ideal image of the diaspora Armenian echo in almost the entire literary output of Hakob Karapents (1925–94), a native of Tabriz, Iran. His characters are ordinary Armenians in the New World struggling to sustain moral integrity and psychological stability. His novels and short stories were published in nine volumes, *Antsanot Hoginer* (Stranger Souls, 1970) to *Mi Mard Ou Mi Erkir* (A Man and a Country, 1994).

Noubar Agishian (1934–), born in Iskandarun, develops an array of diaspora Armenian characters caught in the turmoil of dual identity. They denounce their ethnic heritage and assimilate, or they live a life of hopelessness and frustration: "we are exiles, expelled from earth and heaven, expelled even from life. There is something alien in our existence, something temporary. We wander from one country to another, but we cannot put down roots, strong, deep, and permanent" (*Marde Hoghin Vra* [1987, The Man on the Soil]).

Vehanoush Tekian, (1948–), born in Beirut, on the other hand, struggles to transcend the psychology of a massacred nation and to stand upright despite her grandfather's sad stories of the Armenian past. In her case the awareness of the Armenian past is transformed into resolution to fight for national goals.

Boghos Kupelian (1936–), born in Iskenderun, brings the experience and the worldview of an Armenian wandering from Africa to the Middle East and America to the Armenian American literature. His own quest for an Armenian identity reconciled with a variety of favorable and alien environments gives his characters their idiosyncrasies and puts their sufferings and the burden of history they carry on their shoulders in the context of world suffering.

The literature discussed here in this brief inquiry is only a schematic representation of Armenian American literature. Many names have been omitted; many important aspects of that literature have remained unattended. The Armenian American literature as a body bears all the attributes and effects of a diaspora. It is part and parcel of the Armenian diaspora literature. But it is also a component of the American ethnic literature, for the bare reason that it is produced by an ethnic minority in America. Is this a valid categorization? Where does the ethnicity come into play? In the case of the Armenian American literature in English, it is the flavor of Armenianness, which is made of the Armenian past and the American present. Or as William Saroyan has characterized, it is "the English tongue, the American soil, and the Armenian spirit."

Further Reading

Bedrosian, Margaret. *The Magical Pine Ring*. Detroit: Wayne State UP, 1991.

Peroomian, Rubina. "New Directions in Literary Responses to the Armenian Genocide." *Looking Backward, Moving Forward*. Ed. Richard G. Hovannisian. New Brunswick, London: Transaction Publishers, 2003. 157–80.

———. "The Transformation of Armenianness in the Formation of Armenian American Identity." *Journal of the Society for Armenian Studies* 6 (1992–1993): 119–45.

Shirinian, Lorne, ed. *Armenian-North American Poets: An Anthology*. St. Jean, Quebec: Manna Publishing, 1974.

———. *Armenian-North American literature*. Lewiston: Edwin Mellen Press, 1990.

Tololyan, Minas. *Dar me grakanutiun*. Vol. II. New York: A Publication of the Prelacy of Armenian Apostolic Church of America, 1980.

Rubina Peroomian

ARMENIAN GENOCIDE   The genocide of the Armenians in Ottoman Turkey has been justly proclaimed the first genocide of the twentieth century. Perpetrated by the government of the Young Turks (who came to replace the old Sultan rule in Ottoman Turkey in 1908), this genocide represented the culmination of decades of pogroms and persecution of the Armenian population.

Armenia Major (also known as Western Armenia) was conquered in 1514 by the Ottoman Turks, and since then has remained under Turkish rule. Despite some hardships, Armenians coexisted with the Ottoman Turks in relative peace until the second half of the nineteenth century when external and internal factors contributed to a dramatic shift in the relationship between the two groups. As the Ottoman Empire deteriorated and most of the nations it controlled declared independence, Armenia remained the only substantial Christian minority within the territory of the Empire. In 1908, Sultan Abdul Hamid II was deposed and the Union and Progress Party of the Young Turks came to power, bringing with it more brutality toward the Armenian minority. The Armenian demands for reforms rose to a crescendo. In January 1914, Turkey signed an agreement whereby specific reforms would be carried out in the six Armenian *vilayets* [provinces] of Anatolia, under the observation of foreign inspectors. However, with Turkey's entrance into World War I in November 1914, the agreement was annulled. Fearing that an allied victory would enable the Armenian secession and cause the complete disintegration of the already weakened Empire, the Young Turks, led by Talaat, Jamal, and Enver Pashas, masterminded the massive extermination of the Empire's Armenian subjects and the cleansing of historic Armenia in Eastern Anatolia of its indigenous population.

On April 15, 1915, the plan went into effect. All Armenian males between the ages of eighteen and fifty-five were "drafted" into the Ottoman army and killed either immediately upon departure or in prison camps, leaving behind a defenseless population of women, children, and elderly. The Armenian population was thoroughly disarmed. Lastly, under the pretext of war, Armenian villages and towns were isolated from one another to prevent organized resistance.

On the night of April 24, 1915, the brightest representatives of the Armenian intellectual elite of Constantinople, including writers, musicians, politicians, and scientists, were arrested and brutally massacred. Similar acts of violence against the Armenian intellectuals then spread to other towns and provinces. On June 11, 1915, the Turkish Gendarmes began the brutal deportation of the remaining Armenians from their territories. The inhuman conditions and the violence of the Turkish soldiers against the defenseless Armenian population left few alive. Those who survived the death marches were "relocated" to the Syrian desert of Der Zor and either killed or left to die of heat exposure and starvation. Many Western dignitaries and missionaries working in Turkey reported the atrocities committed by the Turks and the brutal tortures to which they subjected the Armenians. However, the international community remained practically uninvolved despite these reports. Only the United States provided substantial support to Armenian refugees, setting up the so-called Near East Relief Fund to alleviate the sufferings of the survivors. The carnage of Armenians in Turkey continued until the end of World War I.

In 1918, after the fall of the Young Turkish government, documents and plans confirming the premeditated genocide of Armenians were revealed. The masterminds of the genocide, Talaat, Jamal, and Enver Pashas, were tried and sentenced to death *in absentia* by local Turkish courts for crimes committed against the Armenians. The Turkish government never succeeded in capturing them; all three were eventually assassinated in different parts of the world. Significantly, Soghomon Tehlirian, who assassinated Talaat Pasha in Berlin in 1921, was acquitted by a German court. Only one culprit Kemal Bey, vice-governor of one of the provinces, was hanged for masterminding the murder of 68,000 Armenians.

After these early attempts to bring justice to the Armenian people, Turkey adopted an official state policy that refused to acknowledge the occurrence of the genocide; it continues to deny it to this day. Moreover, it actively resists the attempts undertaken by different countries to formally accept the genocide of Armenians in 1915. The entire territory of Western Armenia, parts of it now desolate, remains in possession of Turkey, along with the Armenian national symbol, the biblical Mt. Ararat, located twenty-five miles outside Armenia's capital, Yerevan, but inaccessible to

Armenians. To this day, April 24 remains a day of official mourning in Armenia.

Along with losing most of the territory of their three-thousand-year-old homeland, Armenians suffered other immense losses. Before the genocide, 2,660,000 Armenians lived within the territory of Ottoman Turkey. More than 1,500,000 of them died during the massacres, and fewer than 50,000 Armenians remain in current Turkey. In addition to human lives, Armenians lost many of their most treasured cultural and historical monuments, some dating back thousands of years. During the massacres and in the years that followed years, 2,050 Armenian churches and 203 monasteries were destroyed in Turkey. Western Armenia became entirely Turkish. Those Armenians who survived, barred from returning to their homes, scattered around the world, forming new Armenian communities or joining the already existing ones. There are about six million Armenians living outside Armenia today; the Armenian diaspora in the United States remains one of the largest in the world.

The traumatic memory of the genocide and the unfulfilled desire for justice have also left their mark on Armenian art and literature. While the diaspora Armenians established themselves as successful members of the society, the catastrophic events of 1915 and the subsequent exile and loss of homeland continue to have a special role in Armenian literature, especially in the genres of autobiography and memoir. Some of the topics of early diaspora literature, such as fear of losing cultural **identity**, difficulty adjusting to the host cultures, nostalgia, sorrow, and others, have moved to the background of Armenian American literature, but the genocide and its sociocultural consequences continue to influence writers today.

Further Reading

Dadrian, Vahjakn N. *History of the Armenian Genocide: Ethnic Conflict from the Balkans to the Caucasus.* Providence: Berghahn Books, 1995.

Hovannisian, Richard, ed. *Remembrance and Denial: The Case of the Armenian Genocide.* Detroit: Wayne State UP, 1998.

Margarit Tadevosyan

ARTE PÚBLICO PRESS   The oldest and largest publisher of contemporary and historical literature written by American Hispanics. Through its publication of thirty books per year, Arte Público Press (APP) showcases Hispanic literary creativity and facilitates the entrance of Mexican American, Puerto Rican, Cuban American, and other writers of Hispanic heritage to mainstream publishing. Arte Público Press had its origins in 1972, the year that Nicolás Kanellos founded *Revista Chicano Riqueña* in Gary, Indiana. This quarterly literary magazine won praise and recognition nationwide, including the 1986 and 1987 Citations of Achievement from the Coordinating Council of Literary Magazines. Building on the magazine's successes, Kanellos, who is of Greek and Puerto Rican heritage, founded APP in 1979 to further provide a national American forum for Hispanic literature. The following year, when he was offered a teaching position at the University of Houston, he was invited to take the press with him and to continue his role as the director of APP. In the mid-1980s, *Revista Chicano-Riqueña* evolved into *The Americas Review* with Julián Olivares as its editor. In 1997, on its twenty-fifth anniversary, the review was officially closed under the premise that it had served the purpose for which it had been founded.

By then, Kanellos had started to expand the activities of the press into three new areas. In 1992, with initial funding from the Rockefeller Foundation, he created a national board of well-known Latino critics, professors, and librarians and launched the Recovering the U.S. Hispanic Literary Heritage Project, the first nationally coordinated attempt to recover, index, and publish lost Hispanic writings that date from the American colonial period and the early Spanish settlements through 1960. Two years later, APP created Piñata Books, an imprint dedicated to the publication of literature for children and young adults. With its bilingual books for children and its entertaining novels for young adults, Piñata Books made giant strides toward filling an urgent public demand for books for children that accurately portray Hispanic culture in the United States. In the late 1990s, APP began to publish much-needed documentation of the Hispanic Civil Rights Movement (1965–80) through the creation of the Hispanic Civil Rights Series. Highlighted in the series are such topics as women's activism, **immigration** reform, equity in education, the participation of citizens in a democratic society, civic culture, and racial/cultural relations.

The press has collaborated closely with teachers, librarians, and administrators to include its books in the curriculum. It has also actively partnered with literacy organizations around the country, including Reach Out and Read, Reading Is Fundamental, and Vuela con Libros. As the largest licensor of Hispanic literary materials to the U.S. textbook industry, with works by its authors included in hundreds of anthologies, APP has published books and authors that have been the recipients of hundreds of awards, including several Before Columbus Foundation American Book Awards, several Multicultural Publishers Exchange awards, a PEN award, several Southwest Book Awards, and the Premio Aztlán. Authors published by APP include the Obie Award–winning playwright and filmmaker Luis Valdez, playwright Miguel Piñero, winner of the New York Drama Critics' Award for Best American Play, **Tomás Rivera**, **Rolando Hinojosa**, Tato Laviera, and bestselling author **Victor Villaseñor**. Arte Público Press has also successfully published a wide array of women writers including **Lorna Dee Cervantes**, **Denise Chávez**, **Sandra Cisneros**, Lucha Corpi, **Roberta Fernández**, **Graciela Limón**, **Nicholasa Mohr**, **Pat Mora**, **Judith Ortiz Cofer**, and Evangelina Vigil Piñón.

Through APP's multipronged efforts to highlight the literary efforts of Hispanic writers in the United States, Kanellos and Marina Tristán, APP's assistant director, and the rest of the able staff at the press, have challenged the boundaries of both American and Latin American literature. APP has demonstrated that size (or lack of it) is not proportionally related to success in the commercial book market. Still, in the early years of the twenty-first century, APP finds itself ranked as one of the largest of the small presses in the United States.

Roberta Fernández

ASAYESH, GELAREH (1962–) Iranian American journalist and writer. Asayesh represents the second generation of Iranian American writers who deal with their dualistic identity as Iranians and Americans through the genre of memoir. As a journalist for many years writing for the *Miami Herald* and the *Baltimore Sun*, Asayesh published several articles that dealt with her own experience as an immigrant, some of which are included in her memoir, *Saffron Sky: A Life Between Iran and America* (1999).

Asayesh came to the United States as a child in 1977. Her family settled in Chapel Hill, North Carolina, a year before the Iranian Revolution. Her book recounts some of the events during the period of the revolution and the hostage crisis as she watched them unfold in the U.S. media. She writes about the prejudice she and other Iranians encountered during this period. *Saffron Sky* is part memoir, part diary, and a travel log that reflects on several return visits to Iran after nearly a decade and a half of separation. Asayesh writes about her life "between" the disparate cultures of the United States and Iran, and attempts to grapple with her alienation from and love for both countries. *Saffron Sky* deals not only with those pivotal events that shaped her perspective as an immigrant but also the ways that Iran has become abstract and more a place of nostalgia because of the difficulties of traveling there after the revolution and the development of an increasingly hostile relationship with the United States. When she does eventually return to Iran as an adult, she encounters a country that is unfamiliar. The highly restrictive social codes between men and women and the repressive policies of the Iranian government cause her to reflect on her own desire for an Iran that no longer exists. *Saffron Sky* explores the uneasy spaces of immigrant but also suggests that once one migrates from one country to another, particularly if those countries and cultures are very different, belonging to either culture is a continuous process of negotiation. In addition, Asayesh, like other second-generation Iranian American writers, hones in on the ways that immigrants of Middle Eastern heritage, whether Iranian or Arab, have had difficulty fully embracing American culture since their own cultures of origin have been demonized and oversimplified in the U.S. media over a period of decades. Asayesh's book, like her own biography—a child immigrant educated and raised in the West, married to an American, and the mother of two bicultural children—represents the disparate strands of a tapestry that she attempts to weave into a whole. (*See also* Iranian American Literature)

Further Reading

Bahrampour, Tara. *To See and See Again: A Life in Iran and America*. New York: Farrar, Straus, and Giroux, 1999.

Dumas, Firouzeh. *Funny in Farsi: A Memoir of Growing Up Iranian in America*. New York: Villard, 2003.

Karim, Persis, and Mohammad Mehdi Khorrami, eds. *A World Between: Poems, Short Stories, and Essays by Iranian-Americans*. New York: George Braziller, 1999.

Persis Karim

ASIMOV, ISAAC (1920–1992)   Jewish American author, biochemist, and educator who also wrote using the names George E. Dale, Dr. A, and Paul French. Isaac Asimov was one of the great science fiction writers of the twentieth century. He was a prolific, award-winning author who wrote science books for the layperson, as well as works that dealt with history, literature, the Bible, and other topics. He wrote seven days a week, typed his own manuscripts, conducted his own research, and published more than 500 books.

Asimov was born in Petrovichi, in the former Soviet Union, immigrated to the United States at the age of three, and became a naturalized citizen in 1928. He earned three degrees at Columbia University in New York: BS, 1939; MA, 1941; and PhD in chemistry, 1948. After serving in the United States Army (1945–46), he married Gertrude Blugerman (1948). They were divorced in 1973, and the same year he married his second wife, Janet Opal Jeppson. Asimov taught biochemistry at Boston University's School of Medicine until 1959, when he started to devote his attention to writing full-time. He received numerous awards, some of which include the Edison Foundation National Mass Media Award (1958); Blakeslee Award (1960); World Science Fiction Convention Citation (1963); Hugo Award (1963, 1966, 1973, 1977, 1983); American Chemical Society James T. Grady Award (1965); American Association for the Advancement of Science

Isaac Asimov. *AP/Wide World Photos.*

Writing Award (1967); Nebula Award (1972, 1976); and the Locus Award (1981, 1983). In addition, he wrote several autobiographical works: *In Memory Yet Green* (1979), *In Joy Still Felt* (1980), *I. Asimov: A Memoir* (1994), and *It's Been a Good Life* (2002), edited by his wife Janet Asimov. Some of his other works that include an autobiographical element include *Opus 100* (1969) and *The Early Asimov* (1972). In addition, his brother Stanley Asimov edited a collection of letters titled *Yours, Isaac Asimov: A Lifetime of Letters* (1995).

Asimov's stories began to appear in science-fiction magazines in 1939. More than ten years later he published his first book, *Pebble in the Sky* (1950), which is part of the Empire Series, along with two other novels, *The Stars, Like Dust* (1951) and *The Currents of Space* (1952). The novels deal with the time period before or during the formation of the Galactic Empire and are loosely connected.

Asimov's works that deal with robots have been very popular. The Robot Series comprises novels that take place in the future, when human beings have colonized numerous planets and have created robots. The novels include *The Caves of Steel* (1954), *The Naked Sun* (1957), *The Robots of Dawn* (1983), and *Robots and Empire* (1985). Some of the robot short stories are classics and deal with the "Three Laws of Robotics," which provide a standard for governing the actions of robots. In these tales Asimov presents some of the challenges that exist in a universe that includes both humans and robots. Some of these issues include the following questions: Who is superior, a human or a robot? How does one distinguish between a person and a robot? How does one deal with human resentment of robots? How does one determine what is good for humans? Many of the robot stories are found in such collections as *I, Robot* (1950), *The Rest of the Robots* (1964), *The Bicentennial Man and Other Stories* (1976), *The Complete Robot* (1982), *Robot Dreams* (1986), and *Robot Visions* (1990).

The Foundation Series is based on a trilogy of novels, *Foundation* (1951), *Foundation and Empire* (1952), and *Second Foundation* (1953). The stories focus on Hari Seldon, his invention of psychohistory (a theory of prediction) and the various dilemmas and crises that emerge. Decades later, Asimov published additional novels for this series, including *Foundation's Edge* (1982), *Foundation and Earth* (1986), *Prelude to Foundation* (1988), and *Forward the Foundation* (1993). Although *Prelude to Foundation* was one of the last novels written, it actually sets the stage for the entire series and provides details regarding the life of Hari Seldon and the establishment of the Foundation. Asimov received a Hugo Award for Best All-Time Science Fiction Series for the original trilogy. With the permission of the Asimov estate, science fiction writers Gregory Benford, Greg Bear, and David Brin have written additional novels on this theme that constitute the Second Foundation Series.

Some of Asimov's numerous books on science include *The Chemicals of Life: Enzymes, Vitamins, Hormones* (1954), *Inside the Atom* (1956), *The Human Brain: Its Capacities and Functions* (1964), *Asimov on Astronomy* (1974), and *Exploring the Earth and the Cosmos* (1982). A selection of his works on history includes *The Roman Republic* (1966), *The Shaping of France* (1972), *The Birth of the United States 1763–1816* (1974), and *Asimov's Chronology of the World* (1991). A sampling of his commentary on literature includes *Asimov's Guide to Shakespeare: The Greek, Roman, and Italian Plays; The English Plays* (1970), *Asimov's Annotated "Paradise Lost"* (1974), *Familiar Poems, Annotated* (1977), and *The Annotated "Gulliver's Travels"* (1980). Some of his writings on the Bible include *Words in Genesis* (1962), *Words from the Exodus* (1963), *Asimov's Guild to the Bible: The Old Testament, The New Testament* (1968–69), and *The Story of Ruth* (1972). In addition, he wrote on diverse other subjects included in such books as *Isaac Asimov's Treasury of Humor* (1971) and *Lecherous Limericks* (1975). He also edited numerous books, wrote works for children, and contributed to the field of mystery writing.

Asimov utilized his vivid imagination, keen intellect, and knowledge of science and other subjects to create an enormous collection of works. Through his obsession for writing he left behind a plethora of books, which continue to educate, stimulate, and entertain readers of different age groups. His contribution to the field of science fiction alone singles him out as an extraordinary writer who broke new ground and provided unique ways to envision the future.

Further Reading

Green, Scott E. *Isaac Asimov: An Annotated Bibliography of the Asimov Collection at Boston University*. Westport, CT: Greenwood Press, 1995.

Gunn, James E. *Isaac Asimov: The Foundations of Science Fiction*. Rev. ed. Lanham, MD: Scarecrow, 1996.

White, Michael. *Asimov: The Unauthorized Life*. London: Millennium, 1994.

Deborah Weagel

ASSIMILATION   Broadly defined as the conformity of a minority or immigrant group to the customs and attitudes of the dominant culture, assimilation is a common theme in American literature. While often implicating ethnic or cultural **identity**, assimilation may also refer to other differences from the dominant group, such as religion, language, or sexuality. It is a process that varies depending upon the community in question, the historical moment, and differences *within* groups such as generation, gender, and class, for example. We can view assimilation positively as a means for cultural integration despite ethnic differences from the majority or more negatively as the rejection of one's ethnic community and ancestry through complete absorption into the prevailing culture. It may be most helpful to consider assimilation as collections of choices made by minority groups within contexts delimited by national, regional, and local authority, as well as by popular sentiment. Assimilation in American literary history has meant hope and disappointment, accommodation and resistance, and gratitude and rage in complex relationship to one another.

Official policy and public opinion regarding the assimilability of different ethnic groups in the United States has been inconsistent, resulting in unique symbology depending upon the historical circumstances and the ethnic groups in question. During World War I, for example, there were heightened tendencies to view new immigrants as suspicious foreigners due to fears of divided loyalties for European Americans, resulting in policies intended to ensure conformity rather than ones that might encourage unique identities for different groups. In *Theories of Ethnicity: A Classical Reader* (1996), Werner Sollers refers to this attitude toward assimilation, prevalent in American policy especially from 1914 to 1918, as "Anglo-conformity." In fact, institutions such as schools, health care providers, and law enforcement became agents of assimilation to American culture, or "Americanization." The short-lived experiments in Americanization from this period included many ethnic groups, and, in 1913, the Commission of **Immigration** and Housing began to develop strategies for transforming immigrant values and to ease the integration of such groups as Mexican American women into labor markets in places like California.

In response, writers such as Norwegian American **Waldemar Ager**, in published essays in his journal *Kvartalskrift* (1916–20), and Jewish American **Abraham Cahan**, particularly in the novel *The Rise of David Levinsky* (1917), became among the first to criticize the expectation that immigrants would discard their cultural histories and practices in favor of new American identities. In later twentieth-century writing published by Latin American and pan-Caribbean authors, it is clear that, even when assimilation projects are not so systematic as in this earlier period, almost all aspects of immigrants' cultural practices come under scrutiny, including accents and linguistic practices, culinary habits, and work ethics. In this regard, members of other, supposedly "model" minority groups have ironically been praised for achieving the American dream through hard work and have been used as examples to chastise other minorities who have not experienced upward mobility in the same way. South Asian American writers, including **Bharati Mukherjee** in her novel *Jasmine* (1989), examine the "benefits" of such thinking for immigrants from countries like India, who may seem assimilable because they are considered unthreatening and perhaps also because they fulfill exotic fantasies of the "East."

In the context of historical differences in perceptions of immigrants and racial minority groups, writers from many different backgrounds in the United States have grappled with the questions of if, how much, and with what consequences do immigrants assimilate to the cultural expectations of governing forces, even British immigrants in the eighteenth and nineteenth centuries. For example, John Harrower, whose diary (1773–76) is included in Tom Dublin's *Immigrant Voices: New Lives in America 1773–1986* (1993), describes his transition from a sojourner—an indentured servant who emigrated to the United States because of dire poverty—to a man with grander aspirations and the aim of his wife becoming a true Virginian lady by following him across the ocean. Immigrants like Harrower had hope that they might improve their lots in life and be integrated into the pre-existing societies of British colonialists; we must not forget, however, that they faced discrimination as newcomers and that their individual experiences were affected by differing gender roles that generally ascribed greater authority and mobility to men than women.

Through marriage and other familial connections, British immigrant women *might* yet have had the opportunity of assimilating to mainstream culture, but this was not often the case for the indigenous groups already present when Europeans settled the continent. Indeed, Native Americans have long been the subjects of heated disagreement among members of Congress and other governmental groups attempting to ascertain their place in the American nation. While colonial policies such as the Northwest Ordinance of 1787 guaranteed "decent" treatment of Indians, subsequent legislation such as the Indian Removal Act of 1830 and the creation of reservations in the 1870s and 1880s resulted in coercion, often military in nature, to restructure tribal patterns to favor the interests of whites. Literary depictions of Native American histories include accounts of forcible assimilation to Western education, religion and spirituality, and mores about land use and ownership, to name a few. In 1936, **D'Arcy McNickle**, an adopted member of the Flathead tribe and a man of Cree and white parentage, published *The Surrounded*, revealing the pressures to assimilate to white America that alienated Native Americans from their own communities.

Themes in D'Arcy's writing have been reiterated by other prominent Native American writers including **N. Scott Momaday**, **James Welch**, and **Leslie Marmon Silko**. In her novel *Ceremony* (1977), for example, Silko narrates the return of the half-Indian protagonist Tayo from World War II and Japanese imprisonment to a persistent malaise, or "white smoke," that makes him feel invisible and unable to connect with the people around him or the expectations of daily living. Eventually, he participates in a traditional Laguna Pueblo ceremony and achieves a reconciliation of his multiple cultural influences. Silko thus challenges expectations of Native American assimilation, through the enactment of supposedly lost cultural practices that she shows can still "heal" individuals of this minority community in the United States. More recently published Native American writers such as **Sherman Alexie** continue to invoke, while simultaneously problematizing, the symbol of the "the rez" for Native American experiences of assimilation *and* exclusion.

In African American literary traditions, meanwhile, tensions have existed between possibilities for true integration into dominant culture, on the one hand, and the potential *necessity* for a separate black nation on the other. These tensions are a result of the paradox of assimilation within a nation that historically denied basic liberty and humanity to blacks through the institutions of **slavery**; furthermore, even after the Emancipation Proclamation of 1863, conditions for many African Americans continued to be defined by rampant **racism** and bigotry. Literary debates about black separatism have taken dramatic form, such as in exchanges between

Booker T. Washington and **W. E. B. Du Bois**. Whereas Washington in his autobiography *Up from Slavery* (1901) advocated acceptance of American exclusion of blacks and suggested that blacks construct their own separate programs for racial uplift, Du Bois used the metaphor of "double consciousness" in his *The Souls of Black Folk* (1903) to suggest that such plans only colluded with racist traditions. Du Bois contended that African Americans internalized the negative views of themselves held by whites in power—views that persisted, for example, even after blacks fought for the American cause in the Revolutionary War.

African American writers have historically weighed the different sides of this question, noting throughout the possibility of some African Americans to "pass" for white. In her novel from 1900, *Contending Forces*, Pauline Hopkins narrates the choice of a mixed character, Jesse Montfort, to live as a black man within a black community rather than choosing to take advantage of his ability to be presumed white. In this and later works of African American literature, authors narrate a wide range of responses taken by characters facing pressures to assimilate by "passing," or through other means. During the **Harlem Renaissance**, writers such as **Langston Hughes**, **Zora Neale Hurston**, and Claude McKay focused on a search for shared black cultures in America rather than advocating inclusion in white America. Hurston's *Their Eyes Were Watching God* (1937) is considered significant for her depiction of a black character within all-black contexts rather than in relation to white America, although this choice was the subject of controversy among other African American writers of the time. Some readers considered the author's use of black dialect in the novel to be an affirmation of white people's **African American stereotypes**, but others saw it as a refusal to assimilate to particular expectations of American literary form.

African American writers took even more militant stances after World War II, when blacks fought for America but found that they were still denied the supposed benefits of assimilation. Novels including those by **Ralph Ellison** and **Richard Wright**, as well as poetry by **Amiri Buraka**, **Nikki Giovanni**, and **Sonia Sanchez**, reflected black demands for racial justice and equality, problematizing earlier requests for the chance to assimilation to white norms. Ellison's *Invisible Man* (1952), for example, traces the narrator's search for a viable black **identity** among mentors who advocate everything from grateful submission to white cultural expectations to revolutionary and violent upheaval. Later in the twentieth century, these issues continued to shape African American literature, notably in a work like **Toni Morrison**'s *The Bluest Eye* (1970), the story of the existential damage done to Pecola Breedlove by the dream of assimilation when she becomes convinced that a pair of blue eyes will solve the tragedies of racism and poverty that structure her life.

As Morrison does in *The Bluest Eye*, Asian American writers have questioned if assimilation is even possible, given the visible differences of some ethnic minorities from hegemonic cultural traits. In particular, the "Yellow Peril" and "inscrutable Asian" phenomena of the late nineteenth and early twentieth centuries reflected a popular perception that Asian immigrants, especially Chinese and Japanese male laborers arriving in the country in significant numbers in these periods, were too culturally different to ever be fully incorporated into the mainstream. This influenced policies such as the **Chinese Exclusion Act** of 1882 and the National Origins Act of 1924 prohibiting Japanese immigration at the same time that European immigrants were allowed into the country, albeit with specified quotas. In the early twentieth century, **Sui Sin Far** captured such attitudes in her autobiographical writing in "Leaves from the Mental Portfolio of an Eurasian" as well as in her fictional stories, collected in *Mrs. Spring Fragrance and Other Writings* (1995). In these, she reported that North Americans doubted that Chinese immigrants were humans like themselves with equivalent spiritual depths beneath their supposedly stolid expressions.

Such perceptions and accompanying exclusions led to the development of ethnic enclaves such as Chinatowns, as well as to the relocation of particular Asian Americans under certain international contingencies. **Fae Myenne Ng**'s *Bone* (1993), for example, describes bachelor hotels in San Francisco's Chinatown, similar to those created in several American cities when Chinese female immigration was restricted so as to limit family reunification and the growth of this community. Meanwhile, sentiments about Asian inassimilability led to the creation of relocation or **internment** camps beginning in 1942 for Japanese Americans when the United States found itself at war with Japan in World War II, after the bombing of Pearl Harbor. Stories such as those collected in **Hisaye Yamamoto**'s collection *Seventeen Syllables and Other Stories* (1988) describe the fractured existence of Japanese American families during this period, revealing how precarious the possibility of actual inclusion in the American nation has been for some Asian groups at particular historical moments.

In the twenty-first century, assimilation continues to be a concern for American writers, for immigrants of all backgrounds, as well as for ethnic minorities. Previous models of wholesale Americanization, such as Israel Zangwill's "melting pot" from his play of the same name (1909), have come under considerable scrutiny and criticism by writers because of the implicit assumption that all differences will be eradicated and transformed into one (white) uniform culture. Problematizing the notion of a homogeneous American cultural norm, decades of multiethnic American literature has called for more nuanced and hybridized understandings of identity. (*See also* Ethnicity, Race)

Further Reading

Antin, Mary. *The Promised Land.* Boston: Houghton Mifflin, 1912.

Chu, Patricia P. *Assimilating Asians: Gendered Strategies of Authorship in Asian America.* Durham, NC and London: Duke UP, 2000.

Freedman, Jonathan. *The Temple of Culture: Assimilation and Anti-Semitism in Literary Anglo-America*. Oxford: Oxford UP, 2000.

Overland, Orm. "From Melting Pot to Copper Kettles: Assimilation and Norwegian-American Literature." *Multilingual America: Transnationalism, Ethnicity, and the Languages of American Literature*. Ed. Werner Sollers. New York: New York UP, 1998. 50–63.

Sanchez, George J. "'Go After the Women': Americanization and the Mexican Immigrant Woman, 1915–1929." *Unequal Sisters: A Multicultural Reader in U.S. Women's History*. Ed. Vicki L. Ruiz and Ellen Carol DuBois. New York: Routledge, 1994. 284–97.

Sollors, Werner. *Beyond Ethnicity: Consent and Descent in American Culture*. Oxford: Oxford UP, 1986.

Anupama Jain

ATTAWAY, WILLIAM (1911–1986) African American novelist, scriptwriter, composer, and arranger. Attaway was born in Greenville, Mississippi, but moved with his family to Chicago when he was five years old. In an interview Attaway gave to the *Daily Worker* in 1937, he explained that his father, a physician, feared that his children might internalize Southern racist estimates of their abilities. The Attaway family, then, anticipated the Great Migration of African Americans to the North in the years surrounding World War I. In the 1930s, inspired by the work of Langston Hughes, Attaway began to write short stories and one-act plays while attending the University of Illinois at Urbana. When his father died, he abruptly left school and traveled the country as a laborer and hobo; his experience riding the rails during the Great Depression informed his first novel, *Let Me Breathe Thunder* (1939). Attaway reentered university in 1933 and graduated with a BA in English. During this time he also became involved with the Illinois Federal Writers' Project and invited Richard Wright, who joined the Project in 1935, to read to his college literary society. In 1936, Attaway moved to New York City, where he did various jobs while writing his first novel.

Let Me Breathe Thunder tells the story of two white men—itinerant farm laborers—who in their travels west informally adopt an orphaned Mexican boy who, in the end, dies of a wound he inflicts on himself in order to prove he has the necessary courage and stamina to travel with his older companions. Like John Steinbeck's or **Ralph Ellison**'s Depression-era work, the novel captures the desperation and the resourceful spirit of displaced workers; like Hemingway's work of the same era, Attaway's language is detached and unadorned, his perspective documentary and naturalistic.

With the support of a Rosenwald Fellowship, Attaway began work on his second novel. *Blood on the Forge* (1941) is the story of three brothers—sharecroppers—who flee Kentucky in 1919 after one of them attacks the overseer. Recruited to work in a volatile and eventually strikebound Pennsylvania steel mill, the men undergo the journey north in a sealed boxcar, a journey which critics note, evokes the Middle Passage. In their encounter with industrialization, their folk culture—developed as a strategy, as Ralph Ellison would write, to survive the land and the white masters—undergoes a metamorphosis, if not dissolution. At its publication, the novel was most extensively reviewed by Ellison who would, in the course of his career, continue to document the outcome of migration and the changes in African American culture and consciousness. Although the novel has a tragic end—one brother becomes a strikebreaker and is killed, another is blinded in a horrific industrial accident, and the last is unable to adapt his music to the new rhythms of life—it is a powerfully-rendered account of the Great Migration, Northern America working-class life and the resilience of African American folk culture, particularly oral storytelling and music.

Attaway largely abandoned fiction writing and, in the 1950s, became a writer for television. A film script he wrote in the late 1960s was never produced. However, his interest in music led him to arrange songs and write liner notes for several Harry Belafonte albums, and he published two other books, *The Calypso Songbook* (1957) and *Hear America Singing* (1967). He died in Los Angeles in 1986.

Further Reading

Barthold, Bonnie J. *Black Time: Fiction of Africa, the Caribbean, and the United States.* New Haven, CT: Yale UP, 1981.

Campbell, Jane. *Mythic Black Fiction: The Transformation of History.* Knoxville: U of Tennessee P, 1986.

Condor, John. "Selves of the City, Selves of the South: The City in the Fiction of William Attaway and Willard Motley." *The City in African-American Literature.* Ed. Yoshinobu Hakutani and Robert Butler. Madison, NJ: Fairleigh Dickinson UP, 1996.

Foley, Barbara. *Radical Representations: Politics and Form in U.S. Proletarian Fiction, 1929–1941.* Durham, NC: Duke UP, 1993.

Garren, Samuel B. "Playing the Wishing Game: Folkloric Elements in William Attaway's *Blood on the Forge*." *College Language Association Journal* 32.1 (1988): 10–22.

Hamilton, Cynthia. "Work and Culture: The Evolution of Consciousness in Urban Industrial Society in the Fiction of William Attaway and Peter Abrahams." *Black American Literature Forum* 21.1–2 (1987): 147–63.

Margolies, Edward. *Native Sons: A Critical Study of Twentieth-Century Black American Authors.* Philadelphia: Lippincott, 1968.

Waldron, Edward E. "William Attaway's *Blood on the Forge*: The Death of the Blues." *Black American Literature Forum* 10.2 (1976): 58–60.

Yarborough, Richard. Afterword. *Blood on the Forge.* William Attaway. New York: Monthly Review Press, 1987. 295–310.

Robin Lucy

AUSTER, PAUL (1947–)   Jewish American author. Auster has written fiction, memoirs, literary criticism, essays, screenplays, and poetry. He has

Paul Auster. *AP/Wide World Photos.*

translated a number of French texts, especially Modernist poetry; his own work has been translated into more than nineteen languages and is especially popular in Europe. Variously described as a postmodern writer, an existentialist, and a "European American," Auster's novels also invoke popular genres, including Gothic, nineteenth-century Realism and detective fiction. His work expresses his enthusiasm for European literature—Knut Hamsun's *Hunger* is the inspiration for his main critical work, *The Art of Hunger* (1997)—but the techniques of **canonical** American authors are equally important to an understanding of his work: Poe's suspenseful storytelling, Hawthorne's empathic observations, Melville's sense of the extraordinary in everyday life. Auster's writing style and range of concerns remain consistent and recognizable across his several volumes of fiction and are often rooted in aspects of his own life, much of which he has revealed in autobiographical essays and memoirs.

Born in Newark, New Jersey, and educated at Columbia University, Auster spent much of his young adulthood traveling, especially in Europe; he lived for four years in France, making a meager living as a translator. *Hand to Mouth* (1997), Auster's chronicle of the difficulties of making a living from writing, is revealing, poignant, and comic. Auster returned to New York and, after publishing four volumes of poetry, he suffered from writer's block and his career entered a crisis. At the same time, his marriage collapsed. The unexpected death of his father provided Auster with the financial freedom to focus on his writing and the subject he needed to break his block. He gave up poetry and produced "Portrait of an Invisible Man," a memoir of his father, which became the first part of *The Invention of Solitude* (1982), paired with "The Book of Memory," a meditation on writing, parenthood, and loss. The concerns of these autobiographical pieces inform much of Auster's fiction, as he questions the nature and stability of identity, the relationship between reality and fiction, and coincidence. This last concern has extended into Auster's nonfiction: he has collected his own "true stories" of chance events in *The Red Notebook* (2002) and those of the American public in *I Thought My Father Was God* (2001).

Despite the positive reception of *The Invention of Solitude*, Auster struggled for some time to find a publisher for what became his breakthrough novel, *The New York Trilogy* (1987). Comprised of *City of Glass*, *Ghosts*, and *The Locked Room*, the trilogy was considered too avant-garde, too "European," for an American audience, but because it found great success in Europe, it eventually established Auster's name in the United States. The trilogy makes significant, if subversive, use of the detective genre, presenting a crime, a victim, an investigator, and an extensive set of clues. However, some "clues" are misleading, and the narrative twists do not follow the conventions of the genre. *The New York Trilogy* explores the extent to which a sense of identity relies upon the perceptions of those around us, rather than being a matter of individual choice. The trilogy typifies Auster's fiction in the sense that it is characterized by a playful postmodern manner, but simultaneously explores serious issues of contemporary urban life.

In 1982 Auster married the author Siri Hustvedt; the relationship has featured literally and metaphorically in Auster's fiction ever since. In *City of Glass*, a character called Paul Auster, with his wife Siri and son Daniel, try to help the bereaved protagonist, and in *Leviathan* (1992), the hero, Peter Aaron, meets his wife Iris on the same date that Auster met Hustvedt. There is no doubt that this second marriage has had a huge impact on Auster's life and work: throughout his career he has explored the impact of bereavement on men, and Auster has made clear that, through these characters, he voices his own fears of losing his partner and family. At least half of Auster's novels feature a main character like the protagonist in *City of Glass*, a man who finds himself alone, having lost his family, with his sense of identity and the value of his life rapidly diminishing, or the protagonist of *The Music of Chance* (1991), a bereaved man on an endless road trip who, having fallen in with a petty criminal, finally finds relief from his unhappiness through enforced labor. The recent work seems better able to picture these men as potential survivors of loss, however deep their despair.

Auster's fiction is perhaps best understood as a body of work, patterned by recurring images, names, and stories, each novel a new variant on his key themes. However, his habitual concerns do not mean that the novels are identical: *In the Country of Last Things* (1988) features the quest of Anna Blume to find her brother in a disintegrating city, and *Timbuktu* (1999) presents the first-person narrative of a stray dog. Characterized by a mixture of wry humor and eerie detachment, his fiction presents a narrative voice that communicates the uncanny, touching, and absurd in a given situation. His work has been criticized for its apparent archness, for having a dazzling surface that, whilst entertaining, fails to contain the depth it gestures toward. However, a sprawling novel like *Moon Palace* (1989) links the adventures of its orphaned hero and the history of the United States, while *The Book of Illusions* (2002) connects the familiar lone protagonist to the legacy of American cinema, invoking death and sacrifice as much as survival. There is also, in Auster's work, a sense of the magical: The demotic *Mr Vertigo* (1994) is at its most effective when describing the eponymous protagonist's experience of levitation, and the multiple narratives of *Oracle Night*

(2003) are enhanced by its sense of the fantastic, as a blue notebook (red and blue notebooks recur throughout his oeuvre) provokes extraordinary occurrences.

Auster's surreal and playful fiction is firmly engaged with lived experience, and his work is more human and accessible than his early reputation implied; he is now widely considered one of the most important and influential of contemporary authors.

Further Reading

Barone, Denis, ed. *Beyond the Red Notebook: Essays on Paul Auster*. Philadelphia: U of Pennsylvania P, 1995.

Bilton, Alan, *An Introduction to Contemporary American Fiction*. Edinburgh: Edinburgh UP, 2002: 51–93.

Sarah Graham

AUSTIN, DORISJEAN (c. 1949–1994)   African American novelist, short story writer, anthologist, and newswoman. DorisJean Austin was born in Alabama but grew up in Jersey City, New Jersey. When she was six years old, her family moved to the North but transported with them many of the cultural values so cherished by African Americans of the South. Chief among those values was a strong commitment to home and family and a strong commitment to what black Americans refer to as "a church family" and "a church home." Thus, the Monumental Baptist Church in Jersey City became the church family and church home of DorisJean and the other members of her family.

Austin was first inspired by her high school English teacher, the Reverend Ercell F. Webb, to become a writer. Webb and Austin remained friends throughout her lifetime. Austin's admiration and respect for Webb caused her to select him as the officiant for her first marriage ceremony.

Distinguishing herself in a number of different professions, Austin is most remembered for her work as a novelist. Although *After the Garden* (1987) was the first and only novel that Austin wrote, it placed her in the ranks of African American women writers like **Terry McMillan** and **Gloria Naylor**, who, like Austin, published their first novels in the 1980s. Austin's novel received excellent reviews. Numerous reviewers were impressed by Austin's attention to intra-class conflict among African Americans.

Many readers tend to see *After the Garden* as autobiographical. Set in Jersey City, New Jersey, this work centers on the tumultuous life of fourteen-year-old Elzina who, at fifteen, is impregnated by Jesse James, a young man from the wrong side of town. Unlike Elzina's church-going grandmother, who raised her after her parents died, Jesse's mother embraces a "worldly" lifestyle. She enjoys drinking, playing cards, and other such activities, all of which, according to Elzina's grandmother, place Jesse and his family in a social class lower than hers and Elzina's. Adding to the grandmother's disapproval of Jesse's class standing is that his mother has given birth to several children to different fathers.

When Jesse and Elzina marry, Elzina must choose between moving to her new husband's home on Kearney Avenue and remaining in her own home on Astor Place. To leave Astor Place would be to leave "the garden" and be thrust among "the weeds" on Kearney Avenue. The two decide to remain in their own individual homes, a decision which emphasizes the difficulty, or impossibility, of successfully integrating two classes that differ on moral and religious issues.

Elzina's grandmother dies. Elzina experiences a mental breakdown. With the help of Jesse's out-of-wedlock daughter, Elzina recovers. This out-of-wedlock birth is yet another example of what Elzina's grandmother would regard as further proof of Jesse's inferior class standing.

Austin published several short stories in the 1990s. However, her best-known short piece appears in *Streetlights: Illuminating Tales of the Urban Experience,* an anthology which she coedited with Martin Simmons and to which she contributed one story. "Room 1023" is set in New York and centers on the plight of Lee, a middle-class African American woman who is evicted from a residential hotel for women. She had been a victim of spousal abuse and fled her home after her husband broke her arm. Lee is unemployed and must depend upon court-ordered monthly checks from her husband in order to pay her rent at the hotel. His payments are sporadic; because they are, Lee is forced into the streets of New York.

Austin, in her short life, worked as a journalist, a critic, and as a newscaster. She also was an instructor for Columbia University's advanced fiction workshops between 1989 and 1994. Austin was a member of the Harlem Writers' Guild and a cofounder of New Renaissance Writers' Guild, for which she served as executive director. Austin died of liver cancer in 1994 in New York City.

Further Reading

Austin, Doris Jean, and Martin Simmons, eds. *Streetlights: Illuminating Tales of the Urban Black Experience.* New York: Penguin, 1996.

Joyce Russell-Robinson

AUTOBIOGRAPHY OF MALCOLM X, THE   The *Autobiography* (1965), "as told to **Alex Haley**," remains the core text to the work and life, significantly inseparable, of African American activist **Malcolm X**. The book, dictated to Alex Haley over the course of three years, reveals the discipline, rhetorical force, and unflinching honesty that characterized Malcolm X's devotion to the cause of African American unity. The book revolves around two key transitions in Malcolm's life: his conversion, in prison, to Islam, and his later break from the Nation of Islam and its leader Elijah Muhammad. Thus, a central theme of the book is redemption; also, however, Malcolm's life story reveals the connections between action and social responsibility.

Alex Haley used the impetus of a 1962 interview with Malcolm to propose the autobiography. While highly suspicious of the media and skeptical about the project, Malcolm agreed, and eventually he and Haley developed a working relationship that allowed Malcolm to reveal details of his criminal past in forthright detail, while demonstrating that experience can, and should, lead to self-awareness and, eventually, personal enlightenment.

The book breaks, roughly, into three sections: Malcolm Little's penurious childhood and criminal life; Malcolm's arrest and imprisonment, conversion to Islam, and his life as Elijah Muhammad's disciple; and his split with Elijah Muhammad, his *hajj* and, taking the name El-Hajj Malik El-Shabazz, the reformulation of his segregationist politics and his focus on unity among African Americans, resulting in his formation of the Organization for Afro-American Unity. The book concludes with the circumstances, still somewhat mysterious, surrounding Malcolm X's assassination on February 21, 1965.

Alex Haley wisely remains transparent in the narrative, giving the book the force of Malcolm's own eloquence. Though Malcolm retained the right of final approval of all material, he corrected little of the manuscript; Malcolm never mitigated his criminal life, or the depths of his own debasement, before his religious conversion. In allowing the record to stand unencumbered by conventional narrative strategies of the ghostwriter, the text remains intense and still relevant. Malcolm agreed to let Haley compose an epilogue, without his editorial approval, to be attached to the text. This epilogue allows Haley to emerge as Malcolm's transcriber and further asserts Malcolm's desire that the book reveal his true life as an activist, father, husband, and faithful Muslim.

The Autobiography of Malcolm X became a best-seller, selling 50,000 copies in hardback and about five million paperback copies and became required reading in many college courses. The assassination of Malcolm X increased interest in the text and helped it gain wide readership. The book is still perceived as a formative text in the **Civil Rights Movement**, and a profound description of a man's struggle to reclaim his African **identity**. The book was successfully filmed by director Spike Lee in 1992. (*See also* African American Autobiography)

Further Reading

Bloom, Harold. *Alex Haley's and Malcolm X's "The Autobiography of Malcolm X."* Philadelphia: Chelsea House, 1996.

Lee, Spike. *By Any Means Necessary: The Trials and Tribulations of Making Malcolm X.* London: Vintage, 1992.

Bill R. Scalia

AUTOBIOGRAPHY OF MISS JANE PITTMAN, THE Published in 1972, this historical novel by African American author **Ernest Gaines** received wide attention when it was published and later when it was developed into a major motion picture. So compelling and authentic was Gaines's writing that many readers were deceived by the title and assumed the work was an authentic **slave narrative** rather than a work of fiction.

Miss Jane herself narrates most of the text, an act occasioned by the inquiries of an history teacher who asks to hear her story to correct and amplify the information conventional histories had ignored. Many interpret the history teacher as a stand-in for the author, Gaines, whose own experience growing up in rural Louisiana led him to appreciate the value of oral testimony.

While the text participates in the individual slave narrative tradition, the author's invitation of an oral history—his call for Miss Jane's response—invokes a principle of communal relationship characteristic of the other great aesthetic form that emerged out of **slavery**, the **spirituals**. Set in Gaines's home state, the novel is divided into four parts: The War Years, Reconstruction, The Plantation, and The Quarters. Episodic in structure and epic in its sweep, the novel spans nearly one hundred years, from the 1860s to the 1960s. Miss Jane's longevity allows her a unique appreciation of the development of black life after slavery. Despite her age, however, her credibility is never in question as her recitation of events both personal and public is received by the reader as authentic.

In the opening chapter Miss Jane abandons her slave name and, despite resistance, adopts a new one, signaling Gaines's interest in **identity**, a major theme in African American literature. This act also establishes heroic qualities of the protagonist that she will exhibit throughout her life, including determination, integrity, tolerance, and fairness. Major events in the novel, however, do not always include Miss Jane as the main character. She understands that her experience alone is not an adequate representation of black history, so she promotes a communal picture of black life as emerging out of the experiences of many with whom she comes into contact, including several white characters—public figures and personal acquaintances—who influence and shape her experience. Violence against African Americans trying in various ways to assert their identity advance the narrative, including the assassination of Ned, Jane's adopted son, and the murder of Jimmy, a civil rights worker from Jane's community. That act, however, fails to prevent Jane from participating in a protest—and inspiring others from her community to do the same—that concludes the novel. These moments are indexed against violence and suffering among whites, including the suicide of Tee Bob, who desired to cross racial boundaries. In this manner Gaines reveals the destructive consequences of **racism** for American society as a whole.

Also significant throughout the novel are the folkways of black culture that Gaines introduces to illustrate his text, including religious sentiments, manners of speech and style, and important influences on black life derived from society at large including political elections, weather-related events, technological advancements, and sporting moments in boxing and baseball. These elements not only lend authenticity to the novel but also underscore the unconventional places in which one can locate essential aspects of historical meaning.

Further Reading

Byerman, Keith E. *Fingering the Jagged Grain: Tradition and Form in Recent Black Fiction.* Athens: U of Georgia P, 1985.

Connor, Kimberly Rae. *Imagining Grace: Liberating Theologies in the Slave Narrative Tradition.* Urbana: U of Illinois P, 2000.

Kimberly Rae Connor

B

BACA, JIMMY SANTIAGO (1952–)   Chicano poet. From New Mexico, Jimmy Santiago Baca is best known as a poet who draws not only on his ethnicity but also significantly on his time in prison to articulate spiritual renewal and possibility. Like **Malcolm X** and others, Baca learned to read and write while in prison, and the transformation is vividly portrayed in the imagery of metamorphosis that populates his poems.

Baca is of Chicano, Apache, and Anglo descent. In his recent autobiography *A Place to Stand* (2001), he tells of the racial tension in his family, his father's drinking and failures, and his mother's abandonment of him and his siblings. As a result of his mother's departure, Baca lived with his grandparents until he was placed in an orphanage at the age of five. In his autobiography, he recounts his alienation in the institutions, as well as his learning to live on the street, traffic drugs, and make his own way. At twenty, he was convicted of selling drugs (although he makes it clear that he did not commit the specific crime for which he was convicted in *A Place to Stand*), and then spent six tumultuous years in jail.

He learned in prison that by not acting but taking a position of passive resistance he could break the systematic degradation of his experience; he learned to stand up for himself by not standing up to be counted by the guards. Although he ended up being placed in isolation, the lesson he learned is one of independence and strength. He began writing while in prison, sending out his poetry to *Mother Jones*, where **Denise Levertov**, the poetry editor at the time, not only read and published his poetry but also aided Baca in obtaining a publisher for his first book. Deeply autobiographical, *Immigrants*

Jimmy Santiago Baca. *Photo by Kent Barker. Courtesy of Jimmy Santiago Baca.*

in Our Own Land (1979) was Baca's first major book of poetry and was very well received. The poems combined the brutality of his life experiences with lyrical flashes and an overall sense of possibility. It signaled the emergence of a significant new voice.

Baca's noteworthy collection *Martin and Meditations on the South Valley* (1987) won the American Book Award in 1988. The book is a series of poems that tell the tale of Martin based on Baca himself. By the end of the book, Martin comes into his own putting his abandonment by his mother and other tribulations behind him. *Black Mesa Poems* are the poems of Baca-the-poet, showing not only his poetic confidence but also his personal success in finding stability in his life; Baca was married and had two children by the time of the publication. With his success as a poet, Baca has been invited to teach and speak at numerous schools. In some of the lectures, before and after reading lyrical poems about fatherhood or living in New Mexico, he admonishes the audience to pay attention to the booming if invisible prison system.

Along with *A Place to Stand*, Baca has also published *Working in the Dark: Reflections of a Poet of the Barrio* (1992). From the title alone, one gets a sense of Baca's desire to speak for the poor, which shines through in these loosely connected essays. Their worth comes not from his autobiography but from his explanations of himself as a reader—showing how language liberated him, how reading the works of Octavio Paz, Pablo Neruda, and others enabled his imagination to take flight. They prove crucial in understanding Baca's own poetry and ambition; he wants to fire our imaginations in the same manner such poets fired his.

Released at the same time as *A Place to Stand*, his collection *Healing Earthquakes* (2001) contains five sections of poems all devoted to the poet's quest for love. Nearly all therapeutic in some fashion, the poems range from communal to personal, mixing the thorniness of failure with regenerative and ultimate fulfillment. Baca has since published *The Importance of a Piece of Paper* (2004), a collection of eight short stories that cover emotional and personal territory found in much of his poetry.

Although barely affiliated with **Gloria Anzaldúa**'s political project, Baca can be seen as a *mestiza* voice—that is, a voice of mixed cultural heritages.

His writing is deeply rooted in the experiences of the people of the southwestern part of the United States, detailing not only discrimination but also most significantly determination and success.

Further Reading

Cochran, Stuart. "The Ethnic Implications of Stories, Spirits, and the Land in Native American Pueblo and Aztlán Writing." *MELUS* 20.2 (Summer 1995): 69–91.

Magill, Frank, ed. *Masterpieces of Latino Literature.* New York: Harper Collins, 1994.

Perez-Torres, Rafael. *Movements in Chicano Poetry: Against Myths, Against Margins.* New York: Cambridge UP, 1995.

Thomas H. Kane

BACHO, PETER (1951–)   Filipino American writer. Peter Bacho grew up in Seattle's Central District, graduated summa cum laude from Seattle University in 1971, and earned a law degree from the University of Washington in 1976. Bacho's work has appeared in the *Christian Science Monitor, Amerasia Journal, Oregonian, Tacoma News Tribune, Seattle Review,* and *Zyzzyva.* Since 1988, he has taught Asian American history and literature at the University of Washington's Tacoma campus. Bacho has received the Washington State Governor's Award, the Murray Morgan Book Award, and the Before Columbus Foundation's 1992 American Book Award.

In Bacho's first novel, *Cebu* (1991), Ben Lucero, a Catholic priest from Seattle, makes his first visit to the Philippines to accompany and bury the body of his recently deceased mother Remedios. During his stay he learns from his mother's childhood friend Clara about their experiences during World War II, visits the site of a crucifixion, and breaks his vow of chastity with Clara's assistant Ellen. Confounded by his experiences abroad, Lucero returns to Seattle to minister to a transforming Filipino community racked by tension and violence. *Dark Blue Suit* (1997) consists of twelve interconnected short stories that over the course of nearly half a century follow a group of tight-knit characters: Buddy, his father Vincent, uncles Leo and Kikoy, and childhood friends Rico, Stephanie, and Aaron. In their stories a fictionalized oral history emerges of Seattle's Filipino community through union struggles, education and labor conditions, and the Vietnam War.

For more than thirty years, Bacho has been an avid observer, student, and practitioner of boxing and martial arts, which also figure prominently in his work. *Boxing in Black and White* (1999) features portraits of ten famous boxers (from Filipino champion Sammy Santos to Mohammed Ali) and their broader cultural and political significance. In Bacho's fiction, boxing is a significant reminder of the scrappiness, pride, and resiliency of elder Filipino immigrant laborers. In "A Manong's Heart," Bacho writes, "Our boxers of the past have all but disappeared, as have most of their fans—our fathers, uncles, and friends. But among the remaining few who saw them, certain imprints remain. . . . Is it any wonder, then, that one of the quickest ways to a Manong's heart is to talk fights and fighters?"

In both his fiction and nonfiction, Bacho encourages continuity across generations from immigrants of the 1930s to their American born children to more recent arrivals whose varied class, educational, and linguistic backgrounds threaten to disrupt Filipino American communal bonds. Bacho's spare and bluesy chronicles of the hopes, decisions, and frequent disappointments of his characters act at once to record the rich textures of Filipino American community during the twentieth century and cultivate an historical self-awareness among those who follow. (*See also* Filipino American Novel)

Further Reading

Pisares, Elizabeth. "Payback Time: Neocolonial Discourses in Peter Bacho's *Cebu*." *MELUS* 29.1 (Spring 2004): 79–97.

Alex Feerst

BAKER, HOUSTON A., JR. (1943–)   African American poet, literary critic, and cultural theorist. With a taste for theoretical inquiry and an abiding commitment to African American expressive culture, Houston A. Baker Jr. stands as one of the most perceptive and provocative readers of black literature in the world today.

Born in Louisville, Kentucky, in a thoroughly segregated socioeconomic milieu and educated at Howard University and the University of California in Los Angeles in the 1960s, Baker began his academic career as a Victorianist but turned his attention to African American literary study as a young professor deeply affected by the **Civil Rights Movement** and concomitant changes to humanities curricula. After stints at Yale University and the University of Virginia, Baker moved to the University of Pennsylvania in 1974, where he eventually became the Albert M. Greenfield Professor of Human Relations and director of the Center for the Study of Black Literature and Culture. In 1999 Baker joined the faculty at Duke University, where he is currently the Susan Fox Beischer & George D. Beischer Arts & Sciences Professor of English and editor of the journal *American Literature*.

Baker's early monographs—*Long Black Song* (1972), *Singers of Daybreak* (1974), *The Journey Back* (1980)—outline the distinctive traits that characterize African American expressive culture through readings of major black authors such as **Frederick Douglass**, **W. E. B. Du Bois**, and **Richard Wright**. Heavily influenced by structuralist and semiotic inquiry, these studies affirm the cultural and academic standing of the African American literary tradition. At the same time, they avoid recourse to essentialist paradigms of racial understanding by teasing out the linguistic and discursive contradictions immanent to that tradition. The variety and richness of black literature is such that African American texts stand in dynamically contrasting relation to mainstream (white) literature and to each other.

In 1984 Baker published his renowned model of a theory-oriented African American literary criticism *Blues, Ideology, and Afro-American Literature*.

Here Baker employs critical methodologies ranging from Hegelian dialectics to French poststructuralism to the aural "matrix" of a blues vernacular to situate African American expressive culture at the juncture of the oppressive socioeconomic forces that have shaped black life in the United States. Though some critics, such as Joyce A. Joyce, have criticized him for dubiously integrating "high" (white) theory into analyses of black literature, Baker's project in this book shows how theory can productively delineate the historical and material conditions of an African American expressive culture always already in flux.

In recent years Baker has focused his work on major trends in theoretical inquiry and cultural studies: phenomenology and black feminist thought in *Workings of the Spirit* (1991); the politics of the culture wars in *Black Studies, Rap, and the Academy* (1993); public sphere theory and masculinity studies in *Critical Memory* (2001); and regional studies and autobiographical criticism in *Turning South Again* (2001), a penetrating recasting of his 1987 study *Modernism and the Harlem Renaissance*. As his critical vision grows ever more expansive and daring, Baker continually challenges the field of African American literary study to question its methodological and pedagogical borders.

Further Reading

Adell, Sandra. "The Crisis in Black American Literary Criticism and the Postmodern Cures of Houston A. Baker, Jr., and Henry Louis Gates, Jr." *Double-Consciousness/Double Bind: Theoretical Issues in Twentieth-Century Black Literature*. Urbana: U of Illinois P, 1994. 118–37.

Bérubé, Michael. "Hybridity in the Center: An Interview with Houston A. Baker, Jr." *African American Review* 26.4 (1992): 547–64.

Napier, Winston. "From the Shadows: Houston Baker's Move Toward a Postnationalist Appraisal of the Black Aesthetic." *New Literary History* 25.1 (1994): 159–74.

Kinohi Nishikawa

BAKER, NIKKI (1962–) African American writer. Nikki Baker is the author of several mystery novels chronicling the adventures of Virginia Kelley, a charismatic black lesbian stockbroker who often finds herself at the center of intrigue and murder. Baker uses the popular techniques of suspense fiction to present vivid, realistic characters, and to explore the unique issues surrounding contemporary black lesbian life.

Baker was born in Greene County, Ohio. She received a BS from Purdue University and an MBA from the University of Chicago. Since Baker was not formally trained as a writer, she relies upon her imagination and her experiences as a young, educated, black lesbian of affluent means to fuel her fiction.

Much of Baker's fiction demonstrates her commitment to the concept of "free agency," which she describes as a sense of individual frustration resulting from a feeling of alienation from community institutions. Her novels highlight a vibrant and largely marginalized social group, and describe characters who challenge conventional norms and expectations. Baker's first novel, *In the Game* (1991), introduces readers to Virginia Kelley, a securities analyst who deals with risk assessment. A likable and impulsive protagonist, Ginny and her group of girlfriends face both frustration and success in a world where they must work twice as hard to gain the respect and stature of their white peers. *In the Game* opens with Ginny's old friend Bev who is traumatized by the murder of her lesbian lover Kelsey. After discovering some surprising information about Kelsey, Ginny finds herself entwined in the mysterious death and also threatened by a former lover. In *The Lavender House Murder* (1992), Baker's second novel, Ginny stumbles into a mystery while vacationing at a lesbian-run hotel in Provincetown, Massachusetts, with her friend Naomi. Baker describes an eclectic group of women at the quiet resort, which is upset by the machinations of a ruthless killer. Ginny must again rely on her quick wit and sharp insight to solve the mystery. In the next installment of the Virginia Kelley series, *Long Goodbyes* (1993), Ginny returns home for the Christmas holiday and a high school reunion. Although at first it appears that nothing has changed in her Midwest hometown, Rosalee, Ginny's first love, attempts to rekindle their relationship, and the wife of a local teacher mysteriously drowns. Baker's most recent novel, *The Ultimate Exit Strategy* (2001), describes a perplexing intrigue at Ginny's own investment firm. After her office is threatened by a proposed hostile takeover by a competing firm and her boss is murdered, Ginny learns that many of her coworkers harbor secret motives.

Although Baker's work has not achieved mainstream success, her mystery novels document an important facet of African American life and explore issues critical to the community at large. Baker works as a financial analyst and is a volunteer for Horizon's Youth Services, an organization dedicated to the needs of the gay and lesbian community.

Further Reading

Breazeale, M. Kenon. "Review Essay: The Postmodern Politics of the Lesbian Mystery." *The Lesbian Review of Books* 1 (1994): 14–16.

Stephanie Li

BALDWIN, JAMES (1924–1987)   African American novelist, essayist, autobiographer, dramatist, scriptwriter, poet, speaker, and civil rights activist. James Baldwin's life and work brought him an international reputation by the early 1960s. Although his legacy has not been without its detractors, there is no doubt his eloquent and incisive critique of the national character, as it has been formed and distorted by questions of race, sexuality, and religion, make his work important to the entire enterprise of American literature as well as to the shape of African American literature in the second half of the twentieth century. The theme that most differentiates Baldwin from **Richard Wright** and **Ralph Ellison**, the most prominent African American novelists when Baldwin began writing in the fifties, is

Baldwin's insistence on the fundamental connection between racial and sexual oppression in American experience. More than any other writer of his time, Baldwin challenged the national discourse around race from its preoccupation with "the Negro problem" to an analysis of "the white problem," which Baldwin described as a false "innocence" that involved various levels of denials, collective and individual, of both history and the self. In fiction and nonfiction Baldwin explored the ways in which blacks have paid the price for white denial by becoming symbols of both deviance and desire in the white imagination, and also the ways that whites have paid a price for self-deception. Baldwin's work, however, is not only important for its challenges to white racial ideology but also just as important for its representations of intraracial experience within black families and black communities. In her eulogy, **Toni Morrison** credited Baldwin with making "American English honest— genuinely international" while making it available for black people to express "our lived reality" and "our complicated passion" (Troupe 76).

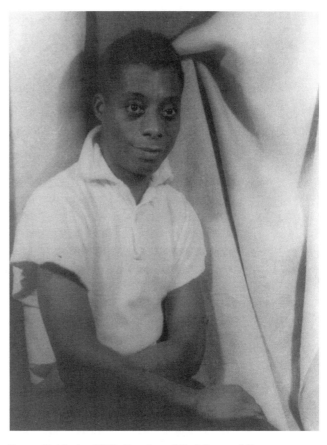

James Baldwin, 1955. *Courtesy of the Library of Congress.*

Major Themes

The complexity of Baldwin's life and work and the politically charged atmosphere in which he wrote have posed significant challenges to scholars and critics, who have frequently emphasized one aspect or period of his work while ignoring or disparaging others. Much of Baldwin's complexity results from his ability to articulate certain seemingly paradoxical positions and themes. Baldwin insists on both the aesthetic and the political value of art, describing the artist as both lover and disturber of the peace. He is severely critical of the Christian church for hypocrisy and for its historical role in the subjugation of blacks; but, at the same time, he shapes his moral vision in the Old Testament language of the Jeremiad and in New Testament images of revelation and salvation. He draws on both interracial themes and subjects and on black nationalist concerns, and thus critiques some of the limitations of both integrationist and segregationist positions in American race relations. He writes openly and movingly about homosexual love, while arguing against the idea of a homosexual identity. He consistently critiqued categories of identity, white and black, gay and straight, as denying the complex reality of individual experience and as creating and maintaining power relationships.

Early Life

James Baldwin was born August 2, 1924, in Harlem, New York, to Emma Berdis Jones, a young, single woman. Three years later Berdis married David Baldwin, and eventually James became the eldest of nine children. David Baldwin, a former preacher who had come north during the Great Migration looking for work and for escape from southern violence, was the deacon of a Pentecostal church. The struggle to support his large family in conditions of acute poverty and racial discrimination took its toll. He was harsh and judgmental. Baldwin said that his father had scared him so badly that no one else could scare him again. When Baldwin learned as a teenager that David Baldwin was not his biological father, this knowledge helped explain his father's hostility and rejection of him. Baldwin's troubled relationship with his stepfather is central to the semiautobiographical first novel, *Go Tell It on the Mountain* (1953), and to the early essay "Notes of a Native Son" (1955). Baldwin came to see his father's self-destructive rages as an object lesson—what happens when a black man believes the white world's judgment about himself. All of Baldwin's work blends autobiography and social commentary. He presented his life metaphorically—his illegitimacy symbolic of the condition of being black in the New World, "a kind of bastard of the West."

Influences

Important early influences that informed Baldwin's art and subject matter included the church, his reading, his family, and mentors. When Baldwin was fourteen he experienced a religious conversion and became a child preacher. He would fictionalize this experience in *Go Tell It on the Mountain* in one of the most powerful descriptions of a religious conversion in American literature. At the climax of the novel, the protagonist John Grimes falls to the threshing floor in the Temple of the Fire Baptized and undergoes a religious crisis that is both a reaction to and a temporary solution for the conflict with his father and with his feelings of dread and guilt over his awakening sexual desires. Ten years later Baldwin spoke directly about the psychological and social forces that drove him into the church in *The Fire Next Time* (1963). Despite his negative assessment of the church, he also testified to the enduring power of spirituals and gospel music that came from the black church and that would always be present in Baldwin's literary language, especially as titles, epigraphs, and allusions. From early childhood, Baldwin was an avid reader. Harriet Beecher Stowe's *Uncle Tom's Cabin* made a particular impression on him. In "Everybody's Protest Novel" (1949), the controversial early essay that would serve as Baldwin's literary manifesto, Baldwin compares *Uncle Tom's Cabin* with Richard Wright's **Native Son** as protest novels, which, he argued, do more to shore up the status quo than to change it because they deny the complexity of Negro life in America by representing blacks as either victims or socially constructed monsters. Baldwin's favorite nineteenth-century novelist was Henry James, whose influence can be seen in Baldwin's style and in his subject of the American abroad.

Important people in young Baldwin's life included his mother, who was a source of spiritual and moral strength, and his siblings, whom he helped raise. Strong female characters, close relationships between siblings, particularly between brothers, and the importance of the family in the struggle to resist oppression and to achieve self-expression are important subjects of his later fictions *If Beale Street Could Talk* (1974) and *Just Above My Head* (1979) and of his widely anthologized short story "Sonny's Blues" (1957). Baldwin was recognized as a precocious child from the time he was in elementary school. A white teacher, Orilla Miller, took him under her wing and introduced him to theater and movies. Fascinated by theater and film from an early age, Baldwin would go on to write two plays, *Amen Corner* (1954) and *Blues for Mister Charlie* (1964); a screen play of the life of **Malcolm X**, *One Day When I Was Lost* (1972); and a cultural critique of American film, *The Devil Finds Work* (1976). The hero of his fourth novel, *Tell Me How Long the Train's Been Gone* (1968), is an internationally known actor who becomes a spokesperson in the **Civil Rights Movement**. At Frederick Douglass Junior High, Baldwin received invaluable guidance from two African American male teachers, the poet **Countee Cullen**, and Herman Porter. During high school, Baldwin met Beauford Delany, an African American artist who became a surrogate father and lifelong friend. Delany introduced Baldwin to secular black music and taught him how to see light and shadow with the eye of the artist.

Transatlantic Commuter and Activist

As a young man Baldwin lived in Greenwich Village and began writing book reviews for the *Nation* and *New Leader*. In 1948 *Commentary* published his first major essay, "The Harlem Ghetto," and the short story "Previous Condition." Also during this period Richard Wright helped Baldwin win a Saxton Foundation Fellowship after reading an early draft of *Go Tell It on the Mountain. Another Country* (1962) draws from Baldwin's years in the Village. The novel follows the lives of seven characters whose interracial and bisexual relationships suggest the limits and the possibilities of healing the divisions of race and sex through intimate encounters. In November of 1948 Baldwin left for Paris with forty dollars in his pocket to escape the pressures of life in New York where he felt targeted as a black and a homosexual. The next ten years were immensely productive. Baldwin wrote all the work that gained him an international reputation while living abroad. *Go Tell It on the Mountain* was completed in a tiny Catholic village in the Swiss mountains where he went with his lover Lucien Happersberger. This village, where none of the residents had ever seen a black person before Baldwin's arrival, also became the subject of an important essay on the relationship of the American Negro to European culture, "Stranger in the Village" (1953). Baldwin's first collection of essays, **Notes of a Native Son**, was published in 1955. Baldwin's second novel, *Giovanni's Room* (1956), about homosexual love between a white American, David, and an Italian, Giovanni, who meet in Paris, has become a foundational text for gay and lesbian studies. Initially Baldwin's agent told him to burn the novel because he was a Negro writer and it would alienate his audience, but Baldwin refused to be limited by stereotypes of the role of a Negro writer. David, the first-person narrator whose ancestors "conquered a continent," represents Baldwin's interpretation of the flaws in white American society. David flees to Europe trying to escape himself and the American version of masculinity only to betray his lover Giovanni. This betrayal is part of a larger failure of love that Baldwin understood to be endemic to American society.

In 1957 Baldwin returned to the United States to travel south, interviewed Dr. **Martin Luther King Jr.**, and reported on the Civil Rights Movement. Over the next decade, Baldwin became an important figure in the movement, describing himself as a witness rather than a spokesperson. His years in the pulpit had trained him well as a powerful and eloquent speaker. Now his impressive rhetorical skill was put to use appealing to the American conscience to transform race relations in the United States. In 1963, a watershed year in the struggle for civil rights, Baldwin published *The Fire Next Time*, met with Attorney General Robert F. Kennedy, and appeared on the cover of *Time* magazine. Calling himself a "transatlantic commuter" rather than an expatriate, Baldwin returned to Europe and to Istanbul to write because he found it impossible to work in the United States. By the late sixties and early seventies, after witnessing the worsening conditions in American ghettos and the murder of key black leaders, Medgar Evers, Malcolm X, and Martin Luther King, Baldwin became increasingly disillusioned with the American government and the will of the people to bring about social change. His work published after the mid-sixties reflects his disillusionment and anger, but it also reflects his interest in the revolution of black consciousness taking place and his increased willingness to represent homosexual themes in a black context, especially in his last novel *Just Above My Head*.

Baldwin's oeuvre includes six novels, seven collections of essays, two plays, two collections of poetry, a collection of short stories, a phototext, a children's story, a screenplay, and many published interviews and dialogues. About three years before his death, Baldwin said, "I certainly have not told my story yet" (Miller 10), which poignantly suggests the extent to which he understood his work as a continuous and unfinished autobiographical project. Baldwin died December 1, 1987, at his home in Saint Paul-de-Vence in southern France. (*See also* African American Novel, African American Autobiography)

Further Reading

Harris, Trudier, ed. *New Essays on "Go Tell It on the Mountain."* New York: Cambridge UP, 1999.

Leeming, David. *James Baldwin: A Biography.* New York: Alfred A. Knopf, 1994.

McBride, Dwight A., ed. *James Baldwin Now.* New York: New York UP, 1999.

Miller, Quentin D., ed. *Reviewing James Baldwin: Things Not Seen.* Philadelphia: Temple UP, 2000.

Porter, Horace. *Stealing the Fire: The Art and Protest of James Baldwin.* Middletown, CT: Wesleyan UP, 1989.

Scott, Lynn Orilla. *James Baldwin's Later Fiction: Witness to the Journey.* East Lansing: Michigan State UP, 2002.

Troupe, Quincy, ed. *James Baldwin: The Legacy.* New York: Simon and Schuster, 1989.

Lynn Orilla Scott

BAMBARA, TONI CADE (1939–1995)   African American writer and activist. Born Miltona Mirkin Cade in Harlem, New York City, fiction writer Toni Cade Bambara is most well known for her attention to specifically African American modes of expression—from dialect to oral traditions of storytelling to African American musical forms such as **jazz**. The diversity in the settings of her stories and novels, which range from the urban north to the rural south to the seas near Vietnam, matches the diversity of her creative output as a fiction writer, screenwriter, and documentary filmmaker. Bambara's screenwriting credits include *The Bombing of Osage Avenue* (1986), the documentary on the Philadelphia police bombing of the activist organization MOVE in 1985, and part three of the series *W. E. B. Du Bois: A Biography in Four Voices* (1995). Her espousal of the Black Aesthetic Movement's move away from the dominant cultural modes of representation also play a role in the style and message of her fiction. Beyond writing and film, Bambara was also a professor at Rutgers, Duke, and the City College of New York, an artist in residence at Atlanta's Spelman College, and an activist in feminist and black liberation movements. She died of cancer in 1995.

Bambara published her first story, "Sweet Town," in *Vendome* magazine after graduating from Queens College in 1959 with a BA in English and theater. She completed her master's degree in modern American fiction at the City College of New York while working as a social worker in Harlem and a coordinator of social programs in Brooklyn. From there, she edited two anthologies: *The Black Woman* (1970), containing short stories, poems, and essays by black women writers and activists; and the collection of juvenile fiction *Tales and Stories for Black Folks* (1971), a collaborative project with her students at Rutgers University. Her first solo publication, *Gorilla My Love* (1972), contains fifteen short stories written between the years 1959 and 1972. The stories, whose locales range from urban to rural settings and whose characters encompass all ages, are unified by the use of first-person narration and Bambara's attention to the specifics of African American dialect and experience. Four of the stories, "My Man Bovanne," "Gorilla My Love," "Raymond's Run," and "Happy Birthday," are also united in the recurrence of different characters named Hazel. As with the stories in *Gorilla My Love*, the ten short stories in her next collection, *The Sea Birds Are Still Alive* (1977), focus most often on female protagonists (notable exceptions are "The Tender Man" and the multiplicity of voices in the title story), but here Bambara's expansions in terms of locale reflect her travels to Cuba and Vietnam and her move to Atlanta in 1974. In the title story, for example, the reader drifts on a boat with refugees lost near Vietnam.

The Salt Eaters (1980), the only novel Bambara published during her lifetime and the recipient of an American Book Award, is set in the fictional town of Claybourne, Georgia. The title refers to the African myth that slaves who ate salt couldn't fly back to Africa (Wilentz 62), and also to the faith healing belief that eating salt can cure poison (Walker 181). The protagonist, former activist, Velma Henry seeks healing at the infirmary after an attempted suicide. Her story is told by a mixture of flashbacks, omniscient narration, and the perspectives of multiple characters. The novel's settings include the Southwest Community Infirmary, the nearby Academy of Seven Arts, a local bus, and the Avocado Pit Café. In her prominence in the resolution of the novel's engagement with cultural and spiritual sickness, the faith healer Minnie Ransom comes to symbolize folk wisdom and communities of women as the key to recovery, over the technology of the male-centered medical community represented by Doctor Meadows (Butler-Evans 182).

After Bambara's death, her friend and editor, novelist **Toni Morrison**, published two additional works by Bambara. *Deep Sightings and Rescue Missions* (1996) contains six previously unpublished short stories and a group of six essays, movie reviews (including a chapter on Spike Lee's *School Daze* [1988]), cultural criticism, and interviews. One interview, "How she came by her name," gives modern readers a clear glimpse into Bambara's early life and her philosophy about the relations between politics and art. In this interview conducted by Louis Massiah, Bambara labels herself not as a writer but rather as "a community person who writes and does a few other things." She also traces the journey that moved her from the name given to her by her father who named her after his employer to the discovery of the name "Bambara" while traveling with her mother to visit her grandmother's grave in 1970. Bambara connects herself with novelist Toni Morrison and poets **Maya Angelou** and **Audre Lorde** as sisters in the "spiritual practice" of gaining independence through choosing one's own name.

After Bambara's death, Toni Morrison edited and published a long manuscript for a novel she considered to be Bambara's greatest life's work. Bambara worked on the novel *Those Bones Are Not My Child* (1999) for twelve years before her death. *Those Bones Are Not My Child* is a carefully researched novel about the search of Marzala Rawls Spencer for her missing child, Sonny. For her story, Bambara draws on interviews and journalistic accounts of the Atlanta child murders of 1979–81 in which more than forty children, most young black boys, became victims. Bambara also wrote about these murders in the short story "Madame Bai and the Taking of Stone Mountain" published posthumously in *Deep Sightings and Rescue Missions.*

Bambara and her works play a part in several communities of African American writers, artists, and activists. Her work relates to the community of artists and critics in the Black Aesthetic Movement (also known as the **Black Arts Movement**) arising in the 1960s and 1970s. Members of this movement, such as **Amiri Baraka**, **Larry Neal**, and Ron Karenga, sought to create a "counter-discourse" of black consciousness and to incorporate politics and community engagement into art (Butler-Evans 20, Perkins 154). In her attention to concerns and moments of healing among African American women, Bambara's work is compared with that of **Alice Walker** and Toni Morrison. For Bambara, the social function of art was most often healing. In the essay "Salvation Is the Issue," Bambara ends by saying, "I work to produce stories that save our lives" (Bambara 47). (*See also* African American Novel)

Further Reading

Bambara, Toni Cade. "Salvation Is the Issue." *Black Women Writers (1950–1980): A Critical Evaluation*. Ed. Mari Evans. New York: Anchor, 1984.

Butler-Evans, Elliott. *Race, Gender, and Desire: Narrative Strategies in the Fiction of Toni Cade Bambara, Toni Morrison, and Alice Walker*. Philadelphia: Temple UP, 1989.

Hull, Akasha (Gloria). "What It Is I Think She's Doing Anyhow: A Reading of Toni Cade Bambara's *The Salt Eaters*." *Home Girls: A Black Feminist Anthology*. Ed. Barbara Smith. New Brunswick and London: Rutgers UP, 2000. 124–42.

Perkins, Margo V. "Getting Basic: Bambara's Re-Visioning of the Black Aesthetic." *Race and Racism in Theory and Practice*. Ed. Berel Lang. Lanham, MD: Rowman & Littlefield, 2000. 153–63.

Walker, Melissa. *Down from the Mountaintop: Black Women's Novels in the Wake of the Civil Rights Movement, 1966–1989*. New Haven and London: Yale UP, 1991.

Wilentz, Gay. *Healing Narratives: Women Writers Curing Cultural Dis-ease.* New Brunswick: Rutgers UP, 2000.

Melissa S. Shields

BAMBOO RIDGE   Literary journal focusing specifically on contemporary Hawaiian and Pacific American literature. Founded in 1978 by poets **Eric Chock** and **Darrel H. Y. Lum**, the stated purpose of *Bamboo Ridge* has been to

JOURNAL OF HAWAI'I LITERATURE AND ARTS

bamboo ridge

25th

Anniversary Issue

featuring:
25th Anniversary
Contest Winners

On-line
Master Workshop
Selections

Kalapana,
A Hawaiian Place
a photo essay by
Mary Ann Lynch

Founding editors Darrell H. Y. Lum (left) and Eric Chock (right) and the twenty-fifth anniversary issue of *Bamboo Ridge. Courtesy of Bamboo Ridge Press.*

foster and promote literature reflective of the local culture, specifically that which runs counter to established stereotypes. Publishing poetry, prose, and literary criticism, the journal has become the centerpoint of a Hawaiian literary renaissance, achieving cultural as well as literary significance.

The formation of *Bamboo Ridge* was an outgrowth of a local literary conference held in 1978 known as the "Talk Story" conference ("talk story" being local vernacular for a free and easy exchange of ideas). One of the notable issues raised by the conference was the paucity of truly local literature by local writers reflecting the concerns of a local audience. *Bamboo Ridge* and the associated Bamboo Ridge Press launched as an attempt to fill that void. The success of the venture was quickly evident, and a number of significant writers first came to prominence through publication in *Bamboo Ridge*, including **Cathy Song**, **Garrett Hongo**, Wing Tek Lum, Rodney Morales, Gail N. Harada, and **Lois-Ann Yamanaka**.

Through the publication and nurturing of such writers, the journal held to its concept of developing local literature as distinct from a generic **Hawaiian literature** dominated by outsiders, most notably James Michener and Mark Twain. According to the journal's founders, the concept of local literature also sought to reach beyond the concept of Hawai'i as a cultural "melting pot" and to instead reflect the multifaceted concerns of a multiethnic society in which language, family history, and geography combine to form what the editors refer to as an "island sensibility." This is particularly evident in the journal's development of writers who emphasize local dialects in both dialog and narrative.

Although *Bamboo Ridge* has been the cornerstone of local literature in Hawai'i since its inception, the late 1990s saw the journal falling into a bit of an eclipse. Critics began to accuse the journal of having a predominantly Asian American focus, to the exclusion of other ethnic literatures, and some saw stasis rather than progress in the journal's history. Alternate journals began popping up in an attempt to rectify these perceived inequities, one of the most notable being *'Oiwi*, which focuses largely on writing by ethnic Hawaiians, a population *Bamboo Ridge* had often been accused of ignoring.

These concerns notwithstanding, *Bamboo Ridge* celebrated its twenty-fifth anniversary in 2003, and at that time was still the focus of local literary activity. The significant local controversy over the work of Lois-Ann Yamanaka (first published in *Bamboo Ridge* and considered part of the "Bamboo Ridge" group of writers) is ample evidence of the primacy of the journal in the literary life of modern Hawai'i.

Further Reading

Sumida, Stephen. *And the View from the Shore: Literary Traditions of Hawai'i*. Seattle: U of Washington P, 1991.

Wilson, Rob. *Reimagining the American Pacific: From South Pacific to Bamboo Ridge and Beyond*. Durham, NC: Duke UP, 2000.

William Curl

BARAKA, AMIRI (1934–) African American poet and writer. A highly influential poet and cultural leader, Amiri Baraka helped define the political and artistic aims of the **Black Arts Movement**. With his confrontational verses and strident social criticism, Baraka has sought to awaken his readers to contemporary social ills and the deplorable state of American **race** relations. Despite the numerous and varied stages of his creative development, his work is consistently marked by its experimental style, innovative use of imagery, and rigorous engagement with black culture.

Baraka was born Everett Leroy Jones in Newark, New Jersey. As a child, he wrote comic strips and science fiction. After graduating from high school at the age of fifteen, Baraka entered Howard University. Despite working with such noted black intellectuals as E. Franklin Frazier and **Sterling Brown**, Baraka flunked out in 1954. He served briefly in the U.S. Air Force, and then moved to New York City.

Baraka joined the community of Beat poets in Greenwich Village. Along with **Allen Ginsberg**, Frank O'Hara, and **Gilbert Sorrentino**, Baraka shared the belief that poetry is a journey of discovery involving innovation and experimentation rather than strict adherence to conventional expectations and forms. In 1957 he married Hettie Roberta Cohen with whom he founded *Yugen*, a magazine of Beat poetry, and Totem Press. During this time, Baraka also studied philosophy at Columbia University and the New School for Social Research.

Amiri Baraka. *AP/Wide World Photos.*

Baraka received critical acclaim for his first collection of poetry *Preface to a Twenty Volume Suicide Note* (1961). The book was hailed for its vivid imagery, eruptions of humor, and innovative style. These experimental verses demonstrate his bohemian influences while also describing aspects of black culture.

In 1959 Baraka traveled to Cuba where he began to formulate new ideas about the purpose of art and his responsibilities as a writer and poet. In Cuba he met a number of artists from Third World nations who shared a commitment to fighting poverty and oppression. Their political involvement forced Baraka to reevaluate his own relationship to the social problems plaguing America.

Baraka's increasing concern with social and political concerns is demonstrated in his award-winning play *Dutchman* (1964). First performed Off Broadway, this one-act play presents an extended dialogue between Lulu, a white woman, and Clay, a middle-class black man. Lulu is depicted as a temptress who ravages black men like Clay who have repressed their sexuality and ethnic **identity**. Although Clay at last expresses his deep frustrations and murderous impulses, Lulu kills him and then awaits the arrival of her next victim.

Dutchman propelled Baraka to the national stage as critics discussed the social and political ramifications of his provocative portrayal of race and gender relations. As Baraka received more public attention, he became increasingly vociferous in expressing his opinions of white culture, the direction of the **Civil Rights Movement**, and the need for black revolution. Baraka attacked white liberals for their hypocrisy, referred to the Beat generation as politically ineffective, and decried the poverty and injustice plaguing the black community. He articulated many of these radical opinions in *Cuba Libre* (1961) and *The Dead Lecturer* (1964). In the latter book, Baraka urges the black community to reject the comforts of an assimilated life, and to take pride in their racial identity while also working for a more just and equitable society. Baraka's dedication to uniquely African American forms of artistic expression is also evident in the landmark *Blues People: Negro*

Music in White America (1963). This highly influential historical study describes the development of black music from **slavery** to contemporary **jazz**, and established Baraka as an important social critic.

In 1965 Baraka left his Jewish wife and moved to Harlem, where he dedicated himself to teaching art and promoting **black nationalism**. That same year he also published *The System of Dante's Hell* (1965), an autobiographical novel that describes an isolated young man's search for value and spiritual wholeness. Although Baraka received a grant from the National Endowment for the Arts in 1966, these funds were withdrawn after authorities learned that guns and ammunition were being stored at the Black Arts Repertory Theatre, a program founded by Baraka. Soon thereafter he moved to Newark where he established the Spirit House Theatre and married Sylvia Robinson, who later changed her name to Bibi Amina Baraka.

Baraka's next book of poetry, *Black Magic* (1969), includes a preface signed by "Ameer Baraka." Baraka adopted this Muslim name, which along with the title "Imamu" translates as "spiritual leader blessed prince." In *Black Magic*, Baraka describes his separation from white culture and espouses black nationalist ideals. With their violent, confrontational tone, these poems lack the irony and humor of his previous work. Critics responded by calling Baraka's work more an expression of social rage than of artistic sensibility. However, in books such as *Home: Social Essays* (1966) and *Black Art* (1967), Baraka expressed his disdain for "white" standards of beauty and value. According to Baraka, art should be a vehicle of revolutionary change, not simply an aesthetic medium. He urged young poets to portray the ills of society in order to create a new America. In later poetry collections such as *It's Nation Time* (1970) and *Hard Facts* (1975), Baraka explores black dialect and other forms of African American cultural expression. During the late 1960s and early 1970s, Baraka linked his exhortations on art and community with political activism. A major spokesman of black cultural nationalism, he helped organize the Congress of African Peoples in 1970 and campaigned for Kenneth Gibson, the first black mayor of Newark.

Baraka dropped the name "Imamu" in 1974, signaling a major transformation in his political views. Aligning himself with third world socialism, Baraka embraced Marxist thought and denounced black nationalism as a dangerous form of **racism**. Baraka has come to view his role as an artist in a larger international context that is not limited to the development of a single ethnic tradition. He continues to view poetry as an important social weapon, but he now seeks to raise the collective consciousness of the working class beyond boundaries of race and national origin. This new approach to art and social change is apparent in such pro-socialist plays as *S-1* (1976), which dramatizes the conflict between American capitalism and the Community party.

Many critics have suggested that Baraka's recent poetry and drama lack the artistry of his previous work. *Poetry for the Advanced*, which was published in *Selected Poetry of Amiri Baraka/LeRoi Jones* (1979), has been characterized as propagandistic in its fervent support of Marxist dogma. Despite this critique, Baraka maintains his commitment to artistic innovation as he explores new forms of creative expression. Recently he has focused more on spoken word and now composes poems that are meant to be read aloud. Baraka has also experimented with video technology, incorporating film and slides in such plays as *Boy & Tarzan Appear in a Clearing* (1981).

Baraka has continued to write and speak out on topics of national concern. Most recently he garnered controversy when the New Jersey state senate abolished the position of poet laureate after Baraka refused to leave that post following a public uproar and charges of **anti-Semitism** concerning a poem he wrote about the September 11 terrorist attacks. (*See also* African American Poetry)

Further Reading

Benston, Kimberly W., ed. *Imamu Amiri Baraka (Leroi Jones): A Collection of Critical Essays.* Englewood Cliffs, NJ: Prentice Hall, 1978.

Watts, Jerry Gafio. *Amiri Baraka: The Politics and Art of a Black Intellectual.* New York: New York UP, 2001.

Stephanie Li

BAROLINI, HELEN (1925–)   Italian American writer, translator, and editor. Barolini's prodigious body of work is both impressive and inspirational. An advocate of Italian American women writers, she restored women's voices to the multicultural literary canon by publishing her landmark, award-winning collection *The Dream Book: An Anthology of Writing by Italian American Women* (1985). The title comes from an old manual called the *Dream Book* that helped Italian immigrant women in the early twentieth century interpret their dreams. Concern about the absence of Italian American women writers led Barolini to her search and research. Even though she did find a few published writers during her search, she also found that recognition of their work had been minimal. Barolini theorizes that Italian American women writers were silenced because of poverty, poor or nonexistent education, the traditional Italian cultural model that values family, and lack of advocacy in the publishing industry.

Barolini takes us on her journey of self-discovery in *Chiaroscuro: Essays of Identity* (1999) from Syracuse, New York, to Rome, Italy, and back to New York State's Hudson Valley. First generation Italian Americans, her parents tried to shed their Italian skin. As a child, Barolini followed her parents' lead and struggled to fit in despite the subtle discrimination she suffered from her peers and teachers. It was not until she was in college that she realized she could choose not to assimilate, so she began to learn about and celebrate her heritage. Accompanying Barolini on her contemplative journey is pleasurable because as she stockpiles experiences her insight clarifies. "How I Learned to Speak Italian" is a tribute to Mr. de Mascoli, the man whose benevolence Barolini credits for her enlightenment. He not only taught her to speak Italian, but also taught her to embrace Italian culture. With her newfound confidence and interest in her heritage, she traveled to Italy where she met her husband, the Italian poet Antonio Barolini. Together they lived the writing life—he wrote in Italian and she translated his work into English. After Antonio's premature death, Barolini realized that she had been focusing on her husband's writing and ignoring her own. So she received a grant from the National Endowment for the Arts, delved into her own writing, and published her first novel *Umbertina* in 1979.

Barolini believes that the grandmother figures prominently in the fiction of Italian American women writers because she is often the farthest one's American heritage can be traced. *Umbertina* (reissued in 1999) is an epic novel of four generations of an Italian American family from the matriarchal perspective that brings to life Barolini's theories about Italian American culture, as each subsequent generation continues the journey toward selfhood that Umbertina initiated. Marguerite, Umbertina's granddaughter, is introduced in the prologue as she struggles to become an independent individual in accordance with the American tradition. As she ponders her life choices with her husband, Marguerite realizes that such a quandary is a luxury Umbertina never enjoyed. Rather, Umbertina's goal, though more arduous, was simple.

Umbertina, a young goat girl in Castagna, a small mountainous village in Calabria, who is oppressed by poverty and patriarchal traditions, has an indomitable spirit. Her marriage to Serafino Longobardi, a man who has already been to America and returns with the cash to prove his success, is arranged by her father. Although Umbertina had hoped to marry Giosue, the charcoal maker, she resigns herself to the arranged union with dignity and begins preparing for married life. She orders a handmade bedspread from Nelda, an artisan in Castagna, to adorn her marriage bed and asks Nelda for some rosemary to plant outside her door. Folklore predicts that the woman who plants rosemary will be the strength of her household. She and Serafino have three sons in Castagna before emigrating to New York City with a group of fellow émigrés who become *paesani*—people as close as family. The Longobardis live in a cramped and filthy tenement that is brightened by the colorfully, intricate bedspread, which bolsters Umbertina's spirit. After the death of their fourth son, however, the family decides to relocate to Cato, New York, near their *paesani*. To pay for the trip, Umbertina sells the bedspread. Though saddened by the loss of her only connection to her homeland, that simple gesture becomes the catalyst for her family's success. What had once been a symbol of her independence from and connection to Castagna frees her from the oppression that tied her to Castagna. In Cato the Longobardis have more children, achieve tremendous success as grocers, and raise their large family.

Their children, first generation Italian Americans, defy their Italian traditions and seek the trappings of middle-class America. Marguerite, a member of the second generation, however, is mystified by her parents' denial of their heritage. She is enchanted by her grandmother Umbertina, even though the difference in their native tongues prevents them from communicating orally. She also demonstrates the same resolve, resiliency, and strength as her grandmother. After graduating from college, Marguerite moves to Italy, marries an Italian poet, and struggles to find her identity— she feels neither Italian nor American. By the time her daughter Tina becomes an adult, Umbertina's purpose comes alive again. Tina is able to balance her Italian heritage and her American ideals. A Dante scholar, she marries and settles in Cape Cod, where Tina sees Umbertina's bedspread on display in a museum. Although she does not know that it belonged to her great-grandmother, she is reminded of Castagna by the colorfully intricate images. The book ends with Tina planting rosemary outside her new home in Massachusetts, suggesting that she, like Umbertina, will be the strength of her household.

Helen Barolini, the god-mother of Italian American women writers, is like Umbertina. Her diligent labor in the field of literature created a legacy for writers for many generations to come. (*See also* Italian American Novel)

Further Reading

Giunta, Edvige. "Afterword." *Umbertina*. Helen Barolini. New York: Feminist Press, 1999. 425–53.

Suzanne Hotte Massa

BARRAX, GERALD (1933–)   African American poet. Born in Attala, Alabama, Gerald Barrax graduated from high school in Pittsburgh, Pennsylvania. Following a hitch in the U.S. Air Force, he worked for a decade as a mail carrier. After completing a BA at Dusquesne University in 1963 and an MA at the University of Pittsburgh in 1969, he taught at North Carolina Central University. Since 1970 he has been associated with the English department at North Carolina State University. Twice married, Barrax has often treated in his poetry his relationships with his wives and with his children from both marriages. In effect he has presented his own family as a microcosm of the African American community. Barrax has tried to find a synthesis between the confessional and the topical modes, and his poems technically combine elements of radical, formal experimentation within the structural frameworks of fairly conventional lyrics.

In his first collection of poems, *Another Kind of Rain* (1970), Barrax juxtaposes the tensions within his own family, particularly between him and his sons, with conflicts within the African American community and between that African American culture and the broader American culture. The style of the poems is marked by Barrax's mixing of black urban slang with allusions to works across the breadth of the literary canon. His second collection, *An Audience of One* (1980), extends this juxtaposition of personal and communal interests and issues. Barrax considers how the contentment he has found in his own life through a second marriage might suggest possibilities for renewal within the African American community. In his third collection, *Leaning against the Sun* (1992), Barrax extends his poetic reach to a transcendental interest in how intimate personal relationships and the social connections within people of a community might suggest the presence of the divine in our lives. Although Barrax's basic materials remain autobiographical details and other details of African American life, his themes clearly have a much broader application.

The publication of *From a Person Sitting in Darkness: New and Selected Poems* (1998) demonstrates Barrax's continuing interest in certain materials and themes while also showcasing his notable technical and thematic growth as a poet. The title is taken from a poem by Emily Dickinson, and although Barrax's poems stylistically do not pointedly suggest Dickinson's influence, the two poets share the ability to focus with an almost obsessive intensity on situations that suggest a very similar range of themes: the emotional complexities of seemingly staid lives and the domestic routines that define them, the implications of even small acts of terrible violence, the meaning of mortality, and the peculiar manifestations of the divine within ordinary experiences.

Further Reading

McFee, Michael. "'Dazzle Gradually': The Poetry of Gerald Barrax." *Callaloo* 20 (Spring 1997): 327–40.

Moore, Lenard D. "On Hearing Gerald W. Barrax." *Black American Literature Forum* 21 (Fall 1987): 241–42.

Pettis, Joyce. "An Interview with Gerald Barrax." *Callaloo* 20.2 (Spring 1997): 312–26.

Martin Kich

BARRESI, DOROTHY (1957–)   Italian American educator, scholar, and poet. Dorothy Barresi has secured a distinguished place in Italian American literature with her award winning poetry collections. Clearly influenced by Italian American tradition, she uses it as a springboard to forge her own poetry that speaks about the vicissitudes of life, both past and present, in a voice that is both original and modern in consciousness and spirit.

Barresi's first significant poetry collection, *All of the Above* (1991), received the Barnard Women Poet's Prize. As its all-inclusive title suggests, this work grapples with many facets of the human experience through a diverse array of speakers—a backup singer, a yet unborn child, a spouse, a lover, a friend, a parent, an observer, and others—who muse philosophically about life, remember deceased loved ones, discuss relationship woes, and even turn their attention toward the trivial or mundane—a hole in the ceiling, mold, formica, and miniature golf. The settings of the poems are just as wide-ranging, spanning from the 1920s to the present. This eclectic collection is enriched by provocative imagery, thought-provoking declarations, and a variety of tone.

In her next collection, *The Post-Rapture Diner* (1996), winner of the American Book Award, Barresi examines many of the same subjects she did in her earlier collection. This time she focuses on life's religious and philosophical underpinnings and reveals its ultimate precariousness. Other recurring themes include food, eating, and cooking, the presence of which are hinted at in the word *diner* in the collection's title. These poems, which have a certain heaviness and solemnity, can occasionally lapse into impenetrability, but they remain poignant due to Barresi's masterful use of language.

In *Rouge Pulp* (2002) Barresi shifts her focus away from the philosophical to the more earthbound realities of the home. Poems dealing with motherhood, parenting, and children predominate, with many others devoted to religion, famous people, past events, beauty, and artifice. Although death casts a pall over many of these poems, it is not a nebulous one, for the poems are generally concrete and accessible, their expressive power undiminished. A testament to Barresi's burgeoning talent, this last collection demonstrates the dynamic nature of her poetry, which is not only versatile but also responsive and capable of great growth.

Throughout these collections, Barresi's indebtedness to the Italian American tradition is clear, especially in her choice of themes: the primacy of the family, mother-daughter relationships, food, looking at the past, realistic depictions of life, and the importance of religion. Her poetry also breaks with the past in its rejection of *omertà*, a code of silence that has traditionally discouraged Italian women from speaking out. Instead, Barresi's poetry openly questions the world, its inhabitants, their actions, and even their belief systems in an attempt to make sense of them all. The result is poetry that is incisive, timely, and utterly compelling. (*See also* Italian American Poetry)

Further Reading

Tamburri, Anthony Julian, Paolo A. Giordano, and Fred L. Gardaphé, eds. *From the Margin: Writing in Italian Americana.* 2nd ed. West Lafayette, IN: Purdue UP, 2000.

Larry Sean Kinder

BASQUE AMERICAN LITERATURE   Any discussion of Basque American literature should inevitably begin with the impact of **Robert Laxalt**'s *Sweet Promised Land* (1957) on the general image of the Basques in America. The publication of this intimate tale of **immigration**, dealing mainly with the return trip of the author's father (Dominique) to his Basque homeland in the Pyrenees Mountains after forty-seven years as a sheepherder, put an end to the invisibility of the Basques in America. *Sweet Promised Land* often has been described as an affectionate memoir of a son to his father. However, the book goes beyond its personal level to illustrate the experience of Basque immigrants in the United States. These immigrants identified with Dominique's story and felt encouraged to display their ethnic pride at a time, previous to the "roots" phenomenon, in which Basques were neither well known nor popular in America.

The new visibility of the Basques after *Sweet Promised Land* also extended to the American literary field where until then Basques had been often neglected as protagonists. Although the first large groups of Basques came to the United States during the California Gold Rush and played prominent roles in the settlement of the American West, few authors seemed to be interested in this immigrant group prior to the publication of Laxalt's work. In fact their identification with the sheep industry, one of the least prestigious economic activities of the West, often relegated them to a secondary social and literary role. Certainly, a few western authors such as Harry Sinclair Drago and H. L. Davis seemed to be interested in this ethnic community. However, in most cases they utilized Basque characters in a superficial and unconvincing way, subordinating their presence to the stereotyped structure of the formula western. It is also worth noting that literary activity was almost nonexistent among Basque immigrants during the first half of the twentieth century. Actually, in this period we need only mention two books written by the Basque American author Miriam Isasi: *Basque Girl* (1940), an autobiography set primarily in Spain and England, and *White Stars of Freedom* (1942), a novel coauthored by Melcena Burns Denny and focused on a young Basque sheepherder's growing to maturity and his becoming an American citizen. This novel is mainly aimed to promote the Allied cause in the context of the early months of World War II.

After the success of *Sweet Promised Land*, Laxalt displayed his versatility as a writer in later books dealing with the history of Nevada, with traditional western subjects as well as his war experiences in Africa. However, he also established himself as the most talented American author writing on the experience of Basques both in the United States and in Europe. Thus, his Basque era consists of nine books in which he shows his skill to combine the views of the Basques who emigrate to the United States with the views of Basque Americans who return to their parents' homeland searching for their roots. In those books focused on the experiences of the *Amerikanuak* (the Basques in America), such as *The Basque Hotel* (1989) and *The Governor's Mansion* (1994), Laxalt often highlights a series of common themes: the endurance of the Basque sheepherders, their hard work, their lean and solitary lives, their pioneering spirit, the existence of certain ethnic prejudices toward these immigrants, the power of family bonds, and the benefits and risks of **assimilation** for the Basque Americans. In those books set in the Basque Country, Laxalt portrays a traditional society from a modern American perspective. These works often reveal his affection for the lifestyle of the Basques in the 1960s, though he also deals with the drama of social poverty and with moral taboos in their ancient villages in books such as *A Cup of Tea in Pamplona* (1985) and *Child of the Holy Ghost* (1992). Laxalt usually emphasizes the most traditional aspects of Basque lifestyle, disregarding recent socioeconomic transformations or contemporary political events in the Basque Country. Thus, these books offer multiple insights on such issues as the close relationship between the Basques and their past, the influence of the Catholic Church, the strong family ties, and the Basque conception of time.

Most of Laxalt's Basque books verge on the autobiographical, and in both his fiction and nonfiction Basque stories he demonstrates his firsthand knowledge of the life and the idiosyncrasies of Basques. Laxalt tells his Basque tales with extraordinary economy, but their formal simplicity turns out to be deceiving because these books contain a carefully crafted style in which attention to detail becomes essential. His Basque works also display his powerful descriptive ability and his concern with authenticity. His commitment to presenting a faithful and convincing portrait of the Basques is perceived, for example, in his decision to include several Basque words or expressions in most of these books. Overall, Laxalt's Basque works reveal his artistry in depicting the traditional lifestyle of the Basques, whether in the Old World or in the American West. The books demonstrate his ability to capture the essence of time, place, and character in two different worlds.

Following the success of Laxalt's works, the new visibility of Basques in the last few decades has stimulated a growing interest in the culture among American authors. This new literary curiosity in the Basques is represented, for example, by the consolidation of the Basque sheepherder as an attractive literary archetype for writers of the American West, including some Basque American authors. In fact *Sweet Promised Land* itself set the pace for other personal memoirs by Basque Americans, most of them dealing with their experiences as sheepherders in the American West. This is the case with two books published in the 1970s: Louis Irigaray and Theodore Taylor's *A Shepherd Watches: A Shepherd Sings* (1977) and Beltran Paris's story, as told to William A. Douglass, *Beltran: Basque Sheepman of the American West* (1979). The first book chronicles the past of the folk singer Irigaray in the California sheep camps of his father and his own struggle for identity, whereas the second book offers a lively depiction of Beltran Paris's life as an immigrant herder in Nevada. We may also find a few other autobiographical accounts where the main story is not related to the sheepherding world, such as Joseph Eiguren's *Kasphar* (1988) and Maita Floyd's *Stolen Years* (1996). Thus, Eiguren's book includes some references to the author's immigration to America and his early days as a sheepherder in the West, but its main emphasis is on his fighting experience in Europe during World War II. Similarly, Floyd's work centers on the writer's late adolescent years living under German occupation in the French Basque Country. Although these writings provide interesting insights into the lives of their protagonists and the most recent past of the Basques, both in America and in the Old World, none of them has been able to achieve the literary recognition and sociocultural impact of *Sweet Promised Land*.

The expansion of literary interest in the Basques is also illustrated by the new prominence of younger Basque American writers such as Frank Bergon, Monique Laxalt (Robert Laxalt's daughter), and Gregory Martin. Frank Bergon, a Nevada author of Basque ancestry, is regarded as one of the most significant voices in contemporary western writing due to his brilliant novelistic definition of Nevada's character in books such as *The Temptations of St. Ed and Brother S* (1993), *Wild Game* (1995), and above all his renowned *Shoshone Mike* (1989). This historical novel has won wide critical acclaim because of Begon's outstanding skill to recreate the so-called "last Indian battle" or "last Indian massacre" (both names refer to a tragic Nevada event in 1911 in which Shoshone Mike and part of his band were killed in revenge for the murder of four stockmen, three of them Basques). Bergon's novel focuses on the conflicting views of Shoshone Mike originated by the cultural collision between whites and Native Americans in the West. The myth of the West with its profound ethnocentric dimensions relegates the Indians to the role of dangerous savages and encourages their annihilation. The novel also offers interesting insights into the extension of prejudice and discrimination against the Basques in the first decades of the twentieth century. In his novel Bergon utilizes a rotating point of view in which one of the most relevant roles is played by Jean Erramouspe, the Basque son of one of the murdered stockmen. Bergon emphasizes Jean's sense of loss and his inability to come to terms with his ethnic heritage. Thus, he not only resents his confinement to the work typical of Basques in that time (sheepherding, working the mines, etc.) but also his immigrant label. He symbolizes in the novel the struggle for acceptance of descendants of Basque immigrants in the American West. Bergon's commitment to provide the reader with an authentic portrait of the Basques in Nevada is illustrated by his interesting insights into their work, his vivid description of their life at the Basque hotels, and his use of a few Basque words and expressions. These Basque terms exemplify the vanishing legacy of the Basque language in the American West in the early twentieth century.

Bergon's second novel, *The Temptations of St. Ed and Brother S*, does not contain a lot of Basque elements, and its major focus does not lie on Basque ethnicity, but on environmental issues. Nevertheless, the main character is a half-Basque monk struggling with the temptations of the modern world in the Nevada desert. His Basque origin is not a mere anecdotal point in the novel but a matter of pride, which increases his personal sense of individuality in mainstream contemporary American society. In his most recent novel, *Wild Game*, Bergon again fictionalizes an actual event—the hunt for survivalist and convicted killer Claude Dallas, an episode that dramatizes the conflict between Old West values of individualism and independence and New West notions of environmentalism and interconnection with the natural world. Its protagonist is a contemporary Basque American, Jack Irigaray, a wildlife biologist and game warden who represents Bergon's own generation, a generation which due to its cultural assimilation by mainstream American society was raised almost unaware of its ethnic consciousness. The novel includes two other major Basque characters, as well as references to Basque rituals, religious beliefs, ethnic features, places, and even an old western movie dealing with Basque pioneers. This film is used by Bergon to illustrate the widespread misrepresentations of ethnic minorities in the West by the Hollywood industry until recently. *Wild Game* also reflects the increasing prosperity of the Basque Americans in the second half of the twentieth century, particularly represented by the new job opportunities offered to them and their replacement in the sheepherding business by more recent and poorer immigrants. Overall, these two novels exemplify Bergon's artistic talent to write first-rate fiction and his ability to go beyond the archetypal figure of the sheepherder, dealing instead with contemporary Basque Americans in the New West.

Another interesting literary approach to the new generations of Basque Americans is *The Deep Blue Memory* (1993), a semiautobiographical novel published by Monique Laxalt under the name of Monique Urza. In this book Laxalt examines the role of the ethnic legacy in contemporary American society. She draws on the experiences of her own family to describe the way in which different generations of a Basque family in Nevada come to terms with the immigration experience. The book emphasizes the conflict between the rewards brought by assimilation and acceptance into American society and the price to be paid for integration and success. This subject also plays a pivotal role in her father's Basque-family trilogy. Nevertheless, Laxalt uses a different generational point of view, a female perspective, and an unusually skillful lyrical tone. *The Deep Blue Memory* can be regarded as the result of Laxalt's need to explore her identity and, in particular, the twin condition of an American upbringing laced with a Basque heritage. Actually, the book portrays the process of exploration of one's ethnic **identity** as a never-ending experience—progression forward, while at the same time remaining sensitive to remembering and understanding the past.

One of the most recent examples of the new prominence of contemporary Basque American literature is Gregory Martin's *Mountain City* (2000), a nonfiction memoir which takes a boom-and-bust Nevada mining town and its thirty-three residents as its subject. Martin is a third-generation Basque American, a descendant of Basque sheepherders and Cornish tin miners. The Basque story of Martin's family occupies a significant portion of the book, a moving tribute to his relatives and, in general, to those who remain loyal to the decaying Mountain City. In the book, written in spare, unsophisticated prose, Martin illustrates his own learning process about growing old, emphasizing the power of home against the backdrop of a vanishing place.

The increasing vitality and recognition of Basque American literature cannot hide the fact that serious limitations still remain in this writing. Thus, we cannot forget that we are dealing with a reduced body of literature, almost exclusively limited to prose works, with very few exceptions, such as Trisha Zubizarreta's *Chorizos, Beans and Other Things: A Poetic Look at the Basque Culture* (1987). Furthermore, too many stereotypical views of the Basques, with a particular emphasis on the sheepherder archetype, still prevail in this literature. Thus, the figure of the Basque woman, both in the American West and in the Old World, still remains underrepresented in Basque American literature.

Life in the modern, industrial Basque country and the experiences of contemporary Basque Americans in multicultural urban communities have not received proper treatment yet. Despite these shortcomings, recent Basque American literature, as exemplified by the remarkable achievement of authors such as Robert Laxalt, Frank Bergon, Monique Laxalt, and Gregory Martin, contains notable artistic values and illustrates both a distinctive culture of its own and the complexity of contemporary ethic American writing.

Further Reading

Douglass, William A., and Jon Bilbao. *Amerikanuak: Basques in the New World.* Reno: U of Nevada P, 1975.

Douglass, William A., and Richard W. Etulain, eds. *Basque Americans: A Guide to Information Sources.* Detroit: Gale Research Co., 1981.

Etulain, Richard W. "The Basques in Western American Literature." *Anglo-American Contributions to Basque Studies: Essays in Honor of Jon Bilbao.* Ed. William A. Douglass, Richard W. Etulain, and William H. Jacobsen Jr. Reno: Desert Research Institute, 1977. 7–18.

Morris, Gregory L. *Frank Bergon.* Western Writers Series 126. Boise, ID: Boise State UP, 1997.

Rio, David. "Basques in the Contemporary Literature of the American West." *The Basque Diaspora/La Diáspora Vasca.* Ed. William A. Douglass, et al. Reno: Basque Studies Program (U of Nevada P), 1999. 274–83.

———. "Basques in the International West: An Interview with Frank Bergon." *Western American Literature* 36.1 (2001): 55–72.

———. "Monique Laxalt: A Literary Interpreter for the New Generations of Basque Americans." *Amatxi, Amuma, Amona: Writings in Honor of Basque Women.* Ed. Linda White and Cameron Watson. Reno: Center for Basque Studies (U of Nevada P), 2003. 86–98.

David Rio

BECKHAM, BARRY (1944–) African American novelist and biographer. Born in Philadelphia, Pennsylvania, Beckham grew up in New Jersey and graduated from Brown University in 1966. In 1970 he accepted a teaching job at Brown and ten years later became the director of the Graduate Writing Program. In 1987 he began teaching at Hampton University. Two years later Beckham left academic life to found a publishing company. He remains active as a publisher and he is currently at work on his autobiography.

My Main Mother (1969) was Beckham's first novel in which the theme is matricide. Mitchell Mibbs, the novel's young protagonist, reconstructs his life and that of his mother whom he has murdered. At times riveting, the novel is a psychologically insightful study of a young man who feels deeply betrayed and abandoned by his uncaring and selfish mother who runs off to New York City to pursue her musical career. The novel received generally favorable reviews.

Beckham's next novel, *Runner Mack* (1972), was much more successful both critically and commercially. Arguably the "first full-length portrait of the black athlete in American fiction," *Runner Mack* is the "first American novel by a black writer to draw an organized sports experience as a means of ordering fictional meaning and purpose" (Umphlett 73). Beckham uses baseball, the quintessential American sport, to offer an incisive critique of the inequalities inherent in American public life. The protagonist Henry Adams aspires to be a major-league baseball player. Though an immensely gifted athlete, his dream remains thwarted by racist institutions and individuals. A disillusioned Adams joins the army and there he meets Running Mack, a politically radical, black soldier. Adams aligns himself with Mack in an ill-conceived revolutionary attempt to overthrow the government of the United States. Mack commits suicide and Adams is left to fight for himself—"he had to run, search, look, fight—but more than anything, not give up."

Double Dunk (1980) is Beckham's slightly novelized biography of Earl Manigault, a legendary basketball player from Harlem. A supremely gifted athlete, Manigault never became the professional basketball player that he longed to be. Instead, he ended up a drug addict and criminal. As in *Runner Mack,* Beckham, with his naturalistic view of the world, finds in his protagonist's environment the roots of his destruction.

Further Reading

Pinsker, Sanford. "A Conversation with Barry Beckham." *Studies in Black Literature* 5 (Winter 1974): 17–20.

Umphlett, Wiley Lee. "The Black Man as Fictional Athlete: *Running Mack,* the Sporting Myth, and the Failure of the American Dream." *Modern Fiction Studies* 33.1 (Spring 1987): 73–83.

Weixlmann, Joe. "The Dream Turned 'Daymare': Barry Beckham's *Running Mack.*" *MELUS* 8.4 (Winter 1981): 93–103.

Trevor A. Sydney

BEHRMAN, S. N. (1893–1973)   Jewish American playwright, screenwriter, biographer, memoirist, essayist, and novelist. A man of many talents, S. N. Behrman is best known for his work in the theater, where he Americanized high comedy of manners. His signature drama contrasts sharply with the social realism and political commentary that prevailed on the American drama stage prior to World War II.

Behrman's is a theater of character rather than plot. As one of his critics noted, he was more interested in the effects of the world on his dramatis personae than in their effect on the world. Many of the plays, beginning with *The Second Man* (1927), are set in elegant drawing rooms where cultivated people of ready wit and informed opinions converse eloquently. Because underneath the frequently mordant repartee lie pointed comments on human behavior and social conditions, Behrman was dubbed "the Congreve of American letters."

Behrman's own background was decidedly more modest. He was born into a lower-middle-class family in Worcester, Massachusetts, and named

Samuel Nathaniel Behrman. His father, more devoted to studying the Talmud than to running his grocery store, taught his son to cherish books. Behrman became a compulsive, comprehensive reader, a habit that fed his creative imagination until he went blind months before his death. He was drawn to the stage early; by twenty he had written and acted in a vaudeville sketch. He studied playwriting first in George Pierce Baker's famous 47 Workshop at Harvard, then as a graduate student at Columbia University under the tutelage of Brander Matthews, a founder of the distinguished theater club The Players. From his first position with the *New York Times Book Review*, Behrman turned to short fiction, essays—especially for *Smart Set*—and shortly, plays.

The polished carapace of works about difficult life choices and competing amours such as *Serena Blandish* (1929), *Brief Moment* (1931), *Biography* (1932), and *End of Summer* (1936) does not conceal the playwright's genuine concern for humanity and the integrity of political and social structures. His anger with the growing totalitarian crisis and his anxiety about those made vulnerable by their activities or affiliations became increasingly visible. For example, one of the guests at the house party at the center of *Rain From Heaven* (1934) is an exiled part-Jewish music critic who decides to return to his native Germany to fight with the underground. When the refugee is attacked by another guest, a budding fascist, he is roundly defended by their sympathetic, worldly hostess. The Jewish plot element, inspired by an actual incident, manifests the playwright's outrage at Germany's abuse of those who had contributed so heavily to her civilization. Though Behrman remained essentially loyal to his genre, the very title of his 1939 *No Time for Comedy* expresses his awareness of the anomaly of high comedy in a world darkened by war clouds.

Behrman treated **anti-Semitism** most extensively in his reworking of Austrian dramatist Franz Werfel's *Jacobowsky and the Colonel* (1944). The plot concerns a Jewish refugee and a Polish officer forced to become traveling companions by their mutual haste to escape the Nazis. During the flight, the Colonel's prejudice melts as he benefits from Jacobowsky's resourcefulness and warmth.

In *The Cold Wind and the Warm* (1958), a stage adaptation of his memoirs, Behrman departs markedly from his characteristic focus and style. Modest western Massachusetts parlors and New York City walk-ups replace fashionable salons; aspects of traditional Jewish life—arranged marriages, the interaction of members of a tight-knit community—supplant cosmopolitanism. *The Cold Wind* had no roles for the chic and sophisticated actors typically found in Berhman works, such as Alfred Lunt and Lynn Fontanne. Its first cast included individuals whose reputation had begun with their association with the largely Jewish Group Theatre: director Harold Clurman and actors Morris Carnovsky and Sanford Meisner.

Although Behrman wrote the last of his twenty-some plays, *But for Whom Charlie*, in 1964, he remained actively engaged in a variety of literary projects, including screenplays. He published his first novel at age seventy-five. In 1938 Behrman joined fellow dramatists Elmer Rice, Maxwell Anderson, Sidney Howard, and Robert E. Sherwood in founding The Playwrights Company. It operated until 1960, producing some of the era's most successful and artistically important plays. Theater historian Allan Lewis saluted Behrman and Rice as "the elder statesmen of the Broadway stage" (18).

Further Reading

Gassner, John. *Masters of the Drama*. New York: Random House, 1940.

Krutch, Joseph Wood. "The Comic Wisdom of S. N. Behrman." *The American Theatre as Seen by Its Critics*. Ed. Montrose J. Moses and John Mason Brown. New York: W. W. Norton, 1934. 272–77.

Lewis, Allan. *American Plays and Playwrights of the Contemporary Theatre*. New York: Crown, 1975.

Ree, Kenneth T. *S. N. Behrman*. Boston: Twayne, 1975.

Ellen Schiff

BELL, JAMES MADISON (1826–1902) African American lecturer, poet, and **abolition**ist. Called the "Bard of the Maumee," James Madison Bell's place in African American history rests on his spirited reading tours and his political awareness of and involvement in the abolitionist movement. Through his poetry and recitations, Bell infused a sense of awareness and urgency during America's reconstruction.

Bell was born in Gallipolis, Ohio, and remained there until he was sixteen years old. He became involved in the plastering trade, a work that remained his primary source of income, and worked throughout the country and in Canada. Bell eventually left Gallipolis and traveled to Cincinnati, taking a job as a plasterer. It was in Cincinnati that he met his wife, Louisiana Sanderlin, with whom he had several children. He worked in Cincinnati until 1853, when he moved to Canada, working there until 1860. Bell migrated west to San Francisco, California, working there and in a few other towns for five years, eventually returning to Toledo, Ohio, around 1890.

During his period of traveling and working, Bell was involved in many artistic and political activities. He wrote and published poetry, read his work on reading tours, and lectured on the abolitionist movement and educational and legal equality for African American people. During his stay in Canada, he met with and befriended the noted abolitionist John Brown. Bell was also a lay worker for the African Methodist Episcopalian Church. During the 1870s, he served for a brief period of time in the Republican political scene.

Topics in Bell's poetry consist largely of the American Civil War and the events leading to it and after it, such as emancipation and restoration. Critics often describe his poetry as orations in verse because his poems are long, most ranging in the area of 750 to 950 lines. Some of his most readable poems appear in his *Works* (reprinted in 1901), which contains a dozen short poems. One of these poems, "Modern Moses," is replete with humor and irony as Bell satirizes Andrew Johnson. He varied some, but little, from the iambic tetrameter verse, most often by altering the stanza length. But Bell is best known for his spirited poetical readings. Like drama, Bell's longer poems appear somewhat flat on the page, but he infused a sense of spirit in his poetry. On his reading tours, Bell gave rousing renditions of his longer works, and his two most well-known orations in verse celebrate the Emancipation Proclamation. In "A Poem Entitled the Day and the War," which he wrote to mark the first anniversary of the Emancipation Proclamation, Bell recounts the time from slavery to 1865. His poem marking the third anniversary, "An Anniversary Poem Entitled the Progress of Liberty," recounts liberty's triumph, President Lincoln, and the period between this time and emancipation. The poem, like many of his others, depicts the struggle of African Americans and urges for continuing effort. In Bell's life and poetry we see a vision of the future with a nod toward the past; a life spent voicing the concerns, struggles, and triumphs of African American liberation.

Further Reading
Redmond, Eugene B. *Drumvoices: The Mission of Afro-American Poetry.* New York: Anchor, 1976.

Michael Modarelli

BELL, MARVIN (1937–) Jewish American poet. Although his poetic achievement has been recognized with a number of important awards, including the Lamont Award from the Academy of American Poets in 1969 and a Literature Award from the American Academy of Arts and Letters in 1994, Marvin Bell remains one of the most underrated poets of his generation.

In part, this circumstance is the result of the difficulty in classifying his work. Although his poems contain many passages of remarkable lyricism, his style is not technically flamboyant. Though his poetic voice is very colloquial, it is, characteristically, not entirely straightforward or wholly accessible. His poems often have an anecdotal frame, but much of the "story" is typically left untold. Even though his poetry often concentrates on the details of the natural world, it does not convey an easily defined "attitude" toward nature but, instead, chases the boundaries between the physical and the metaphysical. His poetry is very personal, but it is not confessional. And although his poetry is very much concerned with his family history and cultural heritage, it does not give those subjects such primacy that it can be described as having an ethnic focus.

Born in New York City to Jewish immigrants from the Ukraine, Bell was raised on Long Island when much of the land was still given over to agriculture rather than suburbs. So, from the start, his perspective has been more rural than urban, more broadly American than cosmopolitan. He received a baccalaureate degree from Alfred University, a Master of

Arts from the University of Chicago, and a Master of Fine Arts from the University of Iowa. After completing two years' service in the armed forces, he returned in 1965 to the University of Iowa as a visiting lecturer in the Writer's Workshop. Although he has held a number of visiting professorships at other institutions, as well as several prestigious fellowships, he has remained on the faculty of the Iowa Writer's Workshop for the whole of his academic career. He was promoted to a full professorship in 1975 and was named the **Flannery O'Connor** Professor of Letters in 1986. One of his most significant contributions to American letters has been the profound influence he has exerted as a teacher upon many American poets of subsequent generations. Moreover, among his essays on the craft of poetry, he has contributed a series of widely read columns to the *American Poetry Review*.

Bell's most important books have been *A Probable Volume of Dreams* (1969), *Stars Which See, Stars Which Do Not See* (1978), *These Green-Going-to-Yellow* (1981), *Iris of Creation* (1990), *The Book of the Dead Man* (1994), and *Arbor: The Book of the Dead Man, Volume 2* (1997). Several volumes of his selected and collected poems have appeared, most recently *Nightworks: Poems 1962–2000* (2000).

Further Reading

Jackson, Richard. "Containing the Other: Marvin Bell's Recent Poetry." *North American Review* 280 (January–February 1995): 45–48.

McGuiness, Daniel. "Exile and Cunning: The Recent Poetry of Marvin Bell." *Antioch Review* 48 (Summer 1990): 353–61.

Martin Kich

BELL, THOMAS (1903–1961)   Slovak American novelist, political activist, social reformer. Born Adalbert Thomas Belejcak, Thomas Bell is remembered most as the author of *Out of This Furnace* (1941). In this naturalistic and loosely autobiographical novel, Bell weaves together the narratives of three generations of an immigrant Slovak family as they work to survive life in a Pennsylvania steel mill before the industry was unionized.

Born in the steel town of Braddock, Pennsylvania, Bell was the son of Michael and Mary Belejcak. Michael was the first of his family to leave the Slovakian province of Saris in 1890 to come to America, followed by his three younger brothers in subsequent years. Bell's father probably began his new life in the steel mills that provide the setting for *Out of This Furnace*, but the newcomer's desire for a better life eventually led him to service and retail business positions in the community. Two of his three brothers were not so lucky. They died early in accidents associated with work for the mill. Having already experienced the long, mill shifts as a teenager, and perhaps conscious that he should make his leave of Braddock to avoid a similar fate, Bell entered the merchant marines at the age of nineteen, and a short time later made his way to New York City to pursue his ambition to be a writer. It was there that Bell, without the benefit of much formal education and even less literary training, wrote six novels and an autobiographical memoir over the course of his life.

Bell's first two attempts were *The Bread of Basil* (1930) and *The Second Prince* (1935), but his literary reputation truly began with the publication of *All Brides Are Beautiful* (1936), *Out of This Furnace* (1941), and *Till I Come Back to You* (1943). *Brides*, set during the Great Depression, was adapted for film in 1946 as *From This Day Forward*, and *Till I Come Back to You*, with its World War II backdrop, was staged on Broadway. Between these two popular successes came *Out of This Furnace*, which presents a critique of the exploitive capitalism, social injustice, and unfair labor practices that came with American industrialization. The Dobrejcak family chronicle consists of three episodic narratives, each representing one generation: Djuro Kracha's journey from a Hungarian village to Pennsylvania by way of New York; his daughter Mary's marriage to the steelworker Mike Dobrejcak and their family's attempt to survive in the face of the heartless demands of the steel mill bosses; and their son Dobie's growing social activism and resolve to vindicate the abuses of a largely immigrant proletariat through organized labor. Bell's final two works were a novel *There Comes a Time* (1946) and a memoir *In the Midst of Life* (1961), which he finished shortly before succumbing to cancer. Although two of his works were adapted for stage and screen, the fact that *Out of This Furnace* regularly appears on university American history reading lists attests to its final importance and will remain Bell's legacy. (*See also* Slovak American Literature)

Further Reading

Berko, John. "Thomas Bell (1903–1961), Slovak-American Novelist." *Slovak Studies* 15 (1975): 143–58.

Coles, Nicholas. "Mantraps: Men at Work in Pietro Di Donato's *Christ in Concrete* and Thomas Bell's *Out of This Furnace*." *MELUS* 14.3–4 (1987): 23–32.

Demarest, David P., Jr. "Afterword." Ed. Thomas Bell. *Out of this Furnace*. Pittsburgh: U of Pittsburgh P, 1941. 415–24.

Robert W. Rudnicki

BELLOW, SAUL (1915–2005)   Jewish American novelist, short story writer, playwright, translator, and essayist. Saul Bellow's preeminent place within the context of Jewish American fiction has been secured by his rigorous pursuit of the deeper, universal truths of human existence in a rapidly changing modern world. Bellow's novels utilize the contexts of his Jewish American **identity** and heritage to question the very being or purpose of humanity in a world of mass production, rapid industrialization, massive population movements, shifting moral virtues, and a lack of genuine human communication and connectivity. His writings bring together a firm belief in modern intellectual humanism, particularly a love of psychology, with a deep reverence and respect for the orders of the past. His genius comes from his ability to intelligently portray complex characters confronting the intellectual, moral, and psychological dilemmas of the modern world in a conscientious

Saul Bellow. *AP/Wide World Photos.*

and stylistically advanced way. Bellow attempts to affirm the innate dignity of all people, and his novels defend the ability of humans to make meaning in a world that appears chaotic, intimidating, and at times evil. His novels can be darkly funny and charming, but they also provide haunting glimpses of the disillusioned, dejected, and neurotic on the verge of self-destruction and total societal estrangement.

Bellow's writings have widely influenced all of American literature after World War II. He has been awarded numerous prizes in the United States and throughout the world for his achievements. Most notably Bellow was the first American to win the International Literary Prize in 1965, was a recipient of the Croix de Chevalier des Arts et Lettres award from France in 1968, received the B'nai B'rith Jewish Heritage award for literary excellence, is a Pulitzer Prize and National Book award winner, and received the Nobel Prize for Literature in 1976 "for the human understanding and subtle analysis of contemporary culture that are combined in his work."

Born in the Montreal suburb of Lachine, Quebec, in 1915, to parents recently emigrated from Russia, Bellow relocated with his family to Chicago in 1924. He was educated at the University of Chicago and at Northwestern University, where he received his BS in 1937. He has served as a professor or writer-in-residence at Bard College, the University of Minnesota, the University of Chicago, Princeton, New York University, and Boston University.

One of the most intriguing aspects of Bellow's early educational and literary development was his learning of Yiddish, Hebrew, English, and French. This cross-section of languages is a good indication of the influence of ethnic and cultural education on Bellow's fiction and the many genres of writing that he would attempt throughout his career. Bellow is a gifted writer because of his special attention to the beauties and distinctiveness of language in its various forms. He is a talented stylist with an ear for lyrical prose, a gift for irony, and a subtle mastery of dialect.

Bellow's early knowledge of Jewish cultural traditions can be seen as a foundation for his writing career. At home the family spoke Yiddish, and Bellow later translated several stories from Yiddish into English. One notable example is fellow American Nobel Laureate **Isaac Bashevis Singer**'s brilliant story "Gimpel the Fool." Bellow attended Hebrew school in his youth, and his family desired nothing more than for their son to become a Talmudic scholar. In all of Bellow's work, there is the distinct presence of his Jewish training, which inevitably intermingles and occasionally clashes with the modern mass movements of American culture. His work bears a distinctive Jewish bearing for it resists much of the romantic and self-indulgent inclinations of twentieth-century fiction. Human nature is not a hopeless void for Bellow, and the world is not a lost place waiting for sure annihilation. Bellow's Jewish **ethnicity** brings forth a picture of a sacred earth—one that rests its hope in the faith, morals, and goodness of humankind. Instead of fragmented cogs in the machine-like processes of technology, Bellow's characters in a self-conscious way call attention to the struggle to overcome the adversities of the modern world by striving for grace, harmony with others, and living through the mysteries of chance and human possibility.

Bellow incorporated his sense of an ideal world from his Jewish legacy with a keen awareness of America's literary landscape. Most of his works deal with heroes attempting to confront the darkness caused in their own souls by casting off the past. These figures all seek to find the essence of what it means to be human beings in a world that has lost its sense of culture and history. Bellow's literary works reject the cultural relativism of twentieth-century literature. His novels, particularly, stand as beacons of light and hope in a sea of despondency and confusion. This does not mean that his fictive worlds are uplifting; on the contrary, most of Bellow's works delve into the pits of human despair and frailty. However, unlike writers such as William Burroughs, **Allen Ginsberg**, **Jack Kerouac**, **Vladimir Nabokov**, Harold Pinter, and Jean-Paul Sartre who exemplify and revel in the alienation of the self in modern literature, Bellow explores the darkness and nothingness at the core of human lives, and yet he attempts to revitalize the human spirit with new found faith in the common bonds of human existence and the quest for love. Ironically, this search for fraternity and for communion with others is discovered through characters who find themselves estranged from people throughout their journeys and many times unable to communicate with those they seek to embrace. Readers can also see hints and allusions to American predecessors, such as Ralph Waldo Emerson, Henry David Thoreau, Herman Melville, Walt Whitman, Mark Twain, and Henry James, and American naturalism throughout Bellow, which are seamlessly placed alongside his concerns for the space of Jewish ethnicity and cultural differences.

Bellow rejects the relativity of much of modern writing—notably the nonchalant acceptance of a world on the brink of the abyss. He desired to champion the moral strength of Western civilization as a way to combat the chaos of a postmodern world. His characters grapple with intense feelings of guilt and frustration; they confront the absurdities of an urban, industrial, and forever changing American landscape, which seems to echo and yet expand on the naturalistic tradition of American writing in the nineteenth century. Instead of being controlled and consumed by the world around them, however, Bellow's characters psychologically spiral into themselves as a defense mechanism against the currents of materialistic exploitation and the devaluing of the human spirit. Although his novels acknowledge the void left after T. S. Eliot's *The Waste Land*, Bellow's works attempt to reaffirm the dignity and nobility of the human character through a careful blending of tradition, intellect, and a core belief in human goodness and order.

A small snapshot of Bellow's most noted novels, a genre which he is most widely recognized for in his career, reveal only a hint of his literary genius as a transcendent Jewish American thinker. His first novel, *Dangling Man* (1944), presents the story of Joseph, a character noted for his philosophical moral focus. The character waits between worlds as he balances his civilian life of intellectual pursuits and his induction into the military. *The Victim* (1947) portrays the struggles between Jews and Gentiles and gives a strong sense of Jewish persecution. *The Adventures of Augie March* (1953), a National Book Award winner, is a novel concerning the "Huck Finn" travels of a young Chicago Jew. *Seize the Day* (1956) is a masterful novella centered around a day in the life of Tommy Wilhelm, a character caught on the brink of self-despair as he struggles with his identity in a world of consumerism and broken bonds. Tommy has abandoned his ethnic name Adler and consistently struggles between the creation of a new self and the pulls of his past. *Henderson the Rain King* (1959) is a highly symbolic recasting of the Don Quixote tale, as Eugene Henderson, a middle-age millionaire, attempts to satisfy his idealistic dreams of self-fulfillment by voyaging off to Africa. *Herzog* (1964) tells the story of a middle-aged Jewish intellectual attempting to ward off insanity as he comes to grips with his own past and his failures in friendships, relationships, parenting, and careers. The movement in the novel pushes Moses Herzog from desperate individuality to neurotic introspection to the verge of suicide, only to eventually lead the hero back to the world of relations and community. *Mr. Sammler's Planet* (1969) leads the reader into a fictional critique of modern society told through the lens of a **Holocaust** survivor in New York. *Humboldt's Gift* (1975) was a Pulitzer Prize winner. The novel brilliantly captures the moral crisis of the intellectual narrator/dramatist struggling to understand his relationship with the world around him and particularly his deceased and estranged mentor, the poet Humboldt. Much of this novel was inspired by Bellow's own life and his strained relationship with New York Jewish intellectual Delmore Schwartz.

In each of these works, Bellow presents main characters that are distinctly Jewish character types. His works powerfully capture characters that endure pain and suffering with an ironic sense of humor; they depict human beings who negotiate through feelings of guilt, powerlessness, and oppression in order to transcend and find a sense of purpose, beauty, and happiness in their everyday lives.

Bellow continued to write with success until his death in early 2005. His writings display the realities and the complexities of human life.

Although Bellow can obviously be classified in ethnic tradition of Jewish American writing, his goal in writing was to move his readers to see the common connections between all human beings. His journey as a writer led him to value his unique place as a Jewish American writer and yet it also moved him to push those ethnic boundaries for universal acceptance as a gifted, intellectual upholder of Western culture. (*See also* Jewish American Novel)

Further Reading

Bloom, Harold, ed. *Saul Bellow*. New York: Chelsea, 1986.

Bradbury, Malcolm. *Saul Bellow*. New York: Methuen, 1982.

Braham, Jeanne. *A Sort of Columbus: The American Voyages of Saul Bellow's Fiction*. Athens: U of Georgia P, 1984.

Clayton, John J. *Saul Bellow: In Defense of Man*. Bloomington: Indiana UP, 1979.

Cohen, Sarah B. *Saul Bellow's Enigmatic Laughter*. Urbana: U of Illinois P, 1974.

Dutton, Robert R. *Saul Bellow*. Boston: Twayne, 1982.

Fuchs, Daniel. *Saul Bellow: Vision and Revision*. Durham, NC: Duke UP, 1984.

Hyland, Peter. *Saul Bellow*. New York: St. Martin's, 1992.

Newman, Judie. *Saul Bellow and History*. New York: St. Martin's, 1984.

Opdahl, Keith M. *The Novels of Saul Bellow*. University Park: Pennsylvania State UP, 1967.

Porter, M. Gilbert. *Whence the Power?: The Artistry and Humanity of Saul Bellow*. Columbia: U of Missouri P, 1974.

Rovit, Earl H., ed. *Saul Bellow: A Collection of Critical Essays*. Englewood Cliffs, NJ: Prentice Hall, 1975.

Trachtenberg, Stanley, ed. *Critical Essays on Saul Bellow*. Boston: G. K. Hall, 1979.

Ian S. Maloney

BELOVED   Remarkable for its thematic complexity and stylistic brilliance, **Toni Morrison**'s fifth novel, *Beloved* (1987), earned her a Pulitzer and no doubt paved the way for the Nobel Prize in Literature. Employing techniques of flashback and multiple points of view, this nonlinear novel confronts the painful and avoided history of **slavery**. With great specificity it chronicles the racial, sexual, and psychic violence endured by African American ancestors. Dedicated to the "sixty million or more" who perished in the **Middle Passage** of the trans-Atlantic slave trade, the novel urges us to remember . . . and then, to move on.

The novel is based on a true story of Margaret Garner, a fugitive slave from Kentucky, who when hunted down by slave catchers in 1856 intended to kill her children and herself rather than be returned to slavery; she was prevented from doing so after she took the life of her daughter. Modeled after Garner, Sethe is the novel's central character who flees the Kentucky plantation ironically called "Sweet Home" and when facing captivity kills her baby daughter named Beloved.

The novel opens in post–Civil War Ohio with Sethe's sad and haunted house eighteen years after Beloved's death. Ostracized by the black community for the infanticide, Sethe and her lonely daughter Denver put up with the restless ghost of Beloved. The spiteful ghost that drove Sethe's two sons to flee their home is driven out by Paul D, a fellow-fugitive from "Sweet Home" who returns to Sethe's life after eighteen years. His return stirs Sethe's memories and the two recount to each other their traumatic memories: Sethe's abuse as a mother reproducing for the plantation; the madness and death of her husband, Halle, whose spirit is broken by the brutality of School Teacher, the plantation overseer; wistful memories of her long-suffering but valiant mother-in-law, Baby Suggs; Paul D's chain-gang experiences in Alfred, Georgia.

Paul D and Sethe's companionship is short-lived as an intruder who answers to the name of Beloved occupies Sethe's house and takes over her life. Sethe believes this homeless young woman is the ghost of her baby daughter Beloved coming back for reparation. But Beloved is hard to appease. After she seduces and drives out Paul D, who is alienated from Sethe when he learns of the infanticide, Beloved cannot have enough of Sethe's attention. Increasingly isolated, wracked by guilt and remorse, Sethe withdraws into herself. Her adolescent daughter Denver is forced to venture out of the house in search of help from the community. Eventually the community of black women rescues Sethe from her torment. Beloved leaves, vanishing mysteriously. Paul D, wiser, comes back to befriend Sethe, who is finally released from her past into the present.

Beloved takes up literally and metaphorically the theme of possession and exorcism. Constructed by different characters recalling their difficult pasts, these collective narratives of "rememory" take us into the very heart of slavery: the gendered nature of the oppression of black men and women and their resistance to it; the intergenerational impact of the pervasive loss and suffering; and the necessity of healing for both the individual and the community by remembering and working through this trauma.

Further Reading

Andrew, William L., and Nellie Y. McKay, eds. *Toni Morrison's Beloved: A Casebook*. New York: Oxford UP, 1999.

Bloom, Harold. *Modern Critical Interpretations: Beloved*. Philadelphia: Chelsea House Publishers, 1999.

Grewal, Gurleen. *Circles of Sorrow, Lines of Struggle: The Novels of Toni Morrison*. Baton Rouge: Louisiana State UP, 1998.

Peterson, Nancy J. "Toni Morrison and the Desire for a 'Genuine Black History Book'." *Against Amnesia: Contemporary Women Writers and the Crises of Historical Memory*. Philadelphia: U of Pennsylvania P, 2001. 51–97.

Gurleen Grewal

BELTON, DON (1959–)   African American gay novelist, editor, and professor. Belton was born in Philadelphia, Pennsylvania, but spent his early years with his grandmother in the Hill district of Newark, New Jersey, which became the setting for *Almost Midnight* (1986), the only novel he has published thus far. A graduate of Bennington College—one of the most elite liberal arts colleges in the United States—Belton worked briefly as a reporter for *Newsweek* before turning to fiction writing. The success of his debut novel earned him a series of academic positions at various universities; he has taught creative writing at the University of Colorado, the University of Michigan, the University of Alabama, and the University of Massachusetts, among many others. In 1995 he edited *Speak My Name: Black Men on Masculinity and the American Dream*, which includes his own autobiographical essay titled "Voodoo for Charles."

Almost Midnight is a magical tale set mostly in the Hill district of Newark. At the center of the narrative is the Reverend Sam Poole, now an impoverished old man on his deathbed. He speaks very little but his life story is reconstructed largely through the recollections of three women who have been abused by Poole in various ways: Sarah Anderson, one of Poole's numerous mistresses, offers a faintly romanticized version of his past; Peanut, an ex-prostitute and also one of Poole's former mistresses, provides a blunt and resolutely unsentimental summation of his life; and Martha, Poole's youngest daughter whom he has sexually abused for several years, paints a picture of the man whom she simultaneously loves and hates. Their recollections collectively reveal Poole's extraordinary history. An orphan who grew up in New Orleans, Louisiana, Poole moves to New Jersey during the 1920s and founds the Metaphysical Church of the Divine Investigation. His various churches, however, are essentially fronts for prostitution, gambling, and bootlegging. Soon he becomes a millionaire and a darling of the white establishment. Along the way he sexually exploits and abuses dozens of women who seem helpless when faced with his immensely charismatic personality and enormous power. "A story of female powerlessness that spans three generations" (Meyer 11), *Almost Midnight* chronicles the lives damaged by Poole. Yet the novel does not provide an entirely convincing rationale for female victimization. Why, for example, Martha continues to support her sexually abusive father with her meager welfare checks remains essentially unclear. Nevertheless, the novel's larger-than-life characters, its magic realist quality, and its exquisitely crafted monologues make *Almost Midnight* a compelling work.

Belton's *Speak My Name* is an important collection of essays. Among the contributors to the anthology are some of the most distinguished contemporary African American writers, such as **Amiri Baraka**, **John Edgar Wideman**, and **August Wilson**. Belton's essay "Voodoo for Charles" is a poignant meditation on his own life as an African American gay male artist and academic to his moving recollection of his phone conversations with Charles, his nineteen-year-old nephew, who awaits sentencing for attempted murder.

Further Reading

Meyer, Charlotte M. Review of *Almost Midnight* by Don Belton. *American Book Review* 8.5 (1986): 11.

Quinn, Mary Ellen. Review of *Almost Midnight* by Don Belton. *Booklist* 82.15 (April 1, 1986): 181.

Emmanuel S. Nelson

BENNETT, GWENDOLYN (1902–1981)   African American poet, fiction writer, artist, illustrator, journalist, teacher. A figure of the **Harlem Renaissance**, Bennett's visual and written art carry themes of racial pride, a longing for Africa, a celebration of blackness, and the black body. Her interests in art and poetry reflect the versatility of her artistic vision.

Born in Giddings, Texas, and raised on a Nevada Indian reservation, in Washington, DC, in Pennsylvania, and in New York, this artist and writer came of age at the dawning of the Harlem Renaissance. She studied art at Columbia University, Pratt Institute, and in Paris, France, and taught art at Howard University. Her circle of friends included such Harlem Renaissance notables as **Langston Hughes**, **Countee Cullen**, **Richard Bruce Nugent**, **Helene Johnson**, and **Zora Neale Hurston**, a group that constantly encouraged her to write and publish her own work. She joined Nugent, Hughes, and others in putting together *Fire!*, a literary arts journal for the younger generation of Harlem Renaissance writers.

During her most productive years, the mid-1920s, Bennett found her art, poetry, and articles in *The Crisis*, *Opportunity* and in other African American journals of the times. For several years she maintained "Ebony Flute," a column in *Opportunity* that served as a sort of "informant" of the whereabouts and involvement of celebrity African Americans.

Though a prolific writer, Bennett never collected her works into a single volume. Bennett crossed artistic lines as a writer and a visual artist. Her penchant for the visual is evident in the vivid and sensual images she offers in her poetry.

Her most widely anthologized pieces are "Heritage" and "To a Dark Girl." In these two pieces Bennett honors Africa's past glory and her future promise through the African American present. Through these pieces she also celebrates "dark skin" and "dark Africa" and redefines myths of blackness. By doing so, she serves as a forerunner to the **Black Arts Movement** of the 1960s and 1970s, which embraced "Black is beautiful" as its theme and mantra.

Poems, such as "To a Dark Girl," reveal Bennett's visual astuteness. In "Heritage" she evokes a sense of a pristine and untainted Africa. Though Bennett begins with exoticized and romanticized images of Africa, she subverts such objectification through willing her subjects to act and rise above their "given" fate. The tools of oppression, such as the minstrel smile, become the instruments of subversion.

Comfortable crafting free verse, Bennett was equally adept at working with classic forms, such as sonnets and elegies. She infuses these forms with an African American spirit.

Further Reading

Bates, Gerri. "Bennett, Gwendolyn." *Black Women in America: An Historical Encyclopedia*. Vol. I. Ed. Darlene Clark Hine, et al. Bloomington: Indiana UP, 1993. 106–09.

Chandra Tyler Mountain

BENNETT, HAL (1930–)   Expatriate African American novelist and short story writer. Bennett was born in Virginia but grew up mostly in New Jersey. Shortly after graduating from high school, he joined the U.S. Air Force and served in Japan as well as in Korea in the early fifties. In 1956 he relocated in Mexico City and he continues to live there in self-imposed exile. So far he has published five novels and a collection of short stories; however, Bennett is yet to receive any substantial critical attention.

Bennett, first and foremost, is a satirist. The racial pathologies and sexual hypocrisies of the American society remain the primary targets of his often devastatingly accurate satire. And neither the blacks nor the whites escape his satiric eye. In his first novel, *A Wilderness of Vines* (1966), for example, Bennett confronts—bluntly and unapologetically—a theme that was considered politically too sensitive in the 1960s: internalized racism among African Americans. Set in an imaginary, all-black neighborhood in the South, the novel relentlessly exposes the deep-rooted self-hatred of its African American characters. Life in this black community pivots on a self-evident and unchallenged hierarchy: the light-skinned African Americans are deemed superior and those with the darkest complexions are perceived as entirely worthless. Bennett probes the attitudes and assumptions that govern this hierarchy in an attempt to demonstrate the extent to which white racism damages the black psyche. As a satirist, however, Bennett's goal is reformist: He makes it clear that it is the responsibility of African Americans to decolonize their racial consciousness and transcend their self-loathing. In his second novel, *The Black Wine* (1968), Bennett debunks the notion that the North is a Promised Land for those fleeing the South. Genuine emancipation, according to Bennett, cannot be accomplished simply by geographical relocation; it is possible only through psychological rehabilitation that results from political self-enlightenment.

Lord of Dark Places (1970) is perhaps Bennett's most provocative novel. Here he argues that Christianity in the hands of white racists has historically functioned as an instrument of domination and a tool of pacification. The novel systematically inverts the central Christian symbols and precepts to expose their insidious collusion in the construction and perpetuation of racist belief systems. Bennett's fourth novel, *Wait until the Evening* (1974), further explores this theme. In *Seventh Heaven* (1976), Bennett's fifth and final novel, he takes on yet another sensitive and controversial subject: the stereotypes attached to black male sexuality. In his attempt to collapse those stereotypes, Bennett at times grossly exaggerates them—a strategy that some reviewers have found offensive. Bennett's most recently published work is *Insanity Runs in Our Family* (1977), a collection of his short stories published in various venues over a period of fifteen years. The idea that animates many of the stories collected here is that madness, in its myriad manifestations, is the logical outcome of America's moral failure to confront its racism.

Bennett has not published any works of fiction under his name since 1977. However, it is generally believed that he may have published six more novels using two different pseudonyms: Harriet Janeway and John D. Revere.

Further Reading

Meyer, Adam. "Hal Bennett." *Contemporary African American Novelists: A Bio-Bibliographical Critical Sourcebook.* Ed. Emmanuel S. Nelson. Westport, CT: Greenwood Press, 1999. 36–41.

Newman, Katherine. "An Evening with Hal Bennett: An Interview." *Black American Literature Forum* 21 (1987): 357–78.

Emmanuel S. Nelson

BERNARDI, ADRIA (1957–) Italian American writer and translator. Adria Bernardi is among the best known of Italian American writers whose work has appeared near the end of the twentieth century. In her writing she strives to connect the lives of earlier generations in Italy with their twentieth-century descendants in America and ultimately to evaluate the immigrant experience.

Bernardi is best known for two books, *The Day Laid on the Altar* (1999), a novel, and *In the Gathering Woods* (2000), a collection of related stories that reads like a novel. Both have received prestigious awards: the Bread Loaf Writers' Conference Bakeless Nason Fiction Prize for first books and the 2000 Drue Heinz Literature Prize, respectively. She has also won an A. E. Coppard Award for Short Fiction (1998) and a James Fellowship from the Heekin Group Foundation (1995).

Both books share subject matter, characters, and lyrical style. The earlier book is set entirely in late Renaissance Italy and concerns itself with three characters who struggle to define themselves through art, one of Bernardi's main concerns. Two are fictional and one is historical, the famous Venetian painter Titian. The two fictional characters reappear in the later book's stories, along with various descendants, both in Italy and America, over the course of the following five centuries.

Bernardi seems ambivalent about the ultimate result of this **immigration**. This is illustrated in "Working the Clock" where in spite of a good life in 1970s America—husband, children, house, health—the protagonist suffers from a vague depression only temporarily relieved by middle-class comforts. It is reflected in the earlier book as well in the character of Bartolomeo, a poor peasant shepherd. Although he does not have the gumption to emigrate from the mountains like so many others, he creates an artistic masterpiece literally inside a mountain—a masterpiece that is the connection to sanity that the final character in the later book grasps at for meaning beyond her successful, scientific life in America.

Bernardi's hometown is near Highwood, Illinois, a working-class Italian enclave in the suburbs north of Chicago along Lake Michigan. There she was nurtured into Italian culture and language, specifically the Romagnole dialect of north central Italy spoken by her family. The language, both in word and feeling, figures prominently in these two books as well as in her other major work, an oral history, *Houses with Names: The Italian Immigrants of Highwood, Illinois.* Here the source of Bernardi's ideas and love for her heritage is made abundantly clear: several dozen *immigranti* describe how in the early decades of the twentieth century they built cities, dug coal, sewed clothing, and cleaned houses in the New World in order to leave physical, but not spiritual, poverty behind in the Old World.

Bernardi, who has an MA in Italian literature from the University of Chicago, has also produced several translations: *Adventures in Africa* (2000) by Gianni Celati, a popular Italian writer, and *Abandoned Places* (1999) by Tonino Guerra, an Italian poet and screenwriter.

Christina Biava

BERNSTEIN, CHARLES (1950–) Jewish American poet and critic. Charles Bernstein is one of the leading voices in the contemporary movement known as Language poetry. Born and raised in New York City, Bernstein graduated from Harvard in 1972 and began publishing his poetry in independent literary magazines. His numerous publications include the notable *Poetic Justice* (1979), *Controlling Interests* (1980), *The Sophist* (1987), and *With Strings* (2001). In addition to his poetry, he has authored three collections of critical work: *A Poetics* (1992), *Content's Dream: Essays 1975–1994* (1996), and *My Way: Speeches and Poems* (1999). Starting in 1978 he coedited with Bruce Andrews the influential magazine devoted to Language poetry, *L=A=N=G=U=A=G=E*. In 1989 Bernstein became David Gray Professor of Poetry and Letters at the State University of New York-Buffalo. He is currently Professor of English at the University of Pennsylvania.

Bernstein's poetry invariably returns to the subject of language, calling the reader's attention to the very stuff of which poems are made. For Bernstein, poetic language does not express the thoughts and feelings of the poet, but appears as an object in the world. Language becomes concrete and sensual. It comes to life. His work demonstrates this in a style at once critical and playful. If such inventions can seem to be so much nonsense, closer readings show carefully constructed occasions of language. With his gathered and overlapped words and phrases, assembled bits of sentences, and overheard conversations, Bernstein continually challenges the conventions of much verse, where words are used as if they could simply represent something outside themselves. His innovative poetry, by contrast, explores how meaning is made, how words are assembled everyday in all social contexts.

Well known for energetic readings where words can be felt as sound, Bernstein stresses the way language shapes perception by making one perceive language. Words become objects of study. When he turns to repeated patterns of speech, found sounds, and the stock phrases that act as replacements for creative thought, he shows how much we traffic in worn out language. By language he means all meaning that emerges from social transaction, be it poems on a page or movies on a screen. Bernstein relentlessly studies the process whereby meaning is made by our inherited language. How are we asked to read? How do we see? What do we hear? What are our concerns as a collective as we are bound to each other through language? How might social life be different?

One of his dominant metaphors is absorption, and to discharge language is get it out—to see it, to hear its power and workings carefully and critically. Bernstein's poetry may try to objectify language, but he keeps it alive through puns, creative play, and breaking and rearranging of syntax and structure. All of his experiments show the lived experience of reading, thinking, and writing. As suggested by the title of his early collection *Poetic Justice*, Bernstein sees language's power reflects his interest in society: social values, political rhetoric, and forms of cultural expression.

Bernstein's poetic interventions show the capacities of language to reorient the world by the roles language plays in shaping what we see. His greatest skill as a poet is in making the reader see the effect and use of words on reality. The goal is a sustained demonstration of what language does and what it might yet accomplish. There is no question that the playfulness, lightness, and humor in Bernstein's poetry keeps it humane and leads it gently toward its possibilities. If there remains the incisive criticism of failing to see what words do—how they inscribe the body politic with the cuts of history—there is also a perpetual stress on human connection, human endeavor, and humane possibility. His collection *Republics of Reality* suggests just that: Poetry may show the words in action, but it remains for us to use them in a new way, to build a new world. Language poetry is about poetic form and its possibilities, but also about the possibilities of public culture—the space of shared language.

Further Reading

Altieri, Charles. "Avant-Garde or Arriere-Garde in Recent American Poetry." *Poetics Today* 20.4 (1999): 629–53.

Auster, Paul. "Twenty-Five Sentences Containing the Words 'Charles Bernstein'." *Why Write?* Providence, RI: Burning Deck, 1996. 33–35.

Lazer, Hank. "Charles Bernstein's *Dark City*: Polis, Policy, and the Policing of Poetry." *American Poetry Review* 24 (1995): 35–44.

Daniel Listoe

BERRYMAN, JOHN (1914–1972) Jewish American poet and Fellow of the Academy of American Poets, Chancellor, 1968–72. John Berryman was born John Smith Jr. Berryman's father, a banker, committed suicide after a failed land speculation when John was ten. Following his mother's remarriage, John Smith took his stepfather's surname but remained depressed by his father's death. Alcohol and family history complicated by the national economy weave a haunting thread through the poet's work, shadowing Berryman's entire career and contributing to his attempted suicide in 1931 and his death in 1972.

In the midst of national economic crisis, still haunted by the past, Berryman became a college student. Graduating Phi Beta Kappa in English, Berryman studied in England and won the Oldham Shakespeare Prize. He taught at Wayne University (Wayne State University) in Detroit, Harvard, and Princeton. Berryman's critical work established him professionally among academic colleagues. His personal history suggests that even after winning the American Academy poetry award in 1950 he saw poetry not as a path to prestige but as a compelling search for meaning and purpose

A major figure in the Confessional school of poetry, Berryman also represents the complexity of the twentieth century. His poetry, like that of Robert Lowell, Sylvia Plath, Anne Sexton, and W. D. Snodgrass, reflects the guiding conventions of the time, but the work also brings to the conventions a compelling originality that boldly resists convention. Berryman's poetry clearly reflects this duality of poetic imagination, representation, and resistance. While probing the extremes of variation in language and emotion, Berryman's life and poetry similarly illustrate the extremes by refusing to be anything if not extraordinary.

The intensity and brilliance of the poet and poems were acknowledged by the National Institute of Arts and Letters Award and the Levinson Prize in 1950 and a Guggenheim Fellowship in 1952. Berryman's first major work *Homage to Mistress Bradstreet* (1953, 1956) was nominated for a Pulitzer Prize in 1956, and *77 Dream Songs* won the Pulitzer Prize in 1964, securing Berryman's literary recognition. Another volume of *Songs* followed in *His Toy, His Dream, His Rest* (1968).

Berryman's fame increased internationally between 1956 and 1961, while his personal life alternately surged and declined through divorce, remarriage, the births of a son and two daughters, a promotion to associate professor, and a lecture tour of India. Exhausted and relentlessly troubled by alcoholism, Berryman was frequently hospitalized, but he continued to teach and publish. Interviews indicate that with his singular exclusion of senile dementia Berryman psychologically courted death as a medium for creativity.

The poet's exploratory engagement with theology emphasizes his preoccupation with the soul and psyche, and in *Homage to Mistress Bradstreet* Berryman explores poetic identity as gender, generation, and inspiration. *The Dream Songs*, 385 songs arranged in sonnet-like sequence, produces a monologue-that-would-be-dialogue between ego and alter ego, with dialectical shifts and psychological projections framing the fragmented conversation. The speakers explore issues clearly familiar to Berryman: suicide, unrestrained sexuality, and alcoholism, obstacles that increasingly alienated him from colleagues, injuring his earlier literary success. In *The Dream Songs*, Berryman's dialectical shifts and projections enable him to approach his preoccupation with death from a literary distance.

Berryman's personal and professional deterioration complete a somber pattern of loss and surrender, more accurately, an obscure dance between surrender and resistance to reality. Berryman seems stranded between the worlds of his parents and his posterity, unable to fully participate in either.

A revealing letter to Berryman from William Meredith, written in 1970 (Connecticut College, Charles E. Shain Library, Special Collections) in response to the poet's request for Meredith's critique of several poems, reveals the changing patterns of Berryman's life and work. Meredith kindly chides Berryman for requiring external commentary, while ignoring his own "considerable" status, earned by taking the difficult, "pig-headed" and "roundabout" path to that recognition.

Meredith's evident friendship and admission of "misgivings" regarding the quality of Berryman's late poems effectively symbolize the characteristic contrasts of Berryman's history. The letter characterizes Berryman's audacity and insecurity as "a contradiction," one that theology, psychology, and poetry evidently could not resolve. Characterized as perhaps a manic genius, and continuously haunted by his father's suicide, Berryman jumped from a bridge in Minneapolis, Minnesota, and died on January 7, 1972.

Further Reading

Mariani, Paul L. *Dream Song: The Life of John Berryman*. New York: William Marlow, 1990.

Thomas, Harry. *Berryman's Understanding: Reflections on the Poetry of John Berryman*. Boston: Northeastern UP, 1988.

Stella Thompson

BERSSENBRUGGE, MEI-MEI (1947–) Chinese American poet. Mei-Mei Berssenbrugge was born in Beijing of Chinese and Dutch American parents and grew up in Massachusetts. She received her BA from Reed College and her MFA from Columbia University. Recipient of two NEA fellowships, her books include *Summits Move with the Tide* (1974), considered one of the first books of poetry by a Chinese American; *Random Possession* (1979) and *The Heat Bird* (1983), both of which won American Book Awards from the Before Columbus Foundation; *Hiddenness* (1987), an artist book collaboration with Richard Tuttle; *Empathy* (1989), winner of the PEN West Award; *Sphericity* (1993), with paintings by Richard Tuttle; *Endocrinology* (1997), an artist book collaboration with Kiki Smith and winner of the 1997 Asian American Literary Award; *Four Year Old Girl* (1998), winner of the 1999 Western States Book Award; and *Nest* (2003). She also has collaborated on theater works with Frank Chin, Blondell Cummings, Tan Dun, Shi Zhen Chen, Alvin Lucier, and Theodora Yoshikami.

Berssenbrugge may be considered a phenomenological poet, investigating the processes of perception and the textures of experience. Science (especially biology), philosophy, visual art, natural landscapes (primarily the New Mexico desert, where she has lived since the 1970s, but also the Alaskan tundra), her Chinese heritage, romantic love, motherhood, and family are some of the predominant materials of Berssenbrugge's work. A sense of wonder toward physical existence, both human and natural (and a strong sense of the interconnection of the two), pervades her poems. In keeping with her belief in Buddhism, which promotes a state of mindfulness to and within the world, Berssenbrugge's work enacts an accurate attention to this world's objects and structures. Her engagements with science and with visual art show the shared commitment of these endeavors to see and grasp the world both in relation to human knowledge and as an entity in its own right, which resists the meanings we project onto it. As evidenced by the title of *Empathy*, Berssenbrugge's investment in the question of knowledge extends to our knowledge of other people, our connections and disconnections; much of her work explores the ways in which we read and misread each other. This is a particularly prominent aspect of *Nest*.

Berssenbrugge was a companion to Georgia O'Keeffe in her youth and is married to the painter Richard Tuttle; her engagement with visual art is vividly present in her poetry. There is a spatial, painterly quality to much of Berssenbrugge's work, and a sense of simultaneity rather than linear progression; the poems tend to spiral and eddy rather than to move forward toward a conclusion. The long, meditative lines of her work since *Empathy* enact this spatial quality, treating the page almost as a canvas. Repetition and variation wind through many of the poems: verbal and visual elements weave in and out; themes (in a musical sense) counterpoint one another. Berssenbrugge's work combines an innovative impulse to expand the frame of what poems can do and be with a strong commitment to beauty. Hers is a quiet but important voice in contemporary American poetry.

Further Reading

Hinton, Laura, and Cynthia Hogue, eds. *We Who Love to Be Astonished: Experimental Women's Writing and Performance Poetics*. Tuscaloosa: U of Alabama P, 2001.

Rankine, Claudia, and Juliana Spahr, eds. *American Women Poets in the 21st Century: Where Lyric Meets Language*. Middletown, CT: Wesleyan UP, 2002.

Reginald Shepherd

BESSIE, ALVAH (1904–1985) Jewish American novelist, screenwriter, and journalist. Born in New York, Bessie's work has been somewhat overshadowed by his extraordinary life as a strident fighter for left-wing causes. A graduate of Columbia University, he wrote his first short story, "Redbird," in 1925, and was a staff member of *The New Yorker* magazine when his first novel, *Dwell in the Wilderness*, was published in 1935. He left America for Spain in 1938 to join the Abraham Lincoln brigade, which was made up of three thousand Americans who fought alongside the Spanish Republican army, against Francisco Franco's fascist forces in the Spanish civil war. While in Spain he encountered many other leftist intellectuals, including Ernest Hemingway who expressed admiration for his prose. With the defeat of the Spanish republicans, Bessie returned to America and wrote a novel chronicling his experience in Spain, titled *Men in Battle* (1939). He also worked as a drama critic and film reviewer for the magazine *The New Masses* (1939–43).

Alvah Bessie, testifying before the House Un-American Activities Committee. *Courtesy of the Library of Congress.*

Bessie moved to Hollywood to begin work as a screenwriter and had several screenplays produced by Warner Brothers, including *Northern Pursuit* (1943), *The Very Thought of You* (1944), *Smart Woman* (1948), and *Hotel Berlin* (1945). He was nominated for an academy award for *Objective, Burma* in 1945, but his career was disrupted shortly after World War II when the House Un-American Activities Committee (HUAC) began investigating the Hollywood film industry for suspected anti-American activity and links to communism. The purpose of the HUAC was to prove that the Screen Writers' Guild had been infiltrated by members of the communist party and that these writers had the ability to insert communist propaganda into Hollywood films, thus threatening the American way of life. Although none of these claims were ever proven, the HUAC was able to subpoena many people who worked in the entertainment industry, who were subsequently forced to leave their jobs by employers who were either suspicious of their possible involvement with communism or afraid of being accused by the HUAC themselves.

In 1947 Bessie was one of nineteen "unfriendly witnesses" called to appear before the HUAC. Of these, eleven people were eventually forced to testify; only German playwright Bertolt Brecht actually gave any information to the Committee, claiming that he was not a communist before returning home to East Germany. The remaining ten became known as the famous "Hollywood Ten." One of them was the director Edward Dmytryk and the other nine were screenwriters: John Howard Lawson, Dalton Trumbo, **Albert Maltz**, **Samuel Ornitz**, Herbert Biberman, Adrian Scott, Ring Lardner Jr., Lester Cole, and Alvah Bessie. Many of these men were Jewish and had been involved in liberal political activities before World War II and the developments of the cold war. As a group they decided to refrain from answering any of the HUAC's questions and plead their Fifth Amendment right to remain silent. As a result of this action all of them received a $1000 fine and were sentenced to one year in prison.

Unfortunately, their problems did not end with the completion of their prison terms; most of their careers were ruined as they found themselves blacklisted in Hollywood for the next ten years, along with over three hundred other people who had been named as suspects of being communists. Bessie, now unemployable in the film industry, wrote about his ordeal in an autobiographical novel titled *Inquisition in Eden* (1965), and he was to revisit the subject in a later work, playing himself in the film documentary *Hollywood on Trial* (1976). His other novels of this time period include *The Un-Americans* (1957), *The Symbol* (1966), and *One for My Baby* (1980). Bessie spent most of the rest of his life in relative obscurity working various jobs, including being a stage manager and sound man at a nightclub in San Francisco's North Beach and later an editor of a union newspaper published by Harry Bridges, the head of the International Longshoreman's Union. American public opinion continued to regard the activities of the HUAC with great favor until the late 1950s, when several prominent members of the committee were involved in corruption scandals and were accused of being overzealous. Bessie's son Dan directed a movie titled *Hard Travelling* (1986), which was based on his father's early novel *Bread and Stone*, as well as wrote the introduction to his father's posthumously published notebooks from the Spanish civil war, *Alvah Bessie's Spanish Civil War Notebooks* (2001).

Further Reading

Barzman, Norma. *The Red and the Blacklist: The Intimate Memoir of a Hollywood Expatriate*. New York: Thunder's Mouth Press/Nation Books, 2003.

Bentley, Eric. *Are You Now or Have You Ever Been: The Investigation of Show Business by the Un-American Activities Committee, 1947–1958*. New York: Harper & Row, 1972.

Dick, Bernard. *Radical Innocence: A Critical Study of the Hollywood Ten*. Kentucky: UP of Kentucky, 1989.

Michelle Erfer

BIBB, HENRY (1815–1854)   African American writer and fugitive slave. Henry Bibb is best known for his autobiography, *Narrative of the Life and Adventures of Henry Bibb, An American Slave* (1849), which documents his experiences in bondage and his repeated attempts to escape. His account is notable for its sensitive exploration of the tension between individual liberty and family unity. Bibb also was active in the abolitionist movement, and he urged blacks to emigrate as he did to Canada.

Born in Shelby County, Kentucky, Bibb was the son of state senator James Bibb and Mildred Jackson, a slave who worked on a nearby plantation. Jackson had seven children who were all sold to different slave owners. As a child Bibb was often hired out to neighboring slave owners and had little opportunity to see his mother.

At the age of eighteen Bibb married Malinda, a **mulatto** slave, and together they had one daughter, Mary Frances. In his autobiography Bibb writes of his frustration and rage at seeing his wife abused. With the hope

Henry Bibb, 1875. *Courtesy of the Yale Collection of American Literature, Beinecke Rare Book and Manuscript Library.*

of eventually freeing his family, Bibb made several attempts to escape **slavery**. He was successful in 1837 and returned six months later to bring his family to the North. However, they were caught and sold to a slave owner in Vicksburg, Ohio. Bibb was soon after sold to a group of Native Americans. He again escaped and renewed his ultimately unsuccessful efforts to rescue his family.

In 1842 Bibb established himself in Detroit and began working as an **abolition**ist. He lectured on the abuses of slavery and campaigned for the Liberty Party. During a lecture tour he met Mary Miles, a Boston woman, and the two married in 1848. The following year his autobiography, *Narrative of the Life and Adventures of Henry Bibb, An American Slave*, was published by the Anti-Slavery Society. His autobiography is considered to be one of the most reliable accounts of slave life, and it is marked by thoughtful reflections on family attachments and the abuses caused by human bondage. Bibb describes his reluctance to get married because such a deep emotional attachment would impede his ultimate goal of freedom. His deep commitment to his family is demonstrated by his dangerous and unsuccessful return to the South to free them from slavery.

After the ratification of the Fugitive Slave Act of 1850, Bibb declared that he would sooner die than return to slavery, and he moved to Canada with his second wife. A year later he founded the *Voice of the Fugitive*, Canada's first black newspaper. Bibb urged blacks, both free and slave, to come to Canada. He also formed the pan-African society, the American Continental and West India League, to unite free blacks. Due to his prominence as a writer and lecturer, Bibb was at last reunited with three of his siblings who also escaped to Canada. (*See also* African American Slave Narrative)

Further Reading

Andrews, William L. *To Tell a Free Story: The First Century of Afro-American Autobiography, 1760–1865*. Urbana: U of Illinois P, 1986.

Stephanie Li

BILINGUALISM   On a basic level, bilingualism in U.S. ethnic literature entails the systematic use of two distinct languages in a given piece of literature as a way locating the author (as well as the characters) in a particular position in relation to mainstream culture. More generally, bilingualism can be seen as a means of expression that has been an important and ever-present element in the production of ethnic literature in the United States. In addition, bilingualism in the United States can be described as a literary practice aimed at documenting a (sub)culture, and as a way of using a subordinate language to contest (fight) the imposed (and imposing) constraints of the monolingual, mainstream (and thus, dominant) culture. In particular, bilingualism in ethnic literature documents the process(es) by which determined communities change/adapt to and learn or negotiate their new lives or realities. Theoretically, bilingualism also serves as a bond or a bridge between immigrant groups and those of the same heritage who have lived in the United States for generations. By the same token, bilingual literature in the United States also documents the clashes between the new immigrants, those who have lived in the United States for one or more generations, and the mainstream Anglo culture. In the end, bilingualism contests mainstream efforts to eradicate the mother tongue from those communities. Or in many cases, that which has become the second tongue, as second and third generations of U.S.-born minorities oftentimes learn their parents and grandparents' mother tongue as a second language. In any case, U.S. ethnic writers from different backgrounds have countered for decades (purposely or not) "English only" efforts and initiatives by unabashedly expressing themselves in their literature with words that are "foreign" to the English language, but are reflective of their ethnic backgrounds (i.e., see the works of Puerto Rican writers **Esmeralda Santiago** and **Sandra Estévez** or Chinese American **Maxine Hong Kingston**) and ways of thinking (i.e., see the works of Chicana writer **Cherríe Moraga** where she argues that Spanish, beyond a way of communicating, is a way of living). In many cases authors write entire texts in a bilingual format (e.g., see the works of Chicana writer **Gloria Anzaldúa**, more specifically, her book *Borderlands/La Frontera*).

As a practice, bilingualism signifies a moving in and out of determined linguistic structures in order to communicate a personal state of mind and a collective reality. (Something to remember here is that culture—whatever that culture may be—is learned and transmitted through language). Language (in this case bilingual language) serves as conduit by which an oftentimes hybrid culture is expressed. Indeed it is precisely this cultural reality that differentiates a U.S. ethnic author using Spanish or Chinese or Ebonics from an Anglo author using Latin or French to spice up their texts or make them seem more sophisticated. Moreover, U.S. ethnic literature provides a unique perspective (unique to a particular community) by using English in conjunction with another distinct language and by sometimes merging both languages, as in the case of Spanglish. For instance, Chicano/a and U.S. Puerto Rican authors use English and Spanish (and in many instances Spanglish) in their pieces as a way of positioning the author (and those like her/him) in the interstices of mainstream Anglo culture and Puerto Rican or Chicano/a culture. In many cases the texts are written primarily in English with some passages in Spanish. In these cases the words in Spanish used by the authors are meant to establish two specific links: (1) a connection with a specific ethnic group at a personal level (and thus establishing a particular heritage); and (2) a broader cultural connection between the author, the community to which he or she belongs, and their heritage. For instance, on a personal level, **Piri Thomas** uses Spanish words in his autobiography *Down These Mean Streets* to establish an overt connection with his Puerto Ricanness, even though the book narrates the struggles he faced as an American "of color" in the United States. On a cultural level, however, the use of those words in Spanish (mainly quotidian expressions) was a conscious effort of connecting himself and his community (Spanish Harlem) to a Puerto Rican ethos that is symbolized by the island in the Caribbean and that can only be expressed in one language—Spanish. Some examples of the expressions used by Thomas are: "Dios mío," "hijo," "caramba," "muchacho," "sí," and "suerte." Though the majority of these expressions have linguistic equivalents in English (i.e., "my God," "son," "darn," "kid," "yes," and "good luck"), there is an element of cultural baggage that is claimed by using them in Spanish—a baggage that would be lost if the expression were to be written in English. As **Ana Castillo** argues in her book *Massacre of the Dreamers*, "Words reflect conceptions of reality and do not simply translate literally" (221). Those conceptions of reality (whatever they may be) are the ones to which bilingual authors seek to remain loyal by keeping them as they are expressed (in this case, in Spanish). Thus, it is not necessarily a refusal of the author to translate, but rather a necessity to convey s specific cultural meaning.

Bilingualism, consequently, serves to highlight the paradox by which these authors belong to two distinctive cultures (e.g., Anglo and Puerto Rican in the case of U.S. Puerto Ricans or Anglo and Mexican in the case of Chicanos/as), yet they also belong to neither. This point is brilliantly illustrated by **Sandra María Esteves** in her poem "Puerto Rican Discovery #3 Not Neither."

In addition to establishing a direct link to a specific (sub)culture and the ethos of a country, bilingualism in U.S. ethnic literature also documents the creation and maintenance of a new hybrid culture that communicates using a "new" language, a language that reflects the experiences of this in-between culture. An illustration of this phenomenon is the poetry of **Lorna Dee Cervantes**. In her poem "Poema para los californios muertos" (Poem for the dead Californios), Cervantes weaves English and Spanish, using Spanish mainly to emphasize the historical commotion and sense of loss of the original Mexican settlement in the state of California. For instance, she uses Spanish when talking about the land: "Husbands de la tierra" (husbands of the land) and "tierra madre" (mother land). She also uses it when talking about ancestors and their struggles.

Regardless of the reason for the "other" language, each bilingual text (and bilingual literature in general) must be studied as a whole—not just the English in it, or the "other" language, or the combination of both, but the content as a solid unit. As Judith Hernandez Mora writes, "I wonder if we could think of [bilingual ethnic literature] as an interpretation, a cultural translation of the English [with another language]" (196, my translation). This cultural translation becomes a language code that allows the authors to (re)invent themselves as members of a subordinate group with a rich culture and distinctive experiences living by the rules of a dominant group. Paradoxically the experiences narrated by the authors are similar to the experiences lived by the members of each group (i.e., subordinate and dominant). However, the fact that the authors are simultaneously living the experiences of two different groups makes their experiences unique. For instance, in her memoir *Almost a Woman*, Esmeralda Santiago writes, "Four days after my twenty-first birthday, I left Mami's house, the rhyme I sang as a child forgotten. . . . Martes ni te cases ni te embarques, ni de tu familia te apartes." The cultural code of this old saying (which she wrote in Spanish) would be lost had Santiago translated it into English. At the same time, the reference to her twenty-first birthday is also important for it marks a rite of passage within Anglo culture—a culture with which she is painfully familiar as a Puerto Rican, who was raised in the United States. Both sets of codes work in this piece to position the author within both cultures. Finally, bilingualism (as a practice in U.S. ethnic literature) provides a tool by which the lives of the members of ethnic communities are highlighted and the reality they live within the broader society is problematized.

Further Reading

Castillo, Ana. *Massacre of the Dreamers: Essays on Xicanisma*. New York: Plume, 1994.

Esteves, Sandra María. *Contrapunto: In the Open Field*. New York: No Frills Publication, 2001.

Hernandez Mora, Judith. "La literature Chicana: Mas alla del ingles y el espanol." *Double Crossings: Entrecruzamientos*. Ed. Mario Martin Flores and Carlos von Son. New Jersey: Ediciones Nuevo Espacio, 2001. 193–98.

Moraga, Cherríe. *Loving in the War Years: Lo que nunca pasó por sus labios*. Cambridge: South End Press, 2001.

Carmen R. Lugo-Lugo

BLACK ARTS MOVEMENT   The Black Arts Movement (BAM) lasted from approximately 1965 until 1976. Its inception has been associated with poet-social critic **Amiri Baraka**'s 1965 founding of the Black Arts Repertory Theatre in Harlem and with Fisk University's 1967 Second Black Writers' Conference, at which many BAM writers first connected. The BAM was the second major twentieth-century movement, after the **Harlem Renaissance** (HR), in which African American writers and visual artists sought to define black creativity. Both the BAM and the concurrent Black Power Movement operated under the auspices of a black aesthetic. Black Power participants were committed to the concrete ways, such as the Black Panther Party's free-breakfast program in which black solidarity enabled independence from mainstream institutions. BAM members argued through their writing and visual creations that art was a means of affirming black cultural elements. Both groups articulated their notion of a black aesthetic through political statements, distinctive rhetoric, and black-nationalist sentiments. For the BAM creative activities served to publicize debates about black **identity** and American **race** relations.

In part the BAM extended the work of the HR. Commentators have described it as both a project that started where HR efforts ended and an attempt to revise the assimilationist attitude of some 1920s artists. BAM participants shared social perspectives with HR artists, including beliefs in the unique qualities of black creativity and in art's potential for expressing political views. Writers from both movements experimented with linguistic and thematic innovations, as in **Jean Toomer**'s *Cane* (1923) and poet **Sonia Sanchez**'s *We a BaddDDD People* (1970). However, BAM writers, particularly the poets, found public performances of their works and broadsides of individual pieces an effective way of communicating with a large audience.

Poetry dominated BAM writing, perhaps because it was relatively short and easy to publish. It also represented a malleable forum for political critique. The **Civil Rights Movement** of the 1950s forms an important historical backdrop to the BAM. The social and legal advances gained during that period seemed to lessen in the face of following events: the assassination of **Malcolm X**, the crimes committed against Mississippi's Freedom Riders and voter registration organizations, and FBI investigations of writers with "seditious" leanings. Sonia Sanchez was under surveillance after she supposedly taught subversive materials, although in 1969 she helped to found the country's first Black Studies Department and taught the first college seminar on literature by African American women. BAM poets explored the limits of American democracy and defied conventional decorum in books such as **Nikki Giovanni**'s *Black Feeling, Black Talk/Black Judgment* (1968), **Haki Madhubuti**'s *Don't Cry, Scream* (1969), **Larry Neal**'s *Hoodoo Hollerin' Bebop Ghosts* (1968), and **Carolyn Rodgers**'s *Songs of a Blackbird* (1969).

Several BAM poets participated in writing collectives. The Umbra writers' workshop, a short-lived group that included **Tom Dent**, Calvin Hernton, and **Ishmael Reed**, emphasized the productive directions in which writing could shape the black aesthetic; they published *Umbra Magazine* and introduced live performance to BAM associates. Some members of the Beats, such as **Jack Kerouac**, imitated the performance techniques popularized by Baraka and Sanchez, unconsciously parodying as well as paying tribute to BAM innovations. Such innovations also overlapped with the experimental creations of high-modernist and Language poets. BAM writers provided a structural bridge between avant-garde movements and unsettled the concept of "black poetry."

The BAM included dramatists, novelists, and essayists who interrogated the movement's politics. **Adrienne Kennedy**'s play *Funnyhouse of a Negro* (1964) examines the spiraling effects of racist social relations. Several books also commented on the BAM's effectiveness: Ishmael Reed's novel *Mumbo Jumbo* (1972), **Alice Walker**'s novel *Meridian* (1976), and Michele Wallace's cultural study *Black Macho and the Myth of the Superwoman* (1978). These works identify the sources of BAM activism and its drawbacks. In the mid-1970s a split between political activists and artists as well as government manipulations led to the BAM's dissolution. Its legacy endures in the efforts of later African American writers to reconcile past social and creative triumphs with future goals.

Further Reading

Salaam, Kalamu ya. "Black Arts Movement." *The Oxford Companion to African American Literature*. Ed. William L. Andrews, Frances Smith Foster, and Trudier Harris. New York and Oxford: Oxford UP, 1997. 70–74.

Smith, David Lionel. "Black Arts Movement." *Encyclopedia of African-American Culture and History*. Vol. I. Ed. Jack Salzman, David Lionel Smith, and Cornel West. New York: Simon & Schuster Macmillan, 1996. 325–32.

Thompson, Julius E. *Dudley Randall, Broadside Press, and the Black Arts Movement in Detroit, 1960–1995*. Jefferson, NC, and London: McFarland, 1999.

Jennifer D. Ryan

BLACK BOY   **Richard Wright**'s *Black Boy* (1945 [expurgated], 1991 [unexpurgated]) is one of the most distinguished autobiographies ever written by an American author. Its plot centers on the author's experiences from childhood to early adulthood, as those experiences were shaped and interpreted by Wright's powerful imagination. As a child growing up in a family abandoned by his father, Wright relied largely on himself to fight off a world that tried to control him. For instance, he took his father's words to make a cat that was keeping him awake shut up literally, to gain a victory over someone who was more powerful than he, but his mother cited hellfire as a possible punishment for his deed. Also particularly notable in the early part of the book are: his jumping ahead twenty-five years to report that he did not turn out like his father (an ignorant sharecropper in Wright's view); his insulting his maternal grandmother by telling her to kiss his ass; his rejection of her Seventh-Day Adventism; his early efforts at becoming a writer; his experiences at an optical factory; and his brief sexual adventure with Bess Moss in Memphis, Tennessee.

Part Two, perhaps less inspired than the first part, concerns Wright's experiences in Chicago, where he joins the Communist Party and begins his writing career in earnest. He is surprised when a Jewish couple he works for is hurt when he lies about why he was absent one day—in the South his white employers would have expected him to lie. In another job, after witnessing the Finnish cook spit in the soup, he debates with himself whether he should report it or not, and then decides to tell a young black woman who also works at the restaurant to report the incident, because he knows she is more likely to be believed than he is. Crucial to Wright's literary development during the early stage of his career is his joining the John Reed Club, which provided him with a sympathetic audience for his early work and also espoused a political philosophy, communism that embraced racial equality. Unfortunately, the Communist Party began telling the young author how to write, which eventually led to his resignation from it.

Major themes in *Black Boy* include his struggle for selfhood against the white and the black communities—Wright accepted very little external authority, particularly when it was contrary to his own desires or based on something other than truth. For example, he rejected the authority of his maternal grandmother's church because he felt it was based on wish-fulfillment rather than evidence. He rejected his relatives' authority because it was based on tradition. Perhaps the presiding theme in the book is hunger (it was originally titled *American Hunger*), hunger not only for food but also for life itself—knowledge, love, experience, travel, friends, language, education. Because so much in his environment thwarted these desires, Wright was constantly struggling to satisfy what it did not. Another key theme is literacy, which he early realized, as so many other black writers have, would greatly increase his leverage on the white world. An unfortunate subconscious theme is the author's concern that his white readers not identify him with poor black people, whom he sometimes seems to see through white eyes; that is, he sometimes looks *at* rather than *with* poor black people, especially poor black women. Another key theme is his complete rejection of the white South's construction of him as subhuman; it claimed to know him but it misconstrued his silence as agreement on Wright's part, whereas it was only a survival strategy.

Black Boy has had a profound impact on subsequent writers. In particular Wright's condemnation of the black community early in Chapter 2, although placed within parentheses in two paragraphs, has drawn comment from other writers, including **Ralph Ellison** and **Houston A. Baker Jr.**, both of whom have taken strong issue with Wright. Ellison pointed out that he found the black community a rich source for his own writing; Baker also challenges the accuracy of Wright's view. In any case, Wright's autobiography is well worth reading and is in many ways his best book. (*See also* African American Autobiography)

Further Reading

Andrews, William, and Douglas Taylor, eds. *Richard Wright's "Black Boy": A Casebook*. New York: Oxford UP, 2003.

Fabre, Michel. *The Unfinished Quest of Richard Wright*. 2nd ed. Urbana: U of Illinois P, 1993.

Felgar, Robert. *Student Companion to Richard Wright*. Westport, CT: Greenwood Press, 2000.

Robert Felgar

BLACK ELK [HEHAKA SAPA] (1863–1950) Oglala Lakota Spiritual Healer. Black Elk is most widely known for his memoir *Black Elk Speaks*

(1932) narrated to poet John G. Neihardt. Although not widely read at first, the memoir became a major cultural staple in the 1970s, crucial both to young Native American activists and counter-cultural Euro-American youths. *Black Elk Speaks* is considered the most important religious text of the twentieth century.

Black Elk met John G. Neihardt in 1930 while the Nebraskan poet was seeking information about the Ghost Dance. Black Elk agreed to talk with him if Neihardt would return the following summer to record the older man's memoir. Black Elk wished to share his life story and vision with the world.

Although Black Elk's memoir includes his observations of key historical events of the nineteenth century, the vision he experienced as a child is considered the most significant portion of the book. In the memoir Black Elk explains that around the age of six he began hearing voices. This was not particularly unusual since he had been born into a long line of *wicasa wakan*, or spiritual healers. At nine Black Elk fell into a twelve-day coma, during which he experienced "The Great Vision."

In this vision, Black Elk is approached by two spirit beings who provide him with a beautiful bay horse to ride and four dozen horses, whose colors correspond to the four cardinal directions of the compass, that accompany him on his spiritual journey to the center of the world. When he arrives he meets with six old Grandfathers who reveal to him the destiny of the Lakota people through a series of four ascensions up a sacred mountain, which Black Elk understands to mean he is seeing four generations into the future. The old Grandfathers provide him with a series of sacred objects and give him instructions to help him ensure that the tree of life would continue to flower.

In addition to describing this vision and working out its interpretation throughout his life, Black Elk recounts many other key episodes in his life. In 1876 at the age of thirteen he participated in the defeat of General Custer at the Battle of Little Big Horn. At nineteen he consulted with an older *wicasa wakan* who helped him better understand the vision that had haunted him for ten years. Following the advice of this healer, Black Elk performed the necessary rituals and took his place as a healer among his people.

In 1886, restless and still haunted by what he had seen in his vision, Black Elk joined Buffalo Bill Cody's Wild West Show to learn more about Euro-American culture and compare it with his own. He traveled to New York and to England, where he performed before Queen Victoria. Black Elk continued his travels through Italy, Germany, and France, twice reporting back to his people through letters that were published in the local Lakota language newspaper.

Upon his return to South Dakota in 1889, Black Elk participated in the Ghost Dance, the religious revival that was sweeping across the plains, and he witnessed the massacre at Wounded Knee in 1890. In the wake of this tragedy, Black Elk rode with the warriors seeking revenge and later partici-pating in the eventual surrender.

In addition to his memoir, Black Elk later provided Neihardt with stories about Lakota history and culture, which was published as *When the Tree Flowered* (1951). Religious scholar John Epes Brown also interviewed Black Elk and published *The Sacred Pipe* (1953), which outlines seven of the major rituals central to Lakota spiritual life.

Much critical debate surrounds *Black Elk Speaks*. One aspect of this debate focuses on the degree to which Neihardt intervened in Black Elk's narra-tive. The publication of interview transcripts in Raymond DeMallie's *The Sixth Grandfather: Black Elk's Teachings Given to John Neihardt* (1984) allows contemporary students of Black Elk to compare the two texts for them-selves. Another aspect of the debate involves the degree to which Black Elk's memoir was influenced by his conversion to Roman Catholicism in 1904. The many parallels Black Elk draws between Christianity and Lakota religious tradition in *The Sacred Pipe* suggest he viewed both belief systems as compatible and consistent with broader spiritual truths. (*See also* Native American Autobiography)

Further Reading

Deloria, Vine, Jr., ed. *A Sender of Words: Essays in Memory of John G. Neihardt*. Salt Lake City: Howe, 1984.

Fleck, Richard F. "Black Elk Speaks: A Native American View of Nineteenth-Century American History." *Journal of American Culture* 17.1 (1994): 67–69.

Jennifer A. Gehrman

BLACK NATIONALISM It is an ideology that developed from African Americans' realization of a shared history of origin, enslavement, degrada-tion, oppression, and **racism** in America. Positing the existence of a white and black America, different versions of black nationalism aimed to forge a collective **identity** among African Americans; achieve **race** consciousness, pride, and unity; and preserve a distinct cultural heritage. In the antebellum period, **slave narratives** described Africans' removal from Africa and their ensuing enslavement, exploitation, and alienation in America as well as their escape from bondage to freedom. The end of the Civil War and the ratifica-tion of the Thirteenth, Fourteenth, and Fifteenth Amendments to the U.S. Constitution failed to bring a real sense of freedom and justice to blacks. The first thrust of nationalism emerged in a number of self-help organizations that later developed true ideologies of black nationalism in search of social, economic, and political rights. For example, in 1881 **Booker T. Washington** founded the Tuskegee Institute, a technical and vocational school focusing on self-help, manual labor, and trades. For him, blacks needed to achieve economic development before they could agitate for political rights. His contemporary **W. E. B. Du Bois** disagreed with this ideology and con-demned what he called Washington's accommodationist approach, on the ground that it amounted to denying blacks their constitutional rights, undermining their self-worth, and perpetuating the stereotype of black inferiority.

During the **Harlem Renaissance**, black writers and artists promoted the idea of a new black person. **Alain Locke**'s "The **New Negro**" (1925), considered the manifesto of the movement, maintained that the Negro was a new person having undergone transformation as a result of transplantation, generally from the South to northern cities, especially to Harlem. Through this transformation the black person had also gained more race consciousness and pride. In the same period, **Marcus Garvey**, a native of Jamaica, promoted the idea of self-help and black nationalism in America and the African diaspora. Through his organization, the Universal Negro Improvement Association, he advocated black unity, race consciousness and pride, self-help, and a return to Africa. The use of the black vernacular, folklore, and themes by the likes of **Langston Hughes** and **Zora Neale Hurston** signaled a sustained effort to establish a cultural black nation within the larger American culture.

In the 1940s and 1950s, **Richard Wright, James Baldwin, Ralph Ellison**, and **Lorraine Hansberry**, among many others, showed in their works that blacks lived in segregated communities away from white neighborhoods. Crossing from one to another was like crossing dangerous borders—in *Native Son*, **Bigger Thomas** learned this reality at his own expense. These writers did not profess separatism, but they certainly explored the reality of cultural, economic, and political separation between black and white America.

The end of World War II, to which African Americans had contributed significantly, brought a strong sense of disappointment, which translated into multiple social forces agitating for civil rights. This struggle known as the **Civil Rights Movement** culminated in the 1960s. This was also a period during which associations, movements, and groups driven by militant black nationalism flourished. The **Black Arts Movement** (BAM), for example, was a nationalist literary movement that celebrated blackness in its diverse manifestations. In its demand for social justice, equality, and end to oppression, it called for black unity with a strong sense of urgency best expressed in **Amiri Baraka**'s short poem "SOS," potently sounding a distress message calling all black people to unite in order to fight for their rights because, it is suggested, it is now a question of life and death. The BAM rejected the white aesthetic, strongly advocated cultural separatism, and called black artists to be at the service of the black community.

Founded in 1930 by Wallace Dodd Fard, the Nation of Islam was another organization with a strong following in the 1960s. Appealing to race consciousness and pride, it promised to solve the socioeconomic problems facing blacks. Under its second leader, Elijah Muhammad, the organization preached black superiority and separation from white America (described as fundamentally evil) and rejected Christian manipulation of blacks. **Malcolm X** was one of its best-known spokespersons in the 1950s and early

1960s, until he separated from the organization to form his own. Since then he rejected the characterization of all whites as evil and welcomed their help but gave them no membership in his organization. In a speech he delivered in Cleveland, Ohio, in 1964, Malcolm X articulated his view of black nationalism. In "The Ballot or the Bullet," he called for unity among blacks, regardless of religious affiliation, in the fight against the white man's oppression. He affirmed that he did not consider himself and other blacks as Americans, but Africans who happened to be in America. He defined his ideology from the political, economic, and social angles. On the political aspect, he meant that blacks had to be educated in how to choose politicians who would truly represent their aspirations. From the economic perspective, blacks had to control the economy of their community by owning its stores, businesses, and industries and by spending their money there. On the social level, Malcolm X asked blacks to get rid of social evils such as alcoholism, prostitution, and drugs that diminished their dignity and destroyed the black community.

After the revolutionary 1960s, cultural separatism continued to play a role in African American culture, life, and literature. Even though writers such as **Ishmael Reed**, **Toni Morrison**, **Alice Walker**, **Charles Johnson**, **John Wideman**, **Ernest Gaines**, **Terry McMillan**, and many others in the period after 1970 cannot be said to be separatists, they nevertheless show unprecedented concern for African American communities, focusing on African American history, culture, and life as these were shaped by the shared past of **slavery**, segregation, and racism and creating a broader sense of blackness that encompasses the African **diaspora**.

Further Reading

Carlisle, Rodney P. *The Roots of Black Nationalism*. Port Washington, NY: Kennikat Press, 1975.

Robinson, Dean E. *Black Nationalism in American Politics and Thought*. Cambridge: Cambridge UP, 2001.

Aimable Twagilimana

BLAESER, KIMBERLY M. (1955–) Native American Indian poet, fiction writer, essayist, editor, and scholar. Widely published not only as a poet, but also as a writer of short fiction and personal and scholarly essays, Kimberly Blaeser was named 2002 Wordcrafter of the Year by the Word Craft Circle of Native Writers and Storytellers. Of mixed Anishinaabe and German descent, Blaeser grew up on the White Earth Chippewa Reservation in northwestern Minnesota. She earned her doctorate at the University of Notre Dame in 1990 and teaches literature and creative writing at the University of Wisconsin-Milwaukee. Blaeser is the author of two collections of poetry, *Trailing You* (1994), winner of the First Book Award of the Native Writers Circle of the Americas, and *Absentee Indians and Other Poems* (2002). She also has written the first book-length scholarly study of a single Native American Indian author, *Gerald Vizenor: Writing in the Oral Tradition*

(1996) and edited *Stories Migrating Home: A Collection of Anishinaabe Prose* (1998). Her work has been included in such important anthologies as *Returning the Gift* and *Earth Song, Sky Spirit*.

Blaeser is profoundly concerned with what it means to write Native American literature in the contemporary world of Barbie dolls and diamond engagement rings. For Blaeser, this does not mean restricting herself to recognizably or stereotypically Indian subjects such as boarding schools or fetal alcohol syndrome. Rather it means connecting through language to life as she finds it, whether on her way to a powwow or in bed with her cat. Blaeser's poems are often linked to the natural world. Grounded in the tribal oral tradition, they are filled with voices and relationships—the voices of family, neighbors, strangers, friends, and even voices of ice. "Speaking Those Names" offers a key to the Native world view that finds expression in her work. Blaeser begins with a series of self-images,

Kimberly Blaeser. *Photo by Vance Vannote. Courtesy of Kimberly Blaeser.*

verbal snapshots of the many people she has been since her childhood. Then she recites her life-list of nicknames, continuing a tribal tradition that finds a story in every name and a new name in a better story. Each name calls a specific self into being and celebrates a quintessential moment of relationship with the name's remembered speaker. More than this, the poem celebrates the process of change that is life itself.

In her first book Blaeser confronts the ironies of contemporary Indian life, including its total invisibility to many Americans. She moves casually between the reservation and urban America, but as she does so, she affirms fundamental, but not unbridgeable, differences between them. In "Waking to Dreams" she explores the difference within the context of her own marriage, as her husband slowly comes to understand the reality of dreams in the Native world. Time is circular, not linear, and Blaeser sees history return in the present moment, not only in "Living History" when she is mistaken for her mother, but also when, like naturalist John Muir, she punctures her eye in Muir's beloved Sierras. Blaeser celebrates her mixedblood **identity** forged through a nexus of family ties, but her most profound concern is to locate human life in the context of the greater web of life. How, she wonders in "Don't Send Me Any Surveys," can she pin her identity down in the fixed categories of a questionnaire any more than a butterfly, whose life, beginning as a cocoon, is a continuing transformation? An amateur nature photographer, Blaeser shares in her poems her careful regard for the natural world, a world that all living beings ultimately disappear into.

In her second book, Blaeser claims her identity as an Indian who, like so many others, lives off the reservation and returns only for visits. As the text evolves, Blaeser's definition of *absentee Indian* expands to include many who have died, including all the suicided Indians. She understands the traditional power of the word to give them tangible presence. Seldom using the pronoun *I*, she remains almost an absent presence in poems that touch the most intimate moments of a woman's life—the death of her mother and the birth of her first child. Life, she suggests, is never more precious than when it is entwined with death, part of a continuing cycle. In "Your Old Lost Loves" she shares her mother's identity. It is a bittersweet prelude to a series of poems celebrating her new motherhood and the voice of her infant son. As Blaeser ends her book, poems of presence and absence begin to alternate, vibrating like complementary colors until afterimages appear. (*See also* Native American Poetry)

Linda Lizut Helstern

BLATTY, WILLIAM PETER (1928–)   Arab American novelist, screenwriter, producer, and director. Prior to gaining international success with his first major foray into horror and the occult with his novel and screenplay *The Exorcist* (1971), Blatty tuned into the complex problems of ethnic identification in an American entertainment industry known for commodifying **Arab American stereotypes**.

The youngest son of Lebanese immigrants, Blatty was raised in New York City primarily by his mother, a woman who attempted to support the family by selling jars of her homemade quince jelly to the rich and powerful. In his first major work, *Which Way to Mecca, Jack?* (1960), Blatty turns to his upbringing to give an autobiographical account of his humiliation at being from a working-class immigrant family and feeling like an outsider in his own country. Always couched in comedy, satire, and verging on the burlesque, Blatty describes being the victim of racial and ethnic slurs as a child, and then going to Hollywood as a young adult, only to be turned away for not looking "American" enough. Like other texts written by ethnic minority authors—**James Weldon Johnson**'s *Autobiography of an Ex-Colored Man* (1912) and **Nella Larsen**'s *Passing* (1929), for example—in Blatty's early autobiography, attempts to "pass" into white culture were hypostasized challenges to both the dominant order as well as his own sense of tradition, lineage, and culture. He writes, "I've got a big fat scar on my id from that time Hollywood rejected me. Now I've got to make them accept me. I want to be 'in'! Only I have no intention of undergoing plastic surgery and looking like the All-American boy. It's Will-yam the Arab I want them to dig." Blatty poses as a famous Arab prince, complete with an alias, and tropes on conventional orientalist stereotypes of the exotic Arab entrepreneur in order to enter into dialogue with notables in the movie industry. Having displayed his ability to play the part, Blatty, according to the autobiography, convinces his Hollywood interlocutors to take a second look at his screenwriting talents.

One can locate an intriguing hinge in Blatty's work in which the early satiric investigations of ethnic **identity** get linked with the thick interrogation of religious morals that dominate his later work. His 1963 comedic novel *John Goldfarb, Please Come Home* tells the story of a former football coach for Notre Dame, turned American pilot, crash-landing in a mythical Arab country. The pilot is forced to train the king's football squad, a team whose description is laden with orientalist stereotype, so they can challenge Notre Dame in a football face-off. At a subtextual level, not only are the Arab figures satirized, but so too are the religious morals at the heart of the Roman Catholic university. Blatty's screenplay was turned into a major motion picture in 1965, but was entangled in a series of suits brought by officials at Notre Dame and ended up being a commercial failure.

Blatty's next major project *The Exorcist* is the one for which he is most widely known. The novel and subsequent film leave behind the world of comedic satire in which burlesque representations of ethnic stereotype challenge conventional cultural norms. Instead, Blatty plumbs the depths of religious belief, representing the ways the scientific and the spiritual are often at odds. He constructs a narrative in which a young girl is possessed by the devil and turned into a murderous monster. The bulk of the tale revolves around the means utilized by the girl's family and several Roman Catholic priests to exorcise the devil.

The novel and film have both been massive commercial successes, and have shaped the popular genre where the supernatural and the horrific are intertwined. *The Exorcist* is a long way from Blatty's earlier comedic work. However, as he notes in his recent books on the making of *The Exorcist*, the money that Blatty used to support himself while writing the novel was won during an episode of Groucho Marx's "Quiz Show" in the late 1960s. On the show Blatty again posed as a stereotypical Arab sheikh. He completely fooled Marx, came away the champion of the show after revealing his true identity, and promptly began work on the novel of a lifetime. (*See also* Arab American Novel)

Further Reading
Shakir, Evelyn. "Arab Mothers, American Sons: Women in Arab-American Autobiographies," *MELUS* 17.3 (Autumn 1991): 5–15.

Keith Feldman

BLESS ME, ULTIMA   First published in 1972, **Rudolfo Anaya**'s *Bless Me, Ultima* remains a seminal text in Chicano literature. A modified Mexican

American bildungsroman, the novel tells the story of Antonio Márez Luna from the age of six (almost seven) to eight and his first two years of schooling. The setting is Anaya's own New Mexico in the post-war 1940s with its dense mixture of Anglo and Mexican cultures. Narrated in the first person in young Antonio's voice, the story is told through flashbacks from the adult Antonio's memories and through his childhood dreams, indicated in the text by italics.

The novel begins with the arrival of Ultima. Ultima (the "last") is a *curandera*, or folk healer, though some would call her a witch. Indeed, religion versus witchcraft is one of the novel's themes. Antonio and his family are Catholics, and his mother is particularly devout, yet they respect the ancient wisdom that Ultima exemplifies and teaches to Antonio.

Preoccupied with his future, Antonio reflects on the warring factions in his heritage—the land-loving Lunas from his mother's side and the wandering Márez from his father's side, or the "moon" versus the "seas" (*mares*). His mother sees him as a priest, while his father dreams of moving to California with his sons. Antonio's three brothers have just returned from the war, disenchanted, embittered, and unbelieving. Antonio attends mass faithfully and makes his first communion, but he also learns to honor the natural world, most strongly symbolized by the "golden carp," a pagan "god" occasionally sighted in the local river.

The Spanish-speaking Antonio fearfully begins school and soon realizes that he is an outsider, someone who brings a lunch wrapped in tortillas instead of bread. But he finds a group of friends and quickly learns the "magic in the letters." He is a successful student, but his learning through experience with Ultima is even greater. She teaches him the use of medicinal herbs and uses him as a medium for curing his uncle Lucas. In her battle with the witch Tenorio and his devil-worshiping daughters responsible for the curse on Lucas, Ultima resorts to rites of the Catholic Church as well as the rituals of her trade. She demonstrates a power beyond that of the local priest. Ultima wins, but Tenorio destroys her by shooting her magical owl. He is killed in turn by Antonio's uncle Pedro. Despite his youth, Antonio experiences death and witnesses many battles: the battle between the Lunas and the Márezes, between Ultima and Tenorio, and between good and evil.

In 1971 *Bless Me, Ultima* received the second annual Quinto Sol national Chicano literary award. The novel remains the best-selling Chicano novel ever published. Widely used in both high school and college classrooms, the novel has received and continues to garner substantial critical attention.

Further Reading

Mitchell, Carol. "Rudolfo Anaya's *Bless Me, Ultima*: Folk Culture in Literature." *Critique* 22.1 (1980): 55–64.

Vasallo, Paul, ed. *The Magic of Words: Rudolfo A. Anaya and His Writings.* Albuquerque: U of New Mexico P, 1982.

Linda Ledford-Miller

BLOOM, HAROLD IRVING (1930–)   Jewish American essayist, literary critic, and university professor (currently Sterling Professor of Humanities at Yale University, Berg Professor of English at New York University, and a former Charles Eliot Norton Professor at Harvard). Although his defense of the High Romantic poets gave him a great reputation as a critic, his controversial *The Western Canon* (1994) definitely made him a household name. He regards Northrop Frye as the model and precursor of his theorizations and argues that the study of literature has incorrectly displaced seminal authors such as Shakespeare, Dante, and Cervantes under the pretext that they do not belong to ethnic or minority groups from where people can obtain a sense of self-identification. In *Shakespeare: The Invention of the Human* (National Book Award finalist in 1998), he elevates the English playwright to the highest place in literature and considers him as the most multicultural author, since he has been translated to almost every language, his works have been widely staged, and his stories told throughout the world.

Bloom lived in the East Bronx until he began his undergraduate years at Cornell University (BA in 1951), and earned his PhD from Yale University four years later. That same year he was offered to stay as a faculty member and started a prolific career as a scholar with more than twenty books ranging from anthropology to literary criticism. He has been awarded several fellowships and received distinctions for his career contributions, namely the Guggenheim Fellowship, the MacArthur Foundation Fellowship in 1985, and the American Academy of Arts and Letters Gold Medal for Criticism in 1999.

In 2000, after the venture of his both highly praised and criticized canonical theory, came *How to Read and Why* (a title indebted to an essay by Ezra Pound), which the author considered as the necessary complement to his 1994 project on what to read. For Bloom, the new literary education unfortunately aims at a "Theory of Resentment," an asseveration that has provoked many accusations of **racism** rooted in the issue of minority segregation. There is a big pressure, he pointed out in an interview, exerted on black and Hispanic students who isolate themselves as a group instead of following his statement that authentic literature doesn't divide people since it addresses itself to the solitary individual or consciousness. Although he frequently expresses in his interviews a hope for future reexamination of aesthetic values, he is still highly critical of the current state of academia and his colleagues. He has spent bitter words to describe academics as charlatans, self-deceivers, and the deceivers of others.

A fierce scholar of the **canon**ical cultural heritage, he entwines his ideas from the theory of literature to the study of religion. He ascribes the very essence of Judaism that directly or indirectly reached the first Rabbis to the writings of Plato. *Kabbalah and Criticism* (1983) and *Literature of the Holocaust* (2003) show the critical train of thought that Bloom has developed throughout the last two decades. In one of his best sellers, *The Book of J* (1990), he coedited with David Rosenberg a translation of some parts of the oldest books of the Bible and an analysis that supports the hypothesis of their female authorship by J, an initial that has conventionally stood for God as Jahweh, Yahweh, or Jehovah and that Bloom attributes to an aristocratic woman in the generation after King Solomon's death.

Among the traditional genres, poetry constitutes Bloom's primary object of initiation in literature. In *The Anxiety of Influence: A Theory of Poetry* (1973), he described the need to reach the sublime and the agonistic as the necessary step in order to truly appreciate literature. From his point of view, only under these conditions is the reader able to discover preferences for one or another poem, a process that he equals to the act of creation since within a poem the ability to exclude other poems constitutes its main strength. Generally his works pay tribute to individualism and has declared that history has provided us with three prophecies about the death of individual art whose authors' legacy (Hegel, Marx, and Freud) is impossible to overcome.

An enthusiast of literary rankings, in 2003 Bloom considered Portuguese writer Jose Saramago as the most gifted novelist alive in the world today (*Genius: A Mosaic of One Hundred Exemplary Creative Minds*) and has ranked four Americans—Thomas Pynchon, Philip Roth, Cormac McCarthy, and Don DeLillo—as those who defend "the Style of our Age."

Further Reading

Allen, Graham. *Harold Bloom: Poetics of Conflict*. New York: Harvester Wheatsheaf, 1994.

"*Choice* Interviews: Harold Bloom Interviewed by Terry Farish." *Choice* 32.6 (February 1995): 899–901.

Moynihan, Robert. *A Recent Imagining: Interviews with Harold Bloom, Geoffrey Hartman, J. Hillis Miller, Paul De Man*. Hamden, CT: Archon Books, 1989.

Yolanda Morató

BLUES, THE   A form of African American vocal music, the blues started out rural but later turned urban. As its name suggests, the general character of this music is sad and mournful. Because the blues reflect the uniqueness of the African American experience, they have exercised a profound influence on black literature. Poets have written blues poetry, fiction writers and dramatists have used blues musicians as characters, and critics have developed a "blues aesthetic."

Form

The following is the first verse of the "St. Louis Blues" (1914) written by an anonymous composer at a time when the blues were still a form of folk music. The melody and words were first transcribed by the black cornet player and bandleader W. C. Handy.

> I hate to see de ev'nin' sun go down,
> Hate to see dat ev'nin' sun go down,
> 'Cause ma baby, he done lef' dis town.

This verse illustrates the standard twelve-bar blues pattern consisting of three lines (AAB), with the first line repeated with a slight variation and the third line resolving or explaining the first two. Early blues also came in two other forms, some in an eight-bar AB pattern and some in a sixteen-bar AAAB pattern; but all blues shared a call-and-response structure, that is, two-bar vocal statements alternating with two-bar instrumental responses. Originally, the instrumental responses were played by the blues singers themselves on their guitars; in later blues they were played by accompanying musicians on their horns.

Melodically the two unique traits of the blues are a standard chord progression and the use of so-called blue notes. All twelve-bar blues follow the same basic chord progression, which in the key of C looks like this:

C / C / C / C7 / F / F / C / C / B-flat / B-flat / C / C

Blues singers and instrumentalists tend to stress "blue notes" to give the blues their mournful character. They are the flatted third and flatted seventh notes of a diatonic scale. In the key of C, they are E-flat and B-flat. Moreover, blues musicians like to squeeze these notes so that they wind up either a quarter step sharp or flat.

The themes of the blues fit the mournful character of the music. Early country blues deal mostly with unhappy love and personal misfortune, while later urban blues often reflect social injustice and white oppression. For example, the first urban blues ever recorded, Mamie Smith's "Crazy Blues" (1920), begins like a typical unhappy love number with the singer saying that she can't sleep at night because the man she loves doesn't treat her right. But this blues ends with a vision of racial violence because in the next-to-last verse the singer releases her frustration by fantasizing that she might get herself crazy on hop (opium), get herself a gun, and shoot herself a cop.

Although the lyrics of Mamie Smith's "Crazy Blues" reveal black people's dislike of the white police, they do not refer to any particular social injustice. However, many blues do. An example is Bessie Smith's "Poor Man Blues" (1928). The singer of that blues addresses a rich man who lives in a mansion but pays his workers so little that they are practically starving. She reminds the rich man that the poor man fought in World War I for him, and she ends by asking, "If it wasn't for the poor man, mister rich man, what would you do?"

History

In their early development, the blues were intimately connected with **jazz**; in fact, the first recorded blues was the instrumental "Livery Stable Blues" (1917) by the Original Dixieland Jazz Band. Moreover, classic blues singers were usually accompanied by jazz musicians, and to this day instrumental blues continue to be an important part of jazz. Nevertheless, vocal blues and jazz eventually parted company.

Musicologists believe that the first blues were sung in the 1890s by itinerant male musicians who accompanied themselves on guitars. However, this kind of country blues was not recorded until the late 1920s. Major early blues figures were Charlie Patton, Blind Lemon Jefferson, and Huddie Leadbetter. In the early 1920s, most of the recorded vocal blues were sung by female singers. The blues now became very popular; in fact, during the late 1920s and early 1930s, a veritable blues craze swept the country, and singers such as Ma Rainey, Bessie Smith, and Ida Cox sold millions of records. Bessie Smith even appeared in an early sound movie. But in the middle 1930s, big band Swing music became the new fad, and the blues lost much of their popularity. However, the black big bands of Jay McShann, Fletcher Henderson, and Count Basie continued to feature "blues shouters" such as Jimmy Witherspoon, Jimmy Rushing, and Joe Turner who mostly sang up-tempo blues.

During the 1940s when Swing turned into Be-Bop, vocal blues separated from jazz and turned into rhythm and blues. Over the years the rhythm and blues designation has been applied to a number of different kinds of popular black music. The originators of rhythm and blues were the former jazz musician Louis Jordan and his Tympany Five whose trademark sounds were a stomping beat, a wailing electric guitar, and a screeching saxophone. Other early rhythm and blues musicians were Fats Domino, Little Richard, and Chuck Berry. Their music had a great influence on Elvis Presley, Jerry Lee Lewis, and other white musicians who transformed black rhythm and blues into white rock and roll. This is why we can find twelve-bar blues patterns in many songs of later rock and roll bands such as the Beatles, the Rolling Stones, and even the Beach Boys.

When the more popular forms of black music in the 1960s and 1970s—soul, funk, and Motown—moved far away from the blues, musicians such B. B. King and Muddy Waters tried to keep the traditional twelve-bar blues alive. This was not easy. B. B. King reports that at a 1960s concert, when he was opening for the rhythm and blues star Jackie Wilson, the black audience tried to boo him off the stage. They simply had no interest in traditional blues because they considered them a backward form of music. But since the 1980s and 1990s, there has been a small revival of the blues. Black blues musicians can again find work in small clubs, both black and white; but at blues concerts, the audiences are mostly white.

The Blues and Literature

Unlike the African American community at large, black literary artists have always been aware of the cultural importance of the blues. Beginning in the 1920s and 1930s, the poets **Langston Hughes** and **Sterling Brown** have tried to create interest in the blues by writing blues poetry. Both wrote poems that have the classic three-line AAB format with an aaa rhyme scheme, and they also developed two other stanza forms. One of them breaks up each of the traditional three lines into two parts for a six-line stanza with an ababcb rhyme scheme. For another stanza form, Hughes and Brown eliminated the repetition of the first line in the traditional blues, and broke up the remaining two lines into two parts each. This resulted in a four-line stanza with an abcb rhyme. In some poems, Hughes and Brown used both the four-line and the six-line stanza forms, and they also inserted blues stanzas in some longer poems whose overall structures are not patterned after the blues. This happens in Langston Hughes' "Weary Blues" (1926) and in Sterling Brown's homage to the blues singer "Ma Rainey" (1931).

Because of the pioneering work of Langston Hughes and Sterling Brown, the blues have become an important part of African American poetry. There is hardly a black poet who has not used the word "blues" in the title of at least one poem. In addition, during the second half of the twentieth century many poets have written blues poems in three-line, four-line, or six-line formats. Among them are **Henry Dumas**, **Michael Harper**, **Robert Hayden**, LeRoi Jones (aka **Amiri Baraka**), Don L. Lee, **Sterling Plumpp**, **Sonia Sanchez**, A. B. Spellman, and **Al Young.**

The blues have also influenced African American fiction. Many stories and novels of black writers have a blues feeling to them, and some actually employ characters who are blues singers. For instance, in **Ralph Ellison's** *Invisible Man* (1952), the protagonist has an encounter with a blues singer who identifies himself as Peter Wheatstraw, an actual person who has over 160 records to his name; in **Alice Walker's** *The Color Purple* (1982), the protagonist's best friend Shug Avery is a blues singer; and in **Albert Murray's** *Train Whistle Guitar* (1974), **Gayl Jones's** *Corregidora* (1976), and **Clarence Major's** *Dirty Bird Blues* (1996), the protagonists themselves are blues singers.

African American drama is tinged with the blues as well. In LeRoi Jones's **Dutchman**, the central character makes this observation about the anger that he thinks smoldered inside the blues singer Bessie Smith: "If Bessie Smith had murdered some white people she wouldn't have needed that music." (35). A friend of LeRoi Jones's, the playwright Ed Bullins likes to specify that blues music be heard in the background of his plays (e.g., see *How Do You Do*, 1968); and **August Wilson,** who wrote a play about blues singer Ma Rainey that was produced on Broadway (*Ma Rainey's Black Bottom* [1984]), has said about himself that even though he doesn't play an instrument, he is "cut from the same cloth" as the great blues musicians.

The Blues Aesthetic

All along, black scholars have stressed the cultural importance of the blues, and they eventually developed a concept that has been called the "blues aesthetic." This is the idea that the blues express the racial feeling and vision of life that arises out of the collective life experiences of the African American community.

The most eloquent early expression of the blues aesthetic occurs in a 1945 essay by the novelist Ralph Ellison titled "Richard Wright's Blues." In that essay, Ellison says, "The blues is an impulse to keep the painful details and episodes of a brutal experience in one's aching consciousness, to finger its jagged grain, and to transcend it, not by the consolation of philosophy but by squeezing from it a near-tragic, near-comic lyricism" (90). This notion is expanded and given the status of an indigenous American aesthetic by Ellison's good friend, the scholar and novelist Albert Murray in his book *The Blue Devils of Nada: A Contemporary American Approach to Aesthetic Statement* (1996).

Another influential study of the blues aesthetic is **Houston Baker Jr.**'s *Blues, Ideology, and Afro-American Literature*. Baker gives a semiotic twist to the blues aesthetic when he says that "the blues . . . exist, not as a function of formal inscription, but as a forceful condition of Afro-American inscription," that is to say, "as a code radically conditioning Afro-America's cultural signifying" (3–4). Baker demonstrates how this code operates by analyzing prose works from **The Narrative of the Life of Frederick Douglass** (1845) to **Toni Morrison**'s *Song of Solomon* (1977).

More recently, Barbara Baker has studied manifestations of the blues aesthetic in the fiction of four Southern writers, three of them black and one of them white. In her book *The Blues Aesthetic and the Making of American Identity in the Literature of the South* (New York: Peter Lang, 2003), Baker includes the white antebellum humorist George Washington Harris because she believes his white characters can be understood only in terms of their interaction with African Americans. They therefore illustrate "the convergence of racial identification inherent in the national character" (5). Baker claims that her work extends a concept developed earlier by Ralph Ellison and Albert Murray. That concept is the "diffusion of blackness within whiteness which Ellison and Murray argue that blues music reflects" (5).

Further Reading

Baker, Barbara. *The Blues Aesthetic and the Making of American Identity in the Literature of the South.* New York: Peter Lang, 2003.

Baker, Houston, Jr. *Blues, Ideology, and Afro-American Literature.* Chicago: U of Chicago P, 1986.

Davis, Angela. *Blues Legacies and Black Feminism.* New York: Pantheon, 1998.

Ellison, Ralph. *Shadow and Act.* New York: Signet, 1964.

Jones, LeRoi. *Blues People: The Negro Experience in White America and the Music that Developed from It.* New York: Morrow, 1963.

———. *Dutchman.* New York: Morrow, 1964.

Oakley, Giles. *The Devil's Music: A History of the Blues.* New York: Taplinger, 1977.

Tracy, Stephen. *Langston Hughes and the Blues.* Urbana: U of Illinois P, 1988.

Eberhard Alsen

BLUEST EYE, THE   The first novel by Nobel Laureate **Toni Morrison**, *The Bluest Eye* (1970), scrutinizes the influence of a white-dominated culture and its politics of **racism** on the life of a young African American girl. Intent on exposing the absurdity of one group's imposition of unrealistic "beauty" standards on a community that can never measure up to such a benchmark, Morrison underlines the destructive notion inherent in a criterion that spurns "difference." Pecola Breedlove's obsession with blue eyes stems from her belief that if her eyes were "different, that is to say, beautiful, she herself would be different." Ironically enough, the "difference" Pecola longs for is, in fact, "sameness," a sameness that will enable her to escape the "ugliness" of the African American community and be absorbed into the "sanctity" of the dominant culture.

The Bluest Eye opens with an excerpt from a grade school primer painting a Rockwellean portrait of the perfect nuclear family. But as the passage is repeated, the ideal becomes distorted, the illusion broken. The lack of punctuation and spacing reflect just how far removed the black family is from the white experience. As the novel progresses, the disparity between the primer world and Pecola's own becomes glaringly obvious. In stark contrast to the "pretty" green and white primer house, the Breedlove house is an abandoned store littered with old furnishings. Pecola's mother, Pauline, is the antithesis to Jane's "nice," happy mother. Contrary to Jane's mother's idealized contentment, Pauline never laughs and her self-hatred is projected onto her daughter. Pecola's detachment from her mother is exemplified by the fact that she calls her "Mrs. Breedlove," even though the little Fisher girl affectionately refers to Pauline as "Polly." A far cry from the "strong," protective father figure of the primer, Pecola's father, Cholly, uses his strength to brutalize the innocent child he is supposed to shield from abuse. Raped and impregnated by her father, Pecola turns inward, and in her madness is convinced that she has been granted the gift of blue eyes.

Pecola's self-hatred and the African American community's rejection of her, Morrison contends, are symptomatic of a much larger issue—internalized racism. Taught to believe that the dominant culture is superior to their own, African Americans such as Pauline and Geraldine disparage anyone who does not typify the white ideal. So indoctrinated into white culture is Geraldine that she makes fracturing distinctions between members of her own **race** based on such spurious attributes as skin pigmentation and demeanor. The one character in the novel who does not internalize such false judgments is Claudia MacTeer.

Unlike Pecola, Frieda, and other characters in the novel, Claudia does not fall under the spell of white America. Not only does she resent the blue-eyed Shirley Temple's association with the African American Bojangles, but her hostility toward all little white girls culminates in her desire to torture their soft, pink flesh in childish retribution for the affection adults shower upon them and not her. Similarly, the young black girl is plagued by a need to dismember her white baby doll in an effort to discover its "dearness," to find in it the beauty that seems to elude only her. What Claudia discovers, however, is that the doll's beauty is, in fact, an illusion. Despite her young age, Claudia recognizes that the contempt she feels for the doll and all white or light-skinned girls is dictated by forces beyond her control. It is, in fact, Claudia's unmasking of the evils of the dominant culture, coupled with her tenacious and defiant nature, that enable her to escape Pecola's tragic fate.

Further Reading

Bouson, J. Brooks. *Quiet as It's Kept: Shame, Trauma, and Race in the Novels of Toni Morrison*. Albany: State U of New York P, 2000.

Otten, Terry. *The Crime of Innocence in the Fiction of Toni Morrison*. Columbia: U of Missouri P, 1989.

Carol Goodman

BODENHEIM, MAXWELL (1892–1954) A prolific, yet wildly uneven writer, Maxwell Bodenheim embodied the myths, dreams, and dubious trajectory of American literary bohemia in the twenties and thirties. A poet and novelist who received early acclaim—Ezra Pound considered him T. S. Eliot's possible successor as the most important voice of American modernism—he soon became a casualty of the Depression and his own dissipated lifestyle. Although largely forgotten now, Bodenheim typified a spirit of idealism and urban romanticism that reveals itself impressively in several works of his prodigious output. Indeed, the self-publicizing hedonist, buffoon, and gadfly should be remembered more than merely as the caricature of the Greenwich Village artist he has become.

After a brief stint in the military, where he went AWOL after assaulting an anti-Semitic officer, Bodenheim drifted to Chicago and then to New York City, where he quickly established himself as a formidable literary presence. Before he was thirty, he was showcased in numerous literary magazines, including *Poetry* and *The Nation*; founded two journals, *Others* and *The Chicago Literary Times* (with **Ben Hecht**); collaborated with **Eugene O'Neill** on writing short scripts; and published two poetry collections. He was included in the first edition of Louis Untermeyer's anthology, *Modern American and British Poetry* (1919), but later omitted—an early indication of how this promising writer would soon drift out of favor with the literary establishment.

But before the decline and fall, Bodenheim managed to merge astute political and cultural analysis with witty, sometimes manic, literary aplomb. In both the poetry and his prose his most interesting subjects are modern women and their striving toward personal fulfillment and social freedom. His chief importance lies with this proto-feminist sensibility, an outlook that reveals a sensitivity to women's struggles without condescension or naiveté. The novels *Replenishing Jessica* (1925) and *Georgie May* (1928) portray women on the brink of possibility and devastation. The former chronicles a woman's quest for sexual enjoyment; the latter gives voice to a Southern prostitute who, disgusted with the indignity of her life, commits suicide. Both succeed in capturing a female consciousness with artfulness usually lacking in male modernist writers. Likewise, the poems are usually either addressed to women or represent them in various vocations and attitudes. Bodenheim's combines this feminine focus with a characteristic *saevo indignatio* with society's puritanical mores and hypocrisies. In "To a Revolutionary Girl," originally published in the leftist journal *The New Masses*, he writes of how society erodes itself with its lack of feeling and, in turn, the individual becomes a ghost of her unrealized self.

Bodenheim's flowering was brief. After the productivity of the twenties and early thirties (in total he published ten poetry collections and thirteen novels), he became an alcoholic and a beggar in Greenwich Village, selling photocopies of his work for money or food. This downturn in his career is responsible in part for not being taken seriously and being largely forgotten. The appearance of *Selected Poems* in 1946 did little to save his reputation. His last work, *My Life and Loves in Greenwich Village* (1954), sometimes thought to be largely ghostwritten, relays his experiences with the eccentrics, cons, and writers of his generation. Unfortunately his critical reputation rests with this self-mythologizing persona and less on the work itself.

Maxwell Bodenheim was murdered in a Bowery rooming house in 1954 by an ex-mental patient. At the time, he had not published anything of any significance for over fifteen years.

Further Reading

Moore, Jack B. *Maxwell Bodenheim*. New York: Twayne Publishers, 1970.

Jonathan Curley

BONNER, MARITA ODETTE (1898–1971)   African American essayist, playwright, and short story writer. Writing during the **Harlem Renaissance**, a black cultural movement of the 1920s and 1930s, Marita Bonner can be considered the literary precursor to **Ann Petry** and **Richard Wright**. She depicted Chicago's black urban poor in the 1920s and 1930s when her female contemporaries **Nella Larsen** and **Jessie Fauset** portrayed the black middle class and when her black male contemporary **Claude McKay** penned black women's insatiable desires. A Boston native who never resided in Harlem, Bonner published most of her works in *Crisis* and *Opportunity*, official publishing outlets for Renaissance writers and from which she received first and second prizes for her works. *Crisis* awarded her first place for "On Being Young—A Woman—and Colored" (1925), an essay that offers survival advice to black women who live in a stifling environment. The essay functions as an umbrella for Bonner's later works on African American women.

From 1922 to 1930 Bonner lived in Washington, DC, where she published three plays: *The Pot Maker* (1927), *The Purple Flower* (1928), and *Exit, an Illusion* (1929). Intended to be read, Bonner's plays document the plight of poor urban black women and the healing measures that they resort to. *The Pot Maker* (1927) recounts the infidelity of a poor black preacher's wife who eases the pain of living with her husband and his parents. *The Purple Flower,* an allegory, dramatizes the revenge tactic of Old Woman, whose life of hard labor has brought her no reward. *Exit, an Illusion* documents a colored woman's passing for white. Bonner's interest in drama was nourished by her association with the "S" Salon, a black literary group that included playwrights Georgia Douglass Johnson, **May Miller**, and Mary P. Burill and met at Georgia Douglass Johnson's Washington, DC home located at 1461 S Street.

Bonner's short stories continue the theme of black women's disillusionment. "The Prison-Bound" (1926) details a black woman's disappointment with poverty. At supper with her husband in a greasy, sooty, bug-infested northern tenement, the woman wants to improve her living conditions, but fails to confer with her husband for fear of his rejection. Racial discrimination and little education add to her misery. "Nothing New" (1926) recounts a black mother's bitter disappointment in sending her son to an integrated art school after he falls in love with a white student and kills the girl's prejudiced white suitor. These stories are set on Frye Street, a mythological, multiethnic Chicago community that Bonner uses in her later stories.

In 1930 Marita Bonner married William Occomy and moved to Chicago, where she started her family. Between rearing three children and teaching in various Chicago schools, Bonner wrote short stories, including "A Sealed Pod" (1936), "Hate Is Nothing" (1938), "Patch Quilt" (1940), and "Reap It As You Sow It" (1940–41). Her third child and only daughter, Marita Joyce, has made Bonner's works accessible to researchers.

Further Reading

Brown-Guillory, Elizabeth. "Marita Bonner." *Black Women in America: An Historical Encyclopedia*. 2 Vols. Ed. Darlene Clark Hine. New York: Carson, 1993.

Harris, Laura Alexandra. "Troubling Boundaries: Women, Class, and Race in the Harlem Renaissance." Dissertation. University of California, San Diego, 1997.

Rita B. Dandridge

BONTEMPS, ARNA (1902–1973)   African American poet, novelist, playwright, historian, editor, and anthologist. Arna Bontemps was a prolific writer and a dedicated chronicler of African American literature and culture. Although Bontemps was an award-winning poet, a skilled editor, and an author of several works for children, his best-known work is probably his historical novel about a Virginia slave rebellion, *Black Thunder* (1936). Today he is remembered as an important figure of the **Harlem Renaissance** whose influence rests on his entire body of work rather than a single text or even a single genre.

Bontemps was born in Alexandria, Louisiana, but was raised in Los Angeles, California, where his family moved when he was three. His upbringing was shaped by his family's conversion from Catholicism to the Seventh Day Adventist faith, as well as his mother's early death, which left him under the care of his father. After his graduation from Pacific Union

College in 1923, Bontemps moved to New York City to take a teaching job at the Harlem Academy.

Bontemps's move to Harlem came in the midst of the literary and cultural movement which would come to be known as the Harlem Renaissance, a movement that he would later document as editor of the anthology, *The Harlem Renaissance Remembered* (1972). Soon after his arrival in New York, Bontemps gained attention for his talents as a poet. His poetry was published in the journals *Crisis* and *Opportunity* and he won the *Crisis*'s poetry prize in 1926 for "A Black Man Talks of Reaping," as well as *Opportunity*'s Alexander Pushkin poetry prizes in 1926 and 1927 for the poems "Golgotha Is a Mountain" and "The Return," respectively. In 1926 Bontemps married Alberta Johnson, with whom he would have six children.

In 1931 Bontemps left Harlem for a teaching position at Oakwood Junior College in Huntsville, Alabama. The same year, he published his first novel, *God Sends Sunday* (1931), which he would later adapt in collaboration with **Countee Cullen** into the play *St. Louis Woman* (1946). Bontemps wrote productively during his years in Alabama, producing the first of his many children's books, *Popo and Fifina* (1932), in collaboration with his lifelong friend, the poet **Langston Hughes**, as well as the award-winning short story, "A Summer Tragedy" (1932).

In 1934 Bontemps was forced to resign from his teaching post at Oakwood and moved with his family into his parent's house in California. It was in California that Bontemps finished writing the historical novel, *Black Thunder* (1936). A complex representation of Gabriel Prosser's attempted 1800 revolt near Richmond, Virginia, a slave insurrection that failed due to a combination of treachery and bad weather, the novel was well-reviewed but only modestly successful commercially. *Black Thunder* would enjoy something of a resurgence during the changed political climate of the 1960s and the book was reissued with a new introduction from the author in 1968. Critics have recognized the novel for its representation of a microcosm of the institution of **slavery** at the turn of the nineteenth century as well as its contribution to the vernacular tradition.

After a brief stay in California, Bontemps moved his family to Chicago and worked as a teacher at Shiloh Academy as well as a writer for the WPA Illinois Writers' Project before receiving a Rosenwald Fellowship to work on his final novel, *Drums at Dusk* (1939). After receiving a master's in library science from the University of Chicago, he became head librarian at Fisk University, a position that he would hold until 1964. During Bontemps's time at Fisk, he produced a number of children's books and collaborated once again with Langston Hughes on two anthologies, *The Poetry of the Negro* (1949) and *The Book of Negro Folklore* (1958). He also published his collected poems under the title *Personals* (1963).

After leaving Fisk, Bontemps taught at the University of Illinois at Chicago Circle and was named curator of the **James Weldon Johnson** Collection of Negro Arts and Letters at Yale University. When he died in 1973 he left behind a lifetime's work as not only a creator but also a chronicler of African American literature and culture. The recent publication of his long correspondence with Langston Hughes provides readers with an opportunity to understand the important and sometimes overlooked role that Bontemps played in twentieth-century African American literature.

Further Reading

Jones, Jacqueline C. "Arna Bontemps (1902–1973)." *African-American Authors, 1745–1945: A Bio-Bibliographical Critical Sourcebook*. Ed. Emmanuel S. Nelson. Westport, CT: Greenwood Press, 2002. 179–84.

Scott, William. "To Make Up the Hedge and Stand in the Gap: Arna Bontemps's *Black Thunder*." *Callaloo* 27.2 (Spring 2004): 522–41.

Todd Dapremont

BORDER NARRATIVES   A term used to describe the writings of those immigrant groups who have come to feel caught between their native cultures and the culture of their new home country—they are tied to both, but do not properly belong to either. The term border narrative may be applied equally to photojournalism, short story, essay, novel, poetry, or cinematic genres. Oftentimes there is a crossing over and blending of genres. These narratives generally display a tension between the past, present, and future as the ancestral ties to the native culture become severed and the ties to the adopted country become stronger. Frequently there is also a strong generational gap—the immigrants' offspring often do not have a direct connection with the culture within which their parents were raised. Social, economic, political, historic, and cultural themes are common among border narratives.

In the United States the term is applied to much of the writing of Mexican and Mexican American authors living along the U.S.-Mexico border. Their writing is characterized by a conscious blending of English and Spanish languages and to a lesser degree traditional Aztec vocabulary. Like the lives of those who write these narratives, the writings are a product of American and Mexican societies coming together to form a new and distinct culture, which has elements of the others but which cannot be precisely termed either.

The Treaty of Guadalupe Hidalgo of 1848, signed by the United States and Mexico to end their war, ceded roughly 55 percent of Mexico's land (present-day Texas, Arizona, New Mexico, parts of California, Colorado, Nevada, and Utah) to the United States in exchange for $15 million as reparations. Mexico's new northern border would from that point forward follow the following route: from the Gulf of Mexico starting at the Rio Grande, up the Rio Grande to the southern border of New Mexico, westward along the southern border of New Mexico, then north following the first branch of the Gila River, then along the Gila River until its intersection with the Colorado River, and then westward following the Spanish-Mexican division of Upper and Lower California. Articles eight and nine of the treaty included provisions for the protection of the property and civil rights of Mexican nationals who would be in U.S. territory after ratification of the treaty. Furthermore it offered Mexican nationals up to a year to decide whether they wished to retain the Mexican citizenship or to become U.S. citizens. If after a year's time any of those Mexican nationals had not responded, they were to automatically become citizens of the United States. However, the reality of the treaty did not match up with what the document stated legally, as evidenced during the Gold Rush, during which time many former Mexicans living inside the new U.S. boundary were evicted from their lands due to lack of physical deeds to the land they claimed as their own. Many Mexican nationals living in the new U.S. territories were questioned as to whether they actually had been living in these areas prior to the signing of the treaty or if they had immigrated there illegally.

Border narratives often describe the "in-between-ness" of those living on the border, the dangers of living there, the hazards of crossing the border, and the instability often felt by those living along the border. Although not exclusively applied to the U.S.-Mexico border region, border studies, a branch of cultural studies, looks strongly and actively at the U.S.-Mexico border to gain insights into the new culture being created there.

Much of what is currently happening in the literature and culture of these groups is a transformation of the border. The border as a dividing line between cultures is giving way to the border as the connection, the one place where two cultures are connected or even fused. For instance, the line that runs from Southern California to Texas is the one place that the United States and Mexico are constantly joined. This is perhaps the largest departure from previous (pre-1970) studies of the border. **Liminality**, the theoretical concept developed by anthropologist Arnold van Gennep, as a theoretical construct allows cultural theorists to probe some of the dynamics disallowed by other modes of research. To take one example, the tejano culture, established along the Mexico-Texas frontier, is a culture that is no longer Mexican nor is it properly mainstream American. These are its parents, but tejano culture has its own rules, codes, and traditions taken from and blended with elements of native Mexican and Texan societies and cultures.

Some of the authors associated with border narratives include **Américo Paredes**, a journalist, creative writer and scholar; **Gloria Anzaldúa**, a scholarly writer, children's book author, and frequent speaker on border studies whose book *Borderlands/La frontera* is a classic in Chicano/Chicana studies; Oscar Martínez, a scholarly writer of life on the border; Devon Gerardo Peña, whose book *The Terror of the Machine: Technology, Work, Gender, and Ecology on the U.S.-Mexico Border* is a border study about the working conditions of border residents, particularly women working in the infamous *maquiladoras*, factories along the U.S.-Mexico border that have gained much attention due to their sometimes abusive and inhumane working conditions; **Sandra Cisneros**, a chicana poet and writer; **Julia Álvarez**; Adriana Ocampos; and **Tomás Rivera**, a Mexican American author, whose book . . . *y no se lo tragó la tierra / . . . And the Earth Did Not Devour Him* details the life of a 1950s Mexican American family who work as migrant workers as seen from the perspective of a boy.

Mexican American border narratives often employ the use of multiple genres, including prose, poetry, photography, paintings, and drawings. These narratives are equally rife with the triumphs of coming to grips with an unstable social **identity** as they are with the troubles associated with living on the border—run-ins with the Border Patrol, poor economic conditions, abuse at the workplace, struggles to balance traditional family customs, and practices with a modern world and many other similar issues.

There are geographic centers along the U.S.-Mexico border that serve as nuclei for particular border groups (tejanos and Chicanos to name just two) and these typically spring up in and around the larger U.S. and Mexican cities along the border. Each of these border groups maintains its own cultural norms (dress, speech, codes of conduct), but what unites them all is the struggle to gain a sense of identity where one is fleeting, a struggle to find a home in a region between two countries that could embrace them as their own, but instead reject them as wetbacks in the United States and pochos in Mexico.

Traditionally focusing on the geographic border region between the United States and Mexico, recently border studies scholars have begun to use the term "border" more loosely, applying it wherever a large group of Mexican Americans settles and begins hybridizing within the community. For example, many border scholars look at the Mexican American population of Chicago. The border there is seen to be carried with their culture, even though the actual U.S.-Mexico frontier is geographically quite distant.

Further Reading

Anzaldúa, Gloria. *La frontera/Borderlands*. San Francisco: Spinsters/Aunt Lute, 1987.

Cisneros, Sandra. *The House on Mango Street*. Houston: Arte Público Press, 1985.
———. *Women Hollering Creek and Other Stories*. New York: Vintage Books, 1992.

Henderson, Mae, ed. *Borders, Boundaries, and Frames: Cultural Criticism and Cultural Studies*. New York: Routledge, 1995.

Hernández, Irene Beltrán. *Across the Great River*. Houston: Arte Público Press, 1989.

Michaleson, Scott, and David E. Johnson, eds. *Border Theory: The Limits of Cultural Politics*. Minneapolis: U of Minnesota P, 1977.

Paredes, Américo. *Between Two Worlds*. Houston: Arte Público Press, 1991.

Rivera, Tomás. . . . *y no se lo tragó la tierra/. . . And the Earth Did Not Devour Him*. Trans. Evangelina Vigil-Piñón. Houston: Arte Público Press, 1987.

Ulibarrí, Sabine. *Tierra Amarilla: Stories of New Mexico/Cuentos de Nuevo México*. Trans. Thelma Campbell Nason. Albuquerque: U of New Mexico P, 1971.

Valdés, Gina. *There Are Madmen Here*. San Diego: Maize, 1981.

Vila, Pablo. *Crossing Borders, Reinforcing Borders: Social Categories, Metaphors and Narrative Identities on the U.S.-Mexico Frontier*. Austin: U of Texas P, 2000.

Villarino, José, and Arturo Ramírez, eds. *Chicano Border Culture and Folklore*. San Diego: Marin Publications, 1992.

Alexander Waid

BORN IN EAST L.A. (1987)   *Born in East L.A.* by Cheech Marin has attracted substantial attention from Chicano film studies scholars. After its debut as the second highest grossing film in the United States, it managed a notable degree of box office success. In fact the profitability of *Born in East L.A.*, *La Bamba* (1987), and *Stand and Deliver* (1988) seemed to reveal the marketability of Latino films.

Prior to *Born in East L.A.*, Marin had made a number of films and comedy albums with his comic partner, Tommy Chong. As a result of the sexual and drug content of these films and albums, Marin earned a reputation as a bawdy humorist. The equation of "Cheech and Chong" with raunchiness eclipsed, however, the savvy countercultural politics of their work. With *Born in East L.A.*, which Marin made after splitting from Chong, Marin offers an intelligent and crafty intervention into 1980s debates about Mexican **immigration**.

The film is inspired by a true story about a Mexican American who was wrongly deported to Mexico. Rudy Robles (Marin) finds himself caught up in an immigration raid in a Los Angeles toy factory and "returned" to Tijuana. The rest of the film follows his efforts to gather enough money working odd jobs to pay a smuggler to transport him back into the United States. Although the film presents Rudy in various silly situations, it effectively challenges racist figurations of Mexican Americans as outside of the American national community. For example, immigration officers' rejection of Rudy's assertions of his American citizenship reflects some individuals' blatant refusal to accept people of Mexican descent as fellow citizens. Ultimately, as Rudy proclaims he is "Born in East L.A.," Marin reminds audiences that Mexican Americans are American citizens, too, because they, too, are "Born in the USA."

The political milieu of *Born in East L.A.* is crucial to any appreciation of Marin's project. In the late 1980s nativist sentiments in the United States precipitated obvious hostility toward Mexican immigrants. Widespread calls for stricter immigration controls and proposals to legislate English as the official language of the United States index the acuteness of the anti-Mexican xenophobia that existed in the United States at the time of the film's release. By portraying the racist denial of a Mexican American the rights and protections that citizens deserve, Marin challenges audiences to reassess the validity of antagonistic sentiments toward citizens who happen to be of Mexican descent. Incidentally, he fails to dismantle resentment of immigrants themselves.

Marin's strategy for recuperating Mexican Americans' status as equal citizens includes representing their Americanization. For Rudy, who can trace the presence of his family in the United States several generations back, the United States is his geographic and cultural home. His familiarity with American popular culture and his experience of dislocation in Mexico align him with American society and counter preconceptions of Mexican Americans as incompatible with American society.

Further Reading

Fregoso, Rosa Linda. *The Bronze Screen: Chicana and Chicano Film Culture.*
    Minneapolis: U of Minnesota P, 1993.
List, Christine. *Chicano Images: Refiguring Ethnicity in Mainstream Film.* New York:
    Garland, 1996.
Noriega, Chon. "'Waas Sappening?': Narrative Structure and Iconography in
    Born in East L.A." *Studies in Latin American Popular Culture* 14 (1995): 107–28.

Phillip Serrato

BOUDINOT, ELIAS (c. 1803–1839)   Native American orator, essayist, and journalist. Originally named Gallegina, or "Buck" Watie, Elias Boudinot was the firstborn child of Oo-watie and Susanna Reese Watie, prominent citizens of the eastern Cherokee Nation.

In 1811 Buck's parents enrolled him in a Moravian mission school at Spring Place (near present-day Chatsworth, Georgia), where he remained until he was twelve years old. At that time, Elias Cornelius, a missionary with the American Board of Commissioners for Foreign Missions, invited Buck and several other promising young Cherokee scholars to travel with him to Cornwall, Connecticut, to enroll in the ABCFM's mission school there.

While en route to Connecticut, Buck Watie met Elias Boudinot, the elderly president of the American Bible Society and one of the mission school's benefactors. In honor of the old man, Buck Watie took his name, enrolling in the Cornwall Mission School as Elias Boudinot—the name by which he is still remembered today.

Although Boudinot converted to Christianity and became a model of "good citizenship," he soon learned that **racism** against Indians was as strong as ever. For example, in 1826 when Boudinot married Harriet Gold, a white woman from a prominent New England family, the townspeople burned the couple in effigy. In fact their interracial marriage caused such a furor in Cornwall that the school eventually had to close its doors.

Upon returning south with his bride, Boudinot was authorized by the Cherokee Nation to travel throughout the United States to solicit money for buying a printing press, starting a newspaper, and establishing a Cherokee academy. It was during this fundraising tour that Boudinot published his now widely anthologized speech, "An Address to Whites. Delivered in the First Presbyterian Church on the 26th of May, 1826." The purpose of his speech was to persuade his audience that Indians are intelligent human beings, capable of the same accomplishments as their Euro-American counterparts.

In October 1827 Boudinot published the prospectus of the *Cherokee Phoenix*, a biweekly, bilingual (Cherokee and English) newspaper. Within a year the first newspaper published by American Indians had subscribers from several states and was being read by people as far away as Germany. Boudinot published national and world news reports, as well as Cherokee news and announcements, in the *Phoenix*.

In addition to public addresses and newspaper editorials and essays, Boudinot translated and published the New Testament, a Cherokee hymnal, and a tract titled *Poor Sarah, or the Indian Woman* (1833).

In spite of his strong advocacy for Cherokees, Boudinot eventually decided that assimilating into white society was his people's only hope for survival. In 1836 he joined some twenty other Cherokees in signing the Treaty of New Echota—an act that resulted in the cession of all Cherokee land east of the Mississippi River. That same year his wife Harriet died; within a year Boudinot had remarried and moved west to Indian Territory (Oklahoma).

On June 22, 1839, while building a new house for his family, Boudinot was assassinated by anti-Removal Cherokees. He is buried in Worcester Cemetery, Park Hill, Oklahoma. (*See also* Native American Oratory)

Elias Boudinot. *Courtesy of the Library of Congress.*

Further Reading

Perdue, Theda. *Cherokee Editor: The Writings of Elias Boudinot.* Athens: U of Georgia P, 1996.

Ginny Carney

BOURJAILY, VANCE (1922–) Arab American novelist. In the course of his long career, Vance Bourjaily has never written a bad novel, despite the fact that he has taken pains never to write essentially the same book twice. Still he has not produced a novel that has achieved such critical and popular success that it has singularly defined the spirit of its period.

Bourjaily was born in Cleveland, Ohio. His father was a Lebanese immigrant and his mother a citizen of Welsh descent. Both parents were journalists, and his mother achieved some success as a romance novelist. During World War II, Bourjaily served first as a volunteer in the American ambulance service in Syria and Italy, then in the American army stationed in Hawai'i. While in the army he sought to make literary use of his experiences with the ambulance service and drafted what would become his first novel, *The End of My Life.* It would not be published, however, until after he had completed his studies at Bowdoin College in 1947. In the 1950s Bourjaily tried his hand at writing in a variety of genres and was

Vance Bourjaily. *Courtesy of the Library of Congress.*

a prominent figure in the literary-magazine scene. From 1958 to 1980 he was a faculty member with the University of Iowa's Writer's Workshop, and he has subsequently taught at Louisiana State University and the University of Arizona. As a teacher, he has had a major influence on a long list of younger writers, from Kent Haruf to Virgil Suarez.

Bourjaily's first four novels have typically been grouped together. *The End of My Life* (1947) is pointedly autobiographical but has a literary model in John Dos Passos's *One Man's Initiation: 1917.* Bourjaily's protagonist Skinner Galt serves as an ambulance driver during the war. Galt is representative of all of those young men of his generation who are profoundly affected by their wartime experiences but lack the emotional and intellectual depth to take any measure of those experiences beyond a sort of reflexive cynicism. In *The Hound of Earth* (1955) a scientist who has helped to develop atomic weapons goes AWOL just before their employment. In his attempt to disappear into the American landscape, he reconnects with fundamental American values. In its themes the novel is very comparable to Frank Waters's *The Woman at Otowi Crossing.* With *The Violated* (1958), Bourjaily may have come closest to writing his "big" novel. A reaction against the social and intellectual conformity of the 1950s, the novel explores the ways in which its characters abuse their intimates at least in part in response to the realities that oppress them in their public lives. In retrospect the novel seems a male counterpart to **Mary McCarthy**'s *The Group.* In *Confessions of a Spent Youth* (1960), Bourjaily returned to the basic materials of *The End of My Life,* but approaches them with a much freer style. The protagonists' names are themselves pointedly suggestive of the difference in approach: Skinner Galt becomes Quincy Quince, making the echo of Thomas DeQuincy's *Confessions of an English Opium Eater* into a sort of **Nabokov**ian conceit.

In his subsequent six novels, Bourjaily has experimented more freely with form and has brought a more complex sense of the novelist's function to the treatment of his characteristic themes. In *The Man Who Knew Kennedy* (1967), Bourjaily attempts to explore the vague but nonetheless compelling connections between the public trauma of the president's assassination and the more personal crises in the lives of his characters. Echoing Sinclair Lewis's *The Man Who Knew Coolidge*, the novel is very comparable to Wright Morris's *One Day*. Nominated for the National Book Award, *Brill among the Ruins* (1970) treats a lawyer's midlife crisis, exhibited in this case in an archaeological excursion among the ruins of Mexico. The well-defined central character, Bourjaily's restraint in handling the novel's themes, and some beautifully rendered incidents make this novel his most polished effort.

Now Playing in Canterbury (1976) and *The Great Fake Book* (1987) represent Bourjaily's nod to the metafictional experimentation of the period. Ostensibly concerned with the staging of an opera at a midwestern college and with a young man's attempt to reconstruct his father's life from the written record, these novels are amalgams of literary and extra-literary forms. Interestingly, in his other two late novels, Bourjaily has treated much more conventional subjects in much more straightforward narratives. *A Game Men Play* (1980) focuses on Chink Peters, a veteran of World War II. Chink's training and violent instincts may serve him well in an ever more violent world, but they are not enough to come to peace with that world or to achieve any sort of meaningful self-understanding. Comparable to John Hersey's *The War Lover*, this novel may be Bourjaily's most completely realized effort. *Old Soldier* (1990) explores the relationship between two brothers, one of whom is dying of AIDS. (*See also* Arab American Novel)

Further Reading

Francis, William A. "The Motif of Names of Bourjaily's *The Hound of Earth*." *Critique: Studies in Modern Fiction* 17.3 (1976): 64–67.

McMillen, William. "The Public Man and the Private Novel: Bourjaily's *The Man Who Knew Kennedy*." *Critique: Studies in Modern Fiction* 17.3 (1976): 86–95.

Muste, John M. "The Second Major Subwar: Four Novels by Vance Bourjaily." *The Shaken Realist: Essays in Modern Literature in Honor of Frederick Hoffman*. Ed. Melvin J. Friedman, John B. Vickery, and Philip R. Yannella. Baton Rouge: Louisiana State UP, 1970. 311–26.

Towner, Daniel. "Brill's Ruins and Henderson's Rain." *Critique: Studies in Modern Fiction* 17.3 (1976): 96–104.

Martin Kich

BOYESEN, HJALMAR HJORTH (1848–1895) Norwegian American novelist, poet, educator, and critic. Hjalmar Hjorth Boyesen was an unlikely constituent of the mid-nineteenth-century "Teutonic" stage of American **immigration**. On the one hand this stage was comprised mainly of Scandinavians, Northern Germans, and Czechs who migrated to the United States in order to reinvent Old World agricultural lives on the Western plains. On the other hand Boyesen was a highly educated and wealthy product of the Victorian era, and he emigrated to the New World for its promise for academic and literary opportunities rather than social mobility and land grants. Though he died of lung disease at the early age of forty-seven, Boyesen was a prolific author, having written eight novels, eight volumes of short fiction, eight books of literary criticism, and scores of articles. He regularly contributed to the nation's most prominent literary periodicals, including *Lippincott's*, *North American Review*, *Harper's Weekly*, *Scribner's Monthly*, and *Atlantic Monthly*, and held professorships in language and literature at Cornell University and Columbia College. Boyesen is best known as a leading figure in American literary realism and naturalism, but mainly for his efforts to introduce continental European authors to the American scene and his promotion of American authors who emulated them, rather than for his own fiction.

Boyesen was born in Fredrikvaern, Norway, to Captain Sarolf Boyesen, an army officer who taught Mathematics at the Norwegian Naval Academy, and Helga Tveten Boyesen, whose father was a prominent, socially conservative judge. In 1868 he received a degree from Royal Fredericks University and a year later emigrated to Ohio. There he received his first teaching position at Urbana University in Urbana, Ohio. Urbana was a Swedenborgian college, however, and the staunch philosophical leanings of the school ultimately drove him away—first to Chicago, where he served as an editor for the Norwegian journal *Fremad*, then back to Ohio. In 1871, discouraged by what he perceived as the stifling, unromantic atmosphere of the Midwest, he moved to Boston, which was then the nation's literary capital and home to the *Atlantic Monthly* editor and future "Dean of American Letters," William Dean Howells.

Boyesen and Howells met soon after his arrival, and subsequently Boyesen's first novel, *Gunnar: A Tale of Norse Life* (1874), was serialized in *Atlantic Monthly* in 1873. *Gunnar* is a highly romantic treatment of Norse life, but over the course of his career, Boyesen developed into a near fanatical advocate for realistic fiction, not only as an aesthetic movement but also as a philosophical one. He wrote his three best novels, *The Mammon of Unrighteousness* (1891), *A Golden Calf* (1892), and *Social Strugglers* (1895), well after this conversion, and each employ social Darwinism and other scientific philosophies as tools to comprehend the effects of industrialization on American culture. As a result, scholars often approach Boyesen as a fascinating "in-between" figure, transforming as he did from romanticist to realist and finally naturalist. In his social history *Main Currents in American Thought* (1927), Vernon L. Parrington wrote at length about Boyesen in the context of the sociological turn in 1890s American fiction; he rightly considers Boyesen a forerunner of what he termed the new school of sociological fiction. Boyesen's fiction might appeal to students of realism and naturalism, but his writing often contains sentimental ingredients that might disappoint realism devotees and sound antiquated to nonspecialists.

His volumes of literary criticism, including *Goethe and Schiller: Their Lives and Works* (1879); *Essays on German Literature* (1892); *A Commentary on the Writings of Henrik Ibsen* (1894); *Essays on Scandanavian Literature* (1895); and

Literary and Social Silhouettes (1894), which includes his famous essay on pandering to American audiences, "The American Novelist and His Public," are enormously influential contributions to American letters, as they successfully introduced the continental European avant-garde to a nation that traditionally followed Great Britain's cultural lead. He continues to be well regarded by specialists for his integral role in the movement to infuse American fiction with social theory and science in the mode of European realists such as Henrik Ibsen and Ivan Turgenev and naturalists such as Emile Zola. Over the course of his expansive career, Boyesen counted many literary giants among his elite circle of friends, including Henry Wadsworth Longfellow, William Dean Howells, Henry James, Mark Twain, Ivan Turgenev, Victor Hugo, and Henrik Ibsen. (*See also* Norwegian American Literature)

Further Reading

Frederickson, Robert S. *Hjalmar Hjorth Boyesen*. Boston: Twayne Publishers, 1980.

Glasrud, Clarence A. *Hjalmar Hjorth Boyesen*. Northfield, MN: Norwegian-American Historical Society, 1963.

Robert M. Dowling

BRADLEY, DAVID (1950–)   African American novelist and author of two novels, *South Street* (1975) and *The Chaneysville Incident* (1981), which won the 1982 PEN/Faulkner prize and an award from the American Academy and Institute of Arts and Letters. In addition, Bradley was awarded a Guggenheim Fellowship and a fellowship from the National Endowment for the Arts. He has published essays in various venues, including the *New York Times*, the *Washington Post*, the *Village Voice*, and *Esquire*.

Descended from a line of preachers, Bradley was born in Bedford, Pennsylvania, received his BA from the University of Pennsylvania (1972), and an MA in United States Studies from the University of London (1974). From 1976 to 1997, he taught at Temple University. He currently heads the program in creative writing at the University of Oregon.

Bradley's first major publication, *South Street*, is a decent debut novel. It is a book about inner-city experience, but not, as one blurb writer has claimed, "about Black America," since black America cannot be summarized or subsumed by an articulation of "ghetto" life alone. This is made abundantly clear in Bradley's second novel, *The Chaneysville Incident*, upon which his reputation largely and justly rests.

Bradley's rural Pennsylvania birthplace is the site that provided the inspiration for the book that many consider his masterpiece. Inspired by some real but obscure local history, *The Chaneysville Incident* also has as its subject the limits of historicism when confronting and seeking to resolve the problems of the past. In this novel, Bradley is exploring the "mystery" of history—not, in this case, the lack of clarity resulting from distortions and misrepresentations (a history that *writes over* certain realities), but rather, what happens when the facts are incomplete or yield no conclusion.

In other words, how do we address the gaps in what we know, in what we *can* know? One answer is to rely on empathy and imagination. Thus the argument has been advanced that in such instances the novel may be more suitable than documentary approaches in recreating the past, in revealing its psychology, its human depth.

Bradley has said that he was thinking of his father, who was an historian as well as a preacher, when he conceived of John Washington, the narrator of *The Chaneysville Incident*. But it was from his mother that he learned of the discovery of the graves of runaway slaves on a farm near Chaneysville, in the county where Bradley was born. According to local legend, thirteen slaves, escaping to the North on the **Underground Railroad** and about to be recaptured, had committed suicide rather than be forced to return to the South. It is important to note that the Mason-Dixon line, which traditionally divided the North from the South, and thus the free from the enslaved, is very close to Chaneysville.

Bradley began writing about this occurrence in the form of a story while he was a freshman in college but realized at that point that he wasn't up to the task. *The Chaneysville Incident* eventually took him a decade of work, involving numerous drafts.

John Washington, in his capacity as an academically trained historian, cannot make the facts he has accumulated add up to a coherent picture or a definitive interpretation. In the end, he resorts to storytelling. Indeed, *The Chaneysville Incident* foregrounds oral tradition, and, like black experience itself, the book is double-voiced: there is the vernacular of Jack, John Washington's informally educated mentor, and there is the "standard" English of John himself.

In John's eventual conceptualization of the incident, the slaves are buried by a white man who has taken pains to figure out who cared for whom in his arrangement of the graves. This, along with the fact that John has a white girlfriend, opens the possibility of black-white understanding and reconciliation that John's own father, Moses, and *his* father, C.K., could not have conceived of, therefore enabling or at least implying a break with the racist past.

Bradley's long-awaited novel in progress is entitled *The Book of Wisdom*, and he is also at work on a nonfiction project, *The Bondage Hypothesis: Meditations on Race and History*.

Further Reading

Bradley, David. "Bringing Down the Fire." *Going on Faith: Writing as a Spiritual Quest*. Ed. William Zinsser. New York: Marlow, 1999. 83–106.

Kubitschek, Missy Dehn. "'So You Want a History, Do You?': Epistemologies and *The Chaneysville Incident*." *Mississippi Quarterly* 49 (Fall 1996): 755–74.

Pavlic, Edward. "Syndetic Redemption: Above-Underground Emergence in David Bradley's *The Chaneysville Incident*." *African American Review* 30.2 (Summer 1996): 165–84.

Robert Elliot Fox

BRAGA, THOMAS J. (1943–)   Portuguese American scholar and poet. Thomas J. Braga's place in the Portuguese American tradition of life writing rests on his compelling collection of poems in *Portingales* (1981) and *Borderlands* (1994). Braga is the grandson of Portuguese immigrants from the island of São Miguel in the Azores. He was born on June 13, 1943, in Fall River, Massachusetts. After graduating from Providence College in Providence, Rhode Island in 1966, he completed his graduate studies at Rice University in Houston, Texas, in 1970, where he earned a PhD degree in French. Currently retired, he has taught courses in French language and literature at the State University of New York, Plattsburgh, since 1972. This was preceded by a two-year appointment at California State College in San Bernardino. He has secondary interests in other Romance languages (Spanish and Italian) including Portuguese, the language of his grandparents. He is remembered for his enthusiasm for Montréal and his guided tours of the local Notre Dame Basilica and, at Plattsburgh, for his walking tours, his poetry readings and voice recitals with several choirs, and his contributions to the Campus Poets Series.

Braga's poems address emotional states with two reference points—the Portuguese American experience and Roman Catholicism. Braga may be considered a Language poet since he is quite interested in the "shape" and "music" of words. His poems are eminently oral and intended to be recited aloud. Unlike José Rodrigues Miguéis and Jorge de Sena, who wrote about their impressions of the United States in Portuguese, Braga focuses on Portuguese American issues mostly in the English language. In *Portingales*, however, four poems have Portuguese versions, which reflect his attachment to the language of his ancestors.

The poems in *Portingales* can be grouped into three major categories. The first deals with life in an ethnic community ("Below the Hill"); the celebration of Portuguese American heroes such as John Phillip Sousa in "Independence"; a Portuguese reaction to mainstream values and beliefs ("Chants Fugitifs"); a critique of the practice of anglicizing foreign names, the role of Portuguese Jews and their contribution to the American whaling industry in Nantucket and New Bedford in the nineteenth century, and their foundation of the Touro Synagogue, in Newport, Rhode Island ("Judith Melo"). The second category focuses mostly on Portuguese traditions and how they are kept alive within a dominant culture. "Ash Wednesday," "Codfish Cakes," and "Bacalhau" highlight the preservation of specific Catholic beliefs, traditions, and foods. The last category deals with the country and culture of Braga's ancestors. "Cravo" stresses the importance of the democratic revolution in Portugal on April 25, 1974, and celebrates Portugal's glorious past during the discoveries in the sixteenth century. The stories narrated by his grandmother, which have crystallized in the poet's mind, are alluded to in "In the Glass Dome." The grandmother figure in this poem—as in most ethnic literatures in America—is the one who caters to the writer's need for ethnic materials. In "Portuguese Lullaby" Braga pulls together different allusions to Portuguese culture while focusing on the Azorean fishermen's contributions to the New England whaling and fishing industries.

The poems touching upon Portuguese American issues in *Borderlands* range from pieces on immigrants refusing **assimilation** and consumerism ("'Mérica, Mané, Maria"), to those on the preservation of ethnic foods and tastes ("Sweet Bread," "Doughboys," and "Caldinho"), and, finally, to the poems on the tensions between those immigrants who wish to assimilate American ways and forget the ancestral culture and language versus the third-generation American-born who wishes to trace his or her ethnic roots, as in "Providence Prose."

Braga has also published *Chants Fugitifs* (1981), where his muse speaks French, still a reflection of Braga's graduate school days. In *Coffee in the Woodwinds* (1990), Braga was inspired by the habitués of a coffee shop in Plattsburgh, where he got to hear the concerns and sounds (accents) of the locals over coffee and donuts. This was followed by *Crickers' Feet* (1992), in which Braga again attempts to capture the rhythms of American speech, still viewing the activities of locals from the "catbird's" seat. In *Litotes* (1997), Braga wrote in a sensuous and, on occasion, homoerotic style. This was followed by *Motley Coats* (2001), where Braga departed from the purely ethnic theme to embrace a wider worldview. Although the subtext is still one of personal identity and sensuality, the language has now been honed. *Inchoate: Early Poems* (2003) includes Braga's very first poetic attempts as a student. His most recent project, *Amory: Six Dialogues and Six Poems*, is still in manuscript form. One of the first Portuguese American voices to write about the complexities of being born a hyphenated American in the English language, Braga's *Portingales* will remain a cornerstone in Portuguese American writing for years to come. (*See also* Portuguese American Literature)

Further Reading

Silva, Reinaldo Francisco. "Representations of the Portuguese in American Literature." *Dissertation Abstracts International* 59.4 (October 1998): 1170. New York University, 1998. DA 9831767.

———. "Thomas Braga's *Portingales*: A Celebration of Portuguese American Culture." *Ethnic Studies Review* 27.1 (2001): 57–77.

Reinaldo Francisco Silva

BRAINARD, CECILIA MANGUERRA (1947–) Filipina American essayist, novelist, and editor. Having won awards for both her writing and her service to the Filipino community, Cecilia Brainard has earned her reputation as a very original and versatile Filipina writer. She grew up in Cebu City on the island of Cebu in the Philippines. An idyllic childhood gave way to chaos following the death of her engineer father, and Brainard escaped into books and journal writing. In 1969 Brainard immigrated to the United States to pursue graduate work in film at the University of California at Los Angeles (UCLA), one of many who fled the dictatorship of Ferdinand Marcos. Following her marriage to Lauren Brainard, a former Peace

Corps volunteer she had met in the Philippines, she began a six-year stint writing the bimonthly column "Filipina American Perspective" for the *Philippine American News*. The columns were eventually collected in the book *Philippine Woman in America* (1991).

From her first book of short stories, *Woman With Horns and Other Stories* (1987), Brainard returned to the Philippines and their history for her source of inspiration. Her thoroughly Westernized education forced her to have to hunt for ties to her heritage, and the impact of colonialism on the Philippines is a recurring theme in her work. Brainard's novels do not focus on Marcos's regime, as much recent Filipino American literature does, but instead return to the experiences of her childhood to explore the impact of foreign wars on her people's soil and spirit.

Her first novel, *Song of Yvonne* (1991), was originally published in the Philippines, and subsequently came out in the United States under the more well-known title *When the Rainbow Goddess Wept* (1994). Internationally acclaimed for its lyric tone and writing style, the book follows the young narrator, Yvonne, as she comes of age during the brutal Japanese occupation of the islands during World War II. Weaving together myth and folklore into her play, and thus into her interpretation of events, Yvonne unwittingly places her family's experiences in the larger context of Filipino history. She highlights the endurance of the Filipino people throughout not just this war, but every war.

Brainard's father's death resurfaces as Yvonne and her mother learn that Yvonne's father may have died in the fighting. While not a biography, the novel does borrow from Brainard's own experiences, including her desire to write. Ultimately, Yvonne comes to terms with all that she has seen and endured by embracing her own life as epic—as epic as the stories she is so fond of—and claiming her story as one that she will grow up to tell herself, in her own words, so that it will never be forgotten.

Brainard's second novel, *Magdalena* (2002), ranges in time from 1912 to 1968 to tell the stories of three generations of Filipina women. Again the presence of foreigners is everywhere, as the Americans use the Philippines as a base while fighting in Vietnam. Juana, a young woman about to give birth to her first child, has decided to write down what she knows of her family's history in order to pass it on to her unborn child. A series of vignettes flows seamlessly to trace the lives of her mother and grandmother through their unhappy marriages and forbidden loves, their lives shaped constantly by war. Brainard integrates the **race** and class prejudices that structure Filipino society with a sense of what duty a woman owes first to her father's and then her husband's position. For her characters, the desire to escape becomes a secret both possessed and possessing.

In addition to her short stories and novels, Brainard also works as an editor. As such, she has published compilations of Filipino American fiction for readers of all ages, and coedited *Journey of 100 Years: Reflections on the Centennial of Philippine Independence* (2000) with Edmundo Litton. A collection of entries from her teenage diary, spanning the years 1962 to 1969, was released in 2003.

In her time not spent writing or editing, Brainard teaches at UCLA–Extension and the University of Southern California. (*See also* Filipino American Novel)

Further Reading

Casper, L. "Four Filipina Writers: Recultivating Eden." *Amerasia* 24.3 (Winter 1998): 143–59.

Grice, H. "Artistic Creativity, Form, and Fictional Experimentation in Filipina American Fiction." *MELUS* 29.1 (Spring 2004): 181–98.

Huebler, D. "An interview with Cecilia Manguerra Brainard [with excerpt from *When the Rainbow Goddess Wept*]." *Poets & Writers* 25 (March/April 1997): 96–101.

Ty, Eleanor. "Cecilia Manguerra Brainard." *Asian American Novelists: A Bio-Bibliographical Critical Sourcebook*. Ed. Emmanuel S. Nelson. Westport, CT: Greenwood Press, 2000. 29–33.

Shannan Palma

BRAITHWAITE, WILLIAM STANLEY (1878–1962) African American editor, critic, poet, and author. William Stanley Braithwaite, child of an ex-slave and a physician's assistant, helped usher African American poetry into the modern era. Braithwaite, who emulated the Romantic poets, especially Keats, wrote of universal issues in his own poetry, mostly staying away from narrower racial confrontations. Although he wrote fiction and criticism in addition to verse, he is best known for his work as an anthologist and editor of poetry journals and compilations.

Braithwaite was born on December 6, 1878, in Boston, living most of his life there. His father, a British New Guiana native, attempted to keep Braithwaite, a frail child, and his four siblings away from the African American culture. Because of this, Braithwaite led a reclusive early childhood, and his father home schooled him, keeping Braithwaite segregated from other African American children. After his father died, Braithwaite attended school until he was eleven, and then dropped out to help his mother. He married Emma Kelly in 1903 when he was twenty-four, and together they raised seven children. Throughout his professional life, Braithwaite mostly edited journals and anthologies while composing his own poetry. He edited the *Poetry Journal* from 1912–14 and the *Poetry Review* from 1916–18, and later served as a literature professor at Atlanta University from 1935–45, where he met **W. E. B. Du Bois**, Mercer Cook, and others.

When he wrote and published, Braithwaite concealed his **race**, striving to gain acceptance simply as a writer rather than a writer of racial distinction. He wrote short fiction, nonfiction prose, and poetry, but Braithwaite was mainly known as an anthologist, editing a variety of compilations of poetry, including the *Anthology of Magazine Verse*, which yearly collected the best magazine poetry, and published many significant poets, such as Robert Frost, Wallace Stevens, **James Weldon Johnson**, and others.

Of his own writing, Braithwaite remained an anonymous voice in poetry, wanting to be judged as an author who touches a universal vein in a wide audience rather than some kind of mission poet. He composed numerous poems that were printed in periodicals and journals, and he published three volumes of poetry: *Lyric of Life and Love* (1904), *The House of Falling Trees* (1908), and *Selected Poems* (1948). Braithwaite's verse style resembles his favorite authors, the Romantics, especially Keats, with its inclusion of dreams, impending doom, and the universal and eternal truth. His poetry often resounds with images of the sea and stars as representative icons or markers of boundaries between the eternal and temporal worlds. Although his short fiction remains secondary to his poetry, one story, "The Quality of Color," published in 1902, stands out as an attempt to address the theme of race through a story of interracial love. Although he stayed away from the color line, some of Braithwaite's criticism touches on light issues of race as well.

Braithwaite holds an essential place in African American literature because of his support in the dissemination of both African American poets and poetry, assisting their entry into the modern age. Braithwaite's poetry knew no color lines, and his ideas resonate with eternal questions that remain relevant today. (*See also* African American Poetry)

Further Reading

Bloom, Harold, ed. *Black American Prose Writers before the Harlem Renaissance.* New York: Chelsea House, 1994.

Butcher, Philip. "Introduction." *The William Stanley Braithwaite Reader.* Ed. Philip Butcher. Ann Arbor: U of Michigan P, 1972. 1–7.

Michael Modarelli

BRER RABBIT   **Trickster** character, like the tortoise, spider, or jackal, brought from Africa and India to North America, which appears as the clever hare in numerous stories. Ostensibly a friend or "brother" to the other animals, he is in reality their nemesis.

The typical plot of these stories involves a contest instigated by a small animal that wishes or needs to outwit a larger, more powerful one. Neither superhuman nor possessing magic powers, Brer Rabbit is quite frequently all too human, guilty at times of foolish and prideful actions, at other times of illegal or amoral ones. Yet always he survives, for small and defenseless as he is, his more powerful opponent invariably exercises less intelligence.

The earliest published examples in America were stories told by Joel Chandler Harris (1848–1908) in *Uncle Remus, His Songs and Sayings* (1880) and *Nights with Uncle Remus* (1883), about an underdog trickster who survives and triumphs over adversity. In Harris's stories, the rabbit trickster uses several varieties of survival tactics: evasion, excuses, false statement that induces negative reaction, songs involving a hidden warning, and entrapment. In the famous Tar Baby story, the fox sets a trap for the rabbit—a tar baby, totally silent and immobile, that reacts to Brer Rabbit's bluster, threats, and physical

Brer Rabbit. Illustration in Joel Chandler Harris, *Uncle Remus and His Friends*, 1892. *Courtesy of the Library of Congress.*

attack with passive resistance—and the rabbit does not escape the stick-fast trap. Later he must outwit the fox with the "Do Anything But . . ." statement (a ploy to deceive the villain about the victim's capabilities). Deception is the major underpinning of these stories; the rabbit often plays dead, shams sickness, and invariably lies.

In his own day, Harris's stories reached a predominantly white audience; later black authors began to publish their own collections of animal tales. Books such as William J. Faulkner's *The Days When the Animals Talked* (1977) and Julius Lester's *The Knee-High Man* (1972) provide all children with standardized speech patterns and spellings, unlike Harris's earlier attempts to replicate the sound and syntax of the slaves who told him the tales. Most recently, readers have **Virginia Hamilton**'s spirited and humorous rabbit tales in *The People Could Fly* (1985), *A Ring of Tricksters* (1997), and *Bruh Rabbit and the Tar Baby Girl* (2003).

Thematically all these stories set forth a code of behavior for the underdog, in which cunning and subterfuge replace open resistance, neither debate nor compromise being a possibility with the master-slave relationship. "It needs no scientific investigation," said Harris in the introduction to his first book of stories, "to show why he [the slave] selects as his hero the weakest, the most harmless of all animals and brings him out victorious in contests with the bear, the wolf, and the fox. It is not virtue that triumphs, but helplessness; it is not malice but mischievousness."

Further Reading

Keenan, Hugh. "Twisted Tales: Propaganda in the Tar-Baby Stories." *Southern Quarterly* 22 (Winter 1984): 54–69.

Mikkelsen, Nina. "When the Animals Talked—A Hundred Years of Uncle Remus." *Children's Literature Association Quarterly* 8 (Spring 1983): 3–5, 31.

Nina Mikkelsen

BRESLIN, JIMMY (1930–)   Irish American journalist and novelist. Jimmy Breslin was born in 1930 in Queens, New York. He attended Long Island University during the 1940s and worked as a copy boy for the *Long Island Press*. He left the university to pursue a career in journalism and worked as a sportswriter for the *New York Journal-American* and the *New York Herald Tribune*. In 1963 he published *Can't Anybody Here Play This Game?*, a critically acclaimed account of the 1962–63 New York Mets. The book, however, came under fire years later when Breslin admitted that the title, initially attributed to Mets manager Casey Stengel, was fabricated by Breslin himself. Breslin ultimately became a columnist for the *Tribune* and from 1965 to 1969 he wrote columns for other New York newspapers. During this period, the focus of his writing changed from sports to New York politics and social issues such as police brutality. In 1969 he published his first novel *The Gang That Couldn't Shoot Straight*. A best seller, it was a sometimes-comic story of "regular guys" who happened to be mobsters and enjoyed rather limited success at their various criminal endeavors. He also worked as a special commentator for ABC News, leaving that post after a few months to mount an unsuccessful campaign for New York City Council president (along with **Norman Mailer**, who ran for mayor). *Running Against the Machine: The Mailer-Breslin Campaign* (1970), an edited collection, features Breslin's own account of the election campaign. He returned to writing fiction in 1973 with the publication of *World Without End, Amen*. Breslin was the subject of some degree of notoriety when he published columns about receiving letters from the "Son of Sam" serial killer, David Berkowitz. He won

the Pulitzer and George Polk awards in 1986 for his columns and, in 1988, began a long relationship with *Long Island Newsday*. More recent works include a biography of Damon Runyon (1991), a memoir about being stricken with an aneurysm (*I Want to Thank My Brain for Remembering Me*) in 1996, and *The Short Sweet Dream of Eduardo Gutierrez* in 2002. This last book marked a return to the sort of investigative journalism that marked Breslin's early work. The book recounted the story of Gutierrez, an illegal immigrant from Mexico, who was killed working on a New York construction site. Breslin wove details of New York City building code violations and political corruption throughout the story of Gutierrez's journey from Mexico to New York.

Jimmy Breslin. *AP/Wide World Photos.*

317

Breslin's journalism and nonfiction are marked by features of the "new journalism" and are similar in many ways to the work of Tom Wolfe, the novelist and perhaps the best known practitioner of "new journalism." Breslin actively eschews any pretense of objectivity placing himself and his points-of-view squarely in the middle of whatever event he happens to cover. Breslin's worldview is an unapologetically urban one. His political views range from New Deal liberalism to contemporary progressivism. Novels such as *World Without End, Amen* and nonfiction such as *I Want to Thank My Brain for Remembering Me* both depict a grudging admiration for the Catholic Church.

Further Reading

Newfield, Jack. *Somebody's Gotta Tell It: The Upbeat Memoir of a Working-Class Journalist.* New York: St. Martin's, 2002.

William Carney

BROADSIDE PRESS   Founded in 1965 by Detroit poet and librarian **Dudley Randall** (1914–2000), the Broadside Press became an important institution of the **Black Arts Movement**. Major publishing outlets had virtually excluded the work of black poets. Between 1945 and 1965, only thirty-five poetry books were published by African Americans and only nine of those were published by presses with a national distribution. Randall's mission was to publish, promote, and distribute quality black poetry in inexpensive but attractive broadsides and books, to "help create and define the soul of black folk, and to know the joy of discovering new poets" (Randall qtd. in Boyd 134). Between 1965 and 1995, the Broadside Press published over 400 African American poets, 94 broadsides, 101 books, 5 posters, and 27 tapes and albums of poetry. Broadside publications reached a largely black audience through small bookstores, mail orders, libraries, and educational and community programs. The press published an illustrious group of poets including **Langston Hughes**, **Gwendolyn Brooks**, **Margaret Walker**, **Melvin Tolson**, **Amiri Baraka**, and **Robert Hayden**. But more significant was the central role Broadside played in first publishing and promoting the careers of virtually all of the newer black poets who gained a national reputation in the late sixties and early seventies, including Don L. Lee (**Haki Madhubuti**), **Nikki Giovanni**, **Etheridge Knight**, and **Sonia Sanchez**.

Randall began his publishing venture out of his Detroit home with twelve dollars. His own "Ballad of Birmingham," about the 1963 bombing of the 16th Street Baptist Church in Birmingham, Alabama, was the first broadside. Randall's "Dressed All in Pink" about the assassination of John Kennedy soon followed. After attending the First Black Writers Conference at Fisk University, Randall got the idea of publishing an anthology of poems in honor of **Malcolm X**. *For Malcolm X* (1967), edited by Randall and Margaret G. Burroughs, contains the work of a number of prominent African American writers and became important to the growth of the press. Randall credited the early success of the press to the commitment of individuals, especially Gwendolyn Brooks, who left Harper and Row to publish with Broadside, and to Hoyt W.

Fuller, editor of *Black World*. Don L. Lee's books, *Black Pride* (1968), *Think Black* (1969), and *Don't Cry, Scream* (1969) sold particularly well. Although primarily publishing poetry, Broadside also published autobiography (including Audre Lorde's *From a Land Where Other People Live* [1973]), essays, criticism, children's literature, and a cookbook. Between 1971 and 1976 Gwendolyn Brooks edited Broadside's *The Black Position*, an annual periodical containing essays on the political, economic, and historical condition of black people.

Despite Broadside's success at publishing a greater variety of poets and a larger number of broadsides and books than any other black publisher in the United States during the sixties, Randall was forced to sell Broadside to the Alexander Crummell Center to avoid bankruptcy in 1976. The press never had adequate capital, and the inflationary economy of the mid-seventies, the increasingly repressive political atmosphere, and the decline in black cultural enthusiasm all impacted the press negatively. Randall did not operate the business on profit principles. Credit to bookstores and poets was overextended and books were underpriced. Randall never paid himself a salary or royalties, although unlike some other small presses, he did pay royalties to authors. Between 1982 and 1985 Randall regained ownership and organized the press as a nonprofit organization. However, in 1985 economic reverses again forced Randall to sell Broadside. The new owners, Hilda and Donald Vest, published an anthology of Detroit poets, *HIPology* (1990), and *Reflections: An Oral History of Detroit* (1992) among other books. Randall received several writing fellowships during the 1980s and was appointed the first Poet Laureate of Detroit by mayor Coleman Young. After Randall's death in 2000, the University of Detroit Mercy established the Dudley Randall Center for Print Culture. The archives of the Broadside Press are now part of the Special Collections Library at the University of Michigan. Under the co-ownership of Willie Williams, the Broadside Press continues to promote Detroit poets.

Further Reading

Boyd, Melba Joyce. *Wrestling with the Muse: Dudley Randall and the Broadside Press.* New York: Columbia UP, 2003.

Thompson, Julius E. *Dudley Randall, Broadside Press, and the Black Arts Movement in Detroit, 1960–1995.* Jefferson, NC: McFarland & Company, Inc., 1999.

Lynn Orilla Scott

BRODSKY, JOSEPH (IOSIF) (1940–1996)   Joseph (Iosif) Brodsky, Russian American poet, essayist, translator, and playwright, was born in Leningrad (now St. Petersburg) in the Union of Soviet Socialist Republic (USSR) to an assimilated Jewish family. Brodsky left school at fifteen and changed jobs many times from 1956 to 1962. Brodsky's earliest poems exhibited overtly modernist influences. In the 1960s the poet engaged in a hot fusion of Baroque and Neoclassical elements with the heritage of the Silver Age and early Soviet modernism.

Arrested in 1964 in Leningrad and charged with "social parasitism," Brodsky set a new standard for literary martyrdom during his infamous trial. He

Joseph Brodsky. *AP/Wide World Photos.*

was sentenced to five years of administrative exile in the Archangelsk Province where isolation, not agricultural work, was the main punishment. Brodsky's greatest lyrics, such as the cycle "A Part of Speech" (1975–76), emerged out of a poetic distillation of his northern exile. Brodsky read Jonn Donne and Louis Untermeyer's anthology of modern Anglo American poetry. After eighteen months Brodsky's sentence was commuted, and Brodsky returned to Leningrad. A Russian-language volume, *Longer and Shorter Poems*, was published in 1965 in Washington, DC. Brodsky's poems were published abroad in many languages. Brodsky's second Russian collection, *A Halt in the Wilderness*, appeared in 1970 in New York.

By the late 1960s Brodsky had developed a unique poetic style. In the Soviet Union he only managed to publish a handful of poems and translations; he refused to compromise with the Soviet regime. In May 1972 the authorities insisted that Brodsky fill out an application to emigrate to Israel, and he arrived in Vienna on June 4, 1972. In Austria Brodsky finally met his hero, W. H. Auden, who wrote the introduction to Brodsky's *Selected Poems* (1973), translated into English by George L. Kline. Brodsky spent nine years at the University of Michigan, and in 1981 he moved to a professorial position at Mount Holyoke College, dividing his time between New York City and western Massachusetts.

A number of collections and volumes of Brodsky's Russian verse appeared in the West, including *A Part of Speech: Poems 1972–1976* (1977), *The End of a Beautiful Epoch: Poems 1964–71* (1977), *New Stanzas to Augusta: Poems to M. B., 1962–1982* (1983), *Urania* (1987), *Annotations of the Fern* (1990), and *Landscape with a Flood* (1996). In English, Brodsky's poems were collected in *A Part of Speech* (1980), *To Urania* (1988), *So Forth: Poems* (1996), and the posthumous *Collected Poems in English* (2000). Brodsky's *Nativity Poems* have appeared as a book in Russian (1992) and English (2001). The Anglo American renderers of Brodsky's poetry include **Anthony Hecht**, Derek Walcott, and Richard Wilbur. Brodsky cotranslated some of his own poems.

In the 1970s Brodsky began to write nonfiction, and his essays were collected in two English-language volumes, *Less Than One: Selected Essays* (1986) and *Of Grief and Reason: Essays* (1995). Brodsky's book-length essay about Venice, published in English as *Watermark* (1992), is simultaneously a fictional memoir and a treatise on time, exilic memory, and beauty.

In 1981 Brodsky received a MacArthur Foundation "genius" award; in 1986, a National Book Critics Circle Award; and in 1987, the Nobel Prize for Literature. An American citizen since 1977, Brodsky was the fourth writer in Russian—and the second Russian Jew after Boris Pasternak—to have been awarded the prize. From 1991 to 1992 Brodsky was the United States Poet Laureate. An official return of Brodsky's poetry to the USSR occurred in 1987, though poisoned by some xenophobic statements in the Soviet press. Brodsky never visited Russia, where he remains a cult figure. On January 28, 1996, Brodsky died in New York of heart failure.

The lyrical and the epic, the confessional and the didactic, competed in Brodsky's verses. Among the Anglo American poets who played a formative role in Brodsky's development were W. H. Auden, Thomas Hardy, and Robert Frost; among the Russian were Anna Akhmatova, Eduard Bagritsky, Nikolay Kluyev, Osip Mandelstam, Vladimir Mayakovsky, and Boris Slutsky. "[Marina Tsvetaeva] was the only poet . . . with whom I decided not to compete," Brodsky stated in 1979.

"When people try to bring [Brodsky's] immense verbal brilliance into English, what you often get is almost pyrotechnics, and almost brilliance, so partly you read his poetry in English as an act of faith," stated Robert Haas in 1996. Given the circumstances under which Brodsky mastered the English language, as a writer in English he lacked perfect pitch, treating English prosody as though it were Russian in translation. Some of Brodsky's Anglo American admirers and critics failed to acknowledge how much he had done for the preservation of poetry as an *art form*. (*See also* Russian American Literature)

Further Reading

Bethea, David M. *Joseph Brodsky and the Creation of Exile*. Princeton, NJ: Princeton UP, 1994.

Polukhina, Valentina. *Joseph Brodsky: A Poet for Our Time*. Cambridge: Cambridge UP, 1989.

Maxim D. Shrayer

BRONER, E(STHER) M(ASSERMAN) (1930–) Scholar, feminist, novelist, author of short stories, articles and plays. Broner has written deeply moving stories, mostly about Jewish women and families. She is well known for her feminist *Haggadah*, the story of the Passover *seder*, written with Naomi Nimrod. Her work challenges observers of Jewish rituals to include women in meaningful ceremonies. Broner contributes to a growing corpus of Jewish American feminist literature that focuses on community, family, and spirituality.

Broner's *Weave of Women* (1978) is visionary and provocative in terms of women's spirituality and political relations with Israel. Her imagined, perhaps utopian, community develops rituals and relations in a commune based in a Jerusalem home. Written in the 1970s, probably primarily for U.S. feminists, the book emphasizes the Jewish component of women's liberation. She continued to approach North American feminists in a consciousness-raising method of changing Jewish worship, including saying *kaddish* (the mourner's prayer) for her father. She tells her story of this practice, unheard of for a woman in the Orthodox community, in *Mornings and Mourning: A Kaddish Journal* (1994).

In *The Telling: The Story of a Group of Jewish Women Who Journey to Spirituality through Community and Ceremony* (1993), Broner narrates the story of the "seder sisters" who celebrated Passover for nearly twenty years, beginning in 1976. *The Telling* includes *The Women's Haggadah,* written by Broner and Nimrod in Israel during the 1970s. This text was reprinted in *MS Magazine* in the United States and became a touchstone for feminist creativity in revising rituals to incorporate women's spirituality. The group, including Gloria Steinem, Bella Abzug, and Phyllis Chesler, integrated traditional text as well as inclusive prayers and rituals reminding the participants of Jewish women's roles in the community's history. Another sourcebook based in Jewish ritual is *Bringing Home the Light: A Jewish Women's Handbook of Rituals* (1999).

Broner's unusual narrative forms captivated and challenged readers. In *Journal/Nocturnal* (1968) she wrote in two columns, one side featuring the daily observations of a wife and mother and the other side, a secret night or dream diary told in the third person. Her subject matter often focused on the mother-daughter relationship, and her work on this in literature resulted in a collaboration with Cathy Davison in *The Lost Tradition: Mothers and Daughters in Literature* (1981) and *Mothers through the Eyes of Women Writers: A Barnard College Collection* (2001).

Her first published short story, "Sudvick the Nudnik," appeared in the *Auburn Review* in 1949. "New Nobility" won an O. Henry Prize in 1968. Other works include *Her Mothers* (1975) and *Ghost Stories* (1995). Awards include a National Endowment for the Arts fellowship and a Wonder Woman Foundation award. Her works are included in *The Norton Anthology of Jewish American Literature*. Broner was a teacher and writer-in-residence at Wayne State University, Sarah Lawrence College, Columbia University, University of California, Los Angeles, and Haifa University. Her collected writings, correspondence, and recordings are archived at Brandeis University. (*See also* Feminism)

Further Reading

Glazer, Miriam. "Orphans of Culture and of History: Gender and Spirituality in Contemporary Jewish-American Women's Novels." *Tulsa Studies in Women's Literature* 13.1 (1994): 127–41.

Omer, Ranen. "'O, My Shehena, Who Shall Live in Your Tent?': Gender, Diaspora, and the Ambivalence of Return in E. M. Broner's *A Weave of Women*." *Frontiers—A Journal of Women's Studies* 23.1 (2002): 96.

Kristine Peleg

BROOKS, GWENDOLYN (1917–2000) African American poet, novelist, and autobiographer. A prolific poet and an important force in Chicago's black community for more than fifty years, Brooks wrote verse recording the experiences of this community where she lived all her life. The first African American of either gender awarded the Pulitzer Prize for poetry, she served as poet laureate of Illinois from 1968 until her death.

Brooks's dedication to the community that served as her central source of inspiration has been manifest throughout her career. She had little formal training in writing but was encouraged by her working-class parents when she expressed a love for words from early childhood. As a teenager she wrote to the African American writers **James Weldon Johnson** and **Langston Hughes**, both of whom generously responded and with whom she met in person. Remembering the importance of this encouragement, she taught writing workshops and gave readings for aspiring writers of all ages in prisons and other unconventional locations as well as in schools. She sponsored numerous poetry competitions, often donating her own money as prizes. The tribute volume *Say That the River Turns* (1987), containing the poetry of young writers inspired by Brooks, testifies to her impact as a mentor.

In 1967, when Brooks was already a highly established and celebrated poet, the experience of attending a black writers' conference at Fisk University prompted her to fundamentally alter her view of race in America, moving from a belief in integration toward a celebration of black culture. The first part of her autobiography, *Report from Part One* (1972), movingly details how her interactions with young writers influenced by the Black Power Movement shaped this transformation. Her continued dedication to these goals can be seen in her support for black institutions such as the Detroit-based **Broadside Press** and the Chicago-based Third World Press and David Press as well as her own Brooks Press, all

Gwendolyn Brooks, c. 1948. *Courtesy of the Library of Congress.*

of which published her work for many years. She has been cited as a kind of literary mother to the Black Arts poets, especially Don L. Lee (later **Haki Madhubuti**) and Walter Bradford. Her own work can be understood as bearing an important relation both to this tradition and to the work of Afro-Modernist poets like **Robert Hayden** and **Melvin Tolson**. Her work also contains important commonalities with that of black women poets and writers who have gained increased critical attention since the 1970s, including **Mari Evans**, **Audre Lorde**, **Alice Walker**, and **Ntozake Shange**.

It would be a mistake, however, to see this transformation as delineating a "before" and "after"' in Brooks's work. Her dedication to recording the daily lives of those around her forms a common thread throughout her work. Although later poems make less use of certain forms such as the sonnet and the ballad, her dedication to craft remains paramount. She has been particularly successful in writing poetry that is both intricately complex and accessible to a wide audience, including those not accustomed to reading poetry, although she has sometimes described the difficulty of doing so. She has remained specifically committed to the black audience, insisting that black artists work on their own terms and not overly concern themselves with criticism from outside. The titles of her collection *Primer for Blacks* (1980) and anthology *Blacks* (1987) underscore her belief in the value of black culture ("black" being a term she feels speaks more to cultural **identity** and pride, as well as to an international identity, than the label "African American") and her desire that it not be dissolved in the name of integration or universality.

An overview of some of Brooks's most acclaimed work reflects these continuities. Her first collection of poetry, *A Street in Bronzeville* (1945), began the portrait of Chicago's black community that would continue to develop throughout her career. Although rooted in the particular geography of the neighborhood, Brooks has noted that her poems begin less with places than with people. Indeed, the reader of *A Street in Bronzeville* is left with the vivid image of the title characters of poems such as "the mother," who in fact never becomes a mother because of multiple abortions, "the preacher: ruminates behind the sermon," whose thoughts wander to the loneliness of God, and "Sadie and Maud," women who make opposite choices with ambiguous results.

Annie Allen (1949), the work for which Brooks won the Pulitzer Prize, offers an imaginatively rendered depiction of black experience during World War II. Using the unusual genre of mock epic, Brooks explores her title character's longings and dissatisfaction, using the language of fairy tale to see how family life, romance, and marriage are not only interrupted by war but disappoint in and of themselves. Like much of her work, *Annie Allen* links the experiences of its central figure to a wider context, suggesting the possibilities of transformation available to the larger community of which Annie is a part. Brooks continued her experiments with form in her novel *Maud Martha* (1953). In this work Brooks uses her own highly poetic prose to tell a coming-of-age story that draws heavily on her own experiences, with a particular emphasis on marriage and motherhood, themes that recur throughout her work.

Although published before Brooks's experience at the Fisk conference, *The Bean Eaters* (1960) marks a turning point in her work and anticipates much that was to come. The collection, which Brooks has noted that she prefers to the prize-winning *Annie Allen*, contains many memorable poems that mix the everyday with a wider context, beginning with a dedicatory poem to her father. "We Real Cool" succinctly distills the swagger of young pool players and is perhaps Brooks's most famous poem, while "The Lovers of the Poor" humorously sends-up delicate do-gooders. In "The Last Quatrain of the Ballad of Emmet Till," Brooks turns her attention to the historical figure of a young boy killed in a racist attack and attempts to imagine a mother's grief.

In the Mecca (1968) continues this concern with important black historical figures with "Medgar Evers" and "**Malcolm X**," both of which turn the poet's eye for detail onto these larger-than-life figures while retaining a sense of awe in their presence. The collection draws on Brooks's experience of working for a "spiritual advisor" in a large Chicago housing complex as a young woman during the Depression. The title poem is a long weaving together of the stories of residents of the Mecca, the form emphasizing the difficulty and claustrophobia but also the possibility of these lives. Later sections include a sequence evoking the Blackstone Rangers, a street gang with whom Brooks herself had conducted writing workshops; dedications at two very different Chicago locations; and the first and second variations on "The Sermon on the Warpland," direct addresses Brooks has continued to rework throughout her career. Her poetic concern with specific historical events and figures continued in *Riot* (1969), which addressed the national crisis that followed the assassination of **Martin Luther King Jr.**, and in later works including *Mayor Harold Washington and Chicago, the I Will City* (1983), *The Near-Johannesburg Boy and Other Poems* (1986), and *Winnie* (1988), a long poem dedicated to Winnie Mandela, wife of South African leader Nelson Mandela and in Brooks's estimation an estimable freedom fighter in her own right. (*See also* African American Poetry)

Further Reading

Gayles, Gloria Wade, ed. *Conversations with Gwendolyn Brooks*. Jackson: UP of Mississippi, 2003.

Mootry, Maria K., and Gary Smith, eds. *A Life Distilled: Gwendolyn Brooks, Her Poetry and Fiction*. Urbana: U of Illinois P, 1987.

Laura Tanenbaum

BROUMAS, OLGA (1949–) Greek American poet and translator. Olga Broumas meshes allusions to Greek mythology and history with contemporary idiom to create verse that explores sensation, emotion, and modes of linguistic and physical expression. Her intense curiosity about the relationship between human beings, their bodies, language, and the environment invests her poetry with vitality and mystery. Broumas's passion for lyric is paralleled by her interest in music and movement. Her diverse occupations reflect these: Broumas is also a translator, a **jazz** musician, and a licensed massage therapist. During her undergraduate and graduate study, Broumas also took up modern dance and printmaking. She is currently poet-in-residence at Brandeis University.

Born and raised on the island of Syros in Greece, Broumas came to the United States as a Fulbright exchange student. She attended the University of Pennsylvania and received a BA in architecture in 1970. Broumas's first book of poetry, *ANHΣYXIEΣ (Restlessness)*, was written in Greek and published in 1967. Pursuing her interest in verse, Broumas earned an MFA in Creative Writing at the University of Oregon in 1973. After teaching at the University of Oregon from 1973 to 1976, Broumas served as the poet-in-residence for Goddard College in Vermont and for the Women Writers Center in Cazenovia, New York.

Her volume of poetry titled *Beginning with O* (1976) won the Yale Younger Poets Prize. Broumas was the first nonnative English-speaking poet to receive the accolade. She was awarded a grant from the National Endowment for the Arts in 1978 and a Guggenheim fellowship in 1981. Broumas also helped to establish Freehand Inc., a learning community of women writers and photographers in Provincetown, Massachusetts. She has published a number of other poetry collections, including *Soie Sauvage* (1980), *Pastoral Jazz* (1983), and *Perpetua* (1989), as well as *Black Holes, Black Stockings* (1985), a collaboration with American poet Jane Miller. Broumas has also translated three volumes of poems and a volume of essays by Odysseas Elytis.

The social condition of women is at the center of Broumas's poetry. In the 1980s, her interest in lyric has given way to more direct narration, which has allowed for a more powerful depiction of lives. Notions of love and family are challenged by her feminist standpoint and her concentration on lesbian experiences. So, too, does Broumas challenge formal and stylistic requirements, embracing experimentation in versification. *Caritas* (1976), a chap-book, was Broumas's first work published in the United States. Unbound and defying poetical convention, the work framed a woman's declaration for a female lover. Broumas chose the Greek word meaning "affection" for her title because it seemed free of conventional (i.e., heterosexual) connotations inherent in the English language.

The poet and literary critic **Stanley Kunitz** recognized Broumas's force when he chose *Beginning with O* as the seventy-second winner of the Yale Younger Poets Prize in 1976. In his introduction, Kunitz celebrates the freedom of Broumas's openly erotic verse and her desire to investigate the possibilities and limitations of language. The volume presents revised Greek myths, which lead into a central section devoted to her former husband, and it concludes with celebrations of lesbian experiences and explorations of the mother-daughter relationship. Politically and poetically, Broumas's work is strident in its appeal to subvert conventions, and yet it recognizes the poet's ancestry, noting Broumas's debt to Sappho, the sixth century B.C.E. Greek poetess. In *Sappho's Gymnasium* (1994), Broumas collaborated with T. Begley to create a volume that paid homage to Sappho as well as Odysseus Elytis, the 1979 Greek Nobel laureate. The volume explores the aural and etymological possibilities available to the poets through appropriation and subversion of poetic conventions.

Broumas's focus on lesbian love broadened in her later volumes. In *Rave: Poems 1975–1999*, Broumas collected verse from her major volumes. The poems vary tremendously in form: some present a mythic quality in their employment of ocean imagery; others blast their critique of destructive attitudes towards nature. (*See also* Greek American Poetry)

Further Reading

Dalven, Rae, ed. *Daughters of Sappho: Contemporary Greek Women Poets.* Toronto: Associated UP, 1994.

McEwen, Christian, ed. *Naming the Waves: Contemporary Lesbian Poetry.* London: Virago, 1988.

Van Dyck, Karen. *Kassandra and the Censors: Greek Poetry since 1967.* Ithaca, NY: Cornell UP, 1998.

Michele Gemelos

BROWN, CECIL M. (1943–) African American novelist and playwright. Cecil Morris Brown's works often include recurring themes of society's systematic suppression of expression from disenfranchised minorities and of minorities' ability to survive in a not so friendly or just world. Nowhere is this sentiment as visible as in Brown's first published work, *The Life and Loves of Mr. Jiveass Nigger* (1970). Here he introduces readers to Mr. George Washington, a young black man who leaves the United States for Copenhagen in an attempt to escape the harshness of black life and establish himself anew, yet finds such reinvention impossible. Mr. Washington's experiences abroad inspire him to write his memoirs upon his inevitable return home to America. Reactions from critics to the novel were mixed; some compared his work to James Joyce and **Ralph Ellison,** whereas others felt the novel lacked plot.

Brown's works are reminiscently autobiographical, and his second and third novels, *Days Without Weather* (1983) and *Coming Up Down Home* (1993), unquestionably provide glimpses into his life that are mesmerizing and humorous. *Days Without Weather*, winner of the Before Columbus Foundation American Book Award, draws upon Brown's Hollywood experiences as a writer for Universal and Warner Brothers. A young black comedian, Jonah, attempts to cinematize a friend's script about a historic slave revolt, but encounters sabotage at the hands of the producer and his uncle. Reminiscent of Spike Lee's *Bamboozled*, Jonah's protests lead to a riot at the studio. The riot is filmed, released, and garners high praise. *Days Without Weather* and *The Life and Loves of Mr. Jiveass Nigger* demonstrate Brown's natural penchant to combine humor with tales meant to question human morality and decency. Brown's knack for humor is further evident in *Coming Up Down Home: A Memoir of a Southern Childhood* (1993). In this novel, Brown presents a vivid self-portrait of growing up amid the racial strife in the rural South. He invites readers to share in his joys and pains as he and his brother confront abandonment, separation, and brutality, and yet it is poignantly understood that many were dealt such fates and had to either perish or prevail.

Influenced by the works of **James Baldwin**, **Richard Wright**, and Ralph Ellison, Brown chronicles in *Stagolee Shot Billy* (2003) the life of a literary and musical legend that transcends accepted attitudes toward African American males, including unprovoked clashes with the police. In this work, which grew out of his dissertation, he revisits St. Louis on Christmas Eve, 1895. This is the event that would etch the mythologized legend of Staggerlee, or Stack-A-Lee, into the catacombs of African American musical folklore. Using variants of the song "Stack Lee," Brown recalls Lee Shelton's murder of Billy Lyons, the brother-in-law of an influential black Republican.

In addition to novels, Brown penned several plays, independent films, and the screenplay for *Which Way Is Up?* (1977), in which Richard Pryor played the lead role. He has also written numerous articles and received numerous awards and recognitions, including a fellowship from the **W. E. B. Du Bois** Institute at Harvard University, University of California at Berkeley's Mentor Fellowship, the Besonders Wertvoll Film Preises German Prize for Film, the Berlin Literary Fellowship, and the Professor John Angus Burrell Memorial Prize. His teaching stints have primarily been in California, but he also taught in France and in Germany.

Further Reading

Margolies, Edward. "Cecil Brown, *Stagolee Shot Billy*." *African American Review* 38 (2004): 171–72.

Clarissa West-White

BROWN, CLAUDE (1937–2002) African American autobiographer, essayist, and activist. Claude Brown's most important contribution to African American literature is his autobiography *Manchild in the Promised Land* (1965), which offers a wrenching portrait of growing up on the streets of Harlem in the 1940s and 1950s. *Manchild in the Promised Land* became a best seller almost instantly, and to date there are an estimated four million copies in print. At the time of its publication, Brown was heralded as the voice of his generation, and *Manchild* as the harbinger of important transitions in African American literature. Curiously, the book has received little sustained critical attention in literary circles since its appearance, but has been widely read as a social history. This lack of critical attention may be due to the view of it more as a social record than as a literary text that transcends the decade of its composition.

A member of a notorious street gang at age nine, Brown had been a thief and drug dealer for eleven years when he left street life at seventeen to pursue an education. He worked his way through high school and entered Howard University, where he began to study writing and submit pieces to magazines. Brown's autobiography grew out of an article about Harlem that he wrote for *Dissent* at the urging of Ernest Papanek, a white educator who had mentored Brown during his stay at the Wiltwyck reform school for boys. The article caught the attention of editors at Macmillan, who offered Brown an advance to complete a book about Harlem. Having never written anything like the book he wanted to produce, Brown turned to **Frederick Douglass**'s *Narrative* and **Richard Wright**'s *Black Boy* and *Eight Men* as guides.

Like Douglass and Wright, Brown positions himself as one of the fortunate few to make it out, and therefore one in a position to help others by telling his story. However, *Manchild* is not tightly focused on the steps that led to Brown's escape from the ghetto. His intention is not to offer his path as a model. Neither is his aim to indict the white community for its failure to offer legal and economic assistance to those struggling upward, although there are many examples of this failure in the book. In recounting his life history, Brown is more concerned with presenting a realistic portrait of Harlem than with promoting a specific social agenda. Ultimately, *Manchild in the Promised Land* is not a criticism of the forces that limited opportunities for the children of the great migration, nor is it a defense of the lost generation's choices, but a text that asks for understanding and acceptance of them. Brown introduces readers to a host of juvenile delinquents, thieves, junkies, and prostitutes in order to explore a community's self-destruction and analyze the lure of criminal life for a generation of African Americans who felt ostracized from American freedoms and opportunities.

In his second book, *The Children of Ham* (1976), Brown again depicts Harlem teenagers struggling to find their way in a world defined by drugs, crime, and prostitution. Here he tells the story of thirteen young people who have formed a "family" in an abandoned building as a means of escaping the drug-defined world in which they live. Having run away from parents who are junkies and alcoholics, they encourage each other to stay clean and pursue their dreams. In this book, Brown adopts the persona of a social worker who visits the runaways, a choice criticized by many reviewers who thought that his language was stiff and distant. Perhaps for this reason, *The Children of Ham* never became as popular or influential as *Manchild in the Promised Land*, but the book is important for its depiction of those determined to survive amid the crushing forces of urban life.

In addition to writing *Manchild in the Promised Land* and *The Children of Ham*, Brown published articles in magazines such as *Esquire, Life,* the *Saturday*

Evening Post, and the *New York Times Magazine*. He also became a noted lecturer and activist, speaking about his experiences and establishing programs designed to help kids escape street life. (*See also* African American Autobiography)

Further Reading

Baker, Houston A., Jr. "The Environment as Enemy in a Black Autobiography: *Manchild in the Promised Land.*" *Phylon* 32.1 (1971): 53–59.

Amanda M. Lawrence

BROWN, FRANK LONDON (1927–1962) Novelist, short story writer, and social activist. Born in Kansas City, Frank London Brown was an important figure among black writers and artists in Chicago in the 1940s and 1950s. A committed leftist in the era of Joseph McCarthy, Brown's life work is a testament both to his energy and to his conviction that art and activism can and should be inextricably linked. Although he died of leukemia at age thirty-four, he had, in addition to writing fiction, worked as a journalist (notably covering the murder of Emmett Till in 1955), been a regular contributor to literary magazines, held positions as a union organizer and as an associate editor of *Ebony*, and had nearly completed a PhD in political science at the University of Chicago, where he had been a fellow of the Committee on Social Thought and director of its Union Research Center. Finally, Brown, who was also a musician, is also noted for his enthusiastic support of bebop and for pioneering the reading of literature to jazz accompaniment.

Although both of Brown's novels, *Trumbull Park* (1959) and *The Myth Maker* (posthumously published in 1969), are influenced by **Richard Wright**, the former as an example of social realist fiction and the latter for its interest in existentialism, Brown's writing is distinct and far from derivative. *Trumbull Park* deals with resistance to the integration of a formerly all-white Chicago housing development called Trumbull Park, and is based on Brown's own experience. Perhaps the novel's semiautobiographical nature is the reason Robert E. Fleming asserts "Brown's picture of Negro life is more thorough than Wright's because it emphasizes the humanity of black people by presenting their daily lives" (79). The novel tells the story of the family of Buggy and Helen Martin, who decide to leave the filth and unsafe conditions of their South Side apartment building and move into a white community where one other black family already lives. Met by an intensifying campaign of intimidation by angry whites, Buggy Martin fears that he lacks the courage to stand up to his oppressors; however, inspired by his wife's courage, he ultimately finds the strength to embrace nonviolent resistance; he walks singing through a white mob to enter his house. *The Myth Maker* tells the story of a young black man, Ernest Day, who is driven by self-hatred to commit an unprovoked murder. Day kills an old man who smiles at him, justifying his act by insisting that in a racist society, the man, who is also black, had no reason to live. Day realizes by the novel's end that in murdering the old man, he has also killed a part of himself.

Brown is known primarily for *Trumbull Park*; his other writings have been largely ignored. Well received upon publication, *Trumbull Park* sold 25,000 copies and garnered good reviews. However, it has received little critical attention since. Despite a recent essay by Mary Helen Washington calling for the reconsideration of Brown as a radical voice in African American letters, he remains underappreciated.

Further Reading

Fleming, Robert E. "Overshadowed by Richard Wright: Three Black Chicago
 Novelists." *Negro American Literature Forum* 7.3 (1973): 75–79.
Graham, Maryemma. "Bearing Witness in Black Chicago: A View of Selected
 Fiction by Richard Wright, Frank London Brown, and Ronald Fair." *CLA Journal*
 33 (1990): 280–97.
Washington, Mary Helen. "Desegregating the 1950s: The Case of Frank London
 Brown." *Japanese Journal of American Studies* 10 (1999): 15–32.

Stephanie Brown

BROWN GIRL, BROWNSTONES Paule Marshall's *Brown Girl, Brownstones* (1959) is one of the earliest Caribbean American coming-of-age novels. The loosely autobiographical story follows the adolescence of Selina Boyce, who, like Marshall, grew up the daughter of Barbadian immigrants in Brooklyn in the 1930s and 1940s. As Selina grows up, she learns to understand her individual **identity** in relation to her family and her community. She comes to terms with being a black girl in the United States, acknowledging her connections to the African American community through the experience of **racism**, and her connections to all immigrants through the experience of leaving home in search of greater opportunity.

As a girl, Selina felt closest to her father, Deighton. She spent long hours listening to him reminisce about Barbados and develop plans to one day return. Selina finds herself estranged from her mother, Silla, who throws her energies into the American dream of buying a house and seeing her daughters rise above her socially and economically. The increasing conflict between Selina's parents reaches its apex in a tragic series of deceptions involving a piece of land in Barbados and the money for a downpayment on a brownstone in Brooklyn, and culminates in Deighton's suicide. The suicide devastates Selina and heightens her distrust of her mother, but it also initiates a new bond between mother and daughter. The two must rely on one another. Selina begins to understand her mother and even to repeat her mother's recourse to devious, unsympathetic means to attain her goals. Selina becomes a young woman when she strikes out on her own, in much the same way that Silla did in her time.

At once tragic and hopeful, *Brown Girl, Brownstones* depicts the failings of the American dream even as it describes the emergence of an ethnic American subject. Selina epitomizes the first generation of Caribbean Americans who maintain a connection to the parents' Caribbean heritage, but understand that they are themselves firmly rooted in their American surroundings. *Brown Girl, Brownstones* describes the passage, through the process of immigration and in the course of one generation, from an identity based on one particular nationality, that of the Barbadian, to an identity based on a combination of race and regional or diaspora culture, that of the brown girl.

Since its republication in the early 1980s, *Brown Girl, Brownstones* has generated substantial critical attention as an exemplary black female coming-of-age novel. (*See also* Caribbean [Anglophone] American Novel)

Further Reading

Buma, Pascal P. "Paule Marshall's *Brown Girl, Brownstones*: A Nexus Between the Caribbean and the African American Bildungsroman." *CLA Journal* 44.3 (2001): 303–16.

Byerman, Keith E. "Gender, Culture, and Identity in Paule Marshall's *Brown Girl, Brownstones.*" *Redefining Autobiography in Twentieth-Century Women's Fiction*. Ed. Janice Morgan, Colette Hall, Carol Snyder, and Molly Hite. New York: Garland, 1991. 135–47.

DeLamotte, Eugenia C. *Places of Silence, Journeys of Freedom: The Fiction of Paule Marshall*. Philadelphia: U of Pennsylvania P, 1998.

Keja Lys Valens

BROWN, JOHN (1800–1859)   **Abolition**ist John Brown was not an ethnic American nor was he a writer. Yet his influence on American literature—by or about African Americans—is vast. Essayists, historians, novelists, playwrights, and poets have found Brown to be a symbol of commitment to the cause of black freedom. Although Brown's personal life was marked by poverty, family deaths, and failed business ventures, he found enduring success as a martyr to the cause of equality, as a voice for resistance, and as a prophet of racial relations. Brown died convinced that he was acting on behalf of God and enslaved African Americans. Unlike even the most sympathetic northern white people, Brown was distinguished by his extraordinary identification with Negroes among whom he lived and worked. Brown's militant opposition to **slavery** first arose while defending the free-soil settlers in Kansas and culminated in October 1859 when he led his followers on a raid of the federal arsenal at Harpers Ferry. Convicted of treason, Brown was hanged on December 2, 1859, a day that became holy for many.

At the time of his death, John Brown drew tributes from notable white authors who saw him as a sign of white America's potential for redemption. Henry David Thoreau, Ralph Waldo Emerson, William Lloyd Garrison, and others published defenses of his actions and character. Brown was the subject of poetry by Henry Wadsworth Longfellow, William Dean Howells, and John Greenleaf Whittier. The song "John Brown's Body" was created and sung in tribute by Union soldiers, and eventually led Julia Ward Howe to compose "Battle Hymn of the Republic." **Frederick Douglass**, among Brown's African American contemporaries, admired Brown's passion and commitment. In subsequent years, Brown's reputation as a champion of African American causes continued to rise in the African American community and was espoused by leaders like **W. E. B. Du Bois** at the beginning of the century and later by **Malcolm X** during the Black Power Movement. Writers like Lerone Bennett Jr., **Michael Harper, William Blackwell Branch**, and Stephen Butterfield have used Brown as a figure in their works.

At his trial defending his actions, Brown made explicit his identification with people of color: "The Bible . . . which teaches me that all things whatsoever I would that men should do to me, I should do even so to them. It teaches me further to remember them that are in bonds as bound with them. . . . Now if it deemed necessary that I should forfeit my life for the furtherance of the ends of justice, and mingle my blood further with the blood of my children and with the blood of millions of this Slave-country, whose rights are disregarded by wicked, cruel, and unjust enactments, I say let it be done" (qtd. in Peterson 14).

John Brown, 1859. *Courtesy of the Library of Congress.*

Further Reading

Aptheker, Herbert. *Abolitionism: A Revolutionary Movement.* Boston, G. K. Hall and Co., 1989.

Du Bois, W. E. B. (1973 reprint). *John Brown.* Millwood, NY: Kraus-Thomson, 1909.

Peterson, Merrill D. *John Brown: The Legend Revisited.* Charlottesville: UP of Virginia, 2002.

Kimberly Rae Connor

BROWN, LINDA BEATRICE (1939–) African American poet and novelist. Publication of *Love Song to Black Men* (1974) gave Brown entrée to the generation of African American writers and poets emerging out of the 1960s whose experimental forms and celebration of being black, coupled with their outrage at the injustice of **racism,** signified a new aesthetic in literature.

Brown began writing short stories at fourteen, but in later interviews confided that lyrical poems suited her youthful sensibilities better. Excelling in this form, her first poem was published in 1958. In her thirties she returned to writing fiction, exploring issues that had fashioned her inner life and developed her sense of right and wrong.

As a writer, Brown placed herself within the continuum of African American women authors creating sacred texts and sacred writings. However, Brown resisted being pigeonholed as either an African American or woman or American writer and defined herself in humanitarian terms.

While attending Bennett College in Greensboro, North Carolina, in the early 1960s, Brown heard **Langston Hughes**, **Sterling Brown**, and **Martin Luther King Jr.** speak on her campus. Her growing political awareness is reflected in her early poem "Precocious Curiosity," published in the collection *Beyond the Blues* (1962).

Love Song to Black Men (1974) was a culmination of a decade's creative work. Described as lyrical and quiet, Brown's work merged reflections of her personal spirituality with her growing sense of civic responsibility.

With her fiction debut, *Rainbow 'Roun Mah Shoulder* (1984), Brown won the North Carolina Cultural Arts Coalition Prize, and the National Endowment for the Arts selected the novel as one of few titles suitable to embody the new American writing. Although Brown's father moved his family from Mississippi to Akron, Ohio, where she was born, Brown's fiction is set in the South. *Rainbow* narrates an African American woman's self-discovery, spanning from 1915 to 1954. Brown developed themes of healing, metamorphosis, and redemption as her character followed her calling to serve the Lord despite the desertion of her husband and being called a witch by her congregation.

In *Crossing Over Jordan* (1995) Brown elaborated on social conditions once again in the South, this time in Georgia. By employing several points of view, Brown followed cycles of oppression and **slavery**'s legacy of familial dysfunction through four generations of mother-daughter relationships.

With Brooke Davis Anderson she wrote *Forget-Me-Not: The Art of Mystery Jugs* (1996), which commented on the meanings behind African American funerary customs as represented by the crude beauty of decorated clay vessels. Brown published a biography of her aunt, *Long Walk: The Story of Willa B. Player as President of Bennett College* (1999), in which she documents the achievements of the first African American woman to serve as president of a four-year college. Brown detailed Player's role in backing the burgeoning **Civil Rights Movement** in Greensboro.

Further Reading

Narisn, Brigham, and Stanley, Deborah A., eds. "Elizabeth Cook-Lynn." *Contemporary Literary Criticism*. Vol. 93. Detroit: Gale Research, 1996. 114–32.

Rebecca Tolley-Stokes

BROWN, ROSELLEN (1939–) Jewish American poet and novelist. Much of Rosellen Brown's work draws on her experiences living in the

South during the **Civil Rights Movement**, and a focus of her work is the relationship between the individual and the community. She is a highly respected author of both poetry and fiction.

Born in Philadelphia on May 12, 1939, Brown moved with her family several times during her youth. Consequently, Brown felt somewhat alienated at school. She used her free time to write, and in high school she was devoted to journalism, which resulted in a scholarship to Barnard College. She earned her BA in 1960, then an MA from Brandeis in 1962. Brown then received a Woodrow Wilson Fellowship in 1965 and moved with her husband to Mississippi, where she taught at Tougaloo College (an African American school). The Civil Rights Movement was in full force, and this influenced Brown's first poetry collection, *Some Deaths in the Delta and Other Poems* (1970). Brown then moved to Brooklyn, New York, for three years, and Brooklyn became the setting for her second work, *Street Games: A Neighborhood* (1974). This autobiographical connection continued as Brown later moved to New Hampshire, which in turn became the setting for *Cora Fry* (1977).

Brown has received numerous awards and grants for her work, including two grants from the National Endowment for the Humanities, a Guggenheim fellowship, and a Best First Novel award from the Great Lakes College Association, for *The Autobiography of My Mother* (1976). She has taught at Tougaloo College, Goddard College, Boston University, University of Houston, Northwestern University, and the School of the Art Institute of Chicago.

The exploration of relationships is Brown's primary concern in her writing. *Some Deaths in the Delta* examines **racism**. *Street Games*, a collection of linked short stories, explores further the relations between people of different races and beliefs. In Brown's first two novels, *The Autobiography of My Mother* and *Tender Mercies* (1978), familial relationships take center stage, the latter being about a family's struggle to cope with a terrible accident. The poem collection *Cora Fry* focuses on a housewife's marital relationship and Brown continues this story nearly twenty years later in *Cora Fry's Pillow Book* (1994). In *Civil Wars* (1984), Brown revisits the South, the Civil Rights Movement, and its aftermath through Jessie and Teddy—an unhappily married couple still clinging to their 1960s ideologies, which seem outdated and awkward in their 1980s community.

Brown's best-known work is her fourth novel, *Before and After* (1992), which became a *New York Times* best seller. It, too, centers on relationships, as an examination of the Reiser family's experience after the teenage son murders his girlfriend. The narrative pays little attention to the murder itself, focusing instead on the individual attempts of the mother, father, and sister to cope with it and with the murderer—their son and brother, Jacob—in their small community.

Further Reading

Lee, Don. "About Rosellen Brown." *Ploughshares* 20.2–3 (Fall 1994): 235–40.

J. P. Steed

BROWN, STERLING (1901–1989)   African American poet and literary critic. Through his poetry, criticism, and teaching, Sterling Allen Brown illuminated the vibrancy of the black folk aesthetic and its centrality to African American literature and American literature as a whole. Influenced by the realism and regionalism of Edwin Arlington Robinson and Robert Frost, and by the efforts of J. M. Synge and **Carl Sandburg** to capture the speech of the people, Brown expands the traditions of black folk portraiture and dialect poetry as developed by **Paul Laurence Dunbar**, **Charles Chesnutt**, and **James Weldon Johnson**. Furthermore, Brown's work broadens the geographical, temporal, and political boundaries of the "**Harlem Renaissance**," a term that Brown rejected in favor of the term "**New Negro** Renaissance" in order to emphasize that this movement went beyond Harlem and the 1920s, and that it was integral to the development of American literature.

Brown was born in Washington, DC, in 1901 to Rev. Sterling Nelson Brown, a minister of Lincoln Temple Congregational Church and professor of religion at Howard University, and Adelaide Allen Brown, a valedictorian of Fisk University who fostered her son's appreciation of poetry and his cultural heritage. At Dunbar High School, Brown studied English with **Angelina Weld Grimké**, French and Latin with **Jessie Fauset**, and history with Haley Douglass, grandson of **Frederick Douglass**. Brown received scholarships to Williams College and Harvard, where he earned a master's degree in 1923. For the next three years, Brown taught English at Virginia Theological Seminary and College; there his pursuit of writing coincided with his immersion into the culture of the surrounding rural communities, including their spirituals and **blues**, stories and aphorisms. In particular, Brown's encounter with an itinerant guitarist named Calvin "Big Boy" Davis inspired several of Brown's best poems. Brown continued to seek the *raconteurs* of his people while teaching at Lincoln University (1926–28) and Fisk University (1928–29). In 1929 Brown returned to Howard, where he taught for over forty years, and the period from 1929 to 1945 was his most productive as a writer.

Brown's first collection of poems, *Southern Road* (1932), deftly incorporates the structure, rhythm, and tone of the spirituals ("When De Saints Go Ma'ching Home"), the blues ("Ma Rainey"), the work song ("Southern Road"), and the ballad ("Odyssey of Big Boy") in order to depict the heroic resilience as well as the hardships of black life. This theme is also conveyed by the book's metaphor of black experience, the road, which is variously manifested as the river, the railroad, and the road to Glory. Brown's poetic range is further evidenced by the book's last section, comprising his earlier work in traditional Euro-American forms. Despite the critical success of *Southern Road*, Brown could not publish his second collection of poetry, *No Hiding Place*, possibly due to its Marxist perspective. Mostly written from 1932 to 1937, *No Hiding Place* presents Brown's class as well as racial consciousness, expressed as ever with irony, wit, and Brown's keen ear for folk speech. Brown's next book of poetry, *The Last Ride of Wild Bill and Eleven Narrative Poems* (1975), explores the African American heroic tradition. It appeared only after his work had been rediscovered as a result of the Black Power Movement. In 1980, Michael Harper edited *The Collected Poems of Sterling A. Brown*, which presents the poetry from all three collections.

Brown's contributions to African American literature extend beyond his groundbreaking poetry. Throughout the 1930s, Brown wrote a column for *Opportunity*, "The Literary Scene: Chronicle and Comment," which examined developments in literature by and about African Americans. From 1936 to 1940, Brown served as the editor of Negro affairs within the Federal Writers' Project (FWP). In this capacity, Brown coordinated all FWP studies on black life, including the collection of oral histories of ex-slaves, and the representation of African Americans in the FWP state guidebooks. Brown shaped black literary studies through critical work such as *Negro Poetry and Drama* and *The Negro in American Fiction* (both 1937), and the important anthology *The Negro Caravan* (1941), edited with Arthur P. Davis and Ulysses Lee. Brown's poetry, criticism, teaching, and scholarship enabled more truthful representations of African Americans, while demonstrating the influences and histories that African American and European American literatures share. (*See also* African American Poetry)

Further Reading

Callaloo 21.4 (Fall 1998) [special issue devoted to critical assessments of Sterling A. Brown's work].

Gabbin, Joanne V. *Sterling A. Brown: Building the Black Aesthetic Tradition.* Westport, CT: Greenwood Press, 1985.

Sanders, Mark A. *Afro-Modernist Aesthetics and the Poetry of Sterling A. Brown.* Athens: U of Georgia P, 1999.

Cheryl Higashida

BRUCE-NOVOA, JUAN (1944–)   Chicano writer, translator, critic, teacher, and scholar. Juan Bruce-Novoa, or as he prefers, Bruce-Novoa, is a prominent figure in Chicana/o literary criticism, and a tireless supporter of Chicana/o studies in the United States, Mexico, and Western Europe. Born in Costa Rica, where his father worked in the coffee industry, Bruce-Novoa spent his childhood and early adult years in Texas and Colorado. He obtained an MA (1968) and a PhD (1974), the latter in Latin American literature, from the University of Colorado, Boulder. He currently teaches in the Department of Spanish and Portuguese at the University of California, Irvine.

Bruce-Novoa's essays—many collected in *RetroSpace* (1990)—have been highly influential in the development of Chicana/o literary trends and criticism since the 1960s. This role is exemplified by the wide impact of Bruce-Novoa's argument that Chicana/o writers occupy an interstitial and intercultural "literary space." That is, Chicana/o literature forms a neo-national body of writing that emerges in the gaps between U.S. and Mexican literary terrains, and that, nonetheless, argues both national traditions.

More controversial was Bruce-Novoa's advocacy of the need for Chicana/o writers to overcome parochial and minority literary concerns and seek themes, styles, and literary models that would have appeal beyond a purported Chicana/o-only reading audience, as befits a "world" literature. In addition to these concerns, Bruce-Novoa was perhaps the earliest critical champion of Chicana/o gay and lesbian writers, hence his strong defense of **John Rechy** and **Sheila Ortiz Taylor** and their formative contributions to the Chicana/o literary canon.

Paralleling Bruce-Novoa's long-standing critical reputation is his output as a creative writer, which includes the bilingual book of erotic and metaphysical verse, *Inocencia perversa = Perverse Innocence* (1977), and a collection of stories originally published in literary magazines and journals over a twenty-plus year period, *Manuscrito de origen* (1995). Bruce-Novoa has also published a novel, *Only the Good Times* (1995). This experimental, episodic, and self-consciously melodramatic narrative spans the era from the late 1950s to the 1980s, and follows the career of Paul, a Chicano cinematographer who cannot separate his desires from his artistic production and aesthetic themes. The protagonist's lifelong obsession for Ann Marisse, which informs and inspires his cinematic output for decades, is framed by a host of intertextual references to popular music, film, and literature, and is punctuated by the narrator's aside footnotes about his editorial discussions, organization of material, and the reliability of his memories. Yet, like Bruce-Novoa's creative work in general, this novel—at once a romance and a memoir of the post–World War II era from a Chicano perspective—has not attracted the level of critical attention paid to his theoretical writing.

Further Reading

Bruce-Novoa. *RetroSpace: Collected Essays on Chicano Literature, Theory and History.* Houston: Arte Público Press, 1990.

Pérez-Torres, Rafael. *Movements in Chicano Poetry: Against Myths, Against Margins.* Cambridge: Cambridge UP, 1995.

Paul Allatson

BRUCHAC, JOSEPH (1942–) Native American author, editor, musician, teacher, and storyteller of mixed ancestry. Joseph Bruchac's father's family was Slovak, and his mother's was English and Abenaki. Born October 16, 1942, in New York, Bruchac grew up in the Adirondack foothills town of Greenfield Center, New York. He has written short stories, poems, novels, and essays. He has also recorded music and stories on *Abenaki Cultural Heritage* and *Alnobak*, Good Mind Records. He earned a BA from Cornell University, an MA in literature and creative writing from Syracuse University, and a PhD in comparative literature from the Union Institute of Ohio. From 1966 to 1969, Bruchac lived and taught English and literature at Keta Secondary School in Ghana, West Africa. Upon returning to the United States, he taught creative writing and African and black literatures at Skidmore College, Saratoga Springs, New York. Bruchac has also taught creative writing for the Great Meadows Institute in Comstock Prison.

Through his literary work, he has managed to preserve Native American culture, language, and traditions. He has also worked toward creating a space for the works of other cultural groups as well. In 1977 he edited (along with Roger Weaver) *Aftermath: An Anthology of Poems in English from Africa, Asia, and the Caribbean*, and in 1984 he edited *Breaking Silence: An Anthology of Contemporary Asian American Poets*. Bruchac's work leans heavily on his own personal experiences, as well as on intense research and data collection on Native American folklore, legends, and individuals. Along with his wife, he created and organized Greenfield Review Press, an independent publishing house. From 1969 to 1990 they published *Greenfield Review*, a magazine committed to publishing multicultural poetry

Joseph Bruchac. *Photo by Carol Bruchac.*

and stories. Greenfield Review Press has published books by Bruchac and other writers who might not have otherwise had their voices heard. His literary works include Native American and universal themes such as reverence for nature, unity with the land and all living things, and spirituality, as well as love of family, friends, and community. Bruchac's family has joined him in his endeavors to preserve culture, history, and the voices of those traditionally silenced. His sons and his sister are all working toward preserving traditional Native American culture, history, and language via specific projects they are developing, as well as through performing in the Dawn Land Singers band.

Bruchac has edited a number of highly praised anthologies of contemporary poetry and fiction, including *The Next World: Poems by Thirty-Two Third-World Americans* (1978), *Songs from This Earth on Turtle's Back: Contemporary American Indian Poetry* (1983), *The Light from Another Country: Poetry from American Prisons* (1984), *New Voices from the Longhouse: An Anthology of Contemporary Iroquois Writing* (1989), and most notably *Smoke Rising: The Native North American Literary Companion* (1995). His poems, articles, and stories have been anthologized in various publications, such as *North Dakota Quarterly, American*

Poetry Review, Studies in American Indian Literatures, Parabola, Smithsonian Magazine, National Geographic, Paris Review, Akwesasne Notes, and *Hudson Review.* He has authored more than eighty books for adults and children, including *The First Strawberries: A Cherokee Story* (1993) (coauthored with Michael Caduto); *A Boy Called Slow* (1998, orig. 1994), illustrated by Rocco Baviera; *The Circle of Thanks: Native American Poems and Songs of Thanksgiving* (1996), illustrated by Murv Jacob; *Between Earth & Sky: Legends of Native American Sacred Places* (1996), illustrated by Thomas Locker; *Squanto's Journey: The Story of the First Thanksgiving* (2000), illustrated by Greg Shed; *Pocahontas* (2003); *Our Stories Remember: American Indian History, Culture, and Values Through Storytelling* (2003); and *The Warriors* (2003).

Other notable books for young people include *Eagle Song* (1995), illustrated by Dan Andreasen. *Eagle Song* tells the story of Danny Bigtree, who moves from a Mohawk reservation to a Brooklyn tenement with his parents. *The Heart of a Chief* (1998) also focuses on a young Native American boy. The protagonist, Chris, a Penacook Indian, becomes a school leader. He encourages others to see that the use of Indian names for school sports teams is dishonorable and offensive. He is also a leader within his community as he protests and argues against allowing a casino on the reservation. Both *Eagle Song* and *The Heart of a Chief* are drawn from Bruchac's experiences working with Native American youth. Cultural **identity** development, resistance, political action, and ecological responsibility are common themes in Bruchac's literature for young adults. *The Earth Under Sky Bear's Feet: Native American Poems of the Land* (1995), illustrated by Thomas Locker, is a collection of twelve Native American poems that celebrate nature, and *Many Nations: An Alphabet of Native America* (1997), illustrated by Robert F. Goetzl, is an alphabet book that identifies numerous Native American tribes and some of their beliefs and traditions. Equally important is *Pushing Up the Sky* (2000), illustrated by Teresa Flavin, a collection of seven traditional Native American tales of Abenaki, Ojibway, Cherokee, Cheyenne, Snohomish, Tlingit, and Zuni origin, restructured into plays for children.

In his picture-book autobiography, *Seeing the Circle*, a part of the Richard C. Owen biography series, he describes his writing process and his heritage; in his book-length autobiography, *Bowman's Store: A Journey to Myself*, reprinted by Lee & Low Publishers in 1997, Bruchac writes of his childhood and his emergence as an author and storyteller. He has performed as a storyteller throughout the United States and in Europe at elementary and secondary schools, organizations, and universities. He does research around Native stories, often collecting them both orally and from various books. He also travels around the country talking to Native people and learning stories, history, and traditions of various tribes. For Bruchac, storytelling, oral or written, seems to be about developing cultural understanding within and outside of cultural groups. As a young boy, his own family was silent about their cultural heritage, leaving Bruchac with a plethora of questions about his cultural identity. Because of Bruchac's contribution to children's and young adult literature, hopefully today's youth will be more knowledgeable of Native American heritage.

Bruchac has received numerous grants, fellowships, and awards, including a New York State CAPS poetry fellowship, a Rockefeller Humanities fellowship, and a National Endowment for the Arts Writing Fellowship for Poetry. He received the American Book Award from the Before Columbus Foundation in 1984 for *Breaking Silence: An Anthology of Contemporary Asian American Poets*; IRA Young Adults and Teachers Choice Award in 1993 for *Thirteen Moons on a Turtle's Back: A Native American Year of Moons*; Young Readers Book Award, Scientific American, in 1995 for *The Story of the Milky Way*; Parents' Choice Honor Award in 1995 for *Dog People: Native Dog Stories*; Notable Children's Book from the American Library Association and Mountains & Plains Booksellers Association Regional Book Award in 1996 for *A Boy Called Slow*; and Nonfiction Honor, Boston Globe-Horn Book, and Notable Children's Book, from the American Library Association, both in 1996, for *The Boy Who Lived with the Bears: And Other Iroquois Stories*. Bruchac's other honors include a Parents' Choice Award, the Skipping Stones Honor Award for Multicultural Children's Literature, the Cherokee Nation Prose Award, Benjamin Franklin Person of the Year Award, the Knickerbocker Award, the Hope S. Dean Award for Notable Achievement in Children's Literature and both the 1998 Writer of the Year Award and the 1998 Storyteller of the Year Award from the Wordcraft Circle of Native Writers and Storytellers. In 1999 he received the Lifetime Achievement Award from the Native Writers Circle of the Americas. As the numerous accolades he has earned suggest, Bruchac has done much to make quality literature about Native American experiences available to readers. (*See also* Native American Poetry)

Further Reading

Andres, Linda R. "Joseph Bruchac." *Children's Literature Review* 46 (1998): 1–24.

Bruchac, Joseph. *Bowman's Store: A Journey to Myself*. New York: Lee & Low Books, 2001.

KaaVonia Hinton-Johnson

BRYANT, DOROTHY (1930–) Italian American novelist and short story writer. Born February 8, 1930, in San Francisco, Dorothy Calvetti Bryant has written prolifically in several genres, including novels, short stories, plays, and nonfiction. Bryant's ancestors were born in Balangero, a village thirty miles northwest of Turin, where her Piemontese relatives worked in the factory town, often laboring fourteen hours a day, six days a week, in the woolen mill. Escaping the rural industrial poverty of their native town, both of Bryant's grandfathers immigrated to America, eventually bringing their families around 1910. Working sporadically in the coal and copper mines, both grandfathers, each suffering from silicosis, wended their way to California. Dorothy Bryant, born in 1930, "along with the

Great Depression," as she says, is the daughter of Joseph, a mechanic, and Judith Chiarle Calvetti, a bookkeeper.

Having grown up in San Francisco's Mission District, a working-class area of factories and small houses with many European and Asian immigrants, Bryant's earliest literary influences may very well have been the pre-war District. Many of her novels, including *Confessions of Madame Psyche, A Day in San Francisco,* and *The Garden of Eros,* portray characters from a variety of ethnic backgrounds. The first of her family to graduate from college, Bryant early considered the local public school and library the "religious temples of [her] childhood." Bryant earned a BA in music in 1950 and an MA in creative writing in 1964 (at San Francisco State University), and her early love of school and abiding respect for the art of teaching were reflected in her career as a high school English teacher and, later, as a college instructor of English and writing in San Francisco. In Bryant's first novel, *Ella Price's Journal* (1972), the female protagonist is herself a working-class woman who returns to college at age thirty-five, developing a commitment to writing through the journal experience. Bryant's second novel, the utopian *The Kin of Ata Are Waiting for You* (1976), became her largest-selling book to date.

Frustrated by marketing considerations, Bryant and her second husband founded ATA Books in 1978, which remarkably kept Bryant's books available through the 1994 publication of *Anita, Anita,* a historical novel about Anita Ribeiro de Duarte, a Brazilian who fought beside Garibaldi in South America and Italy. In 1990 the Feminist Press approached Bryant and reissued four of her novels: *Ella Price's Journal, Miss Giardino, Confessions of Madame Psyche* (for which she won the American Book Award from the Before Columbus Foundation in 1987), and *The Test.* The winner of the Bay Area Circle Critics' Best New Play award for *Dear Master* (about George Sand and Gustave Flaubert) in 1991, Bryantdisplays her strength in writing dialogues, monologues, and her ongoing fascination with historical figures and events. Bryant's *Tea with Mrs. Hardy* (1992) and *The Panel* (1996) were also produced in California.

Bryant's nonfiction book, *Writing a Novel,* comprises, in the author's own words, the "essential three parts of me—the reader, the teacher, the writer." Wide-ranging dramatic narratives emerge out of the richness of Bryant's cultural and regional heritage. An inveterate experimenter in forms including fantasy, historical novels, and fictionalized confessions, Bryant variously populates her landscapes and gives voice to the marginalized. Included are stories of convicts (*Prisoners*), gay men (*A Day in San Francisco,*) a retired schoolteacher (*Miss Giardino*), an old man (*The Test*), and a blind woman (*The Garden of Eros*). For Dorothy Bryant, marginalization is a site of radical narrative possibility, as she gives voice to issues as far ranging as inner-city education, the gay revolution, family relationships, and senility. For Dorothy Calvetti Bryant, fiction does not solve problems; it states them. (*See also* Italian American Novel)

Further Reading

Bryant, Dorothy. *Writing a Novel*. Berkeley: ATA Books, 1979.

———. "Dorothy Bryant." *Contemporary Authors Autobiography Series*. Detroit: Gale Research, 1996. 47–63.

———. "How Many Hyphens Do You Need to Define an Italian-American Writer?" *Adjusting Sites: New Essays in Italian American Studies*. Ed. William Boelhower and Rocco Pallone. New York: Forum Italicum, 1999. 275–281.

Contemporary Authors. Gale Literary Databases. Entry Updated: 2000.

Horn, Barbara. Afterword, "The Tests of Time." *The Test*. Dorothy Bryant. New York: Feminist Press, 2001. 147–170.

Mary Jo Bona

BUDY, ANDREA HOLLANDER (1947–) Jewish American poet, teacher, and essayist. Born in Berlin, Germany, to American parents, Andrea Hollander Budy grew up primarily in the urban northeast of the United States. She was educated at Boston University and the University of Colorado, where she earned an MA in comparative literature and oral interpretation. Since 1977 she has lived in the Arkansas Ozarks. A narrative poet with a gift for finding musicality in ordinary speech, her work is set firmly in the world of sensory detail, often in scenes of domesticity. Budy has said she creates poems by "scooping up from ordinary life, small moments tinged with beauty and grief." Beauty she finds inherent in the world, and grief, eminent, "because we will inevitably lose something or someone, and the beauty will be changed forever" (personal interview, May 21, 2001).

Budy spent twenty years teaching herself to write before publishing her first book at the age of forty-six. *House Without a Dreamer* (1993, 1995) won the 1993 Nicholas Roerich Prize.

Although her Jewishness is not a frequent subject, it informs and colors her work. The recurring themes of beauty, grief, loss, the celebration of marriage, and the examination of creativity that are present in her first volume of poetry are explored more deeply in the second, *The Other Life* (2001). Here the unifying idea that all of us have "other" lives, those of the imagination and those that lie along roads not taken, prompts Budy to draw more directly on her Jewish heritage in some of the poems. "History" and "A Tree Like This One" reference her ancestors' escape from the European pogroms. In the deeply moving "Goodness," she imagines Anne Frank's life had she survived to have a family.

But even these political poems focus on the personal, and therein lies their strength. Though her work recognizes that the quotidian can be interrupted by the horrible—her mother's cancer and her father's Alzheimer's disease are recurring subjects—she rejects anger and helplessness. Instead, she draws from these horrors, realized and escaped, a determination to revere life, the presence of loved ones, and the small joys of daily existence.

Most of Budy's poems are free verse, but she handles form with ease. Internal rhyme, slant rhyme, and echo give structural cohesion to all her poems, which are characterized by skillful line breaks. Her study of oral interpretation makes her an adept and popular reader throughout the United States and abroad.

In 1991 Budy became writer-in-residence at Lyon College (Batesville, Arkansas), where she was awarded the Williamson Prize for Excellence in Teaching (1998). Among her other awards are fellowships from the National Endowment for the Arts and the Arkansas Arts Council, the D. H. Lawrence Fellowship (2002), and a Pushcart Prize for memoir (2003). Individual poems have been chosen for the Ellipsis Poetry Prize (2002) and the Runes Award (2004).

Further Reading

Chappell, Fred. *A Way of Happening: Observations of Contemporary Poetry.* Picador Press, 1998. 273–292.

DeToye, Kate, Matthew Schmitz, and Jason Braun. "An Interview of Andrea Hollander Budy." *Sou'wester* 31.2 (Spring 2003): 8–23.

Suzanne Evans Blair

BUKIET, MELVIN JULES (1953–) Jewish American fiction writer. Melvin Jules Bukiet has published four novels and three story collections, and he has edited two important collections of Jewish writing, *Neurotica: Jewish Writers on Sex* (1999) and *Nothing Makes You Free: Writings by Descendents of Jewish Holocaust Survivors* (2002). His work has been translated into at least six other languages.

Little is publicly known about Bukiet's biography. He was born in New York City, he received a BA from Sarah Lawrence College in 1974 and an MFA from Columbia University in 1976, and he taught writing for the Mount Vernon Public Library and the Writer's Voice before becoming the fiction editor at *Tikkun* (1992–96). Presently, Bukiet teaches creative writing at Sarah Lawrence College.

Bukiet's first novel, *Sandman's Dust*, appeared in 1986 and drew comparisons to Ray Bradbury with its portrayal of a small town visited by an unusual circus. *Sandman's Dust* was followed by two collections of short stories focused on the Jewish community and Jewish themes. *Stories of an Imaginary Childhood* (1992) is set in pre-Nazi Poland, and some reviewers noted the influence of **Isaac Bashevis Singer**. Most of the stories in *While the Messiah Tarries* (1995) are set in New York City. The former collection won the Edward Lewis Wallant Award for best Jewish American fiction, but the latter was more widely praised by critics and reviewers. Notably, it was through these stories that Bukiet began to earn a reputation for his use of humor and satire.

One of Bukiet's central concerns in his fiction is Jewish life in a post-**Holocaust** world. In an essay that appeared in *The Chronicle of Higher Education*, Bukiet wrote, "In the beginning was Auschwitz." His novel *After* (1996) is set in Europe in 1945, as Allied forces are trekking through the countryside, freeing Jews from Hitler's camps. It follows the less-than-admirable lives of a handful of survivors and was called by one reviewer "a brilliant investigation into the possibility of moral life" after the Holocaust. Bukiet's next novel, *Signs and Wonders* (1999), is also set in Germany, but this time at the turn of the twenty-first century. The novel is "purposefully offensive," according to one reviewer, as it portrays Ben Alef, a miracle-performing messiah figure who attracts followers and is later betrayed by one of them and assassinated. *Publishers Weekly* called this examination of Jewishness in the German landscape a "searing, bitterly satirical novel."

Bukiet's most recent novel is *Strange Fire* (2001). It traces Nathan Kazakov's investigation of an assassination attempt on the prime minister of Israel, and it too incorporates Bukiet's Jewish wit and satirical humor. The *Washington Post* remarked that its place might lie "somewhere between Salman Rushdie's *The Satanic Verses* and the late Stanley Kubrick's *Dr. Strangelove.*"

A Faker's Dozen (2003), another collection of short stories, is Bukiet's most recent work. It has been praised for its "dark humor and sly wickedness" but overall has drawn mixed reviews.

Further Reading

Martin, Michael J. "The Ethics of After: Melvin Jules Bukiet, Holocaust Fiction, and the Reemergence of an Ethical Sense in the Post-Holocaust World." *Shofar: An Interdisciplinary Journal of Jewish Studies* 22.3 (2004): 43–55.

Pinsker, Sanford. "Revisiting the Grand Inquisitor: Melvin Jules Bukiet and Theo-Fiction." *Studies in Jewish American Literature* 19 (2000): 49–51.

J. P. Steed

BUKOSKI, ANTHONY (1945–)   Polish American short story writer, essayist, critic, and university professor. Beginning with the publication of his first collection of short stories, *Twelve Below Zero* (1986), Anthony Bukoski has led a virtual renaissance of Polish American literature written in English by the children, grandchildren, and even great grandchildren of immigrants. In addition to *Twelve Below Zero*, Bukoski has published three other collections of short stories: *Children of Strangers* (1993), *Polonaise* (1999), and *Time Between Trains* (2003). His essays have appeared in various anthologies. A fifth collection of short stories, tentatively titled *The Midsummer Fires*, is in preparation and is expected to be completed by the fall of 2005. Bukoski has also begun work on a novel. His reviews have appeared in *Forkroads, Canadian Literature, Studies in the Novel, Southern Humanities Review, Polish American Studies*, and elsewhere.

Most of Bukoski's short stories communicate a clear and evocative sense of place and address powerful themes of painful loss. Both of these features of his work are imbued with strong dimensions of **ethnicity**. The regional quality of Bukoski's writing has led many to compare his work to that of **Flannery O'Connor** and Sherwood Anderson. In Bukoski's case, the region most frequently treated is northwestern Wisconsin, a region that Bukoski firmly regards as worthy of serious literary attention but as sadly neglected in the world of American letters. Even more specifically, Bukoski generally focuses his stories on the East-End Polish American community of Superior, Wisconsin, although he has also studied other parts of the region and of the country and has treated a wide range of other ethnic groups, such as Native Americans, Finnish Americans, Slovak Americans, and even Vietnamese newcomers to the region— groups that, in his estimation, are usually seen as outsiders. Similarly, the themes of loss that he studies typically center on the passing of a community or at least some dimension of community life and are presented through the experience and identity of a specific individual. Even when the loss is more deeply personal, such as death or shattered relations, an ethnic dimension is almost always involved.

These features of Bukoski's fiction are easily illustrated by any number of stories. In "The Children of Strangers," for example, Bukoski deftly captures the powerful emotions of Ralph Slipkowski, a resident of the East-End Polish community of Superior, as he gradually acknowledges not only the passing of his aging generation, but also the steady decline of his ethnic neighborhood and, perhaps most painfully, the difficult surrender of his Polish Roman Catholic parish to strangers. The loss anticipated in "Tango of the Bearers of the Dead" is at once more individual and more tangled. Suffering through the pain of a death vigil for her husband of fifty years, a grandmother attempts to dismiss agonizing thoughts of youthful adultery, while an adult grandson strives to recapture the past as he deals with the imminent death of his grandfather and attempts to understand his family's history and heritage. The final story on Bukoski's latest collection, "President of the Past," connects many of Bukoski's themes in one piece. Buck Mrozek, the middle-aged president of Superior's Polish Club, struggles to come to terms with the dwindling membership of his fraternal club, the dying heritage of his community, his dead father's role in both, and his own mortality. In stories such as these, Bukoski deals with aspects of the Polish immigrant experience and Polish American ethnicity that other writers have either overlooked or misunderstood. Polish Catholic spirituality, the importance of a sense of turf, Polish-Jewish relations in Europe and America, family dynamics, and Polish **feminism** are examined with the eye and emotions of an insider.

These stories also illustrate nicely some of Bukoski's particular skills as a writer. Of these, three stand out: a deft handling of "magical realism" learned from the works of Gabriel García Márquez and William H. Gass; a rare sensitivity to the language of ethnic Americans; and a depth of characterization, especially of ethnic characters.

In taking the risk of focusing on a segment of society largely invisible in American literature and insisting that his community will not pass away "unheard," Anthony Bukoski has perfected his own voice and encouraged a new generation of Polish American writers to follow his example.

Further Reading

Bowen, David. "The Land of Graves and Crosses: An Interview with Anthony Bukoski." *Main Street Rag* 8.3 (Fall 2003): 9–16.

Longrie, Michael. "Replaying the Past: An Interview with Anthony Bukoski." *Wisconsin Academy Review* 42.1 (Winter 1995–96): 29–33.

Thomas J. Napierkowski

BULLINS, ED (1935–) African American dramatist, scholar, and activist. Ed Bullins (Kinsgley B. Bass) was born in Philadelphia, Pennsylvania, on July 2, 1935, to Edward and Bertha Marie (Queen) Bullins. His mother was a civil servant who tried to instill middle-class values in her son. He attended a largely European American elementary school, where he was a very good student, and he spent his summers vacationing in Maryland farming country. However, as a junior high student he was transferred to an inner city school, where he became involved in a street gang, and in one confrontation he was stabbed in the heart and was miraculously resuscitated after dying.

Eventually, he dropped out of Benjamin Franklin High School and served in the United States Navy from 1952 to 1955. While he was in the Navy, Bullins won a lightweight boxing championship and embarked on a self-education program through reading. After his discharge from the Navy, he moved to Los Angeles in 1958, earned his GED, began writing fiction, essays, and poetry, and resumed his formal studies at Los Angeles City College. In 1964 he moved to the San Francisco Bay area, and while he was registered in a college writing program at San Francisco State College, he began to write plays.

Although he would later go on to earn a bachelor's degree at Antioch College in Yellow Springs, Ohio, in 1989 and an MFA from San Francisco State University in 1994, in the late 1960s he emerged as one of the leading and most prolific playwrights of the **Black Arts Movement**. This was an aesthetic movement that sought to define an "authentic" black aesthetic based on the politics of **black nationalism** and a skillful reconstruction of African American folklore. This movement involved scholars and writers like Addison Gayle, **Larry Neal**, **Nikki Giovanni**, **Sonia Sanchez**, Hoyt Fuller, and **Amiri Baraka,** among others. It was a reaction against the tyranny of the Western cultural aesthetic and its overly harsh judgments of any artistic creation that was non-European in its origin or expression.

Bullins's life and writing are both strongly influenced by all of the major themes from the Black Arts Movement: community, love, power, and revolution. In his seminal essay called "Towards a Black Aesthetic," Hoyt Fuller says that in the 1960s the young black writers of the ghetto set out in search of a black aesthetic. This black aesthetic would be a system of isolating and evaluating the artistic works of African Americans that reflect the special character and imperatives of their experiences. Hoyt Fuller goes on to say that this Black Arts Movement was a way of perceiving African American

347

art forms as containing more than aesthetic beauty. After hundreds of years of being told that they are not beautiful, African Americans began to realize and reclaim their beauty through their art. According to Larry Neal's "Visions of a Liberated Future," drama was a prime vehicle for the expression of this black aesthetic.

Bullins made his theatrical debut in San Francisco at the Firehouse Repertory Theater in August of 1965 with three one-act plays: *How Do You Do, Dialect Determinism or The Rally*, and *Clara's Ole' Man*. He also founded a black militant cultural-political organization with Bobby Seale, Huey Newton, and **Eldridge Cleaver** called Black House, and he briefly aligned himself with the Black Panther Party. After being purged from the leadership of the Black House, he was appointed Minister of Culture for the Black Panther Party by Eldridge Cleaver and Emory Douglass. Bullins wanted to promote a form of cultural nationalism called Kawaida, championed by Maulana Karenga. Kawaida simply stated that African Americans could achieve liberation through a careful reconstruction of their lost African culture, but Cleaver and his fellow Black Panthers wanted a revolutionary ideology promoted in African American art that called for armed rebellion.

This philosophical disagreement mainly between Bullins and Cleaver over the role of art in a revolutionary struggle caused Bullins to consider briefly leaving the United States before he moved to New York City to become playwright-in-residence and associate director at Robert Macbeth's New Lafayette Theater in Harlem. For the next ten years Bullins was one of the most powerful and controversial voices on the off-Broadway stage, and along with Amiri Baraka and Larry Neal, he became one of the most influential playwrights of the Black Arts Movement. He also headed the Black Theater Workshop at the New Lafayette Theater and edited Black Theater Magazine, which was housed there. Later, he directed the Writer's Unit Playwrights Workshop for Joseph Papp at the Public Theater and the Playwrights Workshop at **Woodie King**'s New Federal Theater in New York City. His first full-length play, *In the Wine Time* (1968), examines the scarcity of options available to African Americans, especially the urban poor.

In the Wine Time is the first in a series of plays he called the *Twentieth Century Cycle*. These plays all focus on a group of young friends growing up in America in the 1950s. Other plays in this cycle included *The Corner* (1968), *In New England Winter* (1969), *The Duplex* (1970), *The Fabulous Miss Marie* (1971), *Homeboy* (1976), and *Daddy* (1977). In 1975 he received critical acclaim, including an Obie Award and the New York Drama Critics Award for *The Taking of Miss Janie*, a play about the failed alliance of an interracial group of 1960s political idealists. He has also received the Vernon Rice Desk Drama Award, Guggenheim Fellowships, and Rockefeller Foundation and National Endowment for the Arts playwriting grants. True to his black nationalistic aesthetic leanings, Bullins' naturalistic dramas incorporate elements of African American folklore, especially "street" lyrics with interracial tension.

His other notable works include *Goin' a Buffalo* (1968), a short story collection titled *The Hungered One* (1971), and a novel *The Reluctant Rapist* (1973). In *Ed Bullins: A Literary Biography* (1997), Samuel Hay says, "Bullins is a playwright with a revolutionary bent who, despite this inclination, became an artist who has displayed some of the more deeply recessed representations of African American life" (2).

In 1995 Bullins was appointed professor of theater at Northeastern University in Boston. His most recent work, *Boy X Man* (2002), is a memory play about a man looking back on his childhood and the process of growing up. He strains to come to grips with not ever having understood his mother and with having failed to say thank you to a stepfather who had been as much of a father to him as any man could have ever been. Bullins remains continually concerned with getting across to his audience themes that he considers vital to the survival of African Americans; and he continues to insist theater must be revolutionary in order for African American art to be successful. (*See also* African American Drama)

Further Reading

Branch, William B., ed. *An Anthology of Contemporary African American Drama*. New York: Penguin, 1992.

Hatch, James V., ed. *Black Theater USA: Plays by African Americans*. New York: Free Press, 1996.

Hay, Samuel. *Ed Bullins: A Literary Biography*. Detroit: Wayne State UP, 1998.

Raymond E. Jannifer

BULOSAN, CARLOS (1911–1956)   Filipino novelist, poet, and labor organizer. Bulosan was one of the first and most famous Filipino writers in the West to depict the Philippines under U.S. **colonialism** and to present the experiences of Filipinos who immigrated to the U.S. in the 1920s and 1930s.

These subjects constitute the bulk of Bulosan's novel, *America Is in the Heart* (1946), his best-known work. In addition to being loosely autobiographical, the novel is collective, in that its protagonist, Allos, is representative of the approximately 45,000 Filipinos on the mainland in 1930. The book is divided into four parts, the first of which follows Allos as his peasant family struggles to keep their land, to send their sons to school, and to subsist in the Philippines in the wake of World War I. The remaining three sections portray Allos's life after he has immigrated to the U.S. There, Allos hopes to create a better life but instead encounters racist violence and economic exploitation in the Alaskan canneries and the fields of the West Coast. As he develops class and racial consciousness in the course of his experiences, he organizes with other migrant laborers to fight for their rights. The novel ends with Allos's affirming his faith in America as the U.S. enters World War II. Thus, some reviewers and critics have claimed that *America Is in the Heart* shows Allos's **assimilation** and realization of the American dream, but others have argued that the novel's careful documentation of the exploitation of Filipinos undermines

Allos's idealism. The narrative's form has also drawn critical attention. On one hand, its nonlinear plot presents the directionless lives of men forced to follow the crops and prevented from establishing homes. On the other hand, it is possible to trace the trajectory of Allos's political development through the sprawling narrative. Finally, gender and sexuality are thematically significant since the "good" America that Allos seeks is often embodied by the various white women—writers, teachers, and prostitutes—whom he encounters.

As aforementioned, *America Is in the Heart* is loosely autobiographical; like Allos, Bulosan was born in the village of Mangusmana, Pangasinan province, on the island of Luzon in the Philippines. At this time, the Philippines was only nine years removed from the end of the Filipino-American War, in which the U.S. had crushed the native struggle for sovereignty; the Philippines was thus an American "territory." Because his colonial education had taught him about American democracy, Bulosan immigrated to the United States in 1931 in order to escape his country's dire poverty. However, the Great Depression spurred anti-Filipino violence as white workers saw Filipinos taking away previously unwanted but now desirable jobs. Unlike Allos, Bulosan was never healthy enough for fieldwork, but he did become a labor organizer and a writer, and throughout his life, his activism and art fed each other. As Bulosan relates in *America Is in the Heart*, he gained his real education in literature while hospitalized from 1936 to 1938 for tuberculosis after years of impoverished living; soon thereafter, he became a prolific writer.

Unfortunately, *America Is in the Heart* has overshadowed his other work, including his poetry, short stories, and second novel. Bulosan's poetry covers a range of genres and subjects, from his political poems about the Spanish Civil War or the Italian anarchists, Sacco and Vanzetti (and Bulosan once claimed that his poetry constituted the most concrete expression of his politics), to his lyrical poems for Josephine Patrick, his companion late in life, to his Whitmanesque free verse on the meaning of democracy. A long poem, *The Voice of Bataan* (1943), was written for the U.S. Office of War Information, which broadcast the poem overseas, but even this work retains Bulosan's characteristically critical perspective on the exploitation of the poor who, in this case, are made to fight wars not of their making. Of Bulosan's short stories, his collection *The Laughter of My Father* (1944) was a best seller that was eventually translated into more than a dozen languages. Part of its success was due to its being seen as an exotic, humorous portrait of Filipino peasants that confirmed stereotypes of their backwardness. This view, however, missed the nuances of Bulosan's appreciation of folk wit and culture, as well as his satire directed against the Filipino bourgeoisie and the capitalist underdevelopment of the Philippines. Many of Bulosan's other stories address facets of the sociohistorical experiences of the Filipino immigrant that we see in *America Is in the Heart*. Along with *America Is in the Heart*, *The Voice of Bataan* and *The Laughter of My Father* made Bulosan a highly popular writer in the 1940s, especially after Americans saw that they and the Filipinos shared a common enemy in the Japanese.

The cold war dramatically changed Bulosan's fortunes. Although it is unknown whether Bulosan ever joined the Communist Party, he worked with many of its members, and he believed this was why he was blacklisted from writing for Hollywood. In his last five years, Bulosan composed his second novel, *The Cry and the Dedication* (1985, 1995). *The Cry and the Dedication* is about the Hukbalahap ("People's Liberation Army"), Filipino peasant guerillas fighting Japanese and U.S. imperialist forces in the 1940s. This novel presents Bulosan's revision of his earlier faith in the revolutionary potential of American democracy and his embrace of indigenous Filipino radicalism—a move prefigured even by *America Is in the Heart*, where he acknowledges the need to recover his country's history and folklore. Although Bulosan never physically returned to the Philippines, *The Cry and the Dedication* constitutes a literary and political return and a final affirmation of his unflagging belief in working-class and Third World struggle. (*See also* Filipino American Novel)

Further Reading

Evangelista, Susan. *Carlos Bulosan and His Poetry: A Biography and Anthology.* Seattle: U of Washington P, 1985.

Roe, Jae H. "Revising the Sign of 'America': The Postcolonial Humanism of *America Is in the Heart.*" *Journal of English Language and Literature* 49.4 (2003): 905–20.

San Juan, Jr. E. *The Philippine Temptation: Dialectics of Philippines-U.S. Literary Relations.* Philadelphia: Temple UP, 1996.

Wong, Sau-ling Cynthia. *Reading Asian American Literature: From Necessity to Extravagance.* Princeton, NJ: Princeton UP, 1993.

Cheryl Higashida

BUMBALO, VICTOR (1946–) Italian American gay playwright. Bumbalo's multifaceted contribution to gay theater began in 1979. His plays focus on three defining themes of gay life: coming out, relationship woes, and the effects of AIDS on victims and their loved ones.

Niagara Falls (1979) is a two-part comedy in which the nameless gay son is the ghostly hero. The story revolves around sister Jackie's wedding and how some members of the family come to understand themselves because of the crisis their gay son creates when he comes home with his lover to attend Jackie's wedding.

The play opens in Connie and Johnny Poletti's kitchen the morning of Jackie's wedding, as the characters discuss the dilemma their gay son's arrival with his lover poses. Bumbalo renders the stereotypical Italian American couple with genuine affection and hilarious precision: they are melodramatic, superstitious, devoutly Catholic, and strongly patriarchal. However, since family is of paramount importance, somehow the Polettis will learn how to venture into and navigate difficult new territory, thus liberating themselves from self-imposed cultural confines.

Meant to invoke and mock a tired but hilarious stereotype, Part Two takes place on Jackie and Vinnie's wedding night at the less than Edenic Shangri-La Motor Inn. Jackie is grieving and saying her rosary because she regrets having married Vinnie, a stereotypical Italian American. Eventually, with the help of Fred, the gay desk clerk, Vinnie capitulates to Jackie and their marriage is salvaged. The gay brother has inspired the women to voice their own desires and find more joy in their lives.

Adam and the Experts (1990) is about the ramifications of AIDS in the gay community. Eddie is HIV positive, and Adam is his best friend and neurotic caregiver. Both men are angry and afraid. When Eddie breaks the news to Adam, Eddie ends up consoling Adam. Since there is no manual for how to cope with the crisis caused by AIDS, Adam attempts, frenetically, to prolong Eddie's life by reading all the literature available on AIDS cures and locating expert after expert. Eddie dreads Adam's suggestions. He wants dignity and peace in what remains of his life. The play ends with Eddie's death and the lingering tragedy of lives cut short.

Kitchen Duty (1981) depicts a broken love affair and the struggle of being homosexual in a heterosexual world. *After Eleven* (1983) is an examination of a gay couple trying to sustain their relationship during the throes of a midlife crisis. Two short plays, *Show* (1992) and *Tell* (1993), also deal with AIDS.

What Are Tuesdays Like? (1994) takes place on the Tuesdays reserved for HIV-positive patients in the waiting room of a hospital. The patients' conversations demonstrate the plight of AIDS victims and the incremental bond that forms among people who share the same fate. Each character experiences denial, courage, anger, and fear, which sometimes give way to madness. All of them "used to" do or be something else; now they are only AIDS patients, fighting for survival.

Bumbalo honestly and humorously presents relevant issues, providing a point of reference for and validity to gay life, which is an important contribution to gay writing as well as to the literature of AIDS. (*See also* Italian American Gay Literature)

Further Reading

Massa, Suzanne Hotte. "Victor Bumbalo." *Contemporary Gay American Poets and Playwrights: An A-to-Z Guide.* Ed. Emmanuel S. Nelson. Westport, CT: Greenwood Press, 2003. 54–60.

Suzanne Hotte Massa

BURK, RONNIE (1955–2003) Mexican American poet, AIDS activist, and artist. Ronnie Burk's place in contemporary American poetry is marked by his membership in the Surrealist Movement in the United States and by his collaboration with the Chicago Surrealist group. He was an AIDS activist and a constant crusader for social justice and racial equality.

These themes formed a basis for his work and were consistently manifested in his writings, art, and activism.

Besides being a poet, critic, artist, and lecturer, Ronnie Burk was also known as an outspoken member of the controversial group ACT-UP San Francisco. Criticized for their skepticism of AIDS treatment drugs, members like Ronnie Burk insisted that medicines created to combat the HIV virus were actually the source of many AIDS-related illnesses. He was highly critical of the way AIDS organizations used the money they raised to help and service their clientele. To express his outrage over such issues, Burk once dumped cat litter on the Chief Executive Officer of the San Francisco AIDS Foundation. The act created a storm of controversy in which ACT-UP activists were attacked and marginalized for their aggressive tactics. However, for Ronnie Burk the protest was just another battle in a lifelong fight for justice.

Burk's activism was also an integral part of his artistic production. Working as a collage artist, Burk produced pieces that were also deeply critical of AIDS treatment medications and the exploitation of people living with HIV. Thought-provoking and creative, Burk's collages could be shocking and even deeply troubling. Reactions to his work could be strong when he targeted specific people or organizations, and in 2001 the San Francisco AIDS Foundation took Ronnie Burk and several others to court for collages he had created attacking that organization; the Superior Court of California eventually fined Burk.

Originally from Texas, Ronnie Burk began work as a poet in the 1970s after studying literature and philosophy with **Allen Ginsberg** at the Naropa Institute of Disembodied Poets in Colorado. Burk became involved with the Chicago Surrealist Group and published his first book in 1978 after his studies at the Naropa Insititute. He then became an active member of the Surrealist Movement in the United States that grew out of the Chicago Surrealist Group. He moved to New York in 1979, where he continued his surrealist writings and become associated with the artists of the **Nuyorican** Poets' Café. Writing in both English and Spanish, Ronnie Burk published several volumes of poetry and many articles and book reviews. In the 1990s Burk relocated to San Francisco, where, after receiving services from the San Francisco AIDS Foundation, he became involved with ACT-UP San Francisco.

Ronnie Burk was HIV positive and died after complications from a stroke on March 12, 2003, in San Francisco. He was forty-seven years old. Remembered after his death by members of ACT-UP San Francisco as a person who committed his life to fighting against **racism** and for social justice, Ronnie Burk's commitment and dedication demonstrate how one concerned individual can make a significant difference in the way we live. (*See also* Mexican American Gay Literature)

Further Reading

Hernandez-Avila, Ines. "Ronnie Burk." *Dictionary of Literary Biography.* Vol. 209. Ed. Francisco A. Lomeli and Carl R. Shirley. Detroit: Gale, 1999. 20–28.

Staven Bruce

BURNSHAW, STANLEY (1906–)   Jewish American poet, critic, biographer, novelist, playwright, editor, publisher, and translator. Burnshaw's careful craftsmanship marks an exceptional literary career. His widely referenced work has publication dates ranging from the 1920s.

Burnshaw's parents emigrated from Eastern Europe to the United States, where his father directed a home for Jewish orphans. *My Friend, My Father* (1986) provides further biographical information. Burnshaw initially planned to become a teacher, but writing and politics redirected his career. His concern for the poverty of the working class inspired an interest in Marxism that influenced his writing. Burnshaw's name still appears on lists of leftist critics. After publishing his own magazine, *Poetry Folio*, in 1926, Burnshaw went to Europe, where he studied at the Sorbonne and associated with French poet Andre Spire. In 1928 he returned to the United States and completed graduate studies at New York University and Cornell University. Following graduation in 1933, with a master's degree, Burnshaw worked as an editor, reviewer, and critic, with a continuing interest in the economic problems of industrial workers. During this period his focus shifted further toward publishing, resulting in a career that continued for three decades.

The publication of Burnshaw's long poem *The Revolt of the Cats in Paradise* (1945) represents another significant adjustment of focus. This satirical poem indicates the writer's disillusionment with Marxism. The poem also corresponds with an evident transfer of interest, from political activism to critical scholarship. Meticulous analytical skill is evident in Burnshaw's English translations of poetry from other languages. This work maintains for English readers the original writer's art by preserving the original use of nuance, idiom, and allusion (see the Ransom Collection). Burnshaw's special interest in Jewish studies and issues is reflected in *The Modern Hebrew Poem Itself* (1965) and *Mirages* (1977).

In *Robert Frost Himself* (1986), Burnshaw writes about one of the most significant influences on his literary career. The writer's connection with Robert Frost began with an introduction to Frost's poetry when Burnshaw was fifteen years old. Frost and Burnshaw exchanged letters, and in 1958 Burnshaw joined Henry Holt Publishers, where he served as Frost's editor. *Robert Frost Himself* makes an important contribution to the recovery of Frost's credibility after critics' damaging attacks on his character. Burnshaw's biography of Frost, a highpoint for both writers, also symbolizes the potential influence of literature and literary lives.

In 1984 the British journal *Agenda* published a special issue in Burnshaw's honor, and a few weeks before his ninetieth birthday the City University of New York awarded Burnshaw an honorary doctor of letters degree. Among Burnshaw's best-known works are *The Poem Itself* (1960), *The Seamless Web* (1970), *In the Terrified Radiance* (1972), *My Friend, My Father* (1986), and *Robert Frost Himself* (1986). *A Stanley Burnshaw Reader* (1990) and

The Collected Poems and Selected Prose (2002) provide an overview of Burn-shaw's work.

Further Reading

McHale, Brian. "The Red Decade and the Blue Guitar." *Poetics Today* 18.1 (1997): 113–16.

Stella Thompson

BUSLETT, OLE AMUNDSEN (1855–1924) Norwegian American writer. Buslett came to Wisconsin as a thirteen year old. He worked on farms, read in his spare time, and wrote verse. At the age of twenty-six, he decided to become an author, attended lectures at the University of Wisconsin, and published his first two books. In the following ten years he published verse and obscure allegorical dramas, such as *De to veivisere* (1885; The two guides), without popular success. He then turned to three years of journalism, editing several short-lived newspapers. The novel *Rolf Hagen* (1893) included both murder and free love, but still did not sell.

Discouraged, he wrote little until 1908, when he began his late but prolific period with the substantial *Sagastolen* (The saga seat) with the subtitle "A Novel of the Norwegian North America." In his preface he claimed that it was about "social issues that are becoming more and more important in our time," but the novel confused reviewers with its three apparently disparate parts: a love story in a realistic rural setting, a narrative of the rise and fall of a socialist commune, and, finally, a brief vision of an ideal society with a fantastically advanced technology. Another important work is the fantasy novel *Glans-om-sol og hans folks historie* (1912; Splendor-of-Son and the story of his people). The novel's premise is the turn-of-the-century political controversy over a gold-based versus a silver-based currency. It creates an imaginary world with its own history and religion where the family of an Old Testament–like prophet are the bearers of forgotten ideals and are opposed to a gold-worshipping priesthood. In the end the people, led by a female descendant of the prophet, are victorious. *Glans-om-sol* is related to the many utopian fictions of this period, such as Ignatius Donnelly's *Cæsar's Column* (1891) and Edward Bellamy's *Looking Backward* (1888). The allegorical *Veien til Golden Gate* (1915; translated as "The Road to the Golden Gate," 2000) is a response to the World War I Americanization hysteria and a vision of a multicultural United States.

His most satisfactory achievement is the autobiographical novel, *Fra min ungdoms nabolag* (1918; From the neighborhood of my youth), based on his teenage years of hard labor as provider for his family. At the age of twenty-one, he leaves home for work in the logging camps where his first job is "to raft lumber and run the river." His careful attention to detail in evoking the nature of this work makes the account of the rafting process, from the building of the rafts at Stevens Point to the sighting of St. Louis, the best writing of his career. When Buslett died in 1924, he was involved in the periodical publication of a revised collected edition of his work with critical and autobiographical introductions. (*See also* Norwegian American Literature)

Further Reading

Hustvedt, Lloyd. "Ole Amundsen Buslett." *Makers of an American Immigrant Legacy.* Ed. Odd S. Lovoll. Northfield, MN: Norwegian-American Historical Association, 1980. 131–58.

Øverland, Orm. *The Western Home: A Literary History of Norwegian America.* Northfield, MN: Norwegian-American Historical Association, and Champaign: U of Illinois P, 1996. 120–42.

Orm Øverland

BUTLER, OCTAVIA ESTELLE (1947–) Heralded as the foremost African American writer of science fiction. Octavia E. Butler has been awarded the highest honors in science fiction writing—both the Hugo and the Nebula Awards. She received the Hugo Award in 1984 and 1985 for her short fictions, "Speech Sounds" and "Blood Child," respectively, and "Blood Child" garnered the Nebula Award in 1985. Also in 1995, Butler won the MacArthur Foundation's coveted "genius grant," which provides a generous monetary prize in recognition of the winner's contribution to his or her field. Butler has long been a staple in the libraries of literary critics and science fiction fans, who are equally fascinated with and overwhelmed by her understanding of human nature.

In 1976 Butler published the first novel in her Patternists series. *Pattern Master* lays the foundation for the series, which demonstrates Butler's fear of and enthrallment with the human **race**'s potential for evolution and predilection for domination. In the series, selective breeding has created a race of superhumans whose telepathic abilities make them dangerous because they can control normal human beings. The series is best known for Doro, an African immortal, who in his godlike consciousness desires immortal children who will worship him. *Wild Seed*, which was the fourth in the five-book series, won the James Tiptree Award in 1980. Anyanwu is Butler's shape-shifting, immortal African woman whose abilities make her Doro's greatest breeder, but whose maternal instincts make her his worst enemy.

Butler may be better known for her Xenogenesis trilogy. Beginning with *Dawn* (1987), humans have finally detonated nuclear weapons, destroying most of the earth and the majority of mankind. A group of alien gene-traders arrive, and as payment for saving the few humans who survive the destruction, they require not only what is left of the earth, but genetic exchange. As a result, the human beings are forced to evolve into a species far beyond their own understanding or their recognition of humanity. A black woman named Lilith becomes the mother of the new earth children. At issue is Lilith's loyalty to mankind since she is the liaison between the humans and the aliens. As with many of Butler's heroines, Lilith's ability to procreate is also at issue in the series. It is her body that gives birth to the species and she has had little choice in the matter.

Kindred, published in 1979, is the story of Dana, a twentieth-century black woman who is pulled back in time to save her white male ancestor—who is also the slave master of her black ancestors. Butler demonstrates an incredible ability to intertwine African American culture and history with strands of science fiction. The novel is fraught with the implications of Dana's inability to stop her ancestor from moving her through time and space. Whenever his life is in danger, Dana is drawn to him and must save him, or she risks terminating her own lineage. Thus, like her own ancestors bound by **slavery** and like many of the female protagonists in Butler's novels, she has no charge over her body, her space, or her time.

Perhaps the most well known of Butler's heroines is Lauren Olamina in *The Parable of the Sower* (1993). Lauren is the daughter of a minister living in an America decimated by global warming, a collapsed economy, a failed public school system, and a lack of representative leadership. In the midst of the chaos, Lauren sows Earthseed. Earthseed is a new and dangerous philosophy/religion that teaches that God is change and the only real hope for mankind is to re-establish themselves among the stars. *Parable of the Sower* is a warning against a human consciousness that refuses to acknowledge change. These changes are both in the earth itself, such as changes in atmosphere or temperature, and in the people. The refusal to acknowledge changes in demographics, mores, and values proves detrimental to society. Lauren's discovery and categorization of God, human will, and human destiny are presented as the only way through the chaos. The story continues in *Parable of the Talents* with Lauren's daughter, who is given the task of narrating the ending of her mother's story and the beginning of "earthseed."

Although Butler's works are many and her subjects varied, she always returns to a central theme of mankind's inevitable destruction of itself without some kind of extraordinary intervention. Whether the intervention comes in the form of aliens with extra-sensory arms or a black girl teaching change and reaching for the stars, Butler is concerned with humanity's ability to desire change and then to adapt to it. In addition, her ability to weave her theses from a uniquely Afrocentric perspective makes her truly one of the most important writers of science fiction of any racial or gender category. Butler has the unique ability to make slavery in general and the ghost of African American slavery in particular take shape in the contemporary mind. Butler's legacy is that she is both a weaver of fantasy and a collector of history. Her work culminates at the nexus of both these talents. (*See also* African American Science Fiction)

Further Reading

Beal, Frances M. "Black Women and the Science Fiction Genre: Interview with Octavia Butler." *Black Scholar* 17.2 (1986): 14–18.

Bedore, Pamela. "Slavery and Symbiosis in Octavia Butler's Kindred." *Foundation: The International Review of Science Fiction* 31.84 (2002): 73–81.

Bonner, Frances. "Difference and Desire, Slavery and Seduction: Octavia Butler's *Xenogenesis.*" *Foundation: The Review of Science Fiction* 48 (1990): 50–62.

Dubey, Madhu. "Folk and Urban Communities in African-American Women's Fiction: Octavia Butler's *Parable of the Sower.*" *Studies in American Fiction* 27.1 (1999): 103–28.

Hampton, Gregory Jerome. "Octavia Butler and Virginia Hamilton: Black Women Writers and Science Fiction." *English Journal* 92.6 (2003): 70–74.

Melzer, Patricia. "All that You Touch You Change: Utopian Desire and the Concept of Change in Octavia Butler's *Parable of the Sower* and *Parable of the Talents.*" *FEMSPEC* 3.2 (2002): 31–52.

Tarshia L. Stanley

C

CABRERA INFANTE, GUILLERMO (1929–2005) Cuban writer in exile, film critic and journalist. Guillermo Cabrera Infante is the chief example of a classic Latin American writer in exile who looks back to the mother country with the melancholy of times past. Dividing his time between the United States and Europe, Cabrera Infante has been one of the foremost critics of Cuba's Castro regime, although his main works predate Castro's coming to power. Cabrera Infante's *Tres tristes tigres* (1967), his most celebrated work, tells of the author's longing for a pre-Castro Havana. In it, one sees the sexual awakening of an adolescent, the sweltering climate, the brothels, the small gangsters, and the poverty common to 1950s Havana.

Cabrera Infante was born in the hamlet of Gibara in the Orient province, also the birthplace of Fulgencio Batista and Fidel Castro. Cabrera Infante moved with his family to Havana when he was twelve years old. The sudden change from village life to the big city deeply impressed him, and his experiences have been a theme throughout his work. Although family life was characterized by extreme poverty, Cabrera Infante found Havana to be a new world ready to be discovered. The movies, the city life, the cabarets, and the street life began to consume and mold the adolescent Cabrera Infante, who was eager to learn.

After a brief stint at the university, Cabrera Infante began his career as a journalist. He became an editor for *Bohemia* and a film reviewer for *Carteles*. Later, he founded the magazine *Nueva Generación* and helped to establish the Film Library of Cuba. His first mature work, *Asi en la Paz come en la*

Guerra (1960), is a series of short stories which chronicle the political upheaval of Batista's Cuba.

An early sympathizer of Castro's government, Cabrera Infante worked on *Lunes de Revolucion,* a progressive weekly that provided an account of the early days of socialist Cuba. His support for the revolution, however, soon weakened due to a problem of loyalties. It was Cabrera Infante's support for his brother's film, *P.M.,* that provoked his downfall from grace in Castro's regime. By 1961 Castro had officially declared Cuba a socialist country, and a film depicting Havana's nightlife was deemed decadent. After a short-lived clash with governmental censors, Cabrera Infante was soon banished to Brussels as a cultural attaché. After briefly going back to Cuba, Cabrera settled temporarily for an unwelcoming stay in Spain, later seeking refuge in London. In Cuba, Cabrera Infante became a traitor to the revolution.

Tres tristes tigres is a chronicle of pre-Castro Havana. It reflects the peoples' talk, their worries, their dreams, the nightlife, the sea, and the rhythms of the city. All the characters seem to be making up a world whose time has passed. What is revealing in *Tres tristes tigres* is its experimental form; it is a satire peppered with linguistic puns and different temporal sequences. There is a theme, however, that emerges throughout the novel. It is human betrayal. The novel, despite its unorthodox form, is also a parody of life in which life is an artifact of writing. It seems that for Cabrera Infante, life hardly predates art. For him, life is a construction achieved through writing, and this is masterfully achieved in the intertwined stories that make up the novel.

In *Vista del amanecer en el tropico* (1964), Cabrera examines Cuban history in a series of historical vignettes. Another of his works, *La Habana para un infante difunto* (1979), serves as a more autobiographical account—full of memories and observations of Havana's daily pulse. In the book, Cabrera Infante celebrates once again the vanished childhood that seems to be a staple of most of his writings.

Exile has provided Cabrera Infante a chance to experiment with nonfictional writing as well. Perhaps his age and years of exile have prompted Cabrera Infante to publish his first book written in English. *Holy Smoke* (1985) is not about his beloved Havana, but is rather a historical account of the history of tobacco and the cigar and their roles in history, politics, and cinema.

Further Reading

Merrin, S. "A Secret Idiom: The Grammar and Role of Language in *Tres tristes tigres.*" *Latin American Literary Review* 8 (1980): 96–116.

Peavler, T. J. "Cabrera Infante's Undertow." *Structures of Power: Essays on Twentieth Century Spanish-American Fiction.* Ed. T. J. Pavler and P. Standish. Albany: State U of New York P, 1996. 125–43.

Jorge J. Barrueto

CAHAN, ABRAHAM (1860–1951)   Jewish American author, labor leader, educator, and senior editor of the periodical *Jewish Daily Forward.*

Abraham Cahan, a Lithuanian Jewish immigrant, was a major cultural force in the United States at the turn of the twentieth century, a time when few immigrants of the "second wave" of **immigration**—mainly Eastern and Southern Europeans—had the time, money, or education to pursue a literary or political career. Cahan pursued both careers. Though many novels and sociological tracts depicted immigrant ghetto culture from the mainstream perspective, Cahan's novella *Yekl: A Tale of the New York Ghetto* (1896) was one of the first book-length accounts of the urban immigrant experience from an insider's point of view; as such, he stands as the Father of Jewish American literature, with Nobel Prize winners **Isaac Bashevis Singer** and **Saul Bellow** and Pulitzer Prize

Abraham Cahan. *Courtesy of the Library of Congress.*

winners **Philip Roth** and **Michael Chabon** among his progenitors. Cahan's masterwork, *The Rise of David Levinsky* (1917), is the most comprehensive fictional treatment of Jewish immigration in American literature; and as the editor of the *Jewish Daily Forward*, he endowed the Yiddish-speaking population with a vital cultural mainstay for over forty years (1903–46).

Abraham Cahan was born in Vilna, Lithuania, in an isolated Jewish community, or *shtetl*, named Podberezya on July 7, 1860. His parents, Schachne Cahan and Sarah Goldarbeiter, were both Hebrew scholars and teachers, and as such, they educated their son at orthodox cheders. In 1881 Cahan graduated from the Vilna Teacher's Institute, where he adopted the political beliefs of the anti-czarist movement. After Cahan transferred to a school in Velizh, Czar Alexander II was assassinated, and the czarist authorities threatened Cahan with conspiracy charges. He fled to the United States in exile, and on June 6, 1882, Abraham Cahan landed in the poverty-stricken Lower East Side of New York City, where the massive tide of Eastern European Jews was still in its early stages (two million would arrive on U.S. shores between Cahan's arrival and World War I). After some factory work, which fueled him with material for his fiction and political activism, Cahan, now fluent in Yiddish, Russian, and English, accepted a position at the Young Men's Hebrew Association. Even in the United States, Cahan was as virulent an anti-czarist as he had been in Lithuania; he also increasingly affiliated with the socialist party, became a powerful voice for the labor union movement, and, in 1890, while an editor at the weekly *Arbeiter Zeitung* (Workers' Newspaper),

Cahan traveled as a delegate to the Second International Socialist Congress, where he met Frederick Engles.

For many years, Cahan published feature stories about the immigrant experience and the ensuing labor troubles in both Yiddish-language publications and highly circulated newspapers like the New York *World*. In 1897 the soon-to-be (in)famous muckraker Lincoln Steffens hired Cahan full time as a feature writer for the New York *Commercial Advertiser*, and Cahan found himself a lone Jew in a crowd of privileged gentiles, most of whom were recruited straight from Harvard University. As scholar Moses Rischin writes, Cahan's time at the *Commercial Advertiser* constituted "a seminal period in his journalistic apprenticeship" ("Abraham" 10). That same year, he cofounded the *Jewish Daily Forward*, a publication of central importance in Jewish American history, which published feature stories about the immigrant experience, guidelines for survival in the New World, editorials championing socialist and progressive politics, and fiction by early Jewish American writers like Isaac Bashevis Singer.

In his early fiction, notably *Yekl* (1896) (an expanded treatment of "A Providential Match" (1892), his story of marriage and **assimilation** in the New World), *The Imported Bridegroom and Other Stories* (1898), and *The White Terror and the Red: A Novel of Revolutionary Russia* (1905), Cahan freed his Jewish characters from the roles assigned them on the popular stage. Instead, Cahan realistically portrayed newly arrived Jews on the Lower East Side absorbing the influences of the Anglo-German mainstream, struggling with the English language and the marketplaces, and taking in new and exciting forms of entertainment that were not offered back home. In *Yekl*, later adapted into the film "Hester Street" (1975), immigrant protagonist Gitl initially renounces the unorthodox lifestyle of American Jews, but she recognizes over time that for her and her son Yosselè to survive in the new world, they must shed socially limiting traditions while at the same time maintain some old world values that are critical for survival in a foreign, more modern society. William Dean Howells, the most influential literary critic in American history, took note of Cahan's achievements early on: In one New York *World* review, titled "New York Low Life in Fiction" (1896), Howells praised Cahan along with Stephen Crane as "a new star of realism."

The storyline of Cahan's masterpiece, *The Rise of David Levinsky* (1917), which first appeared in a shorter form in *McClure's* magazine as "The Autobiography of an American Jew" (1913), is reversed in its author's actual biography, *The Education of Abraham Cahan* (1926). In *The Rise of David Levinsky*, Cahan's fiction portrays the "external rise [of his narrator] as an internal fall" (Sollors 171); but rather than reaching millionaire status through assimilation like Levinsky, Cahan himself employed his ethnic identity in the role of a political activist. In a later review of Cahan's stories, Howells significantly remarked "it will be interesting to see whether Mr. Cahan will pass beyond his present environment out into the larger American world, or will master our life as he mastered our language. But of a Jew, who is also Russian, what artistic triumph may not we expect?" (*Literature,* December 31, 1898; qtd in Richards vii). But this artist's career was not destined for the assimilationist "triumph" Howells imagined. Instead, Cahan upheld his role as Socialist leader, editor of the *Jewish Daily Forward*, and widely read author of his column "Bintel Brief," and he persisted as a staunch advocate for immigrant communities and labor until his death in 1951. (*See also* Jewish American Novel)

Further Reading

Chametzky, Jules. *From the Ghetto: The Fiction of Abraham Cahan.* Amherst: Massachusetts UP, 1977.

Howells, William Dean. "New York Low Life in Fiction." *World* (July 26, 1896): 6–7.

Marovitz, Sanford E. *Abraham Cahan.* NY: Twayne, 1996.

Richards, Bernard G. "Abraham Cahan Cast in a New Role." *Yekl and the Imported Bridegroom and Other Stories of the New York Ghetto.* New York: Dover Books, 1970.

Rischin, Moses. "Abraham Cahan and the New York *Commercial Advertiser.*" *Publications of the American Jewish Historical Society* xliii (September 1953): 10–36.

———. Introduction. *The Spirit of the Ghetto.* Hutchins Hapgood. Cambridge, MA: Harvard UP, 1967 [orig. pub. 1902].

Sollors, Werner. *Beyond Ethnicity: Consent and Descent in American Culture.* New York: Oxford UP, 1986.

Robert M. Dowling

CALCAGNO, ANNE (1959–)   Italian American fiction writer. Anne Calcagno is one of the growing number of Italian American women writers to gain notice in the 1990s.

Born in San Diego to an Italian father and American mother, Calcagno moved with her parents and younger sister to Italy in the 1960s with American companies during Italy's "economic miracle"—the period when the Italian economy finally rebounded from the devastation of World War II. She was raised in Milan and Rome, only returning to the United States to begin college at the age of eighteen. After college, she remained in the United States, becoming a professor of creative writing at DePaul University in Chicago and the university's writer-in-residence.

Calcagno's fame rests mainly on a collection of stories, *Pray For Yourself* (1993), which won the James D. Phelan Award and was supported by fellowships from the National Endowment for the Arts and the Illinois Art Council. Similar to work of other late-twentieth-century Italian American women writers, most of the stories have American settings and more general American, rather than Italian American, themes. Many of the stories have at their core a modern relationship somehow dysfunctional, yet always presented tenderly. As alone in the world as some of her characters seem to be, Calcagno evokes a caring sentiment in the reader for all of them, and she accomplishes this at least partly through her use of the Italian language. Calcagno is bilingual and bicultural, and Italian cadences and nuances are often in her character's voices and sensibilities.

Still, a feeling common to most of the stories is an unsettling anxiousness that is often vague. "Water in the Aquarium," for instance, hints at a possible gang rape. This and another story with an Italian setting both present an idyllic Italian scene—with something sinister just waiting to happen. "Martine" depicts, through the eyes of the child Martine, a summer afternoon at a Mediterranean beach gone wrong. When a huge wave comes crashing unexpectedly on the beach, she loses hold of her little sister—and doesn't seem to understand why people are angry at her.

Calcagno explores Italy in more detail in a collection of travel essays that she edited, *Travelers' Tales Italy: True Stories of Life on the Road* (1998). Part of the Travelers' Tales Guides, it won ForeWord Magazine's Book of the Year award for best travel book of the year. Although she did not contribute a story of her own to the collection, Calcagno's preface advises the reader: Italy is incredibly multilayered and magnificently beyond the imagination of the uninitiated, or bored, tourist.

Calcagno shows her range with more recent work. The story "What's Yours?" (2002) returns to an American theme, compulsive shoplifting; it won an Illinois Arts Council Literary Award in 2003. One unpublished novel looks at modern Italian history (fascism and colonization in east Africa), and another one, in progress, deals with dog fighting in Chicago.

Christina Biava

CALDWELL, BEN (1937–) African American playwright. Ben Caldwell was born in Harlem on September 24, 1937. Heavily influenced by the Black Power Movement, Caldwell's plays make sharp commentary on the unfavorable conditions of African Americans' lives. His work mainly consists of short one-act plays, satirical in nature, with few characters. In 1965 Caldwell began writing seriously with a circle of artists and writers in Newark, New Jersey. During this eighteen-month "Newark Period," he wrote his most famous and critically acclaimed play, *Militant Preacher* (later titled *Prayer Meeting, or the First Militant Minister*) (1967). This play was published along with works by **Ronald Milner**, **Ed Bullins**, and Leroi Jones/**Amiri Baraka** in *A Black Quartet* (1970). The summer 1968 special issue of *Drama Review*, "4 Plays," featured four of Caldwell's plays: *Riot Sale, or Dollar Psyche Fake Out*; *The Job*; *Top Secret, or a Few Million after B.C.*; and *Mission Accomplished*. Two of Caldwell's plays, *The King of Soul, or the Devil and Otis Redding* and *All White Caste (After the Separation)*, were performed in 1973 at the New Federal Theatre in New York City. Caldwell produced *World of Ben Caldwell* at the same theater in 1982. Running for twelve days only, this monologue collection and sketch comedy brought Caldwell vast critical response. His most recent play, *Birth of a Blues!* (1989), was published in a collection, *New Plays for the Black Theatre* (1989), edited by **Woodie King Jr.** Powerfully talented, Caldwell was presented with the Harlem Writer's Guild Award in 1969 and the Guggenheim Fellowship for Playwriting in 1970. Though he still writes plays and essays, Caldwell's attention is currently focused on the fine arts.

Caldwell's brilliant use of satire to criticize black complacency toward white oppression is exemplified in *Prayer Meeting, or the First Militant Minister*. In this brief play, a minister arrives home, unaware a burglar is robbing his well-furnished home. Hearing the minister, the burglar hides behind a dresser. Caldwell's elaborate stage directions portray the minister as shallow and insincere. As the preacher prays for guidance as to how he can subdue his angry congregation after the murder of a black man by a white police officer, the burglar becomes angry and voices his disgust. Thinking that he has heard the word of God, the minister proceeds to listen fearfully to the burglar's inspiring message of black power. By the end of the play, the minister is a changed man, urging his congregation to stand up to the suffering, murder, and exploitation to which the white man subjects them.

A science fiction piece, *All White Caste (After the Separation)*, employs white characters to depict the second-class citizenship forced upon blacks. The play's setting is Harlem, after the Third World War, in which blacks overthrew their white oppressors and returned to Africa. A handcuffed prisoner is led into a shabby, desolate living room by a white guard, who tells him this is his new home. The prisoner, a writer who sympathized with the Black Power Movement during the war, is baffled by the terms of his imprisonment. He is given a shipping clerk position at fifty-five dollars a week, confined to live in a run-down apartment (which the guard intermingling calls a "cell"), and is given a list of ambitions he is allowed to consider. Caldwell satirically uses the white sympathizer's new life to portray the lives of African Americans. Ironically, the Harvard-educated prisoner who preached black equality is mortified by the living conditions imposed upon him, revealing his privileged status as a white man. At the end of the play, as the white guard is leaving, he advises a black guard to teach the prisoner some **blues** if he resigns to his fate.

In *Birth of the Blues!* Caldwell not only pokes fun at blues musician and **African American stereotypes**, but also criticizes the white entertainment industry's exploitation of black performers. In this hilarious play, a young white reporter attempts to interview an elderly black blues musician, who is playing on a street corner. The ignorant reporter asks B. B. B. B. B. King (the musician) if people confuse him with B. B. King, if he is related to Dr. **Martin Luther King Jr.**, and if he has been blind his whole life, because of his sunglasses. These questions, answered negatively, reveal the media-induced, stereotypical image of blues singers. After telling the story of how he was used for profit making by the white-run music industry, B. B. B. B. B. King explains that the source of his blues is actually his tight, painful shoes.

Ben Caldwell's satirical plays are valuable to the **canon** of African American drama. Through his creative plotlines, biting dialogue, and unfailing wit,

Caldwell sends a powerful message to blacks to reject complacency. (*See also* African American Drama)

Further Reading

Bowman, Kenneth. "The Revolution Will Not Be Televised nor Staged; An Interview with Ben Caldwell." *Callaloo* 22.4 (1999): 808–24.

Ladwig, Ronald V. "The Black Black Comedy of Ben Caldwell." *Players* 51 (1976): 88–91.

Danielle Angie

CALISHER, HORTENSE (1911–) Jewish American author. Calisher is a serious, skilled, and prolific writer. Her first work, *In the Absence of Angels,* appeared in 1953, followed by a succession of essays, reviews, autobiographical writings, collections of short stories, and fifteen novels. Despite such impressive output, her work is not widely read. One reason lies in Calisher's cultivation of an elliptical, neo-Jamesian writing style. Such writing is not affectation. Calisher uses complex language to reveal the subtle intelligence and multifaceted perceptions of her protagonists. Whatever its uses, Calisher's style limits her audience.

Another possible reason for neglect is the disengagement of Calisher's fictive universe from the social concerns of mid- and late-twentieth-century America. The war in Vietnam, for example, receives only brief mention in *Eagle Eye* when Bunty Bronstein goes abroad to avoid the draft (1973); homelessness and poverty are opportunities for self-discovery in *Survival Techniques* (one of the short novels in *Saratoga Hot* [1985]). For Calisher's protagonists, struggles are primarily internal. Hester Elkin, a fictionalized version of Calisher who appears in many of the early autobiographical short stories (see, for example, "Old Stock" in *In the Absence of Angels* and "May-ry" in *Tales for the Mirror: A Novella and Other Stories* [1962]), is repeatedly engaged in the process of formulating an independent self beyond the loving but stifling confinement of her family. Hester is a typical Calisher protagonist, and Calisher's treatment of her illustrates how self-centered Calisher's writing is.

The selves Calisher constructs are frequently Jewish. The Calisher family is the source of Calisher's religious and ethnic preoccupations. In *Herself* (1972), Calisher describes the comfortable upper-middle-class New York Jewish family into which she was born. Although both parents were Jewish, their cultural baggage was different. Calisher's mother was a recent immigrant from Germany and her father came from an old Virginia slaveholding family. These nuances of Jewish **identity** are featured in Calisher's work. Characters like Judge Simon Mannix in *The New Yorkers* (1969) and Zipporah Zangwill in *Sunday Jews* (2002) maintain the residual Jewish consciousness associated with assimilating New York Jews. Their Jewishness is not a matter of religious practice, nor do they inhabit exclusively Jewish worlds. Friends, colleagues, companions, spouses, and hangers-on are a diverse mix of other, sometimes competing, ethnicities. **Assimilation** for Calisher's Jewish characters is an exercise in inclusivity. They take on the attributes of the dominant culture, but the non-Jewish world in which they flourish and flounder shows the influence of their Jewish presence. That Jewishness is a composite of family attachments, cosmopolitan interests, intellectual acuity, emotional intensity, verbal glitter, financial acumen, and pervasive guilt. Hester Elkin, Simon Mannix, Zipporah Zangwill, and Calisher's other Jewish characters are always aware of, frequently amused by, and occasionally regretful about the erosion of their ancestral beliefs. They are also sensitive to and annoyed by the small social embarrassments and disjunctions their Jewishness creates. They nevertheless insist on maintaining some sense of otherness in a society that will never in any case let them forget their difference. What Calisher achieves in her Jewish work, then, is a Judaizing of the Jamesian drama of consciousness.

Further Reading

Hahn, Emily. "In Appreciation of Hortense Calisher." *Wisconsin Studies in Contemporary Literature* 6 (1965): 243–49.

Ingersoll, Earl, and Peter Marchant. "A Conversation with Hortense Calisher." *Southwest Review* 71.2 (1986): 186–93.

Reich, Tova. "Sunday Jews." *The New Leader* 85.3 (May/June 2002): 36–37.

Snodgrass, Kathleen. *The Fiction of Hortense Calisher*. Newark: U of Delaware P, 1993.

———. "Hortense Calisher: A Bibliography, 1948–1986." *Bulletin of Bibliography* 45.1 (March 1988): 40–50.

———. "On Hortense Calisher." *Iowa Review* 24.3 (1994): 185–87.

Bernice Schrank

CALOF, RACHEL BELLA KAHN (1876–1952) Jewish American autobiographer. Rachel Calof wrote her memoir in Yiddish in 1936. The manuscript was translated into English about twenty years after her death and compiled into a typed manuscript, which was distributed to family members and Jewish archives. *Rachel Calof's Story: Jewish Homesteader on the Northern Plains* (1995) was edited by J. Sanford Rikoon and published by Indiana University Press. Calof's story contributes to scholarship in women's studies, western studies, and immigrant literature by focusing on the individual context, revealing daily and prosaic details and adding information on less well-known ethnicities on the frontier. *Rachel Calof's Story* is used extensively in college courses as an eloquent and powerful narrative of the hardships of homesteading.

Although Rachel Calof focused her writing on her life as a homesteader between 1894 and 1917 in Devils Lake, North Dakota, she began her story by telling of her life as an orphan in the Ukraine. Her siblings were dispersed among their relatives and Rachel lived with her grandfather, a religious fanatic. She then moved to her aunt's home as a maid. An inappropriate romance resulted in an arranged engagement to Abraham Calof, who was already living in the United States. Rachel wrote a detailed description of her journey, meeting with Abraham, and moving to North Dakota. Her story is one of poverty, crowding, and deprivation, with Calof relatives surrounding her on the nearby homesteads. Rachel Calof wrote about her wedding, the winters, and some of her nine children's births. She elaborated upon a postpartum depression and her mother-in-law's rituals for protecting the mother and newborn child. Circumcision and dietary laws imposed difficulties on the desperately poor families, but Rachel Calof also conveyed religious observance as satisfying, and she took pride in her role as a Jewish homemaker. She documented crises of sickness and accidents and eventually economic success. The story ended abruptly: After twenty-three years on the farm, the Calof family moved to St. Paul.

The Indiana University Press publication includes a preface by J. Sanford Rikoon and an epilogue by Jacob Calof. Supplementary articles provide background information on farming and Jewish communities. Tracing this manuscript from inception to publication reveals significant translation divergences between the Yiddish and English texts. Research at the Jewish Historical Society of the Upper Midwest (JHSUM) shows that the Yiddish manuscript is 255 pages and not 67 pages, as is suggested in the Indiana publication. Archival evidence also indicates that Rachel Calof submitted her manuscript to *The Forward*, suggesting she was not writing for a family audience as the published version claims. The original Yiddish manuscript is held by the family, though the JHSUM archive holds a photocopy. Since differences between the Yiddish manuscript and the English publication prove to be significant, questions of translation, editing, and collaboration arise. *Rachel Calof's Story* is probably a hybrid text, integrating both oral histories and written texts to portray a more complete, if idealized, picture of life on that homestead. (*See also* Yiddish Literature)

Further Reading

Peleg, Kristine. "In Search of Rachel Calof's Original Manuscript." *Jewish American History* 92.1 (March 2004): 103–12

Kristine Peleg

CAMPO, RAFAEL (1964–)   Cuban American poet, doctor, and social critic. Campo, a member of the Latino gay community, infuses a deep sense of humanity into his evocation of the doctor-patient relationship, recognizing the complexity of both racial and gendered cultural identities.

Born in New Jersey, but with native fluency in Spanish as well as English, Campo possesses a dual cultural **identity**. Campo studied at Amherst University and Harvard medical school, where he is now a faculty member. He worked as a resident at the University of California in San Francisco, an experience which allowed him to come into contact with a diverse range of patients, many of whom were Hispanic, gay, and suffering from HIV. It is the experiences of these marginalized groups that form his key poetic focus.

Campo's intention is to inject a greater realization of human dignity and suffering into what he perceives as the cold environment of medicine. His work is a reaction against the development of a business ethos within the world of medicine, which has prompted him to find a method of creating a more personal relationship with his patients. Campo achieves this partly by conducting the unorthodox practice of teaching poetry to his colleagues and patients. His roles as doctor and poet have evoked comparisons to other U.S. poets, including William Carlos Williams, and his embracing of the body as his central metaphor is reminiscent of Walt Whitman.

Campo's first book of poetry, *The Other Man Was Me: A Voyage to the New World* (1994), won the National Poetry Series 1993 Open Competition. The poems introduce a strong sense of realism into the creation of the hospital environment, in contrast to the somewhat glamorized world constructed by popular contemporary hospital television shows. In one of his best-known poems from the collection, "The Distant Moon," Campo focuses on a gay patient who is dying from HIV. He presents the doctor's affinity and responsibility for his patient, on both an immediately physical plane and a more broadly conceived symbolic plane.

What the Body Told (1996), Campo's second collection, won him the Lambda literary award. Here he makes extensive use of formal structures such as the sonnet. Campo is an advocate of formally structured poetry, which he feels can communicate directly to the patient, as opposed to more open-ended contemporary experimental forms. Furthermore, Campo has indicated that the sonnet in particular appeals to him because of the way that it has been deployed in a number of different languages, making it culturally hybrid, and because of its erotic and physical nature, in that its meter and rhythms emulate the body's heartbeat and breathing. In addition, the sonnet is a form that typically adheres to various rules and then breaks them; it therefore encapsulates the concept of cultural and gendered boundary crossing appropriate to Campo's poems about the problems experienced by the Latino and gay communities. Other innovations include the use of half rhymes and sentences that push beyond the limits of the poetic line.

Campo's memoir, *The Poetry of Healing: A Doctor's Education in Empathy, Identity, and Desire* (1997), is strikingly open about his own sexual responses to his patients, exploding the myth of the doctor's detachment from the patient's personal situation. His subsequent poetry collection, *Diva* (1999), explores his contradictory attitudes toward Cuba, and it was the finalist for the National Book Critics Circle award. Campo continued to explore conflicted cultural identities in his next poetry book, *Landscape with Human Figure* (2002). His most recent essay collection, *The Healing Art: A Doctor's Black Bag of Poetry* (2003), outlines the ways in which the act of reading and writing poetry can be used as a method of healing patients who are suffering from illnesses such as depression and AIDS.

A large number of Campo's poems and essays have appeared in journals such as *The Kenyon Review*, *The Nation*, *The New York Times Magazine*, and *The Paris Review*. Campo is a PEN Center Literary Award finalist and the recipient of a Guggenheim fellowship, and he has also been honored with the National Hispanic Academy of Arts and Sciences Annual Achievement Award.

Rafael Campo continues to write poetry while practicing medicine at the Beth Israel Deaconess Medical Center in Boston. (*See also* Cuban American Poetry, Cuban American Autobiography)

Further Reading

Campo, Rafael. "Formalism, Foreignness, and Friction: The Uses of Poetry." *Hopscotch: A Cultural Review* 1.2 (1999): 40–51.

Henderson, S. W. "Identity and Compassion in Rafael Campo's 'The Distant Moon'." *Literature and Medicine* 19.2 (2000): 262–79.

Helen Oakley

CANDELARIA, CORDELIA CHÁVEZ (1943–)   Mexican American poet, multimedia artist, scholar, activist, and higher education admininstrator. Originally from New Mexico, Candelaria now lives and works as a professor in Arizona. She earned a doctorate in American literature and structural linguistics. As an author of path-breaking studies of Chicana/o poetry, literature, and cultural studies and an academic, Candelaria has built an exemplary career as a scholar, educational leader, and public figure. A pioneering intellectual, she has edited and published extensively in numerous literary and academic journals with national and international readerships. She has consistently held to a core belief in the value of American pluralism in education, culture, and society.

Candelaria's publication credits are voluminous. She has published three volumes of creative writing: *Ojo de la Cueva/Cave Springs* (1984), *Arroyos to the Heart* (1993), and *Cursing Fujimori and Other Andean Reflections* (2003). In addition, her first full-length literary critique, *Chicano Poetry: A Critical Introduction* (1986), has become a classic in the field, and in 1989, she published *Seeking the Perfect Game: Baseball in American Literature*, an unprecedented study that inspired a wave of scholarly interest in American popular cultural studies, including ethnic studies. By the late 1980s Candelaria had become a highly distinguished Chicana scholar, and since then, she has gone on to spearhead many publication efforts to bolster the literature of the Southwest United States and particularly that of Chicana/o and Latina/o writers.

In the 1980s Chicana writers gained voice and visibility in public literary, artistic, and performing venues, and Candelaria was in the forefront of this development. Candelaria believed that Chicana women should not subordinate their quest for individual rights to the Chicano movement, and she proposed that the movement would suffer if it did not hold up the rights of Chicanas or validate women's perspectives. Her desire to highlight women's roles in political activism and discourse led her to edit the first exclusively Chicana issue of *Frontiers: A Journal of Women Studies*. Not unlike other early Chicana feminist projects, this issue of *Frontiers* was a communal effort, coedited by Cordelia Candelaria, Kathi George, and the

Frontiers Editorial Collective; its publication was a watershed moment since the issue featured contributions by major figures, thus galvanizing the Chicana intelligentsia in a new way. The path-breaking 1980 *Frontiers* issue also included lesbian testimonios excerpted from an (at that time) unpublished manuscript titled *Las Mujeres: Conversations from a Hispanic Community* (1981). The issue enjoyed several printings as it quickly became a cornerstone of women's studies and other reading lists that dared to intersect Chicana/Latina **ethnicity** with feminist frameworks and inclusive sexualities before this intersection of studies was as widespread as it now is in the twenty-first century.

Candelaria has edited or coedited several major works in Chicana/o studies, including: *Estudios Chicanos and the Politics of Community* (1989); *Multiethnic Literature of the United States: Critical Introductions and Classroom Resources* (1989); *Community Empowerment and Social Justice* (1991); *Women Poets of the Americas: Toward a Panamerican Gathering* (1999); *The Legacy of the Mexican and Spanish-American Wars: Legal, Literary, and Historical Perspectives* (2000); and *Encyclopedia of Latina and Latino Popular Culture(s) in the United States* (2004).

In addition to having built an illustrious record as a writer and editor, Candelaria has been an innovator in higher education administration. Keeping with her philosophy of intellectual and political pluralism, she was one of the first women to chair an academic ethnic-focused program, and she cofounded the Center for the Study of Ethnicity and **Race** in America at the University of Colorado in Boulder where she served as Founding Director from 1986 to 1988. She has served as chairperson of ethnic studies and literature departments at the University of Colorado, Boulder and Arizona State University, where she carried out the mission of increasing the number of Chicano/Latino faculty. She has also actively participated in Chicana/Latina feminist organizations, social activism, and cultural empowerment, and her participation has included being the first Chicana ever elected to the Ignacio, Colorado Town Council (1968–70) and being elected Chair of the South Bend, Indiana Human Rights Commission (1972–76). (*See also* Mexican American Poetry)

Further Reading

Goldbeck, Janne. "Home in Ojo de la Cueva." *Rendezvous: Journal of Arts and Letters* 22.2 (Spring 1986): 51–52

Kanthak, John F. "Feminisms in Motion: Pushing the 'Wild Zone' Thesis into the Fourth Dimension." *Literature Interpretation Theory* 14.2 (April–June 2003): 149–63.

Edith M. Vasquez

CANE Published in 1923, **Jean Toomer**'s *Cane*, after many years of being out of print, is now widely regarded as the most accomplished literary text of the **Harlem Renaissance**. An intricate composite of poems, sketches, and a play-cum-character dialogue, the book's being called a "novel" is primarily a matter of academic convention. This collage of narrative, poetic, and dramatic voices adopts impressionistic form to depict rural and urban black life at the peripheries of legitimated desire.

Inspired by Toomer's brief tenure as acting principal of a school for African Americans in Sparta, Georgia, in 1921, *Cane* is divided into three parts. The first explores the tragic intersections of female sexuality, black manhood, and industrial modernization in the South. Bearing illegitimate children makes pariahs out of Karintha, an alluring black woman initially admired for her sexual naïveté, and Becky, a white woman guilty of the "crime" of miscegenation: the former becomes a prostitute after killing her baby and the latter lives in abject seclusion with her two mixed sons. Herself the illegitimate child of a black woman and a Jewish man, Fernie May Rosen confounds infatuated suitors with her languid, even spiritually detached, disposition. And in "Blood-Burning Moon," a black field hand, Tom Burwell, murders Bob Stone, the white rival for Louisa's affection, when Bob challenges Tom's right to share intimate space with her. Tom is subsequently hauled to a gutted-out cotton factory and lynched by a white mob.

The second part of *Cane* relocates the setting of both lyric and narrative to Washington, DC, and Chicago. Here, unrequited black and interracial desire takes on a more subdued but no less psychically tragic tone. In "Theater" the difference in class position that exists between Doris, a dancer, and John, the light-skinned and sexually repressed brother of the theater manager, forecloses a romantic bond. The way racial passing defuses such a bond is the subject of "Bona and Paul." Southern students at a Chicago physical education school, the white Bona Hale longs for Paul Johnson precisely because of his mixed racial heritage. But Paul's tortured self-policing of his "dark skin" and his aversion to the exoticization of his shadow doom the relationship to failure.

The third and final section consists of a short, never-staged drama, "Kabnis," whose loosely autobiographical title character dreams of promoting progressive Northern ideals through his work as an educator of rural Southern blacks. Ralph Kabnis soon discovers, however, that the locals are not so much content with the status quo as they are unable to break free from the past with the sort of individuated agency he champions yet fundamentally lacks himself. Embittered and defeated by this realization, the dialogue ends with Kabnis literally bowing to the force of his people's history.

Certain critics, such as Alice Walker, have lamented *Cane*'s lack of "authentic" grounding in the folk culture in which it was conceived; they have also been troubled by the way the mixed Toomer often elected to pass as white and identified foremost as an "American." But the radically experimental form of his book hardly eschews the complexities of racial identification and belonging in the segregated United States. Prior to its publication, themes of thwarted black and interracial love, complemented by the paradoxical logic of passing, had never been so richly portrayed. (*See also* African American Novel)

Further Reading

Gates, Henry Louis, Jr. "The Same Difference: Reading Jean Toomer, 1923–1983." *Figures in Black: Words, Signs, and the "Racial" Self*. New York: Oxford UP, 1987. 196–224.

McKay, Nellie Y. *Jean Toomer, Artist: A Study of His Literary Life and Work, 1894–1936*. Chapel Hill: U of North Carolina P, 1984.

O'Daniel, Therman B., ed. *Jean Toomer: A Critical Evaluation*. Washington, DC: Howard UP, 1988.

Scruggs, Charles, and Lee VanDemarr. *Jean Toomer and the Terrors of American History*. Philadelphia: U of Pennsylvania P, 1998.

Kinohi Nishikawa

CANO, DANIEL (1947–) Mexican American novelist and professor. Daniel Cano's work has been critically acclaimed and recognized as unique in its representation of the lives of Mexican Americans. Cano's novels demonstrate his ability to vividly portray the complexities of cultural **identity** in the face of adversity.

Daniel Cano's first novel *Pepe Rios* (1991) is a story set against the backdrop of the Mexican Revolution of 1910. The novel follows the hero on a journey through war-ravaged Mexico after the death of his father. Finding identity amid chaos is an idea that resurfaces in Cano's work. Having served himself as a soldier during the Vietnam War, both of Cano's novels revolve around the extraordinary circumstances created in times of conflict. In his second novel *Shifting Loyalties* (1995), Cano again uses a war torn backdrop as the context in which his characters struggle. Creating an environment that is constantly in flux is crucial to Cano's writing. He suggests that the surrounding environment is indicative of larger realities. It becomes an external representation of the characters' interior modes. Cano's fascination with environment is evident in his academic pursuits as well. Cano teaches writing at Santa Monica College where he is an active part of the university's environmental studies program. He has also published several short stories in various anthologies.

In addition to his writing, Cano has distinguished himself as a professor. His pedagogical career has been as recognized as his writing career. Cano was awarded the position of visiting lecturer at the University of California, San Diego and received a fellowship from the Institute for Educational Leadership in Washington, DC. In 2003 Cano was honored by the League of United Latin American Citizens (LULAC), Santa Monica-Venice Bay Area Council 2010, at their Community United Awards. Cano has also held the position of Visiting Associate Professor and is currently a professor of English teaching Mexican American literature, literature of Mexico, and creative writing.

Daniel Cano continues to teach and write about environmental and urban studies, and his writing has been recognized for its thoughtful meditations and careful insights. Cano's contributions to his community and dedication to teaching have brought him recognition and praise, and he demonstrates the possibility of advancing beyond adversity in order to discover oneself. Cano's careful writing, character development, and meditative stories have been highly acclaimed by critics, and his writing style and subject matter are part of his unique storytelling abilities. He writes stories that touch upon the broader subjects that synthesize the community, and he has been praised for his fictional topics as well as the social realities with which he grapples. As a result, Cano's work is fresh, relevant, and intriguing to his readers, and his work is considered important by critics for wrestling with themes of identity within a larger community.

Further Reading

Bustamante, Nuria. "Daniel Cano." *Dictionary of Literary Biography.* Vol. 209. Ed. Francisco A. Lomeli and Carl R. Shirley. Detroit: Gale, 1999. 29–33.

Staven Bruce

CANON   Until modern times, the word "canon" was used exclusively in an ecclesiastical context. The canon is still the set of rules, assumed divinely ordered, by which the church (primarily the Christian church in its various embodiments) governs itself. Compare the application of this denotation with the Pali canon, which forms the doctrinal foundation of Theravada Buddhism. Appropriated from the ecclesiastical use to define tenets of practitioners in genres or communities in many areas of the fine arts, such as music, the word is used in literature to denote a list of books accepted by most of a given community as definitive of the rules and mores of that group. Therefore any group of recognizable qualities may, in the field of literature, give rise to a canon. For example, by examining the elements of the type of eighteenth century novel labeled Gothic, that is, by looking for the supernatural or for horror within the text, we may recognize this kind of narrative in English literature and be able to replicate the genre, if necessary, in the future. Although a contemporaneous replication of that novelistic form (using the Gothic as an example) would not share in the actual historical canvas against which this genre was first written, our new renditions would carry the patina of our particular experience. We may recognize the influence of this specific genre on twentieth century writers such as **Octavia Butler**, the science fiction writer, whose novels, such as *Kindred*, although not strictly Gothic, contain elements of the supernatural. This transference of the elements of a particular genre and, therefore, the elements of the respective canon into the literature of another period admits of one paradox of the canon as a grouping: the canon should not, indeed cannot, be closed. Elements of one literary expression flow into those of a later literary and historical period.

In the case of the United States of America, given the present emphasis on diversity and **multiculturalism**, there is an impetus toward inclusion that is driving the reexamination of the canon. It should seem obvious that the canon as it is conceived is also a reflection of literacy, literary theory, and socioeconomic factors. Pronouncements such as **Harold Bloom**'s tome, *The Western Canon: The Books and School of the Ages*, add to the ongoing question as to who controls the canon. And as Trevor Ross writes in *The Making of the English Canon: From the Middle Ages to the Late Eighteenth Century*, "canons make clear the values of great literature and valued modern work" (92). He also joins the commentary that current tradition and definition of self form part of the impetus for the production and control of literature. Clearly there are aspects of power in this state of affairs. Questions of value and valuation arise, particularly in a system such as this where there is no guideline as to who can decide what is of value or not. An example of this occurred at a major university toward the end of the last century. In a debate concerning the list of writers to be studied in its English Department, voices representing new paradigms were raised. George Sweeney reported on September 22, 1997, in the *Daily Bruin* of the University of California at Los Angeles (UCLA), that Ali Behdad, professor of postcolonial studies, stated the English canon was not invented for England. It was invented as part of colonization, in order to shape and form a certain culture in India and other British colonies. Indeed the jingoism of the poetry of Rudyard Kipling and the cautionary precepts in the so-called folk tale "Little Black Sambo," which were dispersed through reading texts to areas of the British Empire as various as the Caribbean, South America, and Australia, were indicative of two sides of the imperialist coin: on one hand, the fortitude of the colonizers was being upheld and on the other, the childlike comicality of the colonized was being reinforced. Arguments at academic institutions such as UCLA contended that the subscribed canon, seen as primarily Western and imperialistically dictated, has traditionally been exclusive and has resisted the influx of multicultural literature. As a result the two forces of traditional literature and new twenty-first century literature are trying to find a balance. Nevertheless the question remains as to the identities and qualifications of those who compose the body that chooses and inserts texts into the canon.

To write about the contents of the canon is then fraught with indecision and redolent of the old imperialist structure. In any contention against the inclusion of, for instance, the rhymes of jingoism and adventures of Little Back Sambo, that same tendency to imperialism would surface, as, through the designation of the canon, the community is told how to act, what to read, and what to believe from a set of books that purports to define excellence for the entire community. **Irving Howe** comments that this is all balanced by teachers who are allowed to speak freely. Thus teachers are assigned the role of arbiter and arbitrator in a system that is already slippery by context, in a country in which, by constitutional definition, all opinions carry the note of validity. And this system, by an unwritten process of checks and balances, identifies writers who appeal to a broad societal base without necessarily questioning old inclusions like "Little Black Sambo." A version of the canon emerges.

To be chosen for the canon is to be anthologized by one of the major presses, such as Norton or Oxford, and thus have one's works placed before a public as the arbiters of literary excellence. These are the writers whose works are important, who have something to say. This list of writers and their works is then perpetuated of itself and, as may be deduced, remains highly dependent on the selection committees of such lists. Therefore, for example, if one considers the works of **Rosa Guy** one would find that she is memorialized as an insightful, searing young adult fiction novelist. This characterization would be one of her claims to fame since she is seen as a pioneer in the exploration of adolescent feelings in an urban setting. These are universal themes. Compare her *Ruby* with Goethe's *Suffering of Young Werther*, in which, although the latter protagonist is not as young as Guy's Ruby, the struggle for self-definition and the exploration of a youthful psychological landscape share commonalties and appear in print at a fortuitous moment in a community's history. In contrast, a dramatist-poet, such as **Owen Dodson**, may be avoided as an exponent on adolescent or young adult soul-searching and discovery, although his autobiographically based *Boy at The Window* was hailed by respected critics as sensitive and honest.

There is the question then of how to resurrect the dead or distinctive works without discrimination and to do so not just during an Asian Heritage Month or African American Heritage Month celebration. Through what mechanism does anyone in a community find those narratives that are important to and for the culture of the United States, at the same time inserting new voices and retaining the others? The canon wars, aided by the publication of Harold Bloom's aforementioned text containing its impressive appendices, Sven Birkerts's anthology *On Literature: The Evolving Canon* (1995), and even the Modern Library's list of the hundred best books of the twentieth century, smack of **whiteness** and deservedly created an uproar. Each of these promulgated an idea of the superiority of literature produced by white writers, with some tokenism by inclusion of writers such as **Toni Morrison**. These were the writers who were touted as representative of the thought and experience of the community. Completely ignored was that subtext, and the implications of that subtext, to the canon: literacy. For literacy to thrive, the reader has to be engaged. In 1997, one of a series of researches proposed that students became more active and thorough readers if they were given texts that reflected their own experience. The typical reading list of a public school district would admit a text such as **Carolivia Herron**'s critically acclaimed children's story, *Nappy Hair*, and have it trounced. Careful examination of so-called relevant texts for the young, and this is where the canon making with its effect does start, has revealed that stereotyping and some degree of lessening of self-esteem are reinforced by these texts (Grice and Vaughn, 1992). This is an argument dismissed by Howe. Howe, in his introduction essay on the subject of the canon, questions whether the function of the humanities is to inculcate self-esteem. The canon of children's literature, one of the many subcanons, starts a student's educational road. What the student reads in school is important. If one reads "Little Black Sambo," or *Nappy Hair,* or if one reads the slave narratives, one is exposed to their characterizations, and their language, tone, and action. This statement, of course, takes any other outside reading encouraged by parents or other interested parties into consideration. By the time the student is likely to graduate, the choice of books may have impacted his or her life. The question is to what degree and to what purpose. Outdated texts, denigrating texts, all have their impact on the future. Thus, for example, if the student is familiar with Nathaniel Hawthorne's work, "The Maypole of Merry Mount," and all that the celebration of Spring connotes, he or she is learning about the culture of those who colonized modern North America. If he or she is not exposed simultaneously to the Juneteenth festival, then a valuable part of the African American experience and, therefore, the American fabric is pushed into the background. And it is this consideration of the American experience that currently is influencing thought on the literary canon as it is delineated in the United States. The American version, to be inclusive, must acknowledge simultaneously its Western stratum and those other components derived from the history of movement into and within the country politic.

There is the danger of stretching the literary experience and output too thin and this is why judiciousness is necessary in this area of openness and diversity in America. Many an excellent writer, not promoted, has waited to be discovered. Many others have flamed and died without fulfilling their promise, and others with no talent have flourished owing to astute marketing. We cannot ignore the impact of the large press, or the importance of wealth in the process of the canon composition. Significant publishers, such as Norton, influence by their magnitude and imposition of texts and not necessarily by their correctness or relevance of choice. The writer has to be published to be read, read to be appreciated, and appreciated in order to be considered for inclusion in the canon. Even in the area of poetry, by tradition the most declaimed of words, the poem written is more permanent and less subject to change than the poem spoken. A poem that answers the needs of the community enters libraries, school texts, and the marketplace and assumes a place in the status quo, its place concretized by the multiplicity of sensibilities to which it appeals. Thus, with multiculturalism, diversity, and ethnic differences on the forefront of educative political programs, the canon is beginning to reflect the works of the several constituents of the American community. With publishers such as **Arte Público Press** and Griffon House Publications, with the proliferation of independent printing via the Internet, and with book festivals and reading groups, writers and critics such as Molefi Asante Jr., **Maxine Hong Kingston**, **Edwidge Danticat**, and Oona Kempadoo are placed on reading lists and mentioned in a one or more versions of what, combined, serves as the literary canon.

Further Reading

Anzaldua, Gloria. *Borderlands/La Frontera: The New Mestiza*. San Francisco: Aunt Lute Books, 1987.

Baker, Houston, Henry Louis Gates Jr., and Joyce A. Joyce. "The Black Canon: Reconstructing Black American Literary Criticism." *New Literary History* 18.2 (Winter 1987): 335–44.

Bloom, Harold. *The Western Canon: The Books and School of the Ages*. New York: Harcourt Brace, 1994.

Eliot, T. S. *The Sacred Wood: Essays on Poetry and Criticism*. London: Methuen, 1920.

Ervin, Hazel Arnett. *African American Literary Criticism*. New York: Twayne, 1999.

Fetterley, Judith. *The Resisting Reader: A Feminist Approach to American Fiction*. Bloomington: Indiana UP, 1978.

Gates, Henry Louis, Jr. "The Master's Pieces: On Canon Formation and the Afro-American Tradition." *Conversations*. Ed. Charles Moran and Elizabeth Penfield. Urbana, IL: National Council of Teachers of English, 1970. 55–75.

Grice, Mary Oldham, and Courtney Vaughn. "Third Graders Respond to Literature for and about Afro Americans." *Urban Review* 24.2 (June 1992): 149–64.

Howe, Irving. "The Value of the Canon." *New Republic* 204.7 (1991): 40+.

Jay, Gregory. *American Literature and the Culture Wars*. New York: Cornell UP, 1997.

Lauter, Paul. *Canons and Contexts*. New York: Oxford UP, 1991.

Morrison, Toni. *Whiteness and the Literary Imagination*. Cambridge: Harvard UP, 1993.

Peters, Cynthia. *Deaf American Literature: From Carnival to Canon*. Washington, DC: Gallaudet UP, 2002.

Ross, Trevor. *The Making of the English Literary Canon: From the Middle Ages to the Late Eighteenth Century*. Montreal and Kingston, Canada: McGill-Queens UP, 1998.

Wimsatt, W. K., and Cleanth Brooks. *Literary Criticism: A Short History*. London: Routledge and Kegan Paul, 1970.

Juliet A. Emanuel

CANTÚ, NORMA ELIA (1947–) Mexican American poet, scholar, folklorist and educator. She earned a doctorate at the University of Nebraska at Lincoln. She has taught and published creative and scholarly works on Chicano/a literature, U.S. Latina/o literature, creative writing, border studies, lesbian sexuality, women's studies, and folklore. Cantú's early life experiences along the Texas/Mexico border caused her to see ambiguities and contradictions as valuable components of her culture, a culture she has sought to record as a folklorist as well as creative writer. Indeed, her literary autobiography, *Canícula: Snapshots of a Girlhood en la Frontera* (1977), interweaves poetic theory with a detailed and visual retelling of Chicana border culture.

Cantú has focused her energies on documenting the stories of Chicana girls as they make their transition into adulthood. She regards the process of becoming a woman in Mexican American families as highly worthwhile of formal investigation and personal discovery. As a folklorist, she has conducted studies of women's rites-of-passage including baptism, quinceañeras, and family intergenerational storytelling. She is committed to the empowerment of Mexican American women.

Cantú has long believed that the empowerment of the Mexican American woman is best achieved through self-knowledge, cultural sharing, and the writing of personal narratives. Cantú's personal ethos has distinguished her in higher education administration; she has served as a university administrator in California and Texas.

Cantú has received many honors including an Award of Merit from the Association of Women in Communications; the Outstanding Alumni Award from the College of Arts and Science, University of Nebraska; a Fulbright-Hays Postdoctoral Research Fellowship as well as a Ford Foundation Chicano Dissertation Completion Grant; and a Fulbright-Hays Research Fellowship to Spain.

Cantú's award-winning publications include *Entre Malinche y Guadalupe: Tejanas in Literature and Art* (1999), *Chicana Traditions* (2002), and *Telling to Live: Latina Feminist Testimonios* (2002). She has published articles in highly esteemed folklore journals, and she has contributed creative works of poetry and fiction to numerous anthologies and periodicals. (*See also* Mexican American Poetry)

Further Reading

Adams, Timothy Dow. "'Heightened by Life' vs. 'Paralyzed by Fact': Photography and Autobiography in Norma Cantú's Canícula." *Biography: An Interdisciplinary Quarterly* 24.1 (Winter 2001): 57-71.

Behar, Ruth. "Sad Movies Make Me Cry." *Chicana Feminisms: A Critical Reader.* Ed. Gabriela F. Arrendondo, et al. Durham, NC: Duke UP, 2003. 109–13.

Betancor, Maria Henriquez. "Photographs and Memory: A Chicana Structures Autobiography." *Revista Canaria de Estudios Ingleses* 37 (November 1998): 225–26.

Cantú, Norma Elia. "The Writing of Canícula: Breaking Boundaries, Finding Form." *Chicana Feminisms: A Critical Reader.* Ed. Gabriela F. Arredondo. Durham, NC: Duke UP, 2003. 7–108.

McCracken, Ellen. "Hybridity and the Space of the Border in the Writing of Norma Elia Cantú." *Studies in Twentieth Century Literature* 25.1 (Winter 2001): 261–70.

Edith M.Vasquez

CAO, LAN (1961–)   Vietnamese American novelist. Lan Cao was airlifted out of Saigon as a teenager in 1975. She earned her BA from Mount Holyoke in South Hadley, Massachusetts, and her JD from Yale University in 1987. She is currently a law professor at the College of William and Mary, where she specializes in International Business & Trade, International Law, and Law and Development.

Cao's first published work was *Everything You Need to Know about Asian American History*, written with journalist and talk show host Himilice Novas. This book, written in question and answer format, relates to the reader information about Asian American religious traditions, holidays, food, and other cultural customs. It also has biographical information on important Asian Americans as well as on racial discrimination faced by those with this ethnic background.

Monkey Bridge, Cao's first novel, is a semiautobiographical story about a teenage girl, Mai, who immigrates to the United States in 1975. Americans are trying to forget the country and war that Mai has left, and this reality is woven throughout the book. From her mother and other older Vietnamese immigrants, who are trying to keep their lives as close as possible to the way it was in their homeland, to the Vietnam Veterans who visit "Little Saigon" for the chance to have someone to talk to about their experiences in the country, this war has been etched in these people's minds and lives forever and is an integral part of who they are. Cao conveys the history of the Vietnam War through the perspective of the Vietnamese using flashbacks from Mai and letters that her mother writes and the stories that she tells her daughter.

The search for Mai's **identity** as a Vietnamese American is at the heart of this novel. Mai is trying her best to assimilate into her new country and culture, but four years after arriving in the United States, she still feels like a visitor. She does well in school and has her sights set on leaving Falls Church, Virginia, and going to college at Mount Holyoke in Massachusetts. But she has become the adult in her mother-daughter relationship since they immigrated to the United States, and she feels guilt about going away. She is her mother's translator and keeper. Her only hope is that either Mrs. Bay, a woman from their village in Vietnam, or Baba Quan, her grandfather, will look after her mother. The problem is that her grandfather was left in Vietnam when her mother escaped and hasn't been heard from since.

Although her mother's suicide and the discovery that Baba Quan was a member of the Vietcong are sensational, their impact on the narrator is important. Mai had spent years wondering and making up stories as to why her grandfather had not been able to meet her mother and escape Vietnam. She had romanticized his role of helping her Uncle Michael and the American soldiers out of danger. Then, at the end of the book, in her mother's suicide letter Mai learns the truth about her family. Mai discovers that her mother was the illegitimate daughter of her mother, Tuyet, and the landowner whom they called Uncle Khan. This fact had eaten away at Baba Quan his entire life, turning him into an alcoholic who sought revenge, and eventually this drove him to join the Vietcong. This history is what Thanh, Mai's mother, calls karma, and this karma is what drives her to commit suicide. In her letter she writes, "I fear our family history of sin, revenge, and murder and the imprint it creates on our children's lives as it rips through one generation and tears apart the next." Her suicide, she believes, will have a cleansing and redemptive effect on the family. (*See also* Vietnamese American Literature)

Further Reading

Coburn, Judith. "Starting Over." *Los Angeles Times Book Review* (September 14, 1997): 10.

Kakutani, Michiko. "The American Dream with a Vietnamese Twist." *New York Times* (August 19, 1997): C13

Schinto, Jeanne. "Monkey Bridge." *Women's Review of Books* (July 14, 1997): 26.

Katherine M. Miller-Corcoran

CAPONEGRO, MARY (1956–)   Italian American fiction writer and essayist. Since her first publication in 1986—the chapbook *Tales from the Next Village*, which included material reprinted in *The Star Café*, 1990—Caponegro has established herself as one of the most interesting of those who break with convention in fiction. Her three collections of novellas and short stories have won the praise of others known for experiments with narrative, such as **Gilbert Sorrentino**, David Foster Wallace, and William Gass. Caponegro is also an occasional essayist and a professor, formerly at Syracuse University and now at Bard College.

Caponegro studied at Brown under John Hawkes, another writer celebrated for nontraditional fiction (for instance, the 1961 novel *The Lime Twig*), and she dedicated *Five Doubts* to Hawkes's memory, declaring that he "never ceased turning doubt into art." Each of Caponegro's stories can be understood as an exercise along those lines, plunging forthrightly into situations and formats that seem unlikely to yield drama. For example, "The Daughter's Lamentation," the lengthy opening story of *The Complexities of Intimacy* (2001), offers little more, at first glance, than a description of a family vacation home and an assessment of how the place may reflect the personality of the narrator's aging father (as well as family dynamics generally). In general, the "action" in a Caponegro story might better be thought of as an assiduous, extended probing into feelings and ideas, within some more or less anxious configuration that is being carefully and slowly established itself. The result always rises to stylistic flourishes and painstaking emotional accuracy, sometimes on an individual level and sometimes within the context of family. But on the other hand, Caponegro's fictions remain frustratingly indifferent to their societal and historical context; "The Daughter's Lamentation" says next to nothing about how the house represents economic status or local history.

Caponegro's meditations tend to run long; each collection has work of novella length, including four of the five stories in *Complexities*. Each piece generally establishes a tone and diction particular to its concerns, with idiosyncratic repetitions and a range of rhetoric defined by the chosen point of view. This stylistic diversity is most prominent in *Five Doubts*, which experiments with such formats as the interview and the instructions for a board game. Yet even given these linguistic differences from story to story, overall Caponegro must be defined as an unusually elegant contemporary writer, rather Jamesian in the sinuosity, subtlety, and sheer length of her sentences. She relies on slang or obscenity far less than most American storytellers, and her work even does without dialogue to a remarkable extent.

Thus, a major risk for this author is that the psychological insight and the aesthetic niceties won't justify the work's protracted and static qualities:

The scrupulous tidiness with which the personal and intellectual discoveries unfold may rob them of emotional impact. Caponegro, a thoroughly self-aware artist, understands this risk and often ends her fictions with some sudden mysterious reversal, or at least a bizarre final development, that in the best cases clarifies the lingering tensions in a fresh way.

Overall, her sensibility may be characterized as coming, over time, into a greater engagement with the realities of her own background. *The Star Café* has no character much like Mary Caponegro (its finest accomplishment is the novella "Sebastian," about British aesthetes), but *Complexities*, with its concern for parents, siblings, and domestic spaces, reads like the book closest to her own experience. Between those two, *Five Doubts* stands as the author's exploration of her ethnic heritage and as her greatest imaginative leap. Each of the stories in *Five Doubts* is inspired by some aspect of Italian culture; the most effective is "Il Libro Dell'Arte," a fantasia of Renaissance painting workshops.

Five Doubts, as Caponegro herself has acknowledged, was inspired in part by her 1994 stay in Rome, on a Prize Fellowship from the American Academy and Institute of Arts and Letters. Her work also won the General Electric Foundation Award for Younger Writers in 1988, and she publishes steadily in literary quarterlies like *Conjunctions*. In 2001 her work was the subject of a special section in the *Review of Contemporary Fiction.*

Further Reading

Goldsmith, Francisca. Review of *Five Doubts*, by Mary Caponegro. *Library Journal* (January 1999): 147.

McLaughlin, Robert L. "Mary Caponegro." *Review of Contemporary Fiction* 21.3 (2001): 111–49.

———. "Time's Arrow." Review of *The Complexities of Intimacy*, by Mary Caponegro. *American Book Review* (March–April 2002): 3.

Sheffield, Elizabeth. Review of *The Complexities of Intimacy*, by Mary Caponegro. *Review of Contemporary Fiction* 21.3 (2001): 196.

Zaleski, Jeff. Review of *The Complexities of Intimacy*, by Mary Caponegro. *Publishers Weekly* (October 1, 2001): 36.

John Domini

CAPOTORTO, ROSETTE (1952–)   Italian American poet, fiction writer, essayist, teacher, and activist. A third-generation Italian American, Capotorto is a key figure of the feminist movement in Italian American literature and the arts. This movement has, on one hand, developed on the margins, rarely receiving the mainstream recognition bestowed upon authors whose works have been published by major publishers; on the other hand, the Italian American avant-garde of which Capotorto is part has helped to propel Italian American literature in the spotlight.

Capotorto's maternal grandparents came from Cerami, a small village near Catania, Sicily, in the late 1800s; her paternal grandparents came from Gioia Delle Colle in the province of Bari, Puglia. Capotorto writes with a distinct awareness of the politics of **ethnicity**, **race**, class, and gender. Born in the Bronx, Capotorto, who has made her home in New Jersey, has become the bard of the Italian American Bronx, as evident in *Bronx Italian* (2002), a chapbook that combines intimate self-exploration and portraits of life in the borough that vibrates in her accent and her writing. Capotorto proclaims herself as inescapably Italian American with a bravado that mocks Italian American machismo. Through her work as a writer, cultural worker, activist, and teacher (she teaches poetry in schools, K–12), Capotorto seeks to establish ties across ethnic and racial divides. Her work as a poet is inseparable from her political commitment to peace and justice.

A student at Hunter College in the 1980s, Capotorto had mentors such as Audre Lorde (to whom she dedicated *Bronx Italian*), Blanche Wiesen-Cook, and **Louise DeSalvo**. She recognizes these mentors and other feminist writers and scholars—such as **Alice Walker**, **Sandra Cisneros**, and **Ana Castillo**—as vital influences on her work. For twenty years, she chose to read—and feed her work with—women writers only, until, she claims, she could counterbalance the influence of all the male authors she had read early in her life and begin reading male writers again. Such a choice signals Capotorto's keen understanding of the relationship between creativity, gender, influence, and recognition as well as how they intersect in authorial emergence and canon-formation.

Capotorto's work has appeared in many journals and anthologies, such as VIA, *Curaggia: Writing by Women of Italian Descent* (1998), *The Milk of Almonds: Italian American Women Writers on Food and Culture* (2002), and *Are Italians White? How Race Is Made in America* (2003). Yet, the heart of Capotorto's work is in the oral realm and comes to life in her many performances and workshops, in which she weaves a multiplicity of personas, voices, and stories. Capotorto's work is both dramatic monologue and memoir, a lyrical but raging indictment of the ways in which systems of power oppress a large silent majority—the people on behalf of whom her poetry speaks. (*See also* Italian American Poetry)

Further Reading

Giunta, Edvige. *Writing with an Accent: Contemporary Italian American Women Authors.* New York: Palgrave, 2002.

Edvige Giunta

CAPPELLO, MARY (1960–)   Italian American lesbian writer, feminist scholar, and professor. Cappello's varied body of work—literary and social essays, collaborative cultural studies, poetry, and a memoir, *Night Bloom* (1998)—is a rich, multicolored tapestry. As she reflects on her family's history, Cappello weaves the emotions, experiences, and revelations into the fabric that is her place in American society. Whether discussing the harsh rigidity of poverty, parochial school, or domestic abuse, Cappello's prose gives way to a beautifully complex sense of promise.

Night Bloom begins with the images of a garden and the rainbow. Indigo, her favorite color at the age of four, is symbolic of the **blues** that define her life: beauty and pain, eternal hope, and emotional distress. She was raised in a working class neighborhood in Philadelphia, where her father tended his fabulous garden while her mother tended the family. Fearful of her father's uncontrollable anger, which erupted in routine beatings of her two older brothers, Cappello distanced herself from him, so knew and loved only the more placid gardener father. Her mother spent many years as an agoraphobic, but found solace in books and is a poet herself. Her grandfather struggled to learn English and suffered from the oppression and disappointment of poverty for most of his life.

Cappello's view of early immigrant life is bleak. Reading her grandfather's words, Cappello discovered that writing the immigrant's history is an arduous, if not impossible, task. Even the style of his writing—squeezed into blank spots on any scrap of paper he could find—reflects the poverty in which he lived. Devising ways to transcend pain, her grandfather left both his history and his legacy on his scraps of paper. His love is evident in the warmth of his words as he sought a cure for his family's ills through writing.

Ethnic, class, and gender biases defined Cappello's youth. Yet she would not be silenced by that oppression. Instead, she continued to cultivate her intelligence in order to overcome her grandfather's personal disgrace and to defy the stereotypes of the Italian American female. She also inherited an ever-present hope for solace. Her grandfather found it by snatching writing moments from his work repairing shoes; her father found it tending his garden; her mother finds it wherever she can, advocating social equality and writing poetry; Cappello finds it by unraveling her history in order to understand it and herself.

Night Bloom's nonlinear narrative meanders through Cappello's memories, hopping from one moment of warmth to another, moments that help Cappello to survive and outwit the oppressive situations that threaten to overwhelm her. Her grandfather's and mother's legacies are resilience and resourcefulness. All three of them, unusual and vigorous, like the Night Blooming Cereus for which the memoir is named, have blossomed amid conditions that might have prevented people less tenacious. The rituals of reading, writing, and remembering are the salvation in which Cappello finds hope, solace, recovery, and discovery. (*See also* Italian American Autobiography, Italian American Stereotypes)

Further Reading

Gillan, Jennifer. Review of *Night Bloom: A Memoir. MELUS* (Summer 2001): 260–63.
Giunta, Edvige. "Italian American Women and the Memoir." *Italian Americana* 18.1 (2000): 61–64.

Suzanne Hotte Massa

CARIBBEAN (ANGLOPHONE) AMERICAN AUTOBIOGRAPHY
Much Caribbean American literature takes the form of loosely autobiographical coming-of-age novels, from **Paule Marshall**'s *Brown Girl, Brownstones* (1959) to **Jamaica Kincaid**'s *Lucy* (1990). **Audre Lorde** speaks to the blur-

ring of lines between autobiography and fiction in Caribbean American literature in the subtitle, "autobiomythography," of her novel *Zami: A New Spelling of My Name* (1982). The story of the author's life, Lorde conveys, combines the tales inherited from her ancestors, the events that she experienced first-hand, and the fictional lives that she has imagined for herself. This blended form of autobiography points to how any autobiography must rely in some way on imagination well as on fact, but also indicates some of the unique features of Caribbean American autobiography. While the autobiography traditionally tells the story of a single and singular self, the one "I" who writes her or his own story, Caribbean and Caribbean American literature remains committed to understanding the individual as always part of a community (a family, a village, a nation, etc.). Thus, autobiographies that blend the protagonist with various other real or imagined people offer an autobiographer whose story is always also that of a community. Nonetheless, the form of the conventional autobiography where a single first person narrator is clearly identified with the author and faithfully represents the author's biography also serves a number of Caribbean American authors.

Because the Caribbean American community is relatively recent and still in the process of establishing itself, many Caribbean American autobiographies tell the story of coming to America or else remain deeply marked by the parents' arrival. They belong to a tradition of American immigrant literature and to a tradition of African American literature. Like African Americans, Afro Caribbeans suffered the **Middle Passage** and **slavery**, but in the Caribbean, during and after slavery, blacks represented the majority of the population. At the same time, after slavery, Afro Caribbeans remained the colonial subjects of the British crown often until they immigrated to the United States. Some Caribbean Americans such as **Claude McKay** and Audre Lorde became major players in African American politics and letters, although others such as **Michelle Cliff** and Jamaica Kincaid continue to understand themselves more as Afro Caribbeans in America than as African Americans.

Born in Jamaica, McKay immigrated to the United States in 1912 and soon became a major figure in the **Harlem Renaissance** with novels such as *Home to Harlem* (1928) and *Banana Bottom* (1933). Like many writers of the Harlem Renaissance, McKay not only lived in Harlem but also traveled extensively. McKay wrote two autobiographies: *A Long Way From Home* (1937) and *My Green Hills of Jamaica* (1979). *A Long Way From Home* follows McKay's twelve years of wandering the globe and his return to Harlem. In his second autobiography, however, written toward the end of his life, McKay returns to his childhood in Jamaica and to an idealized Caribbean past.

To the second generation, the Caribbean is still an ideal but it is only a distant, almost mythic memory. Marshall's *Brown Girl, Brownstones* portrays a girl growing up in the Barbadian immigrant community in Brooklyn between the two world wars. Selina must negotiate the close-knit Barbadian community that is nonetheless deeply committed to the American dream, her father's nostalgia for Barbados, and her own entry into the multicultural world of New York. In *Zami, A New Spelling of My Name*, Audre Lorde similarly describes her childhood as the daughter of immigrants, in her case from Grenada, although the family does not maintain deep ties to any Grenadian community in New York. Lorde/Zami depicts her young adulthood in the 1950s and her coming to terms with her lesbianism in the context of the lesbian and feminist movements, of the African American community, and of her Grenadian heritage.

While second and especially third generation Caribbean Americans increasingly identify with African American communities, newer waves of Caribbean immigrants continue to arrive in the United States. Still living between Caribbean and American identities, Michelle Cliff, **Jamaica Kincaid**, and Patricia Powell continue the Caribbean American autobiographical tradition with novels that blend their own stories with those of their families. Cliff, like Lorde, explores what it is to be a Caribbean American lesbian. In *Abeng* (1984) and *No Telephone to Heaven* (1987), Cliff narrates her forced departure from Jamaica as a child and her struggles to understand her racial, cultural, and sexual difference in the United States and in Jamaica. All of Kincaid's many works retell the stories of her childhood and of her family's past. *Annie John* (1985) and *Lucy* (1990) depict a young girl who grows up in Antigua, comes to the United States to work as a nanny, and discovers herself as an artist. The title of Kincaid's subsequent book, *The Autobiography of My Mother* (1996), foregrounds the complicated identification of the author with the main character of the story. *The Autobiography of My Mother* speaks to the importance of the mother to the identity of the daughter in Caribbean traditions, but it also sets up the autobiography as the story of the person in contrast to whom the author defines herself. Patricia Powell's autobiographical novel *Me Dying Trial* (1993) similarly tells the story of a mother with whom the daughter does not identify.

Mothers also feature prominently in the semiautobiographical short stories and novels of **Edwidge Danticat**, *Krik? Krak!* (1996) And *Breath, Eyes, Memory* (1998). Danticat is from the Francophone Caribbean (Haiti), but writes in English. Her work marks the way in which it becomes increasingly difficult in the American context to separate between Anglophone, Francophone, and Hispanophone Caribbean authors. Indeed, not only Danticat, but also writers of Cuban, Puerto Rican, and Dominican heritage, increasingly write autobiographical novels in English that share many of the characteristics of Caribbean American autobiographies.

Further Reading

Condé, Mary, and Thuronn Lonsdale. *Caribbean Women Writers*. New York: St. Martin's Press, 1999.

LeSeur, Geta. *Ten Is the Age of Darkness*. Columbia: U of Missouri P, 1995.

Paquet, Sandra Pouchet. *Caribbean Autobiography*. Madison: U of Wisconsin P, 2002.

Keja Lys Valens

CARIBBEAN (ANGLOPHONE) AMERICAN NOVEL   Because most Anglophone Caribbeans belong to the African **diaspora**, Caribbean American novels stand at the crossroads of Caribbean novels and African American novels. Authors born in the Caribbean and residing in the United States may be categorized as both Caribbean and Caribbean American, while authors of Caribbean heritage born in the United States may be claimed as both Caribbean American and African American. Close attention to the novels themselves only supports the blurry lines between the different categories, as Caribbean American novels draw on and participate in Caribbean and African American literary traditions. And because both Caribbean and African American literary traditions are themselves composite of African, Euro-American, and many other traditions, it is difficult even to establish hybridity as a mark particular to the Caribbean American novel. A survey of Caribbean American novelists and their works reveals, however, a trend from integration into the **Harlem Renaissance**, the **Black Arts Movement**, and the **Civil Rights Movement** to, in the last quarter of the twentieth century and into the new millennium, greater assertion of ties to the Caribbean and of difference from the African American community.

Jamaican-born **Claude McKay** (1889–1948) wrote the first novel of the Harlem Renaissance to become a best seller. *Home to Harlem* (1928), based in part on McKay's own experience, exemplifies the Harlem Renaissance as it recounts the story of a working-class black man in Harlem in the 1920s. *Banjo* (1929), McKay's second novel, tells of another important aspect of the Harlem Renaissance: the black American community in France. It is only with *Banana Bottom* (1933) that McKay writes explicitly of the Caribbean. The Caribbean often becomes for both first and second-generation Caribbean Americans a place that exists primarily in memory, linked to childhood or to family pasts in ways that are easy to idealize, and *Banana Bottom* offers a typically utopic portrayal of Jamaican village life.

A Caribbean American novelist was also at the center of the Black Arts Movement, to which the Harlem Renaissance gave way. **Rosa Guy** (1928–) was born in Trinidad and moved to Harlem before she was ten years old. Guy cofounded the Harlem Writer's Guild. Her first novel, *Bird at My Window* (1966), charts the struggle of a young black man to hold onto his sanity in the face of a tortuous relationship with his mother and of an increasingly impoverished and polarized Harlem where the Civil Rights Movement is still only a dream. In the 1970s, Guy traveled to Haiti and Trinidad, and when she returned to the United States, began to write novels for young adults, including *The Friends* (1973) and *Ruby* (1976), with West Indian themes. Guy has since published numerous young adult novels, most recently *My Love, My Love, the Peasant Girl* (2002), which follows in the tradition of rewriting Euro-American classics as it resets Hans Christian Andersen's "The Little Mermaid" in the Caribbean, with the major difference between the young lovers being not sea- or land-life, but skin color.

Audre Lorde (1934–92) was born in New York to West Indian immigrant parents, but although Barbadian traditions permeated Lorde's home, like Guy, she grew up in Manhattan surrounded by African American rather than West Indian families. Lorde's novel, *Zami, a New Spelling of My Name* (1982), reflects a deep connection with the African American community and a distant longing for a Caribbean family past. Allusions to the Caribbean frame *Zami*, and the Caribbean stands in the novel as the ideal source of and home for her black lesbian identity, but the great majority of the novel focuses on Audre's coming of age as a black lesbian in the African American and lesbian scenes in New York in the 1950s and 1960s.

With *Brown Girl, Brownstone* (1959), **Paule Marshall** (1929–) became the first Caribbean American writer to focus her work on the growing Caribbean American community that remained largely separate from the African American community. The largely autobiographical coming of age novel follows a young girl growing up in Brooklyn's Barbadian neighborhood. The protagonist finds herself caught between her father's nostalgia for the islands, her mother's intense desire to achieve the American dream of so many immigrants, and her own growing awareness of the African American community. Marshall's subsequent novels, including *The Timeless Place, The Chosen People* (1969), *Praisesong for a Widow* (1983), and *Daughters* (1991) continue to treat the intersection of Caribbean and African American communities and themes. *The Timeless Place* is set on a composite Caribbean island, but in *The Timeless Place* the Caribbean is so rife with the contradictions of its rich and troubled history and its neo-colonial relationship with the United States and Britain that it cannot become a utopia. *The Timeless Place* draws heavily on themes and techniques common to Caribbean literature, highlighting the role of the maroons and finding ways to represent time outside of a linear flow. *Praisesong for a Widow* leans more toward the African American genre of a roots novel, featuring a woman who travels to the Caribbean in search of some sort of connection to her African heritage. But by locating the endpoint of the journey in the Caribbean rather than in Africa, *Praisesong* emphasizes the importance of the Caribbean as a middle point of connection between Africa and African America.

The novels of Elizabeth Nunez also center on Caribbean American characters. Born in Trinidad, Nunez moved to the United States as a teenager. She draws on her own experience to write novels about Caribbean immigrants in the United States. As she writes of love affairs between Caribbean immigrants, African Americans, and Africans, Nunez brings out the differences and also the similarities of their experiences and of their attitudes. *Grace* (2003) and *Beyond the Limbo Silence* (1998) both explore relationships between Caribbean immigrants and African Americans, and *Discretion* (2000) depicts cross-cultural liaisons in New York by focusing on the rekindled love of a married African diplomat for a Trinidadian-born artist.

Although they align themselves less with African American or even Caribbean American communities, many of the most important Caribbean authors of the twentieth century have spent significant parts of their lives living in the United States. Trinidadian Earl Lovelace (1935–), for example, spent more than twenty years of his life studying and teaching in the United States, but all three novels that he wrote during that period, *The Schoolmaster* (1968), *The Dragon Can't Dance* (1979), and *The Wine of Astonishment* (1982), are set squarely in the Caribbean and deal with the classical Caribbean themes of village life and carnival. Lovelace's long residence in the United States, and that of others, such as Belizean novelist Zee Edgell, represent less a desire to become American or to write Caribbean American novels than they do the political and economic realities that force so many people from the Caribbean to leave their island homes.

Other Caribbean authors who have spent the majority of their lives in the United States and see little chance of returning permanently to the Caribbean still maintain primary identification as Caribbean authors but, like Marshall, write novels where the Caribbean becomes a place that has been left behind both in space and in time. The two semiautobiographical novels of Jamaican-born **Michelle Cliff** (1946–), *Abeng* (1985) and *No Telephone to Heaven* (1987), follow the story of a young girl who is forced to move to the United States as a child and who longs to return to Jamaica. In her novels *Annie John* (1986), *The Autobiography of My Mother* (1996), and *Mr. Potter* (2002), **Jamaica Kincaid** (1949–), who left her native Antigua as a teenager, revisits her life and that of her parents in the Caribbean, but in *Lucy* (1990) and *My Brother* (1997), she also describes how life in the United States deeply marks her and her characters' perspectives on family and on the Caribbean. *Me Dying Trial* (1993), the first novel of Jamaican-born Patricia Powell (1966–), details the process of a woman's leaving Jamaica and settling in the United States. After a second novel, *A Small Gathering of Bones* (1994), set in the contemporary Caribbean, with *The Pagoda* (1999), Powell writes a Caribbean historical fiction.

The Caribbean settings and the Caribbean vernaculars of many Caribbean American novels of the late twentieth century and early twenty-first century assert their ties to the Caribbean. But these novels also employ American settings. They continue to parallel African American novels in their connection to the African diaspora even as they also join with the novels of other recent immigrant populations to detail the negotiation of divergent cultural traditions and values. Historical periods and generational differences mark various trends in Caribbean American novels. It remains to be seen if many second and most third-generation Caribbean American novels will continue to merge into the African American **canon**, or whether changing times will lead to the development of more numbered generations of Caribbean American novelists.

Further Reading

Booker, M. Keith and Dubravka Juraga. *The Caribbean Novel in English*. Portsmouth, NH: Heinemann, 2001.

Nelson, Emmanuel S. "Black America and the Anglophone Afro-Caribbean Literary Consciousness." *Journal of American Culture* 12.4 (1989): 53–58.

Paquet, Sandra Pouchet. "Caribbean Fiction." *The Columbia History of the American Novel*. Ed. Cathy Davidson et al. New York: Columbia UP, 1991.

Keja Lys Valens

CARIBBEAN (ANGLOPHONE) AMERICAN POETRY   The United States has served as both a home for immigrant writers from the Caribbean and as a site of literary production for writers who maintain their Caribbean **identity** and focus even as they live outside the region's geographical boundaries. As the Jamaican novelist and poet **Michelle Cliff** has noted, the Caribbean exists all over the world; Caribbean literature is notable for the number of major authors who have made their homes outside the Caribbean itself. Like other genres of Caribbean American literature, then, Caribbean American poetry can be divided into two major categories: the poetry of Caribbean writers living in the United States and the poetry of American writers of Caribbean descent. This distinction may seem slight, but it remains of critical importance.

Whereas London, during the 1950s and 1960s, was the locus of literary activity for Caribbean writers outside the Caribbean, the United States has in recent decades offered Caribbean writers a host of opportunities, notably academic appointments. Meanwhile, the Hart-Cellar **Immigration** Act (1965) made it easier to enter the United States from the Caribbean. The period since 1965 has consequently seen the biggest influx of Caribbean immigrants to the United States.

Of the Caribbean writers in "exile" in the United States, Derek Walcott (1930–) is certainly the most prominent. The St. Lucian poet, playwright, and essayist, winner of the Nobel Prize in 1990, has taught at several American universities, including Boston University and Harvard University. Walcott's *The Arkansas Testament* (1987) derives largely from the poet's experience of living in the United States. The epic poem *Omeros* (1990) is set primarily in St. Lucia, but includes long passages set in North America; the poem is also notable for its critique of American tourism and industry in the Caribbean. Both works address the correspondences between the experience of slavery in the United States and in the Caribbean. Walcott is also fond of noting the ironic relation between American democracy and **slavery**. (Dionne Brand, a Trinidadian Canadian poet, has similarly critiqued the American military interventions in the Caribbean.)

There are other notable examples of contemporary Caribbean writers at home in the United States. The distinguished Barbadian poet (Edward) Kamau Brathwaite (1930–), for example, teaches at New York University; he has previously taught at Boston University, Yale, and other American universities. Michelle Cliff (1946–) was born in Jamaica, but has lived variously in the United States and London as well as in her country of birth. Her writing depicts the experience of growing up in a colonized country, and frequently addresses themes of racial and sexual inequality. Although much of her life has been spent outside Jamaica, her writing, as in *Land of Look Behind: Prose and Poetry* (1985) assumes a Jamaican perspective.

If we expand the definition of poetry to include popular forms, Caribbean poetry has no doubt had its most widespread impact in the United States through the reggae songs of Bob Marley, whose music and Rastafarian beliefs have been absorbed into American popular culture.

It is essential to remember, however, that although these works engage with American culture, they form part of the American literary tradition only tangentially. The borders between national and regional literatures are certainly not fixed, and indeed Caribbean poets draw on American traditions. Yet the cosmopolitan Brathwaite and Walcott are resolutely Caribbean writers despite their time spent in the United States.

In contrast, **Claude McKay** (1890–1948) came from the Caribbean and became absorbed into the American and African American canons. McKay left Jamaica for the United States in 1912 to further his young poetic career. He became a leading figure in the **Harlem Renaissance** and a founding member of the Black Writers Guild. Prior to his emigration, he published two collections of folk poetry, *Songs of Jamaica* (1911) and *Constab Ballads* (1912). Both works are written primarily in dialect; the former depicts peasant life in Jamaica and the latter draws on McKay's own experience as a policeman. Although he was also known as a prose writer in the United States, he continued to publish poetry, including *Harlem Shadows* (1922). His *Selected Poems* appeared posthumously in 1953. Jamaican poet Louise Bennett, who works in the folk tradition that McKay belongs to, has lived in New York (1953–55); she now resides in Toronto.

Caribbean American poetry also includes second-generation writers. **Audre Lorde** (1934–92), for example, was born in New York to parents from Grenada. Although she was a native-born American, hers was a Caribbean immigrant household. Lorde published her first collection, *The First Cities*, in 1968. Her interests in the African diaspora and African mythology are particularly apparent in *The Black Unicorn* (1978).

The poets mentioned thus far all have their origins in the Anglophone Caribbean. But the category of Caribbean American poetry must also include writers from the Spanish Caribbean. New York became an important center in the 1960s for Puerto Rican poets who identified themselves as **Nuyorican**s or Neo-Ricans, that is, first-generation or second-generation Puerto Ricans born or raised in the United States. The Nuyorican Poets' Café, located on Manhattan's Lower East Side (or *Loisaida*), served as a home for writers in this community and produced an anthology, *Nuyorican Poetry* (1975), edited by Miguel Algarín and **Miguel Piñero**. Moreover, poets such as **Judith Ortiz Cofer** and **Aurora Levins Morales** show that poets of Puerto Rican descent living in the continental United State are not based exclusively in New York.

New York has also provided a home to Cuban American poets writing in Spanish, English, or both. The Spanish-language anthology *Poetas Cubanos in Nueva York* (1986) included, for instance, Reinaldo Arenas, who is also known for his poetry in English. Miami, too, has been an important center for **Cuban American poetry**.

Further Reading

Baker, Houston A. *Reading Black: Essays in the Criticism of African, Caribbean, and Black American Literature*. Ithaca, NY: Africana Studies and Research Center, Cornell University, 1976.

Balderston, Daniel, and Mike Gonzalez, eds. *The Encyclopedia of Latin American and Caribbean Literature, 1900–2003*. London: Routledge, 2004.

Burnett, Paula, ed. *The Penguin Book of Caribbean Verse in English*. London: Penguin, 1986.

Nicholas Bradley

CARPATHO-RUSYN LITERATURE   Approximately 1.3 million Carpatho-Rusyn Americans trace their ancestry to the Carpathian Mountain region of Eastern Europe. Most of their ancestors emigrated between 1880 and 1914 from lands that now form part of Slovakia, Poland, and Ukraine. A stateless people for their entire history, Carpatho-Rusyns have also been known as Rusnaks, Carpatho-Russians, Carpatho-Ukrainians, and Ruthenians, and those from the northern slopes of the Carpathians are called Lemkos. Most Carpatho-Rusyns are adherents to eastern Christianity, either Orthodoxy or Byzantine Catholicism, and the church was traditionally the center of Carpatho-Rusyn social and cultural life, along with fraternal societies and brotherhoods, such as the Greek Catholic Union of Rusyn Brotherhoods (Wilkes Barre, Pennsylvania) and the United Societies of the Greek Catholic Religion (McKeesport, Pennsylvania). Today, Rusyn cultural development is supported by secular organizations such as the Carpatho-Rusyn Research Center (Ocala, Florida), the Carpatho-Rusyn Society (Pittsburgh, Pennsylvania), and the Rusin Association (Minneapolis).

Initially, literary works by Rusyns appeared in nearly sixty newspapers and other periodicals published for the Rusyn American community, the most widespread being the *Amerikansky Russky Viestnik* (*American Russian Messenger*, 1892–1952), *Prosvita* (*Enlightenment*, 1917–2000), *Vostok* (*The East*, 1919–50), *Lemko* (1928–39), *Den'* (*The Day*, 1922–26), and the short-lived literary monthly *Niva* (*The Field*, 1916). Rusyn American literature was also published in the annual almanacs put out by the various fraternal organizations, which, in addition to poetry and prose by Rusyn writers, generally included a monthly calendar, popular articles on Rusyn history and culture, and biographies of famous Rusyns. The tradition of the almanac or *kalendar* has recently been revived in the United States with the Carpatho-Rusyn Society's publication of the *Rusyn-American Almanac 2005*. However, the original almanacs and newspapers are now difficult to obtain and for some titles, complete sets are no longer available. There have been few studies of Rusyn American literature and there is no bibliography of Rusyn American publications.

Literary life in the Rusyn homeland had traditionally been preoccupied with questions of language and national **identity**. Situated at a crossroads of culture in Eastern Europe, and subject to competing political pressures, the Rusyns immigrated to America without a cohesive national consciousness and lacking a standardized language. At the time of the largest migration to America before World War I, Carpatho-Rusyns communicated in several dialects that have been classified by modern linguists as part of the Ukrainian language, although as a result of Slovak, Polish, and Hungarian admixtures, Carpatho-Rusyn speech differed markedly from standard Ukrainian. Each writer's choice of written language reflected his own understanding of Rusyn national identity. While some argued that Rusyns were a branch of a larger all-Russian people, others claimed that they belonged to the Ukrainian nationality, and still others insisted that Rusyns were a distinct ethnic group, related to but distinct from both Russians and Ukrainians. Thus, some early Rusyn American literature was written in Russian and Ukrainian. However, most writers supported the distinction of Rusyn culture and used an unstandardized language that followed the patterns of Russian grammar, but included numerous lexical and syntactical borrowings from Carpatho-Rusyn vernacular, as well as from English. Initially, Rusyn writers used Cyrillic, but by the 1930s, most had adopted the Latin alphabet, using a system of transliteration that was based on Slovak orthography. At first, Rusyn American literature was directed solely at the Rusyn community. However, since the 1950s, almost all publications for the Carpatho-Rusyn community have used English, and writers have oriented their works to a broader audience. Third-generation Rusyn American writers have situated their works ideologically in the context of the contemporary Rusyn movement, which defends the identity of Rusyns as a distinct ethnic group. Since the fall of communism, Rusyn culture has experienced a renaissance in the European homeland, which has been nurtured by a reciprocal interest among Rusyns in the United States in their ethnic background.

Most Rusyn American writers of the first generation insisted on their amateur status in literature, contending that it was only love for their people that led them to literature. Many writers were first and foremost Greek Catholic priests, such as Stefan Varzaly (1890–1957) and Basil Shereghy (1918–88), who published occasional poems and plays in almanacs or newspapers. Others were journalists, such as Peter Maczkov (1880–1965), author of a collection of religious poetry (*Vinec nabožnych stichov*, 1958), or Stefan Telep (1882–1965) and Nicholas Cislak (1910–88), who wrote plays for amateur theater groups. The Greek Catholic priest Emilij Kubek (1857–1940) was a prolific writer and is remembered today as the author of *Marko Sholtys*, the only Rusyn-language novel published in the United States. Dymytrii Vyslotskii (1888–1968), known by his pseudonym Van'o Hunjanka, was active in journalism in the Lemko communities of Canada and the United States from 1922 until 1945, and his short stories and plays appeared in the annual almanac he published during the 1930s (*Karpatorusskii kalendar' Vania Hunjanka*, 1930–38).

While most of their stories are set in the new world, Rusyn American authors reveal a certain detachment from the realities of American life, which results from their didactic intent and their concentration on moral and mythic principles. In distinction from most ethnic American literature, little attention is paid to the motivation for leaving the old country, the ocean voyage, or the difficulties of adjustment in the new world. Many Rusyn characters achieve success not by navigating the American educational, social, and political order, but through an intensification of traditional values. For example, in Kubek's story "Palko Rostoka," set in industrial America, which was the reality of Rusyn immigrants, the eponymous hero hides his Rusyn identity and a mysterious past that includes unjust imprisonment. He achieves material success and universal admiration not by leading a strike against the factory's owner, but by urging mediation and compromise. When his secrets are revealed, Palko pays homage to his Rusyn past, but becomes a new man in America, as symbolized by the removal of his beard. The values Kubek expresses in this story are repeated by every Rusyn American author—the keys to success are hard work, modesty, temperance, and economy, and the virtuous man who achieves success is not materialistic, but kind, and most important of all, unpretentious. However, it is clear that Kubek's praise of Rusyn **ethnicity** does not constitute a general endorsement of American diversity, as the author and his heroes cling to old-world prejudices, an aversion to speculation in business, distrust in the efficacy of legal remedies, and suspicion of political action. The heroes of Rusyn American literature are suffering innocents who, in melodramatic turns, prevail against the world's villains by dint of their moral character. Often lacking in realistic and culturally specific details, Rusyn American literature depends on the allegorical mode. The pictures of working-class virtue and the triumph of the good present a kind of wish fulfillment for readers and the prospect of a reorganized society in which they will be able to thrive on moral virtue alone.

The myth is varied only slightly in the work of Vyslotskii-Hunjanka and Cislak, where the Cinderella narrative takes on a political coloring. In these works, the morally virtuous are the pro-Soviet socialists who fight against the aristocracy and the church. In opposition to Kubek, Hunjanka is overtly anticlerical and his heroes espouse explicitly political solutions to their socioeconomic problems. His stories "Starŷ i molodŷ" ("The Old and the Young," 1925) and "Marko Bohach" (1932) and his plays *Sholtys* (1935) and *Petro Pavlyk* (1937) depict the struggles of Lemkos to survive in their homeland under conditions of poverty and political oppression. In "Leško Myrna" (1932) and "Agentŷ," ("Agents," 1928), Rusyn immigrants encounter the Great Depression in the United States, and the author voices support for labor unions. Hunjanka-Vyslotskii also persistently reminds his American readers to offer aid and support to their brothers in Europe.

The most popular literary genres among Rusyn American writers of the first generation were poetry and drama. Short plays provided a sizeable repertoire for the numerous dramatic circles that were centered in local parishes and fraternal organizations. Many are set in the American Rusyn community and deal with its problems—the struggle to become Americans, generational conflicts, and alcohol abuse. *Fedorišinovy* (*The Fedorišins*, 1925) by Valentin Gorzo (1869–1943) is a three-act drama that is based on a true story and that deals with all these issues. American holidays, such as a family Thanksgiving dinner, represent civility to the second-generation of the family but are alien to their religious, tradition-bound mother and their alcoholic father. Despite an appeal to the American legal system, the oldest son is forced to kill his father to defend the family and achieve an "American style" of life. Stefan F. Telep wrote satirical plays that feature a daughter's struggle against patriarchal authority (*Khytra dîvchyna*, *A Shrewd Girl*, 1927) and the witty efforts of Rusyn immigrants to deal with the American legal system (*V sudî, In Court*, 1944). The audience is expected to laugh at the antics of the simple Rusyns, but to heed the judge's admonitions; parents are told to educate their children so they will be an honor to their people, and children are encouraged to remember their roots. *Maria's Problem* (1941) by Judy Mirek, written in a mix of English and Rusyn vernacular, is a lesson addressed to young Rusyns to honor their linguistic and cultural heritage. While Maria's Rusyn-speaking mother tells her "there are no bad ethnicities, only bad people," it is only her Scottish American boyfriend who can influence her, with his reminder that America is "a melting pot of different nationalities." By 1960, plays such as the comedy *Van'o Peperytsia* by Nikolai Tsysliak satirized the immigrant community, which, in the eyes of a recent immigrant, persisted in the same faults and vices that were common in the old country.

While drama was primarily light and entertaining, poetry tended to be serious, religious, and ideological. Lyrical effusions about the beauty of the homeland and the Rusyn experience of suffering fill the work of Sigmund Brinsky (*Stichi, Verses*, 1922) and Ivan A. Ladižinsky (*Karpatorossy v Evropi i Ameriki, Carpatho-Rusyns in Europe and America*, 1940). Of more aesthetic value is the work of two talented poets who began their literary careers in Europe but also published in the United States—the Russian-oriented Dmitrii Vergun (*Karpatskie otzvuki, Carpathian Echoes*, 1920) and the Ukrainian-language poet and Basilian monk, Sevastiian Sabol, who used the pseudonym Zoreslav (*Z rannikh vesen, From Early Spring*, 1963).

Writers of the second-generation used the English language to memorialize the immigrant experience in longer forms. The first Rusyn American writer to seek an audience outside the Rusyn community was Vasil S. Koban, with his novel *The Sorrows of Marienka* (1979), written in the style of sociological realism. Thomas Bell, whose father was of Rusyn background, deals with the fate of Rusyn, Slovak, and other east European immigrants during the Depression in his well-known novel *Out of This Furnace* (1987).

Sonya Jason, the daughter of immigrants from Subcarpathian Rus', incorporates Rusyn-American themes in her memoir *Icon of Spring* (1987). In *Eternal Memory* (1999), Ann Walko interweaves memoirs of immigrant life with songs, recipes, and embedded narratives about the homeland in aesthetically compelling poetic prose. An adaptation of Walko's play *Zhenska shleboda* (*Women's Lib*), originally written in Rusyn, was performed in English at the Andy Warhol Museum in Pittsburgh in 2004. It offers a rare counterpoint to the stereotypical misogyny expressed in traditional male-dominated Rusyn American literature.

Third-generation Rusyn Americans have concentrated on literary and historical scholarship, rather than creative literature, but recently, novels of autobiographical fiction have appeared that reach beyond the Rusyn community. Nicholas S. Karas's novel *Hunky: The Immigrant Experience* (2004) blends history, biography, and fiction as he follows three generations of Rusyns from their home in the Carpathian Mountains to industrial America. *Less Than Diamonds* by Pete Bohaczyk (2002) tells a similar story centered on Rusyn mine workers. Unfortunately, these novels have little aesthetic value and reveal a great deal of confusion about Rusyn history and identity. Another novel in progress, *The Linden and the Oak*, by Mark Wansa, is well researched, historically accurate, and written in a poetic style that captures the spirit of Rusyn folk art.

Further Reading

Magocsi, Paul R. "The Carpatho-Rusyn Press." *The Ethnic Press in the United States: A Historical Analysis and Handbook*. Ed. Sally M. Miller. New York, Westport, CT, and London: Greenwood Press, 1987. 15–26.

———. *Our People: Carpatho-Rusyns and Their Descendents in North America*. Toronto: Multicultural History Society of Ontario, 1984.

———. "Rusyn-American Ethnic Literature." *Ethnic Literatures Since 1776: The Many Voices of America*. Vol. II. Ed. Wolodymyr T. Zyla and Wendall M. Aycock. Lubbock: Proceedings of the Comparative Literature Symposium, Texas Tech University, January 1976, IX (1978): 503–20.

Elaine Rusinko

CASTEDO, ELENA (1937–)   Spanish American novelist and literary critic. Castedo is best known for her fiction, which dramatizes the life of Spanish exiles in Latin America, thereby uncovering class power relationships and exploring conflicted cultural identities.

Elena Castedo was born in Barcelona, Spain, but she can be viewed within a number of different cultural contexts. The exile of Castedo's parents by the Franco dictatorship caused them to depart for Chile, and after this, Castedo lived in a number of locations before finally settling in the United States. The diversity of cultures and work environments that Castedo has encountered has provided her with a range of material to draw on in her fiction. She has worked as a social worker, editor, and salesperson, and she obtained a PhD at Harvard University.

It was the publication of her novel *Paradise* (1990) that brought Castedo's work to a wider public consciousness. *Paradise* was nominated for the 1990 National Book Award, and the Spanish translation has also been subsequently nominated for the Cervantes prize in Spain. The novel is strongly autobiographical in its desire to uncover the experiences of exiled Spanish children, a topic that Castedo feels has not received much attention. The story is narrated from the perspective of a ten-year-old girl named Solita, who has been exiled after the Spanish Civil War and brought up in an unnamed Latin American country. The use of the child's perspective provides a sense of directness to the narrative. Castedo captures the feeling of restlessness induced by the itinerant life of the refugee, whose sense of cultural **identity** is always in a state of flux. Satirical humor is created by the family's visit to a wealthy country estate, during which class-ridden pretensions are exposed.

Castedo has retained strong links with Spain, and she has made several trips to the northern region of Asturias. Having been a U.S. citizen for many years, Castedo has referred to the United States as the land of opportunities. However, she has also expressed disapproval at the emergence of a hybrid form of "Spanglish" (a mixture of English and Spanish) and the dominance of U.S. popular culture in Europe. Castedo is not averse to the interaction of different cultures, but she is a strong supporter of the maintenance of regional traditions and a sense of cultural identity. As well as being a novelist, Castedo has also published a number of critical articles and a study of Chilean theater, titled *El teatro chileno de mediados del siglo xx* (1982).

Elena Castedo now lives in McLean, Virginia, where she continues to write fiction.

Further Reading

Castedo, Elena. "Shifting Contradictions: Or, What Is a Hispanic Writer?" *ANQ: A Quarterly Journal of Short Articles, Notes, and Reviews* 10.2 (1997): 21–24.

Pillado-Miller, Margarita. "Paradise and the Longing for the Father." *Cincinnati Romance Review* 12 (1993): 120–29.

Helen Oakley

CASTILLO, ANA (1953–)   Chicana poet, novelist, and essayist. Considered one of the most prominent, versatile, and innovative Latina writers in the United States today, Ana Castillo creates work known for its feminist stance, sociopolitical commentary, passion, and intelligence. Although Castillo was first known for her poetry, she quickly expanded her creative output to include musical performance, fiction, and criticism.

Born in June of 1953 in Chicago to Mexican American parents who had moved from the Southwest, Castillo is engaged by creative expression through multiple formats. She credits her Mexican heritage with her storytelling abilities and recalls writing her first poem at the age of nine on the occasion of the death of her grandmother. Castillo is also a painter and majored in art education at Northeastern Illinois University, receiving her BA in 1975.

Castillo also found an early interest in social concerns; in her public high school Castillo became involved with the Chicano movement. After graduating from college, Castillo taught ethnic studies at Santa Rosa Junior College in Sonoma County, California, for a year and joined the artistic and activist community of the 1970s, becoming one of the first contributors to the influential literary publication first known as *Revista Chicano-Riqueña* and now known as *The Americas Review*.

From 1977 to 1979, Castillo served as a writer-in-residence at the Illinois Arts Council, and with a grant from that organization, she published her first collection of poems, *Otro Canto* (1977), as a chapbook. Two years later, with a grant from the Playboy Foundation, she published her second poetry collection, *The Invitation* (1979). Castillo continued her education with a master's degree in Latin American and Caribbean studies from the University of Chicago in 1979 and a PhD in American studies from the University of Bremen in Germany in 1991.

Music began to play a central role in Castillo's work and life shortly after her first success in poetry. She created and managed a flamenco dancing performance group from 1981 to 1982. During that time she adapted the poems in *The Invitation* for music, and they were performed at the Soho Art Festival in New York City in 1982. One year later, in June, her play *Clark Street Counts* (1983) was performed by the Chicano Raza Group. The poetry collections *Pajaros engañosos* (1983), published by Cross Cultural Communications, and *Women Are Not Roses* (1984), published by Arte Público Press, demonstrated the maturing voice of the poet.

Changing her creative output's format but not its core themes, Castillo came out with an epistolary novel, *The Mixquiahuala Letters* (1986). Although it was her first novel, *The Mixquiahuala Letters* was widely praised, particularly for its treatment of women, including the struggle between the sexes and its examination of the changing role of women in Mexico and the United States. In 1987 the novel went on to receive an American Book Award from the Before Columbus Foundation and an award from The Women's Foundation of San Francisco, California, in 1988.

My Father Was a Toltec (1988) returned Castillo to poetry and to the expression of the theme of Latina women's existence and gender roles in the Hispanic world. These poems, written in English and Spanish, deal with difficult subjects such as poverty, violence, **racism**, and suicide but resonate with Castillo's passion for language and music.

In spite of her strong poetic voice, it was once again Castillo's fiction that won for her the greatest attention. Her second novel, *Sapogonia: An Anti-Romance in 3/8 Meter* (1990), was nominated for the Western States Book Award, and in 1993 she came out with her third novel, *So Far From God*. Filled with magic, scathing social commentary, and humor, *So Far From God* garnered for Castillo the 1993 **Carl Sandburg** Literary Award in Fiction and the Mountains and Plains Bookseller Award of 1994.

Along with her prolific creative output, Castillo has also served literature as a critic, editor, translator, and anthologist. She made an important contribution as the principal translator of *This Bridge Called My Back: Writings by Radical Women of Color*. The original book was written in English and edited by **Cherríe Moraga** and **Gloria Anzaldúa**, and Castillo, along with **Norma Alacrón** and Cherríe Moraga, translated the influential volume of feminist essays into Spanish as *Esta puete, mi espalda: Voces de mujeres tercermundistas in los Estados Unidos* (1988). Also with Norma Alarcón and Cherríe Moraga, Castillo coedited *Third Woman Literary Magazine: Latina Sexuality* in 1988. One year later, she put together a volume of her own writings, ten feminist essays based on her doctoral work called *Massacre of the Dreamers: Essays on Xicanisma* (1989). The essays comment on the experiences of Latinas, challenge the dichotomy of black/white race relations, and expound on the need for "Xicanisma," a Chicana **feminism** that is socially aware and politically involved. Castillo soon wrote the nonfiction work *Massacre of the Dreamers: Reflections on Mexican-Indian Women in the United States 500 Years After the Conquest* (1995). The anthology she edited the following year, *La Diosa de las Americas/Goddess of the Americas* (1996), collects works, by Octavio Paz, **Sandra Cisneros**, **Denise Chávez**, and others, that discuss the Virgin of Guadalupe and investigate the effect the figure has had on Mexican history, culture, art, and literature.

Castillo published in a new form, short stories, with *Loverboys: Stories* (1996), a collection that explores the experience of love, the positive and the painful, through a wide variety of settings, with W.W. Norton. Castillo continued writing fiction in the following years, publishing the novel *Peel My Love Like an Onion* (1999). Carmen, the protagonist, is an acclaimed flamenco dancer and now at forty years old faces a flare-up of a disease. How Carmen's indomitable spirit enables her to overcome this and the loss of her career and two lovers brings praise to the novel for its powerful yet realistically flawed main character.

With *I Ask the Impossible* (2000) Castillo collected more than sixty poems she wrote between 1989 and 2000. In the collection she affirms the strength of women in the face of the injustice they experience. Also published that year, *My Daughter, My Son, My Eagle, The Dove: An Aztec Chant* (2000) brings together for today's children the advice and affirmations offered in Aztec chants recited by parents and elders hundreds of years ago.

Not only has Castillo's work been widely anthologized in the United States, Mexico, and Europe, but it also has been published both in small, independent presses and mainstream presses, demonstrating that her work finds an audience in a variety of circles. Throughout her career Castillo has contributed to contemporary culture not only through her literary and artistic work but also through the popular press. She has written several essays and columns for regional and national newspapers and magazines on a variety of topics, including the murder of Tejano singer Selena, motherhood, and gender roles in the farm-workers' union. Additionally, Castillo has served as an educator, teaching the history of pre-Columbian civilizations, the United States, and Mexico; women's studies; creative writing; and Chicano literature at a variety of universities.

Castillo's numerous literary prizes include two National Endowment of the Arts fellowships for poetry and a California Arts Council Fellowship for fiction. The Archives of Ana Castillo gave her the honor of being the first Hispanic writer to have a collection at the University of California, Santa Barbara. (*See also* Mexican American Poetry, Mexican American Novel)

Further Reading

Benbow-Pfalzgraf, Taryn, ed. *American Women Writers: A Critical Reference Guide from Colonial Times to the Present.* 2nd ed., vol. 1. Detroit: St. James Press, 2000.

Davidson, Cathy N., and Linda Wagner-Martin, eds. *The Oxford Companion to Women's Writing in the United States.* Oxford: Oxford UP, 1995. 153–54.

Keavne, Bridget, and Juanita Heredia, eds. *Latina Self-Portraits: Interviews with Contemporary Women Writers.* Albuquerque: U of New Mexico P, 2000.

Lomelí, Francisco A., and Carl R. Shirley, eds. "Ana Castillo." *Dictionary of Literary Biography: Chicano Writers,* 2nd ser., vol. 122. Detroit: Gale Group, 1992. 62–65.

Trosky, Susan M., ed. "Ana Castillo." *Contemporary Authors.* Vol. 131. Detroit: Gale Group, 1991. 98–99.

Deborah Owen Moore

CASTILLO, RAFAEL C. (1950–) Chicano writer and teacher. Castillo's fiction forms part of a new wave of Chicano writing that moves on from the social agenda of past authors in order to explore an expanded range of contemporary cultural issues.

Castillo was born in San Antonio, Texas, where he has lived for the majority of his life. The break-up of Castillo's parents' marriage had a profound effect on him and it formed a catalyst for his interest in creative writing, which he began experimenting with while he was still at school. Subsequently, Castillo received a BA in English and political science at St. Mary's University, and he went on to complete an MA at the University of Texas at San Antonio in English and bicultural studies. Since 1985 Castillo has been working as professor of English at Palo Alto Community College in Texas, and he has been the recipient of various teaching awards, including the Palo Alto College President's Award for Teaching (1991).

A key influence who helped to shape Castillo's literary evolution is the Russian writer Fyodor Dostoyevsky, whose evocation of the world of St. Petersburg resonated with Castillo's experience of surviving as a Mexican American in the United States. Castillo's first critical essay, "Chicano Philosophy" (1975), published in the Chicano journal *Caracol* (Snail) discusses Chicano **identity** through the prism of influential political movements such as Marxism. Castillo has also experimented with poetry—"A Variation on a Dostoevski Theme" appeared in the *Arizona Canto al Pueblo* (Song to the People) in 1980. Thereafter, Castillo decided to turn his attention to writing essays and short stories and editing journals such as the *ViAztlán Journal* and *Saguaro*.

Castillo's key work to date is a compilation of eighteen short stories titled *Distant Journeys* (1991), all written between 1980 and 1988. The collection is split into three parts: "Distant Journeys with Strange People," "Distant Journeys to Faraway Places," and "Distant Journeys to Other Cultures." The metaphor of the journey is used in order to place the experience of being Chicano into a multiplicity of cultural contexts, both within the United States and beyond. The stories in the first section of the book explore various characters' confrontations with death, drawing on the devices of magical realism and surrealism. The second part of the book places the Chicano experience in a wider context, investigating themes of human suffering and religious concerns in locations as diverse as Chile and El Salvador. In the final section of *Distant Journeys*, Castillo focuses more specifically on the Chicano experience within the United States, drawing attention to the dilemma of becoming divorced from one's cultural roots, yet not quite being able to become assimilated into alternative cultural possibilities. Castillo affirms the need to maintain cultural connections with the past.

Rafael Castillo's other literary projects include a short story collection titled "Dwarfs and Penitents" and a coauthored novel centering on a World War II veteran.

Further Reading

Rosales, Jesus. "Rafael C. Castillo." *Dictionary of Literary Biography*. Vol. 209. Ed. Francisco A. Lomeli and Carl R. Shirley. Detroit: Gale, 1999. 40–44.

Helen Oakley

CATACALOS, ROSEMARY (1944–)   Greek/Mexican American poet, teacher, scholar, translator, and innovative literary arts administrator. Catacalos, of Greek and Mexican ancestry, was born and raised in San Antonio, Texas. A former newspaper reporter and arts columnist, Catacalos has also worked as a grant writer, publicist, and development officer for nonprofit organizations.

Catacalos has authored two poetry books. One is a handsewn, fine-letterpress chapbook titled *As Long As It Takes* (1984). The other, *Again for the First Time* (1984), is a substantial volume of poetry, which was awarded the 1985 Texas Institute of Letters Poetry Prize. Later that year, she was also awarded the Dobie Paisano Fellowship by the Texas Institute of Letters at the University of Texas at Austin.

Texas has produced numerous Chicano writers, and their subject matter tends to be linked to the heritage of Mexican culture in Texas. According to **Roberta Fernández**, Texas has produced more Chicano writers than any other state in the country. As a whole, Texan writers closely identify themselves with the part of the state in which they spent their youths, even though they may no longer reside there. Writers such as Rosemary Catacalos, Angela de Hoyos, Max Martínez, **Tomás Rivera**,

Carmen Tafolla, and Evangelina Vigil belong to the San Antonio area and tend to follow this pattern.

Although close to her Mexican roots, Catacalos is also an example of the heterogeneous cultural repertoire seen among Latina writers in the United States. Her cultural experience and background include not only her experience as a Chicana, but her Greek ancestry as well. This is apparent in poems such as "Katacalos," in which she portrays her father in a positive light.

Jean Franco has said that Latinas are sensitive not only to the violence of hero myths but also to the violence that takes place in different parts of the world. Catacalos reveals her concern in "The History of Abuse, a Language Poem," where violence is at the core of the private and public sphere. In this poem, both domestic and political violence become her object of representation, along with language.

Catacalos also looks to oral tradition and legend, as do many other Latinas. A good example is found in her poem "A Vision of La Llorona," in which, once again, a Latino writer in the United States reveals her interest for the legend of the weeping woman: the Indian who perpetually laments her drowned children. On the other hand, her poem "Keeping the Vigil" reminds us of the Day of the Dead, the Mexican holiday in which families remember their dead and celebrate the continuity of life. The Day of the Dead continues to be an important subject matter in Latino literature as an ancient festivity that has been transformed through the years, but which was intended in pre-Hispanic Mexico to celebrate children and the dead. Also among Catacalos' cultural activities are her twenty-five years of experience in building altars for the Day of the Dead in both public and private areas.

Catacalos has published widely in national journals, including *The Progressive*, *The Women's Review of Books*, *Parnassus: Poetry in Review*, and *Colorado Review*. Her work was included in *Best American Poetry 2002*, selected by **Yusef Komunyakaa**, and also was collected in *Best American Poetry 1996*, edited by **Adrienne Rich**. Her poems can be found in several trade anthologies and textbooks, and translations of her works have appeared in journals and anthologies in Mexico, Spain, Italy, and Greece.

From fall 1989 to spring 1991, she was a Wallace Stegner Creative Writing Fellow in Poetry at Stanford University, where she received the Patricia Smith Poetry Prize. She received a 1993 National Endowment for the Arts Creative Writing Fellowship in Poetry. Catacalos has also been an affiliated scholar at the Institute for Research on Women and Gender at Stanford University.

Catacalos has worked extensively in support of writers through her leadership, teaching, and advocacy in positions such as executive director of the Poetry Center and American Poetry Archives at San Francisco State University and Literature Program director at the Guadalupe Cultural Arts Center. Her work has been recognized by scholars as well as by other Latina writers in the United States. Authors such as Valerie Martínez have acknowledged the influence of Catacalos in their own work, pointing out the existence of common threads, such as an interest in female relationships, personal struggles, the presence of native language, the redefinition of religion, and the role of women within Latin culture.

Further Reading

Fernández, Roberta, ed. *In Other Words: Literature by Latinas of the United States.* Houston: Arte Público Press, 1994.

María Elvira Villamil

CAVELLO, DIANA (1931–) Italian American novelist and short story writer. Born in Philadelphia in 1931, Diana Cavallo is the daughter of Genuino and Josephine (Petraca) Cavallo. Raised in an Italian American neighborhood in South Philadelphia, Cavallo lived with three generations of her family until the age of ten. In fact, two characters in Cavallo's novel *A Bridge of Leaves*, drawn mostly from life, are the grandfather and grandmother; they spoke the Abruzzese dialect and Cavallo absorbed the language from them.

After graduating from the University of Pennsylvania *Phi Beta Kappa*, Cavallo worked for a year at the Philadelphia State Hospital as a psychiatric social worker. As a witness and observer, Cavallo wrote the case histories for patients in preparation for diagnostic sessions. Not only did Cavallo interview patients at the mental hospital, but she spoke with their family members, too. Such work provided essential backdrop for her 1961 novel, *A Bridge of Leaves*. Begun in Lenox, Massachusetts, the novel took three years to write, much of it written in New Hampshire at the MacDowell Colony, to which Cavallo was awarded a fellowship. A classic novel of development, *A Bridge of Leaves* depicts a young man's rite of passage into adulthood. Divided into three parts, this novel focuses on the protagonist's life as a youngster, a college student, and a worker in an asylum, each section exploring seminal relationships to his grandmother, his twin, and his female lover. Cavallo focuses on the psychology of the questing narrator, who must dig beneath the surfaces of daily life to discover his own profound guilt and grief over the premature death of his twin and his paralyzed inability to mourn his Italian grandmother's death. An abiding concern for Cavallo, the theme of **identity** informs her first novel as the searching self learns to extend himself and commune with a world, constructing a bridge, albeit perishable, but necessary to reach beyond the self.

Cavallo's nonfiction book *The Lower East Side: A Portrait in Time* was published in 1971 and was followed by short stories published in various journals and anthologies, including **Helen Barolini**'s *The Dream Book: An Anthology of Writings by Italian American Women*. After teaching in public schools in Philadelphia, PA, and Clifton, NJ, and in a private school in Brooklyn, Cavallo became an instructor in literature and creative writing at Drexel Institute of Technology (now Drexel University), Queens College, and a lecturer in creative writing at the University of Pennsylvania, beginning in 1980.

403

Between 1969 and 1973, Cavallo was an instructor in literature and creative writing at the University of Pisa (Italy).

In an article on the transformation of experience in the writing of fiction, Cavallo reflects that the narrative voice she has used in her fiction is both male and female, or neither male nor female. In her own attempt to create a bridge that connects author and reader, Cavallo insists on an unanchored quality in the "I" of the author's voice that allows for both the simultaneity and multiplicity of self. In positioning herself in writing from both inside and outside the moment, Cavallo seamlessly merges both states, perhaps simulating the immigrant experience and the experience of duality of many ethnic people in America. (*See also* Italian American Novel)

Further Reading

Bona, Mary Jo. Afterword. *A Bridge of Leaves*. Diana Cavallo. Toronto: Guernica, 1997. i–x.

Cavallo, Diana. "The Transformation of Experience in the Writing of Fiction." *Adjusting Sites: New Essays in Italian American Studies*. Ed. William Boelhower and Rocco Pallone. New York: Forum Italicum, 1999. 267–73.

Contemporary Authors. Gale Literary Databases. Entry Updated: 2001.

Mary Jo Bona

CEREMONY **Leslie Marmon Silko**'s *Ceremony* (1977) is one of the most important novels in contemporary Native American literature. Embracing several key concerns common to many ethnic literatures, including the complex negotiation of racial, national, and ethnic identities, *Ceremony* pushes for a survival strategy that unites the traditional and contemporary strengths of a community and its people.

Ceremony revolves around Tayo, the half-Indian, half-white protagonist, who is sent at a very young age to live with his mother's family on the matriarchal Laguna Pueblo reservation. Marginalized by his community and neglected by his aunt for being an illegitimate half-breed, Tayo later enlists in the army with his cousin, Rocky. Rocky, symbolic of the "new" Indian on the rise who dismisses the old ways and unquestioningly embraces the rhetoric of white, "all-American" values, is killed in the Pacific theater of World War II, and a shell-shocked Tayo returns home with battle fatigue. Tayo's estrangement from the community deepens when he learns that his uncle and mentor, Josiah, died while he was away. However, while other Indian veterans find solace in alcohol and violence, Tayo is driven to seek an alternative resolution to his despair. Sensing that the tradition of battling over the sovereignty of the land has shifted to a psychological war over the hearts and minds of the remaining Indians, he struggles to free himself of the "invisibility" that threatens to engulf his scattered perception of self.

Helped by medicine men, including Ku'oosh and Betonie, and by various women spirit guides including Night Swan and Ts'eh, the "'ceremony" is an exercise in reeducation. Through stories told and memories retrieved, Tayo discovers anew his role in the community's ancient battle against forgetfulness and Indian witchcraft. His understanding of the reasons for Indian degradation is redirected from the convenient scapegoats the white people have become to a deeper examination of his community's own culpability. Thus, the simple dichotomy of **race** is deconstructed; it is a point that is stressed when Tayo narrowly escapes the death planned for him by his reservation mates' murderous bloodlust. Recognizing the changes to the land and hence the need for new healing rituals, Tayo eventually overcomes his sense of loss to center himself and his stories in nature and the human community that make up the land.

Silko asserts that there is a direct link between human misdeeds and the uncertain state of the environment, stemming from historical losses and the active hostility that still threatens the endurance of the Native nations from within and without the reservation. The symbiotic relationship between place and identity is reinforced by the nonlinear, web-like complexity of the novel's structure, which points to the interconnectedness of all events. Inherent in Laguna culture is the quality of adaptability. Tradition is not static but ever-evolving, and Silko's innovative merging of oral traditions and the printed form is in itself a statement on managing change and acculturation in light of retaining traditions. (*See also* Native American Reservation)

Further Reading

Chavkin, Allan, ed. *Leslie Marmon Silko's "Ceremony": A Casebook*. New York: Oxford UP, 2002.

Poh Cheng Khoo

CERENIO, VIRGINIA (1955–) Filipina American poet. Virginia Cerenio, a second-generation Filipina American born in California, earned a BA in English and an MA in education from San Francisco State University. Cerenio's poetry reflects broad Filipina American realities while addressing people and events that have shaped her cultural **identity**.

An involved community activist, Cerenio has been active in Kearney Street Workshop (KSW), an organization that produces art empowering to Asian Pacific American communities, is a founding member of the Bay Area Pilipino American Writers (BAYPAW) collective, and works with the International Hotel Citizen Advisory Committee, a group that promotes senior housing in San Francisco.

Cerenio's poetry has appeared in a variety of Asian American, Filipino American, and multicultural poetry anthologies, including *Without Names: A Collection of Poems* (1985), *Fiction by Filipinos in America* (1993), *New Worlds of Literature: Writings from America's Many Cultures* (1993), and *Returning a Borrowed Tongue: Poems by Filipino and Filipino American Writers* (1997), among others.

Trespassing Innocence (1989), a collection of Cerenio's poetry published elsewhere, recognizes the themes of identity, history, community involvement, cultural legacy, and social justice. As an activist "Flip poet" (American-born or -raised Filipino writer who grew up during the 1960s and

1970s), Cerenio creates a Filipino America that reflects her struggle with identity and loss of culture; her poems often explore rich relationships such as the cultural distance of the *manongs* (older male Filipino immigrants) or her life choices as a second-generation Filipina juxtaposed against the hopes and dreams of first-generation immigrant mothers. Within a traditionally male writing tradition, Cerenio's voice stands out with strong Asian American feminist sensibility.

Cerenio's poetry has also appeared in two landmark anthologies, *Making Waves: An Anthology of Writings By and About Asian American Women* (1989) and *Babaylan* (2000). In 1989 the Asian Women United of California (AWU), an organization promoting positive role models for young women, compiled *Making Waves*, thus completing the first major collection since the 1970s of primarily unpublished works by and about Asian American women. Similarly, *Babaylan* represents the first anthology of Filipina and Filipina American prose and poetry published in the United States.

Cerenio's most recent *Going Home to a Landscape: Writings by Filipinas* (2003) presents a wide range of literary Filipina voices including seasoned writers, such as Cerenio herself, as well as new authors. Arranged in six thematically oriented sections, the poetry and prose of *Going Home* focus on the relationship of Filipina women to place and their consequent struggles to forge their identities.

Cerenio's poetry, shot through with culturally engaging references and socially committed principles, addresses contemporary issues through a perspective that recognizes and celebrates the many cultural and historical challenges of Filipina women. (*See also* Filipino American Poetry)

Further Reading

Moynihan, Susan Muchshima. Review of *Going Home to a Landscape: Writing by Filipinas*. Ed. Virginia Cerenio and Marianne Villanueva. *MELUS* 27.1 (Spring 2004): 294.

Sylvia M. DeSantis

CERVANTES, LORNA DEE (1953–) Chicana poet and activist. An internationally acclaimed poet, Cervantes is the author of two award-winning volumes of poetry, *Emplumada* (1981) and *From the Cables of Genocide*(1991), and her work has appeared in more than 150 anthologies. She is the winner of the Peterson Prize for Poetry, the Latino Literature Award, and the American Book Award and has received two fellowships from the National Endowment for the Arts and a Lila Wallace-Reader's Digest Award. Since 1974 Cervantes has presented at more than one thousand poetry readings, lectures, performances, and panel presentation in such places as the Library of Congress, the White House, and major university campuses. Her work has been translated into German, Italian, French, Spanish, and Czechoslovakian. She currently directs the creative writing program at the University of Colorado, Boulder.

Cervantes began her publishing career not only as a writer, but also as a literary activist, founding Mango Publications in 1974, at a time when most of Chicano publishing was dominated by men. She published the now-famous Chicano Chapbook series and *Mango*, a cross-cultural literary and art magazine. Cervantes coedited and copublished a broadside series of women's art and literature and during the early 1990s, she founded and edited *Red Dirt*, a biannual, cross-cultural poetry journal. She also coordinates an annual writing retreat for women of color, providing space, time, and intensive writing workshops dedicated to developing emerging literary voices.

Chicana/o literary critics have described the connections between Chicana/o poetry and struggles for justice and civil rights. Cervantes clearly fits into this tradition, as well as a Chicana/o cultural tradition shaped by *mestizaje*, a term that originally described the mixing of European and Indigenous elements in Mexican culture, but that is now also used to describe the mixture of American and Mexican elements that make up Chicana/o culture.

Throughout Cervantes's works, from *Emplumada*, through *From the Cables of Genocide* to the forthcoming collection *Drive*, she develops an expanding frame of reference for Chicana poetry. We see a movement from a pride in the indigenous roots of Mexican and Chicana/o culture that is characteristic of classic Chicano literature to a broad engagement with global cultural and political influences. Cervantes's references, which range from the traditional Chicana/o tropes of Meso American images to Hispanophone modernist poetry, from Celtic folklore to Greek myth, indicate a shifting of consciousness. In this collection and in her more recent work, Cervantes extends a Chicana/o poetic tradition across cultural lines to connect very explicitly with third-world feminist concerns.

Questions of aesthetics and history, of literary and cultural tradition are deeply interlinked in Cervantes's work. Cervantes writes poems about Chicanas in gangs, connecting them to Chumash and Greek myths, while describing the realities of their lives. She writes of poverty, combining dignity with righteous anger. Her love poetry acknowledges the influence of Neruda, one of the great love poets of the twentieth century, also famous for his leftist politics. The scope of her poetic vision is vast, intimately connective, and deeply democratic. Cervantes is part of a generation of Latina/o poets, who along with **Martin Espada**, and **Francisco Alarcón**, write powerfully about love and beauty and its importance to struggles for social justice. (*See also* Mexican American Poetry)

Further Reading

Chavez-Candelaria, Cordelia. "Rethinking the 'Eyes' of Chicano Poetry." *Women Poets of the Americas: Toward a Pan-American Gathering*. Ed. Jacqueline Vaught Brogan. Notre Dame: U of Notre Dame P, 1999. 133–29.

Savan, Ada. "Bilingualism and Dialogism: Another Reading of Lorna Dee Cervantes's Poetry." *An Other Tongue*. Ed. Alfred Arteaga. Durham, NC: Duke UP, 1994. 215–24.

Eliza Rodriguez y Gibson

CHA, THERESA HAK KYUNG (1951–1982)   Korean American prose writer, poet, filmmaker, photographer, editor, and performance artist. Cha's best-known work, *Dictee* (1982), has received much critical acclaim since its rediscovery by a group of Asian American scholars in the early 1990s. Critics have focused on her unparalleled experimental writing style of merging various genres, which disrupts literary conventions, along with her unique approaches to the issues of history, **identity**, dislocation, language, memory, and **feminism.**

Dictee is not a conventional autobiographical narrative with a beginning, middle, and end. It is composed of nine parts and each part shows a variety of writing styles, such as journal entries, handwritten letters, dreams, photographs, film stills, diagrams, myths, and calligraphy. As an immigrant herself for whom English is not a first language, Cha demonstrates an extraordinary sensitivity to language as a means of subjugating people and hiding away the history of oppression. The pages of rough drafts, handwritten letters, and side-by-side presentations of French and English language exercises allow readers to understand the meaning of acquiring language via an immigration history. Cha also traces this issue back to the history of the thirty-five-year colonization of Korea by Japan when Koreans were never allowed to speak their own native language. She provides a perspective from which to view the Korean immigrant experience as a continuation of the history of political struggle in Korea. Cha even hints that her own dilemma as a person whose identity is mediated by a hyphen is bound up with the partitioning of Korea as a part of the larger dynamics of the cold war. By illustrating how those who do not qualify for a skillful employment of language are marginalized, Cha explores the inextricable linkage between language and power.

At the heart of *Dictee* are also stories of several women including Cha herself, Cha's mother, and Yu Guan Soon, a young Korean woman who led a resistance movement against the Japanese colonial rule in 1919. The way Cha tells the women's stories disturbs established patterns of writing history. Their stories are not narrated from a neutral and impersonal perspective. For example, in "Calliope/Epic Poetry," Cha's interpolation of the journals of her mother Hyung Soon Huo as a young exile in Manchuria during the Japanese occupation puts readers in a conversation with the author and the contents rather than simply reclaims or recovers the past. The scattered images and calligraphy are also presented without any explanation of specific contexts. Cha never translates or explains but leaves readers who have no cultural and linguistic context continuously pondering over the intended meanings of the images. This strategy brings home to readers how women's voices have been silenced in the name of writing a "universal history." Ironically, through the fragmented stories of women and the fuzzy images, Cha is enabled to argue effectively that the history of female silence is never to be easily appropriated as a subject of oppression but to be the very space from which women's repressed voices can be heard. It is at this point that her central themes of separation and displacement meet up with her ulterior desire for reunification and recovery. At the same time, Cha's thematically and structurally difficult text forces us not to forget that bridging the two conflicting desires can never be easily achieved.

Challenging conventional patterns of historical and autobiographical writing, Cha's text opens up spaces in which Korean American women who have been silenced by their differences of **race**, gender, and language proficiency are enabled to articulate themselves. Each fragmented story written in different styles makes readers continuously conscious of her writing as a progress and how the very act of piecing together fragments to make a coherent narrative sometimes oppresses the voices of the people in "margin." Written at a time when Asian American communities were beginning to shape their social and political consciousness into collective unity, Cha's text calls into question the very assumptions we have about language, history, and identity. Without an equivalent, *Dictee*'s investigation of Asian American women's multiple identities traversing different geopolitical locations, cultures, and several languages, earns its keep in the twenty-first century. (*See also* Korean American Literature)

Further Reading

Cheng, Anne Anling. "Memory and Anti-Documentary Desire in Theresa Hak Kyung Cha's *Dictee*." *Melus* 23.4 (Winter 1998): 119–33.

Kim, Elaine H., ed. *Writing Self Writing Nation: A Collection of Essays on "Dictee" by Theresa Hak Kyung Cha*. Berkeley, CA: Third Woman Press, 1994.

Min-ha, Trinh T. *Woman, Native, Other: Writing Postcoloniality and Feminism*. Bloomington: Indiana UP, 1989.

Seongho Yoon

CHABON, MICHAEL (1963–)   Jewish American prose fiction writer. The thesis Michael Chabon wrote to complete the MFA program at the University of California, Irvine, became his first published novel, *The Mysteries of Pittsburgh* (1983). He is best known for *Wonder Boys* (1995) and the Pulitzer Prize–winning novel *The Amazing Adventures of Kavalier and Clay* (2000). These critically acclaimed works reflect his increasing use of Jewish culture and history as aesthetic resources.

The critical success of both *The Mysteries of Pittsburgh* and *A Model World* (1991), a collection of short stories, earned Chabon an advance for his proposed novel *Fountain City*. After writing 1500 pages over four years, Chabon had to admit that this literary venture had reached a dead end. However, the autobiographical angst of being unable to complete *Fountain City* became the germ for *Wonder Boys*. Grady Tripp, the protagonist of Chabon's second novel, is a creative writing professor at a small college in Pennsylvania and hopelessly mired in his fourth novel, a family saga called *Wonder Boys*. At the outset of Chabon's novel, all parts of Tripp's life are in crisis: Expecting a finished manuscript, his editor has just arrived in town;

Michael Chabon. *AP/Wide World Photos.*

his mistress, the college chancellor, has just announced she's pregnant; his wife has left him; and he suspects that James Leer, a promising but grammatically challenged writing student, is suicidal. Tripp's body reflects the deterioration of his life: Insomnia, combined with the abuse of alcohol and drugs, has resulted in increasingly frequent fainting spells. As a respite from the writing conference that represents the convergence of disasters that Tripp's life has become, he takes James Leer with him to the Passover seder being held at the home of his in-laws.

Tripp's family by marriage is a hybrid and wacky group, and the seder scene at the center of the novel reflects the complexity of family history and current relations. James Leer is the stranger at the table, and his desire to participate in the rituals of the Passover meal adds poignancy to this comical portrait of a dysfunctional clan. Chabon has commented that James's outsider view of this ritual meal was his own writerly attempt to indirectly examine and reconnect with Jewish traditions. In *Wonder Boys*, the ritual marking of the Exodus story precedes and figures Tripp's own liberations. By the end of the novel, an escapade with his editor and low-level gangsters results in the loss of most of the only copy of his manuscript; freed from the burden of this perpetually unfinished novel, he turns his attention to his new wife and son as well as to part-time teaching and new writing projects. Chabon's novel was turned into a successful Hollywood film starring Michael Douglas as Grady Tripp; significantly, the Passover scene and symbolism central to the novel are absent from the film version of *Wonder Boys*.

The Amazing Adventures of Kavalier and Clay is an epic work that puts Jewish cultural history at the center of twentieth-century America. Joe Kavalier and Sammy Clay (formerly Klayman) are cousins who merge their drawing and narrative talents to create the Escapist, a comic book superhero. Joe is a refugee from Prague who becomes increasingly desperate to get the rest of his family out of Nazi-occupied Europe; as one of the cocreators of the Escapist, a figure dedicated to unlocking the chains of oppression, Joe not only strives to make enough money to secure visas for his family but also uses the world of comics to counter imaginatively his sense of powerlessness. Sammy, Joe's Brooklyn-born cousin who struggles with his fatherless state and his sexual confusions, finds a masculine alter ego in the Escapist and in his lover, Tracy Bacon, the man who gives the superhero a voice in the medium of radio. A gay bashing incident perpetrated by the police convinces Sammy not to move with Tracy to California as planned. After Joe's brother, Tommy, drowns en route to New York, Joe joins the navy to fight the Nazis and ends up as the only survivor of a mission in the Antarctic. While Joe confronts literal and figurative ice, Sammy marries Joe's girlfriend, Rosa Saks, who is pregnant with Joe's child. This marriage provides Rosa and her son with security and enables Sammy to defer coming out. By the end of the novel, Joe has staged a dramatic return, Joe and Rosa have reunited, and Sammy has decided that he, like many American heroes before him, must make his westward journey.

In this historically rich novel, Chabon recaptures the Jewish origins of the comic book industry, which was prompted by patterns of employment discrimination that disallowed Jews from becoming respectable commercial artists. Chabon explores the desperation of those working to rescue European Jews and thus to stop—one body at a time—the genocidal project of the Nazis; the **anti-Semitism** and homophobia that mobilized the Senate Judiciary Committee to investigate the supposed connection between juvenile delinquency and comic books in the postwar period; the sting operations used to harass gays in pre-Stonewall America; and the suburbanization of American life post–World War II with its resulting stultification of middle-class women. Moreover, by focusing on the development of the comic book and charting Joe's increasing aesthetic commitments to that form, Chabon challenges critical truisms about the distinctions between high and low art. In addition to winning the Pulitzer Prize, *The Amazing Adventures of Kavalier and Clay* was named one of the notable books of 2000 by the American Library Association and received the New York Society Library Prize for Fiction. Chabon is particularly gratified that *The Forward* included the novel on its list of 100 Great Jewish Books. Like **Saul Bellow**, **Philip Roth**, and **Bernard Malamud**, Michael Chabon seems destined to put Jewish literature at the center of American literary **canons**.

Further Reading

Behlman, Lee. "Michael Chabon." *Holocaust Literature: An Encyclopedia of Writers and Their Work.* Ed. Lillian Kremer. New York: Routledge, 2002. 224–30.

Doherty, Brian. "Comics Tragedy." *Reason* 33.1 (2001): 48–55.

Helene Meyers

CHAN, JEFFREY PAUL (1942–)   Asian American scholar, editor, educator, and short story writer. Jeffrey Paul Chan's importance to the field of Asian American literature began with the groundbreaking *Aiiieeeee! An*

Anthology of Asian American Writers (1974), which he coedited along with **Frank Chin**, **Lawson Fusao Inada**, and Shawn Hsu Wong. The first anthology of its kind, *Aiiieeeee* brought together the writings of Chinese Americans, Japanese Americans, and Filipino Americans in an attempt to define Asian American literature. *The Big Aiiieeeee! An Anthology of Chinese American and Japanese American Literature* followed in 1991.

Chan insists throughout his work on the unique identity of the Chinese American and Asian American. In the 1973 preface to *Aiiieeeee!*, Chan and his fellow editors endeavored to correct America's idea of the Asian American. First and foremost, they stressed that though the anthology did include three different Asian American cultural groups, these three groups represented three very separate cultures. Further, these three disparate cultural groups were also not synonymous with the countries from which they came, nor synonymous with America. Asian American **identity** is inextricably linked with both Asian and white American identity, though distinct and independent from both.

Chan and the other *Aiiieeeee!* editors are also concerned with dispelling **Asian American stereotypes**. In the 1991 preface to the Mentor edition of *Aiiieeeee!*, the editors indict Christian missionaries for the popularization of stereotyping Chinese American men as either the inscrutable "heathen Chinee" or the effeminate, law-abiding, passive, bumbling Charlie Chan. They further take to task those authors they feel further encourage such racist stereotypes through their writings, such as **Pardee Lowe** and Leong Gor Yun.

Within the *Aiiieeeee!* prefaces, as well as in Chan's cowritten article "Asian-American Literary Traditions," Chan argues that revisiting the historical and social realities of Asian Americans should serve to define the as-yet-undefined Asian American literary tradition. He advocates excavating history in order to find the true past of Asian Americans, in an attempt to dispel stereotypes and return to Asian Americans their own identities from which they may in turn form their own literatures.

Chan has also published several short stories in *Asian Pacific American Journal* and *Amerasia Journal*, among other journals. In his short stories as well, Chan endeavors to create for his Chinese American characters an identity separate from Chinese identity. Most recently, his "The Chinese in Haifa" appeared in **Jessica Hagedorn**'s anthology *Charlie Chan is Dead* (1993). Throughout the story, Chan delineates main character Bill Wong's separation from Chinese culture and Chinese American stereotypes: He can't read Chinese, doesn't live in Chinatown like his ex-wife's family, smokes dope, and has an affair with his Jewish neighbor's wife. Ultimately Wong feels more at home with his Jewish neighbors than his ex-wife and her family, who he describes as monkeys, thus creating for himself a new, less-Chinese, identity.

Chan's first novel, *Eat Everything Before You Die*, was published in June 2004. (*See also* Chinese American Poetry)

Further Reading
Kim, Elaine H. *Asian-American Literature: An Introduction to the Writings and Their Social Context*. Philadelphia: Temple UP, 1982.

Anastasia D. Wright

CHANDRA, SHARAT G. S. (1935–2000)   Indian American poet and fiction writer. Author of more than a dozen works during his lifetime, G. S. Sharat Chandra earned a place in American literature through his poetry and short stories that explore the immigrant experience. A graduate of the Universities of Mysore (India) and Iowa, he also held law degrees from India and Canada. In early poetry collections such as the The *Bharat Natyam Dancer* (1968), *April in Nanjangud* (1971), and *Once or Twice* (1974), the reader sees Sharat Chandra developing an ironic and often provocative style to address topics ranging from life in a strange land to the multifaceted nature of human relationships. The culmination of his poetic work came with the 1993 publications of two critically acclaimed collections—*Family of Mirrors* and *Immigrants of Loss*.

Nominated for the 1993 Pulitzer Prize in poetry, *Family of Mirrors* speaks with deep feeling on the expatriate experience. In five sections Sharat Chandra demonstrates the crisis of a man caught between two cultures but not genuinely part of either. Many times surreal, he shows readers what it meant to live in America and dream of India. *Immigrants of Loss* continues the theme of dislocation and location with free verse as well as formal stanzas. Journeying through shifting perspectives, Sharat Chandra reveals the Indian immigrants as both native and alien to their homeland.

The short story collection *Sari of the Gods* (1998) continues the theme of the immigrant condition. Often anecdotal in style, Sharat Chandra uses three sections—"Here," "There," and "Neither Here nor There"—to structure the work and designate settings of his fictional events. At the same time, the sections locate characters at different stages of **immigration**, culturally and psychologically. "Here" represents the difficulties of adjusting to a new land, "There" the longing for India, and "Neither Here nor There" the recognition of the limbo between no longer Indian and not yet American.

Until his death in 2000, G. S. Sharat Chandra was a professor of English at the University of Missouri at Kansas City. (*See also* South Asian American Literature)

Further Reading
Marchant, Fred. "*Family of Mirrors* by G. S. Sharat Chandra." *Weber Studies* 11.2 (1994): 148–50.
McLeod, A. L. Review of *Sari of the Gods*. *World Literature Today* 73.1 (Winter 1999): 212–13.
Miller, Phillip. "*Immigrants of Loss*: The Pleasures of Mixed Prosodies." *Literary Review* 40.2 (Winter 1997): 336–38.
Williams, Janis. Review of *Sari of the Gods*. *Library Journal* 123 (April 15, 1998): 117.

David R. Deborde

CHANG, DIANA (1934–) Chinese American novelist, poet, and painter. Chang was one of the first Chinese American writers and her debut novel, *The Frontiers of Love* (1956), depicted three Eurasians living in pre-Communist Shanghai after World War II. Most of her other works, however, do not have Chinese characters because Chang is more interested in general truths, rather than truths specific to any one culture, and in particular in identity as a universal theme. For Chang, imagination knows no ethnic boundaries, and exoticism can sometimes limit fiction.

Chang, who was born in New York City to a Eurasian mother and a Chinese father and who grew up mainly in China, considers herself an American writer with a Chinese background, and that is why only two of her six novels are about Chinese, Eurasian, or Chinese American characters. *The Frontiers of Love* is actually about Eurasians—people who are European-Asian—and how they deal with issues surrounding their mixed **ethnicity**. While some people within the ethnic movement viewed *The Frontiers of Love* as a metaphor for ethnicity in America, it is, in fact, about multicultural people living in Shanghai. Chang drew on her own background and experiences to explore the conflicts and difficulties for people who do not necessarily belong to one culture or group or one ethnic group. The political situation in Shanghai at this time also plays a role in the novel as their political views help shape the characters' identities. The three main characters, Sylvia Chen, Mimi Lambert, and Feng Huang, who have different backgrounds and views, have in common identity crises and their sense of feeling uncomfortable both in society and within themselves. *The Frontiers of Love* explores issues of **race**, class, and gender, which is all the more impressive because most novels from this time did not.

Her fifth novel, *Eye to Eye* (1974), has as the main character a white, male American artist whose psychoanalysis forms the bulk of the book. The novel is about creativity and Chang has suggested that since the issues she discusses in the work are more important than issues of ethnicity, she chose to

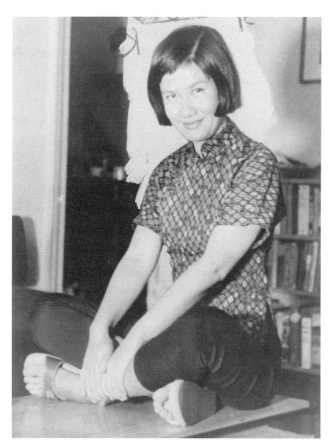

Diana Chang. *Courtesy of the Library of Congress.*

make the main character generic, rather than from any specific culture, as she did with three of her other novels as well. *Eye to Eye* is also interesting as a novel because of its usage of psychoanalysis and its exploration of the way art can reveal emotional and psychological problems of the artist.

In addition to her fiction, Chang has published nearly two hundred poems, both in chapbooks and magazines, and many of these are more personal and also deal more with specific matters of ethnicity. Chang is important not only as the first American-born Chinese person to publish a novel, but also for the fact that she refused to let her ethnicity dictate what she would write. (*See also* Chinese American Novel)

Further Reading

Hamalian, Leo. "A *MELUS* Interview: Diana Chang (Maskers and Tricksters)." *MELUS* 20.4 (1995): 29.

Brett Jocelyn Epstein

CHASE-RIBOUD, BARBARA (1936–) African American sculptor, poet, and novelist. Emphasizing the various cultures of the world in her art, Chase-Riboud utilizes her versatility and range to their fullest potential. She was born on June 20, 1936 (according to one biography it is June 26, 1939), in Philadelphia, Pennsylvania, the only child of middle-class parents. She started sculpting and won many awards for her sculpting and artwork at an early age. In 1957 she earned her BFA from Temple University, where she first exhibited her work. That same year, she received three awards including the John Hay Whitney Foundation Fellowship, which allowed her to study in Rome, Italy. In Rome Chase-Riboud discovered her primary material for sculpting, bronze. After returning to America, she earned her MFA from Yale University in 1960, studying under Josef Albers and Paul Rudolph.

In 1961 Chase-Riboud married Marc Riboud, a French photographer, and they eventually had two children. They traveled all over the world together, allowing her to obtain inspiration for her artwork from diverse cultures, cultures that have appeared in her sculptures. Ultimately, she became the first American woman to visit China after its 1949 revolution. She and Riboud divorced in 1981, and that same year, she married Sergio G. Tosi, an Italian publisher and art dealer. She and her husband live in Paris and Rome. As a sculptor and artist, Chase-Riboud has received numerous accolades and awards for her various exhibitions, including exhibitions at the Museum of Fine Arts in Boston, Massachusetts (1970), the Whitney Museum of American Art in New York (1971), the National Gallery of Art at the Smithsonian Institute in Washington, DC (1971), and the Museum of Modern Art (1971). She received a National Endowment for the Humanities Fellowship in 1973 and the Temple University Alumni Award in 1975. Besides these recognitions, Chase-Riboud has been the subject of many art books.

In the 1970s, inspired by her travels, Chase-Riboud added writing to her increasing artistic repertoire. She published her first poetry collection, *From Memphis to Peking* (1974), and then her first novel, *Sally Hemings: A Novel* (1979). This novel, which chronicles the then-not-proven sexual relationship between Thomas Jefferson and his slave, earned her the Janet Heidinger Kafka Prize for Excellence in Fiction by an American Woman. Her second poetry collection, *Love Perfecting*, appeared in 1980. This work was followed by another novel about **slavery** during the Ottoman Empire, *Valide: A Novel of the Harem* (1986), and *Portrait of a Nude Woman as Cleopatra* (1987), another collection of poems, won her the Carl Sandburg Poetry Prize for best poet in 1988. *Echo of Lions* (1989), a historical novel about the Amistad case, was followed in 1994 by *The President's Daughter*, a book about Sally Hemings and Thomas Jefferson's daughter Harriet who passed for white. Her latest novel, *Hottentot Venus: A Novel*, focused on South Africa, was published in 2003. Through her historical novels, Chase-Riboud blends historical accuracy of little-known figures with sensitivity and depth. She makes the historical subjects approachable and relatable.

In 1990 Chase-Riboud became the artist-in-residence at Pasadena City College in California. At the college, she taught and continued her sculptures in metals and fiber. However, she also expanded her artwork by making multimedia compositions using automated writing.

Chase-Riboud created another controversy in 1997 when she sued Steven Spielberg and Dreamworks SKG for ten million dollars in the United States District Court of California for plagiarism. She claimed that the movie *Amistad*, not yet released at the time, was based on her book *Echo of Lions*. In 1998 she dropped the suit, and the case was settled out of court.

Barbara Chase-Riboud employs her various talents to her advantage. Her multiethnically influenced art and writings stand as a testimony to honoring various cultures and heritages.

Further Reading

Rushdy, Ashraf H. A. "'I Write in Tongues': The Supplement of Voice in Barbara Chase-Riboud's *Sally Hemmings.*" *Contemporary Literature* 35.1 (1994): 100–135.

———. "Representing the Constitution: Embodiments of America in Barbara Chase-Riboud's *Echo of Lions.*" *Critique: Studies in Contemporary Fiction* 31.4 (1995): 258–80.

Devona Mallory

CHÁVEZ, DENISE (1948–) Chicana playwright, poet, actor, and novelist. Having written and produced more than thirty-five plays, Denise Chávez is one of the most prolific Chicana playwrights in the United States. Even so, Chávez has come to be known best for her fiction.

Living in Las Cruces, New Mexico, in the house where she was raised and writing in the room where she was born, Chávez incorporates the Southwestern landscape not only in her plays but also in her numerous poems, short story collection, and novels. Bilingual, Chávez uses both Spanish and English in her works, which draw on her experiences in Mexican and U.S. cultures, and successfully explores universal themes within a regional setting.

Chávez began publishing her plays in the 1970s, and her first play, *Novitiates* (1973), was written during her last year in college. In her plays she often explores the relationship between the New Mexican landscape and the inner world of her characters. Chávez has continued her success as a playwright throughout the 1980s and 1990s with, for example, her acclaimed one-woman play, *Woman in the State of Grace* (1989), which gives voice to nine Chicana characters ranging in age from seven years old to seventy-eight years old.

Although she was first known as a playwright, Chávez has more recently made a name for herself as a fiction writer, and her background in the theater has made her a strong writer of voice and character. She, in turn, is drawn to and influenced by writers who deal with voice and character, such as **Rudolfo Anaya**, Gabriel García Lorca, and **Bernard Malamud.**

Her breakthrough in fiction was *The Last of the Menu Girls* (1986). It contains seven interrelated short stories centered around Rocío Esquibel, a young woman who rejects the traditional roles society imposes on women. During the cycle of stories, Rocío, who works as a "menu girl" distributing and recollecting the hospital's daily menu to and from its patients, compares her life to her mother's and those of other women she meets. Ultimately, Rocío finds and solidifies her own identity. In 1990 Chávez adapted the collection into a play, which was subsequently produced in multiple theaters.

Face of an Angel (1994) was Chávez's first novel and won the 1995 American Book Award and the Premio Aztlán, a prize awarded to an outstanding novel written by a Chicana/o author. Soveida Dosamantes, the focal character of the novel, lives in a fictional town in New Mexico and uses her thirty years of experience working in a restaurant to write a manual for waitresses, called *The Book of Service.* Soveida also takes classes in the Chicano studies department of the local community college and helps on a project to gather the oral history of elderly Chicanas. A multivoiced novel, *Face of an Angel* is told in vignettes, stories within stories, passages from characters' term papers, letters, and extended dialogues. The novel has been praised for its compassion for Chicano culture and its humor.

Six years later, Chávez published *Loving Pedro Infante* (2000), a tragicomic novel revolving around Tere, a Chicana in her thirties who serves as the secretary of the Pedro Infante Club. Tere is an encyclopedia of information about the onetime film star and icon of Mexican popular culture. The book is about relationships and features the fictions Tere tells herself in order to convince herself that it is acceptable for her to continue to see her lover, a married man.

One of the major recurring themes in Chávez's work is the issues women face, including freedom to express themselves. Chávez's social conscience has been a shaping factor throughout her career: frequently she gives workshops to underserved audiences, such as the elderly, developmentally disabled, and the imprisoned. Also, she is deeply rooted in and committed to her community in Las Cruces. She was a founder of and has still served as the artistic director of the Border Book Festival since its inception in 1994, even though it requires a tremendous amount of her time and energy. The festival brings in writers from all over the country and from Mexico.

Chávez earned a bachelor of arts degree in drama in 1971 from New Mexico State University and a master's of fine arts from Trinity University in San Antonio, Texas, in 1974. In 1982 she earned a master's degree in creative writing from the University of New Mexico. (*See also* Mexican American Drama)

Further Reading

Kevane, Bridget, and Juanita Heredia, eds. *Latina Self-Portraits: Interviews with Contemporary Women Writers*. Albuquerque: U of New Mexico P, 2000.

Lomelí, Francisco A., and Carl R. Shirley, eds. "Denise Chavez." *Dictionary of Literary Biography: Chicano Writers*. 2nd series, vol. 122. Detroit: Gale Group, 1992. 70–76.

Trosky, Susan M., Ed. "Denise Chavez." *Contemporary Authors*. Vol. 131. Detroit: Gale Group, 1991. 103–4.

Deborah Owen Moore

CHEE, ALEXANDER (1967–)　Korean American novelist and essayist. Born in South Kingstown, Rhode Island, Chee moved with his family to Korea at the age of nine months when his oceanographer father accepted employment there. When Chee was six years old, his family returned to the United States, moving to Cape Elizabeth, Maine, where Chee lived until attending college at Wesleyan University in Connecticut, which led him to a job at *Out* magazine and eventually to the Iowa Writers Workshop, where he earned his MFA degree. Chee is most known for his debut novel *Edinburgh* (2001), which was published to wide critical and commercial success.

Edinburgh tells the story of a Korean American boy named Aphias Zee, nicknamed Fee, who joins a professional boys choir in Maine and quickly becomes the troupe's star boy soprano. The group is disbanded, however, when authorities uncover that the conductor of the choir is a serial pedophile who has been victimizing his charges for years. Much of *Edinburgh* details the fallout of this incident, as one of Fee's friends commits suicide and another attempts to do so. Fee finds himself engaged in both a sexual and spiritual **identity** crisis, exploring his bisexuality while dabbling in drugs and the religious animism that relates to Fee's Korean ancestry. The book eventually reaches a deadly climax when Fee must confront his attraction to a strange man who turns out to be his former choirmaster's son.

The novel is both a coming of age narrative and an immigrant child narrative, but its frank depictions of drugs, pedophilia, and casual sex ask readers to confront the idea that anyone may harbor a monster within. Chee's complex novel is brought to life through sparse but expressive and lyrical writing that has quickly become characteristic of Chee's unique style. Glowingly reviewed in *The New Yorker,* the *New York Times Book Review, Publishers Weekly,* and *Newsday, Edinburgh* won Chee several awards, including the James Michener/Copernicus Society award and a Lambda Literary Prize.

Foremost among gay and lesbian Asian American authors, Chee actively supports New York's Asian American Writers' Workshop. The son of a Korean father and Caucasian mother, Chee is one of the few gay and lesbian authors who actively explores the Asian **immigration** and **assimilation** experience, especially from the gay and lesbian perspective. His first novel has already established him as a powerful new ethnic voice in contemporary American literature.

Further Reading

Abel, Ann. "In Destiny's Choir." *New York Times* (January 20, 2002): F 19.

Cooper, Michael L. "Alexander Chee's Childhood Feels Like 'A Long Trip by Car, Plane, and Boat'." *Lambda Book Report* (March 2002): 14–15.

Park, Minju. "Homeless." *KoreAm Journal* (April 2004): 37–39.

Michael G. Cornelius

CHERNIN, KIM (1940–)   Jewish American poet, novelist, and memoir writer. Born in the Bronx to Marxist activists Rose Chernin and Paul Kusnitz, Kim Chernin, inspired by the Yiddish oral narratives of her shtetl-born grandmother, rejected political activism in favor of writing narratives of her own experience. Her writing is highly personal and seeks to reconcile the seemingly conflicting components of Chernin's subject position as a Jewish woman, feminist, practicing psychotherapist, and lesbian.

Chernin's writing has perhaps been most profoundly influenced by her relationship with her mother, whose arrest for political insurrection in 1951 created conflict between mother and daughter: Kim was alternately proud of her mother's conviction and hurt by the attention that resulted from the publicity that surrounded the arrest and often caused Kim's peers to ostracize her. She later traveled to Berkeley where she became a poet and mystic, at least in part to differentiate from her mother. She did not begin to reconcile her relationship with her mother until 1967 when her father was killed in a car accident, and Chernin's best-known work, *In My Mother's House: A Daughter's Story* (1983), recounts her journey toward reconciliation as she seeks to create a concept of "home" that includes both daughter and mother.

In fact, mother/daughter relationships in general underlie many of Chernin's works, whether poetry, fiction, psychological study, or memoir—and often these genres seem interchangeable in Chernin's writing. The various themes that are apparent in Chernin's works, including the genres that compose that body of work, often overlap and mesh. Therefore, each of Chernin's works can be read as one part in a larger sequence of writing that explores the role of femininity in traditional and new age religious practice, the role of storytelling as a Jewish and female mode of discourse, eating disorders as problematic female rites of passage, and sexuality—both heterosexual and lesbian—as fluid, unfixed, and alternately sacred.

Chernin has written explicitly about sexuality in *Sex and Other Sacred Games* (1989), a work she coauthored with Renate Stendahl, and in *Crossing the Border: An Erotic Journey* (1994), sexuality is woven into Chernin's autobiographical narrative of her travels to Israel. *My Life as a Boy* (1997) is Chernin's "coming out" narrative in which she examines the social constructions of masculinity and femininity. Chernin has also written explicitly about eating disorders, from both a psychological and personal perspective, in three of her books, *The Obsession: Reflections on the Tyranny of Slenderness* (1981), a collection of poems titled *The Hunger Song* (1982), and *The Hungry Self: Women, Eating and Identity* (1985). In *Reinventing Eve: Modern Woman in Search of Herself* (1987), we see a confluence of all of the aforementioned tropes: mother and daughter relationships, eating, and Jewish feminine **identity.** In this work, Chernin characterizes Eve's consumption of the apple as a desire to connect with a divine femininity—a maternal god figure—that is denied to women in traditional patriarchal religion, and eating what is forbidden becomes a subversive and feminist act in Chernin's revision of the traditional biblical story of Adam and Eve.

Nearly all of Chernin's work expresses the author's desire for community, Jewish, female, or familial. *Crossing the Border*, for example, is a chronicle of Chernin's journey to Israel in 1971 in search of a sense of Jewish communalism, and in *The Flame Bearers: A Novel* (1986), Chernin creates a sect of nontraditional Jewish women who explore the women's experience that has been omitted from traditional Jewish orthodoxy. Chernin's latest novel, *The Girl Who Went and Saw and Came Back* (2002), explores, through the friendship of two female characters, Charlie and Mignon, the precarious distance between madness and religious awakening. Kim Chernin is as much a healer as an author; her life and work deconstruct traditions that have tended to exclude women, and through her writing and psychological practice, Chernin creates—and perhaps restores—a sense of female community. (*See also* Jewish American Lesbian Literature)

Further Reading

Barker-Nunn, Jeanne. "Telling the Mother's Story: History and Connection in the Autobiographies of Maxine Hong Kingston and Kim Chernin." *Women's Studies* 14 (1987): 55–63.

Burstein, Janet Handler. "Recalling Home: American Jewish Women Writers of the New Wave." *Contemporary Literature* 42.4 (2001): 801–24.

Laura Wright

CHESNUTT, CHARLES WADDELL (1858–1932) Novelist, essayist, folklorist, and short story writer. Charles Waddell Chesnutt was one of the first African Americans to gain widespread recognition for his talents as a writer. Born in Ohio in 1858 to free African Americans, Chesnutt was raised in Fayetteville, North Carolina, where he was educated in the public school system. In his early twenties, Chesnutt, having distinguished himself as a leader and educator, was appointed principal of the Normal Colored School in Fayetteville. A few years later, he returned to his birthplace where he established a successful court stenography business. Under the tutelage of a retired judge, he began preparing for the Ohio state bar examination, which he passed in 1887.

In August of that same year, Chesnutt published his first short story in one of the most reputable magazines in the country, the *Atlantic Monthly*. "The Goophered Grapevine" featured Uncle Julius McAdoo, an aged ex-slave who told the tale of a vineyard that had come under the spell of a conjure woman. Chesnutt's work was so well received that he attracted the attention of the prestigious Houghton Mifflin publishing house, which published his first collection of short stories, *The Conjure Woman*, in the spring of 1899. Written in the same vein as "The Goophered Grapevine," which was featured in the collection, *The Conjure Woman* intrigued its predominantly white readership with its tales of conjuring and hoodoo. Chesnutt's unique depiction of African America life and lore earned him the respect of such renowned writers as William Dean Howells, who deemed Chesnutt's stories to be the creation of an honest and original imagination.

Chesnutt's second collection of short stories, *The Wife of His Youth and Other Stories of the Color Line*, was published just a few months after his first. Alarmed by the intraracism that threatened to divide the African American community, Chesnutt demonstrated in *The Wife of His Youth* the perils associated with discriminating against one's own. Drawing on his own experiences as a light-skinned African American, he details the lives and struggles of individuals perched on the socially constructed color line separating black from white. Like his contemporary **W. E. B. Du Bois**, Chesnutt viewed the color line as an obstacle to racial equality and the source of America's "race troubles."

Chesnutt's interest in the color line and the mutability of racial **identity** was the inspiration for his first passing novel, *Mandy Oxendine*, which was published posthumously in 1997. Breaking with the tragic **mulatto** tradition, *Mandy Oxendine* reveals the relative ease with which its "all but white" heroine slips across the color line. That Mandy Oxendine is not destroyed by her "transgression" is perhaps the reason the manuscript was rejected by both the *Atlantic Monthly* and Houghton Mifflin. Chesnutt's subsequent passing narrative, *The House Behind the Cedars*, with its more traditional approach, fared better than *Mandy Oxendine*. Published in 1900, *The House Behind the Cedars* recounts the experiences of two mixed-**race** siblings, John and Rena Walden, who pass in an effort to access the power and privilege not afforded members of their race. Although John Walden emerges from his passing experience relatively unscathed, his sister does not fare as well. Unlike the heroine of *Mandy Oxendine*, Rena Walden meets a tragic end when the secret of her "true" identity is revealed.

Chesnutt's second novel, *The Marrow of Tradition* (1901), was inspired by the 1898 race riot in Wilmington, North Carolina. With its assault on white racist attitudes, *The Marrow of Tradition* alienated some of Chesnutt's earlier admirers, including Howells, who found the novel too "bitter" for his taste. Four years later, Chesnutt published his last novel, *The Colonel's Dream* (1905), which addresses the plight of African Americans in the post-Reconstruction era. Although he continued to devote himself to social and political causes throughout the remainder of his life, Chesnutt's literary career dwindled after the publication of *The Colonel's Dream*. Unable to support himself as a writer, Chesnutt resumed his career as a legal stenographer, publishing only a few more short stories before his death in 1932. Although his popularity had waned, Chesnutt's desire to expose the sophistry of the color line had not. His tireless dedication to improving race relations and his pioneering efforts as a literary artist earned Chesnutt the NAACP's Spingarn Medal in 1928.

Recognizing the power of literature to influence people's perceptions, Chesnutt sought to educate his primarily white reading audience about the evils of race prejudice. Although at times didactic, Chesnutt's works were crafted so as to evoke sympathy in his readers. Through his sensitive depictions of the trials and tribulations of his characters, Chesnutt hoped to cultivate an appreciation for and understanding of the African American community. (*See also* African American Novel)

Further Reading

Andrews, William L. *The Literary Career of Charles W. Chesnutt*. Baton Rouge: Louisiana State UP, 1980.

Duncan, Charles. *The Absent Man: The Narrative Craft of Charles W. Chesnutt*. Athens: Ohio UP, 1998.

McElrath, Joseph R., Jr., ed. *Critical Essays on Charles W. Chesnutt*. New York: G. K. Hall & Co., 1999.

McWilliams, Dean. *Charles W. Chesnutt and the Fictions of Race*. Athens: The U of Georgia P, 2002.

Sundquist, Eric J. *To Wake the Nations: Race in the Making of American Literature*. Cambridge, MA: Harvard UP, 1993.

Carol Goodman

CHIEF SEATTLE (c. 1788–1866)   Native American chief and orator, a.k.a. Seathl. Chief Seattle is most famous for the city that bears his name and for a poignant speech attributed to him. A principal chief among the Duwamish, Suquamish, and other native groups in the Puget Sound region, Seattle remains a prominent and contested figure in the history of the Pacific Northwest. The man the whites called "Seattle" inherited his status as a tribal leader from his father, Schweabe, who was a Suquamish chief, and his mother, Scholitza, who was the daughter of a Duwamish chief. Chief Seattle is credited with uniting native peoples of the Pacific Northwest and encouraging peaceful relations and trade with white settlers, who had begun pouring into the region in the 1790s. His conversion to Catholicism by Jesuit missionaries in the 1830s also contributed to his position as a cultural intermediary. Seattle is said to have combined Christian rituals and traditional tribal beliefs and practices into syncretic religious forms.

In the early 1850s, Dr. David Maynard named a white settlement "Seattle" in honor of the native leader who had advised him to relocate his faltering trading enterprise to a more advantageous point on Elliott Bay. United States officials welcomed the conflation of the man and the trading hub. Having distinguished Seattle as the principal Indian chief of the region, the U.S. government effectively authorized any treaty and land negotiations conducted with the chief as the official relations with Puget Sound Indians. By the time Isaac I. Stevens, the appointed governor of Washington Territory, toured his domain in 1854 to reconnoiter Indian populations, survey land for railway construction, and settle disputed boundaries between the United States and British Canada, Chief Seattle had been confirmed the representative voice of native populations in the region.

The famous speech attributed to Seattle was reportedly addressed to Governor Stevens in late 1854 at the Port Elliott treaty council where the chief ceded native lands to the Americans and agreed to have his people relocated to an Indian reservation. The earliest record of Seattle's speech was published by Henry A. Smith in an 1887 issue of the *Seattle Sunday Star*. Appearing over thirty years after the event, Smith's record of the speech, he admits in his preface, "is but a fragment" of Seattle's entire speech and was derived from "scraps from a diary" he had kept during the treaty proceedings. Nevertheless, because no earlier account of the speech exists, Smith's text remains the closest literary historians have come to a definitive version.

Although some parts of Seattle's speech represent native peoples as obeisant and submissive, other parts resist white encroachment and dominance. On the one hand, Seattle's speech accepts the ideology of the vanishing Indian, repudiates the Indian ethic of revenge, and testifies to the transience of cultures. So too does Smith's preface render a highly stylized, stereotypical portrait of the chief as an imposing noble savage whose dignified presence, grace, and natural eloquence cannot deliver him or his race from inevitable doom. On the other hand, Seattle extols the native beliefs "written in the hearts of our people" and denigrates the laws of the white man's angry God that must be etched in stone lest they be forgotten. In conjunction with Seattle's assertion that "Your God loves your people and hates mine," vastly different attitudes toward the earth separate the "two distinct races." Whereas Native Americans embrace the earth as hallowed ground, whites seek to possess the land temporarily, only so their spirits can "wander off beyond the stars . . . and never return." Seattle insists on the authority of native beliefs in ancestral spirits that shall never depart the earth; the streets of white towns will "throng with the returning hosts that once filled and still love this beautiful land." Try as they might to eradicate Indians, white settlers "will never be alone."

In recent scholarship, questions abound about the authenticity of the speech and the extent to which Smith may have embellished or invented Seattle's words. Aside from the fact that the date of the speech has not been verified, the temporal distance between the treaty council proceedings and the time that Smith published the speech invites doubts about authenticity. Coupled with Smith's reliance on a translator, the flourishes of Victorian diction and classical rhetorical devices in Smith's printed version further complicate matters of authenticity. Yet, though Seattle's native Salishan words are largely lost in translation, Smith's rendering of the speech does evince verbal traces of what a man like Chief Seattle could have articulated. The 1887 text employs some metaphors and turns of phrases characteristic of Salishan dialects and a Chinook pidgin trade language. Beyond these textual matters is the difficulty in placing Seattle, Smith, and Stevens together at a location where such an address likely occurred. It is worth noting too that renewed academic interest in the 1887 text and the historical moment it chronicles has recently prompted scholars to reassess currently circulating variant texts produced in the twentieth century. (*See also* Native American Oratory)

Further Reading

Buerge, David, ed. *Chief Seattle*. Seattle: Sasquatch Books, 1992.

Furtwangler, Albert. *Answering Chief Seattle*. Seattle: U of Washington P, 1997.

Low, Denise. "Contemporary Reinvention of Chief Seattle: Variant Texts of Chief Seattle's 1854 Speech." *The American Indian Quarterly* 19.3 (Summer 1995): 407–24.

Seattle. "Chief Seattle's Speech: The Complete Text of 1887." Trans. Henry A. Smith. *Answering Chief Seattle*. Ed. Albert Furtwangler. Seattle: U of Washington P, 1997. 12–17.

Keat E. Murray

CHILDRESS, ALICE (1916–1994) African American playwright and novelist. Alice Childress was born on October 12, 1916, in Charleston, South Carolina. In 1925 her parents separated and Childress moved with her mother to her grandmother's home in Harlem. Childress's intellect was fostered during her childhood as she was encouraged to feed her appetite for reading and learning. Her grandmother also exposed the young Childress to both the cultural side of the city and the impoverished side, teaching her things that would never leave her. Many of these childhood experiences were later used in Childress's works. Before she entered her senior year of high school, Childress had lost both her mother and her grandmother and was left to take care of herself. One of her first adult decisions was to quit high school without graduating.

Soon after leaving school, Childress married actor Alvin Childress, whom she later divorced. Childress kept both her marriage and divorce dates a guarded secret. It is known that the couple had a child, Jean, Alice Childress's only child, in 1935. Childress remarried, to musician Nathan Woodard, in 1957.

Childress's life as a playwright began in a classical way; she began to act with the American Negro Theater in Harlem in 1943. Six years later she wrote her first play, *Florence* (1949), for this same company. The circumstances surrounding her writing of this one-act play are interesting. Childress wrote the play overnight after engaging in a discussion with a group of other actors, including Sydney Poitier, about how long a good play takes to write. The consensus was that nothing worthwhile could be written in one night. Childress proved the group wrong with her tale of the mother of Florence, the latter of whom is a struggling actress in New York City. Florence herself is never met in the play, which takes place in the waiting room of a train station. Instead we see Florence through the eyes of her mother, Mama, who is at first intent on convincing her daughter to give up her unsuccessful acting career to return home. Mama's conversation with a white actress, Mrs. Carter, ultimately convinces Mama to change her mind and to instead encourage Florence in her acting efforts. It is Mrs. Carter's supposition that Florence would be better suited for a job as a domestic worker than as an actress that riles up Mama's courage to support her daughter's dreams.

Childress continued to work with themes of **racism**, gender inequities, and women's relationships with each other in her subsequent works. Because of the controversial social themes of some of her work, significant time lapsed between her writing and the actual publishing of the pieces. Her play *Trouble in Mind*, for instance, was written and initially produced in 1955 but was not published until 1971. In this play Childress works not only with the theme of racism through lynching but also with the theme of facing the courage of one's convictions as the main character decides she has had enough of the racist treatment doled out by the director and encourages her fellow black actors to rebel as well.

Not long after she wrote *Trouble in Mind,* Childress published *Like One of the Family . . . Conversations from a Domestic's Life* (1956). This series of fictitious vignettes is based on Childress's own experiences with domestic work, something she engaged in to supplement her sparse acting and writing income. *Like One of the Family,* dedicated to Childress's grandmother, presents the views of the protagonist, Mildred, through conversations that she has with her friends about her life. Childress focuses on the problems facing black domestic workers in this book, but she does so in an easy, chatty manner. This foray of Childress's into a nondramatic genre proved successful. The *Baltimore Afro-American* hired Childress to write a column called "Here's Mildred," based on the day-to-day adventures of the book's main character.

Although *Like One of the Family* stands as Childress's sole collection of short fiction, Childress continued to write plays throughout her life, ending with the play *Moms . . . A Praise Play for a Black Comedienne* (1993), which celebrates the life of Jackie "Moms" Mabley. Two of Childress's more controversial plays are *Wedding Band* (1973) and *Wine in the Wilderness* (1973). *Wedding Band* was written in 1966 but did not see a major production until

1972. This play deals with the issue of interracial marriage in South Carolina during a time when such a union was prohibited by law. *Wine in the Wilderness* was first produced in 1969 and deals with both classism and sexism in the life of a young African American woman who turns out to be much wiser than her associates first deem her to be.

Childress began to work with the genre of young adult literature in the 1970s. Her most famous young adult novel, *A Hero Ain't Nothin' but a Sandwich,* was published in 1973. Benjie, the protagonist, deals with both drug addiction and a rough adjustment to a stepfather in this novel. Childress's next young adult novel, *Rainbow Jordan,* was published in 1981 and focuses on the stress the title character faces as he attempts to cope with the lack of a solid parental figure. This novel was followed by Childress's third and last young adult novel, *Those Other People* (1989). In this novel the young protagonist struggles with problems he encounters, especially with his parents, because of his sexual orientation. In all of her young adult fiction, Childress strives to work with themes of racial significance as well as with themes important to the contemporary adolescent experience.

In the midst of her fiction writing, Childress published her only adult novel, *A Short Walk Home,* in 1979. The protagonist here is Cora, who lives through only the first four decades of the twentieth century. In those decades, however, she deals with all of the incredible racial and gender tensions that were truly existent during that time period, continuing the major themes that Childress always found so important to portray in her work.

Childress rounded out her literary **canon** with several nonfiction essays that she wrote throughout her life for a variety of publications, including *The Negro Digest* and *Essence.* She wrote on women in American literature, on black writers, on theater, and on other accomplished artists. She is seen today as a writer who took important thematic chances in her work and who always strove to find the complement between life and literature.

Alice Childress lost her only child to cancer on Mother's Day of 1990. Childress succumbed to her own battle with cancer on August 14, 1994, in New York City. (*See also* African American Drama)

Further Reading

Brown-Guillory, Elizabeth. *Their Place on Stage: Black Women Playwrights in America.* Westport, CT: Greenwood Press, 1988.

Jennings, LaVinia Delois. *Alice Childress.* New York: Twayne, 1995.

Smith, Karen Patricia. *African-American Voices in Young Adult Literature.* Metuchen NJ: Scarecrow, 1994.

Terry D. Novak

CHIN, FRANK (1940–) Fifth-generation Chinese American playwright, short story writer, novelist, and essayist. In a career spanning five decades and multiple genres, Frank Chin is best known as one of the founding editors of *Aiiieeeee!* (1974), among the earliest and most influential anthologies of Asian American writing, published, significantly, by

Howard University Press. In 1991 Meridian reissued a substantially expanded version—*The Big Aiiieeeee!*—suggesting the mainstreaming of Asian American literature from its emergence in the cultural nationalist energies of the late 1960s and early 1970s. Chin also enjoys the distinction of being the first Asian American playwright to be produced off-Broadway at the American Place Theatre in New York with *The Chickencoop Chinaman* (1972) and *The Year of the Dragon* (1974). His most recent work includes a collection of essays, *Bulletproof Buddhists and Other Essays* (1998), and an edited history of the Japanese experience in America, *Born in the USA: A Study of Japanese America 1889–1947* (2002).

The two decades that span the publications of *Aiiieeeee!* and *The Big Aiiieeeee!* witness an instructive shift in Chin's construction of Chinese America, a dislocation that reflects the emergence of a denationalizing global political economy: the nation-based identity politics of the early 1970s located Chinese American **identity** in a heroic tradition of railroad building, but a transpacific swerve by the late 1980s supported an argument for the centrality of Chinese mythology in Chinese American writing. Chin typically elaborates his ethnopolitical critique of American society through the metaphor of the alienated artist/writer; the father-son trope figures prominently as well and assumes a significant political and historical resonance throughout Chin's work. Taken together, Chin's oeuvre strives to articulate an enabling Asian American identity and history in a culture that has historically produced demeaning, Procrustean images of Asian Americans.

Chin's early work sounds a familiar militant rhetoric, a demeanor that owes as much to Sun Tzu's *The Art of War* as it does to the political climate of 1960s America. In Chin's view, whereas African Americans and Latinos enjoy an organic and inherited sense of their American identity through an enabling expressive culture, Chinese Americans are defined by an impotent Chinatown "buck buck bagaw"—hence the title of his first play. This is perhaps Chin's defining polemic, an argument embodied in the multiple meanings of the whimsical signifier *Aiiieeeee!* Ostensibly the mortified cry of the victimized Asian American man, *Aiiieeeee!* simultaneously riffs on a tradition of lyric expression from the Puritan jeremiad to Whitman's *Song of Myself* and **Allen Ginsberg**'s *Howl*. This cry is an assertion of ethnic difference as well as cultural propriety, expressing the right of Asian American writers to a place in the **canon** of American letters.

It hardly surprises then that Chin's first major work *The Chickencoop Chinaman* dramatizes the main character's genesis in an explosion of linguistic mimicry. As the stage directions inform the reader, Tam Lum's speech rapidly shifts from W. C. Fields to American Midwest and Bible Belt holy roller, and his own normal speech jumps between black and white rhythms and accents. In this sequence, Chin brilliantly parodies the opening lines of the Bible, excoriating the missionary dimensions of Christian conversion in the assimilation of Chinese Americans, another of his favorite hobbyhorses. The balance of the play presents Tam and his friend BlackJap Kenji on a quest to find the father of legendary black boxer Ovaltine Jack Dancer, whose life they intend to document on film. But no such father exists, suggesting the failed promise of **black nationalism**, and the play ends with Tam narrating the story of a Chinese ancestor who participated in a heroic tradition of railroad building. Chin revisits this theme in "Railroad Standard Time" (1978) and "The Eat and Run Midnight People" (1976), the lead stories in his award-winning collection, *The Chinaman Pacific and Frisco R. R. Co.* (1988). As a father quest, Tam's family romance resounds on a historical level, symbolizing the journey back—in search of Chinese American history.

Set in San Francisco during the American bicentennial, Chin's second play, *The Year of the Dragon,* analyzes the disposition of Fred Eng's family, whose members' lives narrate the legacy of a traumatic Chinese American history. Central to this history is Fred's father, the ailing patriarch of the Eng family, who cannot imagine for Fred a life beyond the confines of Chinatown. Pa Eng symbolizes all those Chinese sojourners who came to America, the Gold Mountain, and his near death signifies an increasingly obsolescent way of life that imprisons his son Fred, who is culturally a bastard, disenfranchised by a law that bans his biological mother's reunification with his father. An aspiring writer two years into college, Fred must return to Chinatown and support the family as behooves the eldest son, but the cost is high: as top tour guide of the Eng Chinatown tour business, the fortysomething bachelor must perform a minstrel show, donning the mask of a white man playing a Chinaman in order to deliver a Hollywood image of Chinatown to the tourists who come to observe the spectacle of Chinese New Year. Fred embodies a recurring theme in Chin's oeuvre: the writer alienated from his family and society. Fred is reduced to a life of masquerade, consigned to earn a living by perpetuating demeaning stereotypes of Chinatown. That Pa Eng dies before he can deliver the speech his son has scripted for him suggests the cul-de-sac of Fred's artistic ambitions, a fate that leaves him without a usable past and conscripts his identity to a master narrative that haunts his life; thus, the Chinese New Year becomes the bad old year, projecting a future that the past has already rehearsed.

If *The Chickencoop Chinaman* and *The Year of the Dragon* dramatize the predicament of Chinese America, *Donald Duk* (1991) and *Gunga Din Highway* (1994) imagine a potential resolution in a salutary synthesis of Chinese and American culture. Donald Duk, the eponymous, assimilated, twelve-year-old hero of Chin's first novel, aspires to be a dancer like Fred Astaire. At the beginning of the novel, he detests his name and all things Chinese, a denial of his heritage that becomes increasingly charged with the approach of Chinese New Year. But with the help of his progressive friend Arnold Azalea, Donald comes to understand the nature of his self-contempt and gains a sense of ethnic pride and agency. Refusing the chauvinistic omissions of his history teacher and the history books, Donald comes to understand the heroism of Chinese labor in the construction of America's railroads: history and myth converge in Donald's unconscious, a dreamscape that stages the heroic characters and traditions of Luo Guanzhong's *Romance of the Three Kingdoms* (fourteenth century) and Shi Nai'an's *Water Margin* (fourteenth century) on the American frontier. Donald is finally able to construct an identity for himself in the language game of this enabling ancestry, a lineage that comes to life in the preparations of his uncle Donald and father King Duk, who will play the arduous role of the epic warrior-poet Kwan Kung as part of the New Year's Day festivities.

Chin's second novel *Gunga Din Highway* takes its title from the Rudyard Kipling ballad celebrating the Indian water boy who helps the British fight his own people. Here, Gunga Din becomes a metaphor for "fake" Asian American writers who succeed by catering to the tastes and values of a white mainstream audience. The novel itself takes up many of the same themes that *Donald Duk* introduces but on a grander scale, encompassing everything from Hollywood movies and American popular culture to Chinese mythology. The story focuses on the pernicious cultural legacy of Charlie Chan, a screen image that Chin finds especially troubling. Ironically, in the novel, the father Longman Kwan aspires to be the first Chinese to play Charlie Chan. Chin exposes Charlie Chan as the creation of Hollywood's racist love, but also lampoons Longman Kwan and others like him who naively desire to reprise a role that will perpetuate stereotypes of Asian Americans. It remains for Longman's son, the aptly named Ulysses S. Kwan, to invent new images of Asian Americans on the stage.

One of the novel's most comical elements introduces Pandora Toy, Charlie Chan's ardent admirer and the author of *"The Conqueror Woman,"* an unmistakable reference to **Maxine Hong Kingston** and her highly lauded first novel, **The Woman Warrior** (1976). Indeed, it would not be too far off to suggest that *Gunga Din Highway* is Chin's riposte to Kingston's second novel, *Tripmaster Monkey* (1989), whose protagonist Wittman Ah Sing remains one of the most imaginative and sophisticated portraits of Frank Chin to date. Chin's by now familiar diatribe against Kingston, a writer who is his exact contemporary but ideological opposite, typifies the troubling and much commented-on chauvinism of Chin's ethnopolitical project. But the Chin-Kingston schism and the feminist critiques of his work need not blind contemporary readers to Chin's importance in Asian American writing—his intellectual breadth and brilliance as a polemicist make him one of American culture's chief provocateurs. (*See also* Chinese American Novel, Chinese American Stereotypes)

Further Reading

Li, David Leiwei. *"Aiiieeeee!* and the Predicament of Asian American Articulation." *Imagining the Nation: Asian American Literature and Cultural Consent.* Stanford, CA: Stanford UP, 1998. 21–43.

Andrew Shin

CHIN, MARILYN MEI LING (1955–) Chinese American poet, translator, editor, and short story writer. Known for her striking combination of forms, spare prose, and unwavering intensity of voice, Marilyn Chin sets out to capture the **identity** of the Chinese American in her poetry by mediating between East and West. Her three volumes of poetry, *Dwarf Bamboo* (1987), *The Phoenix Gone, The Terrace Empty* (1994), and *Rhapsody in Plain Yellow* (2002), all deal with issues of **assimilation** and retention of culture.

In *Dwarf Bamboo*, Chin seeks to define the Chinese American as an individual within the context of community, through locating the self in the greater ongoing history of Chinese America. She sees this history as inextricably linked to China and incorporates Chinese history into her poetry in order to cultivate and reclaim the history relevant to the Chinese American self and community. Thus, the epigraph of *Dwarf Bamboo* is taken from a poem by the Tang Dynasty poet Bai Jüyi in order to locate her English poetry within a Chinese tradition, melding both East and West into a new poetical form, from which a new cultural self might emerge.

Chin's attention to the Chinese American's plight of mediating a dual heritage is mirrored in her use of both Eastern and Western poetic forms and linguistic choices. Throughout her poetry, Chin incorporates Chinese characters. In "That Half Is Almost Gone" (*Rhapsody*), Chin notes that she plays with both the visual and auditory representation of the Chinese character for love. She also toys with the Chinese *fu* form in the title poem of the same collection. Yet, lest her new cultural form be unintelligible, Chin appends notes for her reader, marginalizing none. Despite Chin's project of creating a new, hybrid cultural form to reflect Chinese American identity, she does not attempt to speak for all Chinese Americans. Thus, Chin invokes satire and irony to create truth in dissonance.

Retention of her Chinese heritage is never easy, as Chin reveals through much of her poetry. In "That Half Is Gone" (*Rhapsody*), Chin fears exile from her Chinese culture and language, as well as the inability to communicate with her own mother. Cultural retention becomes a labor of love, necessitated by sustaining continuity between the past and present generations.

In Chin's later volumes of poetry, she begins to incorporate the stories of Chinese women into her poetry, which allows her to give voice to the silenced, creating dialogue. In the title poem of *Phoenix*, Chin moves through many different historical periods in both China and America, connecting the voices of a concubine and a mother and her daughter. In so doing, she suggests both the continuity and evolution of Chinese American identity. (*See also* Chinese American Poetry)

Further Reading

Gery, John. "'Mocking My Own Happiness': Authenticity, Heritage, and Self-Erasure in the Poetry of Marilyn Chin." *Lit: Literature Interpretation Theory* 12.1 (2001): 25–45.

Anastasia D. Wright

CHINESE AMERICAN AUTOBIOGRAPHY   Although **Maxine Hong Kingston**'s *Woman Warrior: Memoirs of a Girlhood among Ghosts* (1976) was not the first work of Chinese American autobiography, it generated an interest in the genre that, in effect, established the genre as an area of academic interest. Kingston's book is a collection of five narratives, each of which provides a sense of the hazards of being both Chinese and female. In "No Name Woman," Kingston tells the story of an unmarried aunt on her father's side of the family who became pregnant and was so denigrated by her own family and by the other people in her village that she eventually drowned herself. Simply by writing the narrative, Kingston is violating her family's absolute silence on an episode in the family history that they have been determined to forget, as if the act of forgetting can eventually eradicate history and even her aunt's existence. In offering this memoir as an alternative to forgetting, Kingston seems to be highlighting the irony that the oxymoronic concept of deliberate forgetting is itself an assertion of memory. In "White Tiger," Kingston relates a Chinese folk tale about a girl named Fa Mu Lan who becomes an unlikely warrior and defeats the enemies of her village. "Sharman" describes how Kingston's own mother became a doctor, violating just about every expectation of a young woman in her cultural milieu. "At the Western Gate" is another moving narrative about one of Kingston's aunts. In this instance, the aunt travels to America to be reunited with her husband only to discover that he has married another woman and started another family. Finally, in "A Song for the Barbarian Reed Pipe," Kingston describes her own struggles to adapt to America and to synthesize the Chinese and American aspects of her **identity**. The "ghosts" of the title may be understood in multiple ways: they are, at once, the dead ancestors, the people whose stories have been forgotten or repressed, the people who have been left behind in China and are now "alive" to the immigrants only as memories, and the immigrants themselves who feel a profound sense of dislocation and move among their new countrymen with a sense of unbelonging, with the feeling that their presence has at most an ephemeral impact on the American political, economic, social, and cultural landscape.

In *China Men* (1980), Kingston examines the experiences of three generations of men in her family and in the process provides a social, economic, and cultural history of Chinese Americans on the West Coast during the twentieth century.

One of the first widely read Chinese American autobiographies was American-born **Jade Snow Wong**'s *Fifth Chinese Daughter* (1950). The book presents a thoughtful account of her lifelong efforts to find a satisfactory balance between the Chinese and the American elements of her heritage and her experience. The sections dealing with her upbringing are noteworthy not only as a sensitive narrative of maturation but also for the intimate details they provide about Chinese American life in the 1920s and 1930s. Interestingly, Wong's second autobiographical book, *No Chinese Stranger* (1975), was published the year before Kingston's *Woman Warrior*, and so despite the quarter-century between Wong's two volumes, it cannot be said that she was attempting to cash in on Kingston's success. *No Chinese Stranger* concerns Wong's adulthood. The centerpiece of the narrative is the account of her family's trip to China shortly after it was opened to Western tourists.

In *Nine Hundred Years in the Life of a Chinese Family* (1988), Chinese American journalist Francis Ching locates his own experiences within a truly expansive and exhaustive family history. In *Beyond the Narrow Gate: The Journey of Four Chinese Women from the Middle Kingdom to Middle America* (1999), Leslie Chang chronicles the passages of her mother and three of her mother's friends from the political turmoil and warfare that convulsed China in the 1930s and 1940s to very sedate lives in suburban America. At root, Chang is trying to understand how her bicultural identity and her behavior have been shaped by her often very limited understanding of the experiences that created very different needs and expectations among the women of her mother's generation.

A naturalized American citizen, Katherine Wei-Sender has had an impressive career in corporate management. With the novelist Terry Quinn, she wrote the memoir *Second Daughter: Growing Up in China, 1930–1949* (1984). Inevitably, the story of her maturation provides a very personalized corollary to the titanic historical events that completely transformed China during those two decades. Ironically, despite the terrible turmoil of those years, Wei-Sender's narrative is tinged with nostalgic sentiment both for her lost youth and for the China that disappeared with the Communist victory.

Primarily known as a writer of self-help nonfiction titles, former fashion model **Aimee E. Liu** has explored the theme of survival in an autobiographical volume and a family history. In *Solitaire* (1979), she describes her own recovery from a severe eating disorder, and in *Cloud Mountain* (1997), she traces the stories of her grandparents, a politically radicalized Chinese scholar and an American woman who met during the disastrous San Francisco earthquake of 1906. The couple spent most of their married life in China, negotiating a series of great political upheavals from the overthrow of the Manchu rule to the Communist takeover under Mao.

In what amounts to a subgenre of these autobiographies, Chinese Americans have recounted their experiences in China during the Cultural Revolution. In *Life and Death in Shanghai* (1987), Nien Cheng offers a vivid account of her extended persecution at the hands of the Red Guards. Cheng had worked for Shell Oil at the time of the Communist takeover of mainland China in 1949, and she had never found a way to eliminate suspicions that she privately maintained bourgeois attitudes. Because of those suspicions, the Red Guards held her in solitary confinement for more than six years. In *Single Tear: A Family's Persecution, Love, and Endurance in Communist China*, Ningkum Wu explains how as a University of Chicago professor, he responded to a request by the Communist government and returned voluntarily to China to teach. For the next three decades, he and his family would be subjected to recurring periods of persecution that came to a terrible climax during the Cultural Revolution.

In *The Winged Seed* (1995), the poet **Li-Young Lee** recalls his family's escape from China when he was still a very young boy and their subsequent passages through Hong Kong, Macao, Japan, and Indonesia before they secured visas to enter the United States in 1964. Because he has written compelling poems about his family's experiences in Indonesia, Lee has sometimes been identified with a growing group of Chinese American authors with roots in Southeast Asia. Raised in Malaysia, **Shirley Geok-lin Lim** has written creditably in three genres—poetry, the short story, and the novel—while establishing herself in an academic career, producing influential literary criticism, and editing a number of widely used anthologies of literature from East Asia and the Pacific region. In *Among the White-Moon Faces: An Asian-American Memoir of Homelands* (1996), Lim presents a candid account of a tough childhood and adolescence—her mother deserted the family and her father had a harsh personality and fixed expectations of his only daughter. She found an avenue of escape in academic success and pursued it with an almost relentless determination, earning scholarships to universities first in Malaysia and then in the United States. Throughout this time, she often experienced an uneasy awareness of her foreignness and an unsettling sense of dislocation. In response, Lim has embraced the "warrior" persona defined by Maxine Hong Kingston.

In *Falling Leaves: A True Story of an Unwanted Chinese Daughter* (1998), Adeline Yen Mah describes her troubled relationship with her stepmother, a woman with some French ancestry who had, from the beginning, nothing but antipathy toward Mah. Mah's father was a millionaire, and with his wife and all of his children except Mah, he managed to escape from China just ahead of the Communist takeover. Subsequently raised in the relative isolation of a Shanghai boarding school, Mah, like Shirley Geok-Lin Lim, channeled all of her energies into her studies, and after several fortuitous turns of circumstance, she ultimately set up a medical practice in California as an anesthesiologist. As her parents aged, Mah reconciled with them and even helped to care for them, and yet, when her father and then her stepmother died, Mah was betrayed again when she was pointedly denied any share of the inheritance. So Mah's autobiography provides a sort of purgative testimony, permitting her to have the last word on a relationship in which she was always an unequal party. Ironically, her siblings have spurned Mah because of the book, feeling that her chronicle of their stepmother's betrayals has been itself a betrayal of the family's privacy. In the end, *Falling Leaves* is as much about the continuities and the changes within the Chinese family in the mid-twentieth century as it is about the eccentricities of this particular Chinese family.

Further Reading

Lee, Jid. *From the Promised Land to Home: Trajectories of Selfhood in Asian-American Women's Autobiography.* Las Colinas, TX: Ide House, 1998.

Leydesdorff, Selma, Luisa Passerini, and Paul Thompson, eds. *Gender and Memory.* New York: Oxford UP, 1996.

Madsen, Deborah L. *The Woman Warrior and China Men.* Gale Study Guides to Great Literature, Vol. 9. Detroit: Gale, 2001.

Wong, Sau-ling Cynthia, ed. *Maxine Hong Kingston's "The Woman Warrior": A Casebook.* New York: Oxford UP, 1999.

Martin Kich

CHINESE AMERICAN DRAMA   Prior to the 1960s, theater created by Chinese Americans was scarce, generally confined to the occasional revival of classical Chinese operas or the educational theater practices seen in schools and universities, particularly in Hawai'i. With the establishment of the first Asian American theater in 1965 (the East West Players in Los Angeles), the Asian American theater movement began in earnest, offering new opportunities for Chinese Americans interested in playwriting, directing, acting, and design. Since this time, Chinese American playwrights have made significant contributions to the Asian American theater movement, a fact that reflects the community's history of early **immigration** to the United States and its standing as the largest Asian American population today.

Chinese American playwrights garner a number of "firsts" in the broad vision of Asian American theater. For instance, Gladys Li (1910–) was the first Asian American playwright of record in the United States. Writing during the early twentieth century, Li, a Hawaiian-born Chinese American, proved an active advocate for Asian American theater and film during her lifetime, winning both an Academy Award for her documentary film *Kukan* and a Bicentennial Woman of the Year Award by the National Association of Women Artists of America. Writing many years before the Asian American theater movement began, Li emerged from the educational theater venue, writing three plays during her college years at the University of Hawai'i. All of her works, *The Submission of Rose Moy* (1925), *The White Serpent* (1927), and *The Law of Wu Wei* (1928), received production at the Arthur Andrews Theatre of the University of Hawai'i and were published by the school literary magazine *Hawai'i Quill Magazine.*

One of the chief themes of Li's plays is the irreconcilable difference between traditional Chinese and modern American cultures. For example, in *The Submission of Rose Moy,* a young Chinese American woman struggles between her desire for a western education and her parents' wish that she follow the traditional domestic path for Chinese women. Rose Moy finds that there can be no compromise between her quest for American independence and her filial obligations as a Chinese daughter. At the end of the play, she submits to her Eastern ancestral traditions, fainting to the ground as she concludes that there can be no true meeting between East and West. *The Law of Wu Wei* echoes similar sentiments about the conflict between traditional Chinese filial obligations and the Western value of personal freedom. In this play, Li details the failed romance between a Chinese man, bound by family to marry a woman in China, and the Chinese American woman who he prefers.

This assumption that Eastern and Western cultures are eternally separate is echoed in the early dramatic work of Shih-I Hsiung (1902–91). Though Hsiung was born in China and spent his writing career in Hong Kong and London, he reveals a strong kinship to Li in his awareness of the stark cultural divide between China and the West. His plays, *Lady Precious Stream: An Old Chinese Play Done into English According to its Traditional Style* (1934) and *The Romance of the Western Chamber* (1935), were devised to educate Western audiences in the appreciation of the Chinese culture. Toward this end, he created English-language plays based on classical Chinese dramatic traditions, hoping to instill his audience with a respect for the artistic traditions of a "foreign" society.

The first significant wave of Chinese American playwrights rejected Li and Hsiung's assumption of an eternal East-West cultural divide. Emerging during the early 1970s, this generation of playwrights promoted a new vision of the Chinese American **identity**, an ethnic identity that was a unique blending of Chinese and American cultures. Building on the ethnic consciousness-raising of the 1960s, Chinese American dramatists explored the complex and multifaceted experiences of Chinese Americans, often seeking to uncover the lost narratives and invisible lives of their parents, grandparents, and great-grandparents. This initial period of Chinese American playwriting, therefore, is notable for its focus on **immigration**, early life in the United States, the changing Chinese American family, Chinese American identity and cultural traditions, and the issue of **assimilation** into the white American culture.

Furthermore, Chinese American playwriting, as well as Asian American playwriting in general, can be defined in part by its strong consciousness of "otherness," the ethnic stereotyping and abjection enforced by the dominant culture's media and national identity. Responding to this social phenomena, many of these plays attempt to define the Chinese American identity in positive and human terms, often relying on theatrical realism to help develop a sense of on-stage authenticity and realness.

Again, in the broad vision of Asian American theater, Chinese American playwrights may claim numerous "firsts." **Frank Chin** (1940–), a member of the first wave of Chinese American playwrights, is the first Asian American playwright to have received national attention for his dramatic writing. His play, *The Chickencoop Chinaman*, produced by the American Place Theatre in New York in 1972, proved an angry and rebellious investigation into the plight of the socially displaced Chinese American male. His second major play, *Year of the Dragon* (1974), offered a provocative and unsettling view of life in an American Chinatown. Chin, who has worked extensively as an editor, fiction writer, and advocate for Asian American literature and theater, has rallied against what he views as the assimilationist tendencies of some of his fellow writers. Chin has, however, also been subject to sharp criticism for the chauvinism, anger, and offensive language expressed in his plays. A colorful figure in the early stage of Asian American theater, Chin's rise to public attention signaled the beginning of a more public presence for Asian American theater artists.

David Henry Hwang (1957–), another member of the first wave of Chinese American playwrights, is the first Asian American playwright to win a Tony Award for Best Play (1988). A leading playwright in the contemporary theater scene today, Hwang based his groundbreaking play, *M. Butterfly*, on a real-life incident of international espionage and sexual misidentification. In this work, Hwang severely critiques the imperialistic fantasies of Western men toward Asian women, embodying his argument in the relationship between a French diplomat and a Chinese opera singer. Though the French diplomat pursues an oppressive romantic relationship with the Chinese opera singer, who he believes to be the "ideal" woman, the singer is ultimately revealed to be a man.

M. Butterfly is not only Asian American theater's best-known play, it is also one of its most controversial. Given Hwang's characterization of the leading Chinese character Song Liling as a seductive transvestite homosexual, one who is also an undercover Communist spy, Hwang has been accused of reinstating negative stereotypes of Asian males. While Hwang's aim is to deconstruct Western views of Asian gendered identities in the blurred identity of Song Liling, his use of conventional assumptions about Chinese secrecy and sexual exoticism troubles some spectators and scholars seeking more positive depictions of Asian peoples. This ongoing controversy reflects both the political complexity of Hwang's drama and the difficulty in representing Asian characters on Western stages. Made into a feature film starring Jeremy Irons and John Lone in 1993, *M. Butterfly* has been the most widely publicized and discussed of Asian American plays to date.

Less controversial than either Chin or Hwang, Genny Lim (1946–) is representative of many first wave playwrights in her steady quest to uncover the lost narratives of early Chinese immigrants. Known for her careful studies of late nineteenth- and early twentieth-century Chinese immigration and for her unique research at **Angel Island**, Lim has written two significant works, *Paper Angels* (1978) and *Bitter Cane* (1989). Both plays investigate the hardships and personal difficulties suffered by early Chinese immigrants, offering spectators meaningful insight into the immigration process, labor and work conditions, and the isolated living environments of first generation Chinese immigrants.

As a genre, Chinese American drama has proven highly diverse, fostering not only traditional plays but also visual-movement work, solo performance, and dramatized fiction. Theater artists such as **Ping Chong** (1946–) and **Dan Kwong** (1954–) have explored the boundaries and processes of theatrical performance, developing nationally recognized pieces in "theater of images" and solo narrative, respectively. Mainstream stage-versions of successful Chinese American novels such as *The Flower Drum Song*, *The Woman Warrior*, and *The Joy Luck Club* also merit inclusion in the genre of Chinese American drama. Of particular note, the original musical-version of *The Flower Drum Song* (based on a novel by **C. Y. Lee**) was reworked by David Henry Hwang in 2002 to address a more contemporary perspective of Chinese American life, particularly in the area of female gender roles.

Chinese American drama benefits from the continued emergence of new writers. **Chay Yew** (1966–), a self-proclaimed member of the second wave of Chinese American playwrights, is one of the leading new voices in American theater. Known for his innovative stylistic invention, Yew, a Singapore-born Chinese, has achieved international acclaim for *Porcelain* (1992) and *A Language of their Own* (1994), two dramas that investigate the complexities of gay intercultural romance. In his short career, Yew has presented characters with diverse racial and national identities, as well as with differing class backgrounds, sexual orientations, and cultural histories. This dynamic dramaturgy reflects Yew's own transglobal experience and identity.

In many ways, Yew's work is representative of the developing **canon** of second wave Chinese American playwrights. In this new phase of writing, issues of ethnic identity are often superseded by concerns about the Chinese American experience in a multicultural society and the ethics of the post–ethnic-identity political sphere. Clearly, as the Chinese American identity grows and evolves on the intercultural global stage, Chinese American dramas will reflect these changes.

Further Reading

Eng, Alvin. ed. *Tokens*. Philadelphia: Temple UP, 1999.

Lee, Josephine. *Performing Asian America, Race and Ethnicity on the Contemporary Stage*. Philadelphia: Temple UP, 1997.

Moy, James S. *Marginal Sights, Staging the Chinese in America*. Iowa City: U of Iowa P, 1993.

Kimberley M. Jew

CHINESE AMERICAN NOVEL The Chinese American novel emerged as an aesthetic response to a set of specific historical, social, and political circumstances. Like the larger novel tradition, which developed out of an array of genres, such as romance, history, autobiography, and popular journalism, the Chinese American novel assimilates elements of history, autobiography, and myth. Its crowning achievement lies in the imaginative brilliance of **Maxine Hong Kingston**'s widely read novels, *The Woman Warrior: Memoirs of a Girlhood among Ghosts* (1976), *China Men* (1980), and *Tripmaster Monkey: His Fake Book* (1989), a corpus that transcends conventional generic boundaries. Although *Tripmaster Monkey* is regarded as unequivocal fiction, both *The Woman Warrior* and *China Men* are largely autobiographical, narrating history through family stories.

437

The case of Chinese Eurasian sisters **Edith Eaton** and **Winnifred Eaton**, arguably the first Chinese—and Asian—North American writers, exemplifies the complex ways in which literary form shapes and is shaped by the audience, cultural values, and political climate. Edith Eaton wrote primarily short stories and journalistic pieces about Chinese life in the United States and Canada. Although she penned her essays under her given name Edith, she invariably published the fiction under the Chinese nom-de-plume Sui Sin Far (narcissus). Eaton's authorial identifications suggest a canny awareness of her audiences and a process of self-legitimation: In fighting for the rights of Chinese North Americans in articles published in mainstream newspapers, she invokes the cultural authority of "Edith Eaton"; but when writing her short fiction she lays claim as "Sui Sin Far" to ethnic authenticity and insider knowledge of Chinese life.

Edith Eaton's sister Winnifred Eaton engaged in similar performances of identity, exploiting the prevailing cult of japonisme—the West's interest in Japanese culture and art—in order to market her interracial romances. Curiously, as the earliest known Chinese American novelist, she adopted a fictional Japanese persona and wrote books populated with Japanese, Caucasian, and Eurasian characters, but no Chinese. As Onoto Watanna, Winnifred Eaton published more than a dozen novels, one of which, *A Japanese Nightingale* (1901), was adapted for Broadway in 1903. Unlike her sister Edith, who heroically embraced her Chinese ancestry and asserted the rights of the Chinese in the face of rampant Sinophobia, Winnifred, it is argued, exploited the exoticization of the Japanese and sold out her heritage for the ethnic hierarchies of the marketplace. Certainly, the punitive terms of the 1882 **Chinese Exclusion Act**, which prohibited the entry of most classes of Chinese to America, in comparison to the relatively benign 1907 Gentlemen's Agreement (curtailing Japanese **immigration**), would argue for Edith's political stature as a writer who refused to pass. But this approach is perhaps overly simplistic and diverts attention from both sisters' ingenious negotiation of their audiences and a patriarchal publishing industry through ethnic affiliation. Winnifred Eaton's successful performances reflect the importance of sociopolitical context in the literary marketplace—the mirror of cultural taste and value—a circumstance subsequent generations of Chinese American novelists responded to in different ways.

Early Chinese American writers, like the Eaton sisters, confronted a culture that viewed the Chinese as unassimilable aliens. In the face of such pervasive xenophobia, they strove to promote positive images of the Chinese. The changing fortunes of the Chinese during the World War II era witnessed the emergence of the modern Chinese American novel tradition. The Chinese alliance with America and the advent of Pearl Harbor on December 7, 1941, reversed the traditional attitudes toward the Japanese and Chinese: as Japan came to be reviled, Chinese stock rose, along with an increased interest in Chinese culture. The Chinese Exclusion Act was repealed in 1943, although the 1924 quota of 105 remained in place. The new geopolitical alliances and Americans' newfound interest in the Chinese enabled the popular reception of the two most noteworthy works of the period, Pardee Lowe's *Father and Glorious Descendant* (1943) and **Jade Snow Wong**'s *Fifth Chinese Daughter* (1950). In both autobiographies, tradition collides with modernity as the second generation's embrace of mainstream myths of individuality confronts the stiff resistance of the old world embodied in the patriarchal authority of the father.

Jade Snow Wong's *Fifth Chinese Daughter* is an especially compelling testimony to the myth of possessive individualism because of its legacy for future generations of female Chinese American novelists. Born into working-class scarcity in San Francisco's Chinatown, Wong became a scholarship student, successful potter and writer, and cultural emissary for the United States in Asia. Wong's achievements are all the more remarkable given her subordinate status as a woman in a traditional Chinese household, a daughter whose education the father would not support. Her sense of being alienated from agency is epitomized in the title, *Fifth Chinese Daughter*, which is not only her name but also the way she thinks of herself, an identity so subordinate that she does not lay claim to an "I." The irony of an autobiography written from a third-person perspective has not gone unnoticed by Maxine Hong Kingston, who argues for the importance of Wong as a literary model and of the specifically feminist elements of Wong's narrative.

In 1924 Congress passed an Immigration Act that specifically barred Chinese women, wives, and prostitutes, and established an annual quota of 105. This law was dramatically effective in curtailing the Chinese population by eliminating reproduction and led to the unique demographic character of Chinatowns—enclaves of aging Chinese bachelors cut off from their families in Canton province, China, the origin of the Chinese **diaspora**. H. T. Tsiang's *And China Has Hands* (1937) is an early fictional treatment of this bachelor society, but the genre did not achieve fruition until **Louis Chu**'s brilliant novel, *Eat a Bowl of Tea* (1961). Central to the plot is the impotence of Ben Loy, a second-generation Chinese American veteran who is unable to produce an heir with his war bride Mei Oi. Ben Loy's impotence functions as a metaphor for New York's Chinatown, a community of aging, impotent bachelors desperate for new blood. Matters are brought to a head when a rogue seduces and impregnates Mei Oi, but the initial furor and consternation over this transgression give way to celebration when a son is born. Liberated from the oppressive expectations of the parents, Ben Loy and Mei Oi head to San Francisco to begin a new life. A realistic, humorous portrait of a Chinese American community, Chu's *Eat a Bowl of Tea* approaches greatness in its rendition of Cantonese English, an ebullient vernacular that captures the flavor of New York's Chinatown without degenerating into rude caricature.

Chinatown as a specific sociohistorical space functions as the setting for many Chinese American novels; in others, however, Chinatown and its associated history become virtual characters in the novels themselves. These works—which include Lin Yutang's *Chinatown Family* (1948), **C. Y. Lee**'s *Flower Drum Song* (1957), **Gish Jen**'s *Typical American* (1991), **Fae Myenne Ng**'s *Bone* (1993), Sigrid Nunez's *Feather on the Breath of God* (1995), and Canadian Sky Lee's *Disappearing Moon Cafe* (1991 [set in British Columbia and Vancouver's Chinatown])—examine the social and psychological dimensions of place and its connection to Chinese American **identity**. C. Y. Lee's *The Flower Drum Song* was a *New York Times* best seller and was adapted for Broadway by Rodgers and Hammerstein in 1958; in 2001 David Henry Hwang revised the musical to glowing reviews, and in 2002, forty-five years after its initial publication, Penguin Books reissued the novel. Lee's *The Flower Drum Song* introduced mainstream audiences to the social issues of San Francisco's Chinatown and remains as relevant for contemporary audiences as it was in 1957.

The heady liberationist movements of the late 1960s and early 1970s witnessed the emergence of Chinese America's two most influential writers, **Frank Chin** and Maxine Hong Kingston. American-born contemporaries, the dialogue between Chin and Kingston has become foundational to an understanding of Chinese American literature. For both novelists "writin' is fightin'." But ironically, this belief in the power of the written word to effect change has become a bone of contention between them, centering in particular on the significance of myths: for Chin, the essence of myth is its stability over time; for Kingston, however, myths must be renegotiated continually in order to remain relevant. Chin has criticized Kingston for her liberal treatment of received Chinese myths—the story of Fa Mu Lan for example—an orientation that makes her putative autobiographies "fake." But for Kingston the reinterpretation of myths is an important feminist strategy to assert women's agency.

Fifth-generation Chinese American Frank Chin, the first Asian American playwright to be produced off-Broadway, is perhaps best known for his plays, short stories, and as the lead editor of *Aiiieeeee!* (1974), an early and influential anthology of Asian American writing expanded and published as *The Big Aiiieeeee!* in 1991. That he came to the novel late in his career is understandable given his scathing critique of Chinese American autobiography, a genre that he feels has perpetuated a feminized, Christianized, and assimilationist tradition of Chinese American writing ("This Is Not an Autobiography" *Genre* 18 [Summer 1985]: 109–30). Chin attempts to rehabilitate Asian American manhood by appropriating the discourse of **black nationalism** and by excavating heroic images from a Chinese American context, drawing on an epic history of railroad building.

In the late 1980s Chin undertook a transpacific swerve, replacing Asian American cultural nationalism with a Chinese version of cultural nationalism founded on three Chinese classics—Luo Guanzhong's *The Romance of the Three Kingdoms* (fourteenth century), Shi Nai'an's *Water Margin* (fourteenth century), and Wu Cheng'en's *Journey to the West* (sixteenth century).

Abandoning the autobiographical orientation of much Chinese American writing, Chin's novels focus instead on cultural critique, the way that American history and the media construct demeaning images of Asian Americans. Hence, the very titles of his two novels, *Donald Duk* (1991) and *Gunga Din Highway* (1994), exploit images from popular culture to suggest the construction of Chinese America in the American imagination as well as the epic antidote he prescribes. Set in San Francisco during Chinese New Year, *Donald Duk* narrates how the eponymous twelve-year-old protagonist overcomes his alienation from Chinese culture—a self-contempt resulting from pernicious representations of the Chinese in history books and the media—and learns to embrace it. Donald's rehabilitation eventually comes full circle: in his dreams Chinese mythology comes to life on the American frontier as the epic warrior-poet Kwan Kung merges with intrepid Chinese railroad workers.

Chin's second novel riffs on Rudyard Kipling's ballad about the Indian water boy who helps the British defeat his own people. Gunga Din thus functions as an image of Chinese America disseminated through popular culture and symbolizes all those Chinese American writers who promote fake but marketable images of the Chinese to white audiences. In this novel Chin concentrates on Hollywood's construction of Charlie Chan—humble, docile, asexual—as an image of America's racist love. Ironically, the father figure in the novel, Longman Kwan, is lampooned for his naïve aspiration to be the first Chinese American actor to play Charlie Chan, an unworthy ambition because he would be purveying racist stereotypes rather than debunking them. It remains for the aptly named son, Ulysses S. Kwan, to challenge popular stereotypes and introduce enabling images of the Chinese into the American imagination.

Chin himself has identified Louis Chu as a literary forefather, suggesting a masculine tradition of the Chinese American novel inherited by contemporary writers such as **Shawn Wong** and **Gus Lee**. In *Homebase* (1979), Wong narrates the story of fourth-generation Chinese American Rainsford Chan, who, orphaned at fifteen, strives to recover a sense of his parents' love and the history of his male ancestors. *American Knees* (1995), Wong's second novel, examines the pitfalls of interracial romance from the perspective of forty-year-old Chinese American Raymond Ding. Gus Lee's autobiographical first two novels, *China Boy* (1991) and *Honor and Duty* (1994), dramatize the experiences of Chinese American Kai Ting as a youth growing up in San Francisco's rough-and-tumble Panhandle and as a West Point cadet.

If the civil rights era and the legacy of ethnic consciousness-raising accents Frank Chin's cultural nationalism, Maxine Hong's oeuvre exhibits the influence of second-wave **feminism** in the articulation of a Chinese American consciousness and voice. Kingston's *The Woman Warrior* remains among the most widely read texts on university campuses today. One of the work's intriguing features is the way that it revises the genre of autobiography, mingling history, myth, and fiction in a discontinuous narrative in order to dramatize the way that Chinese and family history influence Kingston's contemporary identity. Divided into five sections, the novel dramatizes the subjection of women both in China and America: an aunt's suicide over an adulterous pregnancy; Moon Orchid's (the mother's sister) deterioration into insanity when her husband abandons and rejects her for a younger Chinese American woman; the mute Chinese girl, Kingston's mirror image, whom she bullies. But these examples of Chinese women's oppression are balanced by images of feminine power and autonomy: Fa Mu Lan, the woman warrior; Kingston's mother, the shaman, at once warrior, medicine woman, exorcist, and storyteller who defeats a ghost and liberates a slave girl; Ts'ai Yen, the woman who lived among barbarians for a dozen years and wrote poems about her experience for posterity. That Kingston concludes the novel with an image of Ts'ai Yen in "A Song for a Barbarian Reed Pipe" suggests the blending of the martial Fa Mu Lan with the figure of the artist-poet, the woman warrior who fights through language and art. *The Woman Warrior* itself dramatizes this act of feminist self-realization, moving from the opening vignette of the aunt's tragic suicide to the concluding image of Ts'ai Yen's triumph over bondage and her achievement of a lyric voice. Through *The Woman Warrior* Kingston speaks not only for herself, but for her literary mother Jade Snow Wong and all Chinese women forced into silence.

With her second work, *China Men*, Kingston offers a balancing perspective by dramatizing the history of Chinese men's migration to America, the Gold Mountain. *China Men* begins with a brilliantly comical vignette, "On Discovery," detailing sojourner Tang Ao's feminization in the land of women, a fate that foreshadows the emasculation of Chinese men in America. Simultaneously an analysis of family and a narrative of the nation, *China Men* imagines the stories of her forefathers' migration to the Gold Mountain, the most immediate story being that of her father, whose presence in America is shrouded in silence and mystery. Hence Kingston constructs two different tales of his immigration: in one story, he is the father who immigrates legally according to the laws of the land; in the other, he is smuggled in. Of note is a brief chapter titled "The Laws," which details the history of Chinese exclusion in the United States and provides a stark depiction of the intimate connection between Chinese identity and immigration policy.

If *Woman Warrior* remains Kingston's most popular work, *Tripmaster Monkey* is, incontestably, her most sophisticated text. Set in the heady insurgent milieu of 1960s San Francisco, the novel remythologizes Frank Chin as the signifying yellow hipster Wittman Ah Sing—a clear reference to Walt Whitman—in a brilliantly allusive synthesis of Chinese and American culture. Wittman embarks on a journey to narrate the tale of his tribe, a quest that recapitulates the manifold quest-romances of American and Chinese literature. As a playwright, Wittman imagines a play that will transform an exclusively black and white landscape with a signifying Chinese American difference. Significantly, by the end of the novel, after waging the art of war through epic Chinese American theater, Wittman gives up his imaginative identification with the great warrior-poet Kwan Kung and is transformed into a pacifist.

Just as Frank Chin functions as a conduit between Louis Chu and contemporary Chinese American men's writing, Maxine Hong Kingston's influence has paved the way for a new generation of writers who continue to articulate the issues first raised by Jade Snow Wong, including **Amy Tan**, Gish Jen, Fae Myenne Ng, and Sigrid Nunez. Tan's four novels—*The Joy Luck Club* (1989), *The Kitchen God's Wife* (1991), *The Hundred Secret Senses* (1995), and *The Bonesetter's Daughter* (2001)—dramatize the cultural and emotional estrangement that plagues the relationships among various generations of Chinese women. Thematically, Tan's work is traceable to Kingston's *The Woman Warrior*, and the two writers share the imperative to reinvent received myths so as to shatter conventional representations of Chinese women.

In contrast, Gish Jen's *Typical American*, Fae Myenne Ng's *Bone*, and Sigrid Nunez's *A Feather on the Breath of God*—three highly regarded novels—take up the troubled father-daughter relationship that Kingston examines in *China Men*, a lineage traceable to Jade Snow Wong's *Fifth Chinese Daughter*. In *Typical American*, Jen analyzes the experience of the first generation's immigration to America from the early 1940s to the 1950s, suggesting that while the new world liberates Chinese women from the strictures of traditional Chinese culture, it poses a more ambiguous, potentially mortifying challenge for the father. *Mona in the Promised Land* (1996), Jen's second novel, continues the saga of the Chang clan from the late 1960s to the 1990s; this novel is noteworthy because it portrays the making of second-generation Chinese American identity as a construct mediated through the Jewish experience rather than through an ethnocentric return to roots. In *Bone* Ng connects the broader history of Chinese exclusion in America to its destructive impact on the Leong family: the middle daughter's suicide is symptomatic of the absence of love between father and mother, a condition brought about by the father's humiliating status as an illegal alien, a mere paper son. Similarly, in *A Feather on the Breath of God* Nunez narrates a young woman's poignant struggle to come to terms with her Chinese Panamanian father, a man whose silence symbolizes his feelings of impotence. Having fought as an American soldier in World War II, he returns home with a German war bride only to confront **racism** and disenfranchisement.

For writers like Ng and Nunez, the struggle to come to terms with this traumatic paternal legacy is facilitated through storytelling, the process by which their female protagonists develop a sense of agency and empowerment. By telling their family stories, they assume control over their lives and are able to break with an oppressive past. Leila, the eldest daughter and narrator of *Bone*, comes to recognize that her mother does indeed love her husband, and this knowledge ultimately liberates her from the stifling confines of Chinatown and the history that threatens to suffocate her. Likewise, the nameless narrator of *Feather* works toward a sense of identity through art. By imagining a different father for herself, a parent capable of loving his own daughter, she creates a family story that she can truly inhabit, one fueled by love and desire.

Further Reading

Kim, Elaine. *Asian American Literature: An Introduction to the Writings and Their Social Context.* Philadelphia: Temple UP, 1982.

Li, David Leiwei. *Imagining the Nation: Asian American Literature and Cultural Consent."* Stanford: Stanford UP, 1998. 21–43.

Wong, Sau-ling Cynthia. "Chinese American Literature." *An Interethnic Companion to Asian American Literature.* Ed. King-Kok Cheung. New York: Cambridge UP, 1997. 39–61.

Andrew Shin

CHINESE AMERICAN POETRY   Chinese American poetry consists of multiple and heterogeneous poetic traditions and vastly different, idiosyncratic poetic styles. These characteristics in part reflect the historical conditions, geographical differences, and demographic changes that have shaped the emergence and development of poetry by Chinese Americans. Although the term "Chinese American literature" emerged only during the early 1970s, in the wake of **Civil Rights Movement** and the beginning of multicultural movement, recent scholarship has traced the origins of Chinese American literature to the 1850s when Chinese immigrant communities were established in the United States, especially on the West Coast, and had begun to publish bilingual and Chinese-language newspapers that frequently printed fiction, satire, poetry, and popular Cantonese vernacular rhymes and songs.

San Francisco, also known as "Gold Mountain" among the Chinese, was a gateway of early Chinese **immigration**, and San Francisco Chinatown became a dynamic economic and cultural center of Chinese American communities. In 1854, according to the estimation of a San Francisco–based bilingual paper, *The Golden Hills' News*, no less than 40,000 to 50,000 Chinese had arrived in "Gold Mountain" from China. The number of Chinese immigrants continued to grow over the following two decades partly due to civil war in China and partly because of the Gold Rush and the post–Civil War demand of labor in the United States. The Chinese population declined in the late nineteenth century and remained static for about half a century as a result of anti-Chinese **racism**. Singled out as scapegoats during a period of labor unrest, Chinese Americans became targets of discriminatory laws and racial violence. With the completion of the transcontinental railroad in 1870, the anti-Chinese movement intensified, and eventually led to the 1882 **Chinese Exclusion Act,** which banned immigration of Chinese laborers to the United States and prohibited Chinese from becoming naturalized citizens on the grounds that they were not "white." Not until 1943 did Congress repeal the Chinese Exclusion Act, establishing an annual quota of 105 people for Chinese immigration to the United States and allowing Chinese "aliens" previously barred from citizenship to have naturalization rights. In contrast to the predominantly working-class immigrants to the United States during the nineteenth century and early twentieth century, many of the Chinese immigrants who arrived during and after World War II belonged to the well-to-do, well-educated, or elite class and were able to attend universities and have professional careers in the United States. In 1965 the Immigration and Naturalization Act replaced the national-origin quotas with hemispheric quotas, resulting in a rapid population growth and profound demographic changes in Chinese American communities. These changes became even more dramatic after the normalization of the Sino-U.S. diplomatic relationship following Nixon's visit to China in 1971 and after China's open-door policy began in the 1980s.

The earliest collections of Chinese American verse were written in the local vernacular of the southern province, Guangdong (Canton), where the majority of early immigrants to the U.S. had lived. *Taishan Geyao Ji* (1919, a collection of Taishan [dialect] songs and rhymes) and *Meizhou Guangdong Hau Quiao Liuchuan Geyao Huibian* (1970, a collection of popular songs and rhymes of Chinese Americans from Guangdong) were published in Chinese, but selections from two volumes of *Jinshan Geji* (Songs of Gold Mountain) were translated by Marlon K. Hom and published as *Songs of Gold Mountain: Cantonese Rhymes from San Francisco Chinatown* (1987). The first volume of *Songs of Gold Mountain*, consisting of 808 rhymes, was published in 1911, and the second volume, consisting of an additional 832 songs, was published in 1915. Of those 1,640 pieces, Hom selected 220 for the 1987 volume. All of these rhymes are written in the regulated Cantonese folk song format of forty-six syllables divided into eight lines—5-5-7-7-3-5-7-7—with each line ending in the same consonant or vowel syllable. The predominant themes of these songs are the loneliness of the wives left behind in China, the pain of separation from loved ones, the hardships and struggles for survival in the United States, disappointment at the rarity of chances for of success in the United States, and the disillusionment with the Gold Mountain dreams.

Another important collection of early verses by Chinese immigrants is the bilingual anthology *Island: Poetry and History of Chinese Immigrants on Angel Island, 1910–1940* (1980), translated and edited by Him Mark Lai et al. These poems were written or carved on the wooden walls of the detention barracks on **Angel Island** (in San Francisco Bay), which between 1910 and 1940 was used as an immigration station, where Chinese immigrants were interrogated and examined to screen out the illegal and undesirable aliens. While waiting for the results of their appeals or orders for their deportation, the detainees expressed their anguish, anger, frustration, humiliation, and disillusionment by writing or carving poems on the walls of the detention center. These poems of various lengths are written in variations of five-

and seven-syllable lines and are loosely modeled on the regulated forms of classical Chinese poetry.

The first collection of poems written by Chinese Americans in English, *Chinese American Poetry: An Anthology* (1990), edited by L. Ling-chi Wang and Henry Yiheng Zhao, is a landmark that shows the explosive diversity and development of Chinese American poetry. It consists of selected works by twenty-two poets of two generations with different backgrounds, works addressing a wide variety of thematic concerns in various poetic forms and styles. Poems included in this anthology range from traditional lyrics such as those by **Diana Chang** to difficult conceptual poems by **Mei-mei Berssengrugge**, from Nellie Wong's capacious, meditative lines about Chinese American experience to **Marilyn Mei Ling Chin**'s distinct voice of a passionate feminist, from **Li-Young Lee**'s engaging autobiographical lyric to **Arthur Sze**'s multicultural sequence collage poems, from Wing Tek Lum's love poems that evoke Chinese poets to **John Yau**'s surrealist, postmodern language poems. In addition to their thematic and formal heterogeneity, the geographical locations of those poets—San Francisco, New York City, Chicago, Los Angeles, Santa Fe, Portland, Seattle, and Honolulu, among others—and their prominent poetic careers indicate that Chinese American poetry is no longer contained within Chinatown or circulated among Chinese American communities only. Chinese American poets no longer live in the geographically bounded margins of mainstream American society and culture. However, the multicultural aspects of these Chinese American poems are not simply a direct reflection of the poets' **ethnicity** or social positions. Rather, the formal and stylistic characteristics of Chinese American poetry, like its thematic concerns, are the result of the poets' negotiations with multiple poetic traditions in resistance to **assimilation** by Eurocentric culture, in search of new ways of using language and form to engage with social issues and to reinvent poetry. Poems collected in *Paké: Writings by Chinese in Hawai'i* (1989), edited by **Eric Chock** and **Darrell H. Y. Lum**, show that Chinese American poets in Hawai'i have contributed to the diversity of Chinese American poetry by incorporating local color, including pidgin, into their poems.

Given that *Chinese American Poetry* was published in 1991 and that any selection necessarily involves exclusion, it is not surprising that many contemporary Chinese American poets are not included in the anthology. Some of these poets are recent immigrants such as Ha Jin, Wang Ping, and Bei Dao; some are openly gay or lesbian poets such as Timothy Liu, Justin Chin, and Sharon Lim-Hing; some are **diaspora** poets such as the Malaysian-Chinese American poets, Hillary Tham, and **Shirley Geok-lin Lim**; and some are innovative poets such as Tan Lin and Ho Hon Leung, whose poems do no overtly deal with Chinese American experience per se.

Despite the large number of well-published and award-winning Chinese American poets and the rich variety of poetry they have produced, the 1991 *Chinese American Poetry* remains the only anthology of poetry in English by contemporary Chinese Americans. This phenomenon is perhaps largely due to the efforts to establish pan ethnicity in the formation of Asian American literary traditions. Poems by Chinese American poets are collected in anthologies such as *Dissident Song: A Contemporary Asian American Anthology* (1991), *The Open Boat: Poems from Asian America* (1993), *The Very Inside: An Anthology of Writings by Asian and Pacific Islander Lesbian and Bisexual Women* (1994). *Premonitions: The Kaya Anthology of New Asian North American Poetry* (1995), *Quiet Fire: A Historical Anthology of Asian American Poetry, 1892–1970* (1996), *Take Out: Queer Writing from Asian Pacific America* (2000), and *Asian American Poetry: The Next Generation* (2004). These anthologies provide a larger context for reading Chinese American poetry, most of which is published as the works of individual poets. In spite of their vast differences, Chinese American poets share some important similar characteristics among themselves and with other Asian American poets in their resistance to cultural assimilation, in their exploration of identities of race, gender, class, culture, and sexuality, and in their insistence on engaging with social issues through commitment to formal, aesthetic innovations.

Further Reading

Chang, Juliana. "Reading Asian American Poetry." *MELUS* 21.1 (1996): 81–98.

Hongo, Garrett. Introduction. *The Open Boat: Poems from Asian America*. Ed. Garrett Hongo. New York: Anchor, 1993. xvii–xlii.

Tabios, Eileen, ed. *Black Lightning: Poetry-in-Progress*. New York: Asian American Writers' Workshop, 1998.

Uba, George. "Coordinates of Asian American Poetry: A Survey of the History and Guide to Teaching." *A Resource Guide to Asian American Literature*. Ed. Sau-Ling Cynthia Wong and Stephen H. Sumida. New York: Modern Language Association of America, 2001. 309–31.

Wong, Sunn Shelley. "Sizing Up Asian American Poetry." *A Resource Guide to Asian American Literature*. Ed. Sau-Ling Cynthia Wong and Stephen H. Sumida. 285–308.

Zhou Xiaojing

CHINESE AMERICAN STEREOTYPES   As one of the earliest, and largest, groups of Asian immigrants to the United States, people of Chinese descent have had a long history of both troubled and successful attempts at integrating themselves into the larger American populace. Stereotypes purporting to illuminate their "exotic" racial traits and cultural preferences bear witness to the reluctance with which the public greeted these attempts. These surprisingly tenacious images continue to impact Chinese American life via their depictions of gender, family, work, and citizenship.

The first Chinese immigrants to the United States left their villages in order to escape political conflict and hardship. Their arrival in California coincided with that of Anglo workers from the Eastern seaboard, drawn by the promise of the Gold Rush (1849). Thus, international **immigration** and national migration placed two groups lacking a common language into territory known for its economic opportunity. The competition that ensued fueled nationalist desires for racial homogeneity, resulting in an assertion of insuperable difference between Americans and Chinese. This enabled the "natives" (i.e., earlier generations of European Americans) to limit immigrant access to opportunity. California moved to institute a foreign miners' license tax in 1852 that required nonnatives to pay a monthly fee to roaming tax collectors. Made nervous by the continuing influx of immigrants, the federal government later passed the **Chinese Exclusion Act** of 1882, which both ended immigration of Chinese laborers and denied naturalized citizenship to those already in the country. Though many of these immigrants were men, such legal actions also affected women: the 1875 Page Act prevented the immigration of prostitutes, but was enforced in such a way as to curtail national entry by virtually all females, regardless of profession. As a whole, these acts were designed to halt the threat of the so-called "Yellow Peril": the idea that, given the chance, the Chinese would quickly engulf a white majority population.

In spite of widespread and systematic anti-Chinese sentiment, however, a more positive characterization of the Chinese developed at the same time. This was based on the growing necessity for Chinese labor in agricultural and railway expansion. Many immigrants had left farms behind in China, and thus came to the United States prepared to share their agricultural and engineering expertise. Irrigation and botanical advice made Chinese laborers valuable assets but fostered an image of them as subordinate/servile. Their involvement with the Central Pacific Railroad (1865) reinforced this idea. Specifically recruited because they had proven equal to the arduous physical tasks demanded by the railroad's path (e.g., driving steel, blasting passages through mountains), the Chinese accepted tasks for which the company had difficulty obtaining white labor. Nevertheless, Leland Stanford, Central Pacific president, praised Chinese workers far less for their courage and endurance than for their passivity and reliability (Takaki 91–92).

Images of the subservient, passive Chinese persisted throughout the nineteenth century, operating in conjunction with growing competitive and nativist sentiments. Local and national media responded with representations of the Chinese that both grew out of and contributed to these perceptions. Minstrel performances (often associated exclusively with racist characterizations of African Americans) included the figure of "John Chinaman." From the 1850s onward, this "comedic" caricature embodied a host of devious desires and dangerous designs (stealing jobs from white Americans, "overrunning" the country, etc.), as well as numerous cultural differences marking him as utterly foreign and "other" (eating various vermin and domesticated animals, speaking English with a ludicrous accent). Writer Bret Harte's enormously popular poem "The Heathen Chinee" (1870) immortalized such poisonous imagery. Here, Ah Sin, the main character, is repeatedly identified as "childlike" while at the same time he is cheating white men at cards and leaving them "ruined by cheap Chinese labor" (Takaki 105). The accompanying illustrations also underscore conventional stereotypes of Chinese physiognomy. In these, Ah Sin retains his queue, is much smaller than real (white) men, and possesses eyes that are mere slits. Similar visual tropes appear in illustrations for Mark Twain's *Roughing It* (1872), illustrations which portray Chinese men in non-Western dress and lacking pupils. From the beginning, then, nineteenth-century representations of Chinese immigrants offered little aside from caricatures of physical difference as indicative of negative character traits and dangerous desires. Such caricatures solidified into stereotypes over the course of the century.

In the early twentieth century, a number of popular media highlighted racial differences with reference to specific Chinese and Chinese American characters in many ways comparable to Harte's Ah Sin. Comic strips like "Terry and the Pirates" (1934) and "Flash Gordon" (1934), for example, both feature evil Chinese villains—The "Dragon Lady" and "Ming the Merciless," respectively—who instantiate the stereotypical characteristics reminiscent of John Chinaman. The same period also saw depictions of the passive, hard-working Chinese Americans epitomized by the character Charlie Chan. With his elliptical, piecemeal English, the Honolulu detective foiled criminals in numerous movies (1926–49). The onset of World War II helped ease American fears about the Yellow Peril (the post–Pearl Harbor Japanese assumed the role of preeminent Asian threat), which gave rise to idyllic images of Chinese American **assimilation**. The film *Flower Drum Song* portrayed an all-American community thriving in Chinatown. Using two Chinese American female characters to play out the drama (Mei Li, a "traditional" immigrant woman illegally entering the United States, and Linda Low, a native-born exotic dancer), the film popularized a persistent stereotype. As a dyad, the two women exemplified the opposing images of Chinese American women: one innocent and demure, the other hypersexualized. The theme of assimilation, however, continued to circulate in the popular imagination and reappeared in the political sphere late in the century. While the "model minority" stereotype (hard-working, passive, intelligent) attaches to virtually all Asian American groups, President Clinton singled out Chinese Americans specifically in a speech welcoming Gary Locke, governor of Washington, into the legislature.

Sometimes atavistic, often pernicious stereotypes insistent upon the "otherness" of Chinese Americans bear witness to the 125-year history of their involvement with and integration into mainstream American society.

Further Reading

Lee, Robert. *Orientals: Asian Americans in Popular Culture.* Philadelphia: Temple UP, 1999.

Ma, Sheng-Mei. *The Deathly Embrace: Orientalism and Asian American Identity.* Minneapolis: Minnesota UP, 2000.

Takaki, Ronald. *Strangers from a Different Shore: A History of Asian Americans.*
Boston: Back Bay Books, 1998.

Kim Middleton

CHINESE EXCLUSION ACT   The passage of the Chinese Exclusion
Act in 1882 suspended the flow of Chinese immigrants at the time. It is gen-
erally recognized as a high-water mark of anti-Chinese sentiment in the
United States in the nineteenth century.

Of all Asian immigrants, the Chinese were the first group to enter North
America in large numbers. Because of rice shortages and wars in the mother
country, as well as the lure of gold and opportunities in America, many Chinese laborers, through recruiters and contractors, began to journey to the
new world in the 1840s. At the first onset, their presence in America was
met by as much enthusiasm from employers and the government as hostility from white workers. But the anti-Chinese sentiment eventually overran
the need for cheap labor. The Chinese Exclusion Act (1882) put a stop to the
influx of Chinese laborers—including both skilled and unskilled workers—to the United States for the next ten years. Only a small quota for
students, teachers, merchants, and diplomats was granted. Even these
exempted classes had to present a certificate verified by the Chinese government and American consul in China in order to land in the United
States. The act, along with the 1875 act that barred Chinese women from
entering the United States, resulted in a precipitous decline in Chinese
immigration as well as an unbalanced demographic formation of Chinese
American communities. As the anti-Chinese sentiment continued to
worsen, a series of laws were passed over the next dozen years to reinforce
the exclusion. The passage of the Chinese exclusion laws (1904) put an
indefinite ban on Chinese immigration. These laws crippled the formation
of Chinese American communities. For more than half a decade, Chinese
women in general were barred from entering, and men could not legally
bring their wives and children to join them in the United States. Not until
the alliance with China during World War II were the legislative barriers to
Chinese immigration repealed. And not until the 1965 reform was the effect
of the 1882 Act really altered.

Exclusion laws have reinforced the "alien" and "sojourner" images of Chinese Americans. It was not until the Asian American Movement of the late
sixties and seventies that Chinese American activists and writers sought to
change these images. It is this impetus of claiming America and recuperating Asian American history that compels many writers to produce works
such as the famous anthology *Aiiieeeee! An Anthology of Asian American
Writers* (1974), **Maxine Hong Kingston**'s *China Men* (1980), and **Frank
Chin**'s *Donald Duk* (1991) and *Gunga Din Hingway* (1994).

Further Reading
Chan, Sucheng. *Asian Americans: An Interpretative History.* New York: Twayne,
1991.

Hing, Bill Ong. *Making and Remaking Asian America through Immigration Policies: 1850–1990*. Stanford, CA: Stanford UP, 1993.

Takaki, Ronald. *A History of Asian Americans: Strangers from a Different Shore.* Boston: Little, Brown, 1989.

Wong, Sua-ling Cynthia. "Chinese American Literature." *An Interethnic Companion to Asian American Literature.* Ed. King-Kok Cheung. New York: Cambridge UP, 1997. 39–61.

Shuchen Susan Huang

CHMELKA, DONALD F. (1942–) Czech American author and retired engineer. Chmelka's Czech roots are documented in two works, *Matej's Journey to America: The Driving Forces of Our Immigrant Ancestors* (2002) and *Matej's Legacy* (2003). In both works, Chmelka's Czech roots are examined from a historical perspective, tracing back to ancient times in an effort to explain the events that led to his family's emigration to the United States.

Chmelka was born in Nebraska and was raised in a farmhouse with no modern conveniences. His personality and perseverance were thus formed out of hardship and appreciation for small things. His education began at a country schoolhouse and continued with a bachelor's degree in mechanical engineering from the University of Nebraska and an MBA from Pepperdine University. He traveled the world as a Reliability Engineer and thus obtained a superb knowledge of other cultures and peoples. When his career took him to the Space Shuttle Program in Los Angeles, Chmelka became involved with the local Catholic parish, which was sponsoring a Buddhist family from Vietnam. This experience spurred Chmelka's curiosity to find out more about his own family ties, and after retirement, he became determined to investigate his own family's settlement in the New World.

His first work, *Matej's Journey to America*, begins with discussion of the ancient times and places of the Chmelka family within the historical framework of world events. The impetus for this epic story begins with the discovery of an old family chest in the abandoned farmhouse of Matej Chmelka (Chmelka's great-great grandfather). Chmelka's desire to lead his modern-day family on a path dotted with war, ships, railroads, and Nebraska farmsteads is thus born. Chmelka weaves world events in with personal memoir, lending the work a thread of attachment between past and present. Combining archeological evidence with biblical and genealogical evidence, Chmelka expertly traces his family's lineage along a historical path leading up to Matej Chmelka's death in 1902.

Chmelka's second work, *Matej's Legacy*, continues the journey of the Chmelka family through the twentieth century. The focus is on Chmelka's boyhood and his memories of his youth. He also discusses his work and the technological boom that enabled the Space Shuttle to fly and the personal computer to flourish. Chmelka expresses great concern for America's future as the country makes its way through rocky criticism by friends and the preaching by foes of hatred against the land that his Czech family had considered the Promised Land.

Both volumes offer heavy historical documentation and are interspersed with personal reflection. Chmelka captures the pioneering spirit of the early ancients to the early settlers, the latter finally immigrating to the United States, eager to start new lives and create a nation built on the "can-do" strength that has allowed his family to continue into the twenty-first century. (*See also* Czech American Literature)

Further Reading

Chmelka, Rosalyn M. *The Matej Chmelka Family History.* Privately published, 1992.

———. *A Guide to Research for Butler County, Nebraska.* Lincoln: Nebraska State Genealogical Society, 1991.

Cynthia A. Klima

CHOCK, ERIC (1950–) Asian American writer, poet, and editor. Cofounder and coeditor of the influential Hawaiian journal *Bamboo Ridge*, Eric Chock was one of the driving forces behind Hawai'i's "Local Literature" movement of the late twentieth century.

The Local Literature movement was largely an outgrowth of 1978's famous "Talk Story" literary conference, but the conference itself was the result of a growing clamor over the need for local literature by local writers for a local audience. One of the first shots across the bow in this debate was Eric Chock's "Poem for my Father" (1976), which won numerous awards and turned the attention of scholars and critics of Hawaiian literature to a growing body of poets and poetry that addressed current issues of ethnic **identity** through concrete imagery and idioms unique to contemporary Hawai'i.

This thematic preoccupation can be seen throughout Chock's subsequent literary output, notably "Poem for George Helm" (1980), in which the concrete, picture-postcard imagery of "Aloha" spirit and tour guides is sharply contrasted with ethnic tensions, environmental degradation, and the bitterness of great promise turned false. This is not the stereotypical view of Hawai'i gleaned from travelogues, but it was and is immediately recognizable to those who live away from the tourist enclaves.

What Chock strives for in his work, however, is not so much a castigation of outside forces as a recognition of the validity of his own sense of identity. "The Mango Tree" (1979) clearly speaks to this, as Chock experiments with the use of local pidgin dialect in a "serious" literary form; this use of local language in such a form is nothing less than a demand for the recognition and acknowledgement of the uniqueness and validity of local ethnic sensibilities.

In 1978 Chock and fellow Local Literature writer **Darrell H. Y. Lum** founded *Bamboo Ridge*, a literary journal reflecting what the editors called an "island sensibility." The venture proved quite successful, and a number of significant writers first came to prominence through publication in *Bam-*

boo Ridge, establishing Chock as a central figure in the renaissance of contemporary **Hawaiian literature** and the leader of what came to be known as the Bamboo Ridge group of writers.

In the late 1990s, Chock's critics began to charge that in both his creative work and his editorial choices, he was focusing primarily on ethnicities of Asian derivation to the exclusion of others extant in Hawai'i. The ensuing debate led to the formation of other literary journals and sub-movements and somewhat dampened the influence of *Bamboo Ridge* and Chock himself. Nonetheless, Chock remains a significant force in Hawaiian literature, continuing to write and publish, edit *Bamboo Ridge*, and oversee the compilation of numerous anthologies of local writers.

Further Reading

Sumida, Stephen. *And the View from the Shore: Literary Traditions of Hawai'i.* Seattle: U of Washington P, 1991.

Wilson, Rob. *Reimagining the American Pacific: From South Pacific to Bamboo Ridge and Beyond.* Durham, NC: Duke UP, 2000.

William Curl

CHOI, SOOK NYUL (1937–)   Korean American writer of children's and young adult literature. Choi's award-winning autobiographical/historical trilogy—*Year of Impossible Goodbyes* (1991), *Echoes of the White Giraffe* (1993), and *Gathering of Pearls* (1994)—narrates events of twentieth-century Korean history from the point of view of a young girl. Choi was born in Pyongyang, Korea, and immigrated to the United States to attend Manhattanville College, where she earned a BA in European history. As an educator—she has taught creative writing in high schools—she noted the lack of knowledge about Korea by Americans and therefore writes to help young Asian Americans learn about their heritage and to foster a better understanding of Asia and Asian Americans.

Year of Impossible Goodbyes narrates the events of Korean history during World War II and its aftermath. Ten-year-old Sookan Bak lives in Pyonyang and struggles to preserve her Korean **identity** from the intentions of the Japanese colonizers to eradicate it. When the Russians take over after the Japanese defeat, Sookan's mother—alone, as her older sons are in jail and her husband is detained in Manchuria—decides to leave for the American-controlled south with her young children. The novel conveys the young girl's thoughts—her fears and anxieties, her little victories and dreams—as well as the details of daily life in the midst of war. The Korean's pride in her heritage, cultural identity, and family are at the center of the novel. In the context of narratives of war, this text illustrates how civilians become the helpless victims of political struggles. The "goodbyes" of the title refer to the family's exile and the end of Sookan's childhood.

The family's story continues in *Echoes of the White Giraffe*, where Sookan, now fifteen, her younger brother, and her mother leave war-ravaged Seoul to live in a mountaintop refugee hut in Pusan. The novel centers on the family's poverty and the sense of alienation typical of refugees. The separation from the rest of the family also weighs heavily on them, and though Sookan tries to live an adolescent's normal life—school, friends, even a small "forbidden" romance with a local boy—all aspects of her life are indelibly marked by the effects of war and her father's death. The final novel in the trilogy recounts Sookan's **immigration** to the United States and her experiences as a freshman at a small college in New York. It centers on her process of adaptation to her new life and her connection with her family in Korea, dramatizing her evaluation of both cultures and her own position between them. Sookan is now given to uninspiring self-reflection, which detracts from the quality of the narrative. Nonetheless, the trilogy effectively describes an important story of the Asian diaspora, through an evolving child/young adult character faced with significant choices.

Choi's literary production also includes her picture books for younger readers that center on Korean/American heritage and life. *Halmoni and the Picnic* (1993) deals with the relationship of American-born Yunmi with her grandmother, who immigrates from Korea and has difficulty learning English and comprehending American customs. Embarrassment leads to affinity for both, as Yunmi's classmates help her understand her grandmother, Halmoni, by inviting her to chaperone their picnic. The pictures that complement the narrative—realistic color illustrations bordered with Korean textile designs—cleverly convey the complementary process that the main characters undergo. Their story continues in *Yunmi and Halmoni's Trip* (1997), a book about the journey they take to Seoul, where Yunmi experiences culture shock. The granddaughter's difficulty in Korea mirrors her grandmother's earlier problems in New York, leading to a deeper connection between the two. Another picture book, *The Best Older Sister* (1997), chronicles a young Korean American girl's resentment at the birth of a brother and highlights how her grandmother helps her understand and appreciate not only the new arrival but also Korean family traditions.

Choi's writing engages history and the consequences of the Asian immigration by illustrating the choices and difficulties faced by Korean children in Asia and in the United States. Her perspective is positive, and she notes the difficulties of this situation in ways that suggest possibilities for children and young adults and that allow them to attend effectively to the realities of Asian Americans. (*See also* Korean American Literature)

Further Reading

Ling, Amy. "Sook Nyul Choi, Memoirist and Novelist." *Yellow Light: The Flowering of Asian American Art*. Philadelphia: Temple UP, 1999. 46–54.

Scanlon, Mara. "Sook Nyul Choi (1937–)." *Asian American Novelists: A Bio-Bibliographical Critical Sourcebook*. Ed. Emmanuel S. Nelson. Westport, CT: Greenwood Press, 2000. 56–59.

Rocío G. Davis

CHOI, SUSAN (1969–)   American bicultural (Korean/Russian Jewish) fiction writer. Susan Choi is often categorized as a Korean American author and as such represents an emerging voice in contemporary Asian American literature. She is one of a number of young writers who locate their protagonists in settings/situations outside the conventional expectations of this tradition (e.g., urban locations, culture clash, **identity** formation, etc.). Choi's novels and short stories pay close attention to the effects of surprising environs on characters of Asian descent and thus provide readers with new ways to imagine the complexities of the Asian American experience.

After winning Yale University's Wallace Prize for Fiction and the Henfield Foundation Transatlantic Review Award, Choi published several short stories over the course of the 1990s in literary journals such as the *Iowa Review* and *Epoch Magazine*. Her ascent into the mainstream, however, began with the release of her first novel, *The Foreign Student* (1998). In 1950 Chang Ahn is desperate to avoid being drafted by the Korean Army. By 1955, he has escaped the country on an academic fellowship to a university in the American South. Thus, Chang, or "Chuck" as he is soon dubbed, negotiates the expectations of a Southern society before the advent of civil rights reform. His local guide to the customs governing race and class is Katherine Monroe, an heiress involved in a long-term affair with a professor. Disowned by her parents and barely tolerated by the townsfolk, Katherine recognizes some of her own emotional distance and regret in Chang. Choi stages an interracial love affair that maintains cultural and historical specificity while at the same time he gestures toward an empathetic similarity between those whose pasts continue to shape them.

Choi's second novel, *American Woman* (2003), returns to the importance of history in determining character. Here, she focuses on the controversy surrounding Patty Hearst: a young heiress kidnapped by a revolutionary group (Symbionese Liberation Army), only to join their violent political actions. Hearst's interior life has captivated historians and audiences since the 1970s, but Choi chooses to focus instead on a figure ancillary to the incident, a young Japanese American woman who assisted Hearst and her associates during their year in hiding from the Federal Bureau of Investigation. Choi calls her Jenny Shimada and paints her as a political activist herself afraid of prosecution for her involvement in Vietnam War protests. In the novel, Jenny's relationship to the United States, as defined by **ethnicity** and political sympathies, is mapped in juxtaposition to the range of affiliations from which the Patty Hearst character is able to choose.

Throughout her works, Choi reveals the hidden sites and processes that condition Asian American integration into the fabric of the nation. The positive critical responses to both *The Foreign Student* and *American Woman* indicate that the reading public is willing to witness the heretofore-oblique possibilities of national acceptance that she represents. (*See also* Korean American Literature)

Further Reading

Fitzpatrick, Elizabeth. "Susan Choi." *Asian American Novelists: A Bio-Bibliographical Critical Sourcebook.* Ed. Emmanuel S. Nelson. Westport, CT: Greenwood Press, 2000. 60–63.

Kim Middleton

CHONG, PING (1946–) Chinese American theater director and playwright. Ping Chong was born in Toronto, Canada, in 1946. When he was one year old, Chong, his parents, and his brother moved to New York City. His early interest in visual and performing arts was derived from Chinese Opera (his father was a director and librettist; his mother, a diva prior to their emigration to North America). Chong studied visual arts at Pratt Institute and film at the School of Visual Arts. Chong joined the Meredith Monk Dance Company in 1972, performing and choreographing with her for six years. Chong founded his own theater company, Ping Chong and Company (formerly called the Fiji Theatre Company) in New York in 1975. Chong's interest has been in creating multimedia pieces that incorporate multiple art forms such as recorded sounds, slide/film projections, puppetry, and dance. In many of his multimedia pieces, Chong has also visualized political events and people in diverse historical moments and cultural sites. One of his multimedia works from the 1980s is *Nosferatu: A Symphony of Darkness* (1985). This "mask" piece (which takes place in a New York loft) incorporates the F. W. Murnau classic silent vampire film that parallels the narrative of the play. Chong created *Deshima,* another multimedia piece, in Holland in 1990. It deals with Japan's relationships with the West, focusing on both Western and Japanese **colonialism**, and on the collision of different cultures. For this production, Chong utilized visual arts—the influence of Japanese woodcut work on Van Gogh—as a framework. This piece was presented in a huge warehouse, where the audience was seated in a hydraulic movable box, which was placed about twenty feet from the stage. After *Deshima* Chong staged three other historical "poetic documentary" pieces: *Chinoiserie* (about Chinese history, 1995), *After Sorrow* (about Vietnamese history, 1997), and *Pojagi* (about Korean history, 1999). The four independent pieces are now known as the "East-West Quartet."

Chong has also collaborated with colleges and universities. In April 2004, with the School of Theatre and Dance at Kent State University, Chong, with his codirector Michael Rohd, created *BLIND NESS: The Irresistible Light of Encounter.* The piece combines elements from Joseph Conrad's *Heart of Darkness* and Ping Chong and Michael Rohd's original script about Leopold II, the king of Belgium, and includes Leopold's favorite explorer, Henry Morton Stanley, and human rights activists who fought against Leopold's extractions of natural and human resources from the Congo. In this elaborate multimedia (slides, shadow puppetry, and bunraku puppetry) production, Chong investigates the impact of Western colonialism in central Africa from the nineteenth century to the present.

In addition to multimedia works, Chong has also created a community-based oral history series titled *Undesirable Elements*. In this project Chong collaborates with adults and children in various communities throughout the world. Since the first installment of *Undesirable Elements* was staged in 1992 in New York, numerous others have been presented in cities such as Charleston, Cleveland, Minneapolis, Amherst, Seattle, Washington DC, Chicago, Rotterdam, Tokyo, Berlin, and Amsterdam. (*See also* Chinese American Drama)

Further Reading

Auslander, Philip. "Ping Chong." *Postmodernism: The Key Figures*. Ed. Hans Bertens and Joseph Natoli. Malden, MA: Blackwell, 2002. 82–87.

Caroll, Noël. "A Select View of Earthlings: Ping Chong." *Drama Review* 27.1 (1983): 72–81.

Kurahashi, Yuko. "Theatre as the Healing Space: Ping Chong's *Children of War*." *Studies in Theatre and Performance* 24.1 (2004): 23–36.

Lee, Josephine. "Between Immigration and Hyphenation: The Problems of Theorizing Asian American Theater." *Journal of Dramatic Theory and Criticism* 13.1 (1998): 45–69.

Neely, Kent. "Ping Chong's Theatre of Simultaneous Consciousness." *Journal of Dramatic Theory and Criticism* 6.2 (1992): 121–35.

Shimakawa, Karen. "The Things We Share: Ethnic Performativity and 'Whatever Being'." *Journal of Speculative Philosophy* 18.2 (2004): 149–60.

Westfall, Suzanne. "Ping Chong's *Terra In/Cognita*: Monsters on Stage." *Reading the Literatures of Asian America*. Ed. Shirley Geok-lin Lim and Amy Ling. Philadelphia: Temple UP, 1992. 359–73.

Yuko Kurahashi

CHU, LOUIS (1915–1970) Chinese American novelist. Chu's *Eat a Bowl of Tea* (1961) was one of the first works of fiction to present a realistic portrait of Chinatown, a portrait unsentimental yet sympathetic, thereby breaking with the caricatures and exoticized depictions of Chinese American communities that had been propagated by both European American and Asian American writers. In particular, Chu skillfully captures the everyday speech of post–World War II Chinese Americans through his translations of idiomatic Cantonese into English. Furthermore, in depicting the complications that arise from the marriage of Ben Loy, a young restaurant worker, and Mei Oi, his newly arrived wife from China, Chu satirizes the hypocritical mores of Chinese elders while implicitly critiquing the racist laws that ghettoized, impoverished, and emasculated the Chinese in America. For example, Mei Oi is expected by her male elders to conform to patriarchal Confucian ideals of womanhood. When she has an affair, she meets with the disapproval of her father and father-in-law, and yet the dissolute lives of these men are shown to be indirectly responsible for her infidelity. At the same time, the novel shows that the men's failure to meet the moral standards that they apply to the younger generation is shaped by decades of anti-Chinese **immigration** laws that separated husbands and wives, thus creating the Chinatown bachelor societies that only began to change with the War Brides Act of 1945.

Chu's working-class realism was partly responsible for the novel's initial lack of critical or commercial success; readers and critics preferred books that affirmed stereotypical views of the Chinese in America from upper-class perspectives, such as Pardee Lowe's *Father and Glorious Descendant* (1943), **Jade Snow Wong**'s *Fifth Chinese Daughter* (1950), and **C. Y. Lee**'s *Flower Drum Song* (1957). The cold war anticommunism of the 1950s also decimated the progressive Chinatown literary movement that would have supported Chu's social realism (although Chu himself was not involved with the Left). Thus, despite the fact that Chu was reportedly at work on a second novel and planning a play, *Eat a Bowl of Tea* remained his only work published in his lifetime; a short story, "Bewildered," was published posthumously in 1982 in the journal, *The East Wind*. *Eat a Bowl of Tea* gained its rightful place within the Asian American literary **canon** in the early 1970s as a result of the recovery work of writers **Frank Chin**, **Jeffery Paul Chan**, **Lawson Fusao Inada**, and Shawn Wong, who included chapters from Chu's novel in their anthologies of Asian American literature, *Aiiieeeee!* (1974) and *The Big Aiiieeeee!* (1991).

Chu's ability to depict Chinatown in its complexity was due to his own geographical, intellectual, and political rootedness in New York's Chinatown, the setting for *Eat a Bowl of Tea*. Born in 1915 in Toishan, China, Chu immigrated with his family to Newark, New Jersey, at age nine. After graduating from Upsala College in New Jersey with a major in English and a minor in sociology, Chu's lifelong interest in New York's Chinese community became clear when he earned his MA in sociology from New York University with his thesis, "Chinese Restaurants in New York City" (1939). Like Ben Loy, the young man whose marriage is at the center of the novel, Chu served in the Army in World War II for two years and, with the passage of the War Brides Act, was able to go to China to seek a wife. With Kang Wong, the woman he married, Chu returned to New York's Chinatown where he opened a record shop in 1950 to support his family. Despite their financial hardships, Chu pursued postgraduate study in sociology for two years at the New School for Social Research and took creative writing courses. From 1952 to 1962, Chu hosted a weekday radio program, *Chinese Festival*, which he started with Kang Wong and produced with Lyle Stuart, the publisher of *Eat a Bowl of Tea*. The program, which featured news, interviews, commercials, and music, was popular with Chinese workers, and for its duration, Chu was New York City's only Chinese American disc jockey. Chu also served as executive secretary of the Soo Yuen Benevolent Association (a social center), and from 1961 until his death in 1970, he directed a day center for the elderly. (*See also* Chinese American Novel)

Further Reading

Li, Shu-yan. "Otherness and Transformation in *Eat a Bowl of Tea* and *Crossings*." *MELUS* (Winter 1993): 99–110.

Ling, Jinqi. *Narrating Nationalisms: Ideology and Form in Asian American Literature.* New York: Oxford UP, 1998.

Wang, Shunzhu. "Louis Hing Chu." *Asian American Novelists: A Bio-Bibliographical Critical Sourcebook.* Ed. Emmanuel S. Nelson. Westport, CT: Greenwood Press, 2000. 68–75.

Cheryl Higashida

CHRISTIAN, BARBARA (1943–2000)   African American scholar and essayist. In numerous essays and books, Barbara Christian chronicled the development of black women writers, describing a literary tradition that had been previously neglected in academic discourse. A distinguished scholar and passionate teacher, Christian helped bring the work of black women writers to national attention and pioneered the field of black feminist criticism.

Born in St. Thomas, Virgin Islands, Christian received her doctorate from Columbia University in 1970. The following year, she became an assistant professor at the University of California, Berkeley, where she helped establish the African American Studies Department. During her more than thirty years at Berkeley, she became the first black woman in the university to be granted tenure and to be promoted to full professor.

In *Black Women Novelists: The Development of a Tradition, 1892–1976* (1980), Christian traces the origins of black women writers and examines the destructive **African American stereotypes** they worked to debunk. Part one offers an analysis of representations of the "tragic mulatta" in early twentieth-century texts and praises the work of later writers such as **Anne Petry**, **Zora Neale Hurston**, and **Gwendolyn Brooks** for their depiction of ordinary, working women. Part two is an in-depth study of novelists **Paule Marshall**, **Toni Morrison**, and **Alice Walker**, who, according to Christian, create a new definition of womanhood that resists the destructive stereotypes of the past. In their frank treatment of oppression and the sexism that exists in the black community, these writers explore the frustration and creative ability of black women.

Christian's second book, *Black Feminist Criticism: Perspectives on Black Women Writers* (1985), is a collection of seventeen essays written between 1975 and 1984. Christian returns to writers like Morrison and Walker, exploring the role of nature, community, and class in their later texts. Christian's penetrating analysis of themes such as lesbianism, female self-definition, and motherhood in black women's literature offer ground-breaking perspectives on texts by **Audre Lorde**, **Gloria Naylor**, and Buchi Emecheta.

In her influential article "The Race for Theory" Christian disparaged the use of critical jargon that alienates readers and keeps power in the hands of an academic elite. This widely cited essay highlights Christian's belief in the need for meaningful exchange between the university and the community at large. As a vocal political activist, Christian worked throughout her life on issues of both global and local import. She fought to keep Ethnic Studies at Berkeley, voiced her support of affirmative action policies, and spoke out at rallies against U.S. intervention in Central America and the Caribbean as well as against U.S. support of apartheid in South Africa. She was also a beloved teacher who worked with educators at Berkeley High School and ran discussion groups with working class black women. As a result of her passionate approach to literature and academic study, black women writers have gained greater respect and appreciation within the academy and among the public at large.

Further Reading

Cornwell-Giles, JoAnne. "Afro-American Criticism and Western Consciousness: The Politics of Knowing." *Black American Literature Forum* 24.1 (1990): 85–98.

Stephanie Li

CIRESI, RITA (1960–) Italian American fiction writer, essayist, critic, and educator. Rita Ciresi has emerged as one of America's premier comic novelists and short story writers.

Ciresi was born and raised in the Italian American section of Hamden, Connecticut. She began writing fiction and poetry in high school, and by twenty-two had recognized her calling. At twenty-five, she published her first story while attending graduate school in Iowa. After receiving her PhD from Pennsylvania State University in 1992, Ciresi began her career as a college professor at Hollins College in Virginia. A year later, she published her first critical essay on Italian American writing, "Paradise Below the Stairs" (1993), and her first book, *Mother Rocket* (1993), a collection of stories, which won the Flannery O'Connor Award for short fiction. The stories of *Mother Rocket* enact the tragedy and comedy of romantic love, generational conflict, and social discomfort, frequent subjects of Ciresi's fiction. Her characteristic gallows humor and well-plotted, hyper-realistic domestic drama mark stories such as "The Silent Partner," about a couple confronting a serious disease.

This same tragicomic formula is at the heart of Ciresi's first novel and most popular book to date, *Blue Italian* (1997), about a young couple, the wife Italian American, the husband Jewish American, struggling to cope with cultural differences and the young husband's cancer. *Blue Italian* appeared a year after Ciresi took her current position as a professor of creative writing at the University of South Florida. The following year, she published another successful novel, *Pink Slip* (1998), in which appears Ciresi's most memorable character, Lisa Diodetto (Lisa "A. K. A. God"). Lisa is a young Italian American career woman who finds herself part of a corporate world she is satirizing in a novel written on company time. This conflict parallels Lisa's internal conflict between career ambition and desire for traditional family life. The story of Lisa's conflict and her love affair with another in a line of Ciresi's Jewish male characters, Eben Strauss, continues in her latest novel, *Remind Me Again Why I Married You* (2003). In the time between these two novels, Ciresi published another critical article, "Straight Men and Other Ordinary Joes: An Introduction to Richard Russo" (2001), and a collection of linked short stories, *Sometimes I Dream in Italian* (2000), which chronicles the childhood and adult experiences of Angel and Lino Lupo, especially their uneasy relationships with each other and members of their Italian American family. A number of stories from this collection and from *Mother Rocket* appear in various anthologies.

At the time of this writing, Ciresi is at work on two manuscripts: a novel, *How Long Do You Have to Live?*, which tells the story of two cancer survivors who meet and fall in love, and a book of essays, *Hello! I Am an American! Surrender!*, which explores the often-difficult task of being American in the world today. In the near future, she plans to write two more novels, both set in her adopted home state of Florida. (*See also* Italian American Novel)

Further Reading

Giunta, Edvige. *Writing with an Accent: Contemporary Italian American Women Authors.* New York: Palgrave, 2002.

Mannino, Mary Ann. "In Our Ears, a Voice: The Persistence of Trauma of Immigration in *Blue Italian* and *Umbertina*." *Italian Americana* 20.1 (Winter 2002): 5–13.

George Guida

CISNEROS, SANDRA (1954–) Mexican American novelist and poet. One of the foremost Mexican American writers today, Sandra Cisneros has garnered critical and popular acclaim for her genre-defying prose narratives about the life experiences of Mexican American women. Her first work of fiction, ***The House on Mango Street*** (1984), explores the sexual and racial oppression, poverty, and violence experienced by a young Mexican American girl. Praised for its unique voice and deft fusion of poetry and prose, *The House on Mango Street* is a staple in today's multicultural literary **canon**. Cisneros's second work of fiction, *Woman Hollering Creek and Other Stories* (1991), contains stories narrated by adult women as well as children exploring similar themes; it was excerpted in *The Norton Anthology of American Literature* in 1998. Her most recent novel, *Caramelo* (2002), traces three generations of a Mexican American family; it was dubbed a landmark work by one reviewer. Cisneros's poetry, which provocatively challenges the restrictions on Mexican American female sexuality, has also gained recognition in recent years.

Sandra Cisneros was born in Chicago to a Mexican father and Mexican American mother, the only daughter among seven children. Her parents divided the family's time between Mexico and the United States; and Cisneros observed the conflicts of cultural loyalty and feelings of alienation her family experienced as they crossed and recrossed the border. While

Sandra Cisneros. *AP/Wide World Photos.*

attending the University of Iowa's Writers Workshop after college, Cisneros realized that her childhood experiences differed significantly from those of her classmates. Thus she created the distinctive voice of Esperanza, the narrator of *The House on Mango Street*, to explicate life in the barrio for Mexican American women. Written as a series of vignettes, each never more than a few pages in length, Esperanza's observations are painfully honest and stunningly acute. Seen from the burgeoning consciousness of a girl hovering between childhood and adulthood, the barrio is not a nurturing place for women. Instead, women are restricted by poverty, domestic and sexual violence, and racial prejudice. Although it is often the men who hold them back, these women can imagine escape only with the help of another man. Esperanza's classmate Sally, for example, marries young in order to flee her abusive father, only to discover her husband is equally violent and controlling. The lovely Rafaela is locked in her apartment by her husband, but she daydreams about meeting another man who might offer her a different kind of life. It is Esperanza who questions the traditional Mexican categories for women—virgin, wife and mother, or whore—as she begins to imagine new possibilities for the lives of Mexican American women. By the end of the book, Esperanza realizes that to develop her individuality and artistic creativity, she must live independently of men. Thus in the penultimate vignette, she yearns for her own house: "Not a man's house. Not a daddy's. A house all my own." Esperanza's desires for an independent life are echoed by Cisneros in the author note at the end of the Vintage paperback edition, in which Cisneros is described as "nobody's mother and nobody's wife."

Woman Hollering Creek and Other Stories continues Cisneros's exploration of women's lives on both sides of the U.S.-Mexico border. Divided into three sections, this book chronicles the stages of female maturation, portraying the exuberant chatter of young girls and the newly awakened sexuality of adolescents, as well as the sharply cynical and fiercely independent voices of mature women. Cisneros keenly captures the vicissitudes of emotion prevalent in each stage of life. In the first section, she writes unerringly in the voice of the preternaturally wise children who document both the individual and communal struggles of Mexican American women. In "Eleven," the protagonist Rachel is humiliated to tears when she is mistakenly identified as the owner of a smelly, raggedy sweater found in her classroom's cloakroom; and thus Rachel's Anglo teacher is subtly indicted for not distinguishing between her Mexican American pupils. Cisneros paints equally vividly the girlish joy of discovering nearly new Barbie dolls sold cheaply at a sidewalk sale and the deep-set contentment of being carried to bed by one's father after falling asleep in a movie theater. In the second section of the book, Cisneros considers the emergent sexuality of teenaged girls, a theme only briefly developed in *The House on Mango Street*. "One Holy Night" chronicles the very real danger of sex for a girl who falls in love with a man who visits her pushcart. Calling himself Chaq after the Mayan god of love and life, the man seduces and then abandons her. While pregnant with his child, the girl sees a newspaper photo of Chaq in handcuffs. Her lover, she learns, is a middle-aged drifter with no Mayan blood, and a serial killer of young girls. This story dramatizes the negative consequences of premarital sex for young women in the Mexican American community; but here the expected outcomes of social martyrdom and single motherhood are eclipsed by the real potential of death at the hands of a murderer. Cisneros's focus on female sexuality continues in the stories of adulthood in the last section of the book. In particular, she demonstrates the limited opportunities available to women to experience fulfilling adult relationships in this patriarchal society. In "Eyes of Zapata," Inés must content herself with the sporadic visits of her lover, the father of her two children, rather than demand his fidelity or his presence in her house, lest he leave her entirely. In the title story, Cléofilas anticipates in her marriage the passionate romance she sees on television shows; instead, her husband consistently beats and verbally abuses her. Ultimately, Cléofilas must rely upon another woman to help her and her children return to the safety of her father's house across the border in Mexico. Here and in other stories, Cisneros questions the primacy of marriage and motherhood in Mexican American culture that undermines any other potential accomplishments by women. In *Woman Hollering Creek*, Cisneros writes longer, more plot-centered narratives, though her poetic style of prose writing follows the arc of *The House on Mango Street*. She liberally sprinkles Spanish words within these stories, leaving the reader to comprehend the phrases as best she may. Yet any disconcertion the reader may feel from this **bilingualism** is countered by the concurrent exploration of cultural displacement experienced by Cisneros's characters; those readers unfamiliar with Spanish can thus empathize with the women who struggle with their dual Mexican and American legacies.

Cisneros's novel *Caramelo* is both her longest and most plot-centered work of fiction. Cisneros writes what she calls the archetypical Mexican love story:

the deep ties between parents and children, rather than husbands and wives. Drawing upon the details of her own family history, she explores the tangled relationships between the doting Mexican mother Soledad and her adoring son Inocencio, Inocencio and his American-born daughter Celaya, and Celaya with Soledad, whom the girl dubs "the Awful Grandmother." Cisneros examines the role of storytelling in family histories and the legacies of one's ancestors in forming the individual self. Celaya, for example, has trouble comprehending her grandmother's seemingly irrational demands upon her children until she learns about the traumas of her grandmother's youth that led her to require such devotion and respect from her children. Celaya then better understands "the Awful Grandmother," as well as her own position as the daughter of a Mexican father.

Playing with the conventions of form and narrational integrity, Cisneros includes within the larger plot conversations between the Awful Grandmother and the narrator Celaya, where Soledad objects to her granddaughter's portrayal of the family history. Cisneros also uses multiple footnotes to explicate aspects of Mexican history and culture or to digress from her primary storyline with additional detail about minor characters. Ultimately, *Caramelo* both educates its readers and celebrates the vibrant wealth of Mexican American culture.

Though best known for her fiction, Cisneros has also published several books of poetry, including *Bad Boys* (1980), *The Rodrigo Poems* (1985), *My Wicked, Wicked Ways* (1987), and *Loose Woman* (1994). Cisneros regards her poetry as more personal than her fiction, as it taps deep into her dreams and subconscious; indeed, many of her poems were never intended for publication. Her poems challenge patriarchal limitations placed on female individuality and sexuality, questioning the negative judgments made against women who behave similarly to men. Her poetic style is raw but playful, with short lines and stanzas that emote powerful sentiments. Ultimately, Cisneros's poetry, as well as her fiction, urges a revision of traditional Mexican American female **identity**, one that boldly questions the constraints set again women's psychological and social growth, while also honoring the history and traditions of Mexican American culture. Already the recipient of such prestigious awards as the MacArthur Fellow, Sandra Cisneros is a pioneering figure in Mexican American literature, as well as an essential writer of the American experience. (*See also* Mexican American Novel, Mexican American Poetry)

Further Reading

Madsen, Deborah L. *Understanding Contemporary Chicana Literature.* Columbia, SC: U of South Carolina P, 2000.

Robin E. Field

CIVIL RIGHTS MOVEMENT   For about fifteen years, from the mid-1950s through the late 1960s, the United States experienced an effort by many of its citizens to overturn the long-standing body of law and custom that relegated African Americans to second-class citizenship and to require

Photograph showing civil rights leaders, including Martin Luther King Jr., marching on Washington, 1963. *Courtesy of the Library of Congress.*

the United States to offer full civil and political rights to all the country's citizens, regardless of race. Through its early years, the movement focused on the American South, where a system of racial oppression and exploitation that dated to slavery kept African Americans poor and living in caste-like circumstances. Once the reality of **race** relations and living conditions in northern cities gained wider attention, however, it broadened to include the rest of the country. After 1965, the movement was weakened by its successes, which included passage of laws guaranteeing access to public facilities and voting. It was weakened, too, by the Vietnam War, which sapped the country's spirit and resources; the assassination of important leaders, including **Martin Luther King Jr.**; and a backlash against black militancy and against social activism generally. By the early 1970s, the nonviolent protest that had characterized much of the Civil Rights Movement was only a memory, and the coalition of blacks, labor leaders, educators, clergy, and various other liberals that waged a unified campaign for broader civil rights through the mid-1960s was gone.

Historian Harvard Sitkoff writes that, as with revolutions generally, the Civil Rights Movement was nourished by anger and born of hope. The anger came from the continuing degraded existence of African Americans through years when civil and political rights were being pushed as ideals at home and abroad. The term "**Jim Crow**," shorthand for American racial segregation, hides the humiliation and despair that characterized blacks' experiences and feelings through the middle of the twentieth century. But whence any hope? It came from a government beginning to recognize the extent of blacks' oppression (as it trumpeted freedom in the escalating cold war) and an African American population expecting progress following a global war against a racist tyrant. The federal government at mid-century was leaning toward taking on racial discrimination, one might say, just when African Americans were growing increasingly inclined to give government a shove.

And shove they did, beginning in December 1955, in Montgomery, Alabama, in an already charged atmosphere. In May 1954, the United States Supreme Court had declared unconstitutional, in *Brown v. Board of Education*, the long-held "separate but equal" doctrine that allowed segregation and inequality in public schools. Almost immediately, white southerners organized to resist the decision's implementation (which the court decreed should occur "with all deliberate speed") and defend their racist way of life. Further raising tensions was the August 1955 murder of fourteen-year-old Chicagoan Emmett Till, visiting in the Mississippi Delta, for whistling at a white woman, followed by the acquittal of two white men accused of the crime. So when Rosa Parks refused to relinquish her seat on a Montgomery bus and the city's African American population boycotted the bus lines, it made big news. The boycott's success, ending segregation on the city's busses a year later, made bigger news still. Blacks across the South and beyond saw the grit and bravery of Montgomery's black community and recognized the strength ordinary African Americans could command if organized and determined.

The young minister who led the Montgomery boycott, King, soon formed the Southern Christian Leadership Conference (SCLC) to plan further nonviolent, civil rights activities, but the organization's speed was almost as deliberate as the *Brown* decision's enforcement. Thus, the late 1950s witnessed little more than the integration of one Little Rock, Arkansas, high school, facilitated by federal soldiers, and congressional passage of one weak civil rights bill. As the 1960s dawned, few recognized any concerted movement for civil rights underway.

Young African Americans would change this circumstance almost overnight. On February 1, 1960, four students from all-black North Carolina A & T College, in Greensboro, kept their seats after being refused service at a downtown lunch counter. The next day, twenty-seven others joined them, and before the month was out, similar "sit-ins" were occurring in cities across the South. Barely two months later, like-minded youth formed a Student Non-Violent Coordinating Committee (SNCC) to lend organization and planning to the escalating protests. King's SCLC scurried to keep up. Southern whites marshaled their forces to resist pressures for change, too, so by the summer of 1960, battle lines were drawn. Often below the radar in each skirmish would be the movement's soul, the local African Americans, who were tired of the way they were forced to live and ready to take risks to change it.

The protests of the early 1960s fell into patterns. A "Freedom Ride" of blacks and whites riding busses across the South in 1961 to call attention to segregation in interstate commerce resulted in burned busses, injured riders, and prison sentences, but little integration. One year later, a shooting war broke out in Oxford, Mississippi, over the admission of African American James Meredith to the state's university. Civil rights organizations marshaled their forces in 1963 in Birmingham, Alabama, one of the South's most segregated cities, seeking jobs for blacks and integration. Birmingham's Director of Public Safety, Eugene "Bull" Connor, determined to stand firm and the result was scenes of brutality: police dogs biting, and water from fire hoses nearly drowning, peaceful demonstrators. King and city officials eventually reached a compromise that pleased few who had risked life and limb. In August 1963, at the March on Washington, King continued to speak in pacifist tones, but weeks later a bomb killed four African American girls awaiting choir practice in Birmingham's Sixteenth Street Baptist Church, and before the year was out, President John F. Kennedy, who had been moving toward supporting legislation to end discrimination, was assassinated in Dallas, Texas. As the country mourned its fallen president, blacks lamented that a century after Emancipation, many descendants of slaves still could not exercise a citizen's rights.

Kennedy's successor, President Lyndon B. Johnson, knew Congress's back halls and worked them to insure passage, by July, of the Civil Rights Act of 1964, which outlawed segregation of public facilities. Not resting on this success, SNCC was involved in a "Freedom Summer" for Mississippi, which involved volunteers educating black Mississippians on the intricacies of voting. The June 21st murder outside Philadelphia, Mississippi, of volunteers James Chaney, Andrew Goodman, and Michael Schwerner did not deter others, and under their direction a Mississippi Freedom Democratic Party formed and sought acceptance in the Democratic National Convention in August. In denying the Freedom party anything beyond token representation at its convention, the Democratic Party showed its true colors, which in Mississippi remained white.

The Civil Rights Act of 1964 dealt with segregation, leaving disfranchisement as the focus of efforts in 1965. Aware that violent opposition to their nonviolent tactics gained attention, civil rights leaders selected Selma, Alabama, for a voting rights campaign. There, Sheriff Jim Clark had an unruly posse with a reputation for being quick with the nightstick. Clark's men played their role with full brutality on "Bloody Sunday," March 7, riding in on horseback, clubbing demonstrators who knelt in prayer after crossing Selma's Edmund Pettus Bridge. It was a ghastly sight on the evening news. After federal intervention, demonstrators marched the fifty miles from Selma to Montgomery, bringing their protest to the state capital, where Alabama Governor George C. Wallace blustered and stalled. That night, Ku Klux Klansmen shot and killed Detroit housewife Viola Liuzzo, drawn to Alabama by the struggle against injustice. Later in the month, Johnson sent to Congress a bill authorizing federal examiners to register black voters, and on August 6 he signed this Voting Rights Act of 1965.

Liberals everywhere celebrated this second major piece of civil rights legislation in successive years, but their joy may have prevented their recognizing signs of the movement's disunity. As early as the "long, hot summer" of 1964, young blacks had begun rethinking their goals and tactics, slowly distancing themselves from King's nonviolent efforts to achieve integration and moving toward a more militant approach to gaining control of their own destiny. While King was in Montgomery in 1965, describing the moral universe in optimistic terms, SNCC's James Forman was inviting African Americans to knock the legs off of any table where blacks were not allowed to sit. A year later, noting that power was the only thing respected in the world, SNCC leader Stokely Carmichael advised blacks to get power "at any cost." Moderate black leaders shied away from Carmichael's Black Power stance. Meanwhile, less than a week after Johnson signed the voting bill, blacks in the Watts district of Los Angeles waged a six-day riot that required 14,000 National Guard troops to bring order and left thirty-four dead. Blacks in America's cities, who suffered from lack of jobs, poor education, and the social effects of their culture of poverty, had grown angry at all the attention on the plight of African Americans in the South. The man who some urban blacks looked to for guidance, the enigmatic **Malcolm X**, had been gunned down by Black Muslim opponents in early 1965. Watts was the first big manifestation of urban blacks' frustrations; many more would occur in coming summers.

The fractured Civil Rights Movement after 1965 simply never healed. More moderate African Americans hoped to work with their allies in labor unions, the Democratic Party, and government generally to build on their success and bring greater opportunity to black Americans. Johnson's Great Society programs held potential for improvement—his encouragement of employers to take "affirmative action" to make up for past injustices and hire more African Americans became standard practice in federal hiring—so long as the momentum continued. King, who might have remained the leader of moderates, was distancing himself from them and from government supporters with his criticism of the Vietnam War and his emphasis on economic change to help the nation's poor. More radical elements listened to Huey Newton, Bobby Seale, and **Eldridge Cleaver** of the Black Panther Party for Self-Defense, who encouraged inner-city blacks to arm themselves and take control of their own affairs. The Federal Bureau of Investigation, whose leader, J. Edgar Hoover, considered such activity un-American and dangerous, took on the Black Panthers, killing and incarcerating some and driving others underground or out of the country. By the time of King's assassination in Memphis on May 3, 1968, it was too late for anyone to reunite the movement's various elements. The November election of Richard M. Nixon as the country's president signaled an electorate that was tired of political and social activism. By then, the United States was also a country with a full-blown foreign war on its hands, drawing the attention of many former civil rights demonstrators as casualties mounted.

The Civil Rights Movement's legacy is more than two sweeping pieces of legislation and heightened awareness of the wrongs dealt to Americans of African descent. Out of the effort came a consensus on the legitimacy of civil rights as an issue worthy of national attention and a body of law that continues to be useful in guaranteeing civil, political, and human rights to all Americans. From the movement, too, came greater awareness of women's issues and growth in efforts to insure equal rights on the basis of gender. The movement's shortcomings are evident as well, however. A half-century after the *Brown* ruling, many schools are still segregated, and African Americans remain poorer as a group than American whites. Late in their lives, King and Malcolm X were in agreement that in a capitalist economy, those lacking capital were destined to remain at a disadvantage. The movement tackled the legal basis of segregation and political discrimination, but it failed to alter the economic circumstances, still in existence, that make it difficult for the descendants of former slaves to enjoy equal economic opportunity nearly a century and a half after **slavery**'s end. (*See also* Black Arts Movement)

Further Reading

Dittmer, John. *Local People: The Struggle for Civil Rights in Mississippi*. Urbana: U of Illinois P, 1994.

Sitkoff, Harvard. *The Struggle for Black Equality, 1954–1992*. Rev. ed. New York: Hill and Wang, 1993.

Weisbrot, Robert. *Freedom Bound: A History of America's Civil Rights Movement*. New York: Penguin Books, 1990.

Donald R. Wright

CLARKE, CHERYL (1947–)   African American poet, lesbian-feminist advocate, and theorist. Cheryl Clarke was born in Washington, DC, in 1947, where she grew up, receiving a BA from Howard University. Since 1969, she has been associated with Rutgers University in New Brunswick, New Jersey, where she completed an MA, MSW, and PhD, and was appointed Director of Diverse Community Affairs and Lesbian-Gay Concerns in 1992. Between 1985 and 1988, she was a member of the Board of Directors of New York Women Against Rape, and from 1987 to 1990, was a founding member and fundraiser for New Jersey Women and Aids Network. Between 1981 and 1990, she was a member of the editorial collective of the magazine *Conditions*, and from 1990 to 1992, served as cochair of the board of the Center for Lesbian and Gay Studies at the City University of New York Graduate Center. She is a member of the faculty of the Cave Canem poets group, dedicated to the study and promotion of contemporary African American poetry. She presently lives in Jersey City, New Jersey.

In the contributor notes to the edited collection *I Do/I Don't: Queers on Marriage* (2004), Cheryl Clarke is identified as an "unregenerate lesbian-feminist, poet, and author of four books of poetry." Her commitment to racial and social justice, to **feminism**, and to lesbian resistance has thus not wavered in the roughly twenty years that she has been writing. In all of her work, whether poetry, literary scholarship, or political advocacy, the political and the personal fuse with a broad vision of contemporary history and culture. Autobiography, narrated lives, and the history of communities come together to illuminate the ways society is shaped by **race** and sexuality. Her writings unfurl a vibrant articulation of the importance of struggle, linked to a poetics of affirmed difference and the denunciation of the oppressive forces that beset women in particular.

Clarke's first book of poetry, *Narratives: Poems in the Tradition of Black Women*, appeared in 1983. It was followed by *Living as a Lesbian* (1986), *Humid Pitch* (1989), and *Experimental Love* (1993), which was nominated for a 1994 Lambda Literary Award. The publication of her latest work, *Corridors of Nostalgia*, is announced for 2005.

Clarke's poetry is tense, concise, and pulsating with anger and compassion. It wastes not a single word, and precisely crafts every line, whether in the narrative form with its mixed inflections of quotidian speech and storytelling, or in the elegiac or epic modes. Narrative is recurrent both as form and theme in her work, including *Corridors of Nostalgia*. For instance, in "Women in Uniform." Clarke works innovatively with poetic form; breaking down and freeing syntax, sparsely and effectively using repetition, blending and questioning the categories of prose and verse, for example titling poems "Journal Entry . . ." or "postcard" or "storytelling" (*Living as a Lesbian*). A narrative poem such as "Women in Uniform" takes that form to its ultimate potential, switching from elliptic, almost telegraphic style, to lyrical enunciation, as does "Movement" (*Experimental Love*), a majestic evocation of the movements for civil rights, that raises the descriptive and personal narrative conclusion to the level of the epic. Erotic encounters between women, the ever-present shadowing of male desire and heterosexual norms, the ocean-like strength of desire, collide and intertwine in some of the most powerful sexual imagery written by a contemporary poet. Much like **Audre Lorde**, Cheryl Clarke subscribes to a politics of the erotic that makes the explicit singing of desire and sexual passion a liberating stance for women. Women are everywhere in her poems, and the denunciation of violence against them, daily and historical ("Indira" in *Living as a Lesbian*) is a prominent theme in her work. In addition, historical and biographical reflections on the **Civil Rights Movement** and the Black Liberation Movement suffuse Clarke's poetry with a complex web of anger and sorrowful nostalgia; such complexities are sometimes penned in a few lines, encapsulating the moods and political struggles of an entire era ("Since my lover left the city . . . ," *Living as a Lesbian*). The intertext of black American culture is present everywhere, in particular with the intricate lacing in of famous **blues** lines throughout the poems of *Living as a Lesbian*. Overall, Clarke's poetic production is rich and diverse, militant and grieving, disciplined and impassioned, inspirational and confrontational.

Cheryl Clarke's poetry has been widely recognized in African American, feminist, and lesbian/gay publications. It has been anthologized in a dozen collections, including the authoritative *No More Masks! An Anthology of Twentieth-Century American Women Poets* (ed. Florence Howe, 1993). Her poems and essays have appeared as well in numerous journals including the *Black Scholar, Belles Lettres, Callaloo, Feminist Studies,* the *Kenyon Review,* and *Sojourner.* Her poetry has been highly praised by other prominent lesbian, feminist, and African American writers, from Audre Lorde to **Adrienne Rich**, **June Jordan**, Dorothy Allison, and **Jewelle Gomez**.

As a scholar, Clarke has dedicated herself to a reclaiming of the fundamental impact of black women writers from the post-1968 period, ranging from Audre Lorde to **Gwendolyn Brooks**. She has focused on bringing to light authors who are insufficiently written about in the mainstream. And she has now written a path-breaking study of women and the Black Arts Movement, appearing in 2005 with Rutgers University Press, formulating a new theory of contemporary black poetries in which Gwendolyn Brooks's 1968 "In the Mecca" is a pivotal text.

Clarke is a foundational figure of the black feminist movement, on a par with leading forces such as Audre Lorde, **Pat Parker**, **Barbara Smith**, and Michele Wallace. She has theorized the independent construction of black feminism, associating with such crucial texts as the Combahee River Collective's *A Black Feminist Statement* (*This Bridge Called My Back: Writing by Radical Women of Color,* ed. **Cherríe Moraga** and **Gloria Anzaldúa**, 1981), whose importance continues to be recognized. Cheryl Clarke's role is continually evidenced in the writings of others. Two essays in particular, "Lesbianism: An Act of Resistance" (*This Bridge Called My Back*) and "The Failure to Transform: Homophobia in the Black Community" (*Home Girls: A Black Feminist Anthology,* ed. Barbara Smith, 1983) have been amply referred to in the last five years. In a notable testimony to Clarke's stature and influence, her essay on homophobia is treated as a landmark by scholars addressing the reclaimed history of black gay/queer male writers, and her essay on lesbian resistance remains a defining text for lesbian feminists. (*See also* African American Literature)

Further Reading

Allison, Dorothy. "Rhyme, Women, and Song." Review of *Humid Pitch: Narrative Poetry* by Cheryl Clarke. *Village Voice Literary Supplement* (February 10, 1987): 52.

Campbell, Jane. Review of *Humid Pitch: Narrative Poetry* by Cheryl Clarke. *Belles Lettres* (Fall 1990): 53.

Gomez, Jewelle. "Cheryl Clarke's Narrative Poetry." *Womanews* (April 1983): 11.

———. "The Body Electric." *Lambda Book Report* 10.9 (April 2002): 14.

Mahone, Sydne. "Truth to Be Told." Review of *Living as a Lesbian: Poetry* by Cheryl Clarke. *Womanews* (May 1986): 15.

Randolph, Elizabeth. "Cheryl Clarke (1947–)." *Contemporary Lesbian Writers of the United States: A Bio-Bibliographical Critical Sourcebook*. Ed. Sandra Pollack and Denise Knight. Westport, CT: Greenwood Press, 1993. 122–27.

Francesca Canadé Sautman

CLEAGE, PEARL (1948–)   African American poet, prose writer, editor, columnist, and playwright. Reflecting her strong beliefs in freedom and equality, Cleage's controversial, prolific, and award-winning writing in several genres boasts her cultural prominence as a writer and performer, though selection of her debut novel, *What Looks Like Crazy on an Ordinary Day* (1997), by Oprah Winfrey for her Book Club expanded the audience for her work.

While studying playwriting at Howard University in Washington, DC from 1966 to 1969, Cleage won the *Promethean Literary Magazine's* first prize in poetry in 1968. Two of her one-act plays, *Hymn for the Rebels* (1968) and *Duet for Three Voices* (1969) were produced at Howard University before she relocated to Atlanta, Georgia, earning her BA from Spelman College, where she continued her studies in drama and playwriting. Published the year she graduated from Spelman, *We Don't Need No Music* (1971), a collection of poetry, was overlooked but her play *The Sale* (1972) opened at Spelman.

While she continued writing plays in the 1980s, which were produced professionally in theaters spanning the United States, she also contributed essays and reviews to *Black World*, *Essence*, *Ms.*, and the *New York Times Book Review*. In the meantime, she published another collection of poetry *Dear Dark Faces: Portraits of a People* (1980) and a privately printed chapbook *One for the Brothers* (1983). *Hospice* (1983) was produced Off Broadway at the New Federal Theater, New York, and won five Audience Development Committee (AUDELCO) Awards for Outstanding Achievement Off Broadway in 1983.

Cleage's fiction and poetry were amassed in two publications, *The Brass Bed and Other Stories* (1991) and *Mad at Miles: The Blackwoman's Guide to Truth* (1991). With the production of *Flyin' West* (1992), which premiered at the Alliance Theater in Atlanta, Cleage displayed her knack for bundling **race**, gender, and history with humor to deal with pressing social issues. *Deals with the Devil: And Other Reasons to Riot* (1993) was well-acknowledged and presented over thirty essays of Cleage's take on issues of race, politics, gender, sex, film criticism, and popular culture.

Cleage's recent fiction fuses her affection for African American characters with contemporary issues such as AIDS, substance abuse, and terrorism. In touching on social issues affecting the African American community within her novels, Cleage promotes dialogue about political issues with the intention of spurring societal transformation instead of remanding discussion of her work to the journals of literary criticism.

What Looks Like Crazy on an Ordinary Day; Wish I Had a Red Dress (2001), which won the top fiction honor in the 2002 Literary Awards of the Black Caucus of the American Library Association; and *Some Things I Though I'd Never Do* (2003) reflect Cleage's feminist sensibilities and her skill in writing about taboo topics with humor and spirit.

Further Reading

Giles, Freda Scott. "The Motion of Herstory: Three Plays by Pearl Cleage." *African American Review* 31.4 (1997): 709–12.

Sullivan, Esther Beth. "The Dimensions of Pearl Cleage's *Flyin' West.*" *Theatre Topics* 7.1 (1997): 11–22.

Rebecca Tolley-Stokes

CLEAVER, (LEROY) ELDRIDGE (1935–1998)   African American writer. Eldridge Cleaver is the author of *Soul on Ice* (1968), a collection of autobiographical reflections and political essays that shocked readers with its bold descriptions of prison life and frank assessment of American **race** relations. Cleaver became a prominent voice among the Black Panthers, exhorting radical claims of self-defense and **black nationalism**.

Leroy Eldridge Cleaver was born in Wabbaseka, Arkansas, though he grew up in the Watts district of Los Angeles where he was often in trouble with the law. After being convicted of marijuana possession in 1954, he was sent to Soledad State Prison where he obtained his GED and read the works of **W. E. B. Du Bois**, Karl Marx, and Thomas Paine, among others. He was released in 1957, but was soon after convicted of rape and assault. In Folsom State Prison, he joined the Black Muslims and became a follower of **Malcolm X**.

While in prison, Cleaver began writing some of the essays that would eventually be included in *Soul on Ice*. In 1966, the magazine *Ramparts* published "Notes on a Native Son," Cleaver's infamous attack on **James Baldwin**. Due to his growing fame, Cleaver was able to gather the support necessary to obtain parole. He continued to write for *Ramparts*, and eventually became senior managing editor.

Cleaver was introduced to Bobby Seale and Huey P. Newton, the cofounders of the Black Panther Party for Self-Defense, in 1967. In addition to opposing police harassment and brutality, the Panthers organized free lunch programs for needy children and other community services. Cleaver was especially impressed by their militant ideology and joined the group as their Minister of Information.

Cleaver received widespread national attention with the publication of *Soul on Ice*. The book addresses such issues as prison life, interracial relationships, and Cleaver's own profound sense of racial alienation. It did much to present the claims and ideological development of black nationalists although it also galvanized national concerns about the Black Panthers. While some critics admired Cleaver's frank portrayal of American race relations, others criticized his profanity and radical claims. Despite the mixed responses to *Soul on Ice*, readers recognized the emergence of a new and powerful voice in the black community. In 1970 it received the **Martin Luther King Jr.** Memorial Prize.

Two days after the assassination of Martin Luther King Jr., Cleaver was involved in a gun battle in California. He was charged with violating parole as well as assault and attempted murder. However, a number of prominent intellectuals, including **Susan Sontag** and Gary Merrill, rallied to his defense, and Cleaver was released. He was soon after selected to be the presidential candidate for the Peace and Freedom Party, a radical, interracial organization.

Eldridge Cleaver. *Courtesy of the Library of Congress.*

In 1968 the court ruling following Cleaver's arrest was overturned. Rather than face criminal charges, Cleaver fled the country and lived as a fugitive for the next seven years. He spent time in Cuba, Algeria, and France, and also visited the Soviet Union, China, North Vietnam, and North Korea. He published *Post-Prison Writings and Speeches* (1969) while in Cuba. This collection was scorned by many critics who deemed it a simplistic rationale of Black Panther ideology. During this time, Cleaver also had two children, Maceo and Joju, with his wife, Kathleen.

Cleaver's travels through various communist countries fed his growing disillusionment with his former political beliefs and socialism in general. He found the promised revolutionary spirit of Marx and Lenin to be a fraudulent reality, calling Cuba's policies "voodoo socialism." This political awakening was accompanied by his sudden conversion to Christianity, which was precipitated by a mystical vision.

In 1975, Cleaver returned to the United States and surrendered to the Federal Bureau of Investigation (FBI). The attempted murder charge was dropped after he pleaded guilty to assault and he was ordered to do community service. He published *Soul on Fire* (1978), a collection of autobiographical essays that recount his relationship with the Black Panthers and his spiritual transformation. Although some critics praised his mature perspective, many decried the absence of his passionate rhetoric.

Cleaver was involved in a number of activities prior to his death in 1998. He designed men's trousers, worked with evangelical organizations, and made an unsuccessful bid for Congress in 1984. Though he struggled with addiction and anonymity toward the end of his life, Cleaver will continue to be remembered for his fiery rage and passion.

Further Reading

Warnken, William P., Jr. "Eldridge Cleaver: From Savior to Saved." *Minority Voices: An Interdisciplinary Journal of Literature and the Arts* 1.2 (1977): 49–61.

Stephanie Li

CLIFF, MICHELLE (1946–)   Jamaican American novelist, prose-poet, short story writer, literary and cultural critic. Growing up Caribbean amid a confusion of cultural influences distorted by colonial and postcolonial socio-political realities, Cliff had to negotiate a complex web of privilege and oppression to recover suppressed AmerIndian and African lines embedded in her family's genealogy. Sexist and heterosexist prejudice also presented formidable obstacles to the adolescent lesbian's determination to claim all her identities in writing. In the face of these ambiguities and challenges, Cliff has seized the possibilities for affirming difference and worked out an aesthetics equal to the task. In particular, three remarkable novels—*Abeng* (1984), *No Telephone to Heaven* (1987), and *Free Enterprise* (1993)—have secured Michelle Cliff an important place in postcolonial Caribbean and African American literature. These novels advance Cliff's project of rewriting "official" histories that have erased or distorted colonized and oppressed people's stories of damage, survival, and resistance. Cliff invests her own conflicted experiences of racialized oppression and privilege in Clare Savage, the Jamaican protagonist of *Abeng* and *No Telephone to Heaven*.

Cliff was born a light-skinned creole of European and African descent in Jamaica, still a British Crown Colony in 1946. At age three, Cliff moved with her family to the Unites States, where the light-skinned Cliffs often passed for white but still experienced difficulties assimilating into U.S. culture. In 1956 the family returned to Jamaica and enrolled Cliff at a private girls' school, where she received an anglocentric colonialist education until 1960, when her family moved back to New York. Anne Frank's diaries inspired Cliff to begin writing despite her family's ridicule, and a New York women's writing group encouraged her to launch her writing career with "Notes on Speechlessness" in 1978. In *Claiming an Identity They Taught Me to Despise* (1980) and *The Land of Look Behind* (1985), Cliff experimented in prose-poetry and short fiction, honing her craft and courageously exploring her multiple, conflicted identities. Formal study of languages, comparative history, women's studies, and politics also contributed to Cliff's commitment, in her teaching and her writing, to redressing the misrepresentations of history and educating others in the damaging effects of **racism** and other oppressions.

The bildungsroman *Abeng* enacts Clare Savage's journey to politicized consciousness through experimental layered narratives that recover her maternal AmerIndian roots, and claim legendary Jamaican woman-warrior Nanny as foremother of postcolonial resistance. *No Telephone to Heaven* continues migrant Clare's journey to the Unites States and England, then back to Jamaica and revolutionary action. Her story converges with those of other "crossroads" characters—crossing boundaries of nation, **race**, class, and gender—who unite in rebellion, even if the climactic act is tragically compromised. Influenced by Toni Morrison's *Beloved* (1988) and its fictional reconstruction of untold stories of bondage and resistance, Cliff wrote *Free Enterprise*, set in slave-era and turn-of-the-century United States. Mary Ellen Pleasant, African American entrepreneur and rebel, stands at the center of the novel's layered narratives. Ghosts past, present, and future of the African Americas are raised, scattered images and voices of resistance and complicity from disparate times and cultures are collected together to tell a provocatively different black American history of slavery and its aftermath. Cliff's most recent book is *The Store of a Million Items* (1998), a collection of short stories featuring characters in revealing cross-cultural encounters. (*See also* Caribbean American [Anglophone] Novel)

Further Reading

Agosto, Noraida. *Michelle Cliff's Novels: Piecing the Tapestry of Memory and History. Caribbean Studies.* Vol. 1. New York: Peter Lang, 2000.

Backes, Nancy. "Growing Up Desperately: The Adolescent 'Other' in the Novels of Paule Marshall, Toni Morrison, and Michelle Cliff." *Women of Color: Defining the Issues, Hearing the Voices. Contributions in Women's Studies.* Ed. Diane Long Hoeveler, Janet K. Boles, and Toni-Michelle C. Travis. Westport, CT: Greenwood Press, 2001. 147–57.

Elia, Nada. *Trances, Dances, and Vociferations: Agency and Resistance in Africana Women's Narratives.* New York: Garland, 2001.

Garvey, Johanna X. K. "Passages to Identity: Re-Membering the Diaspora." *Black Imagination and the Middle Passage.* Ed. Maria Diedrich, Henry Louis Gates Jr., and Carl Pedersen. *W. E. B. Du Bois Institute Series.* Oxford, UK: Oxford UP, 1999. 255–70.

Gifford, William Tell. *Narrative and the Nature of the Worldview in the Clare Savage Novels of Michelle Cliff. Caribbean Studies Series.* Vol. 4. New York: Peter Lang, 2001.

Gourdine, Angeletta K. M. *The Difference Place Makes: Gender, Sexuality, and Diaspora Identity.* Columbus: Ohio State UP, 2003.

Macdonald-Smythe, Antonia. *Making Homes in the West Indies: Constructions of Subjectivity in the Writings of Michelle Cliff and Jamaica Kincaid. Literary Criticism and Cultural Theory Series.* London: Routledge, 2001.

Cora Agatucci

CLIFTON, LUCILLE (1936–) African American poet, autobiographer, children's book author, and professor. Lucille Clifton employs a spare and direct style in her poems about African American families, culture, and history. Whether her subjects are historical events or personal experiences, her poems are always imbued with good-hearted irony and resolute optimism.

Lucille Clifton was born Thelma Lucille Sayles in Depew, New York, on June 27, 1936, the daughter of Samuel and Thelma Sayles. Her parents participated in the Great Migration of African Americans north in search of jobs in the early 1900s; her mother came from Georgia and her father from Virginia. Neither parent had the opportunity to complete elementary school, but they instilled their love for language, especially the rhythms of the King James Bible, in their daughter. Clifton's father, a steel worker, also told stories about his great-grandmother Caroline Donald (1823–1910), a woman who was kidnapped from Dahomey, West Africa in 1830, sold into slavery in New Orleans, and walked to Virginia in a slave coffle. Her daughter Lucille, Clifton's namesake, was the first black woman legally hanged in the state after she murdered the white father of her son Genie. Clifton details her family history, including the deaths of her mother in 1959 and her father in 1969, in several poems as well as the 1976 memoir *Generations*.

Clifton, the first member of her family to finish high school, entered Howard University in 1953 as a theater major. At Howard Clifton met several other future writers: **Sterling Brown**, **Toni Morrison** (Chloe Wofford), and **Amiri Baraka** (LeRoi Jones). She transferred after two years to attend Fredonia State Teachers College, but left before graduating to pursue writing. In 1958 she married Fred Clifton, a professor of philosophy. The couple soon had six children, four daughters (Sidney, Fredrica, Gillian, and Alexia) and two sons (Channing and Graham). Clifton continued to write while she was raising a family, but has credited the demands of motherhood with creating her succinct but powerful style. She received the Discovery Award in 1969, and published her first collection of poems (*Good Times*) and her

Lucille Clifton. *AP/Wide World Photos.*

first children's book (*Some of the Days of Everett Anderson*) in the same year. She began writing children's literature at the suggestion of her friend **Maxine Kumin**, the poet and children's book author. Through the years Clifton has published over twenty children's books, many of which feature Everett Anderson, a boy from the inner city with a positive spirit and inquiring mind. Clifton began to accept poet-in-residence positions in 1971 and moved temporarily to California after the death of her husband in 1984. She is currently a professor at St. Mary's College in Maryland. She was appointed the Poet Laureate of Maryland in 1979.

Clifton has maintained a consistent rate of publication since 1969: *Good News of the Earth* (1972), *Ordinary Woman* (1974), *Two Headed Woman* (1980), *Good Woman: Poems & Memoir* (1987), *Next: New Poems* (1987), *Quilting: Poems* (1991), *The Book of Light* (1993), *Terrible Stories* (1996), and *Blessing the Boats: New and Selected Poems, 1988–2000* (2000). She won the National Book

Award for poetry for the last collection, her first major award despite three previous nominations for the Pulitzer Prize.

Many of Clifton's poems are inspired by her family and demonstrate her trademark unadorned free verse and compelling use of repetition, a style reminiscent of the early **Margaret Walker**. Clifton frequently writes about her parents and their turbulent marriage in works like "Forgiving my Father" and "In the Evening." In the poems "She Understands Me" and "the death of thelma sayles" the author mourns the unfulfilled potential of her mother, an amateur poet who battled epilepsy, mental illness, and her husband until her death at age forty-four.

Lucille Clifton's poems also address the experiences of modern African American women. Works like "the thirty eighth year," "homage to my hair," and "homage to my hips" proudly detail the sensual physicality of modern "ordinary" women with their curvy hips, tangled hair, and tired faces. To show the rich complexity present in all women, Clifton frequently alludes to the Biblical Virgin Mary and the Hindu goddess Kali in the "Some Jesus" sequence in *Good News*, the Mary sequence in *Two-Headed Woman*, and the Kali poems in *Ordinary Woman*. With these works Clifton pushes her readers to accept the potential for a woman to be both selfless and destructive in her simultaneous roles as daughter, wife, and mother.

Finally, Clifton is especially adept at utilizing historical events or figures to explore themes of silence, injustice, memory, and prejudice. She defends her attraction to history in poems like "i am accused of tending to the past" in which she argues that history, like a "monstrous" infant, is a living entity. It must be tended and controlled so that it does not threaten the present. In the companion poems "at the cemetery, walnut grove plantation, south carolina, 1989" and "slave cabin, sitterly plantation, maryland, 1989" Clifton testifies for the unnamed slaves whose contributions are evident in the tools, crafts, and structures on the plantations. Clifton returns to the early seventeenth century for "In Salem," a poem that honors the black women who were terrorized during the New England witch trials. Other historical tragedies such as Gettysburg, Nagasaki, Jonesboro, and the Birmingham bombings, figure in Clifton's verse.

Lucille Clifton is one of the nation's most respected poets. Her work shares areas of interest with other prominent contemporary writers: social issues (**Sonia Sanchez, Nikki Giovanni**), motherhood (Toni Morrison, **Louise Erdrich**), fathers (**Janice Mirikitani, Sandra Cisneros, Hisaye Yamamoto**), and spirituality (**Denise Levertov**). Clifton's approachable style and diverse subject matter appeal to a vast audience; she continues to write poetry, memoir, and children's literature.

Further Reading

Mance, Ajuan Maria. "Re-Locating the Black Female Subject: The Landscape of the Body in the Poems of Lucille Clifton." *Recovering the Black Female Body: Self-Representation by African American Women*. Ed. Michael Bennett and Vanessa S. Dickerson. New Brunswick, NJ: Rutgers UP, 2001. 123–40.

Ann Beebe

COBB, NED (1885–1973)   African American autobiographer. Ned Cobb's autobiography, *All God's Dangers: The Life of Nate Shaw*, represents the narrative literary tradition that began in the eighteenth century and continues to evolve today. An illiterate man with a gift for storytelling, Cobb told the story of his life to Theodore Rosengarten, a Harvard University graduate who would capture Cobb's narrative in *All God's Dangers*. In this manner, Cobb's autobiography exemplifies the "as-told-to" tradition of African American autobiography.

Published in 1974, *All God's Dangers* renders the oral history of Ned Cobb, a folk hero in his small, rural home community of Tallapoosa County, Alabama. The book won a National Book Award in the same year. Nate Shaw is the hero of *All God's Dangers*. Cobb chose that name as his pseudonym, hoping to protect his privacy. Shaw begins his story in the late nineteenth century, giving an account of the disappointment he and his family members experienced because they were treated like slaves, despite their freedom. Shaw relates the plight of African American tenant farmers, such as he was, who still were expected to answer to the white landlords.

Shaw, however, wants better for himself. Inspired by his grandmother, he believes that skill and hard work will lead to improved living conditions. By 1931, with a wife and ten children to support, Shaw joined the Share-croppers Union. Just one year later, he opposed four deputy sheriffs' attempts to confiscate his neighbor's property for the benefit of the white landlord. Following a violent struggle with the officers, Shaw was arrested, convicted of a felony in court and sentenced to twelve years in prison. When he regains his freedom, he returns home to find that his wife is dying and that many of his children have left home. Still, Shaw resumes his farming with dignity, hoping still to prosper.

Cobb shared his story with Rosengarten in 1969, at the age of eighty-four. He died just four years later and would not witness the publication of his narrative. Still, having lived from the Reconstruction era of the late nineteenth century through the mid-century **Civil Rights Movement**, Shaw relates the often harsh realities of a time in which African Americans in rural communities struggled for equality during the period of legal segregation in the United States.

In the spirit of **slave narratives** written by **Olaudah Equiano, Frederick Douglass,** and **Harriet Jacobs**, Cobb's story represents the concept of learning through struggle as a source of freedom. Moreover, as Cobb's is an oral history written by a third party, it is comparable to *The Confessions of Nat Turner* (1931) as well as *The Autobiography of Malcolm X* (1965). (*See also* Amanuensis)

Further Reading

Rosengarten, Theodore. "Stepping Over Cockleburs: Conversations with Ned Cobb." *Telling Lives: The Biographer's Art*. Ed. Marc Pachter. Washington, DC: New Republic Books, 1979. 104–31.

Ondra K. Thomas-Krouse

COHEN, SARAH BLACHER (1936–)   Jewish American playwright, critic, editor, and professor. Cohen is a writer who brilliantly combines her complex Jewish faith and culture with the awareness, sensibility, and dark humor of a person with a disability. This humor is always apparent in her character's dialogue as well as her own conversation. Speaking of her youth, Cohen sardonically recalls, "I couldn't run fast, but I could think fast" (Telephone interview, April 20, 2004). Cohen's transformation from scholar to dramatist presents readers and theatergoers with a fascinating and humorous literary journey.

Cohen is the youngest daughter of Mary and Louis Blacher, Yiddish-speaking immigrants from Minsk, Russia. Cohen's father ("Louie the White-Jew" as he was called by his gentile friends) was a junk-dealer in rural Appleton, Wisconsin. Cohen is in the process of completing a memoir titled *Junk-Dealer's Daughter* based upon her singular mid-American Jewish upbringing. Reminiscing about her youth Cohen reveals a major theme of her dramatic work: "I should have been a stand-up comic. My mother told me to be 'adel' or 'genteel,' but I had a loud voice and wanted to speak up. I liked these women who needed to have their voices heard" (Telephone interview, April 20, 2004). These themes of empowering women and giving voice to the voiceless have occupied a prominent position in Cohen's work both on and off the stage.

Cohen began her career as a literary scholar with a well-received book titled *Saul Bellow's Enigmatic Laughter*, published in 1974. Since that first volume Cohen has written and edited nearly half a dozen other books, including *Comic Relief: Humor in Contemporary American Literature, Jewish Wry: Essays on Jewish Humor, Cynthia Ozick's Comic Art*, and *Making a Scene: The Contemporary Drama of Jewish-American Women*.

After having written several highly regarded critical studies, it appeared as if Cohen's career was destined for the academy and not the stage. Despite her many accomplishments as a professor of English at the State University of New York campus at Albany, Cohen's scholarship has taken a less academic turn. In the last few decades Cohen has followed **Cynthia Ozick**'s advice and transformed herself into an increasingly visible and influential playwright. In her foreword to her 1983 collection of essays *Art and Ardor*, Ozick had this to say about Cohen: "I have a conscientious and responsible friend, a professor and a scholar, and also a reputable literary critic; in her heart she is a secret playwright. She wants to make things up: characters, settings, dialogues, plots. . . . She will not permit herself a descent, however alluring, into the region of the trivial. She is a writer of essays" (ix).

Six years later in 1989 Cohen made that "descent" with her first drama, *The Ladies Locker Room*. Still, before creating this autobiographical play, Cohen played the midwife collaborating with Nobel laureate **Isaac Bashevis Singer** on the Off Broadway play titled *Schlemiel the First*. Since then Cohen has cowritten plays of increasing range, beauty, and outrageous humor. *Sofie, Totie and Belle,* a musical about "unkosher" Jewish comediennes, was first produced in 1992 before moving to Off Broadway in 2000. In 1994 Cohen's *Molly Picon's Return Engagement*, a dynamic musical about the most vibrant Yiddish singer of her time, was staged. *Henrietta Szold: Woman of Valor*, sponsored by the New York State Writers Institute, appeared in 2000 and is a rousing tribute to the courageous founder of Israel's Hadassah Hospital. In 2001, *Danny Kaye: Supreme Court Jester*, a musical about America's best ambassador of good wit, had its world premier. In 2004 Cohen's cowritten *American Kezmers* was selected as one of the seven best new musicals to be performed at the New Tuners Stages Festival in Chicago.

More recently Cohen's career seems to be coming full circle. Cohen's current project is titled *Shared Stages: The Drama of Blacks and Jews*, which contains her coauthored play *Soul Sisters*, a multicultural musical celebrating the relationship between African American and Jewish women during the civil rights era. This book seeks to combine both of Cohen's loves: scholarly and dramatic writing. Today, Cohen's plays are being produced across the United States and Europe.

Perhaps it is only fitting that Cohen, who through her late transformation from critic to playwright has overcome years of "dramatic" silence, should have the last word: "As an untamed playwright, I have employed gleeful abandon to make these unorthodox ladies into *vilde chayes* (wild beasts), leaping over the boundaries of Jewish respectability. Yet I have not alienated audiences with their breaches of decency. Rather than offending sensibilities, their big mouths have created an enduring tumult, and their innovative *schmutz* (filth) has left an indelible mark. Meanwhile, as playwright, I am in the process of creating other obstreperous sisters to disturb the peace" (Cohen 203).

Further Reading

Cohen, Sarah Blacher. "From Critic to Playwright: Fleshing Out Jewish Women in Contemporary Drama." *Talking Back: Images of Jewish Women in American Popular Culture*. Ed. Joyce Antler. Hanover, NH: Brandeis UP, 1998. 191–203.

Ezra Cappell

COLEMAN, WANDA (1946–)   African American poet, fiction writer, essayist, and dramatist. Wanda Coleman is a prolific author and outspoken cultural critic who challenges popular stereotypes about black writers. She has sparked public outrage by writing negative reviews of books by **Maya Angelou** and **Audre Lorde**, and she openly criticizes the academy for its marginalization of many African American women artists. In interviews, she advocates a black feminist politics that can account for the specificities of black women's experiences. However, she argues in her essays on American social relations that **race** continues to be the central unresolved issue in the United States. Coleman's unwillingness to accept a status thrust upon her by the coinciding factors of gender, race, economic circumstance, and profession suggests that she is attempting to redefine the field of contemporary African American literature by bringing its unacknowledged geographies to light.

Coleman grew up in Watts, a suburb of South Central Los Angeles. Her work's themes and rhetoric often reflect the frustrations of living in a geography that is invisible to most inhabitants of the United States. She has received little public recognition, other than the 1999 Lenore Marshall Poetry Prize, for her work. This circumstance may stem in part from her unwillingness to project a conformist image of herself. She is unafraid of living a life on the margins even of the poetry community but argues that, because of the rapid development of the Los Angeles literary scene, western cities are supplanting New York and Chicago as the locus for experimental, nonwhite literatures. Coleman's work also interrogates the ways in which the geographically controlled publication and dissemination of texts collude in supporting persistent social problems.

To date, Coleman has published seven books of poetry, including *Ostinato Vamps* (2003) and *Mercurochrome* (2001); two books of poetry and stories; a collection of essays, *Native in A Strange Land* (1996); a novel, *Mambo Hips and Make Believe* (1999); several videos and audio recordings; and numerous articles. Her first book, *African Sleeping Sickness: Stories and Poems* (1990), introduced her first of three ongoing poetic series, "American Sonnets." She originally envisioned this group as a collection of 100 jazz-influenced sonnets but has since published them in various forums. Her transformation of the **canon**ical sonnet form illustrates her revisionist perspective on white American literary traditions, as do her experiments with a range of forms and mixed-genre collections. Finally, Coleman is a well-known participant in the Los Angeles performance-poetry scene. She recorded a segment for the video series *The United States of Poetry* (1996) and has given readings in California and around the country. Her independence of thought and her considerations of the ways in which geography shapes social conflicts render her work an important addition to debates about national **identity**.

Further Reading

Comer, Krista. "Revising Western Criticism Through Wanda Coleman." *Western American Literature* 33.4 (Winter 1999): 357–83.

Magistrale, Tony, and Patricia Ferreira. "Sweet Mama Wanda Tells Fortunes: An Interview with Wanda Coleman." *Black American Literature Forum* 24.3 (Autumn 1990): 491–507.

Jennifer D. Ryan

COLLINS, KATHERINE CONWELL [Also known as Kathleen Conwell or Kathleen Collins Prettyman] (1942–1988) African American filmmaker and playwright. Inspired by **Lorraine Hansberry**'s aesthetic, Collins wrote life as she saw it and did not allow herself to be fettered by constraints placed on African American writers. She looked at African Americans as human subjects and not as mere **race** subjects. When her plays did focus on issues of race, she rendered what she felt were honest portrayals of black life and not portrayals that exaggerated negative aspects or posed overly positive aspects of black existence in America while ignoring the often negative and daunting realities. Rather than seeing black problems as simple manifestations of white oppression, Collins suggests that much of it has to do with the internal dialogue and pressures we impose on ourselves. Her plays are deeply psychological in nature. She integrates certain elements of her personal life into her plays and invites us to go beyond the surface meaning of things and think about the values and the attitudes imposed on us by society and how we choose to deal with them.

Collins was born in Jersey City, New Jersey, March 18, 1942, to Frank and Loretta Conwell. Her father worked as a mortician and afterward became the principal of a high school that is now named after him. He later became the first African American state legislator in New Jersey. After graduating from Skidmore College in Sarasota Springs, New York, Collins followed her father's political lead and became involved in the Student Nonviolent Coordinating Committee's (SNCC) thrust to help register voters in the South. After obtaining her degree in philosophy and religion in 1963, Collins furthered her education at the Sorbonne in Paris, France. There she became interested in telling stories through film. She completed the Master's of Arts degree in 1966 through the Sorbonne's Middlebury graduate program. She then returned to the United States and began her writing career, while working on the editorial and production staff of WNET Radio in New York.

Collins's first stories reflected her experiences in SNCC, France, and the dilemmas of a young married woman. In 1974, shortly after her marriage to Douglass Collins ended, Collins joined the faculty of City College at the City University of New York as a professor of film history and screenwriting. In fact, it was her students, particularly Ronald Gray, who encouraged her to pursue a script she had previously abandoned. Adapting Jewish writer **Henry Roth**'s fiction to film, Collins became the first African American woman to write, direct, and produce a full-length feature film. The screenplay turned film, *The Cruz Brothers and Mrs. Malloy,* about the struggle of three Puerto Rican brothers to survive in a small country town, won first prize in the Sinking Creek Film Festival.

Losing Ground, which led to the first independent feature film by an African American woman filmmaker, followed in 1982 and won first prize at the Figueroa da Foz International Film Festival in Portugal. Other films to her credit include *Madame Flor* (1987) and *Conversations with Julie* (1988). Her films have been shown on the Learning Channel and the Public Broadcasting Station.

Among her plays are *In the Midnight Hour* (1981); *The Brothers* (1982), which was a finalist for the Susan Blackburn International Prize in Playwriting and voted one of the Best Plays of 1982 by the Audience Development Committee (AUDELCO) Awards Committee; and *The Reading*, a one-act play about the conflict between white and black women, commissioned by the American Place Theatre (1984). She also penned *Begin the Beguine* (1985), a collection of one-act plays produced at the Richard Allen Center for Culture and Arts in New York; a play about the first black aviatrix, Bessie Coleman (*Only the Sky is Free* [1985]); *While Older Men Speak* (1986); and *Looking for Jane*. In 1987, Collins married Alfred E. Prettyman and completed her screenplay *Madame Flor.* In spring 1988 Conwell completed a novel, *Lollie: A Suburban Tale,* and in the summer another screenplay, *Conversations with Julie*, about a mother and daughter coming to terms with separation.

Her plays employ such themes as marital malaise, male dominance and impotence, freedom of expression, and the unglorified plight of the black middle class. Her protagonists are typically self-reflective women who move from a state of subjugation to empowerment. Collins's plays followed the "Blaxploitation" era and a number of plays and films that focused on the rise of blacks from poverty or "ghetto" life. She met a great deal of criticism because many feel that her plays have not been black-centered or have lacked the requisite positive representations of black life. Despite such disapproval, Collins continued to write about the complexities of black life, some of which has little, if anything, to do with race, choosing to go "her own way" rather than being overly concerned about how she's perceived by others.

Although Collins wrote and produced a number of plays and films in her lifetime, one gets the feeling that she was only just beginning when she succumbed to cancer. During her short life Collins managed to change the face and content of black womanist film. Her influence extends to other black filmmakers such as Euzhan Palcy and Julie Dash who both honor her fearlessness and presence as a writer and filmmaker. (*See also* African American Film)

Further Reading

Campbell, Loretta. "Reinventing Our Image: Eleven Black Women Filmmakers." *Heresies* 4.4 (1983): 58–62.

Nicholson, David. "A Commitment to Writing: A Conversation with Kathleen Collins Prettyman." *Black Film Review* 5.1 (1988–89): 6–15.

Chandra Tyler Mountain

COLLINS, MERLE (1950–) Caribbean American poet, novelist, short fiction writer, lecturer and educator. A prolific writer, Collins is one of the foremost female writers to explore and fully capture the diasporan experience dominant in all of her creative writing, which is a fusion of racial, political, cultural, and societal concerns. Born on the tiny island of Grenada in the Caribbean, Collins attributes most of her writing philosophy to her childhood in Grenada, where she learned how to intertwine concepts of oratorical media with the formal art of writing. As for her interest in history, politics, and government, she earned a PhD in Government from the University of London, admitting she always had an interest in politics, especially after the tensions surrounding the invasion of Grenada by the United States in 1983.

Collins has written several volumes of significant work. Her first novel, *Angel* (1987), is a bildungsroman or coming-of-age story that traces the life of a young woman, Angel, during the political tensions in Grenada, particularly during the United States invasion of the country. Amid the Grenadian people's struggle to achieve political autonomy, and amid the photographs, holy pictures, religious signs and symbols, signs of the cross, and sayings as part of the traditional culture, Collins captures the cadence and imagery of Grenadian speech and renders a sensitive portrayal of personal and political struggle for change, as Angel grows up rebellious and headstrong.

In *The Colour of Forgetting* (1995), set on the mythical islands of Paz and Eden, Collins writes a lyrical novel of everyday disappointments and triumphs, depicting the never-ending tensions of land disputes, family feuds, political upheaval, and personal trauma. Drawing on her storytelling techniques from her mother and grandmother, who were performers and storytellers, and on the community for whom she writes, Collins conjures up magical stories and weaves together important threads of history and memories of ancestry as the past is slowly threatened by the present.

Collins has also published a collection of short stories, *Rain Darling* (1990), and three collections of powerful poetry, *Because the Dawn Breaks* (1985), dedicated to the people of Grenada; *Rotten Pomerack* (1992), about the ironies and paradoxes of living in such poems as "Chant Me a Tune," "How Times Have Changed!," "Nearly Ten Years Later," and "The Lesson"; and *Lady in a Boat* (2003). At the heart of each work is the voice of a lyrical, passionate storyteller and poet, a voice for the people of Grenada, calling attention to particular experiences, whether personal or political, breaking silences and building bridges that have taken a lifetime to cross.

Interested in performance poetry, Collins joined the African Dawn, a group that blends poetry with African music, in 1985, and has performed on tours throughout Britain and Europe. She has performed and presented her own poetry and prose fiction around the world, electrifying audiences on college campuses, at the Embassy of Grenada, the Bette Noir Poetry Festival, and many others.

Collins, like **Paule Marshall**, who also draws from her West Indian ancestry, has made a significant impact on the literary world through her unique style of writing. She often utilizes the Caribbean dialect, and with her skills as a storyteller and fiction writer, Collins captures the richness of Grenada's folklore and the nuances of everyday life in an environment and world that she is still searching to understand. Her forthcoming novel is *Invisible Streams*. (*See also* Caribbean [Anglophone] Novel)

Further Reading

Bloom, Harold. "Merle Collins." *Caribbean Women Writers*. Philadelphia: Chelsea House, 1997. 45–57.

Booker, M. Keith, and Dubravka Juraga. "Merle Collins: *Angel* (Grenada, 1987)." *The Caribbean Novel in English: An Introduction*. Portsmouth, NH: Heinemann, 2001. 172–78.

Cobham, Rhonda. "Making It Through the Night." *New Beacon Review* 2 (November 1986): 25–77.

Collins, Merle. "Orality and Writing: A Revisitation." *Winds of Change: The Transforming Voices of Caribbean Women Writers and Scholars.* Ed. Adele S. Newson and Linda Strong-Leek. New York: Peter Lang, 1998. 37–45.

Saunders, Patricia Joan. "Merle Collins." *Twentieth-Century Caribbean and Black African Writers.* Third Series. Ed. Bernth Lindfors and Reinhard Sander. Detroit: Gale Research, 1996. 59–66.

Wilson, Betty. "An Interview with Merle Collins." *Callaloo* 16 (Winter 1993): 94–107.

Loretta G. Woodard

COLON, JESUS (1901–1974) American writer of Puerto Rican descent. Jesus Colon was born in Cayey, Puerto Rico, to a very poor family. In the back of their house was a cigar factory that Colon would visit as a young boy to hear the lector (reader) read works of literature and political thought to the cigar makers. Observance of otherwise illiterate workers reciting the classics and being inspired by radical thinkers, and his own early exposure to writers and philosophers like Zola and Karl Marx (which the factory lector provided him), had a profound impact on Colon's intellectual development. As Colon recounts in his own classic series of short essays, *A Puerto Rican in New York and Other Sketches* (1961), when just a school boy, he joined with his classmates to organize a successful strike against a teacher's unjust threat of punishment. In 1917 he witnessed a strike of unarmed factory workers and the subsequent murder of one of the strikers. This incident was another key event that deepened his awareness of class inequity and state power, and laid the groundwork for Colon's lifelong commitment to social and economic justice, and his permanent identification with the collective and public good over individual glory.

Jesus Colon is considered the father of the **Nuyorican** literary and cultural movement. Although *A Puerto Rican in New York and Other Sketches* is his only published book of essays, it stands out as a landmark representation of Puerto Rican immigrant life and Latino experience in general. In 1984 it was posthumously given the American Book Award, Before Columbus Foundation Award, and is referenced by many writers and critics of Latino literature and culture. His work inspired the next generations of writers such as **Piri Thomas, Nicholasa Mohr,** and **Esmeralda Santiago** among others. It is from this largely autobiographical text that one can gain insight into Colon's life, but more significantly gain a greater understanding of the collective experiences in the barrio with its shared poverty and injustices that the vast majority of twentieth-century Caribbean poor people faced (and continue to face). Published in 1961, it is the first such text in English to recount the day-to-day reality of Puerto Rican immigrant life, and with a prose style that reflects the Afro-Caribbean oral tradition, also offers audiences a detailed perspective of the larger Latin and Latin American cultural heritage from a people's point of view, while matter-of-factly critiquing its misrepresentation that the media and Hollywood promote in the interest of cultural **assimilation**.

Like many Puerto Ricans before and after him, Colon left his native Borinquen as a young man to follow the so-called American dream. He stowed away on the SS *Carolina* (which, he points out, was later sunk by the Germans) and landed in Brooklyn around 1918. He would remain in New York for the rest of his life. Colon took many and varied jobs in the city, working as a dishwasher, a dock and railyard worker, a postal worker, and later as a labor organizer. These firsthand experiences of solidarity and struggle with other workers that crossed ethnic lines further solidified his own political position and in 1923 he joined the Socialist Workers Party. He began to write regularly for Spanish-language socialist newspapers in New York like *Justicia* (Justice), *Unión Obrera*, *El Machete Criollo*, and others. By the 1940s he also began publishing articles in English in journals such as the *Daily Worker* and *Mainstream*. He founded the small press, Editorial Hispánica (Hispanic Publications) and participated in the creation of other journals such as "Vae Victis" (whose unfortunate title—woe to the vanquished—hid the fact that it contained many important articles and essays, but as Colon himself asserts it was too obscure a name for any worker to identify with). Colon was a tireless community and cultural activist, organizing and promoting Latino cultural activities through the International Workers Order and other community groups. His activism led him to run (unsuccessfully) for local and state office on the Labor Party and Communist Party tickets. In the 1950s he was called before the House Un-American Activities Committee (HUAC) where he shocked the committee with an eloquent refusal to cooperate.

In *A Puerto Rican in New York*, Colon relates the extreme poverty he and others suffered in the early days with humorous and poignant anecdotes that detail how he survived and how one could survive in such circumstances. In essay seven "Two Men But with One Pair of Pants," Colon tells of how he shared an apartment with his brother who had a night job while he worked days so they could share the same pair of work pants. Similarly, in "How to Rent an Apartment with No Money" Colon gives valuable advice to the poor prospective renter, while also underscoring the importance of community trust and generosity that allows one to take an apartment without really being able to afford it. "I Heard a Man Crying" relates how hunger reduces a robust man to profound hurt and sorrow. In these tales Colon knows what it is like to be destitute, but also finds consolation in the fact that he is one among many in the same circumstance. Throughout his essays is the ever-present optimistic belief that someday, if workers unite, they will prevail.

Colon also confronts U.S. **racism** and ethnocentrism by recounting personal episodes such as the offer of a job on the merits of his literary skills, only to be dismissed on sight because he was not "white." In "Hollywood Rewrites History" he critiques the larger issues of the distorted Latino image, and in other essays takes on U.S.-supported despots like Trujillo of the Dominican Republic or celebrates revolutionary figures like Cuban independence fighter Antonio Maceo and progressive artists like Diego Rivera. Colon's essays educate U.S. audiences, while keeping Puerto Rican and Latino cultural legacies alive. The paucity of published books by this important literary figure is balanced by Colon's unyielding activism and the impact that his sole text *A Puerto Rican in New York* has had and continues to have on generations of readers and writers.

Further Reading

Olivia, Marciela. "Jesus Colon." *Biographical Dictionary of Hispanic Literature in the United States*. Ed. Nicholas Kanellas. Westport, CT: Greenwood Press, 1989. 63–69.

Colleen Kattau

COLONIALISM AND U.S. ETHNIC LITERATURES Colonialism, as it is conventionally understood—namely the practice of exploiting resources and "civilizing" foreign peoples through resettlement and missionary work—became a fairly common practice starting with the European "discovery" of the Americas in the late 1400s and early 1500s. Colonialism was one of the central practices European countries used to attain economic dominance around the world. It reached a peak in the late nineteenth century, began to wane in the earlier years of the twentieth, formally ended after 1945, and has in recent years been refashioned into less formalized practices of so-called neocolonialism. Conventional United States history tends to distinguish itself from the formal colonial projects that originated in countries like Britain, France, Belgium, the Netherlands, Portugal, and Spain. However, recent work in literary and cultural studies has clarified the ways in which such an exceptionalist stance hides what William Appleman Williams has called "empire as a way of life" in America.

By putting into the U.S. frame the terms "colonialism" and "imperialism" (the latter being the economic and political system through which the former is practiced), one can begin to question the ways in which "**ethnicity**" as an American category of **identity** gets understood in relation to national projects of expansion and settlement. "Ethnicity" as a community's cultural tradition or common heritage thus gets put into motion, and becomes a dynamic process of re-articulation: groups migrate from one place to another, either willingly or—as has been more often the case—by force; they come into contact with different belief systems, economic interests, and cultural mores; they are challenged to define their constitutive elements; and they are given less-than-equal status when compared to the dominating culture. Just as the concept of "race" as a category of identity has been understood through the ways it is defined in relation to social constructions of difference and unequal power hierarchies, so too does the concept of "ethnicity"—often considered a more stable category than "**race**"—become linked to particular sociohistorical processes when considered simultaneously with colonialism.

There are at least three major categories from which the experience of colonialism has been captured by U.S. ethnic literature: There are those works written in the context of formal and informal U.S. colonialism abroad, those written in response to the experience of internal colonialism (on the American continent), and those written in dialogue with, or support for, other subjects of colonialism around the world. The first category includes literatures written by authors whose heritage traces back to the foreign sites where the United States has had colonial involvement: Puerto Rico (colonized in 1898; became part of the U.S. Commonwealth in 1952); the Philippines (came under U.S. rule in 1899; gained its independence in 1946); Hawai'i (established as a U.S. territory in 1900 and a state of the Union in 1959); Guam and American Samoa (both formally governed by the United States beginning in 1898; became unincorporated territories in 1950); and the U.S. Virgin Islands (purchased from the Danish in 1917; currently an unincorporated territory). The second category includes literature written by authors from a wide variety of ethnic and racial groups (Native Americans, Chicanos, Japanese Americans, African Americans, and others), all of whom see their relationship to the nation as one structured through dominance, expropriation, displacement, and violence.

Out of both of these contexts (external and internal colonialism) often come dialogues between colonial and postcolonial peoples around the world about commonly held aspirations for liberation. For example, the challenges of migration, displacement, confrontation, and liberation are all traveling themes across postcolonial literatures from sub-Saharan and North Africa, Southeast Asia, and the Middle East. Thus U.S. ethnic literatures often engage broader transnational understandings of larger experiences of colonialism related to but distinct from the U.S. nation-state. They often trace the lived experiences of a globalizing capitalist economy whose wealth primarily resides in Western Europe and the United States, or the difficulties posed by a Western definition of national sovereignty that is often ill-equipped to account for individuals whose tribal or religious affiliations trump claims of national legitimacy.

In what follows, these general categories are given specificity through a brief description of several of the many contemporary texts that grapple with colonialism and its aftermath.

In *Panoramas* (1997), Puerto Rican author **Victor Hernandez Cruz** describes through poetry and prose the dual themes of displacement and bilingualism. From his location as an émigré writer of the **Nuyorican** school (a community of Puerto Rican poets living in New York City), Cruz gives flesh to the problems of traditional autobiography. He represents the traveling musicality of Puerto Rican life, the cultural clash of having to live elsewhere than home, and the aesthetic beauty of the Spanish *ars poetica* of his heritage. Across the book's five sections, Cruz colors the text's imagery with the dislocating metaphors of migration and the ways migration dislodges the individual from his tradition, history, family, and heritage.

In her first novel, *Dogeaters* (1990), Filipino writer **Jessica Hagedorn** describes the messy aftermath of U.S. colonialism—and the country's prior experience with Spanish colonialism as well—in the Filipino capital city of Manila in the early 1950s. The novel depicts the newly independent country as the site of a chaotic blend of violent class divisions, political corruption, rampant commercialism, and squelched dreams. Throughout the novel, there is no single reliable narrator, as event overlaps with event overlaps with event. Instead of a single point of view, character-sketches of a variety of postindependence Filipinos slowly push the narrative forward. The effect thematizes the many ways in which the feeling of national belonging is experienced, challenged, and repressed at different times and for different reasons.

Gloria Anzaldúa, a Chicana poet and professor, in many ways defined what has become known as "mestiza consciousness" with her genre-bending *Borderlands/La Frontera* (1987). Mixing alternative history, autobiography, poetry, lengthy excerpts from other writers, and eight different dialectics (from standard English to Pachuco), Anzaldúa constructs a deep analysis of the effects of internal colonialism on Mexicans, Chicanos, and women. Through the content of her narrative, as well as the complexly hybrid form of the text itself, Anzaldúa offers a means through which to resist the dominant patriarchal structures she claims have been imposed by the United States on Chicanas in particular, and all women of color more generally.

Native American author Young Bear of the Mesquakie tribe writes in *Black Eagle Child: The Facepaints Narrative* (1992) of the complex and challenging obstacles facing Native Americans living on reservation lands parceled out by the U.S. government and administered by the U.S. Department of Interior. Indeed, the Indian experience is plainly an outcome of the practice of internal colonialism. The narrative delicately navigates between Young Bear's honest portrayal of Mesquakie history and personal experience without revealing the tribe's ancestral secrets. Like *Borderlands/La Frontera*, the text is a synthesis of prose, verse, and indigeneous vocabulary, and moves in and out of factual autobiography. The protagonist, a veiled alter ego for Young Bear named Edgar Bearchild, struggles with alcoholism, drug addiction, a failed stint in a California college far from the reservation, and the discomfort of returning to a tribe in which he finds no discernible place.

While several generations removed from the contemporary authors just discussed, the writings of African American **W. E. B. Du Bois** (1868–1963) epitomize the global solidarity-building ethic at play in this literature. From the beginnings of U.S. colonialism abroad, through the dawn of the **Civil Rights Movement**, and into the era of decolonization after World War II, Du Bois always worked to understand the particularity of race relations in the United States (what some would call the product of internal colonialism) as part of a much larger system of racial dominance worldwide. Perhaps one of his most famous statements, repeated twice in **The Souls of Black Folk** (1903), that "the problem of the twentieth-century is the problem of the color-line," has often been thought of as prescient only in a narrow United States context. However, Du Bois first uttered that sentence at an international conference held in London in 1900, and was addressing not just U.S. concerns, but the much larger issues of global Euro-American colonialism and imperialism and its effects on native peoples around the world. In *Darkwater* (1920), Du Bois suggests that an antiracist politics developing in the United States should be in sync with the much wider anticolonial politics emerging in the third world in order to forge a resistance to colonialism's damaging social, cultural, and economic effects. Thus, he lays plain the intimate—and dire—commonalities of the slums of East St. Louis, the rampant lynchings in Alabama, the genocide in the Belgian Congo, and the devastation wrought by World War I, all through a complex overlaying of prose essay, poetry, satire, and melodrama.

Shared across all these texts is a concerted effort by the writers to develop new literary forms through which to represent the hardships of the colonial encounter. Each text attempts to narrate a history from below, and in order to do so, the conventional tools of American literature are put through a rigorous process of revision and hybridization. The outcomes of such reworkings are socially and politically salient cultural documents that reimagine history, tradition, belonging, and indeed language itself in the hopes of assuring that the violence of colonialism's past will not be forgotten, the violence of colonialism's present will come to an end, and life experience in all its density can be given voice. (*See also* Native American Reservations)

Further Reading

Kaplan, Amy. *The Anarchy of Empire in the Making of U.S. Culture.* Cambridge, MA: Harvard UP, 2002.

Kaplan, Amy, and Donald Pease, eds. *Cultures of United States Imperialism.* Durham, NC: Duke UP, 1993.

Kazanjian, David. *The Colonizing Trick: National Culture and Imperial Citizenship in Early America.* Minneapolis: U of Minnesota P, 2003.

Rowe, John Carlos. *Literary Culture and U.S. Imperialism: From the Revolution to World War II.* Oxford and New York: Oxford UP, 2000.

Singh, Amritjit, and David Schmidt, eds. *Postcolonial Theory and the United States: Race, Ethnicity, and Literature.* Jackson: UP of Mississippi, 2000.

Williams, William Appleman. *Empire as a Way of Life.* New York: Oxford UP, 1980.

Keith Feldman

COLOR PURPLE, THE   Published in 1982, presented with the Pulitzer Prize and National Book Award in 1983, and adapted into a major Hollywood film directed by Steven Spielberg in 1985, *The Color Purple* is **Alice**

Walker's third and most controversial novel. In its creative engagement with the epistolary form, the book shows how a poor, uneducated African American woman endures pain and hardship to become, through the nurturing of communal black womanhood, a fully constituted subject of strength, self-confidence, and desire.

The narrative begins with fourteen-year-old Celie's revelation to God that she is physically and sexually abused by a man, Alphonso, who she believes to be her natural father. He later gives away the two children she has by him. When Celie is married off to Mr.___, she worries that her younger sister, Nettie, will have to endure similar abuse from their Pa. Nettie comes to live with Celie and Mr.___, but his intense jealousy over their tight-knit relationship forces Nettie to leave the house and subsequently move to Africa. Incredibly, the missionaries in whose custody Nettie is placed happen to adopt Celie's two children.

Mr.___ only perpetuates the cycle of violence that typified Celie's life with Alphonso, (who later turns out to be her stepfather). Mr.___ also withholds psychic and affective comfort from Celie by hiding the numerous letters Nettie mails to her from Africa. The downtrodden Celie internalizes feelings of abjection and worthlessness to the point where she convinces her stepson, Harpo, to beat his own wife, the defiant and physically imposing Sofia Butler, into submission, which he does not succeed in doing.

The turning point in the narrative comes with the arrival of Shug Avery, also known as "The Queen Honeybee," a spirited, sexy, and flamboyant **blues** singer who lives by her own rules and refuses to obey the dictates of patriarchal authority; the latter, as embodied by Mr.___, is deflated by his submission to her demands. Though an occasional lover to Mr.___, it is Celie with whom Shug eventually develops a deep and meaningful bond. In their emotional exchanges and sexual encounters, Shug enables Celie to recognize her own beauty and self-sufficiency and thus to leave Albert. The couple settles in Memphis, where Celie makes a living by tailoring personalized, seemingly ungendered, pants for those she loves. Imbued with self-determination, Celie later visits a distraught Mr.___, whose first name is revealed to be Albert, upon her stepfather's death. A momentous reunion occurs when Nettie and the children return from Africa; a corresponding reconciliation has Celie and Albert agreeing to be friends.

Walker's novel has elicited vituperative reactions in both academic venues and the popular media. The sections on Africa have been deemed culturally biased; the frank depiction of lesbian sexuality has been summarily censored on moral grounds; and the putatively "harsh" treatment of black men, especially in the film, has been construed as an indication of Walker's selling out to the white establishment. That the book sparked such fiery, if not sometimes misguided, debate underscores the invaluable discursive effect it has had on black women's writing, African American literature, popular culture, and **race** relations in the United States. (*See also* African American Novel, African American Lesbian Literature)

Further Reading

Gates, Henry Louis, Jr. "Color Me Zora: Alice Walker's (Re)Writing of the Speakerly Text." *The Signifying Monkey: A Theory of Afro-American Literary Criticism*. New York: Oxford UP, 1988. 239–58.

Harris, Trudier. "On *The Color Purple*, Stereotypes, and Silence." *Black American Literature Forum* 18.4 (1984): 155–61.

Hernton, Calvin C. "Who's Afraid of Alice Walker? *The Color Purple* as Slave Narrative." *The Sexual Mountain and Black Women Writers: Adventures in Sex, Literature, and Real Life*. Garden City, NY: Anchor, 1987. 1–36.

hooks, bell. "Writing the Subject: Reading *The Color Purple*." *Reading Black, Reading Feminist: A Critical Anthology*. Ed. Henry Louis Gates Jr. New York: Meridian, 1990. 454–70.

Kinohi Nishikawa

COLORED MUSEUM, THE   George C. Wolfe's *The Colored Museum* (1986) is a daring and innovative play that established Wolfe as a significant voice in American theater. Drawing upon the musical revue style, the play comprises eleven "exhibits," set on a revolving stage, that present and challenge **African American stereotypes** through searing satire and farce. The opening vignette depicts the Middle Passage on an airline named "Celebrity Slaveship," which features a "Fasten Your Shackles" sign and a pert stewardess who forbids drumming or call-and-response singing. "Cookin' with Aunt Ethel" satirizes the Aunt Jemima stereotype and down-home cooking through a character who bakes "a batch of Negroes" using ingredients—both real and clichéd—of their cultural heritage; "The Photo Session" features a "gorgeous, black couple" who model for *Ebony Magazine* as a means of conforming, albeit unsatisfyingly; and "Soldier with a Secret" addresses the historical dismissal of blacks in the military while also drawing a parallel to the war conditions that blacks face in their own neighborhoods. "The Gospel According to Miss Roj" features a crossdresser working in a club called "The Bottomless Pit" who spoofs the notion of style through her "snap" power, while "The Hairpiece" debates black identity through talking wigs—an "Afro" and a more culturally acceptable "Barbie doll dipped in chocolate" style. The center of *The Colored Museum* is "The Last Mama-on-the-Couch Play," a send-up of black acting styles as well as of **Lorraine Hansberry**'s *A Raisin in the Sun* and other such realistic socioeconomic dramas. In "Symbiosis," a corporate black man attempts to discard objects from his past in order to assimilate into the white business world; "Lala's Opening" features a Josephine Baker–type chanteuse haunted by a past she has tried to leave behind, and "Permutations" is a monologue by Normal Jean Reynolds that comments on both the stereotypes about and the pride of teenage black mothers through a mutation with the gorgeous, yet deeply unhappy film star Marilyn Monroe. The final exhibit, "The Party," brings together Wolfe's themes and characters through Topsy Washington—a character whose name fuses

Uncle Tom's Cabin with the nation's capital and first president and who makes a distinction between "black/Negro/colored Americans" at an imaginary celebration in Harlem.

Wolfe's play challenges African Americans to consider what parts of their cultural heritage to preserve while discarding the baggage of **racism**, oppression, and **slavery**. Similarly, it charges white audiences to recognize the misguided stereotypes and perceptions, in which they are complicit, that perpetuate these negative images. The play's innovative structure as a series of museum exhibits not only establishes its historical ideas but also suggests that some African American myths and stereotypes should be relegated to such a stark and sterile environment.

Further Reading

Euell, Kim. "Signifyin(g) Ritual: Subverting Stereotypes, Salvaging Icons." *African American Review* 31 (1997): 667–76.

Savran, David. "George C. Wolfe." *The Playwrights' Voice: American Dramatists on Memory, Writing and the Politics of Culture*. New York: Theatre Communications Group, 1999. 347–48.

Simpson, Janice C. "A Jam Session with George C. Wolfe." *Theater Week* 26 October (1992): 18–21.

Karen C. Blansfield

COLTER, CYRUS (1910–2002)   African American novelist, short story writer, and scholar. Cyrus Colter was born in Noblesville, Indiana, in 1910, later moving to Greensboro, Indiana, and Youngstown, Ohio. He attended Youngstown State and Ohio State universities and earned a JD from Chicago-Kent College of Law in 1940. After a brief stint at the Internal Revenue Service, Colter served in World War II as a field artillery captain in the Fifth Army. Returning from Europe, he began practicing law in Chicago in 1946 and in 1950 joined the Illinois Commerce Commission, where he worked for twenty-three years. In 1973 he was appointed professor of creative writing in the nascent African American studies department at Northwestern University, where he then served as chair, and later held the Chester D. Tripp Chair in Humanities.

Colter's contribution to African American literature began after his fiftieth birthday with a self-initiated program of wide reading in Russian literature. Believing the psychological depth he admired in Russian characters to be relatively lacking in African American literature, and spurred on by his wife to try his hand at it, Colter began to draft stories of his own. His first short story "A Chance Meeting" was published later the same year, 1960, in *Threshold*, a small Irish magazine.

His first collection of short stories, *The Beach Umbrella* (1970), won the University of Iowa School of Letters Award for Fiction. The title story recounts a man's trip to the beach where he believes possessing an umbrella will allow him to fit in with the crowd and enjoy his life; unsuccessful, he ends the day resigned to a life of loneliness. Colter's second collection, *The Amoralists and Other Tales* (1988), includes "Moot," the story of an elderly man and his dog who die in quick succession, unmourned, and leave no trace of their coexistence beyond an apartment that is hastily cleared out by strangers. Over the course of his career, Colter published stories and poems in *Chicago Review*, *Epoch*, *Northwest Review*, *University of Kansas City Review*, and *Prairie Schooner*.

Colter's first novel, *The River of Eros* (1972), tells the story of Clotilda Pilgrim, a woman who murders her own daughter, Addie, who she believes has fallen into the same irresponsible behavior that had once led Clotilda to have an affair with her brother-in-law. In his second novel, *The Hippodrome* (1973), an upstanding and religious man, Jackson Yaeger, murders his wife and her lover in a fit of passion and runs from the police. *Night Studies* (1979) follows the lives of three characters in three different centuries—an African American leader, an educated black woman who marries a white man, and a white woman unaware of her own black heritage—as connections gradually emerge among them. Colter's fourth novel, *A Chocolate Soldier* (1988), offers an elderly pastor's fragmented recitation of a murder from the 1940s. As Meshach Barry tells the story of Cager Lee, his college friend who murdered a white woman, Barry's narrative voice becomes increasingly unreliable, calling into question the accuracy of his recollection. Colter's final novel, *City of Light* (1993), portrays the activities of Paul Kessey, an African American in Paris who writes letters to his deceased mother and runs the Coterie, a group with the goal of creating a homeland to which people of the African **diaspora** can return. During the long planning phase of the project, Paul and Cecile, with whom he has been having an affair, die from a racist attack.

Colter's austere themes, contemplative realism, and dense portrayals of wide-ranging African American characters have earned him much admiration among readers and critics; his achievements have been recognized with an honorary doctorate from the University of Illinois—Chicago, and, in 1990, the inscription of his name, along with other distinguished Chicago writers, on the frieze of the Chicago public library.

Further Reading

Fogarty, Robert. "Work: Beginning to Write at Fifty: A Conversation with Cyrus Colter." *Antioch Review* 36 (Fall 1978): 422–26.

Mesic, Penelope. "Visible Man." *Chicago* 40.6 (June 1991): 118–24.

O'Brien, John. *Interviews with Black Writers*. New York: Liveright, 1973: 17–33.

Rao, Raja E. *Beyond Protest: A Critical Examination of Contemporary African American Literature*. New Delhi: Academic Foundation, 1993.

Skramstad, Susan. "Interviewing Cyrus Colter" *Story Quarterly* 11 (1980): 65–73.

Alex Feerst

COMDEN AND GREEN　Comden, Betty (1915–) and Adolph Green (1915–2002). Jewish American lyricists of American musical theater. The team of Comden and Green were the longest-running writing partnership in twentieth-century American theater. In a career that spanned over sixty years, Betty Comden and Adolph Green wrote several commercially successful musicals for the stage and screen marked by fast-paced and witty lyrics with a satirical edge.

Comden was born Basya Cohen to Russian Jewish parents on May 3, 1915, in New York City. Green was born in the Bronx to Hungarian Jewish parents, Daniel and Helen Weiss Green, on December 2, 1915. Both attended New York University and became members of the Washington Square Players. Though they were often assumed to be a married couple, the pair had a purely professional and completely platonic collaboration, separately enjoying long marriages and family lives.

In 1938 Comden and Green began performing with singer Judy Holliday as "The Revuers," a successful New York nightclub act. Holliday was, like Comden, the child of Russian-Jewish immigrants; she would later work with Comden and Green in *The Bells Are Ringing* (1960).

When the creators of the ballet *Fancy Free* (1944) decided to expand the dance about three brash sailors on shore leave into a full-length musical, Comden and Green were hired to write the libretto and lyrics. The resulting play was their first major success, *On the Town* (1944). Comden and Green wrote the book and lyrics and composer Leonard Bernstein wrote the music.

Bernstein was a lifelong friend of Green; they had worked together at a Massachusetts Jewish summer camp for boys in 1937 where Bernstein, the camp music director, cast Green, a camp counselor, in a production of *The Pirates of Penzance*. Later the two men became roommates in New York City.

The success of *On the Town* was followed by *Billion Dollar Baby* (1945) and by Comden and Green's second collaboration with Bernstein, *Wonderful Town* (1953). The team also wrote songs for the popular stage musical *Peter Pan* (1954).

In 1949 Comden and Green won the Screen Writer's Guild Award for their film adaptation of *On the Town*. The team's most noteworthy screenplay, however, is *Singin' in the Rain* (1952), which Comden and Green developed out of several songs and plotlines from the movie musicals of the 1920s and early 1930s. *Singin' in the Rain* has been placed on several lists of the best films of all time and is recognized as an early example of self-reflexive cinema.

In 1952 Comden and Green became subjects of interest to the House Un-American Activities Committee (HUAC), along with *Singin' in the Rain* star Gene Kelly. The leftist politics of Comden and Green, along with their Russian and Hungarian Jewish heritage, created suspicion in the heightened anticommunist environment of Washington, DC. Judy Holliday was called to testify about the members of "The Revuers," though Comden and Green's career did not suffer as much as other artists whose patriotism was challenged by the HUAC.

The politics of Comden and Green show through in their work on the 1967 show *Hallelujah, Baby!*, which traces African American life from the post–

Civil War era to the **Civil Rights Movement**. The show was cowritten by composer Jule Styne, their collaborator on *Two on the Aisle* (1951), *Bells Are Ringing, Do Re Mi* (1960), *Subways Are for Sleeping* (1962), and *Lorelei* (1974).

Comden and Green continued to be active and innovative in the1980s. Their 1982 musical, *A Doll's Life*, is an imaginative sequel to Henrik Ibsen's classic *A Doll's House*. In 1985 they adapted the screenplay for *Singin' in the Rain* for the Broadway stage. And in the 1990s, Comden and Green won the Tony award for their lyrics for *The Will Rogers Follies* (1991).

Throughout their long careers as writers, Comden and Green continued to perform. In addition to appearing in the original production of *On the Town*, they created an award-winning cabaret show called *A Party with Betty Comden and Adolph Green* (1958 and1977).

Noteworthy Comden and Green songs include "New York, New York (It's a Wonderful Town)," "Neverland," and "Make Someone Happy." Adolph Green died in New York City on October 23, 2002. (*See also* Jewish American Musicals)

Further Reading

Comden, Betty. *Off Stage*. New York: Simon and Schuster, 1995.

Green, Stanley. *The World of Musical Comedy: The Story of the American Musical Stage as Told Through the Careers of Its Foremost Composers and Lyricists*. New York: Ziff-Davis Publishing Company, 1980.

Robinson, Alice M. *Betty Comden and Adolph Green: A Bio-Bibliography*. Westport, CT: Greenwood Press, 1994.

DeAnna Toten Beard

CONFESSIONS OF NAT TURNER, THE   Penned by a white lawyer and slaveholder, Thomas R. Gray, *The Confessions of Nat Turner* (1831) was printed and widely circulated in pamphlet form shortly after the trial and execution of **Nat Turner**, the avowed leader of one of the most significant slave insurrections in U.S. history. The revolt, which took place in Southampton County, Virginia, and lasted from August 22–23, 1831, involved as many as eighty insurgents and led to the deaths of approximately sixty white people and a much larger number of both convicted and "suspected" black rebels. Turner himself successfully eluded the authorities without leaving the general area for two months. He was finally captured on October 30 and hanged on November 11.

Gray's document claims to be a faithful transcription, "with little or no variation," of the actual words Turner used to describe his motives in a series of interviews conducted in Turner's jail cell in the days leading up to his trial. But given that the document is equally a product of sensationalistic white reactions to the revolt and Turner's subsequent capture, it should be seen as framing the rebel's voice in very specific ways: Gray's editorial commentary states that Turner is "a complete fanatic, or plays his part most admirably."

The "confession" proper begins with Turner's account of his childhood, which he remembers as being suffused with divine signs that he "was intended for some great purpose" including his innocent revelation of a particular event that had already occurred, "certain marks on [his] head and breast", and his miraculous discovery that he could spell without having been taught how to read. Explaining how he was able to trace God's text in the natural world throughout his life, Turner courts messianic topoi and thought by proposing that the revolt was the fulfillment of his spiritual destiny.

The rest of the document details the home-by-home movement of the rebellion, including Turner's striking the first (hatchet) blow against his master, Joseph Travis, and is structured by Gray's simultaneous disapproval of and fascination with the persona Turner conveys in their exchanges. The latter is perhaps most dramatically ventriloquized in the final episode of the pamphlet, which has the court's judgment rendered in rather overzealous terms: Turner is to be "hung by the neck until [he is] dead! dead! dead!"

Though historians and literary critics have engaged in a heated conversation over the relative degree to which Turner is allowed expressive agency in his own confession, there is widespread agreement that the pamphlet has had a profound effect on the course of U.S. history. Its publication not only provoked a landmark debate on **abolition** in the Virginia legislature in 1831–32, but swelled the tide of both black and white anti**slavery** print culture in the North. The document's contemporary salience has been informed by **William Styron**'s controversial Pulitzer Prize–winning novel, *The Confessions of Nat Turner* (1967), whose white author asks readers to imagine the carnal motives behind Turner's actions.

Further Reading

Aptheker, Herbert. *Nat Turner's Slave Rebellion*. New York: Humanities Press, 1966.

Davis, Mary Kemp. *Nat Turner Before the Bar of Judgment: Fictional Treatments of the Southampton Slave Insurrection*. Baton Rouge: Louisiana State UP, 1999.

Greenberg, Kenneth S., ed. "Introduction" *The Confessions of Nat Turner and Related Documents*. Boston: Bedford, 1996. 1–35.

Sundquist, Eric J. "Signs of Power: Nat Turner and Frederick Douglass." *To Wake the Nations: Race in the Making of American Literature*. Cambridge, MA: Harvard UP, 1993. 27–134.

Kinohi Nishikawa

CONJURE   A syncretistic form of New World African folk belief that involves magic (also known as *hoodoo*, or *obeah* in the Caribbean), supernatural control exercised upon locals by a conjurer, therapeutic medical counsel, the application of charms and spells, and the psychic manipulation of roots. In early African American literature, representations of conjuring are situated largely in the southern states among rural slave populations. Antebellum North Carolina is the site of such works as "The Goophered Grapevine" and "Po' Sandy," both conjure-themed stories consolidated in **Charles**

W. Chesnutt's *The Conjure Woman and Other Conjure Tales* (1899). The recurring figure of Aun' Peggy, a root-working freewoman, situates a source of potentially subversive power on the periphery of the heavily Christianized master/slave discourse.

Attuned to the brutalities of the slaveholding system, **Frederick Douglass**'s *Narrative* (1845) describes the salutary effects of a magic root presented to him by fellow bondsman Sandy Jenkins. A similar desire for protection motivates Min of **Ann Petry**'s neo-naturalistic novel ***The Street*** (1946) to seek the counsel of The Prophet David, a local root doctor. Conjurers are often characterized as being "two-headed" because they exercise twice as much sense as the layperson. Both this conjurer's overtly religious name and the large gold cross he gives to his client suggest the imperative of moving beyond a narrow understanding of conjure as a collection of superstitious practices involving candles, potions, and lucky talismans. Rather, they gesture toward the more porous arena of neo-African spirituality known as *vaudou* (voodoo).

Intrigued by this topic, folklorist **Zora Neale Hurston** embarked on excursions to Florida, Louisiana, Jamaica, and Haiti. Two studies emerged: *Mules and Men* (1935) and *Tell My Horse* (1938). Along with accounts of Hurston's experiences as conjurer's apprentice in New Orleans, *Mules and Men* includes appendices titled "Paraphernalia of Conjure," "Formulae of Hoodoo Doctors," and "Prescriptions of Root Doctors." *Tell My Horse* highlights the rich complexity of voodoo as a mélange of the transplanted animistic beliefs of West African slaves and certain ritualistic elements of Roman Catholicism, a legacy of European colonization.

Such figures as Ajax's mother in **Toni Morrison**'s *Sula* (1973), and Pilate Dead, the ancestral healer in Morrison's ***Song of Solomon*** (1977), complement the herbalists-cum-witches Mama Yaya and Judah White of Maryse Condé's *Moi, Tituba, Sorcière . . . Noire de Salem* (1986). Geographically unbound, but circumscribed by narrowly prescriptive notions of cultural, medical, and religious legitimacy, conjuring remains the work of unconventional individuals who mediate between spiritual and material worlds. Among others, iconoclastic PaPa LaBas, the conjure-man detective of **Ishmael Reed**'s *Mumbo Jumbo* (1972) suggests that (neo)Hoodooism may serve as an interpretive template for a magically empowered hermeneutics of black difference.

Further Reading

Baldwin, Richard. "The Art of the Conjure Woman." *American Literature* 43.3 (1971): 385–98.

Chireau, Yvonne. "Conjure and Christianity in the Nineteenth Century: Religious Elements in African American Magic." *Religion and American Culture* 7.2 (1997): 225–46.

Jaskoski, Helen. "Power Unequal to Man: The Significance of Conjure in Works by Five Afro-American Authors." *Southern Folklore Quarterly* 38 (1974): 91–108.

Nancy Kang

CONLEY, ROBERT J. (1940–)   Native American novelist, poet, and playwright. An enrolled member of the United Keetoowah Band of Cherokee Indians, Robert Conley was born in Cushing, Oklahoma. He attended high school and college in Wichita Falls, Texas. In 1966 Conley completed a bachelor's degree in drama at Midwestern University in Texas, and in1968 he received his master's in English at the same university. He has taught English and Native Studies at colleges in Illinois, Iowa, Missouri, and Montana, as well as in his home state of Oklahoma.

Both of Conley's paternal grandparents were schoolteachers in the Cherokee Nation prior to statehood, so they told their grandson many stories—especially "outlaw" stories—about Indian Territory. Although most of his own writing deals with Cherokee culture, characters, and themes, Conley also admits to having been heavily influenced by the language of Shakespeare, whom he has been reading since he was ten years old. Conley, an accomplished and prolific writer, published his first novel, *Back to Malachi*, in 1986. Since that time, more than forty of his novels have been published. Although Conley's Real-People series, which traces Cherokee history as far back as the year 1500, has attracted a wide reading audience, his most popular work is *Mountain Windsong* (1992), a novel focusing on the separation of two young lovers during the infamous Trail of Tears. In 1995 *Mountain Windsong*, which has been hailed by critics as an "American classic," was adapted into a musical.

In addition to his work as a novelist, Conley is a noted poet, short story writer, and screenplay writer. His poetry has been published in English, Cherokee, German, French, and Macedonian, and he has also received critical acclaim for his collection of short stories, *The Witch of Goingsnake and Other Stories*. Additionally, Conley has written several plays, and has gained a degree of fame in the literary world as the writer of the Columbia Pictures screenplay, "Geronimo: An American Legend." Conley is a member of the Western Writers of America and has won that organization's award for Best Western Short Fiction three times (1988, 1992, and 1995). In addition, he was chosen Wordcrafter of the Year in 1997 and was twice named the Wordcraft Writer of the Year (1999 and 2000) by the Wordcraft Circle of Native Writers and Storytellers. Other awards bestowed upon Conley include induction into the Oklahoma Professional Writers Hall of Fame (1997), Oklahoma Writer of the Year (1999), and the Cherokee Medal of Honor (2000).

Robert Conley, who has been called "the most Cherokee of all Cherokee writers," now lives with his wife, Evelyn, in Tahlequah, Oklahoma (the historic capital of the Cherokee Nation), where he devotes his life to writing full time. (*See also* Native American Novel)

Further Reading

Brill de Ramirez, Susan B. "Walking with the Land: Simon J. Ortiz, Robert J. Conley, and Elma Wallis." *South Dakota Review* 38.1 (Spring 2000): 59.

Bruchac, Joseph. "A More Realistic Picture: An Interview with Robert Conley." *Wooster Review* (Spring 1988): 106–14.

Ginny Carney

COOK-LYNN, ELIZABETH (1930–)   Native American short story writer, scholar, and editor. Possessing one of the most authentic of Native American tribal voices, Cook-Lynn described writing as an essential act of survival for contemporary American Indians. Speaking with the voice of her tribe, but not for them, in *Then Badger Said This* (1977), Cook-Lynn merged the oral tradition of her Dakota heritage with prose and poetry crafting an integrated genre.

Readers gained new ways of perceiving and interpreting history, other than with simple facts, when Cook-Lynn published *Then Badger Said This*, which was greatly influenced by **N. Scott Momaday**'s *The Way to Rainy Mountain* (1969). Within the work, she styled her prose after his lyricism. However, it wasn't until selections from *Then Badger Said This* were included in the anthology *The Remembered Earth: An Anthology of Contemporary Native American Literature* (1981) that the work caught a widespread audience that connected with her universal themes of family and nature treated with her particular style that melds anger with responsibility.

Further exploring social issues that threaten her tribe's spiritual traditions, her chapbook, *Seek the House of Relatives* (1983), was published the same year that she helped found *Wicazo Sa* [Red Pencil] *Review*. As an important American Indian Studies scholar, her literary criticism within the genre continues to inform the work of scholars.

The Power of Horses and Other Stories (1990) presented an extension of her most important themes of tribal unity and sovereignty that she further explored in her novella *From the River's Edge* (1991) by showing legal and tribal conflicts in one man's quest for justice.

Cook-Lynn examines the role that literary criticism plays in the development of Native American **identity** and literature in the controversial collection *Why I Can't Read Wallace Stegner and Other Essays* (1996). She maintains that the Native American perspective is most important in literary criticism of Native American writing and also examines the divide between a concern with nationhood, or tribalism, and the recent trend of universalism that sidetracks cultural identity.

Cook-Lynn collaborated with Mario Gonzalez in writing *Politics of Hallowed Ground: Wounded Knee and the Struggle for Indian Sovereignty* (1998), which documents the Sioux's struggle for justice against the United States government. The same year she published another collection of poems *I Remember Fallen Trees* (1998).

Anti-Indianism in Modern America: A Voice From Tatekeya's Earth (2001) is one of the most important works published in the field of American Indian Studies. In twenty essays Cook-Lynn argues for tribal sovereignty, criticizes Native writers for writing with tribeless voices, and convinces readers that new perspectives are essential for explaining the central issues in American Indian discourse. As with her other writing, within these essays, she cleverly reveals the cultural conflict between white Americans and Native Americans.

In recent years, her writings have been prolifically represented in anthologies covering topics such as writing, poetry, short stories, and research.

Further Reading

"Elizabeth Cook-Lynn." *Contemporary Literary Criticism*. Vol. 93. Ed. Brigham
    Narisn and Deborah A. Stanley. Detroit: Gale Research, 1996. 114–32.

Rebecca Tolley-Stokes

COOPER, ANNA JULIA (1858–1964) African American author, intellectual, activist, and educator. A highly educated middle-class Southerner, Anna Julia Cooper's greatest intellectual achievement over her expansive lifetime—she was born into **slavery** and lived to see the beginnings of the **Civil Rights Movement** of the 1960s—was her book *A Voice from the South* (1892), a volume of protest that marked the nativity of the black feminist movement in the United States. In it, we find the extravagant rhetoric and historical knowledge that was later employed by **W. E. B. Du Bois** in his seminal sociological treatise *The Souls of Black Folk* (1901). Cooper argued that African American women, and women in general, would find political salvation through higher education; at age sixty-seven, she accordingly became the fourth African American woman ever to receive a PhD. In addition, she felt that the only voice that could adequately effect political change for black women was that of black women themselves: "Not many can more sensibly realize and more accurately tell the weight and fret of the 'long dull pain,'" she wrote in her preface to *A Voice from the South*, "than the open-eyed but hitherto voiceless Black Woman of America" (ii).

Cooper was born into slavery in Raleigh, North Carolina, on August 10, 1858. Cooper's mother, Hannah Stanley Haywood, was owned by George Washington Haywood, who Cooper admitted later in life was her father. Following Emancipation, Cooper matriculated into St. Augustine's Normal School and Collegiate Institute. Cooper married George C. Cooper, also a St. Augustine graduate, in 1877, but he died two years later and she never remarried. After her husband's death, Cooper received a bachelor's degree and then a master's at Oberlin College and went on to teach at the M Street School, the only black secondary school in Washington, DC. In 1902 she became that school's principal, though a series of scandals made her appointment morally controversial. In 1914 Cooper began doctoral work at Columbia University, but withdrew a year later after adopting her deceased half-brother's five children. She completed her PhD at the highly prestigious University of Paris, Sorbonne, in 1925 and employed her prodigious intellect on behalf of a number of social causes over the course of her life. Cooper lectured at the 1893 World's Congress of Representative Women and the 1900 Pan-African Congress in London and helped organize the Colored Woman's League of Washington, DC, the National Conference of Colored Women, and the Colored YWCA. In 1930 she became president of the Frelinghuysen University in Washington, DC, an institution dedicated to educating underprivileged blacks.

Cooper resolutely fought for black women's rights, but some critics consider her a social elitist. In a number of paradoxical sections in *A Voice from the South*, she speaks in a derogatory tone about underprivileged blacks and other minorities. Cooper was a "progressive" intellectual, however, making her well-meaning, if often degrading, objective the elevation of the underprivileged to an ideal state of educated, middle-class respectability. But as a black woman born in the slave-holding South who emerged as a leading figure in higher education and civil rights activism, Anna Julia Cooper was by any measure a radical force in American intellectual history. Cooper died of a heart attack at age 105 in 1964, the year Lyndon B. Johnson signed the Civil Rights Act that finally made the segregation of public facilities and discrimination in the workplace illegal in the United States.

Further Reading

Shockley, Ann Allen, ed. *Afro-American Women Writers, 1746–1933: An Anthology and Critical Guide*. Boston: G. K. Hall, 1988.

Sterling, Dorothy, ed. *We Are Your Sisters: Black Women in the Nineteenth Century*. New York: W.W. Norton & Company, 1984.

Washington, Mary Helen. Introduction. *A Voice from the South: By a Black Woman of the South*. Anna Julia Cooper. New York: Oxford UP, 1988 [orig. pub. 1892].

Robert M. Dowling

COOPER, J. (JOAN) CALIFORNIA (193?–)   African American short story writer, novelist, and playwright. Since the early 1970s, J. California Cooper has written six collections of short stories, three novels, and seventeen plays. Her play *Strangers*, also known as *Ahhh, Strangers* (1978), won Cooper the Black Playwright of the Year Award, and her second collection of short stories, *Homemade Love* (1986), won an American Book Award. Cooper's works are late-twentieth-century manifestations of the folk traditions of African American literature; they display a unique mix of oral-tradition immediacy with the importance of family, **feminism**, Christianity, critique of class inequalities that doesn't deny personal responsibility, and a "**blues** sensibility" of optimism under hardship.

It is this unusual, and sometimes quirky, mix of elements conveyed in a quiet intimacy—an intimacy characterized as like listening to a story told by a friend as you and she sit on a porch and snap beans—that has most attracted many readers. Through misspellings, malapropisms, fragments, and other devices, Cooper connects oral intimacy to the vernacular tradition of providing an insider's view of communities whose "nonstandard" languages indicate educational, economic, and political marginalization, yet also a resilience and insightful "folk wisdom" that calls the imputed "superiority" of a "standard" into question. Cooper manifests the African American vernacular tradition of telling seemingly simple stories that show how disenfranchised communities not only survive but can inspire and educate those willing to pay attention.

These characteristics situate Cooper's work as descending from the spirituals, work songs, and folktales that promote African American vitality and coherence while countering the rhetoric of **racism**. To this tradition, Cooper adds both a consistent feminist critique of patriarchy and occasional graphic depictions of sexuality. These depictions range from celebrations of women's sexuality to scenes of degradation. The tone Cooper takes toward women in degrading scenes, however, remains matter-of-fact, maintaining a sort of documentary "distance" that refrains from judging these actions. Cooper's reticence to judge, acknowledges that poverty, racism, and patriarchy sometime leave women with few socially admirable options. What Cooper's stories do not refrain from judging, however, are people's motives, and this sometimes results in a rather old-fashioned moralizing that some critics find heavy-handed.

Criticism has been leveled at Cooper's optimism and belief in the agency of the individual that situates Cooper in the **Booker T. Washington** tradition of unduly minimizing the effects of the racism and poverty into which many African Americans have been—and continue to be—born. From this view, Cooper's emphasis on hard work, frugality, honesty, and belief in God lets the dominant "white" society off too easily. In Cooper's defense, however, her characters are not blind to class and racial injustices, and the "successes" of her characters are often limited. In many ways, Cooper expresses the blues tradition of turning hardship and loss into success, but success that never leaves sorrow behind.

Cooper's work argues that although African Americans struggle under the injustices of racism, and although women struggle under the injustices of patriarchy, individuals cannot be reduced to categories, and the complexities and possibilities of individuals are beyond capture. From this comes an appreciation of others *as individuals*, an appreciation of their quirks and their potentials and a connecting with others as part of an empathy that Cooper calls "love."

Love in Cooper's work intertwines with Christian faith while sympathizing with those disregarded or rejected by society. This is already apparent in her earliest works. The plot, for instance, of Cooper's *How Now?* (produced in 1973 by the Black Repertory Group of Berkeley, which produced most of Cooper's early plays) details the conflict between a disabled girl who wants to continue her education and the girl's mother who wants her daughter to become pregnant to qualify for welfare benefits. *The Unintended* (c. 1983) tells about the love that unexpectedly results when a thirty-five-year-old virgin's need for money leads to her sexual involvement with a hunchback.

Cooper's work not only shows the value of paying attention to—and ultimately empathizing with—those ignored by society, but also shows how things are often not as they seem. We find this in the short story version of Cooper's play *Loved to Death* (date unknown), which appeared under the same name in Cooper's first collection of short stories, *A Piece of Mine* (1984). The ten-page title story is quintessential J. California Cooper. It is conveyed in a modified oral tradition of a narrator speaking to "Mr. Notebook." The narrator is an "all crooked" woman whose sister, Zalina, has the apparent luck of great beauty. But her father tries to rape Zalina, who leaves home and marries; then the white boss of her husband rapes Zalina and kills her husband. Zalina returns home and later dies of alcoholism. The narrator raises Zalina's children and also experiences sex with a local man who had initially come to visit Zalina but then switched to the narrator. In this "oral" story Cooper packs class, **race**, gender, feminist critique, oral sex, the Bible, the importance of education, physical disability, and a counterintuitive understanding of beauty, and then ends with the "blues optimism" of the narrator going outside to run with one of Zalina's children.

Although Cooper has spent much of her adult life in California, many of her stories seem to take place in rural Texas (Marshall) where she lived for a year as a child and for eight years as an adult. Cooper refuses to divulge her age, is vague about how many times she has been married, and is generally reticent with personal information. The broad arc of her work has tended toward increasing "Christian moralizing," but this predominates mainly in Cooper's second novel, *In Search of Satisfaction* (1994).

Cooper's short stories have received more acclaim than her novels, but Cooper's more extended analyses of people and motives in, for instance, the novels *Family* (1991) and especially *The Wake of the Wind* (1998) are historically grounded studies of the horror and complexity of **slavery** and its aftereffects. Both novels add to our understanding of some of the more difficult aspects of African American life since the mid-to-late 1800s. With Cooper's sixth short story collection, *The Future Has a Past: Stories* (2001) Cooper remains a unique, engaging, and under-appreciated ethnic American voice.

Further Reading

Carroll, Rebecca. "J. California Cooper." *I Know What the Red Clay Looks Like*. New York: Crown, 1994. 63–80.

Marshall, Barbara Jean. "Kitchen Table Talk: J. California Cooper's Use of Nommo—Female Bonding and Transcendence." *Language and Literature in African American Imagination*. Ed. Carol A. Blackshire-Belay. Westport, CT: Greenwood Press, 1992. 91–102.

Kevin M. Hickey

CORSO, GREGORY NUNZIO (1930–2001) Italian American poet. Gregory Corso was born in New York City on March 26, 1930. From early infancy, Corso's life was marked by unusual difficulties and restless energy. Abandoned as an infant, he spent his formative years in orphanages and foster homes. He once spent five months in the New York City jail (popularly known as "the Tombs") and was even put under observation at the famous Bellevue mental hospital. In his late teens, Corso was finally convicted of theft and spent three years in Clinton State Prison. Upon release from prison, however, Corso's life took a different turn. He joined up with several icons of the Beat generation—including **Allen Ginsberg**, **Jack Kerouac**, and William S. Burroughs—and began a tumultuous career as a poet and cultural gadfly. By many accounts, Gregory Corso was something of a paradox; his poetry is considered full of "beauty, truth, and respect for all beings" (Morgan, xiii), but the man himself could be rude, insensitive, and given to harmful excess.

Although Corso has written several prose essays ("Poetry and Religion" 1963, "Between Childhood and Manhood" 1965) and a few plays (including "Standing on a Streetcorner" 1962), he is primarily known as a poet. His major publications include *The Vestal Lady on Brattle and Other Poems* (1955), *Gasoline* (1957), *The Happy Birthday of Death* (1960), *The American Express* (1961), *Long Live Man* (1962), *Elegiac Feelings American* (1970), *Herald of the Autochthonic Spirit* (1981), and *Mindfield: New and Selected Poems* (1989). Over the course of his lifetime, Corso managed to explore many aspects of the human condition in his poetry. A favorite topic, one to which he returns again and again, is the seeming inability of America (and Americans) to live up to the very ideals—justice, equality, compassion—so enthusiastically held to be self-evident.

His first volume of poetry, *The Vestal Lady on Brattle and Other Poems*, is but an early foray into this disillusioned view of American life. One critic has described this volume as presenting the motif of "predatory devouring or destruction of innocence and beauty" (Stephenson 11). While this description is certainly true (the title poem, "Sea Chanty," "Song," and "The Sniper's Lament" all present a rather bleak picture), it doesn't completely capture the resigned, passive tone of the work as a whole. "Destruction" and "devouring" suggest an outside force, something that is acting on us. However, Corso's almost playful use of unpleasant imagery is more reminiscent of entropy—a quiet implosion instead of an invasion.

One of Corso's later offerings, *Elegiac Feelings American*, becomes rather harsh in its assault on the disconnect between America's ideals and the actual reality. The opening poem, "Elegiac Feeling American (for the dear memory of Jack Kerouac)," is straightforward in its denunciation of the hypocrisy inherent in much of American behavior during the 1960s. In particular, Corso attacks the veneer of civilization, the superficial comedy and mechanical coldness that America presented. He does this primarily to mourn the passing of Jack Kerouac, who he felt was never truly at home here. The unfettered criticism of American history and culture continues in other poems; including "Spontaneous Requiem for the American Indian," "America Politica Historica: In Spontaneity," and "The American Way." In the latter piece, for example, Corso laments the endless conformity that he saw becoming ever more dominant in our society. At one point he even called the whole of Americans "replicas" with no distinguishing features among them. He saw America as becoming ever more regimented and standardized, wiped out of creativity and freedom of expression.

This is not to say that Corso was either pessimistic or relentlessly dismal in his poetry. On the contrary, his work is shot through with quirky humor, inventive language, and unusual syntax. One senses that Corso was not trying to paint America, or humanity in general, as doomed. Instead, his poetry thrums with frustration that we as human beings and Americans in particular, are not living up to our potential. As to that potential, Corso gives us plenty in which to admire and take comfort.

Further Reading

Morgan, Bill, ed. *An Accidental Autobiography: The Selected Letters of Gregory Corso.* New York: New Directions Publishing Corporation, 2003.

Olson, Kirby. *Gregory Corso: Doubting Thomist.* Carbondale: Southern Illinois UP, 2002.

Skau, Michael. *"A Clown in a Grave": Complexities and Tensions in the Work of Gregory Corso.* Carbondale: Southern Illinois UP, 1999.

Stephenson, Gregory. *Exiled Angel: A Study of the Work of Gregory Corso.* London: Aldgate Press, 1989.

Paul Washburn

CORTEZ, JAYNE (1936–) African American poet, activist, and spoken-word performer. Jayne Cortez was one of the first black writers to read her poetry to the accompaniment of a live **jazz** ensemble. Her first spoken-word recording, *Celebrations and Solitudes* (1975), included the music of bassist Richard Davis. She founded her performance ensemble, the Firespitters, in the late 1970s; *Unsubmissive Blues* (1979) was their first album together. Cortez wrote her first book of poetry, *Pissstained Stairs and the Monkeyman's Wares* in 1969. Here, as in her other poetry collections, she equates political corruption with environmental violations in order to highlight the ways in which human beings can profoundly damage their surroundings. These elements define Cortez's work as a key successor to the political statements of the **Black Arts Movement**.

Cortez's interest in music and issues of racial **identity** can be traced back to her childhood. She attended Los Angeles's Manual Arts High School, where she studied piano, bass, and cello. Her at-home listening included the music of Ella Fitzgerald, Billie Holiday, Charlie Parker, and Thelonious Monk. In addition, she began writing poetry seriously after her involvement with Ornette Coleman, a jazz saxophonist who founded the free jazz movement. In 1954, she attended several of his performances, and they married a short time after their first meeting. Their son, Denardo Coleman, a drummer and longtime member of the Firespitters, was born two years later. Although Cortez and Coleman divorced in 1964, she produces her albums under his label, Harmolodic, and at least three members of the Firespitters have also been members of Coleman's ensemble, Prime Time. Her live performances share with free jazz the traits of loose thematic associations and group improvisations. However, she has also developed a series of signature qualities in her poetry that distinguish her work from that of other avant-garde artists.

Many of Cortez's poems contain cultural allusions that illustrate the historical backgrounds to her work. Her poetry also manifests experimental linguistic features that mimic improvisatory performance and a radical politics that condemns international human-rights abuses. Its scatological themes link her cultural critiques to the efforts of the early-century surrealists. Her use of repetitions-with-a-difference is grounded in African performance traditions and the call-and-response strategies of gospel music. Poems that appear in a recorded form different from the original print version serve as a reminder of the flexibility necessary for live improvisation. This trait resembles recent developments in slam and performance poetry. Finally, the parallels Cortez draws between social and ecological crimes suggest that she has been influenced by the evolving ideas of eco-**feminism**. She often articulates her political views in terms of their relevance to black women's social experiences.

"So Many Feathers," a poem that appears in both *Mouth on Paper* (1977) and *Coagulations* (1984), is a tribute to African American dancer and singer Josephine Baker that repeatedly invokes Baker's physical characteristics as an attempt to understand the contradictions of her character. Cortez describes Baker as beautiful, talented, and, because she agreed to perform for members of the white upper class in apartheid South Africa, indirectly complicit in the oppression of blacks. "If the Drum Is a Woman," a poem included in the collections *Firespitter* (1982) and *Jazz Fan Looks Back* (2002), takes its title from a 1956 Duke Ellington album, *A Drum Is a Woman*. The opening line, "If the drum is a woman," both acknowledges Ellington's artistic heritage and throws into doubt the metaphorical premise of his piece by juxtaposing a revised version of his title to a series of violent action verbs—"pounding," "pistol whipping," and "shooting"—that recall both drumming techniques and domestic abuse. Cortez's poetic treatments of black women investigate the broader resonance of their personal lifestyle choices.

Today Jayne Cortez continues to write poetry, perform with the Firespitters, and give lectures and readings around the world. She has also received several awards for her work, and she has worked with multiple political organizations. To date, she has published nine books of poetry and produced eight albums of music and spoken-word performance. Her activities in the realms of fine arts and politics demonstrate her position as an African American artist committed to the global feminist struggle and the artistic inheritance of the Black Arts Movement. (*See also* African American Poetry)

Further Reading

Bolden, Tony. "All the Birds Sing Bass: The Revolutionary Blues of Jayne Cortez." *African American Review* 35.1 (Spring 2001): 61–71.

Melhem, D. H. "Jayne Cortez: Supersurrealist Vision." *Heroism in the New Black Poetry: Introductions and Interviews*. Lexington: UP of Kentucky, 1990. 181–212.

Jennifer D. Ryan

COVINO, PETER (1963–)   Italian American poet and editor. Covino's poetry, while rooted in the Italian American experience, debunks its mythologies and stereotypes. Born in Sturno, a small town in the province of Avellino, in the southern Italian region of Campania, Covino immigrated with his family to the United States in 1966, though the family frequently returned to their home country. Covino's complicated awareness of hyphenated **identity** brings forth a conception of hybridity as a productive site for creative and cultural exploration. Unlike much traditional immigrant literature that nostalgically evokes the separation from an often-mythologized homeland, Covino's work frequently exposes the devastating experience of growing up within a patriarchal cultural and a familial context where violence and thwarted relationships prevail.

The son of a cabinetmaker and a dressmaker who stressed higher education, Covino graduated from Amherst College, where he majored in English, in 1985. He pursued a master's degree in social work at Columbia University and, after completing his studies there, worked for several years as a social worker. He would later go back to English studies, pursuing a master's in English at City College, New York, and a PhD in poetry at the University of Utah. His parents' background filters into his poetry, for example through images of sewing, building, and planting. On the other hand, his experience as a social worker shapes his concern with depicting a psychological landscape in which gender, class, **ethnicity**, and sexuality intersect in shaping both family and social dynamics. Far from conventionally realistic or narrative, Covino's poetry takes on surreal and experimental traits both in form and content. If his poetry is shaped by immediate autobiographical circumstances, it is also imbued with classical influences. Covino also acknowledges the influence of such modern and contemporary authors as Giorgio Bassani (with whom Covino first studied Italian poetry in 1983), Arthur Rimbaud, Constantine Cavaty, Jorie Graham, and Don Revell, one of his mentors in Utah.

In 2001 Covino published *Straight Boyfriend*, which won the Frank O'Hara Prize in Poetry. His book of poems *Cut off the Ears of Winter* will be published in 2005 by New Issues Press. Covino cofounded the poetry journal *Barrow Street*, which in 2004 began publishing books. Covino's commitment to poetry is evident in his active presence on the New York literary scene, where he has organized countless poetry readings and series, including the prestigious Barrow Street series.

Covino's haunting poems are characterized by an exquisite lyricism and the reliance on distorted syntax as well as diction borrowed from Italian language and dialects, as evident even in his early work, for example, "The Poverty of Language," his first published poem. Italian American male writers have been less willing to expose the dark side of Italian American family and culture and to question its mythologies than Italian American female authors. Often foregrounding queer identity, though never simplistically, Covino has opened the door for others to explore such often unspeakable issues as incest, violence in the family, homosexuality, and the complex ways in which immigrant history and family violence are interrelated. (*See also* Italian American Poetry)

Edvige Giunta

CRAFTS, HANNAH (Dates unknown)   African American novelist. "Hannah Crafts" exists only as the pseudonym of an unidentified writer, and "Crafts" may be a tribute to Ellen Crafts, who escaped from **slavery** in 1848 disguised as a white male. The search for the identity behind the pseudonym began in 2001, when **Henry Louis Gates Jr.** noticed a listing for an unpublished manuscript in an auction catalog. Apparently dating from the 1850s, the clothbound manuscript, called "The Bondwoman's Narrative, by Hannah Crafts, a Fugitive Slave, Recently Escaped from North Carolina," was a "fictionalized biography . . . of the early life and escape of one Hannah Crafts" that had sat for more than fifty years in the collection of the late Dorothy Porter Wesley, the famous Howard University librarian. Gates bought the manuscript, and began a long process of detective work, seeking to authenticate the holograph and determine its author.

Experts examined ink, paper, punctuation, and handwriting, and dated the manuscript between 1853 and 1861. *The Bondwoman's Narrative* is therefore the first novel written by a female fugitive slave and most likely the first novel written by an African American woman. In addition, as Gates explains in his introduction to the 2002 edition of the novel, it is our first "unedited, unaffected, unglossed, unaided" glimpse into the mind of a fugitive slave. The text is not filtered through an abolitionist editor, and complicates traditional abolitionist-approved narratives that tended to present a unified slave community. Instead, Hannah's slave-characters make class and color distinctions amongst themselves, and an internal slave hierarchy emerges. These details, and those of the intimate relationship between mistress and slave, for example, are textual clues that the slave narrator's voice is authentic and her experience of slavery first-hand. Similarly, her tendency to introduce characters as people first, and blacks second, suggests that she is African American.

The author certainly claims in the preface that she has simply "relat[ed] events as they occurred." But this claim is just token and formulaic: *The Bondwoman's Narrative* is a *fictionalized* autobiography, a novel in the first-person, albeit drawing on the author's life-experience. It uses the religious, gothic, and sentimental conventions of mid-nineteenth-century fiction, combining coincidences, heroines and villains, portents, old portraits and cursed trees. "Crafts" borrows from Dickens's *Bleak House*, scatters biblical and classical allusions throughout, and adopts a florid Victorian style to tell the story of Hannah, a light-skinned house-slave who discovers that her master's new wife is a mulatto passing for white. Hannah helps her mistress flee the blackmail of a villainous lawyer, Mr. Trappe, who knows her secret racial **identity** and pursues and captures the pair. After the melodramatic death of her mistress, Hannah works as a maid to the unpleasant Mrs. Wheeler, but escapes when threatened with a forced marriage to a field slave. She eventually reaches safety in the North, where she marries a minister and begins work as a schoolteacher in a free black community in New Jersey.

In writing fiction disguised as nonfiction, the author acknowledges and challenges the demands of the time: "Veracity was everything in an ex-slave's tale, essential both to its critical and commercial success and to its political efficacy within the movement," Gates reminds us in his introduction to the novel. Perhaps feeling trapped by the expectation that she write her "true" story, "Crafts" explores Mr. Trappe's reminder that "words [are] shadows, the very reverse of realities" (97). Her novel destabilizes genre and dwells on the doubleness of language, proposing instead a path to freedom carved variously by imagination, silence, and visual art. She lays out the slave's uneasy relationship with language, as though suspicious of the well-established concept of slaves writing themselves into existence with the tools of the Western literary tradition. Indeed she apparently never tried to write herself into existence publicly: There is no evidence that she tried to publish *The Bondwoman's Narrative*. And though her novel, finally public, reached the *New York Times* best seller list in 2002, her existence and historical identity remains mysterious. The search for Hannah Crafts continues.

Further Reading

Gates, Henry Louis, Jr. "Introduction." *The Bondwoman's Narrative*. Hannah Crafts. New York: Warner Books, 2002: ix–lxxii.

Gates, Henry Louis, Jr., and Hollis Robbins, eds. *In Search of Hannah Crafts: Critical Essays on "The Bondwoman's Narrative."* New York: Basic Books, 2004.

Townshend, Dale, "Speaking of Darkness: Gothic and the History of the African American Slave-Woman in Hannah Crafts' *The Bondwoman's Narrative*." *Victorian Gothic*. Ed. Karen Sayer and Rosemary Mitchell. Leeds: U of Leeds P. 2003: 141–54.

Zoe Trodd

CRASTA, RICHARD/AVATAR PRABHU (1952–) Indian American novelist. Richard Crasta's work forms part of the larger traditions of satirical literature in India, Britain, and the United States, recalling by turns Daniel Defoe, Saros Cowasjee, and Richard Russo. As well, his interest in the psychological, social, and sexual growth of adolescents locates his writing in the line of the bildungsroman (novel of development) along with that of James Joyce, **J. D. Salinger**, and Arundhati Roy.

Crasta was born in 1952 in Bangalore, India, the son of John and Christine Crasta, Roman Catholics of Mangalore, Karnataka, where he grew up. With a BA from Mysore (1972), Crasta was accepted into the Indian Administrative Service. He studied for an MA in the United States from 1979 to 1981 and, after a short return to India, emigrated in 1984 to the New York

City area. In 1987 Crasta received an MFA from the program in creative writing at Columbia University. A marriage in the 1980s to another South Indian emigrant ended in divorce in 2000.

The Revised Kama Sutra: A Novel of Colonialism and Desire appeared in India in 1993, with later editions in Britain, the United States, and Germany. Its title refers to Vatsyayana's manual of erotic love as foil for the life of a sex-starved Roman Catholic boy in 1960s India. A collection of essays, *Beauty Queens, Children, and the Death of Sex*, was published in India in 1997. Finally, in 1998 Richard Crasta edited *Eaten by the Japanese: The Memoirs of an Unknown Indian Soldier,* by his father, John Baptist Crasta. At that time, he began publishing as Avatar Prabhu.

The serio-comic novel *The Revised Kama Sutra* follows the development of Vijay Prabhu and is organized around the four Vedic stages of life: "The Beginnings of Wisdom, or, Encounters with Dharma," "Turning Away the Dogs of God, or, In the Time of Artha," "Delicious Undertakings, or, the Rule of Kama," and "Endless Laughter, or The Moksha Express." So Crasta/Prabhu, unlike Vatsayana, does not limit himself to guiding readers through the realm of sexuality: He "covers" the entire mind-body state. Crasta's polemical collection, *Beauty Queens, Children, and the Death of Sex* covers everything from the Miss World contest held in a puritanical India to the Bush family's imperial pretensions in Iraq. *Eaten by the Japanese* reconstructs the memories of John Crasta, recounting in chilling detail the lives of POWs on Rabaul in the South Pacific.

Several reviews of *The Revised Kama Sutra* have appeared since its release in 1993, the majority in India, and most of those are impressed with the novel's satirical qualities. British reviewers were generally favorable. More recent reviews in the United States were mixed. In addition, there have been several interviews with the author and reviews of *Beauty Queens*. To date, there have been no full-length critical analyses.

Further Reading

"All One Writes Is Autobiographical." Interview by Sumita Thapar. *The Pioneer* (March 22, 1994): 13.

"Hamburgers Can Never Taste the Same As Idlis to an Indian." Interview by Mahesh Nayak with Vikas Kumar. *Mangalore Today* (January 1998): 18–20.

Barry Fruchter

CRAWFORD, JANIE The dynamic protagonist of **Zora Neale Hurston**'s novel *Their Eyes Were Watching God* (1937), Janie Mae Crawford marries three different men before she turns forty but cultivates a genuinely loving relationship only with her last husband, a charming and good-natured blues traveler, Vergible "**Tea Cake**" Woods.

Janie finds that her strong personality and firm commitment to realizing emotional, psychic, and sexual fulfillment with a mate are incompatible with the plans her first and second husbands have set out for her. Janie's brief marriage to Logan Killicks, a landowning farmer, is largely defined by her serving as his workhorse; the relationship terminates when she runs off with the stylish city slicker, Joe "Jody" Starks. But Starks proves to be only a slightly better choice when he excludes Janie from the public life he orchestrates as the preeminent man-about-Eatonville. Storeowner, postmaster, and eventual mayor, Starks consistently dismisses or ignores Janie's appeals to become a more respected figure in their home as well as a more active member in the community. After several years of marriage, Janie one day forcefully talks back to Starks in public. His embarrassment over the incident leads to his declining health and eventual death.

Tea Cake walks into Janie's life soon after she puts Starks, and the suppression of her desire, to rest. What flourishes in their relationship is an intimacy that arrives at mutual understanding and the possibility of Janie leading a self-determining life through open, often playful, dialogue. Though not without occasional reservation and doubt about the relationship, Janie envisions herself as Tea Cake's equal, both as a worker in the bean fields of the "muck" and as a lover in their time alone. Tragedy strikes the relationship, however, when a rabid dog bites Tea Cake as he rescues Janie from flooding caused by a hurricane. Tea Cake's mental faculties erode steadily, and his behavior becomes increasingly erratic and violent. Janie is forced to decide whether to save herself or to have both of them perish. She kills Tea Cake in an act of self-defense and is subsequently tried for his murder.

The extent to which Janie comes to articulate a feminine or even feminist consciousness by the end of the narrative has been a subject of intense critical debate. Some scholars have pointed out that the absence of Janie's "spoken" testimony in the trial scene allows patriarchal authority to return in the form of the acquittal handed down by the all-white, all-male jury. What bears consideration in this reading is the fact that the novel's main narrative is set within a frame narrative that sees a humble yet self-assured Janie recounting her tale to her Eatonville "kissin'-friend," Pheoby Watson: "Mah tongue is in mah friend's mouf." Hurston renders her protagonist a master storyteller in order to underscore the kind of muted agency Janie exercises in strategically displacing or withholding her voice when the unfolding of the narrative, her narrative, requires it.

Further Reading

Kaplan, Carla. "The Erotics of Talk: 'That Oldest Human Longing' in *Their Eyes Were Watching God*." *American Literature* 67.1 (1995): 115–42.

Kubitschek, Missy Dehn. "'Tuh de Horizon and Back': The Female Quest in *Their Eyes Were Watching God*." *Black American Literature Forum* 17.3 (1983): 109–15.

Washington, Mary Helen. "'I Love the Way Janie Crawford Left Her Husbands': Zora Neale Hurston's Emergent Female Hero." *Invented Lives: Narratives of Black Women, 1860–1960*. Garden City, NY: Anchor, 1987. 237–54.

Kinohi Nishikawa

CRÈVECOEUR, J. HECTOR ST. JOHN DE (1735–1813)   French travel writer, soldier, diplomat, surveyor, cartographer, Indian trader, farmer, cultural and social observer. Crèvecoeur's place in colonial American literature rests on an epistolary collection of travel writing and an early piece of cross-cultural reportage from America, *Letters From an American Farmer* (1782). In particular, Letter IV, "What Is an American?", draws attention to Crèvecoeur's collection, as he attempts to profile an average American, extolling the advantages of "that new man," who "melts" the burdensome and divisive European past and builds an industrious and just new nation. Although Crèvecoeur's visions of America are often uneven and uncritical, his images of multiethnic Americans have become a part of the national imagination and have laid foundations for future definitions of the United States.

Crèvecoeur's life follows the trajectory of numerous transatlantic journeys. Born to minor French aristocracy and educated in France and England, Michel-Guillaume Jean de Crèvecoeur sailed for Canada in 1755, where he fought for the French militia in the French-Indian War. In1759, he moved to New York, became a naturalized citizen of the British colonies, anglicized his name to J. Hector St. John, settled on a farm, and worked as a surveyor, befriending and trading with Indian tribes. During this period of calm, Crèvecoeur wrote most of the sketches for his collection. In it, the fictive narrator "Farmer James" reports on idyllic particularities of American rural life, ranging from farming, whaling, frontier life, and life with the Indians to charming descriptions of natural history. Disrupting the flow of the collection and infusing a welcome realistic dimension to Crèvecoeur's representation of the bucolic life in the new world is the often-criticized unevenness of later letters and their disturbing images of **slavery** and intimations of encroaching Revolutionary turmoil. Indeed, in the late 1770s, Crèvecoeur's peaceful paradise was destroyed, and as a loyalist sympathizer, he was forced to flee to France, taking with him the manuscript of the *Letters*. The publication of the collection and its warm reception in England and later in France established Crèvecoeur as an authority on America. Appointed consul, he returned to America after the Revolution (1783) and dedicated himself to building diplomatic relations between the two countries. At the end of his diplomatic career in 1790, Crèvecoeur returned to France, where he lived until his death.

In 1801 Crèvecoeur published another significant work, *Journey into Northern Pennsylvania and the State of New York*, and in 1925, *Sketches of Eighteenth-Century America*, a companion volume to the *Letters*, was selected and published posthumously. Despite stylistic flaws and biased representation, Crèvecoeur's work occupies a significant place in the larger body of early American writing. In particular, *Letters of an American Farmer*, often likened to Thomas Jefferson's *Notes on the State of Virginia* (1785), is significant for its valuable depiction of colonial American life and an early introduction of pressing questions of **identity** formation facing the emerging nation. (*See also* Franco American Literature)

Further Reading

Manning, Susan. "Introduction." *Letters from an American Farmer.* J. Hector St. John de Crèvecoeur. New York: Oxford UP, 1997. vii–xlvi.

Ljiljana Coklin

CRUZ, NILO (1961–)   Cuban American playwright. Cruz was born in Matanzas, Cuba, in 1961 and immigrated with his family to Little Havana in 1970. He began acting, directing, and writing plays in the Miami area in the 1980s, where he was mentored by Teresa María Roja, founder of the Prometeo Theater. He studied drama at Brown University where he received an MA in 1994. Currently he resides in Manhattan and teaches theater at Yale. He has received grants from the National Endowment of the Arts, the Rockefeller Foundation, and the Theatre Communications Group. In 2003 Cruz gained national notoriety by winning both the American Theater Critics/Steinberg New Play Award (given to plays produced outside New York City) and the Pulitzer Prize in drama for his highly acclaimed play *Anna in the Tropics.* Among the dozens of Cruz's earlier works are *Night Train to Bolina,* for which he won the W. Alton Jones Award; *Two Sisters and a Piano; Dancing on Her Knees;* and *A Park in Our House.* Cruz's two most recent plays are *Beauty of the Father* and *Lorca in a Green Dress.*

Cruz wrote *Anna in the Tropics* in 2001–2002 while he was playwright-in-residence with the New Theater in Coral Gables, Florida, where it premiered the following season. *Anna* is the first work by a Latino playwright to win a Pulitzer and one of only a handful to receive the award without being shown first in New York City. The play takes place in Ybor City (Tampa) during the early years of the Depression, and deals with the lives of working-class cigar makers in a *tabaquería* (cigar factory). It draws on a uniquely Cuban tradition where the workers themselves, not the bosses, would hire *lectores* (readers) who would read to them throughout the day while they worked. The *lectores* would have at hand all kinds of print material, from daily newspapers to classic works of literature. In the play, a *lector* comes from out of town and interrupts the calm by reciting

Nilo Cruz. *AP/Wide World Photos.*

from Tolstoy's *Anna Karenina*. Cruz is intrigued by the seemingly contradictory idea of illiterate workers memorizing and reciting the classics by heart. For Cruz, it reflects the central human need for cultural expression to give meaning to life. *Anna* is indicative of Cruz's great interest in focusing on Cuban and Latino themes in his writing, not only as a way to chronicle cultural practices that are fast disappearing, such as in the case of the factory lector, but also to underscore and share the vast cultural contributions and impact that Latino culture has had and is having on Anglo culture.

The spirit of Federico García Lorca is the driving force behind Cruz's two most recent plays, *Beauty of the Father* and *Lorca in a Green Dress*, which give voice to his continuous fascination with the life and work of Spain's most famous twentieth-century poet and playwright murdered by the Fascists at the beginning of the Spanish Civil War. As with Cruz's other work, these plays are marked by their poetry and symbolism. Steeped in the Latin American art of magical realism, they are indicative of Cruz's singular interest in achieving a theatrical language that infuses mind, body, and spirit in order to create altered spaces of meaning.

Further Reading

Caridad Svich, Maria Teresa Marrero. *Out of the Fringe: Contemporary Latina/Latino Theatre and Performance*. New York: Theatre Communications Group, 2000.

Ellis, Roger. *Multicultural Theatre II: Contemporary Hispanic, Asian, and African-American Plays*. Colorado Springs: Meriwether Publishers, 1998.

Colleen Kattau

CRUZ, VICTOR HERNÁNDEZ (1949–)   American poet of Puerto Rican descent. Cruz is a person of many cultures. Born on February 6, 1949, in the mountain town of Aguas Buenas, Puerto Rico, Cruz's poetry asserts a mixture of Spanish, African, and indigenous or Taino roots that define his ancestry. His poetry reflects the movement between and among cultures that informs his experience and acknowledges the layers of history and ethnic diversity that have come before it and that leave their mark on the present.

Cruz is a prolific poet and writer whose collections include *Pappo Got His Gun* (1966), his first publication, a homemade chapbook, that he hand delivered to book stores for distribution, *Snaps* (1969), *Mainland* (1973), *By Lingual Wholes* (1982), *Rhythm Content & Flavor* (an anthology, 1989), *Red Beans* (1991), and *Panoramas* (1997). He also has an unfinished novel called *Time Zones*. Cruz is included in dozens of anthologies, journals, newspapers, and other publications of Latino, African American, and Puerto Rican writing, and has been interviewed extensively about his work. His poems have been translated into five languages, and have been published in Spain and Latin America. In 1968 three of his poems were selected for publication in *Ramparts*. In 1995 he was selected for inclusion in Bill Moyers's Public Broadcasting Service series *The Language of Life*, which chronicles the work of North American poets. He also has participated in the predominantly

African American writers' journal *Umbra* particularly when it was moved to the Bay Area of California. Cruz was crowned Heavyweight Poetry Champion of Taos's World Poetry Bout Association two years running (1987–88). He has taught at San Francisco State University, Lehman College, and University of California campuses at Berkeley and at San Diego. While in Berkeley Cruz worked with junior high school boys on developing themselves as writers; this experience is chronicled in his poem/pamphlet "Doing Poetry," part of which was later used to create an operetta by Hans Werner Henze in 1973. In 1989, after thirty-six years in the United States, he moved back to Puerto Rico. Cruz currently divides his time between Morocco and his native Borinquen.

Victor Hernández Cruz. *Photo by Nestor Barreto. Courtesy of Victor Hernández Cruz.*

While Cruz identifies with all the cultural influences that come to fruition in his poetry, he also considers himself a U.S. or American poet because, although Spanish is his first language in terms of listening and speaking, he writes primarily in English. He is one of the few Puerto Rican poets to identify in this way and to write predominantly in his second language, although he is based much of the time in Puerto Rico. For Cruz, U.S. English is further removed from the crown and thus can be more flexible and rule free. The freewheeling character of Americanized English is a major source of the playfulness and immediacy of much of his poetry, which seems both spontaneous and carefully constructed. His geographical and multicultural heritage also affords him a privileged position from which to write in a way that moves even beyond bilingualism, and that is both within and outside of the U.S. context. Some of Cruz's early influences are William Carlos Williams and Federico García Lorca, whose *Poet in New York* was especially inspirational because of Lorca's infusion of music within his poetry, particularly Flamenco, a musical style born out of Moorish, Latin, and Gypsy influences. He also cites Ezra Pound, **Amira Baraka**, and Rumi as impacting on his poetry, as well as the musical influence of **jazz** music like that of Miles Davis.

Cruz's poetry is in many ways a working out of his early childhood experiences in which one minute he was surrounded by a rural and tropical geography of dirt roads, green lush mountainside, and fruit trees ripe for the picking, and the next abruptly uprooted to a starker, colder, yet exciting land of pavement and skyscrapers. Cruz speaks of how as a child he tried to pull apart the buildings to recover the lost green that he thought they were hiding (Moyers, 100–101). The visceral nature of Cruz's poems can be traced back to his early years in Puerto Rico when he would accompany his grandfather, a tobacconist, to his workplace where he had the opportunity to smell, hear, and feel an integral part of island culture. When he was just five years old, Cruz's family moved to what Puerto Ricans call "Loisaida" or Manhattan's Lower East Side, where he spent his later childhood and adolescence. Along with the blending of predominantly African American and Puerto Rican cultures in that area of New York which created a dynamic and stimulating context within which to grow, Cruz also experienced the ethnocentric bias of "English" only and **racism** based on skin color.

Cruz's writing is marked by constant change, movement, rhythm, and music. It is active and dynamic because he himself is the product of movement. He is very much tied and indebted to his ancestral roots though his poetry does not dwell in the past, but rather explores how the present is informed by cultural movements that are at once linear and twisting, constant and changing. He is interested in the geographical spaces and meshing between the Mediterranean and Caribbean seas, and the cross-fertilization among Spanish, African, Caribbean, and Western cultures. His work explores the northern African presence in southern Spain from which most of the Caribbean has been colonized. In *Red Beans* for instance, a text of both poetry and essays, the opening quotes connect the "*ay lo lay la*" sounds of the *jíbaro* (mountain peasant) music of Puerto Rico with the distant Islamic language that also necessarily defines Puerto Rico's present via Spain. The text's subtitles, meanwhile, reveal the playful (and informative) nature of Cruz's cultural comparisons and contrasts: "The Guayabera Is the Tuxedo of the Caribbean" and "Morning Rooster" boast cultural icons in a radical and recontextualized way. His poetry combines the experiential with more generalized truths. Cruz is deeply aware of the centrality of poetry to life itself in the journey to find what makes community and to discover what is human.

Further Reading

Dick, Bruce Allen. *A Poet's Truth: Conversations with Latino Poets.* Tucson: U of Arizona P, 2003

MacAdams, Lewis. *Victor Hernandez Cruz* (Videorecording). Los Angeles: The Foundation, 1989.

Major, Clarence. *The Dark and Feeling: Black American Writers and Their Work.* New York: Third Press, 1974.

Marzán, Julio. *Inventing a Word: An Anthology of Twentieth-Century Puerto Rican Poetry.* New York: Columbia UP, in Association with the Center for Inter-American Relations, 1980.

Moyers, Bill. *The Language of Life: A Festival of Poets.* New York: Doubleday, 1996.

Shepperd, Walt. "Work with the Universe: An Interview with Clarence Major and Victor Hernandez Cruz." *Conversations with Clarence Major.* Ed. Nancy Bunge. Jackson: U of Mississippi P, 2002. 3–9.

Colleen Kattau

CUBAN AMERICAN AUTOBIOGRAPHY   Due to the relatively recent arrival of tens of thousands of Cuban exiles since the onset of the Cuban revolution in 1959—the largest exodus in the island's history—Cuban American authors have only lately embraced the quintessentially American genre of ethnic autobiography. Out of sixteen single- and multiple-authored autobiographical works noted in this entry, only two were published before 1990. The first of these, *A Book* (1976), by Cuban entertainer Desi Arnaz, describes the vicissitudes of the protagonist upon his arrival in the United States after fleeing civil violence in Cuba in the 1930s—a period that also witnessed Cuban migration to the United States—and his eventual, successful career in the entertainment industry, including his stint as co-protagonist in the comedy series "I Love Lucy." The second, *Contra viento y marea* (Against All Odds, 1978), is not an autobiography per se, but testimonial literature by young Cuban Americans who returned to the island in the late 1970s with the intention of reconnecting with their native land. Influenced by the antiwar and **Civil Rights Movement**s of the late 1960s and early 1970s, these sons and daughters of exiled Cubans sought to experience Cuban society firsthand, and wrote about their positive impressions in this book, the recipient of the prestigious Casa de las Américas award.

The bulk of Cuban American autobiographical narratives began to appear toward the end of the millennium, authored by a second generation of Cubans who came of age in the United States. Unlike the authors of *Contra viento y marea*, however, they emphasize the failed policies of the Cuban revolution. Written in English, these narratives evince the authors' position of straddling two cultures.

The autobiographies of Carlos Eire, **Pablo Medina**, and **Virgil Suárez** are growing-up narratives largely circumscribed to the island. Eire, a professor of religious studies and history at Yale University who uses figurative language like an accomplished poet, offers a poignant tale of a privileged, if vulnerable, childhood in *Waiting for Snow in Havana: Confessions of a Cuban Boy* (2003), winner of the National Book Award for nonfiction. The son of a municipal judge, Eire left Cuba at the age of eleven with his brother through the Peter Pan Airlift in 1962 and never saw his father again. Written in just four months with the urgency of a liberating confession, the book highlights the uplifting magic of childhood as well as the painful consequences of depravity, separation, and exile. A novelist and poet, Pablo Medina also writes about an elitist upbringing in *Exiled Memories: A Cuban Childhood* (1990), while Virgil Suárez, who left Cuba in 1974, delves into growing up in a middle-class home during the revolution in his autobiographical books

Spared Angola: Memories from a Cuban-American Childhood (1997) and *Infinite Refuge* (2002). Especially for authors such as these who have not returned to their native land, memoirs offer a means of symbolically connecting the past with a present that is an unlikely outcome of that past.

Second-generation Cuban Americans **Gustavo Pérez Firmat**, Román de la Campa, María del Carmen Boza, Emilio Bejel, and **Rafael Campo** have also written autobiographies. Published shortly after his celebrated *Life on the Hyphen: The Cuban-American Way* (1994), Pérez Firmat's memoir, *Next Year in Cuba. A Cubano's Coming-of-Age in America* (1995), nominated for a Pulitzer Prize in nonfiction, dwells on the dilemma of a young man torn between his family's obsession with an advantaged past on the island and his need to engage his American surroundings. Laying claim to a hyphenated identity, Pérez Firmat (currently David Feinson, Professor of Humanities at Columbia University) illustrates the personal dislocations occasioned by exile, presenting at the same time a sympathetic portrait of the beginnings of the Cuban enclave in Miami's Dade County, the author's hometown. Román de la Campa's *Cuba on My Mind: Journeys to a Severed Nation* (2000) focuses on the author's reevaluation of the Cuban regime after an initial period of empathy that led him to participate in the Cuban progressive movement. Another subject he addresses is the role of Cuban Americans within the Latino community. María del Carmen Boza's *Scattering the Ashes* (1998), the only book-length narrative by a single woman writer, revolves around an ambivalent father-daughter relationship.

With his openly gay perspective, cultural critic, poet, and professor Emilio Bejel adds a spin to Cuban American autobiography in *The Write Way Home* (2003), a first-person account on the need to come to terms with one's sexual identity and sense of family. Also assuming a homosexual **identity** in *The Poetry of Healing* (1997), Rafael Campo, a medical doctor and published poet, underscores the healing power of medicine and poetry, as well as its limits, in the midst of the AIDS epidemic. A different approach to gay themes is displayed in **Reinaldo Arenas**'s autobiography *Antes que anochezca* (Before Night Falls, 1992), made into a popular film by Julian Schnabel in 2000. What is emphasized in this book, published posthumously, is Arenas's fallout with the Cuban government due to his unconventional behavior. Arenas lived the last ten years of his life in New York City where, having contracted the HIV virus, he committed suicide in 1990.

Acknowledged by critics as relevant are a number of autobiographical essays written in the 1990s by Ruth Behar and Eliana Rivero, women who, because of their feminist perspective, have contributed to diversify the white, male, heterosexual, and upper-middle-class viewpoint only seemingly prevalent in Cuban American autobiographical writings. These writers identify with other Latinas with whom they share many concerns as women of color.

Furthermore, women have figured prominently in testimonial writing akin to the testimonial literature that has flourished throughout Latin

America since the 1980s. Within this tradition in which individuals bear witness to experiences worthy of public attention, three recent books deserve to be mentioned: *Bridges to Cuba/Puentes a Cuba* (1995), edited by Ruth Behar and Juan León; *ReMembering Cuba* (2001), edited by Andrea Herrera O'Reilly; and *By Heart/De memoria* (2003), edited by María de los Angeles Torres. The three books convey the worldviews of diverse sectors of the Cuban American community. In an effort to overcome the historic divide between Cubans on either side of the Florida Straits, Behar and Torres also obtained the collaboration of Cubans on the island with an interest in building bridges.

Finally, Evelio Grillo's *Black Cuban, Black American* (2000) reminds us that Cuban migration to the United States harks back to the mid nineteenth century. The son of dark-skinned cigar workers who had migrated from Cuba, Grillo grew up in the early twentieth century in a black neighborhood in Tampa, Florida. Foremost among Grillo's apprehensions is the racial binary in U.S. society, which urged him to forge an alliance with African Americans. This memoir, with its emphasis on **race**, stands in evidence of the diverse circumstances that have given rise to Cuban American autobiography.

Further Reading

Alvarez Borland, Isabel. "Autobiographical Writing. Negotiating an Identity."*Cuban-American Literature of Exile. From Person to Persona.* Charlottesville and London: UP of Virginia, 1998. 61–87.

López, Iraida H. *La autobiografía hispana contemporánea en los Estados Unidos: a través del caleidoscopio.* Lewiston, New York: Edwin Mellen Press, 2001.

Iraida H. López

CUBAN AMERICAN NOVEL   One of the striking features of what might be called the "history" of the Cuban American novel is its stark refusal to correspond directly to, or in any way simply "represent," what are conventionally taken to be the "histories" of either the Cuban American community, or of some larger Cuban diasporic entity that might include populations both on and off the island that is still called Cuba. That latter history usually traces the conventional line of cause-and-effect, from the 1959 Cuban Revolution to the consequent exodus of that movement's enemies into a decades-long self-styled exile, primarily concentrated in Miami, Florida. The exiles, in turn, found themselves, in spite of their own most dearly held intentions, both assimilating and establishing themselves in a decidedly "Americanized" context, which, by the 1980s, certainly had taken a significant and defining turn away from that initial "exile" to a more familiar "immigrant" mentality, from which was finally born the identifying category of Cuban American. The history of the production and publication of long prose narrative works of literary fiction, either by U.S.-based writers of Cuban descent, or on the theme of U.S.-based Cuban experience, or both, bears little correspondence to that familiar narrative, even when that narrative itself becomes a central trope or point of elaboration in many of the texts collected under the rubric in question.

The starting point for this history of the genre could be, for example, the moment in the late 1980s when two significant publishing events occurred within two years of one another: the appearance in 1987 of *The Doorman* (*El Portero*), Cuban novelist **Reinaldo Arenas**'s only major fictional work to be set entirely in the United States; and the publication in 1989 of Cuban American novelist **Oscar Hijuelos**'s *The Mambo Kings Play Songs of Love*, which that same year became the first novel by a U.S. Latino writer to win the Pulitzer Prize for fiction. The critic Isabel Alvarez-Borland, in 1998's *Cuban-American Literature of Exile* (one of the very few book-length studies of post-1959 off-island Cuban writing), suggests that there is very little novelistic production of note in the Cuban American community before this period. What is striking, therefore, about the phenomenon defined by the near-simultaneous appearance of Arenas and Hijuelos's titles is their utterly tangential relation to the "official" version of Cuban American history. The very openly gay Arenas, for example, had only left Cuba some years earlier as part of the 1980 Mariel boatlift; he was already an established, though severely persecuted, writer in Cuba, and when he finally escaped the country he opted to settle in New York City rather than Miami primarily because of the political and sexual intolerance he saw prevailing in that capital of Cuban America. *The Doorman*, written originally in Spanish and set in late-1980s New York, is bitingly critical of not only Cuban Miami, but also of the United States in the age of Ronald Reagan and AIDS. *The Doorman*, stylistically consistent with the fantastical, experimental qualities of Arenas's major, Cuba-based fiction, suffered considerable overshadowing from the flashier success of Arenas's 1992 memoir, *Before Night Falls*. Hijuelos, on the other hand, was born in New York City in the early 1950s to Cuban parents, lived his entire life in the United States, and set the events of his prize-winning novel primarily in the Cuban musical club-land of 1950s New York, hence before the revolution and well outside the frame of reference of exile-dominated Miami. *Mambo Kings*, which was Hijuelos's second novel, set the standard for Cuban American literary expression in English, demonstrating the appropriateness of this adopted language for the narration of a decidedly lasting, increasingly institutionalized immigrant experience.

While Arenas and Hijuelos were enjoying the privilege of seeing their work appear under the imprints of major New York–based publishing houses (Arenas at Grove Press, Hijuelos at Farrar, Strauss and Giroux), at least one other Cuban American novelist of note was beginning to publish at the same moment but at the much more modestly positioned **Arte Público Press** of Houston, Texas. This was **Roberto G. Fernández**, whose satiric 1988 novel *Raining Backwards* both corrects and completes some of the complicated representational tendencies in the work of the other two writers. Fernández, like Arenas, was born in Cuba, though he left at a much younger age, in the early 1960s, and settled with his family in Miami, where he grew up. His first literary publications were primarily in Spanish. *Raining Backwards*, Fernández's first novel in English, is set in the heart of early-1970s exile Miami; it therefore reflects in its every detail the writer's intimate familiarity with the qualities of political and cultural life in that community, but it mostly exploits that familiarity to satirize those qualities with a degree of incisiveness that only an insider could manage. In *Raining Backwards* and its follow-up (1995's *Holy Radishes!*, also from Arte Público), Fernández strikes a precarious balance between a deep fondness toward and an equally deep cynicism about the community in which he grew up, and which he continues to write about, from his perhaps safer current position as teacher of creative writing at Florida State University in Tallahassee. Since the late 1980s Arte Público Press has been instrumental in publishing a good deal of work by other, less prominent but also quite talented and even prolific Cuban American novelists, including **Elías Miguel Muñoz** (see 1988's *Crazy Love*, 1991's *The Greatest Performance* and 1998's *Brand New Memory*, for example), **Virgil Suárez** (1995's *Havana Thursdays*, 1999's *The Cutter*), and Himilce Novas (1996's *Mangos, Bananas, and Coconuts*). The proliferation of writers and titles issuing from just one small press reflects something of the vitality and urgency of the movement inaugurated by Arenas, Hijuelos, and Fernández in those pivotal years between 1985 and 1990.

Of the novelists to appear on the Cuban American scene in the 1990s, perhaps none has received as much attention and acclaim as **Cristina García**, whose *Dreaming in Cuban* (1992) marked the appearance of the first major fictional work by a Cuban American woman writing on Cuban American themes. *Dreaming in Cuban* therefore both builds on and corrects the work begun by the established male writers in this nascent tradition by augmenting their already profoundly critical fictive interventions into the business-as-usual of telling Cuban American history by a profound, and profoundly feminist, reconstitution of that history. Born in Cuba, raised in Brooklyn, and based in Los Angeles, García too, like Hijuelos and Arenas before her, embodies a history with no direct correspondence to the Cuban-Miamian-American line. Across her three existing novels (including, after *Dreaming in Cuban*, 1997's *The Agüero Sisters*, and 2003's *Monkey Hunting*), García devotes very little space to direct representations of life in Cuban Miami (which mostly occur in the second novel) while she devotes extraordinary energy to reimagining life in Cuba at various stages of its history. In general, her favored American setting, of significant importance in all three novels, is New York City. Of the three, *Dreaming in Cuban* remains perhaps García's best-regarded and certainly most studied; its narrative, across three generations of the women in the del Pino family, also manages to renarrate Cuban American history across most of the twentieth century. Her most recent, *Monkey Hunting*, expands García's range considerably, both historically and culturally. Beginning in the mid-nineteenth century, it tells the story of three generations of a Chinese Cuban family, beginning with the patriarch who arrives in Cuba from China only to be sold into **slavery**, and ending with his Afro-Chinese Cuban American grandson serving the United States in Vietnam.

Perhaps the most telling counter to both García's literary and political ambitions can be found in the work of the mystery writer Carolina García-Aguilera, who, since the mid-1990s, has been producing an impressive series of pulp-style detective novels featuring a recurring detective figure named Lupe Solano. García-Aguilera's titles, which include *Bitter Sugar* (2002), *Havana Heat* (2000), and *Bloody Waters* (1998), are all unapologetically set in the heart of Cuban Miami, and her garrulous, engaging protagonist/narrator Lupe Solano functions very effectively as an informal cultural informant into the defining mentalities of twenty-first century Cuban Miami, a community that manages uncannily to reflect historical changes (like the end of the cold war and the influx of non-Cuban Latinos to Florida) at the same time that it clings tenaciously to its anti-Castro politics as though the revolution had only happened yesterday. *Bloody Waters*, for example, uses the impact of the Mariel Boatlift on Miami's Cuban community as an active factor in the otherwise conventional plot of murder, blackmail, and mayhem with which any reader of postmodern detective fiction would be immediately familiar.

A number of emerging novelists at the turn into the twenty-first century prove that the Cuban American novel has a bright future, one that will continue the work of already-established figures, both major and minor, and in addition will take on new themes, and new strategies, as the political and cultural conditions defining Cuban America continue to shift. In addition to continuing significant work by writers as important as Hijuelos and García, the new century has seen the publication of new work by writers as disparate as Achy Obejas (who followed 1996's *Memory Mambo* with 2001's *Days of Awe*), José Raúl Bernardo (who followed 1996's *The Secret of the Bulls* with 2003's *Wise Women of Havana*), Ernesto Mestre (who followed 1999's *Lazarus Rumba* with 2004's *Second Death of Unica Aveyano*), and Ana Menendez (see 2003's *Loving Che*). Obejas's *Days of Awe* appeared earlier than García's *Monkey Hunting*, but together they embody the rich, challenging cultural and historical complications informing the ongoing elaboration of Cuban American identity. As *Monkey Hunting* explains why there are Cubans of Chinese ancestry, *Days of Awe* explains why there are Cubans of Jewish ancestry; together these novels establish in important, compelling ways how inadequate the national term alone (even when hybridized as Cuban American) can be for the articulation of the always complex, always simultaneous operations of history and identity. Little besides a common interest in the various and complex ways that history can condition identity, especially in the specifically Cuban American context, binds these writers and their works to one another. Their biographies are as various as their literary predilections, and their approaches to the act of narrative are as various as their distinct senses about how exactly history and fiction can and should most productively inform one another.

It is worth noting that significant novels devoted to Cuban American themes have also been produced by some interesting non-Cuban writers, including 1990's *The Perez Family* (by Christine Bell), 1991's *Los Gusanos* (by filmmaker John Sayles) and 1995's *Cuba and the Night* (by journalist **Pico Iyer**), each of which in its own way evinces the same impatience with the neatness of the "line" of official Cuban American history, and which together suggest that the questioning of the authority and logic of that line may be of value to more than just the Cuban American "community" it claims to name, and to define.

Further Reading

Alvarez-Borland, Isabel. *Cuban-American Literature of Exile: From Person to Persona.* Charlottesville: U of Virginia P, 1998.

García, María Cristina. *Havana USA: Cuban Exiles and Cuban Americans in South Florida, 1959–1994.* Berkeley and Los Angeles: U of California P, 1996.

Pérez-Firmat, Gustavo. *Life on the Hyphen: The Cuban-American Way.* Austin: U of Texas P, 1994.

Smorkaloff, Pamela Maria. *Cuban Writers On and Off the Island.* New York: Twayne, 1999.

Ricardo L. Ortiz

CUBAN AMERICAN POETRY   The literature of the Cuban exile enjoyed a long history in the United States well before the generation of the Cuban Revolution of 1959. The notable poetry of nineteenth-century exile, for example, includes José María Heredia's **canon**ical ode "Niágara" (1824), the anthology *El laúd del desterrado* (1858), Bonifacio Byrne's patriotic "Mi bandera" (1899), and José Martí's four books of poems, *Ismaelillo* (1882), *Versos sencillos* (1891), and the posthumous *Versos libres* (1913) and *Flores del destierro* (1933). The Recovering the U.S. Hispanic Literary Heritage project has been instrumental in providing current access to this historical period of U.S. Cuban literature. The project issued a new edition of *El laúd* (1995; ed. Matías Montes-Huidobro) and the first bilingual edition of Martí's complete *Versos sencillos/Simple Verses* (1997; trans. Manuel A. Tellechea). The two compilations that have come out of the first decade of the recovery project, *Herencia: The Anthology of Hispanic Literature of the United States* (2002) and *En otra voz: antología de la literatura hispana de los Estados Unidos* (2003), are indispensable resources on the literature and literary history of Cuban exile in the United States. For the most part, however, this body of exile literature is not relevant for an anglophone readership (with the possible exception of Martí, who has acquired a place in comparative nineteenth-century American letters). The Cuban American literature that is most integral to ethnic American literature began with the first generation of exiles following the revolution of 1959, continued after the Mariel boatlift of 1981, and extends into the twenty-first century with the children of both generations. Numerous literary magazines have given a voice to these writers over the years, including *Areíto*, *Escandalar*, *Exilio*, and *Linden Lane Magazine*. Cuban American literature also has received broad distribution through **Arte Público Press**, Bilingual Press/Editorial Bilingüe, and Ediciones Universal, the three leading publishers of Spanish language and bilingual literature by Latino writers in the United States.

The first generation of Cuban American poets wrote primarily in Spanish and in response to the historical circumstance of their exile from Cuba following the revolution, as opposed to the Chicano and Puerto Rican writers (with whom they are often categorized as the three principal groups of U.S. Latino writers), who found their initial literary expression through the repercussions of the **Civil Rights Movement**. Also in contrast to the English-dominant Chicanos and Puerto Ricans, Spanish was the language of choice for Cubans in the United States in the 1960s and 1970s. As a result, Cuban poetry in the United States of this early period is more likely to be considered Cuban or Cuban exile literature rather than a discrete branch of the growing corpus of multiethnic American literature.

The Cuban American literature anthologies of these two decades reflect such choices of language preference and national allegiance. Early primary and secondary sources confirm that virtually all the poetry of this period was both written in Spanish and regarded as Cuban national literature. These books include two anthologies of exile poets, Angel Aparicio Laurencio's *Cinco poetisas cubanas, 1935–1969* (1970) and Ana Rosa Núñez's *Poesía en éxodo: el exilio cubano en su poesía, 1959–1969* (1970); Matías Montes Huidobro and Yara González's dictionary, *Bibliografía crítica de la poesía cubana (exilio: 1959–1971)* (1972); Orlando Rodríguez Sardiñas's *La última poesía cubana: antología reunida (1959–1973)* (1973); and José B. Fernández and **Roberto G. Fernández**'s *Indice bibliográfico de autores cubanos (diáspora 1959–1979)/ Bibliographical Index of Cuban Authors (Diaspora 1959–1979)* (1983). Four of the *Cinco poetisas*—Rita Geada, Ana Rosa Núñez, Pura del Prado, and Teresa María Rojas—appear in Rodríguez Sardiñas's *La última poesía cubana* and in subsequent compilations over the years (Núñez and Prado as late as the 1990s, in English translation). *La última poesía cubana*, one of the earliest compilations of this type, likewise anthologizes several other prominent Cuban exile writers, including José Kozer, **Dolores Prida**, and Isel Rivero. Most of these poets have continued to write in Spanish (Kozer is especially prolific), although at least one turned to English and even other genres (Prida writes bilingual drama). Still other poets in *La última poesía cubana* (Angel Cuadra, Belkis Cuza Malé, and Heberto Padilla) went into exile in the United States long after the publication of the anthology. More recently, the practice of bringing together island and diaspora writing has continued in León de la Hoz's *La poesía de las dos orillas: Cuba (1959–1993): antología* (1994). Hoz's alphabetical arrangement of poets presumes the primacy of a national-literature focus rather than the geographical fact of residency either in Cuba or in exile in the United States, the "other shore."

Silvia Burunat and Ofelia García's *Veinte años de literatura cubanoameri-cana: antología 1962–1982* (1988) is the single best source of poetry and fiction of those years. (Published by Bilingual Press/Editorial Bilingüe, it is also the most accessible.) The thematic organization illustrates both ongoing connections to island concerns (the opening section treats Afro Cuban **identity**) as well as the tendency to explore—in Spanish—issues of identity, exile, and **immigration** as part of a nascent Cuban American experience. Especially noteworthy in *Veinte años* are the contributions of Lourdes Casal, Uva Clavijo, José Kozer, and Juana Rosa Pita. Despite the rich tradition represented in all anthologies of this kind and in the dozens of discrete volumes published by these poets, however, the language factor has precluded the inclusion of this literature in English-language books. Ultimately, this early Cuban American poetry remains largely invisible to the general reader of multiethnic American literature.

By the 1980s and 1990s, several factors combined to allow broader recognition of Cuban American poetry. English had become the language of choice and these younger Cuban American poets, unlike the first-generation writers, were writing squarely within American literature. They were publishing in mainstream literary magazines like *American Poetry Review, Blue Mesa Review, Kenyon Review,* and *Prairie Schooner,* as well as in the Latino publications *Americas Review, Bilingual Review,* and *Linden Lane Magazine.* Cuban American poets also were included alongside other Latinos in groundbreaking anthologies such as *El Coro: A Chorus of Latino and Latina Poetry* (1997; ed. Martín Espada) and *Paper Dance: 55 Latino Poets* (1995; ed. **Victor Hernández Cruz**, Leroy V. Quintana, and **Virgil Suárez**). Contemporaneous Cuban American anthologies reflect these changed circumstances. Carolina Hospital's *Cuban American Writers: Los Atrevidos* (1988) features the poetry of ten Cuba-born writers who are "daring" for choosing English even as they identify implicitly and explicitly with both the exile experience and Cuban literature (16–17). Hospital, for her part, is equally daring as an anthologist, not only for asserting a place for such writers in Cuban and U.S. literature, but also for bringing together the breadth of these exile and immigrant traditions in a later anthology, *A Century of Cuban Writers in Florida: Selected Prose and Poetry* (1996; coed. Jorge Cantera). The writer and scholar **Gustavo Pérez Firmat** has called these writers born in Cuba but raised and educated in the United States the "one-and-a-half" generation. Many of these daring "one-and-a-halfers" (Jorge Guitart, **Pablo Medina**, Ricardo Pau-Llosa, and Hospital and Pérez Firmat themselves) also appear in Delia Poey and Virgil Suárez's *Little Havana Blues: A Cuban-American Literature Anthology* (1996); still others (**Sandra Castillo**, Adrián Castro, Silvia Curbelo, and Dionisio Martínez) in Hospital and Cantera's Florida anthology. Together these editors have identified a corpus of poets who depict not only the exile experience, but also more universal aesthetic and thematic considerations. The literary criticism by scholars of this generation—such as Isabel Alvarez Borland's *Cuban-American*

Literature of Exile: From Person to Persona (1998) and virtually all of Pérez Firmat's work on Cuban and Cuban American literature and culture—invariably illuminates the development of Cuban American poetry, even though the studies may not directly or exclusively treat poetry per se.

Further Reading

Cantera, Jorge, and Carolina Hospital. "Florida and Cuba: Ties That Bind." *A Century of Cuban Writers in Florida: Selected Prose and Poetry*. Ed. Hospital and Cantera. Sarasota, FL: Pineapple, 1996. 1–28.

Cortina, Rodolfo J. "History and Development of Cuban American Literature: A Survey." *Handbook of Hispanic Cultures in the United States: Literature and Art*. Ed. Francisco Lomelí. Houston: Arte Público; Madrid: Instituto de Cooperación Iberoamericana, 1993. 40–61.

Hospital, Carolina, ed. *Cuban American Writers: Los Atrevidos*. Princeton, NJ: Ellas-Linden Lane, 1988.

Kanellos, Nicolás. "An Overview of Hispanic Literature in the United States." *Herencia: The Anthology of Hispanic Literature of the United States*. Ed. Kanellos et al. New York: Oxford UP, 2002. 1–32.

Lindstrom, Naomi. "Cuban American and Continental Puerto Rican Literature." *Sourcebook of Hispanic Culture in the United States*. Ed. David William Foster. Chicago: American Library Association, 1982. 221–45.

Maratos, Daniel C., and Marnesba D. Hill. *Escritores de la diáspora cubana: manual biobibliográfica/Cuban Exile Writers: A Biobibliographic Handbook*. Metuchen, NJ: Scarecrow, 1986.

Poey, Delia, and Virgil Suárez. Introduction. *Little Havana Blues: A Cuban-American Literature Anthology*. Ed. Poey and Suárez. Houston: Arte Público, 1996. 9–15.

Wall, Catharine E. "Latino Poetry." *Critical Survey of Poetry*. 8 vols. Ed. Philip K. Jason. 2nd rev. ed. Pasadena, CA: Salem, 2003. 4825–32.

Catharine E. Wall

CULLEN, COUNTEE (1903–1946) African American poet. Best known for his frequently anthologized sonnet poem, "Yet Do I Marvel," Countee Cullen's current reputation is based on the poems from his first book of poetry, *Color* (1925), which was written when he was an undergraduate at New York University where he graduated Phi Beta Kappa. He was a major figure of the **Harlem Renaissance** (also known as the **New Negro** Renaissance) movement and seemed its most promising poet, but this promise was never fulfilled. Due to racism, being an African American poet was at best difficult, so Cullen's aim was to be considered a poet, not a "Negro" poet, but his adherence to the traditional poetic forms meant he rejected the major principles of the Harlem Renaissance movement which celebrated and recovered poor black culture, the vernacular forms, and **jazz** and blues. **Langston Hughes** criticized him for scorning black folk culture in his desire to be accepted by white mainstream culture, and Cullen in turn believed Hughes's "jazz poetry" to be an oxymoron and the vernacular forms dangerous.

Cullen's haunting and elegiac lyrics used the formal poetic forms of the Petrarchan and Shakespearean sonnet, Spenserian stanza, and the ballad. Although he rebelled against being labeled a "Negro" poet, he is critically acclaimed for his race-conscious poems in which he explores his ambivalence of being thusly labeled. He begins *Color* with "Yet Do I Marvel" in which he acknowledges the difficulties and struggles of being an African American poet; the autobiographical elements in the book not only focus on his life but also his literary influences. In "Incident," he describes the profound impact of being called a "nigger" by a white boy when he was eight years old. He was greatly influenced by the Romantics, especially by John Keats, and he pays homage to him in "To John Keats, Poet. At Spring Time." Adopted at the age of fifteen by the Reverend and Mrs. Frederick A. Cullen, he was

Countee Cullen in Central Park, 1941. *Courtesy of the Library of Congress.*

reputed to have had a very close relationship with his father who influenced him religiously, and many of his poems incorporate religious allusions and themes. In the title poem of *The Black Christ* (1929), he examines African Americans as Christ-like figures unjustly crucified by whites, an important image in African American literature for lynching.

Cullen's exploration of **race** issues was not tangential to his poetry. In his most critically acclaimed poem "Heritage" also in *Color*, the speaker examines his African heritage and the conflict African Americans have of reconciling a legacy of a homeland far removed in terms of time and culture, so that Africa to them is just a name and a place. He was very interested in primitivism (African American as well as white mainstream interest in Africa), which incorporated the belief that civilization is a façade of an older, primitive self. In this poem as well as others in *Color*, for example, "Atlantic City Waiter" and "Fruit of the Flower," he celebrates what was believed to be a uniquely African American self and **identity** in which Africa represented the roots. He also explores African Americans' struggle for identity through the duality or "double consciousness" of being African and American. He was also innovative in terms of form because he goes against conventions by using rhymed couplets in trochaic trimeter rather than the conventional iambic pentameter.

The Ballad of the Brown Girl: An Old Ballad Retold (1927) focuses on the issue of miscegenation in an allegorical form in which an aristocratic lord marries a "brown girl" rather than the acceptable white lady. Like a traditional English ballad, the story involves a murder (when the brown girl kills her white rival), but also a lynching (when her husband lynches her). The allegorical English setting allowed Cullen to critique **racism** and lynching in a way that was acceptable to his white audience. The poem is competently written, but it was not as well received as he had hoped.

Cullen's work was well received during his time, and he received a Guggenheim fellowship in 1927, which he used to go to Paris where black artists were more accepted. Although he continued publishing until his death, the language and imagery in his later work were frequently mundane. His use of the traditional forms left him outdated at a time when most major artists of the Harlem Renaissance and the Modernist movement were experimenting with form and language, the vernacular, music, and also incorporating popular culture. For these reasons Cullen continues to be neglected by critics in African American literary studies.

Further Reading

Baker, Houston, Jr. "The Poetry of Countee Cullen." *Major Modern Black American Writers*. Ed. Harold Bloom. New York: Chelsea House, 1995. 29–30.

Ferguson, Blanche E. *Countee Cullen and the Negro Renaissance*. New York: Dodd, Mead, 1966.

Lomax, Michael L. "Countee Cullen: A Key to the Puzzle." *The Harlem Renaissance Re-Examined*. Revised and expanded edition. Ed. Victor A. Kramer and Robert A. Russ. Troy, NY: Whitson, 1997. 239–47.

Reimonenq, Alden. "Countee Cullen and Uranian 'Soul Windows'." *Critical Essays: Gay and Lesbian Writers of Color*. Ed. Emmanuel S. Nelson. New York: Haworth, 1993. 143–65.

Shackleford, Dean D. "The Poetry of Countee Cullen." *Masterpieces of African American Literature*. Ed. Frank N. Magill. New York: HarperCollins, 1992. 382–86.

Shucard, Alan. *Countee Cullen*. Boston: Twayne, 1984.

Tuttleton, James W. "Countee Cullen at 'The Heights'." *The Harlem Renaissance: Revaluations*. Ed. Amritjit Singh, et al. New York: Garland, 1989. 101–37.

Ymitri Jayasundera

CULTURE CLASH Latino performance/comedy troupe. The comedy trio Culture Clash has amassed acclaim from mainstream theater critics as well as scholars of Chicano/Latino theater and performance. The group is an offshoot of Comedy Fiesta, a performance/comedy troupe born in 1984 that consisted of Richard Montoya, Ric Salinas, Herbert Siguenza, Jose Antonio Burciaga, Monica Palacios, and Marga Gomez. By 1988, Comedy Fiesta had become Culture Clash and had been whittled to its present core of Montoya,

Salinas, and Siguenza. The influence of the Marx Brothers, Buster Keaton, and Mexican comic actor Cantinflas can be seen in the wit and slapstick that characterize Culture Clash's work. In addition, Culture Clash's use of satire and comedy to comment on an array of social and political concerns reflects the inspiration the trio has drawn from the politically motivated teatro of the Chicano Movement. Armed with intelligence, political astuteness, a sense of humor, a sense of urgency, and a Brechtian sense of theater's potential to raise audiences' consciousness, Culture Clash has consistently managed to provoke critical thinking about various issues.

The group's first two plays, *The Mission* (1988) and *A Bowl of Beings* (1991), brilliantly engage the subjects of Chicano **identity** and the racist organization of the American entertainment industry. In *The Mission*, three Latinos' inability to break into television, film, and stand-up comedy reflects the limited opportunity that is available

The Latino comedy group Culture Clash is featured in a PBS documentary, "The Border." *AP/Wide World Photos.*

to aspiring Latino entertainers. As Richard, Ric, and Herbert, the eponymous characters of this quasi-autobiographical play, look for work, they discover their potential for success circumscribed by the fact that only stereotypical and caricatured roles are available to them. *A Bowl of Beings*, Culture Clash's follow-up piece, consists of a series of sketches that dramatize the difficulty of defining Chicano identity. Through a panoply of characters that includes history's first Chicano, a wannabe Chicano revolutionary, a Chicano in the midst of a mental breakdown, and a Chicano-turned-stoner, Culture Clash maps the ways that the cultural and racial hybridity of Chicano identity complicate efforts to define this identity.

After *A Bowl of Beings*, Culture Clash staged a number of productions that explore the history and social relations of specific locations. The first of these productions, *S.O.S.—Comedy for These Uncertain Times* (1992), examines the ailments that Los Angeles communities and families had to confront in the early 1990s: the beating of Rodney King by Los Angeles police officers, the Los Angeles riots, racial tensions, homophobia, and AIDS.

531

Amid this distressed condition of Los Angeles, *S.O.S.* functioned as a call for change and healing. For *Radio Mambo* (1995), *Bordertown* (1998), *Nuyorican Stories* (1999), and *Mission Magic Mystery Tour* (2000), Montoya, Salinas, and Siguenza interviewed residents of Miami, San Diego, New York's Lower East Side, and San Francisco's Mission District, respectively. In each of these shows, the members of Culture Clash assume the personas of their interviewees in order to provide an insightful snapshot of the various personalities that occupy particular locales. As audiences come face-to-face with the idiosyncratic individuals of these communities, they realize the dignity and pathos of each one. In addition, the unique challenges that stand in the way of these communities' harmony become apparent vis-à-vis the revelation of the conflicts that haunt them. More generally, Culture Clash has managed, through their site-specific pieces, to foreground the fear, anxiety, animosity, and uncertainty that suffuse contemporary American society and that must be negotiated.

Other pieces by Culture Clash include *Carpa Clash* (1993), a tribute to Cesar Chávez; *The Birds* (1998), a musical adaptation of Aristophanes' work; and *Anthems: Culture Clash in the District* (2002), a site-specific show that explores Washington, DC. *Chavez Ravine* (2003) has been Culture Clash's most successful piece. This musical exposes the political story behind the construction of Dodger Stadium by unearthing the human history beneath it. As *Chavez Ravine* portrays the deals that resulted in the bulldozing of Mexican immigrants' houses for the sake of building a southern California home for the Brooklyn Dodgers, the show challenges audiences to acknowledge the shady political machinations that have built Los Angeles. Ultimately, *Chavez Ravine*, like many of Culture Clash's other works, lays out for audiences the unfair ways that power, as it is unequally distributed in the United States, encroaches on individual lives and individuals' dignity. (*See also* Mexican American Stereotypes)

Further Reading

Glenn, Antonia Grace. "Comedy for These Urgent Times: Culture Clash as Chroniclers in America." *Theatre Forum* 20 (Winter–Spring 2002): 62–68.

Kondo, Dorinne. "(Re)Visions of Race: Contemporary Race Theory and the Cultural Politics of Racial Crossover in Documentary Theatre." *Theatre Journal* 52.4 (2000): 81–108.

Phillip Serrato

CUMPIAN, CARLOS (1953–) Mexican American poet. Born and raised primarily in Texas, Cumpian is presently a high school teacher in Chicago and editor-in-chief of March Abrazo Press. Along with other Mexican American writers who identified themselves as Chicano, Cumpian began reading and publishing work in Chicago in the 1970s and shortly after published his first book of poetry, *Emergency Tacos: Seven Poets Con Picante* (1989) with **Sandra Cisneros**, Carlos Cortez, Beatriz Badikian, Cynthia Gallaher, Margarita Lopez-Castro, **Raul Nino**, Carlos Morton, and Marc Zimmerman.

The structural patterns of his poems, although illuminated through performance, can only be fully appreciated once the reader moves past their initial reading of the text. Most of Cumpian's early poetry evokes sounds and rhythms uniquely Mexican/Spanish, yet the majority of his poetry to date encompasses the realities, triumphs, and defeats of inner-city American life, as well as varied social and political issues. He melds multiple facets of his past career experiences and friendships in order to showcase the brilliance found within the complex syntax and verbiage indicative of Cumpian's poetics. Through his poetry he is able to express his views on a range of issues from the economy and racial discrimination to the presidency and environmental concerns.

Coyote Sun (1990), Cumpian's first poetry book to feature only his work, speaks to the figurative homeland of Chicanos, Aztlán, without explanation or apologies. Readers are therefore left to their own devices to decipher and locate the poems in the larger context of human existence. Cumpian also threads a familiar theme—animals and nature—within this collection that is present in others. Cumpian often recalls the destruction of world peace and harmony by European domination. His poetry includes important historical dates and subsequent events: 1492, 1521, the dropping of the atomic bomb in 1945, and the Cuban Revolution of 1959. His second collection, *Latino Rainbow: Poems about Latino Americans* (1994), is an illustrated picture book consisting of twenty rhythmic poems portraying Latino historical events and figures. The poems cover the colonization of California to the first Latina astronaut. Poems found within *Armadillo Charm* (1996) epitomize the interactions between the present and past, the usual and extraordinary, the included and secluded. The poems range in metaphoric topics from the sturdiness, yet impending extinction, of the armadillo to boxing, which echoes the common man's struggle for self-sufficiency despite his best efforts. His denouncement of Anglo American's claim to all that lives and breathes is influenced by the work of Alberto Rio and John Nichols, yet other themes present in the book can be traced to the writings of Chicano writers such as **Rudolfo Anaya**, **Ana Castillo**, and Native American poet **Simon J. Ortiz**. Readers will identify with the gritty, yet timeless, images reflected in the poems found within the collection.

Cumpian has been able to parlay his involvement with Chicano/Latino writing circles into the creation of humorous and well-thought-out pieces that audiences find accessible. Due to the initial lack of exposure and venues to perform, Cumpian founded the La Palabra Reading series at the Randolph Street Gallery in Chicago and has been able to promote and champion the once quelled Chicano/Latino voice via oral performances and productions. (*See also* Mexican American Poetry)

Further Reading

"Carlos Cumpian." *Drumvoices Revue: A Confluence of Literary, Cultural and Vision Arts* 6 (1996–1997): 14–17.

Schandelmeier, Cathleen. "Poetry Profile: Carlos Cumpian." *Letter Ex: Chicago's Poetry Newsmagazine* 95 (1994): 8–9.

Zimmerman, Marc. "Transplanting Roots and Taking Off: Latino Poetry in Illinois." *Studies in Illinois Poetry*. Ed. John E. Hallwas. Urbana, IL: Stormline Press, 1989. 77–116.

Clarissa West-White

CURIEL, BARBARA BRINSON (1956–) Mexican American poet, writer, professor, and feminist scholar. Barbara Brinson Curiel's poetry is minimalist and exact, invoking entire scenes from a single word. She writes in both Spanish and English.

Barbara Brinson Curiel published her volume of poetry titled *Speak to Me From Dreams* in 1989, although she had published her several individual poems in a variety of venues prior to that. The work demonstrates Curiel's ability to evoke profound emotions with very few words. Her minimalist style is at once accessible and challenging. Curiel's unique style as a writer was recognized and applauded when she was awarded the Third Women Poetry Prize from Third Women book publishers in 1986. Eventually Third Woman publishers would go on to publish *Speak to Me From Dreams*. Curiel has also written short stories and published several incisive scholarly articles about Latino/a literature. Currently a professor at California State University at Humboldt, her primary areas of research and scholarship have been in American ethnic literature, Chicano cultural productions, and women's writing. She has also worked as a University of California Humanities Research Institute Postdoctoral Fellow in the Post-national American Studies Research Group and as a Lecturer in Ethnic Studies and Women's Studies at California State University, San Marcos. Curiel's academic research and writings about Hispanic literature have been featured in several anthologies including *Infinite Divisions: An Anthology of Chicana Literature, Literatura Chicana 1965–1995: An Anthology in Spanish, English and Caló* (1997), and *The Floating Borderlands: Twenty-five Years of U.S. Hispanic Literature* (2000).

Curiel received her BA in English and Spanish with honors from Mills College in 1979. She then completed work for an MA in Spanish at Stanford University in 1981. In 1995 she completed her PhD in literature at the University of California, Santa Cruz. Doing her doctoral dissertation on "Sex and the Spirit: the Authorization of Narrative in the Works of Three Women Writers of Color," Curiel began what has been a career-long examination of the texts of women of color. She continues to examine the multifaceted landscape of **race** that comprises American literature and seeks to understand the role of women within that context. Praised by **Lucille Clifton** as a writer with a "magical voice," Barbara Brinson Curiel continues her art and activism through her poetry and scholarship. (*See also* Mexican American Poetry)

Further Reading

Sanchez, Ramon. "Barbara Brinson Curiel." *Dictionary of Literary Biography*. Vol. 209. Ed. Francisco A. Lomelí and Carl R. Shirley. Detroit: Gale, 1999. 61–64.

Staven Bruce

CURRAN, MARY DOYLE (1917–1981)   Irish   American   novelist.
Mary Doyle Curran's primary contribution to ethnic American literature
comes from *The Parish and the Hill* (1948), a novel that poignantly dramatizes the potential loss of community tradition and support inherent in
immigrant **assimilation** and American dream upward mobility.

The Parish and the Hill relates the struggles and shifting group identifications of three generations of an Irish American family from the perspective
of Mary O'Connor, the granddaughter of postfamine Irish immigrants. The
parish of the title refers to an Irish Parish in Holyoke, Massachusetts, where
Mary's grandparents find a supportive, if ethnically exclusive, social network. Their children, however, experience a less cohesive community as
Irish traditions are shattered by poverty, by American politics in the World
War I era, and by growing intra-ethnic class consciousness as some families
attempt to move up to "the Hill," a symbol of assimilation into the mainstream American middle class. Mary's father moves her family to the Hill,
and as she comes of age in the 1920s, the observant narrator must navigate
the conflicting values embodied by her "shanty Irish" mother and "lace
curtain" Irish father. Within the parish community, the shanty Irish uphold
Old World traditions and support each other in a collective stance against
the dominant, prejudiced "Yankee" society. Her father's drive to upward
mobility, alternatively, leads him to deny his Irish heritage. The shift from
shanty to lace curtain identities restructures the community's identifications: Where the former operates on an insider vs. outsider basis, the latter
recognizes splintering class divisions within the Irish American community. The curtain symbolizes emerging class boundaries separating neighbor from neighbor, and the novel views second-generation Irish American
identity as a complex mix of new prosperity and lost unity. Curran's realistic representations of alcoholism, domestic violence, poverty, **racism**, and
class consciousness critique early twentieth-century American culture even
as she develops an alternative vision of an open parish that would unite
and support working class families of all American ethnicities—an ideal
also suggested in her story "Over These Prison Walls I Would Fly."

Like her *Parish* narrator, Curran (née Doyle) was raised in Holyoke by
an Irish immigrant father and an Irish American mother. Financing her
education by working as a waitress, clerk, and housemaid, she earned
degrees from Massachusetts State College and State University of Iowa. She
taught at Wellesley College, at Queens College, and at the University of
Massachusetts–Boston, where she was a professor of literature and director
of Irish Studies. Her literary friends included **Saul Bellow**, Paolo Milano,
and Babette Deutsch. Although her teaching left her little time to publish
during her lifetime, she left numerous completed manuscripts when she died
in 1981. (*See also* Irish American Novel)

Further Reading

Halley, Anne. "Mary Doyle Curran: 'Over These Prison Walls I Would Fly'."
    MELUS 15.3 (1988): 3–14.

Scott, Bonnie Kime. "Women's Perspectives in Irish-American Fiction from Betty Smith to Mary McCarthy." *Irish-American Fiction: Essays in Criticism.* Ed. Daniel J. Casey, Robert E. Rhodes, and William V. Shannon. New York: AMS, 1979. 87–103.

Jacquelyn Scott Lynch

CZECH AMERICAN LITERATURE   The settlement of Czechs in North America can be roughly broken into two periods. Until the end of World War I, the Czech lands were a province of the Austro-Hungarian Empire. The immigrants who came to the United States in the late nineteenth and early twentieth centuries settled primarily in rural areas of the Midwest. There were also significant Czech communities in Chicago and Texas. Czechs were a relatively well-educated immigrant group, and Czech-language periodicals thrived during this period. The poet Josef Václav Sládek traveled around the United States in 1868–70, and his description of life among the Czech immigrants, *My America* (*Má Amerika,* first collected in book form in 1914), is considered a classic work of Czech literature. Chicago was a center of Czech literature as early as the 1890s. Czech poetry, prose, and even drama, such as J. R. Pšenka's play about Czech immigrants, *The Boarders* (*Bordynkáři,* 1911), enjoyed considerable success. However, virtually no works of early Czech American literature have been translated. Czech Americans assimilated relatively quickly into mainstream American culture, and the Czech language (as was the case with other ethnic groups) was usually lost after the first or second generation.

The support of Czech Americans helped Tomáš G. Masaryk win Woodrow Wilson's support for an independent Czechoslovakia in 1918, and this new republic became a model of multicultural democracy in Central Europe. Czechoslovakia was a prosperous state in the interwar period, and immigration dropped considerably. This period also saw closer cooperation between Czech and Slovak immigrant groups, since the two nations had been joined in a single "homeland." However, a second phase of **immigration** from Czechoslovakia took place in several major waves, especially after the Nazi occupation in 1938, the Communist seizure of power in 1948, and the Soviet invasion in 1968. These later Czech exiles were often writers and other intellectuals who had left for political reasons. The Czechoslovak Society of Arts and Sciences (known in Czech as *Společnost věd a umění,* or SVU), founded in 1950, was one of the most important Czech American organizations during the Communist period. SVU's publications, including the journal *Kosmas* (founded in 1982) emphasize the continuity between the earlier Czech American immigrants and the later refugees from Communist rule. In 1989 peaceful protests in Czechoslovakia led to the Velvet Revolution, which ended the Communist regime, and in 1993 the country was divided into the separate Czech and Slovak Republics.

Because the Czech lands were originally known in English as Bohemia, the term "Bohemian" was commonly used until the early twentieth century, to designate both the Czech language and Czech ethnic origin (it is not fully clear why the word took on the connotations of an artistic, unconventional lifestyle, as it is usually used today). By the 1920s, the term "Czech" had become commonly accepted (although the unusual "Cz" spelling actually comes from Polish; it has not been used in the Czech language for centuries). The best-known Czech immigrant in American literature is undoubtedly the title character of Willa Cather's novel *My Ántonia* (1918). Although Cather was not of Czech origin herself, her Czech characters in this and other works are based closely on childhood friends. "Neighbour Rosicky," a widely anthologized 1925 story by Cather, also offers a sympathetic and intimate portrait of Czech American immigrants. Following the usage of her time, Cather almost exclusively refers to her Czech characters as Bohemian rather than Czech. She shows extensive knowledge of the lifestyle of Czech Americans, including their food, music, and relationships with other ethnic groups.

After Czechoslovakia was abandoned to Hitler by the Western powers at Munich in 1938, the situation became dangerous for many Czech writers, especially Jewish writers. One of the few able to reach the safety of the United States was Egon Hostovský, who emigrated from Prague to New York, and spent the war years in America. He settled in the United States for good in 1948, and most of his novels from the 1950s came out in English translation, establishing him as one of the leading Czech writers in the West. Several of his later novels are set in the United States, including *The Midnight Patient* (1954) and *The Charity Ball* (1957), which have been translated into English, as well as *Foreigner Seeks Apartment* (Cizinec hledá byt, 1948), which has only been published in Czech. His last major novel, *The Plot*, came out in English in 1960. Its protagonist, Jan Bares, is a Czech writer whose years of exile have made him indifferent to the question of Czech **identity**: "But what's so terrible about being a Czech? Surely our national soul, forever whining about centuries of oppression, is of no concern to Americans . . . Americans much prefer to scrutinize their own way of life and their own natures." Although Hostovský has been essentially forgotten by American critics, he set a precedent for Czech-language authors in North America in using autobiographical fiction as a basis for describing the exile experience.

Like Hostovský, the novelist and literary critic Milada Součková emigrated to the United States permanently in 1948. Although her fiction was never translated into English, she wrote several important works of literary criticism, including *A Literature in Crisis: Czech Literature, 1938–1950* (1954) and *A Literary Satellite: Czechoslovak-Russian Literary Relations* (1970). Součková's final novel, *The Notebooks of Josephina Rykrova* (Sešity Josephiny Rykrové, 1981, expanded edition, 1993), is an experimental fictionalized memoir that includes impressionistic memories of her childhood in Prague, as well as images from her life as an exile in America.

Other Czech American authors from the 1948 wave of exiles, which included some of the most notable cultural figures of interwar Czechoslovakia, were sometimes less fortunate. Their works, banned in their home country and not translated into English, were thus doubly cut off from their potential readers. Before the war, the novelist Zdeněk Nemeček won a literary prize in Prague for his novel *New York in a Fog* (*New York Zamlženo*, 1932), but after he emigrated to New York and submitted some of his writing, American publishers rejected it as too "foreign" for the American reader. One of the leading journalists of interwar Czechoslovakia, Ferdinand Peroutka, also lived in New York, but his most important novel *The Cloud and the Waltz* (*Oblak a valčík*, 1948) was never translated. Jiří Kovtun, the author of several monographs on T. G. Masaryk, wrote two novels: *Prague Eclogue* (*Pražská ekloga*, 1973) and *Message from Lisbon* (*Zpráva z Lisabonu*, 1979). Kovtun, a researcher at the Library of Congress, also published an extensive bibliography of Czech and Slovak literature in English (1984, updated edition 1988).

The 1960s were a particularly promising period for Czech literature. After the harsh censorship of the Stalinist 1950s, a more liberal political climate allowed a new generation of writers to emerge. By spring 1968, sweeping reforms seemed ready to transform the country into a uniquely democratic form of communism. However, this period (known as the Prague Spring) was quickly cut short by an invasion led by the Soviet Union. In the repressive period that followed, thousands of Czechs went into exile, including some of the best writers of the previous decade. Several notable writers emigrated to the United States, including Arnošt Lustig, a survivor of Auschwitz and author of such novels as *Diamonds of the Night* (1962). Lustig never wrote about his life in America, and in fact wrote almost exclusively about the **Holocaust**. However, he did rewrite several of his novels for American and other Western readers, such as his novel about a concentration camp survivor, *Dita Saxová* (1963, revised editions 1979 and 1993). The short story writer Jan Beneš, a survivor of the Communist labor camps, resettled in California. Beneš's powerful short stories on the experiences of political prisoners, written before his emigration, have been translated into English.

The best-known Czech writer in North America after 1968 was the novelist Josef Škvorecký, who moved to Toronto. Škvorecký was best known for his 1959 novel *The Cowards*. In the 1960s he was a successful translator of English and American literature. In his later work, after his emigration to Canada, his Czech became heavily influenced by "Czechglish," the speech of North American Czechs. Škvorecký's novel *The Engineer of Human Souls* (1984) won Canada's prestigious Governor General Award. It features the autobiographical character Danny Smiřický, who had appeared in several of his other novels and was now (like Škvorecký) a professor of English literature in Canada. Several of Škvorecký's novels are set in the United States and are based on historical characters. *Dvořak in Love* (1986) is a fictionalized account of Czech composer Antonín Dvořak's stay in the small town of Spillsville, Iowa, where he composed his famous "New World Symphony." *The Bride of Texas* (1995) is set during the American Civil War and is based on the real experiences of Czech immigrants who fought for the Confederacy.

Zdena Salivarová, Škvorecký's wife, was also a notable writer; her novel *Summer in Prague* (1973) was critically acclaimed when published in English translation. However, Salivarová devoted much of her energy to the couple's publishing house, 68 Publishers, which printed over 200 banned books during the 1970s and 1980s, including some of the most important works of Czech literature from that period. A number of them were works by Czech authors in North America: from Hostovský to Škvorecký, and, most significantly, a younger generation of Czech Americans who began writing in the United States. For example, Jan Drábek's novel *Whatever Happened to Wenceslas?* (1975) is a humorously autobiographical portrait of a Czech boy who comes to the United States in 1948 and struggles in adapting to American society. Salivarová finally published her own novel about life in exile, *Dung of the Earth (Hnůj země)* in 1994, but only a short excerpt has been translated.

Perhaps the most innovative of the younger Czech American writers nurtured by 68 Publishers was Jan Novák, who left Czechoslovakia with his family after 1968. Novák's *Striptease Chicago* (1983) is a collection of stories set in the Czech community in Chicago. Like Škvorecký, he writes in a Czech American dialect, in this case the "Czechagoese" of Chicago Czechs. In his first novel, *The Willys Dream Kit* (1986), Novák made the remarkable transition to writing in English, with a distinctively original style. Published when the perception of Czechs as dissidents had heightened interest in Czech themes among American readers, the novel was nominated for the Pulitzer Prize. With his second novel, *The Grand Life* (1988), Novák gave up Czech themes entirely to write a story about American corporate life. He returned to Prague after 1989 and spent a year living there with his family, an experience described in his memoir *Commies, Crooks, Gypsies, Spooks & Poets: Books of Prague in the Year of the Great Lice Epidemic* (1995).

The Willys Dream Kit begins during World War II, and follows a thinly fictionalized account of Novák's own family history up to 1968, when they escaped from Czechoslovakia. Although his fictional alter ego appears in the background, the novel actually focuses on his father, who embezzles large amounts of money from the factory in their provincial Czech town (ironically called the "metropolis") and avoids punishment by escaping with his family in August 1968. After a sojourn in the Traiskirchen refugee camp near Vienna, the family is finally given permission to enter the United States. When they land in New York, the mother realizes that they "had just disembarked from a time machine, for in moving from the metropolis to New York, they had traversed a distance of several decades." After a night in a cheap hotel, the family wakes up exhausted, "as if the crushing pressure of countless stories of iron and cement . . . had lain on top of their bodies all night like miles and miles of ocean water. . . . The street, deserted last night, was now crowded with people who seemed little more than pairs of outsized elbows." They are pleasantly surprised when they arrive in Chicago, which reminds them of their hometown. The two children adapt with relative ease to their new life in America, but the adjustment is more difficult for their parents, especially the father, who becomes an alcoholic and is left by his wife. Finally, he is confined to a mental hospital, where he obsessively writes a book that runs for hundreds of pages and is meaningless to anyone else. At the end of his odyssey, he becomes a dark parody of all Czech authors in America, trying to fight a world that has defeated him.

Iva Pekarková's first novel, *Truck Stop Rainbows* (1992), was received enthusiastically by critics as a female counterpart to the predominantly male voices of Czech literature. In her second novel, *The World Is Round* (1994), Pekarková fictionalizes her own escape from Czechoslovakia via a refugee camp in Austria (which also appears in Novák's work). Her fictional alter ego finally reaches New York in her third novel, *Gimme the Money* (2000), which is based on her own experiences as a taxi driver in Manhattan. As an immigrant living and working in the tough neighborhoods of New York, the protagonist Gin (short for Jindřiška) abandons the past and embraces an exuberantly multicultural America: Her roommate is a Puerto Rican lesbian, her green-card husband is a French-speaking West African, and the only other East European character in the novel at all is her Russian boss. As a cab driver, Gin has a privileged insider's view of the New York lifestyle, but most of the Americans in the book appear only fleetingly, in her rearview mirror. Her views of New Yorkers are primarily based on generalizations rather than individual characters.

> In the City of New York a culture shock lay in wait beyond every street corner—those little Park Avenue ladies who screamed bloody murder every time the taxi hit a pothole; "tough" Wall Street businessmen who used silver tubes to stuff cocaine up their noses in the back seat; China-town where she struggled with chopsticks . . . the laws of the Harlem ghetto where the residents decked-out in the latest fashions were begging for attention but at the same time a curious glance was a crime punishable by instant shooting.

Gin's "Czech" perspective remains perceptible through her ironic attitude toward the relentless New York lifestyle. Although she manages to survive, the glamour of the metropolis finally wears thin; although she devours her new experiences with gusto, she seems to have a faint nostalgia for her old life in Czechoslovakia, when she could digest each moment more fully.

A small group of American writers of Czech descent have also explored the question of their ethnic identity. The best known of these is Patricia Hampl, whose award-winning 1985 memoir, *A Romantic Education* (second edition, 1999), examines the connections between her childhood in Minnesota and her experiences as an adult in Communist Prague. Hampl's later work *Spillsville* describes the Iowa town made famous by Dvořak's sojourn there. In fiction, the writer Mark Slouka's debut collection of short stories, *Lost Lake* (1998), depicts life among a small community of Czech immigrants and refugees. Ann Kimmage is not of Czech origin, but her memoir, *An Un-American Childhood* (1996), describes her experiences as the daughter of American communists who were sent to Prague in the 1950s. Kimmage's experience is the mirror image of such Czech immigrants to America as Novák and Pekarková. After almost ten years of living in Prague, she meets an American girl about her age who is visiting the country, and realizes that their experiences are so different that even with a common language, they cannot truly understand each other.

Only since the Velvet Revolution ended the Communist regime in 1989 has Czech American literature been freely and objectively discussed by Czech critics. Czech American writers such as Hostovský and Novák have been reclaimed for the Czech literary tradition after being officially "forgotten" (sometimes for decades). For example, Vladimir Papoušek has written extensively on immigrant and exile literature by Czech writers (unfortunately, his work is not available in English). In the United States, a parallel process of reevaluating the "**canon**" has been taking place in recent years, and many previously neglected writers, particularly those from different ethnic and cultural backgrounds, have been "rediscovered." *The Boundaries of Twilight*, a 1991 anthology of "Czecho-Slovak writing from the New World," includes previously unpublished stories by Škvorecký and Salivarová, as well as an excerpt from Pekárková's *Truck Stop Rainbows*, but nothing by Novák, arguably the most significant Czecho Slovak writer to emerge in the "New World" in the previous decade. As an essential part of this redefining of American literature, writers such as Hostovsky, Novák, and Pekarková, as well as the Canadian-based Škvorecký and Salivarová, should be examined in depth as part of the legacy of Czech literature in North America.

Note: Most of the works listed above were originally written in Czech, but for those translated into English, only the English title is provided. The original titles are listed only for books that have not been translated.

Further Reading

Chroust, David Zdenek. "Václav Alois Jung's 1903 Novel as a Document of Czech- American Immigration History." *Kosmas: Czechoslovak and Central European Journal 16.1* (Fall 2002): 46–62.

Hribal, C. J., ed. *The Boundaries of Twilight: Czecho-Slovak Writing from the New World.* Minneapolis: New Rivers Press, 1991.

Kovtun, Jiri. *Czech and Slovak Literature in English: A Bibliography.* Washington, DC: Library of Congress, 1988.

Machann, Clinton, and James W. Mendl, eds. *Czech Voices: Stories from Texas in the Amerikán Národní Kalendár.* College Station: Texas A & M UP, 1991.

Charles Sabatos